Essentials of Learning

ESSENTIALS OF LEARNING

THIRD EDITION

Robert M. W. Travers
Western Michigan University

THE MACMILLAN COMPANY
New York
COLLIER-MACMILLAN LIMITED
London

Printed in the United States of America

THE MACMILLAN COMPANY
866 Third Avenue, New York, New York 10022
Collier-Macmillan Canada, Ltd., Toronto, Ontario

Library of Congress catalog card number: 77–156836

PRINTING 3456789 YEAR 456789

PREFACE

ATTEMPTS TO REWRITE PORTIONS OF THE SECOND EDITION OF THIS BOOK soon led the author to realize that research had produced radical changes in the point of view of psychologists in the years since the second edition was written, and that a new edition had to be virtually a new book. This third edition is almost entirely new and not just a revision of the previous edition, which reflected thinking of the late fifties and early sixties. Although previous editions had emphasized the operant conditioning point of view, this new edition has had to reflect the upsurge of interest in perceptual aspects of learning, the present fascination with information-processing models of learning, and the new cognitive psychology. Operant conditioning remains a vigorous area of activity, particularly in its applications to the education of the mentally retarded and the treatment of the psychotic, but it has ceased to be the frontier that attracts many academic research workers. An example of the changed emphasis in academic research in learning is found in the fact that although ten years ago operant techniques were widely applied by academicians to the study of attitude change, the social psychologist today seems to prefer to conduct studies of attitude change within a framework of dissonance theory. Another illustration is shown in the fact that the extensive new research on memory, dominated by information processing models, has resulted in a literature that makes only rare mention of the term *reinforcement*. The modern student of learning should have familiarity with the concepts of operant conditioning as well as those of classical conditioning, but his knowledge of learning would be very limited if it were to stop at the boundaries of those fields. Furthermore, the area of research on perception, which was having little impact on our conception of learning ten years ago, is now a branch of knowledge making unique contributions to our conception. The neurophysiologist and the computer specialist are also making unique contributions. Many disciplines contribute to building knowledge about learning. Any attempt to present research on learning as a unified field would provide a false unity. In the place of unity one sees a number of distinct and vigorous approaches that are producing notable advances. The approaches are not necessarily incompatible, but they will probably not be fitted into a unified system in the foreseeable future.

An author of a general textbook on learning, such as the present one, is today faced with problems in writing the text that did not exist just a few years ago. He can no longer prepare himself to write a chapter by reading all the relevant research related to the topic. If he attempted to do this, he would never begin to write the chapter because of the voluminousness of related research. What he has to do, before he writes on any subject, is to begin by reading the excellent reviews that cover the relevant topics and to find out from these reviews what are considered to be the pieces of primary research of crucial importance. He can then turn to this smaller number of significant studies and digest them at leisure. The author cannot possibly avoid reading primary sources, and any primary source cited in this volume has been read, but guidance in writing this text has been derived from works in each area that attempt to organize available knowledge. The reviews and literature surveys also serve the author of a general text in another capacity. Because one can rarely place much reliance on the results of a single study, the review article can indicate the kinds of studies that have been producing consistent findings and those that provide only will-o'-the-wisps. For example, studies of achievement motivation show considerable variability in their findings and it takes a comprehensive review to determine whether there is a sufficient thread of consistency running through them for one to assert that they represent an organized body of knowledge. Several carefully prepared reviews of research on achievement motivation assert that they do. Such reviews and the conclusions they draw are much more than mere compilations of findings, for they are studies in their own right, even though the basic data for them consist of other studies. Such second-order studies, that is to say studies of studies, generally have to be consulted in order to determine what a research area in the behavioral sciences is or is not producing. A book of this kind has to rely to some extent upon the conclusions drawn from studies of studies, and the judgments drawn concerning what are, and what are not, productive lines of research.

The contemporary literature of psychology appears to be organized into printed materials at four levels of detail. First, there are original empirical and theoretical studies which are published mainly in journals. Then, at a second level, there are articles and books that bring together the research on rather narrow topics. A third level is represented by texts covering still broader areas. Finally, at the fourth level, there are very general texts such as those that carry the title of general psychology.

The student starts building his knowledge by working through a general textbook of broad coverage. During this period of his development, he may sometimes make excursions into the literature at the other levels, but the general textbook provides the literature most closely related to his immediate goals. Then he will go on to tackle books at the level of this book. In the study of such a book he may become fascinated with a particular topic and decide to explore it further. His best approach would be to read the review articles that specialize in the particular area he wishes to explore and, if his intellectual appetite is still unsatisfied, he can then turn to the original contributions of outstanding significance that the review articles have identified. Because the author believes that the student should work his way up the hierarchy of the literature, a very large number of the references cited in this book refer to review articles. Such references should be of maximum value to the student and are those to which he should next turn. Previous editions listed large numbers of primary sources of research, but users of the volume reported that they found the list of references of little value for their purposes. They viewed the massive list of references as a device for giving the volume academic respectability rather than academic utility. For this reason, detailed documentation of every point made has been omitted, though the reader can always find the supporting sources listed in the review articles cited. Furthermore, most of the historical references that were so abundant in previous editions have been omitted on the basis that they have little value for most readers and provide only academic adornment. These breaks with the tradition of psychologists of providing prolific documentation have resulted in a textbook that is more like a textbook in biology than in psychology. Documentation practices in the writing of textbooks are, unfortunately, more a matter of tradition than of utility to the student.

Finally, appreciation must be expressed for the extensive help provided by Professor Harwood Fisher of the City College, City University of New York, and Professor Edward A. Nelsen of North Carolina Central University. Each of them undertook a very detailed review of an early version of the revised manuscript and contributed many constructive ideas.

Robert M. W. Travers

CONTENTS

Three: Conditions Related to Learning

Four: Laboratory Research and Teaching

LIST OF FIGURES

PART ONE

BASIC LEARNING PROCESSES

CHAPTER ONE

Orientation to the Study of Learning

THE ONE AREA OF SCIENCE THAT HAS LONG BEEN CONSIDERED TO HOLD the key to the improvement of education is the psychology of learning. The hope has been that, with the development of a science of learning, the pupil would be able to learn more in less time than was ever possible in the past. Some of the more optimistic predictions about the impact of a science of learning have come from psychologists. These predictions promised that the new science of learning would produce a dramatic revolution in education, but the resulting changes in education have not, in fact, been of this character. They have been slow and continuous, though highly significant over the last half century. Neither scientist nor layman need be disappointed, however, that the emerging psychology of learning has not produced an educational revolution, for the slow evolution of education that it has produced has been of great importance.

The gradualness of the change in education through the impact of the psychology of learning has made it difficult for a single generation to recognize the changes that have taken place, but excellent descriptions exist of the way schools were run at the turn of the century, and these descriptions make it clear that the intervening years have produced far-reaching changes. When John Dewey founded his experimental school at the University of Chicago in 1896, he had great difficulty in purchasing movable furniture for the classrooms. Today, it would be difficult, if not impossible, to buy the traditional school furniture that was bolted to the floor. The change in the fixtures is one recognition of the fact that flexibility in the physical arrangements of the classroom provides flexibility in planning instruction. The changes in the appearance of the classroom are but symptomatic of other aspects of the evolution of teaching skill. The child who fails to learn is no longer treated as one who fails because of lack of moral fortitude. Today an effort is made to determine the reasons for the lack of progress of the child who does not learn. It is hard to believe that most teachers at the turn of the century viewed academic failure as moral failure—a failure to try hard enough. The instructional materials to which the modern school child is exposed have been carefully designed in terms of what is known about learning, and the level of difficulty of the reading matter has been checked by the application of a readability formula. The subjects that are taught in the modern school have been selected on some basis other than tradition, and none of the subjects are there because of some vague hope that they may discipline the mind. Research undertaken as early as the turn of the century showed that school subjects, believed to provide a magic formula for disciplining the mind, not only had no magic to them, but often antagonized the student to all learning in school. Schools have changed, and much of the change can be attributed to research undertaken on the psychology of learning.

Numerous other examples can be cited of the impact of research on education. A substantial beginning has been made in discovering the reasons why the child from an impoverished environment has such difficulties in school. A generation ago, teachers often held the opinion that such children could not learn because they were inherently stupid and because they had inherited from their parents genes that made them that way. Armed with this belief, the response of the teacher was often that of attempting to do little more than keep the child out of mischief. If the child could not learn, then the best course of action was to prevent him from interfering with the learning of other children. The solution seen to the problem today makes the assumption that such children probably have as much inherent capacity to learn as have middle-class children, but their problems are of a different nature. What these problems are will be considered in later chapters. Among more recent notable developments has been research on perception that provides considerable knowledge about the nature of such perceptual tasks as reading. Unfortunately, the design of learning situations in which pupils might efficiently acquire this important skill has had to be based, in the past, on speculation. There is now substantial evidence that much of that speculation was wrong and new knowledge about perception is coming into being that may provide a sound basis for teaching reading efficiently. Another area in which substantial scientific progress has been made is that of motor skill learning. One can now say that a substantial body of knowledge exists, as compared with that existing ten or twenty years ago, which can serve as a basis for designing training in many skills involving muscular coordination.

The extraordinary developments in schools that have taken place during the last three quarters of a century have remained unnoticed by most of the public, and research has been given little credit for the educational reform it has brought about. One reason for this is that the young adult, just a few years out of school, is quite unaware of what schools were like two or three generations ago. His limited knowledge makes him concur easily with those who mistakenly, but with a loud voice, claim that the schools are not of the quality they used to be. Another reason for the common failure to recognize progress is that the problems that still remain to be attacked are overwhelmingly great compared with those that have already been solved. Some of the knowledge presented in this volume may suggest solutions to a few of these problems.

There is also another very subtle way in which knowledge of a discipline such as psychology has influenced teaching in the classroom and the entire organization of the school. J. W. Getzels has pointed out on a number of occasions that psychology and the other behavioral sciences develop a conception of man and it is this conception of man that molds the way in which the young are raised. So long as man was viewed as a creature completely the master of his own fate, the child could be held responsible for all of his own shortcomings, including failure to learn, but once the behavioral sciences had demonstrated that man could also be a victim of circumstances, then the child could sometimes be considered to be such a victim also and, hence, in need of help. The ultimate example of the impact of such a conception of man on education is found in the production-line type of education, in which each step in the shaping of the final product has to take place in proper order and has to be completed before the next step is initiated. In such a system of education the central role of the teacher is that of prescribing what educational steps are to be undertaken on the pupil at any time and to make sure that all steps are properly completed before new ones are initiated. Such procedures and the conception of man they imply are at opposite poles from the conception of man developed by other psychologists, as, for example, Jean Piaget, who views him as an active agent engaged from the earliest stages in making decisions about himself. Perhaps no branch of psychology is, at this time, properly qualified to offer a complete picture of the nature of man that should be allowed to dominate education.

How a Science of Learning Improves Education

Now that one can look back on nearly three quarters of a century during which a science of psychology has had an impact on schools, one can begin to see how a basic science of behavior exerts its influence. Surprisingly little change can be attributed to direct attempts of psychologists to do research in school settings. Indeed, the three psychologists who have produced the greatest changes in schools, Edward L. Thorndike, B. F. Skinner, and Jean Piaget never undertook any research in classrooms. Rather their approach was that of developing knowledge in the laboratory. The laboratory knowledge derived by Thorndike was applied to the design of school readers, to the design of dictionaries, to the modification of literary works to make them readable for young children, to the design of procedures for the teaching of arithmetic and algebra, to the design of curricula, and to the design of testing procedures. The most notable applications of the discoveries of B. F. Skinner have been in the development of improved methods of organizing subject matter and the concept of programmed learning, and also in his emphasis on reinforcements in skill learning. Piaget has provided knowledge that has had impact on the design of early education programs. The very substantial impacts of these psychologists has been possible, not because they set out to investigate school problems in school settings, but because they were able to make successful attempts to develop fundamental knowledge of learning phenomena through basic research studies conducted in the laboratory. One can contrast their success with the dismal failure of those who, in recent years, have advocated a direct head-on attack on school problems through conducting investigations in school settings. The hundreds of millions of dollars spent on ventures of the latter type have produced far less change in schools than the investigations of a few laboratory scientists, whose work has brought about most of the significant advances during the present century. A crude direct attack on educational problems, massive though it has been, could hardly be expected to produce the kind of revolution in school practice that has already begun to happen as a result of skilled laboratory investigation.

Too often the educational practitioner expects that the laboratory scientist will produce prescriptions for effective education that can be readily followed. This is not the case. The early physicists, from Isaac Newton on, did not provide prescriptions that engineers designing bridges could follow on a rule-of-thumb basis, but the knowledge they provided made bridge building a much more systematic and effective procedure than it had been in previous centuries. No longer did the bridge designer have to guess where the main stresses in bridges could occur; these could be determined by applying the principles of physics. The physicists provided the engineers with ways of thinking about bridge design and with some general problem-solving techniques. Physics also provided the engineer with a technical language that he could use to describe precisely what happens when a load is applied to a bridge. The bridge builder no longer had to use the vague and fuzzy language of tradition, but was armed with precise ways of describing specifications. Nevertheless, bridge building did not undergo any sudden revolution; the changes in these structures were subtle, more readily noticed by the expert than by the ordinary man.

The impact of a laboratory science of learning has also been slow and subtle, but it has permeated both the curriculum and the entire teaching act. In addition to the kinds of changes noted earlier in this chapter, there has been a steady alteration in the approach taken to educational problems. This is partly because the technical language of the laboratory can be used to describe, with infinitely greater precision than was possible in the past, the nature of the difficulties that are being encountered. Unless one can describe precisely what the problems are, one cannot hope to find solutions to them. Problem identification is always a first step toward progress. Although the lay public is not always impressed by the fact that the problems have been identified, for the public wants nothing short of solutions, there is great progress inherent in being able to identify problems clearly and precisely.

One must readily admit that the development of a science of learning has not produced solutions to many of the most pressing educational problems, though research with implications for education has been moving ahead. Twenty-five years ago medicine had reached the point of establishing that some diseases were due to viruses, but our ability to treat virus infections is still extremely limited. Before anything could be done about virus diseases, the discovery had to be made that virus structures existed. The study of the way in which viruses are produced led to an understanding of how the body manages to cope with virus diseases. This knowledge, in turn, has led to some techniques of prevention and, in a few cases, cure after a virus infection has become established. In the same way, educators and scientists together are slowly identifying the causes of educational failure and the keys to educational success, but new practices that will prevent failure and maximize success are in many cases still far off. Progress in education cannot be measured by changes in school alone; rather one must look at the subtle undercurrents where the new tides of educational ideas are formed.

What Is Learning?

A common definition of learning is that learning occurs when a response *R* shows relatively permanent modification as a result of conditions in the environment sometimes referred to as stimuli or *Ss*. The meanings of the term *stimulus* and the term *response* will have to be sharpened up later in this chapter. For the present, the reader may interpret these terms as they are customarily used in courses in general psychology. Although the emphasis in this definition is on events (the response, the environment) that someone other than the learner can observe, the mechanism of learning lies within the learner and involves changes in the central nervous system. Although the changes involved in learning are internal, the evidence that learning has occurred is found in observing responses, that is to say, in observing the behavior of the learner. One can find out for sure that a child knows how to add fractions by presenting him with a problem involving the addition of fractions and then checking to see whether he can solve it correctly. In such a case one is observing the behavior of that child and deriving from the behavior evidence that he can or cannot add fractions. The psychologist uses the term *acquisition* to refer to the process of acquiring a skill—in this case the addition of fractions.

The psychologist views the term *learning* as embracing a wider range of phenomena than does the layman, who thinks of it largely in terms of school learning. Let us consider an example that illustrates the broad scope of the psychologist's concept of the term. A person stops his car at a traffic light and, a few seconds later, his car is hit in the rear with almost explosive violence by a truck. The person in the car is badly shaken by the impact and is taken to the hospital in a state of shock, but he recovers from the accident. Two weeks later he stops again at the same intersection and a funny thing happens. He turns white, his heart beats wildly, and he breaks out in a cold sweat. During the next year the same thing happens whenever he comes to the place of his original accident. The psychologist would say that he had *learned* all of these responses at the time when his car was hit by the truck. One can learn visceral and emotional responses just as one can learn academic skills. Such learning is a matter of particular interest to clinical psychologists, who often encounter patients who have acquired unwanted emotional responses and wish to learn to gain control over them.

Learning can occur in slow and subtle ways and the learner may be quite unaware that a process of acquisition is in progress. A person who visits Japan for the first time begins by thinking that all Japanese look alike, but as time goes by he becomes more and more capable of differentiating one Japanese from another. The skill he has acquired is referred to as a perceptual skill and the learning involved perceptual learning.

Although the experience of our traveler to Japan is a common one, neither he nor other travelers who have had a similar experience can describe how they learn to differentiate faces in the Orient. However, psychologists engaged in the experimental study of perceptual learning are beginning to understand something about the processes involved.

The definition we have been considering excludes changes produced by fatigue or other transitory conditions, but there are borderline phenomena that may cause one difficulty in deciding whether they should or should not be classified as learning. Let us consider a few of these.

One of the borderline phenomena is known as habituation. A person buys a grandfather clock with a loud tick. The first night he is kept awake by the ticking of the clock. The second night he is less aware of it, and after a few nights he never notices the ticking either by day or by night. He has become habituated. Presumably, this habituation involves a change in the nervous system that blocks the signals from reaching the higher centers. Also, the change is a relatively permanent one, for he can go away on a vacation and, when he returns, will be able to sleep the first night back, and will not have lost his habituation. Habituation falls within the commonly accepted definition of learning, but many psychologists refer to it as habituation rather than as learning. This is a matter of custom rather than of any profound knowledge concerning the difference between habituation and other learning phenomena. Habituation is commonly distinguished from more complex forms of learning by referring to the latter as conditioning, but this, in turn, produces difficulties, for some forms of quite complicated perceptual learning also cannot be classified as conditioning.

A second phenomenon that falls on the borderline of the definition of learning is sensitization. Let us illustrate this phenomenon by considering a dog brought to the laboratory for experimentation. The dog is placed in a harness and an experiment is begun that calls for the dog to make a response every time a faint light goes on, but the dog gives no indication that it is capable of responding to the light at all. The experimenter then gives the dog a strong electric shock, and from that point onward the animal shows responsiveness to the light. The shock has had a sensitizing effect, making the animal more responsive to all stimuli in its environment. The effect may be quite permanent in that when the dog is brought back to the laboratory a year later it may still show the same heightened sensitivity to the light. The sensitization is also likely to be specific to the situation in which it has occurred. The dog will not show the same heightened sensitivity in situations outside the laboratory.

Sensitization falls within the definition of learning given here, although, as in the case of habituation, psychologists typically make a distinction between sensitization and more complex forms of learning.

Transitory modifications of behavior are not generally regarded as representing learning. A person who takes a drink at a party and who becomes highly sociable for the duration of the effect of the alcohol is not considered to have learned sociable behavior. The transitory change in his behavior is explained in terms of the temporary removal of inhibitions that ordinarily interfere with his social life. On the other hand, consider the case of a person who has many sessions with a psychological counselor and who, as a result of the therapy, is able to develop a more satisfactory social life, which he continues to pursue long after therapy ceases. Most psychologists would say that such a person had learned more effective social behavior through his contacts with the counselor. The change in behavior is clearly classified as learning.

Although the last two examples provide a fairly clear distinction between a situation in which there is no learning and one in which learning occurs, many situations cannot be so easily classified. Consider the case of a parent who observes that his child hardly ever opens a book and who decides to correct this situation. He offers his child fifty cents for each book read and tells him that the money will not be given unless he can answer some questions about the book. The scheme works beautifully and during the next two months the child reads ten books, in comparison with zero books during the previous two months. The parent then decides that his child must by now have discovered the inherent rewards of reading, and that he can stop offering him money to read. Accordingly, he stops, but during the next two months the child does not read any books at all. The incentive provided by offering money produced a change in performance, but no permanent change was produced in the child's behavior—as is evident from the results of withdrawing the reward. Some psychologists define learning in such a way that the temporarily changed performance of the child would be classified as learning. Other psychologists, who define learning as it was earlier defined in the chapter, might say that performance had been temporarily changed, but that the child learned from the experiment only that adults sometimes offer rewards and that the same adults are likely to withdraw the rewards arbitrarily. There was certainly no increase in the frequency of reading behavior other than that which was reward-dependent. No permanent change in behavior was evident. Rewards may produce quite transitory or quite permanent changes in behavior depending on the conditions under which they are applied.

Performance is very readily changed by offering money or other rewards, but the production of more permanent changes in behavior is a more difficult matter. In the case of our anecdote, the parent might have done a little better by changing from a condition in which the child was rewarded for every book he read to a condition in which there was only an occasional and unpredictable reward. Even then, one cannot be sure that book reading would have been continued.

Some Basic Elements of a Science of Learning

The physicist limits his observations to certain fundamental characteristics of our very complicated universe. Generally, his observations have to do with mass and space and time. The scientist who studies learning, and attempts to understand it, also limits his observations generally to two main categories, namely, stimuli and responses. These terms were originally derived from the field of physiology, where they have quite precise meanings. A physiologist who has isolated a single nerve fiber may stimulate it with a given electrical charge, the stimulus, and observe the response that occurs in the form of a nerve impulse traveling along the nerve fiber from the point of stimulation. In this case, the stimulus can be described precisely and the characteristics of the response can also be exactly specified. In physiology, stimuli are small, precise, physical events, and the responses are also quite identifiable, but when the same terms, stimuli and responses, are used by the psychologist they generally lack any such precise meaning. Consider the kind of study in which a child watches a film showing an adult engaging in some form of aggression, and the experimenter is interested in determining whether viewing the film will increase the aggressive behavior of the child who views it. Can one reasonably speak of *a* stimulus in such an instance? The picture shown on the screen is immensely complex and in no way comparable with the kind of stimulus used by the physiologist on the nerve fiber. Yet, through custom, the showing of the film would be described as a stimulus, or as a sequence of stimuli.

The complex stimulus of the psychologist and the simple stimulus of the physiologist also differ in another important respect. The physiologist knows exactly how and where the stimulus is being applied. It is being applied to a particular nerve fiber at a particular time and in a particular location. The psychologist showing the film cannot even be sure that it is having any impact on the child at all. Indeed, the child's mind may be wandering in other directions, or his head may be turned away. Although one can use the term stimulus to describe the film shown to the child, it refers only to a general set of circumstances and not to a specific event having specific impact. The example considered is one that involves extreme stimulus complexity. Sometimes the psychologist uses much simpler materials, as when he studies the ability of the child to discriminate the difference in length of two lines; but even in this case the stimulus is much more complex than any used by the physiologists who originated the term. Many psychologists are inclined to believe that the term stimulus is not a very appropriate one in the behavioral sciences, although it is appropriate in physiology where it was first used.

Because stimuli do not generally come in neat packages in the world of daily experience, psychologists often construct simplified stimuli through which they study learning—much as the chemist conducts his experiments with quite pure chemicals in order to overcome the difficulty involved in the fact that naturally occurring chemicals are contaminated with so many unwanted compounds that they do not provide a useful means for studying chemical processes.

Sometimes an attempt is made to measure the characteristics of stimulus materials. For instance, various formulae have been developed for measuring the level of difficulty of children's reading materials. These measures of reading difficulty provide one means of describing the stimulus situation presented by such materials. Whenever materials to be learned are verbal, some attempt is made to measure the degree to which the material includes familiar or unfamiliar words and the complexity of the sentence structure involved. So long as verbal materials are involved the estimation of level of difficulty can be readily made. In studies involving nonverbal materials, however, greater problems are encountered in specifying the characteristics of those materials. In studies of visually presented shapes, one can devise ways of measuring the complexity of the shape if one is dealing with fairly simple figures, but if one were dealing with the ability to remember complex shapes such as are represented by human profiles, then one might have great difficulty in specifying the characteristics of such stimuli.

The present custom in psychological literature is to specify the stimulus situation by the letter *S*. The letter *S*, in itself, is compact, but it is often used to denote quite complex situations. The symbol *S* might better stand for the *situation* confronting the learner rather than a specific *stimulus*, as the latter term is used by the physiologist.

One cannot separate sharply the stimulus presented in a learning experiment from the other conditions prevailing at the time. If one is conducting a study of the factors related to the retention of information about the shape of objects, and shows learners a number of shapes, which they must later try to identify, the length of time that the learner views each shape may be as critical a factor as the characteristics of the shape itself. Also, the context within which the shape is presented may be crucial. A shape presented against a background of other shapes may be more difficult to identify and remember than one presented against a uniform gray background. Other factors to control would be the number of times each shape is viewed, the number of shapes viewed, the time between the presentation of each shape, and whether the time between each presentation of the entire series was of long or short duration. In specifying all of these conditions one may hope to pin down enough factors so that an experiment can be undertaken that some other scientist can reproduce with similar findings in another laboratory.

What often happens is that in designing an experiment one fails to take note of some factor that later studies show to be of substantial significance. When another experimenter then repeats the experiment, he also does not control for this factor, and consequently obtains different results. The author once attempted to reproduce an experiment of another research worker involving the perception of form. The article reporting the previous experiment provided an illustration showing the shapes used and these were meticulously copied, but the results of the experiment were entirely different from those of the original. Lengthy inquiry turned up the fact that the shapes shown in the journal article were about one quarter the size of those used in the original study. The size of the shapes had not been reported because it seemed to be quite a trivial matter, but in psychological experiments apparently trivial factors have an extraordinary way of turning out to be of the greatest significance.

The term *stimulus* represents a broad category of conditions to which the learner is exposed in an experimental study. The term *response* also represents a broad category. If a response is limited to the twitch of a very small muscle, then it is a concise and identifiable happening, but in most psychological experiments it is an aggregate of happenings. Suppose a person engages in learning the German equivalents of twenty English words. After he has repeated the pairs of German and English words three times at a paced rate, he is given the English words one at a time and is asked to write out their German equivalents. The learner sometimes writes out the German words quickly and accurately, but sometimes he is slow and hesitant. A few of the German words are given correctly, but some are slightly distorted. In a few cases he gives one of the German words that appeared, but attaches it to the wrong English word. The response has many significant characteristics. In teaching such a task in a real classroom, the instructor might be interested in several of those characteristics. For example, he would certainly want the student to be able to give the correct German word, but he would also want him to be able to produce the translated word fairly quickly. If the words had been presented through the medium of a tape recorder, the instructor would be interested in determining whether the learner had acquired a correct accent. This might be a very difficult matter to determine with any precision and would be a matter of judgment.

Thus, in a relatively simple learning task, the response to be acquired is complex and has many separate components, some of which are related to one another and some of which are not. The ability to translate a word is almost certainly related to the speed at which this is done. Good translators also tend to be fast translators, but accent may be a more independent characteristic. A person may have complete mastery of a foreign language except for the accent. Another response characteristic is the frequency with which responses occur. In many school situations the teacher is interested in increasing the frequency with which children ask questions. In this case, frequency is the response characteristic with which the teacher is concerned. A teacher may also want to reduce the frequency of responses that are disruptive of learning. Some psychologists have been particularly interested in the latter problem and numerous studies provide simple techniques for reducing the frequency with which pupils aggress against other pupils, the frequency of unnecessary physical movement around the classroom, and the frequency of casual conversation.

There are also other subtle response characteristics that have to be recognized in the planning of any school program. These have often been the target of experimental investigation. Responses also have to be learned in such a way that they can be readily transferred to new situations. The child who learns to say "is not" in school rather than "ain't" has acquired a trivial learning if he uses the correct form only in the school setting. He has to have learned the response so that it will be performed in other settings. This has long been recognized as a problem by speech correction specialists, who have observed that children may often speak well when they are in speech therapy sessions, but that they revert to their older habits as soon as they leave the room. The context of behavior often triggers correct or incorrect behavior. The characteristic of the response considered here is that of transferability to new situations.

Another subtle characteristic of learned responses that is of the utmost significance is resistance to forgetting. Teachers want to produce learning that will be as permanent as possible, but they do not always arrange learning conditions to ensure that this goal is achieved. If the student crams before exams and learns little at other times, the learning conditions are not conducive to good retention. From performance on tests one can say little about the permanence of what is learning. The latter has to be studied through measuring retention after a lapse of time. Although fairly good techniques have been developed for ensuring that what is learned will be learned relatively permanently, these techniques are not typically applied in education, largely because of a lack of interest in this variable.

The point has been made that the psychology of learning has borrowed many of its basic terms from physiology, but there are some contemporary psychologists who find the language of physiology clumsy for their purpose and prefer to use a language more closely associated with computers and information theory. These psychologists are more likely to refer to *inputs* than to *stimuli,* and to *outputs* than to *responses.* They also talk of the *storage* and *retrieval* of information rather than the long-used terms of *retention* and *recall.* Some of the later discussion in this book, which deals with these topics, will bring the reader into contact with this newer language, but the earlier chapters of the book, which handle simpler learning processes, will be developed in terms of the more traditional language of experimental psychology. It may well be that when psychology finds the language best suited to its purpose, that language may not be the one it has taken over from physiology.

Some Basic Categories of Learning

Psychologists have long been concerned with identifying some basic, elementary, and simple forms of learning. The hope has long been embraced that the complex forms of learning engaged in by all human beings could be considered to be a compounding of the basic forms of learning, which involve quite simple processes. Psychology is at a stage at which it has discovered some of these elementary learning processes and can demonstrate them in the laboratory to anyone who wants to witness them. The psychologists can also demonstrate that these processes play a significant part in the lives of both human and nonhuman learners, but he has been much less successful at demonstrating that all learning involves these processes and only these processes. Some psychologists have dedicated much of their lives to producing credible arguments that all complex forms of learning are merely combinations of more fundamental forms, but these arguments, though credible, are a far cry from proof. The fundamental forms of learning considered in the remainder of this chapter are presented because they have significance in molding our lives, but no claim is made that they represent a comprehensive inventory of all learning processes.

There is far from complete agreement concerning the processes that should be regarded as the fundamental categories of learning. Of the four basic processes considered here, the first two are found in most recent classification systems. Let us first consider these two categories together. In the one category a new stimulus comes to produce a response that it did not previously initiate. In the other category, a subject makes a response that, in turn, produces a new stimulus situation. One can think of these learning situations rather loosely as learning involving $S \rightarrow R$ in the first case and $R \rightarrow S$ learning in the second. The arrow can be replaced by the words *leads to*, and thus one can say that *S leads to R* or that *R leads to S*. The reader must note that there are also two other possible combinations of *S* and *R* that could form categories in such a system, namely $R \rightarrow R$ and $S \rightarrow S$. Let us now consider the kinds of phenomena that fall into these four categories.

Learning Involving New S → R Relationships

Classical conditioning experiments reflect this category of learning. Russian physiologists, who first initiated systematic research in this area, typically focused their research on the learning of some familiar response such as salivation, which can be measured easily and quantitatively in terms of the number of drops of saliva produced, or the response involved in the withdrawal of a limb from a noxious stimulus, a response that can be measured in terms of speed of withdrawal. In a typical Pavlovian experiment a dog learns to salivate in the presence of a new stimulus, such as a light or a bell or a tone, which ordinarily does not make a dog salivate. Salivation is produced by food, but if a bell is sounded each time food is presented, the dog eventually comes to salivate whenever the bell sounds. The animal learns the response of salivation to the presence of the stimulus bell, and thus a stimulus that did not trigger the particular response before the experiment began comes to trigger it through the conditioning procedure involved in the experiment.

The essential feature of this kind of learning is that a stimulus occurs in the presence of a response that it does not ordinarily elicit and acquires the property of eliciting the response. Of particular interest is the fact that responses, such as salivation, that are not ordinarily considered to be under voluntary control can be conditioned. The classical conditioning case of learning, or the classical conditioning paradigm, as it is called, is probably a very significant case of learning. Consider the case previously cited of the person involved in an automobile accident. At the time of the accident the person experiences intense fear involving many reflexes including those of the viscera, which produce that well-known sinking feeling in the stomach. Many months later, when that same person is driving past the corner where the accident occurred, he experiences exactly the same sinking feeling in the stomach. What has happened is that the stomach and intestinal responses occurring at the time of the accident became conditioned to the stimuli present at that time. Later, when the person was again exposed to these stimuli, they again triggered the responses. At the time of involvement in the accident the person was conditioned to produce these responses in the presence of these stimuli. Figure 1 shows equipment used to study such problems.

Although classically conditioned emotional responses may be a plague in the life of civilized man, such responses may have been immensely valuable when man was living in a primitive state. Consider, for example, a man living in a primitive society who goes on a hunting expedition and encounters a new animal that has migrated from another region. Our primitive man attempts to capture the animal but discovers that it has extraordinary strength. In the process, he has strong emotional reactions that help his body perform at the peak of strength and

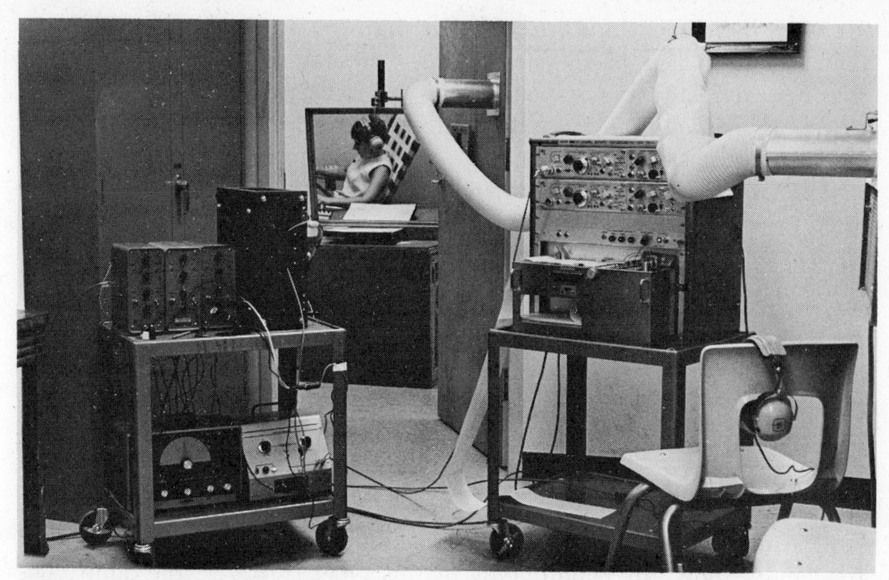

Figure 1. Apparatus used for classical conditioning of emotional responses. The person whose responses are being conditioned is isolated in the inner air-conditioned room. The experimenter operates the equipment in the foreground and observes the subject through a one-way screen in the door, which is closed during the running of an experiment.

perhaps save his life. He also experiences the bodily responses associated with fear. All of these responses become conditioned to the sight of the new species of animal. Several days later, our same primitive man is out again on a hunting expedition and sees the same animal again. Immediately, emotional responses associated with combat and fear are triggered in his system. These prepare him for combat with the creature or for rapid flight—an avoidance response that may this time save his life. These classically conditioned responses were of great survival value to primitive man, though they are a plague to man living in a civilized community. Modern man does not have to respond to most situations with gut reactions and, indeed, such reactions are a disadvantage in that they often interfere with the ability to think calmly about a situation.

In most studies of the classical conditioning type, the scientist must use a response that he can readily elicit. For this reason a reflex is commonly employed. One can very readily elicit a response such as salivation in any animal, including man. The experimenter also has no difficulty in eliciting a response such as the raising of a leg when a shock is applied to the floor on which the foot rests. Such situations have an advantage in that the experimenter can be sure of eliciting the response that he wishes to condition to a new stimulus.

Many psychologists have assumed that any stimulus that occurs at the same time as a particular response acquires some capacity to elicit that response, and the response does not have to be a reflex for it to be conditioned to a new stimulus. Although American psychologists have confined their studies of classical conditioning to studies of eliciting reflexes with new stimuli, Russian psychologists have long been interested in conditioning other forms of response (see Cole and Maltzman, 1969). One technique for doing this is for the child involved in the experiment to first learn to press a key whenever a light goes on. This is accomplished by giving the child instructions to do so. Then another stimulus such as a buzzer, is introduced that always precedes the light. After a few trials involving both the buzzer and the light, the buzzer is sounded alone and the child presses the key. The demonstration suggests that the essential condition for a new stimulus to acquire the property of eliciting a response is for it to occur at about the time when the response is made, and that the response does not have to be a reflex. This kind of conditioning is particularly striking in very young children, but few adults show any conditioning of this type. However, the adult does show classical conditioning of many reflexes, notably those reflexes that are described as emotional responses.

Because learning of the $S \rightarrow R$ type has typically been studied through situations involving reflexes, the learning phenomenon is commonly referred to as the conditioned reflex. Reflexes are innate forms of behavior triggered by a particular stimulus, which is referred to as the unconditioned stimulus. The new stimulus that comes to trigger the response, after learning, is referred to as the conditioned stimulus.

Although one may speak of classical conditioning as though it were a simple phenomenon, it is in fact quite complex. It is a fairly clear-cut form of learning in many laboratory animals and clean experiments can be undertaken with it. When one speaks of a clean experiment in this area one means an experiment in which the results show clear evidences of learning and which can be reproduced, with the same results, in another laboratory. Great care has to be taken in carrying out such experiments if they are to provide clean results. Pavlov found in the early days of his studies that an animal might not learn a conditioned response if some slight distraction were accidentally introduced, such as the sound of footsteps outside the laboratory.

Human learning has sometimes been studied through the conditioned reflex paradigm. The late Kenneth Spence, for example, conducted most of his research on human learning through the study of the conditioned eye-blink response. The advantage of studying learning in such a simple situation is that the important factors related to learning can be readily measured and controlled. One can measure the strength of the puff of air that produces the eye blink. One can measure the delay between the puff-of-air stimulus and the eye-blink response, and one can measure the amplitude and strength of the eye blink. Nevertheless, when the classical conditioning paradigm is applied to human subjects, other factors tend to be introduced which make the phenomenon more complicated than it is in the case of laboratory animals, and also more variable from person to person. This was brought home to the author some time ago when he was interested in conditioning to the sound of a tone, a response that takes place when a person is administered an electric shock. One result of brief electric shock is a response known as the galvanic skin response, which is a marked change in the electrical conductivity of the skin of the hand. When an electric shock is given, and a tone is sounded simultaneously, the galvanic skin response may become conditioned to the tone. In one such experiment several of the students who were the subjects showed no conditioning of the response to the tone. When they were questioned after the experimental session, they volunteered the information that they had seen no connection between the tone and the electric shock and did not realize that the tone had anything to do with the experiment. The conditioning of the galvanic skin response obviously called for something more than the mere response to the shock and the mere response to the tone. The same experiment also demonstrated some other phenomena indicating the complexity of classical conditioning in human subjects. After the conditioning procedure had been followed, most subjects showed well-established responses to the sound of the tone, but the conditioned response would fail to appear on trials on which the subject was told that he definitely would not receive an electric shock. In other words, if the subject did not expect the tone to be followed by a shock, then he showed no galvanic skin response. Many classically conditioned responses can be made to appear or not to appear depending upon what the experimenter tells the person involved.

The classical conditioning paradigm for experimentation with learning has involved many different responses. Some of these, such as changes in heart rate, or changes in respiration, are of obvious significance, but some such as the knee-jerk reflex or the eyelid reflex do not have the same evident importance for daily living. However, the assumption is commonly made that what is learned about the learning process through the study of one reflex will be similar to what can be learned through the study of conditioning another reflex. Research has generally given support to this assumption, although there are some exceptions. For example, studies of the response of the pupil of the eye to light, known as the pupillary reflex, have shown it to be an extraordinarily difficult reflex on which to produce conditioning, a finding that suggests that in order for conditioning or learning to take place the response involved must be under at least indirect control from the higher centers of the brain. The pupillary reflex does not seem to be under such control.

Most psychologists would take the position that many typical unwanted emotional responses have been acquired through classical conditioning in the laboratory of life. Emotional responses are, of course, basically unlearned responses that have value to living organisms. An animal that is frightened shows an increase in blood pressure, a raised blood-sugar level, rapid breathing, and a high pulse rate. All of these emotional responses are of value in placing the body in a state where great physical effort can be exerted either to provide a defense or to lead to an escape. The animal displaying these responses can fight with greater vigor or flee more effectively and rapidly than a relaxed animal.

Man shows emotional responses that are very similar to those shown by higher animals, but he also manifests many inappropriate emotional responses that can plague his life and prevent him from being an effective member of society. For example, although man has reason to be fearful on many occasions, there are also occasions in the lives of most of us when fear responses occur even though we know that the situation should not really be feared. One person experiences fear responses when he has to pass close to a deep lake or river. He knows that these responses are irrational and that he has them because as a boy he nearly drowned. The psychologist would say that during the drowning episode, when he had every reason to respond with the deepest fear, his emotional responses related to fear became conditioned to the stimuli associated with the presence of deep water. Later, when he found himself near to a body of water, the fear responses would become immediately triggered. In this way an irrational and unreasonable emotional response would have been acquired through a mechanism closely similar to that of classical conditioning. The assumption is that most irrational and inappropriate emotional responses are acquired through classical conditioning in naturally occurring situations. The emotional responses first occur on some appropriate occasion, but they subsequently occur also in the presence of other irrelevant stimuli. Later these irrelevant stimuli show the property of eliciting the emotional responses with which they have become associated.

If psychologists are correct in assuming that many of the unwanted emotional responses are acquired through classical conditioning, then the study of this type of learning may be expected to lead to the discovery of ways of getting rid of these responses. Because much of the work of psychiatrists and clinical psychologists is occupied with helping patients rid themselves of bothersome emotional responses, the study of classical conditioning can be considered to be an approach through which some parts of psychotherapy can be given a scientific foundation. Indeed, a type of therapy known as desensitization is based largely on what has been discovered in the laboratory about classical conditioning.

Learning Involving New R → S Relationships

In this learning condition the human or animal subject learns to make a response that produces events or states of affairs of a kind that are much sought after by the organism. Thus, a hungry rat can learn to press a bar which, in turn, delivers a small amount of food into a trough, and a hungry pigeon can learn to peck a small white button on the wall which, in turn, brings the result of a food trough being raised into a position that permits the pigeon to retrieve some grain from it. Although one can designate this type of learning in a simple form as *R* → *S* learning, the process is more complex than this simple designation would indicate.

When the response of the hungry rat has been learned, one can say that the response has been brought under the control of the prevailing conditions, or that it is under stimulus control, that is to say, the animal is very likely to make these responses under these conditions. Classes of responses that are under stimulus control are referred to by Skinner (1938) as *operants*. Sometimes the behavior involved is referred to as *instrumental behavior*. This term introduces an additional concept, namely, that the behavior involved is instrumental in producing a particular state of affairs—in this case a situation involving food. The implication is that the behavior is the instrument through which a highly preferred situation is produced. An operant may also be instrumental in avoiding particular kinds of situations collectively described as aversive.

The learning of operants may take place along two quite distinct lines. Place a rat in a box which contains only a bar and a trough into which pellets of food can be delivered. The rat will explore the box and eventually place its front feet up on the bar in such a way that the bar is pressed down. The rat eventually learns to press the bar down and thus to obtain food, and although at the beginning of the training session this is a rather infrequent form of behavior, once the animal is well trained, bar pressing becomes a very frequent form of behavior. The animal learns to press the bar to obtain delivery of food. Learning involves a change in the frequency with which the animal presses the bar. In technical terms one would say that learning produces a change in response probability, that is to say a change in the frequency with which a response may be expected to occur. Figure 2 shows laboratory equipment used in studying such problems.

Similar kinds of increases in response frequency as a result of its consequences can be observed early in the life of the human infant. Give a hungry baby a few drops of milk every time he kicks a leg, and leg kicking shows an increased frequency of occurrence. The kick of the leg has become an operant. Give a child ten extra points every time his

Figure 2. Equipment developed for recording behavior related to discrimination learning. The subject of the experiment, human or subhuman, is located in a soundproof area separate from the main recording equipment. (Photograph supplied by courtesy of BRS-Foringer, the manufacturer of the equipment.)

homework is neat and clean, and neat and clean homework is more likely to occur.

Sometimes instrumental learning involves far more than a change in the frequency of occurrence of a response. One may train a rat to obtain food by pulling a string suspended from the ceiling of the cage. Although a rat may occasionally push down a bar placed in his environment, rats do not pull pieces of string suspended from the ceiling. Rats may sniff the string, but one might wait through the lifetime of a rat and it would never pull a piece of string. Sometimes in instrumental learning an animal, such as a rat, can be trained in gradual steps to perform such a fundamentally new act as that of pulling the string and thereby obtaining the delivery of food. In such a case the response probability is initially at zero, for the animal does not make the response at all. Training produces a mode of response that did not occur previously.

Parallel cases of learning in young children are easy to find. When an infant is first given a spoon, he clenches the handle of the spoon so that the spoon is held upright and can retain no food. One may help the child by putting the spoon into the food, but the food falls off the spoon as soon as it is left in his unguided hand and the reinforcement of receiving food in the mouth through his own activity does not take place. A better procedure is to give the infant a baby spoon with the handle so bent that, when he naturally grips the spoon, the spoon remains horizontal and the food stays on it. He is then readily able to bring food from the plate to his mouth. One can then slowly adjust the shape of the handle of the spoon until he learns to use a normal spoon. A thoughtful arrangement of the learning conditions permits the child to acquire this important instrumental response.

Changes in behavior produced through instrumental learning are referred to as the *shaping of behavior,* a term introduced by B. F. Skinner some years ago and now widely used. It is applied both to the case in which a response is increased or reduced in frequency and also to the case in which a fundamentally new response is learned. Those who apply what is known about the shaping of behavior to practical situations are often said to be engaged in *behavior modification,* though this is a term applied to any technique which has established effectiveness in changing behavior.

Instrumental learning must be considered to be of some significance in the acquisition of human behavior. Skinner (1957) has taken the extreme position that most significant adult behavior and all verbal is a form of instrumental behavior, but only a few psychologists today would agree with him in this respect.

Within this category fall components of the learnings commonly encountered in schools, though any school task one can name also has components from the other categories of learning considered here, and perhaps also aspects of learning not well described by the basic categories. Thus, children in the first grade in school have to learn to make responses to printed words that will bring praise from the teacher or that will provide them with some piece of information they need to have. The acquisition of appropriate new responses in school often produces the highly sought after state of affairs known as good grades, which, in turn, result in social approval. Teachers generally attempt to control the responses that will or will not be acquired by the pupils. The teacher does this by dispensing sought-after situations such as good grades, praise, and special privileges.

Techniques for the experimental study of what we have called here $R \rightarrow S$ learning are numerous. The situation S, resulting from the instrumental behavior R, has to be some kind of preferred situation, that is to say, a situation that the learner seeks out and chooses in preference to other situations. In the case of preschool children, the preferred situations in experiments related to this kind of learning have commonly involved the delivery of such choice consumables as an *M & M* candy or a small marshmallow. Sometimes the situation for these young children has involved praise, and occasionally opportunity to play with some special toy.

Certain important differences must be pointed out between $S \rightarrow R$ learning and $R \rightarrow S$ learning. In the one case learning begins with a response readily produced in the experimental situation, but in the other case the experimenter is interested in a response that is either very infrequent or nonoccurring. For this reason it has commonly been said that classical conditioning learning involves only the learning of a new stimulus that comes to trigger old behavior, while in instrumental learning a new response is learned. For this reason, the one is commonly called stimulus learning and the other is called response learning. In the one a new significance becomes attached to a stimulus, and in the other a new response acquires significance or an old response acquires new instrumental value. The terms stimulus learning and response learning are convenient because they focus on important central characteristics of what is learned.

Although one can make clear distinctions on paper between $S \rightarrow R$ learning and $R \rightarrow S$ learning, most significant learning involves both categories. Even when the scientist tries to produce pure forms of one or the other kinds of learning in the laboratory, both kinds of processes are generally involved. Liu (1964) has pointed out that when a rat performs the instrumental response of running through a maze to reach the food in the goal compartment, many reflexes related to eating take place along the way and these become conditioned to the stimuli provided by the maze. Thus, while the rat is learning the instrumental response of reaching the food, it is also acquiring classically conditioned responses to the maze. When a rat learns to press a bar to deliver a food pellet, the bar pressing activity comes to trigger all kinds of reflexes related to the intake and digestion of food and these become classically conditioned to the stimuli provided by the box, bar, and food-delivery mechanism. At the human level the child may learn to place a coin in a slot machine to obtain delivery of a candy bar, but soon the mere sight of the coin-operated machine will produce the reflex of salivation, showing that not only did instrumental learning take place but, in addition, the classical conditioning of the salivary reflex also took place at the same time. When a business executive makes an important decision, with either damaging or gratifying consequences, the emotional responses that accompany the decision-making process become conditioned to many features of the decision-making situation. A case of pure instrumental conditioning hardly seems to exist, and pure cases of classical conditioning are difficult or impossible to find. A person shows an eye-blink reflex if a slight puff of air strikes the eyeball and this response has been used in many laboratory studies of classical conditioning in humans, but in such experiments results are often confused by the voluntary eye-blinks of subjects who try to anticipate the occurrence of the puff of air. These anticipatory responses must be considered to be instrumental responses. Incidentally, the puff of air does not have to be noxious to produce the normal reflex or to provide a situation in which conditioning will readily take place. Indeed, conditioning of the response to a light or tone takes place most readily with very mild puffs of air that are no stronger than those of a mild breeze on a pleasant day.

Learning Involving New R → R Relationships

This category of learning pertains to the learning of chains of responses that are rapidly run off, as when a child learns to write a word or whistle a melody. A distinction must be made between making a slow sequence of responses in which the performance of one act provides the stimuli that initiate the performance of the next act in the sequence, and chains of acts that are run off too rapidly for any one response to produce new stimuli that set off the next response. An example of the former is knot tying. In the early stages of learning to tie a knot each stage of tying the knot is followed by a pause, the situation is examined by the person undertaking the task, and then the next step is initiated. After very extensive practice, the knot-tying task may take place at great speed and the dependence of the process on chains of responses in which each component response produces stimuli that initiate new responses becomes much less obvious. In the case of motor skills that are undertaken at great speed, as in the case of playing a fast passage on a musical instrument, it is physically impossible for there to be such a simple chain of stimuli and responses for, as Hebb (1958) long ago pointed out, there would not be time enough for each response to produce stimuli that would initiate the next response. Remember that a musician may play notes at rates of up to five hundred per minute, and under such conditions the stimuli provided by the playing of one note would not have time to set off the next response. The alternative explanation is that the musician's brain sends out a sequence of correct signals to the muscles and that the total performance is monitored only in a very general way. The brain seems capable of running off whole sequences of commands to the muscles without waiting to see what happens to each. This phenomenon becomes particularly evident when one studies motor skills, as Keele (1969) has shown. Even subhuman brains, very remote from man in the evolutionary scale, seem capable of doing this. Consider the flapping of the wings of the hummingbird, which may occur as fast as ninety times per second. In order for this to happen, the brain of the bird would have to emit the proper sequence of commands to the muscles at this enormous speed.

Thus, learning to emit rapid sequences of responses seems to be somewhat different from learning to produce the component responses, or learning to make each response in a sequence in which each component response is triggered by the previous response. Learning, called here $R \rightarrow R$ learning, refers to the production of sequences of responses of the former rather than the latter kind.

Learning Involving New $S \rightarrow S$ Relationships

One way of demonstrating this category of learning is to undertake an experiment involving three stages. In the first step, two stimuli, such as a light and a tone, are presented together a large number of times. Then a response is conditioned to one of these stimuli. In the third step the other stimulus is presented and is found to elicit the conditioned response in the same way as the stimulus to which it was originally conditioned. If a dog were first exposed to the light and the tone for, say, one hundred trials, and the dog were then conditioned to salivate in the presence of the tone, then, later, the light would also be found to have the property of eliciting salivation. This phenomenon is known as sensory preconditioning. An eye blink conditioned in a human subject to occur when a tone is sounded will also be triggered by a light if the subject has been exposed to a pairing of the light and the tone prior to the experiment. In common language, one would say that the tone and the light had become associated. The essential condition for this kind of learning is that the two stimuli enter the perceptual system at the same time. The learning involved is generally described as perceptual learning in order to distinguish it from learning centered on the formation of new responses. This kind of associative learning represents only one form of learning in the perceptual category and there are others which will be considered in the chapter on perception.

There has long been dispute concerning what learning should be considered to belong in this category and what learning should not. Pure cases cannot be found. For example, learning the names of different trees would be considered by most psychologists to be primarily a perceptual task involving the identification of the significant characteristics of each tree and the association of the cluster of characteristics that identify a tree with the corresponding name. Nevertheless, there are some psychologists who would prefer to argue that this learning should be placed primarily in the $S \rightarrow R$ class, in that the person learns to say a particular name when he encounters a particular tree. Although the latter is a common outcome of such learning, there are strong reasons for believing that an individual can learn to associate the appearance of a tree with the sound of the name of the tree or with the printed name of the tree without ever saying the name to himself through slight movements of his vocal cords. We do know that such learning can take place after the muscles involved in speech have been paralyzed—a fact that gives strong support to the idea that the learning involved is essentially perceptual and in the $S \rightarrow S$ category.

The learning discussed in the $S \rightarrow S$ category represents perceptual learning at a very simple level. More complex perceptual learning involves not just the associating together of two items of information, but such complex matters as the extracting of information from a very complex environment, the organizing of information, and the systematic storing of information in memory. Although there is ample evidence that a simple associative type of learning takes place and plays a significant role in the development of the individual, this does not mean that this is the only important perceptual operation involved in learning. Other perceptual learning processes can be demonstrated and there is considerable doubt whether these can be reduced to this category or to the other categories of learning discussed here.

The Significance of the Classification System

Our purpose in presenting a classification of learning activities is not just to show that the writer has an orderly mind and that all these activities can be neatly packaged into four convenient parcels. The categories have considerable significance, in that the conditions that produce the most effective learning in one of these categories are different from the conditions that produce the most effective learning in the other categories. Because a major responsibility of the teacher is that of arranging appropriate conditions so that effective learning will occur, the teacher must also have some understanding of the category or categories of learning involved in the particular tasks that the pupils have to master, so that appropriate conditions for the learning of the tasks can be arranged. Most tasks that pupils have to master have components involving complex combinations of the categories that have been discussed, and the provision of efficient learning conditions requires that many factors have to be taken into account. The next chapter focuses primarily on the first two of the categories. The chapter on perceptual learning focuses primarily on the third category, and the chapter on motor skill learning expands on the fourth category, though emphasizing that motor skills also have components from the other categories.

Mediating Conditions Related to Learning

The classification of learning phenomena considered up to this point has been based largely on observable conditions related to learning, namely, stimuli and responses. Other events, however, which are less accessible to observation, also happen during the course of learning. Pavlov was one of the first to recognize that although learning in his laboratory animals could be well described in terms of the stimuli to which they were exposed and the changes in the responses made, human learning also appeared to involve internal events that were much more difficult to control. Pavlov believed that learning in the human involved, in addition to the familiar mechanism of classical conditioning, another mechanism which he termed the *second signaling system*. This was primarily speech, and included internal speech. Modern technical literature related to learning does not generally refer to the second signaling system, but it does make frequent reference to *mediating processes* in learning. The term *mediating* is derived from the fact that these important events happen between the arrival of the stimulus and the output of the response and can be said to mediate between the stimulus and the response. These mediating responses are particularly evident in human learning and become more evident as the growing individual leaves early childhood and enters the elementary school. Let us consider a very simple type of experiment that illustrates the growing role of mediating process as the human learner matures.

Reese (1968) has summarized numerous experiments in which children, and also various species of animals, have been presented with the problem of choosing between two shapes, such as a square and a triangle. If they press the button below the square, then they are right, and receive an *M & M* candy or a token. If they press the button below the triangle, they are wrong and receive nothing. The problem can be elaborated in various ways to make learning more difficult, but let us consider it in its simplest form. After the child has thoroughly learned that the square is the correct shape to which to respond, the rules are switched but without the child being told. The switch in rules changes conditions so that the triangle now becomes the correct shape and the square becomes the wrong one. When this switch takes place, the very young children have difficulty in learning the new response. They behave as though they must first learn to stop responding to the square and then learn to respond to the triangle. The older children of elementary school age behave quite differently. They quickly stop responding to the square, try responding to the triangle and, as soon as they find that the triangle is now correct, continue to respond to it consistently. The slow change in response of the young children when the conditions are switched is very much like the behavior of lower animals in a similar situation. The quick change in the behavior of the older children when conditions are switched is something entirely different.

In the type of experiment involving a reversal of stimulus-response relationships, the older children are able to solve the new problem quickly because they have internal processes that permit them to take a short cut to the solution. They do not have to go on pressing the button below the square, which produces no results, for a long period of time to know that something has been changed. They can formulate alternative courses of action, such as trying the button below the triangle, and they can then check to see whether the alternative form of behavior produces results. They can concoct within themselves strategies for taking care of the new set of circumstances and can then see how these strategies work. These internal events are generally referred to as mediating processes.

The internal processes related to learning, that is to say the mediating processes, cannot be observed directly; they have to be inferred from data. In the case of the type of study just described, one can reasonably infer from the performance of the older children that they are able to solve the problem more rapidly than the younger children because they are able to formulate within themselves a strategy for coping with the changed conditions that occur when the experimenter switches the rules. Often the mediating processes are verbal and involve what is commonly called talking to oneself.

A subject in a laboratory experiment who is learning to associate the word *tree* with the word *house* may say to himself, "The tree grows by the house." Although the experimenter may be unable to observe this inner verbalization directly, he may find that he can explain some differences in the learning of different subjects in terms of the extent to which they later report that they engage in such mediating processes linking up pairs of words. In such cases, subjects can be helpful in suggesting the kind of mediating process that may be operating. In other tasks, the experimenter himself may have to conjecture what the mediating processes are. First let us consider a common experience that illustrates this point. A person faced with a major problem during his work day may make every effort to solve it but may achieve no success. When he arrives home in the evening, he turns his attention to other matters. There, some hours later, while he is working on a hobby, the solution to the problem suddenly comes to him. Presumably, the solution did not come out of a vacuum but was a result of ongoing mediating processes of which he was not aware.

Now let us consider an example of hidden mediating processes that can be demonstrated only in the laboratory. A whole series of findings reviewed by Neisser (1967) show that when individuals are asked to remember sets of individual letters presented on a screen, and to recall the letters later, those incorrectly recalled tend to be similar in sound to the right letters rather than similar in form. If the letter presented were *E*, it would be more likely to be incorrectly recalled as *D*, which is similar in sound, than incorrectly recalled as *F*, which is similar in form. This finding suggests that when letters are seen and memorized, they are converted into an auditory representation of the letter, but this is a conjecture requiring further substantiation. Another series of studies points to a similar conclusion, for it has been shown that when a person memorizes a set of letters, and then is given a second set to confuse his memory of the first, the confusion is greatest if the letters are similar sounding to the ones in the original list and least when they are similar in appearance. More recent work by Corcoran (1967) also points in the same direction. Corcoran asked subjects to cross out each letter *e* in a page of print and found that when subjects missed one, there was a marked tendency for it to be a silent *e*. The various items of evidence all converge on the same suggestion, namely, that when individuals have to learn or recognize letters, the visual letters are converted (recoded) into an auditory form before they are either recognized or stored in memory. In other words, a mediating process takes place involving the recoding of the visual information into an auditory form. Although the experimenter cannot observe this recoding directly, he infers that this mediating process occurs.

The mediating responses become modified by the consequences of behavior. When behavior results in the achievement of a goal, the mediating responses that led to that behavior are likely to take priority in similar situations over the other mediating responses that were not successful. Some special mediating processes are referred to as perceptual processes. These involve the intake of information through the senses and the interpretation of the information at the higher levels of the nervous system.

Much learning that occurs in schools involves a modification of the mediating processes and the development of new mediating processes. A person presented with a novel problem involving arithmetic may sit in silence for ten minutes until he produces the answer. A long sequence of mediating responses occurs, which culminates in the discovery and announcement of the solution. When similar problems are then given to the same individual, he gives the answer to each with increasing rapidity. Internal processes that are successful tend to be retained, and those that are unsuccessful tend to be eliminated. The mediating mechanisms also draw on the reservoir of past experience that may function in the solution of the problem.

In learning long division, the child brings to the process previously learned skill in the addition and subtraction of single digit numbers and also multiplication skills. These skills can be undertaken effectively only insofar as they can be undertaken in the pupil's head. While the teacher says that the pupil has learned to perform these basic arithmetical processes in his head, the psychologist says that the pupil has learned mediating processes that permit him to perform the arithmetical operations.

Sometimes measurements may be made of the extent to which the pupil can undertake particular mediating processes, as when a teacher finds out the extent to which a pupil can divide numbers, one into another, in his head.

The conditions that exist before the pupil enters a particular learning situation and that influence his rate of learning are sometimes referred to as antecedent conditions, in order to distinguish them from the conditions existing at the time when learning occurs. Antecedent conditions produce characteristics internal to the learner which permit him to perform particular mediating processes.

Let us add at this point another term to the reader's vocabulary. When measurement is made of some internal condition that influences behavior, the psychologist says that he is measuring an *intervening variable*. The teacher who measures the extent to which the pupil can perform in his head some of the basic arithmetical operations needed to perform long division, is said to be measuring one of the intervening variables involved in long division. The variable is one that intervenes between the presentation of a long-division problem to the student and his finding of a solution.

Many of the commonly measured intervening variables related to human learning are related to mediating processes. Most aptitude tests represent attempts to measure some of the mediating processes involved in particular types of school learning, but the term is also used to cover a wider range of internal conditions than are included in the category of mediating processes. Measures of motives are also measures of intervening variables, for motives represent conditions that are internal to the learner and are not directly observable.

Very great scientific difficulties are encountered in disentangling the effect of numerous antecedent conditions on learning, partly because the conditions interact in complex ways to produce learner characteristics. For half a century scientists attempted to find out the extent to which adult intelligence, as measured by intelligence test scores, could be attributed to genetic and environmental conditions, but this turned out to be an impossible task to accomplish because the two classes of antecedent conditions are inextricably interwoven. A portion of the difficulty in handling this problem derives from the fact that one is limited in the extent to which he can experiment with human subjects. Often one cannot deprive a group of children of a particular condition in order to determine whether deprivation is associated with depressed ability to learn certain skills, because such deprivation might permanently harm the child. The best one can do is to search for a group of children who have been thus deprived by an accident of fate. Then the problem arises that such children have generally also been deprived of other conditions that may be associated with effective learning. For this reason, the experimenter often has to turn to the study of animals which can be deprived of various sources of stimulation in the environment. Then, of course, ensues the problem of whether one is justified in generalizing the results to man.

Organizing the Results of Research on Learning and Theorizing

The discussion of mediating processes brings out the point that the psychologist sometimes has to assume that hidden conditions are influencing learning. Motivation is one such hidden condition, for one never observes a motive directly, but only its consequences. A word such as *motivation* is a *theoretical term*. This means that it refers to conditions that cannot be directly observed. Theoretical terms are contrasted with *empirical terms,* which refer to directly observable phenomena. Words such as *stimulus* and *response* are empirical terms, for both stimuli and responses are publicly observable for all to see.

Physicists and chemists have long used theoretical terms successfully in developing their sciences, and psychologists have hoped that they could do the same. The chemist introduced the concept of an atom as a theoretical idea in order to explain his data long before there was any direct evidence of the existence of atoms. J. J. Thomson concluded that the only way to make sense out of his data on cathode rays was to introduce the concept of an electron, a subatomic particle that could not be demonstrated to exist by any direct means. When the concept of an atom and the concept of an electron were first introduced, they were theoretical terms. Later, X-ray photography made it possible to photograph both atoms and atomic structure and the atom ceased to be a theoretical term and instead referred to an observable reality. Today the term *atom* would be described as an empirical term. The electron has also acquired a reality that it did not have when Thomson first introduced the term. The electron cannot be observed directly nor photographed, but the path of an electron can be observed in a cloud chamber and the overall evidence is overwhelming for the existence of such subatomic particles. The valuable theoretical ideas of the scientist slowly become realities if initially they were well chosen.

Psychologists also introduce theoretical terms referring to events that are not directly and publicly observable, but these days they do this with great caution, because past generations found themselves bogged down in a morass of such terms that produced confusion rather than clarification. The theoretical terms of the chemist generally refer to hidden events within the chemical reactions he studies. The theoretical terms of the psychologist who studies learning refer to hidden events within the learner.

A few psychologists, notably B. F. Skinner, have taken the position that the study of learning should involve, at this stage, a language closely tied to data and that the time is not yet ripe for introducing theoretical terms. They say, "Stick with the observables and do not speculate about that which cannot be directly observed by independent observers." These psychologists rightly point out that psychology has had a long history of unproductive and often grandiose speculations about conditions underlying observed behavior, and that success came to the research psychologist when he learned that he had to keep close to his data and avoid theoretical speculation. Coining such theoretical concepts as life instincts, death instincts, libidos, and inferiority complexes represented a useless form of play with theoretical terms. A disciplined scientific endeavor has had to learn to avoid the wild creation of new concepts that lack an adequate foundation. Nevertheless, most modern psychologists would take the position that a few theoretical terms, cautiously introduced, may be of value at this time, particularly if many different lines of research all suggest that these theoretical ideas can be justified. The mistake of psychologists of the past was not in introducing theoretical terms, but in introducing them recklessly and without adequate data to justify their use. Some theoretical terms are used in the remainder of the book but, it is hoped, they will be used sparingly and only where a large body of experimental evidence justifies their use.

Let us now consider briefly the relationship of theoretical terms to scientific theory. Here one immediately encounters difficulties, because what is termed scientific theorizing includes a number of quite different and distinct activities. For our present purposes we will regard a scientific theory, the product of theorizing, to be a set of generalizations that permits the scientist to make predictions. For example, the theory of nuclear physics provides an account of the structure of the atom and the energy changes that take place when there is a change in that structure. Much of this theory is represented by statements written as mathematical equations. The theory does involve a limited number of theoretical terms such as *positron* and *neutron.* These are theoretical terms in that the particles they represent cannot be observed but have to be inferred from other data. Indirect experimental evidence for the existence of these particles comes from many sources and is strong.

Attempts to build comprehensive theories of learning were common during the first half of the present century, but this kind of theorizing, loosely modeled after that of the physicist, was so unsuccessful that it has been abandoned. The early all-inclusive theories of learning such as Thorndike's connectionism, Gestalt learning theory, Guthrie's contiguity theory, Lewin's field theory, and others, all suffered from the same basic defect of attempting to produce too many sweeping generalizations from too limited data. All contained a kernel of truth, but not enough to provide a useful picture of how learning takes place. All introduced theoretical terms on a grand scale, but without the experimental foundation necessary to provide strong justification for their use. Too much theorizing took place too soon, before enough knowledge had accumulated.

The abandonment of attempts to develop comprehensive theories of learning did not lead to all theorizing being abandoned. In place of the immensely ambitious, all-inclusive theories of the past, psychologists began to build very limited theories designed to permit prediction in very limited areas of learning. The new developments in theorizing were vastly less ambitious than their predecessors but perhaps more realistic in what they might accomplish. Examples of such limited theories of learning are scattered through this volume. The chapter on the learning of motor skill illustrates some of the limited theorizing that has taken place in relation to that area of learning. Other examples of productive theorizing, which have led to extensive research, are found in the chapters on attitude learning, perception, and social aspects of learning. These limited theories serve the purpose of summarizing a large amount of experimental evidence and provide a few generalizations that extract the kernel of truth from the mass of material. Even such limited theories must be treated with caution and attempts to apply them must be restricted to the narrow areas in which they have been developed. There is an ever-present danger among psychologists and educators alike to overgeneralize dangerously from sparse findings.

Animal and Human Learning: Continuity or Discontinuity

A significant issue on the contemporary scene is the extent to which human learning reflects processes identical to those found in animal learning. Many psychologists have taken the position that research on learning in animals will succeed in identifying the basic processes involved in all learning and that these same processes will be found to underlie learning in human beings. Indeed, so firm is this belief among many engaged in research on the learning of operants that some have plunged forth to apply their findings, derived mainly from animal research, to such diverse problems as the training of the mentally handicapped, the design of school curricula, and the treatment of mental patients. Such applications have met with some successes and some failures. The successes have often been taken to support the position that there is complete continuity in animal and human learning which are said to differ in complexity and not in the basic processes. The failures have been seized upon by other psychologists to indicate that there is a lack of continuity. However, this kind of evidence throws little light on the problem for, even if there is some discontinuity, one would expect some applications derived from animal behavior to be applicable to human behavior. Even if there is continuity, one would also expect some applications to be unsuccessful, mostly because of underestimating the complexity of the problems involved.

The main argument for continuity is that the nervous systems of all the higher animals are built of the same kinds of components, nerve cells, which all function in very much the same way. The components of the nervous system of the rat or the lizard function in a very similar way to those of man. The human nervous system has more nerve cells, but they are the same kind of nerve cells as those of lower animals. In addition, information in the nervous system is probably stored by much the same mechanism in all creatures that have complex nervous systems. Physiologically, there is complete continuity between the nervous systems of subhuman organisms and the human nervous system. This is a fairly persuasive argument for continuity. One can also add to this argument the fact that an understanding of most organs of the human body has been derived largely through the study of the same organs in lower animals. What has been learned in this way has paved the way for the development of medical knowledge.

This physiological argument is not quite as plausible as it sounds.

There is a long jump from learning the anatomy and physiology of the nervous system to an understanding of behavior. Also two machines may contain the same kinds of components but may function in very different ways. Similarity of components does not mean similarity of function. The human nervous system may have components very similar to those of the rat, but this cannot be taken to mean that they function in similar ways. Indeed, it seems clear that man has components of the nervous system that produce and handle verbal behavior, which have no counterparts in any other living creature. Added to this fact is the widely accepted proposition that the study of subhuman organisms has contributed little to an understanding of human speech.

At the present time, one can say that psychologists have been successful in taking principles derived from the study of lower organisms and applying them to the problems of learning and behavior control in the case of humans who are functioning at relatively simple levels. For example, considerable success has been achieved with the application of such principles to the training of the mentally handicapped, to learning in very young children, and to the treatment of some persons in mental hospitals. Such individuals are not behaving at the full intellectual capacity of the adult human. In their adjustments to their environment they are closer to simpler creatures than to the fully functioning mature human.

Much less success has been achieved in applying the results of research on the behavior of animals to individuals of normal ability, older children, and normal adults who are not in mental institutions. This could be because they function in many ways differently from lower animals, or because their behavior is vastly more complex, although based on the same fundamental learning processes.

Summary

1. Although many research workers in the early part of the present century believed that the development of a psychology of learning would soon produce a revolution in education, the change it has produced has been gradual and subtle, but nevertheless pervasive and, after nearly three quarters of a century, impressive.
2. Not only has the appearance of classrooms changed, but there has also been a complete reorientation of the teacher toward the pupil and toward the problems of providing instruction. Research has produced a problem-solving attitude on the part of the teacher in handling the difficulties of the pupil, and what has been learned about learning has had considerable impact on the

design of the curriculum. Although critics of the schools have often taken a position that there has been little change over the last few generations, nothing could be farther from the truth.

3. Little of the change in schools can be attributed to the work of those who chose to conduct their research in the schools themselves. On the contrary, most of the change has come from the ideas of academicians who gave the appearance of working alone in ivory towers. Men such as Thorndike, Skinner, and Piaget stand out as giants, who worked quietly in their laboratories to produce ideas that changed the course of education. The impact of such ideas is to be contrasted with the lack of impact of much recent research, which represents crash programs supposedly designed to solve critical problems. Such programs have typically had only the impact of a drop of a pin.
4. Learning is far from being the clearly defined phenomenon that it is commonly thought to be. There is a central area of well-defined phenomena, but there is a gray area around the edge where there are phenomena that some would classify as learning while others would not. Habituation and sensitization are two such borderline phenomena.
5. Definitions of learning differ sufficiently that there is often disagreement concerning whether a particular modification in behavior can or cannot be regarded as learning.
6. Psychology has inherited a vocabulary from physiology that the psychologist often has to use with much less precision than the way in which it has been used by the physiologist. Although the terms *stimulus* and *response* may have quite precise meanings in a physiological context, they often lack this precision in the writings of psychologists. The corresponding symbols *S* and *R* generally represent quite complex sets of events and conditions. A stimulus is commonly a conglomerate of conditions to which a learner is exposed and the response is an intricate complexity of muscular and glandular activities. In most studies only a small component of the total response to the learning situation is studied.
7. Psychologists have long sought to find classifications of learning phenomena, but none that have evolved up to this time have shown themselves to be entirely satisfactory. The classification presented in this chapter serves primarily the purpose of showing the range of learning phenomena. It is also a crude classification, in that pure forms of learning in the various categories probably do not exist.
8. The first category of the fourfold classification represents classical conditioning. The essential feature of learning in this category

is that a stimulus comes to produce a response that it did not produce in the first place. The essential condition of this kind of learning is that a response occurs in the presence of a stimulus that does not ordinarily elicit it. After some repetitions of the response in the presence of the stimulus, the stimulus then acquires the property of eliciting the response. Research on learning in this category typically involves a readily controlled response such as a reflex, but the response probably does not *have* to be a reflex. This category of learning is considered to be of significance in that it may encompass the learning that takes place during the acquisition of unwanted emotional responses. There can be no doubt that many emotional responses come to be triggered by all kinds of stimuli through learning as one passes through life, and the necessary condition for such learning may be that the emotional response occurs in the presence of the particular stimulus that comes to trigger it. Such learning had value when man was living under primitive conditions, but its value in a civilized society seems to be largely negative.

9. A second category of learning is the acquisition of responses that lead to the production of a new stimulus situation which can be described as a preferred situation. Such learning is generally accomplished by presenting the preferred situation after the particular response, which then becomes a more and more frequently occurring response. This kind of learning situation has become known as operant conditioning, to distinguish it from classical conditioning. It is also referred to as instrumental conditioning, because the response is an instrument for producing the preferred situation that follows it. Instrumental learning may involve more than a mere change in the frequency with which a particular response occurs and may result in the slow emergence of new responses. Behavior may be slowly shaped to produce behavior different in character from any shown by the learning organism prior to training. Although one would like to think of classical conditioning and instrumental conditioning as involving two entirely distinct categories of learning, this is not the case. Instrumental learning always has included in it some classically conditioned components. Classically conditioned responses also include some instrumentally conditioned elements. The two categories are closely interwoven in practice.

10. A third category of learning is that in which a response becomes part of a sequence of responses. Such learning produces a chain of responses. The learning of chains of activities is essential for the performance of most complex skills. Such chains are different from sequences of responses in which the stimuli produced by

one response initiate the next response, for well-learned chains of responses run off so quickly that such a chain of *S*'s and *R*'s would not have time to occur.

11. A fourth category of learning is that which has been commonly referred to in the past as perceptual learning. It involves associating together two stimuli that enter the perceptual system at approximately the same time. Sensory preconditioning is one example of this category of learning. Many psychologists today would regard paired-associate learning as falling mainly within this category. The latter technique has become one of the most important tools for the study of verbal learning.
12. An account of human learning cannot limit itself to the description of stimuli and responses, for important internal events also take place, which play a crucial role. These internal events are referred to as mediating processes and are particularly evident in human learning. There is evidence that although the learning of very young children can be well described in terms of stimuli and responses, the learning of older children is highly influenced and speeded up by mediating processes. These mediating processes are often essentially verbal in nature and involve, in some cases, the development of strategies for solving problems.
13. Human learners can sometimes report on the nature of the mediating processes taking place, but some of these processes are hidden from the learner and can be discovered only through experimentation. Much of education involves the development of mediating processes. Indeed, the educated, skillful problem solver is a person who has a large repertoire of mediating processes which he can bring to bear on the problems he encounters.
14. Words that refer to hidden processes that cannot be observed directly are said to represent theoretical terms. Mature sciences are characterized by careful and economic usage of theoretical terms. Earlier generations of psychologists made the mistake of introducing large numbers of theoretical terms without having the experimental evidence to support their usage. Modern psychologists introduce theoretical terms sparingly, and they do not introduce them unless experimental evidence from many different directions justifies their use.
15. Most scientific theories involve the use of a few theoretical terms. Psychology, at this time, seems capable of developing only very limited scientific theories of learning. There seems little likelihood that a comprehensive theory of learning will be developed in the near future.
16. Although most of the important technical ideas that have influenced education have come from the laboratory, there are, never-

theless, some real difficulties and hazards in taking the knowledge derived from laboratory research and applying it to the solution of educational problems. The central difficulty stems from the fact that there are conditions influencing classroom learning that have not yet been recognized and that may interfere with the application of knowledge derived under other circumstances. The sociologist has had far more success than the psychologist in conducting research in natural settings in the classroom and in deriving from such research results that have practical application.

17. An important issue in the matter of applying laboratory results to the solution of practical human problems is whether animal and human learning can be considered to represent a continuity, with the one differing from the other only in complexity. Many psychologists take the position that there is a lack of continuity between animal and human learning and that man's capacity to use language represents a function different from any found in subhuman species.

CHAPTER TWO

Reinforcement and Learning

IN THE PREVIOUS CHAPTER, A MAJOR CATEGORY OF LEARNING WAS DEscribed as that in which the organism learns to make a response *R* that produces a particular state of affairs *S*. The state of affairs *S* is always a preferred state of affairs, that is to say one that has a high probability of being selected when the learner has an opportunity of choosing between this and other situations. A hungry rat readily learns to press a bar when the action is followed by such a preferred situation as the presence of food. A child learns to say "please" to obtain a cookie. Learning in this category is commonly discussed in a language that has evolved in the writings of B. F. Skinner, and that is now widely used by psychologists who identify themselves as operant conditioning psychologists or behavior modification psychologists.

Skinner made an important break with tradition when he published in 1938 his classic work entitled *The Behavior of Organisms*. Older conceptions of learning regarded it as a matter of building up connections between stimuli and responses. In such theories all behavior was considered to be a response to some stimulus, and often because no external stimulus could be found to account for the behavior, then an internal stimulus was thought to exist that might produce such behavior. This point of view made many scientists feel uncomfortable, for it really amounts to imagining the existence of stimuli in order to make a behavior theory acceptable. Skinner took the position that only some behavior is the result of specific and identifiable stimuli, and that there is other behavior that simply does not stem from any such identifiable source. This was an important step forward.

As a matter of historical interest, one may note that Skinner classified behavior either as respondent or emitted behavior. Respondent behavior was that behavior which follows some identifiable stimulus and is a result of it. A reflex such as an eye blink, which occurs in response either to a loud noise or to a puff of air on the eyeball, is an example of respondent behavior. Indeed, all reflexes, because they are triggered by specific stimuli, would be classified in the respondent class. Emitted behaviors occur initially without any identifiable stimuli initiating them. A class of emitted behavior such as foot lifting or saying a particular work is referred to as an *operant*. Some operants acquire a complex relationship to stimuli as the individual develops and learns. Let us consider an example of the development of such a relationship.

Anyone who has observed young children knows that vocal behavior in a one-year-old child takes place in a great variety of situations. The infant will spend a part of the day babbling, regardless of where he is or what is happening in his surroundings. The same is not true of the eight-year-old, who is likely to be highly vocal in the presence of other human beings, but relatively silent when he is by himself. The presence of other people is the situation that comes to elicit talking behavior. The relationship of the presence of others to talking behavior is complex in that the young child, placed in a group of children, may often just talk to himself. The precise situation does not determine exactly what he says in the same way that, say, a tap below the kneecap produces the invariable reflex in the leg. The relationship of the social condition to the amount of talking behavior emitted is very complex. In this example, talking behavior is an operant that acquires a high probability of occurring in a social situation.

When an operant appears only in the presence of a certain stimulus, it is said to be a discriminative operant and the stimulus is said to be a discriminative stimulus. If particular stimuli are most likely to elicit a particular form of behavior, then it is said that the behavior is under the control of that stimulus.

The distinction between emitted and respondent behavior is not so clear as it might seem at first glance. When Skinner writes about a behavior that has an identifiable stimulus, he is referring to behavior very closely tied to a particular stimulus. The response of the leg to a tap below the knee satisfies the definition of respondent behavior. Reflexes fall into the classification of respondent behavior, but few other behaviors do. A pupil who pays attention to the teacher and takes occasional notes is not manifesting respondent behavior, and neither is a pupil who applauds at the end of a lecture. Skinner would not classify most of such behavior in the respondent class, for he would say that the relationship of the stimulus to the response is complex and not of the direct nature found in respondent behavior.

In the initial stages of learning based on emitted behavior, the learner shows a very low frequency of occurrence of the behavior to be learned. The child learning to use the expression "Give me" to obtain objects has almost certainly already used the words. Let us not go into the matter of how he has learned to say "Give me," but before he learns to use these words on appropriate occasions he will probably have been heard to say them while he is lying in his crib or on other occasions when the words have little relevance. Learning to use the words appropriately involves an increase in the probability that they will be used on occasions when the child is reaching for some desired object and a decline in probability that the words will be enunciated on occasions when they have no relevance. Learning involves changes in response probabilities in particular situations. When a response is brought under stimulus control it means that the situation determines whether the response will or will not occur. When I meet a friend as I leave for work and say "Good morning," the behavior has a 100 percent chance of occurring under these conditions, that is to say it is under a high degree of stimulus control, and the response has a high probability of occurring.

Skinner and many of his followers have taken the position that learning during childhood slowly brings behavior under stimulus control, that is to say, behavior, through learning, becomes more and more appropriate to the situation in which it occurs. These psychologists view the behavior of the young infant as largely random emitted behavior, such as arm and leg waving, babbling, movements of the eyes, and so forth. Such random behaviors are emitted in considerable quantity, but other psychologists, notably Jean Piaget, have pointed out that much of the behavior of the infant is highly controlled by stimuli provided by the environment. Skinner, of course, would classify these behaviors as respondents and tend to de-emphasize their significance, but Piaget would regard them as the very foundation of all future behavior. One can say, for sure, that the infant has a large repertoire of behavior under stimulus control. The infant in the early weeks of life sucks when any part of its face is stimulated, fixates a bright light and follows the light when it moves, shows a turning movement of the head in the direction of a sound, cries when hungry, goes to sleep when rhythmically patted, and so forth. Whether one regards the behavior of the infant as being largely random emitted behavior or behavior under stimulus control depends on what behavior one happens to observe. Skinner has tended to emphasize emitted behavior as the foundation of learned patterns of responses, and much learned behavior may well find its roots in the emitted behavior of the young infant. However, throughout the discussion the reader must keep in mind that learned behavior may be much more deeply rooted in the great variety of respondent behaviors shown at birth than the followers of Skinner have generally considered it to be.

Up to this point the assumption has been made that learning occurs and that behavior becomes more and more appropriate to the situations in which it occurs, but nothing has been said about the conditions that have to exist in order for learning to occur. A science of learning is concerned to a great extent with the discovery of the conditions under which learning occurs. Until one knows what those conditions are, one can do little to facilitate learning because one does not know what conditions to provide. Most of the remainder of this chapter is concerned with discussing what is known about particular conditions that bring operants under control. The major condition that will be discussed is the occurrence of events known as reinforcers.

Reinforcement of Operants

Generations of psychologists have made the observation that certain kinds of events that follow particular behaviors increase the probability that the behaviors will occur. If a hungry rat is placed in a box equipped with a lever, the depression of which releases a pellet of food, the animal will soon learn to press the lever. The event that follows the pressing of the lever, namely, the release of food, is an event that increases the probability that the rat will press the lever. Other behaviors that occur in the box and that are not followed by this particular event will decrease in the frequency with which they occur. The delivery of the food is described as a reinforcing event or as a reinforcer. The behavior of the rat in the box is shaped by the reinforcing event, and soon the hungry rat directs most of its energies to the pressing of the lever to the exclusion of other forms of behavior. Many other events besides the delivery of food have been demonstrated to reinforce the behavior of the laboratory rat.

In the case of human behavior a large number of different events can be identified as having reinforcing properties. Skinner has pointed out that one of the most common reinforcers used in civilized societies is money, but not all members of such a society are reinforced by money. Young children are not generally reinforced with money because other events are generally found to have better reinforcing properties. The preschool child is typically reinforced for appropriate behavior with adult approval. Adolescent behavior is highly reinforced by the approval shown by other adolescents.

The term *reinforcer* is used here rather than the older term *reward*, though an examination of the research literature shows that the two terms are used as if they were interchangeable. The term *reward* generally carries with it the implication that the event is a pleasurable one, and the term reinforcer is neutral and is used to indicate only that the event increases the probability of occurrence of the behavior it follows.

Learning is typically produced in animals through the control of reinforcing events. Rats will learn a maze by being deprived of food for twenty-two hours before being placed in the starting box of the maze. They then rapidly learn to find the goal box that contains, on each trial, a small amount of food. Hungry pigeons will learn a number of skills through the manipulation of reinforcing events involving the delivery of food. Although consumables represent the core element of reinforcing events used to produce learning in laboratory animals, human learning can be produced and controlled through the manipulation of a great range of other events, including money, approval, and the occurrence of words such as *right*. The teacher who has knowledge of the events that reinforce may be able to exercise control over the learning of pupils.

There is considerable question whether food should be used as a reinforcing event in the case of the young child, as it is when the mother says, "You have been very good, here is a piece of candy." The main argument against such practices is the belief of many physicians that overeating in the adult can sometimes be attributed to the fact that the reward system of the individual was originally tied to food during his childhood. When such a food-rewarded individual reaches adulthood, he may continue to reward himself with food to the point where he grossly overeats.

The impressive part that reinforcing events play in the control of learning in laboratory situations has led some psychologists to take the position that all learning involves reinforcing events and that, conversely, no learning will take place without the occurrence of reinforcing events. Such a generalization extends far beyond the limited laboratory data on which it is based. There is also an increasing body of experimental research supporting the position that learning can and does take place without the occurrence of reinforcers.

Those who maintain that all learning is dependent upon the occurrence of reinforcers refer to this generalization as the *law of reinforcement* or as the *law of effect*. The position taken here is that reinforcing events play an important role in learning, but there is no advantage in taking the extreme position that reinforcement is a necessary condition for learning.

A fact to be kept in mind in evaluating the impressive literature on the manipulation of behavior through the control of reinforcements is that it is based largely on a few species, i.e. the rat, the pigeon, the monkey, and, to a lesser extent, man. One can certainly point to other species in which the role of obvious reinforcers in the shaping of behavior is much less impressive. For example, one does not teach a parrot to speak by carefully regulating the reinforcements and reinforcing any speech activity that approximates what is desired. On the contrary, two factors seem to be important in teaching a parrot or parakeet to speak. One is that the bird has to be exposed to endless repetitions of the desired phrase. The second is that there must not be any other objects or events that compete for the bird's attention. Birds that are caged with other birds do not learn to speak, and the best procedure seems to be to take the bird from the cage and to perch it on a finger. The bird is unlikely to speak while perched on the finger, but after a large number of repetitions of a particular phrase, the bird will sometime later produce the phrase while it is in the cage. Again, although a dog's behavior is often readily shaped by means of reinforcements, there are also aspects of behavior that are more easily learned by other means. For example, a common way of teaching a dog to shake hands is to take the dog's paw in one's hand and to say "Shake." This is done a number of times and at the end of the session a scrap of food is given, though what is supposed to be reinforced by the scrap of food is not clear. After this performance has been performed a number of times, the dog will raise his paw and shake hands when the signal is given. The training does not involve the dog performing some action, for it is the trainer, and not the dog, who raises his paw.

Reinforcement theory generally assumes that certain conditions or events have the inherent property of acting as reinforcers. Thus food and water given to a hungry and thirsty animal may be assumed to function as reinforcers as soon as the nervous system is capable of producing learning behavior. Other stimuli may presumably have the same effect. Such stimuli might include, in the case of a child, a soft touch on the skin, a bright and shiny object, moving objects, and so forth.

A wide range of other phenomena may function as reinforcers. For a child, the process of exploring his environment may, in itself, reinforce the activity. Exploration whets the appetite for exploration. Money represents a generalized reinforcer for most people, although there are some whose behavior would not be reinforced by the offering of money. The commonest and most effective reinforcer in a learning situation is the knowledge that the response made was the correct one. There are also some children who may be much more concerned with obtaining the social approval of their classmates than with knowing that their response is in some way approved by society. Perhaps in a class of the future the teacher will spend the first day of school in determining the conditions that are effective for reinforcing the behavior of each child.

Some books assume that the reinforcers of behavior are known and can be identified. One common statement is that *all* children need social approval, implying that social approval is a major reinforcement. There is little or no evidence to support this point of view, though the behavior of some children under some conditions can be effectively reinforced through social events. Another common statement is that the experience of accomplishment is of particular importance because it will, in and of itself, promote development. In some it may, but here again there is little or no evidence to support this statement as a generalization.

When a reinforcement follows a particular response, rather than other responses, one says that the reinforcement is contingent on the particular response. When one speaks of the reinforcement contingencies in an experiment, one is speaking about the particular forms of behavior that are followed by reinforcements.

Primary and Secondary Reinforcers

A distinction is commonly made between primary and secondary reinforcers. The point has already been made that certain conditions appear to function as reinforcers without any learning taking place. Food will reinforce the behavior of any hungry animal, and from the earliest age. Every professional animal trainer, as well as the amateur training his dog, knows that food can be used to produce learning. Water will do the same for a thirsty animal, and so will any condition that satisfies a basic physiological need. Such a reinforcer is known as a primary reinforcer.

Secondary reinforcers are stimuli that did not originally reinforce behavior but that have acquired this property by having been associated with primary reinforcers. A stimulus that was not originally a reinforcing one can become so through being associated with one that *is* reinforcing.

If a pigeon is fed at ten-second intervals and if a buzzer is sounded before each presentation of the food, then the buzzer comes to acquire the same reinforcing properties as the food. It is then possible to use the buzzer as a reinforcer—that is, the buzzer can be used to provide some modifications in the pigeon's behavior. If each time the pigeon stands on one leg the buzzer sounds, then the pigeon will more and more frequently stand on one leg. In technical language it may be said that the sound of the buzzer has become a secondary reinforcer for the particular pigeon, a property that the sound ordinarily does not possess. A secondary reinforcer may lose its power after it has been used for some time without being paired with the original reinforcer through which it acquired its reinforcing properties. It is possible that some conditions of reinforcement may result in much greater permanence of secondary reinforcing properties than is ordinarily found in typical laboratory experiments. The failure of secondary reinforcers to continue to function as such is one of the difficulties encountered in using this type of mechanism to account for the fact that many different kinds of objects come to have reinforcing properties that remain stable over long periods of time. Money comes to have the property of being a rather general reinforcer, and even small amounts of money, too small to be of real economic significance to the individual, may still reinforce behavior.

Another example of the development of a secondary reinforcer is provided in a classic study by Wolfe (1936), who trained chimpanzees to work for chips which they were then able to insert into a slot machine in order to obtain grapes.

After some training, the chips acquire some properties as secondary reinforcers. They remain weak and transitory reinforcers and do not retain this property without reconditioning. The chimpanzees would even show some hoarding behavior, but difficulty was experienced in arranging conditions so that the animals would hoard as many as twenty chips. Nothing comparable to the extraordinary power that money acquires as a shaper of behavior for many human beings is seen in the property that the chips acquire for the chimpanzees.

Although numerous experiments have been conducted that involve the use of reinforcing procedures with children, nobody has been able to prepare a complete list of what might be considered the primary reinforcers of human behavior. There is no doubt that food will reinforce a hungry child and that water will reinforce a child who is thirsty, but a great range of other events will also reinforce the behavior of children. A child will learn to press a button on the wall with increasing frequency when the only reinforcement provided is a light that goes on each time the button is pushed. Should the light be regarded as a primary or a secondary reinforcing event? One cannot readily see how the light could have acquired secondary reinforcing properties but, unlike most primary reinforcers, it has no obvious relationship to the physiological needs of the child. The light functioning as a reinforcer fits the general rule that any mild and novel event is likely to have positive reinforcing properties.

Just as one can identify fairly clearly some events (such as food and water) that are primary reinforcers in their origin, so too can one identify some events that are essentially secondary reinforcers. The giving of money is one of the most universally effective of secondary reinforcing events. However, just as tastes for particular foods are often acquired, and hence some foods under some conditions may function as secondary reinforcers, so too may money be valued by the adult partly because that same adult as a child liked to play with shiny coins, and the response to bright objects may be largely an unlearned response. So-called primary reinforcers may have learned components to them and so-called secondary reinforcers may have primary components. The distinction between primary and secondary reinforcers is not as clear as one would like it to be.

Information Value and Incentive Value of Reinforcements

The term *reinforcement* represents a general category of events, perhaps much too broad for thinking about educational problems. Some reinforcements are clearly related to quite basic needs of living creatures, as when a hungry rat is trained to run a maze by providing small quantities of food each time the animal reaches the goal box. Under such learning conditions, it is reasonable to assume that an object that can be used as a reinforcer has incentive value, that is to say, it has value in energizing behavior as well as in strengthening responses. The difference between the use of the term *incentive* and the use of the term *reinforcement* is not always clear in current psychological literature. Consider an experiment in which children are shown a series of ten English words and their French equivalents, pair by pair. After the presentation of the ten pairs, the children are then tested on their ability to give the French equivalent of each of the ten English words. Then the pairs are presented together in a new learning trial, and so forth. Now let us suppose that in one of the procedures used in the experiment, the child was given an M & M candy immediately after each correct response. It would be quite customary to refer to the M & M as the reinforcement for the response. Now let us consider another procedure in which each time the child made a correct response he was given a token, and in which he also knew that, at the end of the session, he would be able to turn in the tokens for M & M's. In the latter case, the M & M's would probably be referred to as the incentive. The tokens might or might not be referred to as the reinforcers, depending upon the particular experimenter. The terms incentive and reinforcer are sometimes used virtually interchangeably, a fact that brings out the close relationship between the two.

Consider a child learning to add single digit numbers who is told after each addition whether he is right or wrong. In the latter case, the primary function of the reinforcing event is that of providing information. One cannot entirely separate the incentive-giving and the information-giving aspects of reinforcement, for even in those tasks in which the reinforcement is designed to be strictly informative, it also has incentive value. Numerous studies have shown that even with dull and uninteresting tasks, such as that of drawing a line three inches long over and over again, a person will continue to perform the task over long periods of time and perhaps even without improvement, provided he is told after each trial how well he is doing. Knowing how one is doing will, in itself, maintain behavior as well as serve the function of improving performance. Hence, in such a situation, one can think of knowledge of results as having incentive value, that is to say, it is an event that serves to energize behavior. In the training of animals, the reinforcements are designed largely around the incentives that have to be introduced in order to maintain particular kinds of behavior. In developing a circus act, a lion trainer has the problem of enticing a lion to sit up on its hindquarters on a stool. Now any lion is able to climb on a stool and to sit on its hindquarters, but the problem of the trainer is to introduce incentives so that the lion will do both when a particular signal is given. The reinforcement that he uses in training the lion does this. On the other hand, in teaching a child arithmetic, the child neither knows nor understands the operations to be performed, and considerable information must be given to him in order that learning may take place.

Knowledge of Results—The Information Factor in the Guidance of Learning

If a person were to perform, but never knew how well he was doing, he would have no basis for improving his performance. It is difficult in daily life to find a task that a person can perform without his receiving some information about how he is doing. In the laboratory such tasks can be readily devised. Over half a century ago Thorndike devised one such task in which human subjects were asked to draw a three-inch-long line again and again on separate sheets of paper. The subjects were never told whether their line was too short or too long; hence they had no basis for improving their performance, and they did not improve. After practice they tended to draw lines of more uniform length, but they were not able to make adjustments in the length of the line so that it approximated more closely the required three inches in length. If, on the other hand, the subjects had been able to check the length of each line or had been told in some way how well they were doing, then improvement would have taken place.

The information the learner obtains about the usefulness, or effectiveness, or appropriateness of his response is called *knowledge of results* or *informative feedback*. Sometimes the term *feedback* alone is used. This information falls into the class of events known as reinforcers, because it modifies the probability that a particular behavior will be repeated or inhibited on subsequent occasions. Although knowledge of results can be classified as a reinforcer, placing it in the same category as food given to a hungry animal may obscure the problems involved in designing situations in which knowledge of results is effectively provided.

A first point to be made is that any ongoing activity requires informative feedback for the activity to be pursued successfully, even when no learning occurs. A very simple activity such as that involved in walking down the street requires a very complicated system of feedback for it to occur smoothly and effectively. The brain has to know where the person's legs are so that movements can be coordinated. In the normal individual, sensory information comes from the muscles and joints, giving him information and permitting him to walk in a coordinated manner. However, when a disease of the spinal cord, known as tabes dorsalis, occurs, the tracts of the spinal cord that carry this information are destroyed and the information from the muscles and joints can no longer reach the brain. The person then has difficulty in walking, though he can manage to do so by directing his eyes downward and watching his legs. In this way he manages to keep track of the position of his limbs; in the dark, however, when he cannot see his limbs, he is unable to walk and will fall to the ground when he attempts to do so. One takes this self-monitoring of ongoing activity so much for granted as to be unaware of its importance, but it is vital for the continuing flow of behavior. One of the more dramatic demonstrations of what happens when this feedback is disrupted is shown in the delayed feedback of speech. A person ordinarily hears his speech as it occurs, but it is possible to record a person's speech and then to play it back to him through earphones as he speaks after a second or two delay. The effect of providing this unusual delayed feedback of his own speech is to disrupt the speech mechanism. A person thus receiving delayed informative feedback may stutter and become disorganized. A similar disruption occurs when a person is given a manual task to do with his hands hidden from view, but is allowed to see the image of his hands on a television screen delayed several seconds. Under such conditions he also becomes confused and fumbles the task.

The kind of feedback that has just been discussed is necessary for the production of most long sequences of behavior, and it must take place whether learning is or is not taking place. But for learning to occur, another kind of feedback is also necessary. This is the feedback provided by information concerning the extent to which new behavior is appropriate or correct. This feedback is generally what is meant by knowledge of results.

Knowledge of results may be provided in many different ways and under many different conditions. For example, a person learning to drive a car receives feedback as he drives down the street and sees whether he does or does not stay in his own lane. This is a continuous kind of feedback provided as the task is undertaken. Sometimes it is called concurrent feedback. Then, at the end of the driving lesson another kind of feedback takes place when the instructor tells the pupil the extent to which his performance has been adequate and the errors that he has to correct on the next lesson. The latter may be described as terminal feedback to distinguish it from concurrent feedback. The advantage of concurrent feedback over terminal feedback is obvious. The person receiving information about his performance while he is in action can take immediate steps to remedy deficiencies, whereas when he is given terminal feedback he must wait until the next trial or lesson before he can correct his performance, and by that time he may have forgotten what there was to correct. A person driving a car is likely to learn more by concurrent feedback than by the terminal feedback provided at the end of the lesson. However, one cannot be sure in every case that concurrent feedback will be superior to terminal feedback because there are some laboratory experiments in which the reverse has been the case. However, there are unquestionably certain situations in which concurrent feedback is less efficient than terminal feedback. This can be illustrated at an anecdotal level by the case of a man who learns to travel by jeep between two desert outposts one hundred miles apart. This he does once a week and he keeps track of his position by noting the hills and other landmarks as he goes along. These provide him with concurrent feedback, and arrival at his destination provides terminal feedback. Soon he learns to make the journey without error, but then, one day, he has to make the journey in the dark, and he loses his way because his learned performance was highly dependent on concurrent feedback, which was absent in the darkness. The point to note is that if he had trained himself to make the journey without concurrent feedback, that is to say, in the dark, then he would have been well prepared to make it under any conditions. The use of concurrent feedback is of limited value when the final performance, for whatever reason, is to exclude it.

The identification of the sources of feedback used by learners in a task is not the easy matter that it is commonly believed to be. A lesson in the difficulties involved is provided by research that has been done on the feedback involved in using a typewriter. Expert typists and teachers of typing have long claimed that highly qualified typists watch neither the keyboard nor the material coming out of the typewriter, and that their eyes are fixated steadily on the copy they are typing. They also claim that they can identify errors they make because to type a word wrong "feels" wrong. When West (1967) studied the performance of some expert typists in a situation in which they could see neither the typewriter nor the typewriter roller, they showed a substantial increase in errors. It seems that the expert does depend on visual cues to check his performance and his product and, when deprived of those cues, shows a decline in performance. It seems, though, that he must be unaware of the extent to which he uses vision for him to take the position in teaching typing that the learner should not use visual cues at all.

The latter procedure probably adds immensely to the frustrations of the beginner and is likely to be a hindrance rather than a help.

Holding (1965) has provided a quite elaborate classification of the different conditions under which feedback may be given, and part of the discussion here is based upon his analysis. One distinction he brings out is the difference between intrinsic and artificial feedback. When a person learns to solve a problem and arrives at a solution, the feedback is his knowledge that the problem has been solved. In such a case the feedback is inherent in the solution of the problem and is referred to as intrinsic feedback or intrinsic knowledge of results. This intrinsic feedback is to be contrasted with what Holding calls artificial feedback, as would occur when a person is given a grade for his performance or is given a prize if he has performed particularly well. The most desirable kind of feedback is quite obviously intrinsic feedback because it is highly task-related and tells the person what was good or bad about his performance. Artificial feedback, to be of maximum use, has to be much more closely tied to the task than it usually is.

An example of the effective use of artificial feedback is found in an old World War I procedure for training men to fire a rifle. One of the main difficulties in instructing men in this skill is that of teaching them to fire the rifle by squeezing the trigger and butt with the thumb and first finger. Most men tend to *pull* the trigger, which is a wrong procedure. A simple device can be attached to the gun so that when the soldier squeezes properly a buzzer is turned on (or off). The buzzer provides artificial feedback for the purpose of drawing the attention of the trainee to the cues related to squeezing the trigger. That is to say, the buzzer alerts the individual to what is happening in his hand and how his hand should feel when it is correctly tensed against the butt and trigger. This is what is meant when it is said that the buzzer draws the learner's attention to certain cues. Holding also cites another interesting example in which air-to-air gunners were trained in a simulator in which a buzzer was sounded whenever the gunner had the correct range adjustment. Trainees who learned with such a device made more rapid progress than those who had only more conventional forms of feedback.

Another very interesting example of the use of artificial feedback is found in the various devices designed to train children to stop bedwetting. A typical device for this purpose is described by Van Wagenen and Murdock (1966). The essential feature of this device is a buzzer that sounds as soon as the first drops of urine come into contact with the diaper. The buzzer would appear to serve the purpose of drawing the child's attention to how his body feels when urination is about to occur. If he is sleeping at the time, then the buzzer wakes him and permits him to attend to what is happening. Learning to recognize the cues that precede and accompany urination takes place rapidly with the use of such a device in the case of normal children who have passed the age when bladder control ordinarily occurs.

The Effect of Informative Feedback in Open and Closed Tasks

Until recently, the assumption was commonly made that informative feedback, such as saying "right" or "wrong," would be reinforcing under most conditions, but Nuttin and Greenwald (1968) have found that they are effective as reinforcers only when certain conditions exist. They refer to these kinds of reinforcing events as rewards and punishments, as did Thorndike fifty years earlier, but the modern trend would be to use the term informative feedback. Nuttin and Greenwald have undertaken experiments to show that this kind of informative feedback is most effective on what they call open tasks, and that it is quite ineffective on closed tasks. An open task is one that the person undertakes knowing that he will later have to use the responses learned. A closed task is a one-time task, undertaken by a person on a particular occasion and with the knowledge that he is not going to have to perform the same tasks or similar tasks in the future. The person views the open task as a part of an ongoing activity that extends into the future. This is related to the notion, long stressed by educators, that learning will take place most effectively when it is related to the goals and needs of a child. The findings of Nuttin and Greenwald have been confirmed by research undertaken by Longstreth (1970), who points out that it supports a belief long held by educators that a learner's intentions are crucial in determining how much is learned. Repetition, without expectation that the material will have future utility, produces little learning.

Correlated Reinforcement

A condition of reinforcement widely used in teaching practice is that of *correlated reinforcement.* This condition requires that the quantity of reinforcement be related in some way to performance. The assignment of a grade so that the grade reflects the quality of performance is an example of correlated reinforcement. This phenomenon has not been widely studied by experimental psychologists, although it was mentioned by Skinner as long ago as 1938. More recently, it has been examined within a program of experimental studies by Logan (1960), who has conducted his research with rats in a maze-learning situation. The limited data related to this problem and the fact that studies have been restricted to a single species—the rat—means that few generalizations can be made that apply to the human learner. However, several potential advantages of correlated reinforcement can be pointed out.

First, correlated reinforcement provides the learner with considerably more information than can be supplied through a reinforcement that does not vary in magnitude. If the learner is provided with correlated reinforcement, he finds out not only that his response is generally in the right direction, but also the degree to which it is in the right direction. The reinforcement has more information embedded in it when it is correlated with performance than when it is not so correlated.

Second, the learner may modify his behavior and obtain definitive information concerning the value of the modification when the reinforcement is correlated with performance. Thus, correlated reinforcement enables the learner to have some degree of control over the learning situation, which he would not have with uncorrelated reinforcement.

Third, a numerical grading system provides one form of correlated reinforcement that may have advantages if the competitive aspects of the system are suppressed.

Self-reinforcing Activities

Those psychologists who regard reinforcement as a necessary condition for human learning have long had difficulty in accounting for the fact that some human learning occurs in the absence of observable reinforcers. Certainly, a person can read a book and learn much from the process, but where are the reinforcing events? Such apparent exceptions to the notion that reinforcement is necessary for learning permit two courses of action. One of these is to take the position that not all learning requires reinforcing events; the other is to assert that hidden reinforcers are operating. The second of these two positions has generally been preferred by researchers in the field of reinforcement phenomena, perhaps because they tend to think of reinforcement as representing a general principle underlying all learning. Thus an activity such as reading is said to involve reinforcing events internal to the reader and the activity is said to be self-reinforcing. The purpose of invoking such unobservable reinforcers is to sustain the belief that reinforcement is a necessary condition for all learning; but the possibility exists that some learning may take place without the occurrence of such events, in which case the scientist would be guilty of imagining events that had no real existence at all.

The safest position at the present time is to stay close to the facts. Because there are some learning tasks in which the acquisition of a skill is closely tied to the presence of reinforcers occurring at the appropriate time in relation to the response, one can say that reinforcement is sometimes a condition of learning; but to say that it is necessary for all learning goes far beyond the facts.

Whether learning can take place without the presence of reinforcing events has long been a focus of controversy, which is difficult to settle through experimentation. In order to settle the matter it would be necessary to design experiments in which learning occurred but in which all possibilities of reinforcement were excluded. Some studies have been designed that come close to meeting this requirement, and these have shown that learning occurs when reinforcements are either absent or minimally present. Such studies are considered at greater length in the chapter on perception.

Extinction of Behavior

Learning has two important aspects. On the one hand, it is a positive process that results in the acquisition and emergence of new behavior. On the other, learning may proceed by the elimination of undesirable and unwanted behavior. Both the positive and negative aspects of the formation of behavior involve learning. Both are learning processes.

Teachers often think of learning only in a positive sense, emphasizing the skills that are slowly acquired through contact with the school. They forget that an important problem in school learning is also the getting rid of undesirable behavior acquired elsewhere. The child who is a so-called disciplinary problem in school is one who displays certain unwanted aspects of behavior that interfere with positive learning. The pupil may show high needs to interact with other pupils in ways that are not particularly constructive, and may devote little of his energies to the pursuit of learning as it is done by other children. He may be hostile to the teacher. He may be a bully. He may be interested in affairs outside the school and absent himself frequently. All of these are well-learned habits of behaving that the teacher may wish to see eliminated and may have to eliminate before constructive learning within the school situation can take place. Every teacher knows that this is a difficult task, for attempts to eliminate well-established patterns of behavior are likely to be quite fruitless.

The mental-health worker is faced with even more serious problems of eliminating behavior. The person who comes to the clinic with serious neurotic disturbances is often one who has learned a whole host of worthless responses. Perhaps the problem of the individual who reports at the clinic is that he responds to most of life's situations with anxiety. In other words, he has learned inappropriate anxiety responses to life which the clinician must help him to unlearn; but, as everyone knows, unlearning is a difficult matter.

Psychologists do not refer to the unlearning of behavior, but use the term *extinction* instead. The latter term needs some explanation, partly because it is not used with any uniform meaning among psychologists. Most of those who work in the field of operant conditioning define it in this way: *A response that has been previously learned through reinforcement may be extinguished if it is permitted to occur repeatedly without reinforcement.* This definition has been widely used in the writings of B. F. Skinner (1938, 1953), although the concept itself was originally developed by Pavlov before the turn of the century. In Pavlov's original demonstration of the phenomenon, he showed that once a dog had learned to salivate at the sound of a bell, then salivation would occur to a lesser and lesser extent as the bell was repeatedly sounded but without any food being provided. After enough soundings of the bell, the animal would cease to salivate when the bell rang, for the response had been *extinguished.* Skinner showed a similar phenomenon in the case of operants. A rat that had learned to press a bar that delivered food would press the bar less and less frequently once the food mechanism was turned off. Eventually, the rat would just give the bar an occasional press, as a rat would do even if it had never learned to obtain food in that way. The latter slow rate of bar pressing is called the *base rate.* When behavior has reached the base rate, the response is commonly referred to as having been extinguished.

Up to this point the term extinction is fairly clear in meaning, but confusion arises because some psychologists use the term to cover all phenomena that are commonly called "forgetting," although the evidence seems absolutely clear that much of human forgetting involves very different phenomena from the extinction phenomena that have just been discussed. Just as in current literature the term reinforcement refers to a multiplicity of phenomena, so too does the term extinction. For the purposes of this book, the term extinction will be reserved for those situations in which a response previously learned through reinforcement is permitted to occur without the contingent reinforcement and shows a decline in strength. Not all learned responses show extinction when they occur without reinforcement. The self-destructive behaviors of some children who hit themselves repeatedly or claw themselves until they bleed do not extinguish. Many such children have died from persistent self-inflicted injuries. In hospitals they often have to be placed in restraining harnesses. There are also many behaviors that are assumed to be learned and that do not extinguish. Nail-biting behavior shows great persistence even when allowed to occur freely. The common interpretation is that nail biting reduces some kind of inner tension and that the tension reduction reinforces the nail biting. Also, the self-stimulation itself may be reinforcing. This is falling back on the idea that there are hidden reinforcers. Because one cannot provide the conditions necessary for the extinction of nail biting, other methods have to be adopted to eliminate the habit. One method is to make nail biting punishing. One way of doing this is to make the person bite his nails deliberately in front of a mirror. Another is to paint the nails with a substance intensely unpleasant to the taste.

Extinction is not as widely used by parents and teachers as it should be, partly because their own impulses are often to do the reverse. If a child has a tantrum, the parent may ignore it for a time (extinction), but soon the parent can stand the crying and whining no longer and gives in to the child's demands (positive reinforcement). In this way a behavior that should be extinguished becomes positively reinforced. Mental health workers use extinction extensively. A man who visits a psychiatrist because he has an almost uncontrollable desire to shout obscene words may be asked by the psychiatrist to shout those words in the office and, in this way, slowly extinguish the tendency. Extinction represents one of the few moderately successful ways of eliminating problem behavior.

Because extinction offers so much promise for behavior control, it has been important to find out what kind of a process is involved. At first sight one might guess that it is merely a process of obliterating or washing out learned behavior—perhaps the opposite of learning—but this does not seem to be the case at all. A key to the understanding of extinction is found in a phenomenon known as *spontaneous recovery*, which may be illustrated thus. Let us suppose that a child has learned that a particular candy machine is not working properly and that it will occasionally deliver a ball of bubble gum if the lever on it is depressed. The child continues to depress the lever until the machine has been emptied. Next day, he returns to the machine, which has since been filled and fixed, and begins to press the lever, but after thirty depressions no candy has been delivered and his response becomes extinguished. On the following day, he comes to the machine again, and this time presses the lever ten times before his response is extinguished. Still, the following day he presses the lever six times, and from then on he gives the lever a couple of presses each time he passes by. The latter is now his base rate and represents what he does whenever he comes upon a similar kind of machine. One day he makes one of his occasional presses of the lever and the machine delivers candy. Immediately he begins to press the lever furiously. There has been a *spontaneous* recovery of the response. Now note that a single reinforcement produces a complete recovery of the response in full strength. Extinction has not caused the response tendency to vanish, but merely to be temporarily inhibited. In fact, the overwhelming evidence indicates that extinction is a process of inhibiting a response and is not a process of eliminating the basic learned mechanism on which the response is based.

A second procedure for the extinction of behavior, previously learned through reinforcement, is to arrange the situation so that the behavior would ordinarily occur and then to prevent the response from occurring. In training a dog to sit and wait for a command before coming forward to take a piece of food, this kind of procedure is used. What is generally done is to show the dog the food while another person restrains the animal from advancing and the person with the food says "Hold it." Then the dog is released when the command "Come" is given. Soon the animal learns to inhibit the tendency to approach the food when he is told to "hold it," and no physical restraint is necessary. In such a situation the dog also learns ways of inhibiting the approach tendency. For example, the dog will commonly turn his head away from the food so that it cannot see it during the waiting period. A related procedure for blocking an undesirable response is found in Wolpe's desensitization technique (1958) used for helping patients eliminate anxiety responses. (See also Paul, 1966, for a description of the technique.) In this technique the first task of the therapist is to find out which situations produce anxiety responses. These situations are then listed in order from the one that produces the least anxiety to the one producing the most. Then the patient is helped first to become deeply relaxed and then to think of the least anxiety-producing situation while maintaining his relaxation. The theory is that relaxation is incompatible with anxiety and that, so long as the patient is relaxed, thoughts about the anxiety-producing situation will not produce anxiety. When the patient has learned to tolerate this first situation without an anxiety response, the therapist asks the patient to think about the next situation on the list, and so on, in ascending order. By this procedure the patient slowly becomes desensitized to the range of situations included in the list. The whole technique is nothing more than that of providing the stimulus that has ordinarily produced the unwanted response and then blocking the response. Rachman (1967), who has summarized the research on desensitization, indicates that most results are positive. In addition, he notes that although many psychoanalyists had predicted that unfavorable side effects would result from this form of therapy, these side effects have not occured. One prediction was that the desensitization procedure would be followed by what has been termed symptom substitution, as would happen if a person cured of an uncontrollable fear of the dark were suddenly to find that he now feared being alone, although he had never had this fear previously. Studies of desensitization have found no evidence of symptom substitution happening in those who are desensitized.

Other procedures for eliminating behavior learned under reinforcing conditions do not depend on response inhibition but on increasing the strength of other responses. If a child in a classroom responds positively to almost everything except the ongoing classroom work, the teacher may try and find ways of making the classwork more rewarding for that particular child. In doing this the teacher is attempting to increase the strength of the responses related to classwork so that they will compete favorably with the responses related to other stimuli.

Vicarious Extinction of Avoidance Behavior

The extinction of many undesirable avoidance responses is often best undertaken through indirect means. Teachers and parents have long known that children can be helped to overcome unreasonable fears through being brought into contact with other children who do not display these fears, but only recently has this phenomenon come under experimental investigation. Bandura, Grusec, and Menlove (1967) attempted to help children who were fearful of dogs to overcome this fear by confronting them with situations in which they saw other children behave positively and without fear toward dogs. The fearful children thus exposed to fearless behavior on the part of other children showed a significant reduction in their tendency to avoid approaching or contacting dogs. The crucial factor in the learning situation appears to be the behavior of the nonfearful child toward the dog. If the adult who is present engages in explaining that there is no reason to be fearful or that dogs are nice animals, little is accomplished in reducing the avoidance responses of the fearful child. What is not clear from such studies is whether it is avoidance responses alone that are reduced through the observation of the model or whether the internal anxiety associated with those responses is also reduced. A child could remain intensely anxious in the presence of dogs but, after having seen another child approach a dog fearlessly, might be shamed into doing the same thing, although he might do it under considerable stress. Learning to be brave is quite different from learning to be nonfearful. Perhaps it is more desirable to be brave but fearful than to remain fearful but cowardly.

The Shaping and Modification of Behavior

In training a pigeon to move in a circle when placed in a training box, the first step for the hungry pigeon to learn is that when a buzzer is sounded then a food trough will move up into a position where the food can easily be reached for a ten-second period. The buzzer becomes a secondary reinforcer. Once the pigeon has mastered this lesson, training can be commenced. The experimenter watches the pigeon carefully, while having in his hand a switch that controls the buzzer and food trough, which always work together. The experimenter watches the pigeon until he sees the pigeon make a slight turn in the desired direction. The moment this happens he presses the switch and the pigeon is reinforced both by the buzzer and the opportunity to reach the food. Ten seconds later the food trough moves out of reach and the pigeon begins to engage in what appear to be random movements. Once again the experimenter waits for the pigeon to begin to move in a circle and, with luck, the pigeon will this time make a larger move of a circular kind. This is reinforced by the buzzer/food combination, and so the procedure goes on until the pigeon readily makes a full circle each time. An important point to note in this procedure is that not only are the right moves reinforced but the wrong moves are extinguished through the nonreinforcement. Thus the shaping of behavior involves the strengthening of all behavior involving closer and closer approximations to the desired behavior and the extinction of all competing responses. In this way, behavior is slowly brought under control and the pigeon will immediately begin to walk in circles as soon as it is placed in the training box. Additional controls can then be introduced. For example, the pigeon may learn to walk in circles only when a light is turned on. The latter is relatively easy to teach a pigeon once it has acquired the habit of walking in a circle. From that point on, the pigeon receives reinforcement only when the light is turned on. In a single session the pigeon will learn to walk in circles when the light is on and in other ways when the light is off.

The shaping of the pigeon's behavior involves the use of reinforcements that are not intrinsic to, that is to say, a part of, the pigeon's task. The behavior is manipulated through food, a need-related object in a hungry pigeon, and, according to the interpretation of this aspect of reinforcement given here, the effect of the reinforcer is probably that of providing an incentive effect. The procedure is adopted for the training of the pigeon because it is not possible to produce the behavior by saying to the bird, "Just run in a circle and you will get fed." The operation of slowly shaping behavior by waiting for behavior in the desired direction to occur is pursued only because there is no more efficient alternative procedure available. The general technique does offer promise in the modification of behavior in similar situations involving human beings where there are difficulties in communicating. Examples of humans whose behavior needs to be shaped, but with whom there is often no more communication possible than there is with a pigeon, are found in the cases of persons in mental hospitals, autistic children, and the seriously mentally retarded. In the past, the training of such individuals has been severely limited by the fact that there is virtually no effective means of communicating with them. Operant conditioning techniques have provided a means of improving the adequacy of the behavior of many such individuals who previously would have been considered to be completely untrainable.

An examination of current research literature shows that the most frequently published accounts of the application of operant conditioning techniques are in the treatment of the mentally retarded. The number of studies in this area probably runs in the hundreds. Many of them deal with the problem of toilet training, largely because many institutions for the mentally retarded have assumed that the children confined in them were not capable of mastering this basic skill. The application of operant conditioning techniques, involving the reinforcement of partial success at first, has shown that these individuals are much more capable of being trained than was previously believed possible.

Many studies report that mentally retarded children as old as fourteen years, who had never acquired the rudiments of toilet training, were trained in a matter of weeks. The general nature of the procedure is simple. First, some attempt is made to determine the times at which urination or bowel movements occur. Then the person is persuaded to sit on the toilet at that time. Whenever success is achieved, some reinforcement, such as a piece of candy, is provided. In addition, any attempt by the individual to move toward the toilet on appropriate occasions is rewarded, even if he has an accident on the way. The essence of the technique lies in closely observing the person to be trained so that even minimal behavior in the right direction can be reinforced immediately.

One can also find some examples of the shaping of behavior in typical classroom situations and these examples parallel closely the behavior of the pigeon learning to move in circles. Consider the case of a child learning the pronunciation of a foreign language. The child makes an effort to pronounce the foreign words but, at first, fails to note that foreign words are not pronounced in the same way as English words. Soon he gets the idea that he has to say the foreign words in a different way from the English words, and he makes crude attempts to do so. Each time he shows an improvement in pronunciation the teacher gives a nod of approval or reinforces the improvement in some way. Errors will at first be disregarded, but will be corrected if they persist. In this way the pronunciation of the foreign language is slowly shaped to conform to the pattern of the native. The reader should note that although there is a parallel between training the pigeon to move in circles and training the child to pronounce correctly, there are also differences in the procedure. In neither case can one tell the learner exactly what to do, but the child can be given a demonstration of the correct performance and at least some cues as to what the performance involves and how he can correct his errors.

Similar techniques have also been used for improving the behavior of some classes of mental patients. Because some institution inmates show almost no response to anybody, the first task in treatment is to increase responsiveness to others. This is accomplished also by observing the behavior carefully and reinforcing any signs of responsiveness. If the observer can identify some object to which the patient will respond and which the patient will seek to obtain, then the task is greatly simplified. In one such case, the therapist eventually noted that a patient who seemed to be completely unresponsive would respond to the sight of chewing gum and that he would enjoy chewing it. This suggested that a stick of gum might be a powerful reinforcer of behavior and that it could also be used as an incentive for increasing his responsiveness to others. Armed with this knowledge, the therapist required that the patient show an increased responsiveness to others each time that he was to obtain some gum. After much work, the patient was brought to the point of asking for gum in order to obtain it. This led to the patient being made to understand that other aspects of his needs would be satisfied only if he asked for what he wanted. The case illustrates the fact that with many individuals in mental hospitals, who often operate at a very low intellectual level, the effective reinforcements are often related to very basic primitive needs.

Not all classes of seriously disturbed patients seem able to respond to this kind of approach. Particularly suited to this approach are those who are responsive to external conditions. The more advanced patients can be reinforced with tokens that they can turn in for special privileges or objects more directly related to their needs. Indeed, the tokens may be used to control the economy of a ward in a mental hospital in much the same way as money controls the transactions of the outside community. Patients may have to work to obtain anything beyond the bare necessities of life. If they behave well and earn enough tokens, then they can obtain better foods or even better sleeping accommodations. Such arrangements are referred to as "token economies." A hospital ward run on such a system provides payments in tokens for desirable forms of behavior, and the tokens are used to buy important privileges. Azrin and Allyon (1969) have provided a colorful description of such an economy. In an extreme form, patients living within a token economy are provided with only the minimum facilities for survival. The food they receive is dull, cheap, but adequate. The beds are hard and of marginal quality. The recreations and freedoms they enjoy are the minimum necessary for maintaining health. When they earn tokens for socially acceptable behavior, they may buy with them better sleeping accommodations, or better food, or better recreations. The claim is made by those who run token economies in hospitals that the result of the system is greatly improved patient behavior. The inmates are reported to work hard for the privileges they value, but they also complain that the privileges cost too much in terms of the tokens they have to earn to pay for them.

When hard data are available, they tend to indicate that the phenomena involved in token economies are more complex than the simple reinforcement interpretation might imply. Allen (1970) conducted a study in which sixteen adult retarded mental patients, already living in a token economy system, had the system extended to personal grooming. Once each day the patients were checked against a list of desirable grooming points and the patient was given a token if she either achieved a criterion score or made an improvement over a previous day's score. The token could be used for meals, cigarettes, or candy. The patients did make an improvement in their appearance. However, almost as much improvement took place when the same check list was used and the patient was given a token regardless of improvement. What appeared to be happening was that the checking procedure in itself produced improvement.

Despite the fact that token economies have been used in many mental hospitals, the long-term value of such reinforcement systems to the patients is not known. Even if token economies produce improvement in the behavior of the ward patients, this is no guarantee that the improvement will be maintained after the patients leave the hospital. The behavior-modification psychologists argue that, on leaving the hospital, the reinforcements provided by society will take over and maintain the improved patient behavior, but this is a hope rather than an established fact. The book by Azrin and Allyon is notably lacking in any evidence to show that their token economy was effective and that it achieved the goals set for it.

Although token economies are designed to reinforce the more socially acceptable behaviors and have had some success in this direction, they are not without their problems. Patients compete with one another and begin to show all the conflicts and bitterness that people show when competing in a money economy. Token economies have also been introduced into schools on an experimental basis to provide a reinforcement system, generally for the purpose of reducing the amount of disruptive behavior, but they also have problems.

Other areas in which some success has been achieved include helping autistic children to respond more to others so that learning can be more readily elicited (see, for example, Hewett, 1966). At least one study—Schwitzgebel (1967)—shows that delinquents who were positively reinforced by praise in interviews for making more desirable statements showed improvement in this respect both in subsequent statements made in interview situations and in statements made in natural settings. Nevertheless, universal success has not been achieved.

Enthusiasm for a new technique tends to result in an overevaluation of its merits. A part of the rosy picture results from the fact that much of the data related to the success of the technique comes from articles in which a report is made on a single case. Occasional successes are found with almost any technique proposed for modifying behavior, and these are the cases likely to be published. The failures, the cases where the technique did not work, never reach the literature. For this reason, all techniques have to be viewed with reservation until studies are undertaken on unselected cases and with all cases, not just the successes, reported. There is also another problem associated with the evaluation of behavior modification techniques, which is well illustrated by the claim that stuttering can be treated with operant conditioning techniques with dramatically successful results. What the studies do not report is that the literature of speech pathology is full of reports of techniques that had some temporary success in the treatment of stuttering, but that these techniques generally produced, in the long run, far more problems than they solved. The test of the effectiveness of the treatment of stuttering has to involve a follow-up of the case over a period of years, for remission of symptoms over long periods is common.

The Teacher as a Reinforcing Agent

With the role of positive reinforcements now well established in the laboratory, research workers became intrigued with attempting to demonstrate that the reinforcing behaviors of the teachers have a similar effect on learning in the classroom. Rosenshine (1969) has reviewed available studies that relate teacher behavior to measured achievement and some of these studies include measures of teacher behavior that could be considered as reinforcing. In all the studies reviewed by Rosenshine the learning of students has been measured through some kind of testing device and he excludes studies in which learning was rated by observers. He also distinguishes between assessments of teacher behavior derived from counting incidents, such as incidents involving the rewarding of a pupil for correct behavior, and overall ratings of the same kind of behavior.

Perhaps one of the variables considered by Rosenshine most closely related to positive reinforcement is that described as "teacher use of praise." Rosenshine reviewed fifteen studies that made use of this variable but the relationships of praise to achievement were found to be highly inconsistent. There is a very slight tendency for the correlation between amount of praise and achievement to be positive, but the trend is barely perceptible. Rosenshine also found nine studies in which the teacher's use of student ideas was studied in relationship to achievement, but again no particular trend in the results was discernible. A more promising variable is teacher warmth, generally measured by means of a rating procedure. Of the fifteen studies reviewed, twelve produced a significant relationship between teacher warmth and achievement and three yielded mixed results.

A particularly interesting finding of the Rosenshine review is that disapproval and criticism on the part of the teacher generally correlate more consistently with achievement than does praise. The latter finding does not mean that disapproval is more powerful than praise for it may well be that those teachers who use disapproval use it more consistently than other teachers use praise.

The studies covered by the review give some support to the idea that the teacher who is broadly reinforcing in his behavior and is described as warm provides a good environment for learning. However, there is no reason why a teacher who is warm should not also criticize and disapprove and provide the pupil with the advantages that also come from these forms of behavior.

The studies taken collectively generally show a higher relationship between measures of positively reinforcing teacher behavior and achievement when the former are measured by means of ratings than by counting incidents. The reason for this seems to be that one would have to wait a long time to count enough incidents of, say, teacher approval to obtain a reliable measure. On the other hand, one may be able to rate reliably in a short time a teacher's tendency to devote time to approving of pupils' actions and products. An approving teacher might be expected to provide constructive suggestions, approach pupils in a friendly way, respond constructively to suggestions by pupils, and show other positive behaviors. The observation of behaviors such as the latter might help in rating the teacher for showing approving behavior even though few instances of such behavior could be observed.

The research that has been reviewed by Rosenshine has often been referred to as disappointing. The reason for applying this epithet is that the teacher has long been regarded as almost the sole agent responsible for children learning or not learning. Research showing only small relationships between teacher behavior and pupil achievement seems to demote the teacher from the sovereign role assigned to him by society. The mistake in all such discussion is to assume that the status of the teacher is at stake. Let us consider the role of the teacher as a reinforcer of pupil behavior and see what relationships between teacher behavior and pupil achievement one might expect to find in the Rosenshine type of study.

Teachers do engage in reinforcing pupil behavior, but there are many other sources of reinforcements. Workbook assignments generally permit the pupil to know whether his work is correct or incorrect. Pupils reinforce other pupils in numerous different ways. Parents reinforce pupil behavior. The pupil's world is full of reinforcing events. The school is a rich source of reinforcements and the teacher contributes only a small fraction of those reinforcements. Teachers are probably not very effective at reinforcing pupil behavior related to intellectual accomplishments, partly because they have too many other things to do. They have to find interesting materials that will attract the attention of the pupil. They have to plan and organize. They also have to diagnose the source of pupil difficulties and take steps to resolve these difficulties. Teachers are very busy people and can devote only a small part of their time to reinforcing pupil behavior. If this is a correct account of what teachers do, then one would expect only very small relationships between tendencies for teachers to provide positive reinforcements and pupil achievement.

Material Incentives: A Focus of Controversy

The problem of whether material reinforcements, involving objects desired by the child, are less or more effective than praise or other forms of verbal reinforcement is a matter of both scientific and practical interest. Numerous laboratory studies, reviewed by Benowitz and Busse (1970), have shown that reinforcements involving small trinkets, toys, and other items wanted by children, when used as reinforcers, produce more learning than is produced by verbal reinforcements. Benowitz and Busse (1970) conducted a study in a classroom situation and found similar results. The fact that their subjects were black children from poor families may have played some part in their results, but the weight of the evidence leads one to expect that even with white children from prosperous families a similar effect would be expected. The findings of research have led psychologists to suggest that all learning in school might be expedited by the universal use of material rewards. Some have even gone so far to propose that children be paid to learn in school, much as adults are paid to work. The idea is a radical one, and interesting, but any recommendations concerning its implementation will have to wait until more is known about the side effects of such a system.

interesting idea

Most teachers would take the position that learning activities can be made intrinsically interesting and that when this is done material reinforcers may add little. They also suggest that any small gains produced by material reinforcers may be counterbalanced by undesirable side effects. They argue in this connection that it is very important to make the learning activity so inherently interesting that the children want to engage in further learning for its own sake. They are fearful that the use of material reinforcers may result in some children never acquiring an inherent interest in learning and that such children will learn only the desire to accumulate possessions. Some of these points may be sound. The area needs careful investigation.

Complex Effects of Reinforcements on Human Behavior

It is easy to be lulled into the oversimplified notion that reinforcement operates on human behavior in just the same way that it does on behavior involving simpler organisms. Although differences will become more apparent in the later chapters on perception, problem solving, and transfer, a single example will be discussed here involving what is known as probability learning (see Brookshire, 1970).

Consider a task in which an animal or a human is faced with a task involving two levers (or two doors, or two buttons to press). The subject is confronted with this equipment and learns to press the levers. The experimenter arranges conditions so that the pressing of the right-hand lever is reinforced at random on 70 per cent of the occasions, and the pressing of the left-hand lever is reinforced at random on 30 per cent of the occasions. The reinforcement can be food, or a toy in the case of children, or some other appropriate object. In such a situation, the rational approach which will deliver the maximum number of reinforcements would be to press only the lever on the right, and that is exactly what animals other than man do. Man does something different. When a human is confronted with such a problem, he will settle down to pushing the right-hand lever 70 per cent of the time and the left-hand lever 30 per cent of the time, even though this provides him with fewer reinforcements than he would receive if he stayed with the right-hand lever. The result is that on this problem he does not do as well as other animals. Brookshire (1970) points out that man's behavior when confronted with such a problem reflects a belief that the problem is soluble and that, if he can only find the right system, then he will be able to obtain a reinforcement on every trial. Since the assignment of reinforcements is on a random basis, he cannot do this. Indeed, there is no way of outguessing the system. Other animals do better than man because they do not attempt, in most cases, to outguess the system and do not evolve strategies that attempt to do this. Brookshire does note that in the few cases in which subhuman creatures have shown the behavior typical of man in this situation there is reason for believing that they are trying out strategies to outfox the system.

One is reminded in this connection that Pavlov pointed out nearly a century ago that classical conditioning in man is probably very different from that in simpler organisms, because man possesses a speech system that influences behavior and exerts an influence on the conditioning process.

Negative Reinforcement and Punishment

Living creatures avoid some stimuli and engage in escape behavior if exposed to them. Thorndike referred to these stimuli as annoyers, but in recent times a more common practice has been to refer to them as *aversive* stimuli. Some of these are fairly universally aversive to organisms, particularly if they produce strong stimulation such as is produced by electric shock or hot objects. Some are quite specific to particular species. Many birds and monkeys show panic behavior when snakelike objects come into their field of vision. Young children four or five months old commonly show signs of distress when approached by persons other than their immediate family. At eighteen months they show fear responses when placed alone in a room with an unfamiliar object.

Aversive stimuli have long been used to control behavior, though less so in modern times. A great range of aversive stimuli has been used in this connection. Pain-inflicting stimuli were commonly used in the past, but the trend in recent times has been to produce an aversive situation through the withholding of an expected reward. Teachers and parents commonly undertake the latter by taking away a child's privileges. Thus a child may be punished by not being allowed to go out to play. The withholding of a reward is generally believed to be an effective means of controlling behavior. An interesting point to note is that while the withholding of an expected reward is punishing, the withholding of an expected punishment has not been well established to have a rewarding effect.

All aversive stimuli that actually occur may have two effects. They may inhibit behavior at onset, that is to say, at the time when they are immediately applied, but when they stop, the cessation may have much of the effect of a reward. When one obtains relief from pain, the relief may have many of the consequences of positive reinforcement. Behaviors occurring at the time when an aversive stimulus ceases are strengthened. This is the phenomenon referred to as negative reinforcement. *A negative reinforcer is a stimulus the removal of which increases the strength of a response.*

In the presence of an aversive stimulus, the organism typically shows escape behavior. When an escape behavior is successful, it reduces or removes the aversive stimulus. When this happens, the effective response is reinforced by the reduction or removal of the stimulus. The reinforcement thus operating is negative reinforcement.

Negative-reinforcement phenomena were first explored with classical conditioning. In the typical demonstration, a dog is placed in a harness, a bell is sounded, and, shortly after the bell, an electric shock is applied to one of his paws. The dog then raises his paw and escapes from the shock. After several repetitions of this sequence, the bell is sounded and the dog anticipates the shock by raising his paw. Avoidance behavior has taken the place of escape behavior. Learning has occurred, and the character of the learning is such that it is commonly called *avoidance learning*.

A small child may show behavior parallel to that just described. The child, exploring his neighborhood, meets a larger and very aggressive child who begins hitting him. The smaller child is able to escape from this aversive situation and runs home, but the escape behavior and the resulting removal of the aversive condition does more than just increase the tendency to escape on future such occasions. The escape behavior leads to avoidance behavior and the child simply learns to avoid the stronger aggressive child. Aversive stimuli, the reduction of which originally reinforced the escape behavior, come to reinforce avoidance behavior.

At this point, punishment must be distinguished from negative reinforcement. Punishment is used in society for the purpose of either weakening or obliterating a response. Negative reinforcement occurs when an aversive stimulus is turned off, but punishment has its effect when an aversive stimulus is turned on. A situation involving punishment is one in which an aversive stimulus either accompanies or follows a learned response. In practice punishment and positive reinforcement are used in combination. Consider a situation in which a parent is watching a child play in the front yard. Each time the child shows sign of moving out into the street, the parent voices some mild threat. The latter punishment is designed to inhibit the response of running out into the traffic. The child also discovers that as soon as he settles down again to play in the yard the threats of the parent are turned off. The cessation of threat, like the termination of any other aversive stimulus, has the effect of strengthening the response that accompanies it. In this case, the response associated with the turning off of the aversive stimulus is that of playing in the front yard and hence this response is strengthened by the negative reinforcement. Punishment is likely to be most effective when it leads to an alternative and more desirable response that is strengthened by the turning off of the punishment.

Mowrer (1960, p. 28) distinguishes punishment learning from learning involving negative reinforcement in this way: "It is proposed that so-called punishment be termed passive avoidance learning (learning to avoid by not doing something) and that the contrasting form of avoidance learning (learning to do something as a means of avoidance) be termed active avoidance learning." The distinction is a convenient one.

Aversive stimuli are commonly administered in the anticipation that they will lead to and strengthen desirable forms of behavior. Teachers expect children to walk in the halls in school and not run. If a child runs, then he is punished, sometimes by having to go back to the end of the hall and begin again. After a few incidents of this kind, walking behavior may become established and running behavior is avoided. The teacher may hope to accomplish two goals by making the running situation aversive. On the other hand, he may wish to weaken the tendency to run, and on the other, he may hope to strengthen the tendency to walk in the particular situation. A child might learn always to walk in this situation, not because the tendency to run is any less strong, but because the tendency to walk is relatively stronger.

Society does not always provide punishment under conditions in which there is some clear and feasible set of avoidance responses to the act punished. The person who is punished as a habitual criminal may have no other course open to him than a career of crime, for nobody will give him honest employment. A child who is punished for thumb-sucking may have no other comparably satisfying alternative activity to indulge in when he feels threatened. In such cases, punishment is directed toward the very temporary suppression of behavior, but it cannot provide a negative reinforcement for more desirable behavior.

The assumption is commonly made that a threat of an aversive stimulus will have much the same effect as the aversive stimulus itself. This is likely to be the case when the threat has been followed on some occasions by actual punishment. When it has been thus coupled, it would be expected to acquire some of the properties of the aversive stimulus for the shaping and control of behavior. When a mother smacks a child on the rear and, at the same time, says "No," she can expect that the word "No" will eventually acquire many of the aversive qualities of the smack and will have much the same effects on the child's behavior. Only the idle threat that is never paired with an aversive stimulus fails to have an influence.

Research on the Effectiveness of Negative Reinforcement and Punishment

The effectiveness of negative reinforcement in producing learning has long been demonstrated and studied in the laboratory. Before the turn of the century, Bechterev had shown that dogs rapidly learned to raise a paw to avoid shock and that this simple situation could be used to study a wide range of learning phenomena. The effectiveness of negative reinforcement has never really been questioned and there are some experimentalists such as Dinsmoor (1968) who take the position today that negative reinforcement produces just as effective learning as positive reinforcement and also provides some laboratory advantages. In the study of animal learning using small pellets of food as a positive reinforcer, the food consumed may slowly produce partial satiation of the hunger drive and a resulting change in behavior. On the other hand, if the animal is learning in a situation involving avoidance of electric shock no such satiation has been shown to occur, though some have speculated that living creatures may habituate slowly to aversive stimuli.

The early experiments by Thorndike (1932, 1935) on the effect of punishment on responses produced data suggesting, at first sight, that punishment did not weaken a response; later, when the data were reworked, the effect of punishment was shown to be roughly the opposite of reward. Controversy over the interpretation of the Thorndike data gave the impression that the effect of punishment had to be considered a matter subject to dispute. This impression was strengthened by research by Skinner (1938), who studied the effect of punishment on rats placed in a situation in which they had learned to obtain food by pressing a bar. In such a situation the mechanism that delivers food can be turned off and the rat will continue to depress the bar for some time, but will eventually stop pressing it. Skinner took rats that had learned to depress the bar and turned off the food mechanisms for all of them, but allowed them to continue depressing the bar. Half of the rats were then punished for depressing the bar by the mechanical application of a slap to the paw placed on the lever. Although the rats were slapped during the first ten bar presses the effect was only a temporary slowdown in their bar-pressing behavior. Skinner concluded that the effect of punishment was a temporary interference with the performance of the punished response and that the interference rapidly wore off when the punishment was withdrawn. Quite similar results were obtained by Estes (1944), who gave electric shock as a punishment for bar pressing. Estes did find more positive effects of punishment, though only when the punishment was either severe or prolonged, but the effects of punishment in his research could be described as being generally weak and certainly not dramatic. Later research, however, has shown dramatic effects of punishment in the control of behavior. Far from being the weak and unpredictable phenomenon that it appeared to be in early experiments, it has turned out to be one that can have a powerful effect on behavior when administered under particular conditions. Later research has done much to indicate what conditions must exist for punishment to be effective.

Solomon (1964) has summarized much of the later basic experimentation and has succeeded in identifying the conditions under which punishment does or does not suppress behavior. The first class of situation that he examined was that in which an aversive stimulus is used to suppress a response previously learned by means of reward or positive reinforcement. Many experiments have been undertaken on a wide range of species, but the results did not begin to fit together until research workers began to vary systematically the strength of the aversive stimulus administered. Solomon points out that when that is done, the effects of punishment fall into a clear pattern. Very mild punishment does no more than make the victim a little more alert. As the punishment becomes stronger, then it temporarily suppresses the response punished. Still stronger punishment produces a more marked suppression, and with some lasting effects. Very strong punishment produces a very complete and very permanent suppression of the response. For the punishment to be effective, it must occur very close in time to the response.

Much the same appears to be true of avoidance behavior. Mild aversive stimuli are likely to produce inconsistent and unreliable avoidance behavior, but strong stimuli may produce dramatic effects known as traumatic avoidance learning, a phenomenon reviewed by Solomon and Wynne (1954) and Turner and Solomon (1962). The usual method of demonstrating the phenomenon involves the use of a piece of equipment known as the Miller-Mowrer jumping box. The essence of the phenomenon is that an animal is placed on a grid which can be electrified, and is then given a near-fatal electric shock just after a light is turned on. The animal shows avoidance behavior by jumping off the grid. Without ever receiving another shock, the animal will continue to show escape behavior by jumping off the grid for hundreds of consecutive trials every time the light goes on. Indeed, the behavior virtually does not extinguish.

The results of research on punishment are not without surprises. One would expect that behaviors related to survival would have a resistance to punishment that would not be evident in the case of trivial learned behaviors, which are readily suppressed if a suitable intensity of a punishing stimulus is used, but this is not what has been found. If animals are severely punished several times by means of electric shock for performing actions instrumental in obtaining food and the punishment is subsequently withdrawn, the animals may well starve to death rather than attempt to obtain food through the act that has been punished. In such experiments the animals can obtain food only by means of the punished act and no other. A limited amount of research has also been undertaken on the effect of punishment on other forms of behavior that are considered to be essentially innate. Solomon points out that research generally shows that such innate forms of response can be suppressed by means of punishment if this occurs concurrently with the response. For example, birds that are just hatched tend to follow a moving object, which under natural conditions is the mother, and punishment will suppress that response. Once again it must be pointed out that the fact that punishment will suppress even those responses that are vital to survival indicates the extraordinary power of punishment to modify and control behavior—a conclusion that is quite contrary to the conclusions drawn from earlier research.

The general findings of Solomon are that punishment, if severe, is highly effective in suppressing behavior, but he also cautions the reader from overgeneralizing from limited laboratory data. He points out, for example, that punishment that is very effective in one situation may be quite ineffective if the punished response is followed closely by a rewarded response. An illustration of the latter would be if a child were smacked for running out in the street and then, a few seconds later, were rewarded with candy for playing on the sidewalk. Under such conditions the punished response may increase in strength, perhaps because it has led to a rewarding situation.

A very interesting application of the use of punishment is found in the treatment of children who show self-destructive behavior. These young children are typically hospitalized. If they are not kept in garments that provide physical restraint, they will injure themselves repeatedly, sometimes by hitting their bodies against sharp objects, sometimes by beating themselves with their hands, and by a great variety of other means. Such episodes will run into the hundreds every hour, and many of these unfortunate youngsters are covered with scars and lacerations from what they have done to themselves. Oddly enough, although such behavior is extremely painful to the children, the punishing effect that it has does not suppress the behavior. However, if the occurrence of such behavior is followed immediately by a strong electric shock, the punishment produced in this way by the physician does have an immediate effect of suppressing self-destructive behavior. Bucher, et al. (1968) have described some cases of this kind in which the effects have been dramatic and in which the self-destructive behavior disappeared and remained absent for as long a period as several weeks. These research workers also showed that if the shock were accompanied by the word "No," then this word also could be used to suppress self-destructive behavior. There was some tendency for the learned suppression to occur only in the presence of the experimenter who administered the shock, but the practical problem this presented was overcome by having the shock administered by several different persons. The most general suppression would probably be obtained by punishing the self-destructive behaviors in a great variety of situations with many different persons administering the shock or the restraining word "No." Similar success has been found in the suppression of pathological screaming behavior (see Hamilton and Standahl, 1969).

Some Issues Related to the Use of Aversive Stimuli in the Control of Behavior

There can be no doubt that punishment can be extremely effective, under some circumstances, in facilitating learning but the effectiveness of aversive stimuli for this purpose does not necessarily justify their use.

Modern society generally believes that if control over undesirable behavior can be brought about by pleasant means, the use of aversive stimuli should be avoided. Those who administer education have shown a trend toward reducing the aversive stimuli to which pupils are exposed and, as far as possible, they attempt to control learning by means of positive reinforcers. John Dewey long ago took the position in many of his writings that education cannot be regarded just as preparation for life. Education and childhood are a part of life and should provide experiences that are valued in themselves. Within the framework of such a philosophy, the adult has a questionable right to make life disagreeable for the child.

A real difficulty in arriving at practical educational policy in such matters is that one does not know the extent to which an individual can grow up to meet the demands of the real world without having some profitable experiences with aversive conditions. Painful experiences with hot objects and sharp objects appear to be quite important in enabling the individual to avoid being burned and injured. Animals that do not have these experiences during the growing period (see Hebb, 1958) show an extraordinary incapacity to avoid injury when they are mature. The person who loses sensitivity to pain has difficulty in preventing himself from being harmed. At a very basic level, the aversive stimuli produce learning that prevents injury. The real issue is whether aversive stimuli can be used effectively without undesirable side effects, for promoting social and academic learning. If a child were never punished for hurting another child, would he learn not to hurt other children? If a person were never punished, or never saw another person punished for taking the property of another, would he learn to avoid stealing? The answers to these questions are highly controversial, and so the use of aversive stimuli and punishment in education remains highly controversial.

One argument commonly put forward against the use of aversive stimuli for the control of learning is that the use of such stimuli is believed to have unfortunate side effects. This argument is found in many of the early writings of B. F. Skinner and of others who wrote on the subject before midcentury. Whether there are, or are not, such side effects to punishment as it might be used in educational situations remains a matter for argument. Solomon's review of the problem (1964) takes the firm position that there is no evidence to support the idea that the use of punishment has bad side effects that outweigh the advantages to be achieved through its use. Nevertheless, one can point to studies that show clearly that painful aversive stimuli often produce serious consequences. Brady's primates (1958), which were periodically shocked at random intervals shortly after a given signal, developed stomach ulcers if conditions were arranged so that an alert animal could press a key to turn off the anticipated shock. Maier's rats (1949) which were confronted with an insoluble problem, and, if they made an incorrect response, were physically punished by falling onto a hard surface, showed deep and prolonged disorganizations of behavior. Ulrich, Azrin, and Hutchinson (1965) reported that electric shock produces aggressive behavior in a wide variety of species. Sears, Maccoby, and Levin (1957) found that children who were punished most during early childhood showed at later ages the greatest frequency of behavior problems in the area of aggression. There is much evidence of this kind. The first three of the previous four references could perhaps be written off as irrelevant in that they used very strong aversive stimuli and the Brady and Maier studies involved noxious stimuli over many weeks. In educational situations, it is very unlikely that such intense aversive stimuli would be used for so long. The Ulrich et al. review covered experimental situations using a single electric shock but of extremely high intensity and representing a level of stimulation not used in the control of school learning. The Sears et al. study is not so easily dismissed. There is also evidence that anxiety builds up for a period of several hours after a punishing experience. This is known as the Kamin effect and has been demonstrated on a wide range of species. The review of the subject provided by Geller, Jarvik, and Robustelli (1970) indicates the generality of the phenomenon, though it still has to be demonstrated on man. Perhaps the control of learning through the use of aversive stimuli does have unfortunate side effects.

One additional consideration must be introduced in evaluating the use of aversive stimuli for promoting learning. Dinsmoor (1968) points out that one cannot reject the use of aversive stimuli merely because they may have bad side effects, because positive reinforcers also have side effects and these are not all desirable. The spoiled child is typically one whose life has been overwhelmed by an abundance of rewards. The excessive use of positive reinforcers may have effects just as unfortunate as the excessive use of negative reinforcements and punishments.

Much more needs to be discovered in this area before firm recommendations can be given to the teacher.

Some Effects of Timing and Magnitude of Reinforcements

Delay in Reinforcement and Informative Feedback

Contemporary educational literature frequently states that delay in reinforcement reduces the efficiency of learning in children. The origin of this belief is derived from the early experiments, mainly with rats, on the effect on learning of the delay in time between the behavior to be reinforced and the dispensing of the reinforcement. These experiments generally showed that delay produced a reduction in the amount of learning and that the reduction increased as the delay increased. The results were unfortunately generalized to humans and the belief that delay in reinforcement is damaging to learning soon became well established. Much of the guilt for this overgeneralization of limited results must be assigned to psychologists interested in operant conditioning phenomena and concerned with applications of the knowledge achieved to the design of teaching situations. Indeed, these psychologists promoted the idea that teaching machines were bound to give effective instruction because they provided immediate reinforcement while more typical teaching situations provided only delayed reinforcement.

Renner (1964) has made an excellent summary of the research on delay in reinforcement up to about 1963. A more recent but less theoretically oriented review by Bilodeau (1966), who has been closely associated with much of the research on motor learning, comes to substantially the same conclusions. The generalizations which Bilodeau has derived have been substantiated by subsequent work and some well-supported statements about the effect of delay in reinforcement on learning on both human and subhuman learners can now be made. In the case of animals, Renner points out that several different conditions of delay have been studied. Delay in the reinforcement may be by a constant time interval or by a variable interval. Some experiments have both trials with delay and trials with immediate reinforcement as soon as the terminal behavior is completed. Constant delay and variable delay seem to have quite different effects. In the case of subhuman animals, Renner reaches the familiar conclusion that the introduction of a constant delay retards learning. On the other hand, if the delay is variable, the effects are not as clear-cut, for sometimes there is no effect on acquisition whereas sometimes there is a retarding effect. Variable delay leads to increased resistance to extinction. Delay does not generally retard human learning. Studies have also turned up the finding that some delay may sometimes help retention, although why this is so is quite obscure. The delay in feedback may merely prolong the learning task and thereby provide rather better conditions for learning. In some of the studies the apparent improved retention associated with a delay is an artifact, as Markowitz (1966) has shown. In only one area of human learning has delay been found consistently to have deleterious effects, namely, in discrimination learning with young children (Rieber, 1964).

In the case of discrimination learning in children of elementary-school and preschool age, a few studies have shown an advantage for immediate versus delayed reinforcement, but the data show no clear trend. Rieber (1964), who has conducted a whole series of studies related to this problem, points out that the phenomenon is greatly complicated by the frustration effect produced by a delay in reinforcement. One might perhaps expect retarded children to be particularly susceptible to any delay in reinforcement effect, but this has not been found (see Hetherington and Ross, 1966).

In more recent times, interest in the effect of delay on reinforcement has been focused on problems of verbal learning. Experimental psychologists concerned with this issue have generally used word-association learning (the paired-associate learning technique). A study of Atkinson (1966) uses this technique and also provides some illuminating results. Atkinson started out by taking note of the fact that previous studies on the effect of delay in reinforcement on word-association learning had produced highly inconsistent results. Sometimes the delay increased the effectiveness of learning, but sometimes the results were deleterious. The delay in reinforcement (right or wrong) was typically a matter of a few seconds. Atkinson sought to resolve these discrepancies and to pin down the unidentified condition that was producing them. He presented on a screen combinations of three different letters, referred to as three-letter trigrams. The subject had to respond by giving a number from two to nine. For each trigram, one number was a correct response and any other number given was wrong. The experimenter decided arbitrarily which number was to be called right in the case of each trigram. The subject was presented with a trigram on the screen. He then immediately guessed which was the right number by pressing a key that represented that number. Then, either immediately after his response, or after a delay of up to twelve seconds, reinforcement was provided either by the correct number together with the trigram appearing on the screen or by the subject being told whether he was right or wrong. In addition, during the interval between the making of the response and obtaining reinforcement, some subjects were instructed to count backwards by threes, whereas others were not so instructed. The experiment was in fact somewhat more complex, but the description given here is adequate for present purposes.

The most significant finding of the study was that delay in reinforcement was a condition favorable to learning, provided that the subject did not have to count. If he had to count during the interval while waiting for reinforcement, then the delay was either harmful or had no effect. The combination of delay in feedback and requiring the subject to count backwards was *not* harmful if the feedback given the learner consisted of both the trigram and the right answer. It was harmful if the feedback consisted only of the words "right" or "wrong." The implication is that if the learner makes a response to a trigram and then has to count backwards, he has difficulty in remembering what his response was by the time he is told "right" or "wrong." However, if after counting backwards he is then told what the right response is, and is also shown the trigram, then he can use the information and learn through it. In contrast, if the interval between his response to the trigram and the feedback is a time when he can do what he wants, then it provides a condition favorable to learning. It permits, among other activities, rehearsal. What happens during the delay interval that promotes learning is probably complicated and is given some consideration in the later chapter on retention.

The results of the Atkinson study remind one of the results of a much earlier classic study by Carlton (1954), who showed that delay in reinforcement of maze running in rats did not affect learning, provided that the rats' orientation toward the goal box was maintained during the delay period. The study involved a very simple learning situation in which rats left a starting box, moved down a short alley, and then entered the goal box. Contact with a bar in the goal box resulted in the delivery of a food pellet after a given interval of time. Two different goal boxes were used. In the one goal box the walls were only two inches apart and the ceiling so low that the rat had almost no opportunity to move once he reached the goal. The alternative goal box was seventeen inches wide and provided opportunity for the rat to move during the delay interval. Some rats were run with no delay in the delivery of food in the goal box, but others had to wait ten seconds for the delivery of the pellet of food. The interesting results were that, in the confining goal box, learning was the same whether there was no delay or a ten-second delay, but in the case of the rats free to move about in the goal box delay in reinforcement reduced learning substantially. Confinement kept the rats oriented toward the goal box, but in free movement it was as if they lost track of what they had been doing.

A second type of verbal learning task has also been used in research on delayed and immediate information feedback. Reference is made here to studies that involve materials similar to those used in schools. Sassenrath and Yonge (1968) have reviewed many of these studies as a preliminary to conducting one of their own. They point out that the numerous studies do not come up with a clear answer. Research does not typically show any significant difference between delayed and immediate feedback or learning. However, they also find that a group of studies suggest that delayed feedback may result in better long-term retention than does immediate feedback. In the Sassenrath and Yonge study, students were given sixty four-choice multiple-choice items, one at a time, which they read and then guessed an answer. The initial scores on the test indicated that the students had virtually no knowledge of the subject matter. Those who received what they called immediate feedback were then given the test over again, but with the answers marked. The delayed feedback group did not receive the test with the answers marked until a week later. One should note that in this study, as in many other studies with school-like material, what is called immediate feedback involves a delay of fifteen or more minutes, and bears little relationship to the twelve-second or less delay involved in the Atkinson study. The terms *immediate* and *delayed* are relative and have no absolute significance.

Sassenrath and Yonge administered a test of retention following the feedback material, and gave the same test again a week later. They found that immediate feedback and delayed feedback had no difference in their effects on measures of retention made right after the learning session, but that delayed feedback had an advantage on long-term retention. This finding is consistent with the findings of many earlier studies and also confirms a study by Lintz (1968) undertaken with third-grade boys and involving auditory materials.

One must presume that the effect of delayed versus immediate feedback in the group of studies just discussed is a different phenomenon from the effect found in the paired-associate learning studies. In the Atkinson type of study, delay would appear to facilitate rehearsal, but in the Sassenrath and Yonge study the delayed condition does not provide any particular opportunity for rehearsal of the materials to occur as compared with the immediate feedback condition. A much more likely hypothesis is that the delayed feedback situation in the latter study spreads out learning over a longer interval of time, a condition that generally favors more effective learning. Delay in feedback, in the case of human learning, involves many different phenomena, some of which are favorable to learning.

The difference in the negative effect of delay in reinforcement in animal studies of motor and perceptual learning and the positive effect of delay in many human studies has to be understood in terms of what happens inside the learner. One factor is that, compared with other species, the human has a superior capability of holding information inside himself for future use or until a reinforcing event arrives. Very often, man converts the information to be held in temporary storage into a verbal form to make it more retainable with greater precision. For example, suppose I try to draw a line three inches long, and I make it as nearly as possible one half the width of the paper, by doing this I have found a way of describing my performance accurately to myself. If the experimenter thirty seconds later says the line was a half inch too long, I now know that next time I have to make a line less than half the width of the paper. By translating my performance into words I have *coded* the information for later use. It is this coding that permits me to use feedback that comes at a later time. The coding process does for the human being what maintaining an orientation does for the animal. Holding the animal in position maintains the external situation before it, but in the human, the situation can be held internally and conceptually through the coded description.

In summary, one can conclude that although animal studies show a considerable advantage for immediate in contrast with delayed reinforcement, the same conclusion cannot be drawn from human studies. The human learner may benefit from delays in reinforcement in many subtle ways. Delay may provide opportunity to rehearse the response, and may also distribute learning over a greater span of time, also with an added advantage. One can no longer justify the use of teaching machines on the grounds that they provide immediate reinforcement, for the evidence generally favors delayed reinforcement, particularly when the criterion of learning is retention over some substantial interval of time.

Finally, the point must be stressed that while delay in reinforcement is often critical in the training of animals, there are much more critical problems of timing in the case of human learning. For example, Bourne and Bunderson (1963) found that in a concept-learning task, the most critical matter in the timing of the task was the amount of time allowed *after* feedback or reinforcement before the next problem was presented. What appears to happen is that the subject is given a problem; he attempts a solution; then he is told whether he is right or wrong. After he has received this information, he needs time to assimilate it and perhaps to think over why he was right or wrong. If he is not given time to do this, but is hurried on to the next problem, then learning is retarded. In such tasks as Bourne and Bunderson used, the critical matter is not how quickly the reinforcement or feedback arrives, but whether there is a pause after reinforcement to permit the subject to use the information provided. A later study by Jones (1968) confirmed the finding of the importance of the post-feedback interval and also suggested that this interval was the period during which the information provided by feedback was used by the subject. Jones also found that the length of the post-feedback interval was a much more critical matter than the length of the delay in providing feedback. The conclusion to be drawn is that it is not enough to tell a child whether his solution to a problem is right or wrong. The child must also be given time to think about what makes his answer right or wrong. Too often the teacher provides the child with feedback and then rushes on to the next problem.

Information Given Before Responding Versus Information Given After Responding: Two Methods of Teaching

Very clear evidence of the noncritical nature of delays in providing feedback is seen in the fact that the information provided by feedback can sometimes be given *before* rather than after the response. When this is done, learning may take place just as well as when the usual sequence of response followed by feedback is used. Although this chapter has emphasized that the response-reinforcement model of learning produces efficient results in many learning situations, the reader must not lose sight of the fact that man differs from lower organisms in that he is able to use information provided in advance of action. Lower organisms are much less capable of either obtaining or using such advance information. Only man can be told in advance of attempting to solve a problem how he should go about solving it. This is because man can obtain through verbal communication more information than lower organisms can, and he has a vastly greater capacity for storing information for later use. How much information should be given to a human learner prior to his attempt to solve a problem is a controversial issue in education. Traditional teaching procedures generally advocated giving the pupil substantial information before he, the pupil, attempted to solve the problem. In recent times effort has been devoted to the development of teaching methods in which the pupil himself attempts to discover the principle involved in the solution of particular classes of problems. This is the discovery method of learning, which in many respects follows the response-reinforcement model in that a minimum amount of information is given in advance and the pupil has to make some kind of response before he finds out whether he is right or wrong. Discovery methods provide the pupil with little advance information concerning how he should go about solving a problem, in contrast with more traditional methods that guide the pupil with advance information. Information given before responding can influence behavior only when the information can be stored until needed. Information given after responding can influence behavior only if a knowledge of the response can be stored long enough so that it can be evaluated in terms of the information given.

Instances are certainly accumulating in which information given before the subject makes a response produces learning that is at least as good as when the learning process requires the subject to respond and then find out whether his response was appropriate. In order to compare the effect of giving information before a response is made with the effect of providing information subsequent to the response, von Wright devised an ingenious situation (1955, 1957). The essential feature of the von Wright situation was that the subject had to follow his path through a paper maze presented on a moving band of paper. The apparatus could be arranged so that the subject could see far enough ahead so that he could take the correct turn each time the pathway split. The apparatus could also be arranged so that the subject could see only a small part of the pathway ahead and hence had to make a decision, each time the path split, without knowing whether the choice was correct or not. In the latter case, the subject had to wait until the paper had moved a certain distance before he could find out whether he was on the right path or had chosen a blind alley. It required from three to five times as much time to learn the maze when information followed the making of a choice than when it preceded it. When information is given after the choice has been made, the subject must retain information about the choice he has made, then evaluate that choice in the light of the information later provided, and finally store in his memory the information about what he should have done. The latter is a complicated process in comparison to that of storing advance information concerning a correct response.

A number of studies have been conducted by Annett (1959, 1961), in which a comparison has been made between subjects who were given information in advance of the task and subjects given knowledge of results after they had made a response. An important point to note is that the Annett tasks were perceptual rather than motor. In one experiment the task of the subjects was to estimate the number of dots presented on a screen for a very brief exposure. One group was told the correct number in advance of each presentation; the other group saw the dots presented, guessed the number, and then was told the correct number. (A control group was given no information at all.) Both subject groups improved in their ability to estimate the number of dots, but they did not differ from one another significantly; it made no difference whether information was given before exposure to the stimuli or after responding.

In a second study by Annett (1961) the basic task of the subjects was to identify the occurrence of a tone that was so faint that it could barely be heard (this is referred to as a *near-threshold tone*). One group received a short flash a half second before each signal (tone) occurred; another group received a flash after the signal, to indicate to the subject that he had responded correctly or that he had missed the signal. The group that received the advance information showed a significantly greater gain than the group that received information after responding.

The tasks that have shown some advantage for information given before rather than after responding have been tasks in which the learning involved is better described as perceptual learning rather than motor learning. The central focus of the task is on perceiving rather than on other forms of action.

Magnitude of Reinforcement

An important and significant problem is the extent to which magnitude or quantity of the reinforcer is related to learning. Suppose a person could keep his job only if he learned to speak Spanish, a language important in his business contacts, and let us say that during the period of learning the foreign language, payment was related to how much he learned. Would he learn faster if he were given ten cents for each foreign word learned than if he were given only five cents? In most learning situations the assumption is made by the teacher that minor rewards, such as the pupil being told that he is right, are just as effective as lavish praise. If money or candy were used as reinforcers, then most teachers would bet that a small amount would be just as effective in producing learning as a large amount. Data on this problem have been largely lacking.

As with most problems on learning, the main attempts to find a solution have involved work with animals. The difficulties involved in experimenting in this area stem from the fact that, for there to be any effect, the animals have to be able to discriminate a large reward from a small reward. In the case of a child it is easy to say, "Today you will get a piece of candy for every ten answers correct," or "Today you can get twice as much candy as yesterday, for we will give you a piece for every five answers that are right." A rat might not show any signs of recognizing the difference between one pellet of food and two pellets. We can point out to a child that a reward is larger or smaller than previously, or the child may readily recognize differences in the magnitude of rewards even if they are not pointed out, but subhuman subjects are much less capable of making this discrimination. Special techniques have had to be evolved for the study of the effect of magnitude of reward on the learning of animals.

Much of the knowledge in the area derived from research with animals has been summarized in two reviews. The first of these, by Pubols (1960), summarizes the main well-established empirical findings. The second by Black (1968) is much more theoretically oriented and does an excellent job of pointing up the theoretical issues.

Pubols (1960) finds substantial support for a number of propositions as a result of his review of studies of animal learning. The fact that the findings fit with common experience with human behavior suggests that Pubols' conclusions may well apply in the human field, but this is a conjecture that should be applied with caution. First, Pubols states that studies generally show that an increase or a decrease in incentives or reinforcements does not affect rate of learning. A major exception to this is that the reinforcements or incentives cannot be reduced to zero without a corresponding reduction in learning. Second, as the incentive or reinforcement is increased in quantity, the final level of performance reaches higher levels. Responses learned with larger reinforcements have the appearance of being more resistant to extinction, but this is only because they are learned to higher levels in the first place as a result of the larger reinforcement. When responses are learned to the same level of performance but with different magnitudes of reinforcements, then the rate of extinction is the same.

Black (1968) has summarized some other recent findings of the relationship of reward magnitude to behavior in such situations. First, a reduction in the reward results in a decline in the vigor of the response. Reduce the amount of food at the end of a single-alley straight runway, and the rat runs less rapidly. Second, an increase in the reward increases the vigor of the response. The rat runs more rapidly as the reward is increased. Third, when the reward is reduced, the rat shows a reduced level of performance, but it is reduced below the performance level of rats that are run continuously on the lower level of reward. The latter is known as the contrast effect. This effect is shown only when the level of reward is reduced. There is no corresponding effect when the level of reward is increased.

Black (1968) favors an explanation of the phenomenon very similar to that proposed much earlier by Spence (1956, 1960). The increase and decrease in vigor of the response is attributable to the change in incentive value but this in itself does not mean that a higher reward produces more learning, although it does produce greater vigor of response. The contrast effect is understood as a building up of inhibition that occurs when the level of reward is reduced. Thus a reduction of reward results not only in a reduction in incentive value but also in a building up of inhibition that also reduces the vigor of response.

Most of the recent studies reviewed by Black (1968) are concerned with the effect of reward on the maintaining of behavior, rather than with the acquisition of new behavior. Similar results have been found in studies involving the maintenance of behavior in children. Nakamura and Boraczi (1965) cite a series of studies to which they have contributed showing that the persistence of children's responses is related to the magnitude of the reinforcement involved. They have also demonstrated that children respond more vigorously when the reinforcement is increased and less vigorously when it is reduced. Another study with adults by Toppen (1965) has shown that increasing the pay on a dull repetitive task increased the output, and Leventhal (1964) found that such an increase made the task appear more attractive. These findings, like those just reviewed, are hardly astounding. Although these studies are of some theoretical interest, their practical implications hardly go beyond what the nonpsychologist already knows. In laymen's terms they can be said to suggest what is obvious, namely, that a person jumps more rapidly to pick up a five-dollar bill lying on the floor than he does when the bill is only a one-dollar, and also that a person who occasionally finds a five-dollar bill will engage more in searching behavior than a person who finds only one-dollar bills. These studies do not tell us what, as teachers, we may want to know, namely, whether increasing the size of the reward will increase the rate of acquisition of a skill. This is a very different matter from the matter of maintaining behavior already acquired.

A few early studies (Thorndike, 1935) in the area did attack the problem of interest to teachers and others in education, with results which fit quite well those summarized by Pubols and Black. Some more recent research on the effect of varying the amount of reinforcement on human behavior has been reviewed by Atkinson (in press) and with some interesting conclusions. The research reviewed is mainly that of W. F. Harley, Jr., who has been concerned with tasks involving paired-associate learning. Atkinson points out that the Harley studies, like many of those previously conducted, show that giving the same subject different rewards on different parts of a task results in difference in amount learned. On the other hand, when some subjects are given a large reward, say twenty-five cents, for each item learned, and other subjects are given no money for learning, then there is no difference between the high-reward and the low-reward group. Atkinson explains this difference by suggesting that under the condition in which some items are to be rewarded, if they are learned, by twenty-five cents and the others are not thus rewarded, the subject simply studies those associated with the reward and neglects the others. The low-reward and high-reward items are thus processed differently. In addition, Atkinson suggests that the high-reward items may be rehearsed, while the other items are neglected. The subject is likely to bring to the rewarded items all the learning strategies he has. In addition, Atkinson cites data from an unpublished study by K. Gibson which also suggest that the effect of introducing a reward for performance on a portion of a task results in the adoption of an effective strategy with that portion of the task, but to the neglect of other unrewarded portions of the task. The effects of varying the magnitude of reinforcement seem to be indirect (see also Pihl and Greenspoon, 1969).

The review of the studies that have been made of the effect of varying the magnitude of the reinforcer on the amount of learning suggests how this factor should and should not be used in practical teaching situations. The results fit well with the experience of those who have attempted to introduce a token system or a point system for controlling learning and have found that children under such a system soon take the attitude that they will learn only those things for which they are paid in points or tokens. This behavior is much like those of the subjects in the experiments reviewed who learned only the high-reward items in a list of items. Another finding of interest is that the reinforcements operating in most laboratory tasks are sufficient to ensure learning and that any increment in them is likely to have little effect on learning. One is tempted to generalize from this finding and to suggest that any increment in the reinforcements provided by the classroom will probably have little effect. The latter needs to be investigated.

Partial Reinforcement and Schedules of Reinforcement

In natural settings, there are few very specific behaviors that are followed 100 percent of the time by reinforcement. A predatory animal visits a particular location where food is commonly found but perhaps finds food there on only 50 per cent of the occasions. Whether it finds food or not is largely a result of numerous chance factors operating. One might say that, under such circumstances, the schedule of reinforcement is random. In a sense one might argue that the hunting behavior of an animal is always reinforced on 100 per cent of the occasions, in that the search for food either has to be successful or the animal dies.

Many learned human operants are not reinforced on most of the occasions on which they occur. The nursery-school child who plays gently with another may be complimented from time to time by the teacher. There may also be some rewards intrinsic to the gentle play situation that maintain this behavior, but this kind of play situation seems to be quite dependent upon the incidence of suitable external reinforcement for it to be maintained over any great length of time. The acquisition of social skills, where only some successful performances are reinforced, is to be contrasted with the acquisition of academic knowledge, in which some kind of reinforcement or knowledge of results is provided after every performance.

An important matter is what happens when the frequency of reinforcement is reduced from reinforcement on every trial to reinforcement on only some trials. The rate of learning goes down as the frequency of reinforcement is reduced and this is to be expected. However, another thing also happens. As the reinforcement is reduced, the behavior becomes less and less amenable to extinction. A favorite kind of experimental situation for the study of this phenomenon is the one-armed bandit, the Las Vegas type of slot machine. With such a device a person can be reinforced on every trial or on any percentage of trials that the experimenter may wish. In studies using this kind of equipment, the typical finding is that the most difficult response to extinguish is the one that has been reinforced on about 50 percent of the occasions, though there are some exceptions to this rule. On the other hand, when the subject is reinforced on every trial and the reinforcements are then cut off, the response is readily extinguished. The phenomenon discussed here is known as the partial reinforcement effect. One hundred per cent reinforcement is most effective for rapid acquisition, but the response that is most stable and the most resistant to extinction is one that has been learned with a schedule of reinforcement of less than 100 per cent reinforcement.

Because there are many habits of behavior that one hopes will be permanent and that may be reinforced only rarely after they are acquired such habits should be learned on a schedule of less than 100 per cent reinforcement, or, if they are initially learned on a schedule of less than 100 per cent reinforcement, then they should probably be maintained for a period following acquisition with a tapered-off frequency of reinforcement. Such a rule would appear to apply well in planning the learning of habitual modes of behaving, but there is no evidence that the acquisition of academic knowledge should be learned on this kind of basis. Indeed, most psychologists would unequivocally advocate that in the case of academic knowledge, the pupil be reinforced on every trial.

The partial reinforcement effect, commonly referred to as PRE, is of considerable theoretical interest, a fact that accounts for the continued large numbers of researches that appear on the topic. Excellent reviews of the massive literature published on the subject have been written by Jenkins and Stanley (1950) and by Lewis (1960). These reviews have been mainly directed toward an examination of the theoretical issues and the formulation of a theoretical interpretation of the phenomenon.

No theoretical explanation is entirely satisfactory at this time, and, indeed, there may be no single satisfactory explanation of the partial reinforcement effect. The nearest to a defensible explanation is the discrimination theory. This theory states that resistance to extinction is a function of the difference between stimuli present during acquisition and stimuli present during extinction. The theory argues that when acquisition is accompanied by 100 per cent reinforcement and then the reinforcement suddenly stops, the subject quickly discriminates between the original state of affairs and the new one. If, on the other hand, the subject is reinforced on only 25 per cent of the trials during the acquisition series and then reinforcements are stopped, the change is not as easily identified and behavior continues as though there had been no change in the situation. When reinforcements are provided on only 25 per cent of the trials, there will sometimes be quite long runs of trials without any reinforcement at all, and thus, when the reinforcements are switched off, there are no very dramatic changes in the situation, but just a very long series of trials without any reinforcement. Most, but not all, of the experimental attempts to verify the discrimination theory experimentally have produced supporting evidence. There are also alternative explanations, all of which encounter as much, if not more, conflicting evidence in the studies designed to test them. These alternative explanations all tend to single out some special aspects of the behavior observed during partial reinforcement to account for the phenomenon. The so-called after-effects theory, for example, is based on the fact that at the end of a nonreinforced trial in a maze running in rats, the rat engages in behavior related to searching for food and behavior related to frustration. These behaviors produce stimuli inside the rat which become conditioned to the running response on the next trial. Hence, next time the animal engages in food-searching behavior in the goal box, the internal stimuli tend to produce running behavior as soon as the rat is placed back in the starting box. What the animals essentially learn, according to this theory, is to respond to the frustrations of not being rewarded by further running behavior on the next trial. If the rat is reinforced on every trial, then it does not have the opportunity to learn to respond to the nonreinforcement situation.

There are a vast number of different ways in which reinforcements on less than a 100 per cent basis can be arranged. One may decide to reinforce every second or every third or every fourth instance of the behavior with which one is concerned. This is called a *fixed-ratio* schedule of reinforcement. After each reinforced response there are a number of nonreinforced responses before the next one is reinforced. Sometimes an abbreviation is used in discussing a fixed-ratio schedule. For example, if the sixth response and no other were to be reinforced, the term *FR-6* would be used to indicate that a fixed-ratio schedule was used and that every sixth response in the category of interest was reinforced.

A second schedule of reinforcement is the *variable-ratio* schedule. In setting up such a schedule, the experimenter may decide that 25 per cent of the behaviors are to be reinforced, but that the number of nonreinforced behaviors that lie between two reinforced behaviors may vary from zero to eight. The number of nonreinforced trials between successive reinforced trials may be determined by throwing dice or other means of obtaining a list of random numbers. The variable-ratio schedule under consideration would be denoted as *VR-4* to indicate that, *on the average*, one behavior in four is reinforced.

Schedules of reinforcement may be established not in terms of the number of consecutive behaviors that are nonreinforced following each one that is reinforced, but in terms of the time that elapses from one reinforcement to the next. One might decide, for example, to reinforce a child for the first occurrence of attentive behavior following the end of a five-minute period measured from the last attentive behavior that was reinforced. If one did this, then the reinforcement schedule would be described as a *fixed-interval* schedule or, in this case, a *FI-5* schedule. Finally, the interval of time between reinforcements may be varied and form a random pattern. When this is done, the interval is said to be a *variable-interval* schedule.

There are numerous other schedules that have also been used in rare experimental designs. For example, in one unusual type of schedule, reinforcements always occur in pairs with two successive behaviors being reinforced. There is no limit to the number of patterns or combination of patterns that can be devised.

The effect of these schedules of reinforcement on behavior have been extensively studied in the case of rats, pigeons, and a few other subhuman species, using mainly consumables as reinforcers. The applicability of the results of these studies to problems of learning and maintaining human behavior in natural situations is largely a matter of conjecture, although a few experiments with humans using rather artificial laboratory tasks have produced fairly similar results. Thus many studies have found that a fixed-ratio schedule of reinforcement provided for a pigeon, pecking a small disc on the wall of its training cage, results in a very uniform output of pecking behavior, but pecking stops almost immediately when the reinforcements are stopped. This is very much like a factory worker paid on a piece rate, who receives a dollar for every five pieces he makes. Industry has long found that such a payment plan produces a very uniform output of work. If one wishes to have the behavior continue after reinforcements are terminated, then a variable-ratio schedule of reinforcement is to be commended, but it cannot be introduced in a factory, although it can be used in a school. The latter schedule produces the partial reinforcement effect previously discussed.

Fixed-interval schedules produce a very different effect. Animals reinforced on this basis tend to show a low output of the reinforced behavior except toward the end of the interval, when the reinforcement is about to occur. If a pigeon is reinforced for pecking at a disc on the wall for the first pecking response following the end of each minute, then pecking behavior is likely to be absent during the first forty-five seconds of each minute and then become more frequent as the time arrives when reinforcement is due. The output of work is very variable under the fixed-interval schedule. When the variable interval is introduced, the performance becomes more steady and may even approach that of the variable-ratio schedule.

In the fixed-interval schedule of reinforcement, there are times when the subject can obtain no reinforcement. Such periods are commonly referred to as *time out from reinforcement*. Such time outs represent quite aversive kinds of situations.

Explanations of Reinforcement

Scientists are rarely content to sit back and observe an interesting phenomenon in all its manifestations. Curiosity leads scientists to imagine what is behind the phenomenon, what are the mechanisms that produce it, and how it is related to other phenomena, and then to seek out means of checking on these conjectures. In common language, this is what is called finding explanations. Psychologists have been much more successful in identifying interesting phenomena, of which reinforcement is one, than in finding explanations for them. Indeed, the task of finding explanations has been so unsuccessful that some psychologists take the position that it is a hopeless pursuit at this time. Those who assume this position view the immediate role of the psychologist as that of discovering relationships between conditions of learning and measures of what is learned, that is to say, there is to be no theorizing but only the accumulation of facts. This recipe for progress has some virtue to it, for psychologists have been far too prone to jump ahead with theorizing, even before a substantial body of fact is there to provide a foundation, but on the negative side there is the overwhelming argument that no science has ever shown much progress through the massing of facts alone. Those scientists who have been able to look beyond the facts and devise experiments to check out their conjectures are those who have been able to produce the great advances in knowledge.

Explanations of reinforcement are many (see Reid, Travers, and van Wagenen, 1964), and yet they are unsuccessful as scientific explanations in that it has not been possible to devise many worthwhile experiments to check on their validity. The earliest type of explanation was put forward by Thorndike, who proposed that what he called satisfiers (these are essentially positive reinforcers) acted in some way on stimulus-response connections that just preceded the occurrence of the satisfier. The argument would be that if a child saw a cookie jar and said "Please, cookie!" and then obtained a cookie, that the satisfier, the cookie, functioned in some way by strengthening the connection between the stimulus provided by the cookie jar and the response of saying "Please, cookie!" The supposed strengthening of this connection is alleged to account for the increased tendency for the child to ask for a cookie when he sees the cookie jar. In modern terms, the supposed increase in the strength of the connection is claimed to account for the effect of the reinforcement provided by the cookie.

As a conjecture, the idea is plausible that the reinforcer acts back on the connection between a stimulus and response that has just been used, but it is not a very useful speculation. We know already that a reinforcer, by definition, increases the probability of a particular response in a particular situation, so the explanation does not really add anything or suggest anything that we do not already know. Also, the explanation does not even begin to suggest how one can begin studying the reasons that underlie the reinforcement phenomenon. Indeed, there does not seem to be a single experiment that has grown out of this idea that a reinforcer strengthens a bond. In summary, the explanation is a sterile one.

A very different attempt at explanation is found in the work of Hull (1943), Hull proposed that behavior is always energized by what he called drives, which are strong internal stimuli that result in heightened activity. If an animal is deprived of food, strong internal stimuli are produced that result in a heightened level of activity. Food reduces the drive by reducing these internal stimuli, and this, in turn, lowers the level of activity. Hull's argument is that food functions as a reinforcer because it produces the reduction in a drive and that it is the reduction in the drive that produces the change in the response probability. This explanation has some possibility of being tested experimentally. One can, for example, implant a tube in a vein of a small hungry animal, such as a rat, and arrange that whenever the animal performs a particular act, such as that of pressing down a bar with its forepaws, a small amount of sugar solution is released into the vein. If the drive-reduction theory of reinforcement is correct, then the release of the sugar solution should reduce the hunger drive and have a reinforcing effect. Some evidence has been provided by such experiments to suggest that the release of the sugar directly into the vein does have a reinforcing effect. This indeed supports the drive-reduction theory of reinforcement, but, as often happens, other psychologists have been just as clever in producing other evidence strongly supporting the opposite position. A very simple experiment, now performed innumerable times in many different forms, has shown that a solution of saccharin is an excellent reinforcing agent for a hungry rat. Now the saccharin solution cannot possibly produce drive reduction, in that saccharin is a biologically inert substance, provides no calories, and does not enter into the metabolic processes. The saccharin solution cannot reduce any drive. In such an experiment care has to be taken that the solution does not reduce another drive, such as thirst. Of great significance is the fact that sugar solution and saccharin have essentially the same reinforcing properties, despite the fact that one reduces the hunger drive, while the other cannot.

The outcome of the research generated by the drive-reduction theory of reinforcement is the conclusion that drive reduction may play a part in the functioning of reinforcers but it is clearly not the only mechanism operating. There are other suggested mechanisms, but probably none that have been so carefully and systematically explored as the drive-reduction mechanism.

A third kind of interpretation of reinforcement involves what is called the expectancy hypothesis. This was first advanced as a part of a systematic theory of learning by the late Edward Tolman, but it is also found in writings produced in the last century. The concept of expectancy is derived from personal experience, but many useful and sound scientific concepts have been thus derived. The concept of expectancy, derived from daily living, is still far from being the scientific concept that one would like it to be, but the arguments for attempting to convert it from a crude popular idea to a precisely defined scientific concept are substantial. One does produce much behavior because one expects to achieve certain results. One does place a dime in a Coca-Cola machine because one expects to obtain a Coke. It is much more plausible to state that one deposits a dime in a Coke machine because one expects to obtain a Coke than it is to say that one deposits the dime because one has been reinforced in the past for performing this act. In midmorning one goes to the room where coffee is available because one expects to obtain coffee there—or does one go just because one has been reinforced with coffee by going there in the past? Certainly, the first time one went to coffee one must have gone with some expectancy of receiving coffee, because others in the office had told us about it. If expectancy was an important element the first time, then why might it not be an important element on subsequent occasions? The expectancy argument receives strong support from our daily experience.

The expectancy theorists have argued that what is learned is not responses, as the reinforcement psychologists have argued, but expectancies. This kind of explanation takes the position that when a rat runs a maze, what is learned is not a specific series of responses that come to have a high probability of occurring in the maze situation, but an expectancy on the part of the rat that certain broad categories of action will lead to certain results. The difficulty has been to find evidence for this position. One approach of nearly half a century ago was to find out whether a rat could still run a maze, even though made incapable of performing the responses it had learned during acquisition training. Rats that have been surgically treated after learning to run a maze, and hence can no longer run, will still manage to wriggle through the alleys and reach the goal box. Whatever is learned, it is not the specific set of running responses that have been "reinforced." Such evidence does not argue strongly for the idea that expectancy is a crucial factor in such learning, but only that one cannot account for learning in terms of the acquisition of specific responses alone or even in terms of broad classes of responses.

A rather different approach to the problem of the role of expectancy in learning was evolved by the late Clark Hull and his student, the late Kenneth Spence. Their work, in this respect, stems from the observation that when a hungry animal is performing the task that it has already learned of running a maze for food in the goal box, the animal typically makes what are referred to as fractional anticipatory goal responses during its passage through the alleys. Such an animal will smack its lips and make swallowing movements as it passes along the runway, and these anticipatory responses occur long before the animal reaches the goal box. They are called goal responses in that they involve responses similar to those that the animal makes when it reaches the goal. They are called fractional because they involve only a part of the goal responses. The animal running the maze shows only a part of the behavior involved in eating and not the whole eating routine. In a sense, it seems reasonable to think of these anticipatory responses as being the manifestations of what have been referred to here as expectancy responses. Indeed, some psychologists would say that anticipatory responses *are* expectancy responses and that expectancies are nothing more than components of the goal response. This is all very plausible, but the results of research based on this conception of expectancy have been disappointing (see Logan, 1968).

Despite the fact that experimental approaches to the expectancy interpretation of reinforcement learning have not, as yet, led to the productive line of research needed to develop the concept as an explanation, effort continues because it is a highly favored form of explanation. Many aspects of applied psychology assume the expectancy hypothesis to be true. Most industrial psychology that has to do with incentives assumes that the expectation of rewards has an important effect on behavior, and this is why business and industry have incentive systems. The incentives of which the industrial psychologist speaks are often identical with what other psychologists refer to as reinforcements or reinforcers.

Finally, it must be pointed out that one can often conveniently speak as though reinforcements produced a direct modification of behavior, even though any direct effect is quite implausible. There is a certain convenience in thinking that one can overcome the bad habits of a pupil by providing reinforcements for alternative forms of behavior that are more desirable. At least this way of thinking provides a practical approach to the problem and a well-tried recipe for achieving practical results. However, if the expectancy hypothesis is correct, one may not be just modifying the pupil's behavior in the naïve way suggested by the formula for behavior modification. The expectancy hypothesis suggests that what one may be teaching him is how to obtain certain rewards when the teacher is present; and it also suggests that in other situations, where the teacher is not present, the old bad habits may immediately return. The internal substructure of the habit may not be changed, even though the surface phenomena may show striking change under the immediate circumstances of the changed reinforcement. The followers of Skinner simply say that all one ever has to worry about is surface phenomena, but a great deal more research will be needed if strong support is to be found for this contention.

Summary

1. The language commonly used for discussing the learning of instrumental responses ($R \rightarrow S$ learning) has been derived largely from the work of B. F. Skinner, who distinguishes between respondent and emitted behavior. The former appears as a result of a well-identified stimulus, but the latter cannot be considered to be produced by a particular stimulus.
2. As the child develops, behavior becomes more and more a set of

organized sequences of behavior. This change in behavior through learning is referred to as the shaping of behavior. As behavior is shaped, it shows a linking of behavior with certain situations, that is to say, certain behavior tends to take place in certain situations. These situations are said to provide discriminative stimuli and the behaviors involved are referred to as discriminative operants.

3. A reinforcer is an event following behavior, which changes the probability that the behavior will occur again. The term *reinforcer,* unlike the term *reward,* does not carry with it the implication that the event involved is pleasant or unpleasant. For this reason many prefer to use the term reinforcer, though the term reward is still widely used in such emminently respectable scientific sources as *The Journal of Experimental Psychology.* Some psychologists have taken the position that all learning involves reinforcing events, but this is a position that is becoming more and more difficult to maintain. Much of the research on reinforcement has been undertaken with a few species in which reinforcement plays a very clear, central, and powerful role in learning. The animal psychologist is always in danger of choosing species that fit closely his theoretical position on behavior.
4. Some events acquire their reinforcing properties as a result of learning, while others have reinforcing properties because of the inherent nature of the organism. The former are referred to as secondary reinforcers and the latter as primary reinforcers. There is no agreement at this time concerning the number of different kinds of events that should be included in a complete list of primary reinforcers. If such a list could be made, then it would differ from one species to another. Although some books on education assume that the reinforcers of the behavior of young children have been identified, this is far from the truth.
5. Secondary reinforcing events are those that did not originally have the power of reinforcing behavior. They acquired the property of reinforcement by being paired with events that have reinforcing properties. A whistle does not reinforce the behavior of a dolphin, but after the whistle has been blown every time the dolphin is fed, the whistle acquires much the same reinforcing properties as the food. The sound of the whistle has thus become a secondary reinforcer. However, if the whistle is thereafter never paired with food again, but is used to reinforce the behavior of the dolphin, it will rapidly lose its reinforcing properties.
6. Reinforcement is a complex phenomenon and the single term

covers a very broad category of events. In the case of human learners, events that are reinforcing include those involving preferred consumeables, such as M & Ms, and also events that are verbal and information-giving.

7. The most common reinforcing event in the school-age child's life is that provided by knowledge of results, or informative feedback, as it is commonly called. A chain of behaviors, if it is of any substantial length, requires that the person involved know how he is doing. This requires some kind of concurrent feedback. One could not tie a complicated knot if one did not know the exact position of the cord and of one's hand at each stage. Some of the feedback with which one is concerned in formal training sessions is feedback provided from a source external to ourselves. Such feedback may be either concurrent or terminal, concurrent when it is provided while the task is being undertaken, and terminal when it is provided after completion of the task.
8. Both concurrent and terminal feedback may be either intrinsic or artificial. In educational situations, artificial feedback is often tied too remotely to the task to be of value. An overall grade for work performed during a semester is probably almost useless as a means of improving future performance. The most the person graded can derive from such a procedure is a review of his notion of how much time to spend on schoolwork in the future. However, if artificial feedback is tied closely to the task to be mastered, it can have high utility in producing learning.
9. A crucial factor in determining the extent to which the results of feedback are retained is the learner's knowledge that the information provided by feedback is or is not going to be used later.
10. Just as reinforcement increases the probability of occurrence of the response on which the reinforcement is contingent, so does the withdrawal of the reinforcement decrease the probability of the occurrence of the response. This decline in response probability when reinforcement is withdrawn is referred to as extinction. Once a response has been completely extinguished, it will show a rapid recovery to the strength it had before extinction, if the reinforcing contingency is reintroduced. This well-established fact suggests that extinction is not an erasure process that simply eliminates the learning that has taken place, but that it is a process of inhibition.
11. A second procedure for eliminating a response is to arrange the conditions that ordinarily produce the response and then prevent the response from occurring. The latter mechanism is closely related to the desensitization procedure that has become

widely used by psychotherapists. There is some evidence that the desensitization procedure is effective in controlling unwanted behavior, such as anxiety responses.

12. The term vicarious extinction has been used to describe cases in which a child's anxiety response has been eliminated through contact with nonanxious children.
13. The shaping of behavior occurs through the positive reinforcement of any trend in behavior in the desired direction and the extinction of any trend in the opposite direction.
14. Attempts to shape behavior through the manipulation of reinforcement and extinction have been particularly successful in the cases of young children of preschool age, the mentally handicapped, and certain categories of patients in mental institutions. Such procedures commonly involve the use of token systems of reward, with the tokens being turned in at a later time for desired objects or privileges. The introduction of token economies into institutions is not without problems similar to those involved in the larger token economy in which we all live. Although these behavior modification procedures have had considerable success with human beings operating at rather simple levels, very little application of consequence has been reported in improving academic learning on the part of individuals who fall within what is called the normal range.
15. Stimuli that living creatures typically avoid are referred to as aversive stimuli. Aversive stimuli have an immediate effect of inhibiting behavior, but the removal of an aversive stimulus has much of the effect of a reward. A first response to an aversive stimulus is escape, but the animal may ultimately be able to learn to avoid encounters with aversive stimuli. Escape behavior gives way to avoidance behavior. Punishment is a special case of the use of avoidance behavior. Punishment is generally administered in the hope that it will inhibit a response.
16. Sometimes the effects of negative reinforcement may be dramatic and permanent, as in the case of traumatic avoidance learning, but effects of this kind can be produced only when extremely severe stimuli are involved. With milder stimuli, the learning produced by negative reinforcement is probably comparable to that achieved with the use of positive reinforcers. The effect of punishment on the suppression of a response is highly dependent upon the strength of the punishing agent. Mild punishment may only make the subject punished more alert, but severe punishment may block a response permanently. Moderate punishment has an effect in between. Some quite dramatic effects have been found in the use of punishment to suppress self-destructive

behavior in young children. The side effects of punishment are not clear at this time. Physical pain may produce aggression and, under some circumstances, may produce a complete disorganization of behavior. Parents who punish the most tend to have children with the greatest number of problems in the area of aggression. The main arguments against the use of punishment for the control of behavior are moral and ethical.

17. The effects of delay on reinforcement depend highly on the circumstances involved. If the orientation of the learner to the learning situation can be maintained during the delay period, then the effect of delay is minimal. In most tasks undertaken by human learners the effect of delay in reinforcement is not damaging and sometimes helpful. What happens during the delay interval is probably quite crucial in determining the effect of delay on reinforcement.
18. In the case of subhuman learners, all information and reinforcement has to be provided after responses have been made to the learning situation. In the case of human learners, information can be given prior to the making of a response. In at least some tasks, there seems to be an advantage in providing information before each trial rather than as a terminal point in each trial. An important factor in human learning is the time that elapses between trials, because this is the time during which the information provided by the trial is assimilated.
19. The most consistent finding with respect to the magnitude of reinforcement of learning is that an increase in magnitude tends to be accompanied by an increase in vigor of the response. There is very little evidence that an increase in the magnitude of the reinforcement increases the amount of learning on each trial.
20. Reinforcements may occur on every trial or on only certain trials. The pattern of distribution of reinforcements is referred to as the schedule of reinforcement. The partial reinforcement effect is the name given to the condition occurring when the schedule of reinforcement is reduced below 100 per cent, and administered on a random basis. The rate of learning decreases, but the rate at which the response is extinguished, after the withdrawal of the reinforcement, is also reduced. Various explanations have been offered for this phenomenon but none are entirely satisfactory. Some of the common schedules of reinforcement have been given names such as fixed-ratio schedules, variable-ratio schedules.
21. Although there have been many practical and important applications of the principle of reinforcement, the mechanism

involved is still obscure. There is some evidence to support the drive-reduction theory of reinforcement, but more than drive reduction appears to be involved. The theory that reinforcement learning involves the acquisition of expectancies has long fascinated psychologists, but it has been a difficult one with which to experiment.

CHAPTER THREE

Some Acquisition and Retention Phenomena

A LEARNING CURVE IS A WAY OF REPRESENTING THE PROGRESS OF learning. A beginner at bowling may keep a careful record of his score, week by week, and may plot his scores on a graph to show his progress. The graph is a learning curve. A quite typical learning curve for the acquisition of a motor skill is shown in Figure 3. The performance of the skill shows a typical rapid increase during the early stages of practice and much less progress during the later periods. For a long time psychologists thought that the type of curve represented by Figure 3 was the typical learning curve and, indeed, similar curves were produced in experiments that involved a whole range of tasks including verbal tasks.

More recently, questions have been raised about whether the typical learning curve of the kind that has just been discussed can be regarded as representing the overall course of learning. Learning of most tasks does not start from scratch. The person who bowls for the first time brings to his performance extensive practice with the task of throwing balls and other objects. Although bowling is new to him, it is only new with respect to certain aspects of the task. The ball is likely to be larger than any he has thrown or rolled in the past and also considerably heavier. The targets at which he throws the ball are different. The surroundings are different from those in which he has manipulated balls in the past, for he has been used to throwing and rolling balls in out-of-door situations. Despite these differences, he brings to the situation a range of previously developed skills that permit him to score perhaps as high as eighty the very first time he bowls. He is not so much learning a new skill as transferring the skills he has acquired to a new situation. His learning curve for bowling is a curve reflecting his ability to transfer to the bowling situation the skills he has already learned.

An interesting question is, What kind of a learning curve would be produced in the acquisition of a skill for which the individual came to the learning situation without any previously acquired related skills? Such situations are difficult to find. One source of such learning curves is the learning that takes place in infancy and early childhood. An example of such a curve is presented in Figure 4, which shows the vocabulary acquired by a child during his first six years. This curve represents only the lower portion of the complex learning curve, which would continue to rise but at a decreasing rate and eventually would

Figure 3. Curve representing learning of the skill involved in the control of the performance of a miniature plane, the movements of which are manipulated by means of a set of controls similar to those used in an aircraft. Data from Ammons, et al., 1958. (Reproduced by permission of the American Psychological Association.)

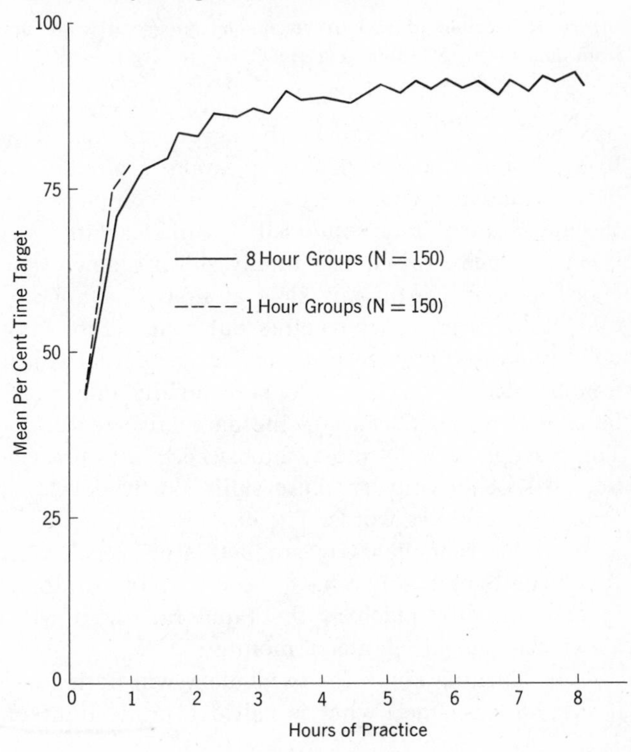

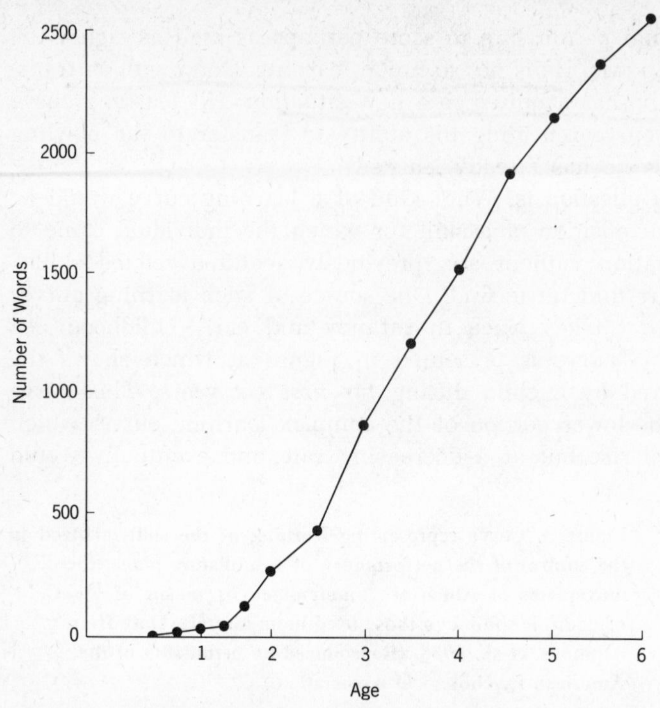

Figure 4. Relation of size of vocabulary to age. (Graph drawn from data by M. E. Smith, 1926.)

become horizontal. Even by the age of six some tendency for the curve to bend toward the horizontal position is already apparent. If data had been available for ages above six, the complete curve would have had the appearance of an extended S, with learning very slow at first, then becoming more rapid, and finally slowing down again. A good question to ask is why learning is slow at first. The answer to this is provided by Gibson (1969), who points out that before language is spoken the child must first engage in extended perceptual learning. The child must first be able to discriminate perceptually one word from another and be able also to differentiate the distinctive features of particular words. The perceptual skills must, almost certainly, precede the actual production of speech. Only as these skills slowly develop can the child begin to produce and use words. The development of these prerequisites makes it inevitable that the early production of speech will be very slow. Once these perceptual skills have been developed, then the acquisition of speech can take place at the rapid rate with which it proceeds after about the age of eighteen months.

The learning curve for vocabulary will flatten out in the teens, when it will have reached what is called a crude limit of learning. The fact that a person may cease to add to his vocabulary after he leaves high school does not mean that he is incapable of making additions. He may have reached the limit of the vocabulary that he needs for performing in life and have no incentive for additional vocabulary learning. The crude limit of learning simply represents the limit occurring under particular conditions; it does not represent any maximum level that cannot be exceeded.

Another source of data that may shed light on the shape of the learning curve is found in animal studies. In the case of both classical conditioning and instrumental conditioning studies one can find cases in which the learning task involved is so novel that the animal cannot be expected to bring to the learning situation any previously mastered skills. The classical conditioning of an eyelid response might be such a case, but few studies of this kind are available because psychologists have been more interested in the factors that modify learning than in the pure form of the learning curve. However, Hilgard and Marquis (1936, p. 190) have provided the learning curves for three monkeys in a classical conditioning eyelid experiment and show curves that are approximately S-shaped. Spence, who became interested in this problem many years later (1956), came to the conclusion that, at least for instrumental conditioning, the shape of the complete learning curve was S-shaped. Some interesting data have been provided, in this connection, by Harlow (1959), who trained chimpanzees to solve very extended series of problems and demonstrated the development of problem-solving skills. The procedure involved presenting the animal with two dishes, upside down and different in some way. The animal had to find out which dish covered a small amount of food. In the first set of trials it might always be the square dish, and not the round one. In the second set it might always be the black dish, and not the white dish. In the third series, the large one and not the small one was correct, and so forth. With each problem, the animal had six trials. On the first trial of each series, he could only guess, but within eight trials he would make considerable progress in solving the problem. In the early learning series, the chimps would be likely to be responding correctly 70 per cent of the time by the ninth attempt at a problem, but after solving thirty to forty such problems, with six attempts on every problem, the chimps would solve a problem 90 per cent correct after a single trial. Learning curves provided by Harlow, shown in Figure 5, make it possible to see how the shape of the learning curve changes from the initial problem, where the problem is highly novel for the particular animal, to the case where a problem is solved after much previous practice with other problems. The learning of the first problem provides a curve resembling a long drawn-out S, but the learning curves for problems late in the series look more and more like the typical learning

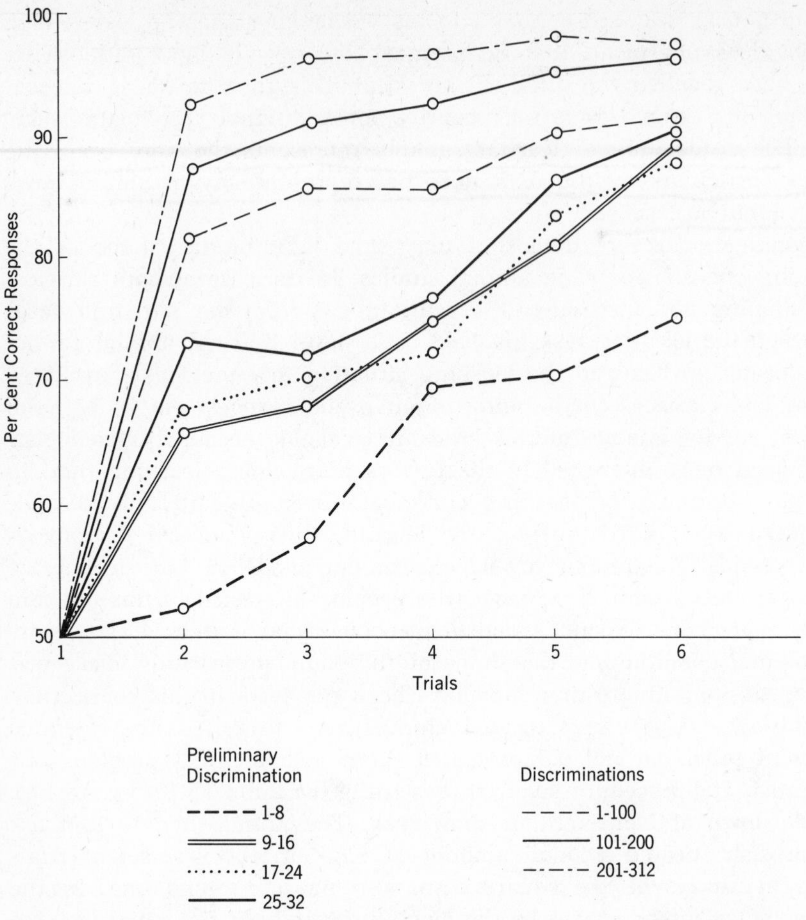

Figure 5. Family of learning curves showing the development of a learning set. (From "Learning Set and Error Factor Theory," by H. F. Harlow, in "Psychology: A Study of a Science," Vol. 2, edited by S. Koch (Copyright 1959 by McGraw-Hill Book Company, Inc.). Used with permission of McGraw-Hill Book Company, Inc.

curves produced by humans on tasks to which they bring many component skills.

The evidence generally points in the direction of suggesting that a learning curve, involving a task that starts the learner off from scratch and does not draw upon what he has learned previously, is S-shaped. The learning curve that shows a sudden rise, right from the beginning, belongs to a task that involves many skills that the person has previously learned. Although the S-shaped curve is simple, it is a product of complex circumstances. A very young child, or an animal, placed in a novel learning situation, may have difficulty initially in differentiating the stimuli to which he must respond. He may also be distracted by novel aspects of his environment. Learning in an unfamiliar world makes for slow learning, but the slowness is likely to be a result of a combination of factors. Once the initial difficulties have been surmounted, learning then proceeds at a much more rapid pace. Finally, a crude limit of learning is reached when incentives no longer exist for further learning.

Some learning curves have been described as showing portions where learning is slowed down, followed by a period when learning takes place rapidly again. Such phenomena were first reported by Bryan and Harter (1897) in their classic study of learning Morse code. Figure 6 reproduces some of the curves from the Bryan and Harter study. The slowed-up portion of the learning curve, seen only in the curves for the receiving code, was referred to by Bryan and Harter as a plateau, but the evidence for the existence of such plateaus was not striking. If the reader will scrutinize the curves in Figure 6, he may well have difficulty in finding anything that looks like a plateau at all. Because the graphs were plotted to show daily performance over a period of forty weeks, it is quite possible that any slight slow-up in the rate of learning during one part of the forty-week training period might be due to short periods of ill-health, difficulties in attending to the task caused by worry, or perhaps even lack of sleep, which may have prolonged effects upon performance. Many writers have attributed to whatever plateaus they could see a much deeper significance. It is claimed, for example, that in learning to type the pupil first learns to hunt and peck letter by letter. When he becomes skilled in striking individual letters, his performance reaches a maximum and learning seems to stop for a time. Then he begins to type by groups of letters and the resulting learning curve begins to go up again. This is a convincing argument, but the writer has been unable to find learning curves that provide convincing evidence that such plateaus exist at all except as artifacts.

Learning curves typically rise and then flatten out, indicating that some kind of limit of learning has been achieved. This limit is commonly referred to as the crude limit of learning. It is a limit of learning under the particular conditions of learning prevailing at the time. Under different conditions, the learning curve might tend to rise again. It has already been pointed out that when larger reinforcements are introduced, or larger incentives as some would say, the learning curve may rise to higher levels. The crude limit of learning rarely, if ever, reflects the limit of performance that the person can achieve, but only the limit reachable under the particular conditions.

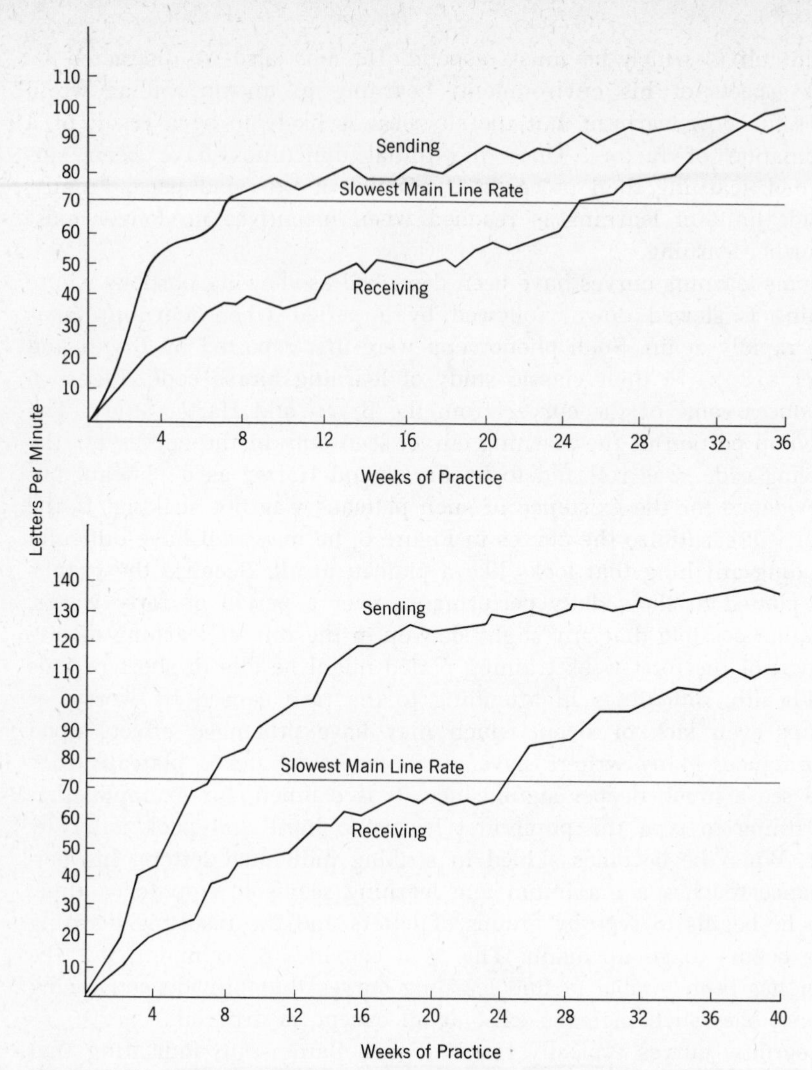

Figure 6. Curves for the learning of Morse code for individual subjects showing plateaus on the receiving curves. (From Bryan and Harter, 1897, p. 49.)

Mathematical Models and Learning Curves

During the last decade, considerable interest has been shown in attempts to derive a learning curve by mathematical methods from assumptions made about the learning process. For example, if the assumption is made that equal amounts of practice produce equal increments in the number of correct responses, then learning would be represented by a straight line on a graph that related the percentage of correct responses to the amount of practice. Such an assumption would not be valid and would not produce a learning curve that corresponded, to any extent, with that produced by real data. The problem is to make assumptions that lead to curves that correspond closely with those produced through the analysis of real data. If a set of assumptions can be made about learning from which mathematical procedures can derive a learning curve that fits closely that derived from real data, one can then say that the mathematical model has validity. This procedure is roughly that followed by scientists in the physical sciences who frequently make assumptions concerning the nature of the phenomena they are studying and then derive mathematical equations from those assumptions. The next step is to find out whether experimental data fits the mathematical functions that have been thus derived. Elaborate computers are often used to calculate the results expected in terms of theory, which are later compared with those from actual data.

Psychologists have attempted to produce theoretical learning curves, starting with many different assumptions about the learning process. Some of the curves thus produced have shown a remarkable degree of correspondence with actual data. An example of such a theoretically derived curve is shown in Figure 7. In this figure the circles represent the points on the curve derived from experimental data. The continuous curve represents a theoretical curve. The data in this case fits well the theoretical learning curve. Indeed, the fit is exceptional. Other cases could be presented in which a much poorer fit was obtained. The Brody (1957) data are presented here to indicate that this approach may well have a bright future.

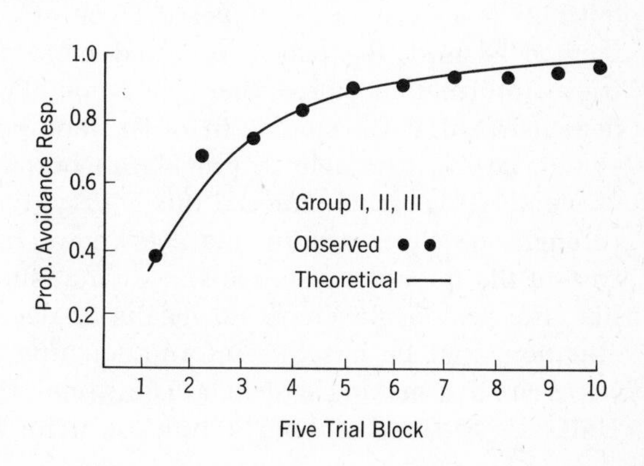

Figure 7. Graph showing the fit of actual data to a theoretical learning curve. (After Brody, 1957, p. 243. Reproduced by permission of the American Psychological Association.)

Retention

A discussion of recording the progress of learning is appropriately followed by a discussion of the related problem of recording the retention of what has been learned. Just as the learning curve is a record of only one aspect of learning measured in a particular way, so too is a curve of retention a record of a product of learning as it is measured at various intervals of time after the learning conditions have ceased to operate. Because retention can be measured in a number of different ways, a graph representing the degree of retention can be drawn for each way in which retention is measured.

Different measures of what has been retained are dependent upon different internal processes. Each involves its own skills. Let us consider the various methods, beginning with what is generally considered to be the least sensitive.

The Free Recall Method. This is the method most frequently used by teachers. The pupil studies the French equivalents of a number of English words and then must show that he can write out the French words when the English words are presented. Although the term *free recall* is commonly used to describe such a situation, the person making the recall has to have some cues in order to know which French words to produce. In the minimum cue situation, the student would simply be told to write out all the English words and their French equivalents from the list he had been studying. Generally, the teacher will provide more cues and he will typically provide a list of the English words against which the student must enter the French equivalents. Still more cues can be provided by measuring retention through a situation in which the French word has to be entered in a blank space in an incomplete French sentence. An essay test approximates a free recall situation, but often in such tests the student is not given sufficient cues to tell him just what he is supposed to be able to recall. When the recall method is used, the person involved must search his memory and retrieve information stored there, but not all information stored can be demonstrated to be stored. In order that he can demonstrate what is stored, he must be able to provide an output related to it. In the case of memory for verbal material this is easy, for he can demonstrate either through speech or writing that he knows the particular words. In the case of the retention of crude visual data, such as what a neighbor looks like, the person may have no means of demonstrating, in a free recall situation, that he has this information unless he has the artistic skills necessary for making a sketch. The same is true of memory for music. Unless a person can hum a tune or write it out in musical notation, he cannot demonstrate through a free recall method that he has stored information about the tune.

The Recognition Method. The recognition method probably involves different internal processes from the free recall method. In the case of learning French vocabulary, a recognition test might involve the presentation of the English words, each followed by a number of French words. The task of the person taking the recognition test is that of selecting the correct French word from the alternatives provided. The person taking this test has certain options. Under some circumstances he may have to do no more than read the several words that follow the English word and determine which word was the one he recently saw during the study period. To do this, he may only have to identify certain attributes of the word. For example, he may note that one of the French words from which he has to choose begins with *w* and is long, and he may also remember that one of the French words he studied began with *w* and was long. Therefore, he chooses that word. In such a case the test would merely show that he had remembered some characteristics of the French word, and not that he could recall the actual word. Recognition measures of memory involve a perceptual analysis of what is presented and then some matching of the results of that analysis with information stored about previous experiences. Recognition may be based on very fragmentary information. Recall requires that very detailed information must have been stored internally. For this reason, it is generally a more difficult process than that of recognition and is dependent upon more complete retention.

The Relearning, or Saving, Method. Some sensitive techniques have been developed that can demonstrate that there has been retention even though all of the ordinary tests of retention used in schools indicate that there has been none. A very sensitive technique widely used in laboratories is known as the saving method. In this method the subject learns the material to a certain standard of proficiency. If he is learning a list of words, then he may learn them to the point where he can repeat the list back perfectly on three *successive* trials. This would generally be done by presenting him with the list of words, permitting him to read it through once, and then asking him to recall the list he has read. This is repeated time after time until he reproduces the list perfectly on three successive occasions. After a period of time, the degree to which he has retained the list is measured by determining how much more learning must take place in order to relearn the list to the point where, once again, it can be repeated perfectly on another three successive occasions. If twenty-five repetitions were required in the original learning series to reach the point of perfect recall, only five repetitions might be required at a later time to reach the same point of learning. And because, on relearning, five instead of twenty-five repetitions were required, one might say that on relearning there was a "saving" of 80 per cent. This is how the method acquired its name. In some studies it has been the only method so far developed that is sensitive enough to provide evidence that there has been some retention of the original information learned.

Curves of Retention

Retention is the continued capacity to behave in a particular way that has been learned. Forgetting is the gradual or rapid loss of a response in the repertoire of the individual. When a child forgets a poem, it means that he has lost the ability to recall the poem—that is, he has lost the capacity for making the responses involved in the recitation of the poem. The word *forgetting* is used here loosely. Although the pupil has forgotten the poem insofar as recitation is concerned, he has not forgotten everything about the poem. He would probably still recognize the poem as one he had learned previously. Even if he had so far forgotten the poem that he did not recognize it, he might still find it unusually easy to learn.

Forgetting is a normal everyday event, and a constant reminder of man's limitations. There are also certain kinds of forgetting that the clinician tries to produce in individuals in order to help them with their problems. To a great extent, the treatment of mental disorders is an attempt to rid the person of certain unwanted aspects of behavior. These unwanted aspects of behavior may vary from minor twitches of the muscles of the face to deep-seated anxiety responses that torture the soul. That such responses are generally very difficult to eliminate is attested to by the fact that therapy is a long and rather unsatisfactory process. Behavior is not eliminated easily. Sometimes there seems to be no method through which unwanted behavior can be eliminated. Oddly enough, fate seems to have decided that the things we want to retain most, such as intellectual knowledge, are not easily retained, but neurotic behavior of which we would like to rid ourselves remains remarkably persistent.

A typical curve of retention is shown in Figure 8. Although the curve is derived from data from this century of Cain and Willey (1939), the general form of the curve was known to Ebbinghaus and to other psychologists of the last century. The reader must realize that only in general features does the curve remain the same from one batch of data to another, the most notable of these features being the rapid

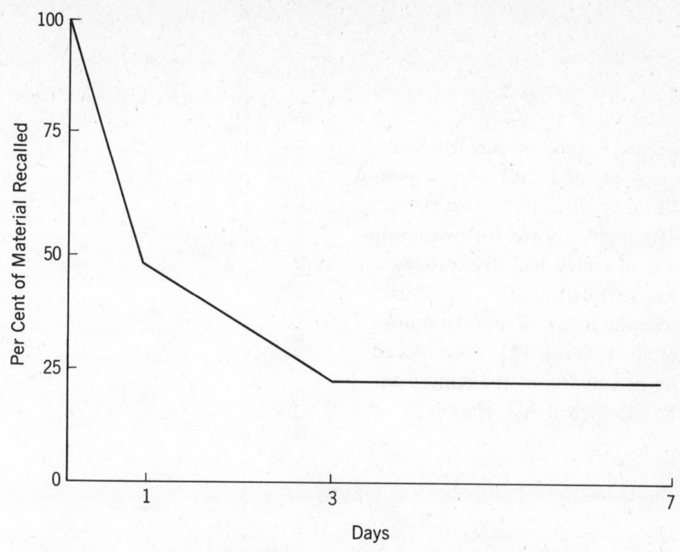

Figure 8. Curve of retention for nonsense syllables. (After Cain and Willey, 1939, p. 211. Reproduced by permission of the American Psychological Association.)

decline in the information or skill retained during the period that immediately follows learning, and then a declining loss as time progresses. Many different conditions determine the extent to which there is an initial rapid loss in what has been learned.

Ammons et al. (1958) studied long-term retention of two skills. One skill was referred to as a procedural skill. It involved the manipulation of a set of controls in the correct sequence by following a chart on the wall. The other task involved the control of the performance of a miniature plane by operating a set of controls similar to that found in an aircraft. Figure 9 shows the loss in skill in the procedural task over a period of two years. The two lines on the graph are for the subjects who had five training trials and those who had thirty training trials. The difference in the percentage of the acquired skill lost is markedly less for the group that had the most training. However, there is a sense in which this graph overestimates the loss, for a large part of the losses tend to be rapidly regained once practice trials are given. The greater the time interval during which no practice took place, the greater was the amount of retraining required to regain the original skill. Figure 10 shows the retraining curves for the airplane-control task for those who had originally been given one hour of practice on the task. An important point to note is that most of the original skill was reacquired after only two trials, even after a two-year no-practice interval.

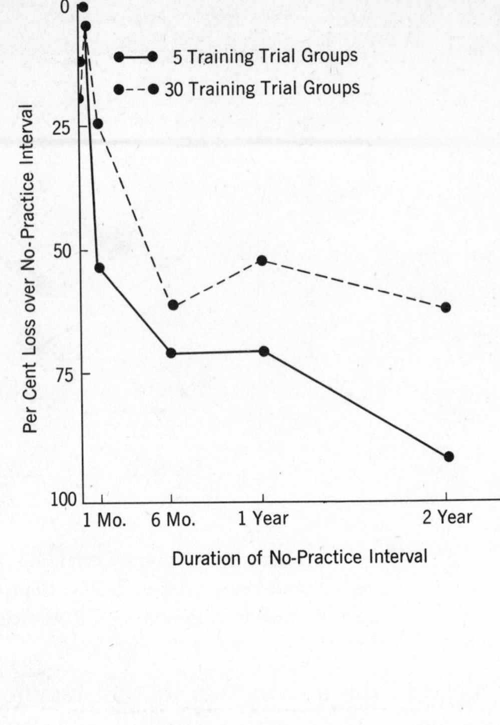

Figure 9. Loss of performance on sequential task over a period of no practice up to two years. The loss is shown for two groups, one of which had five training trials while the other had thirty training trials. (From Ammons, et al., 1958, p. 322. Reproduced by permission of the American Psychological Association.)

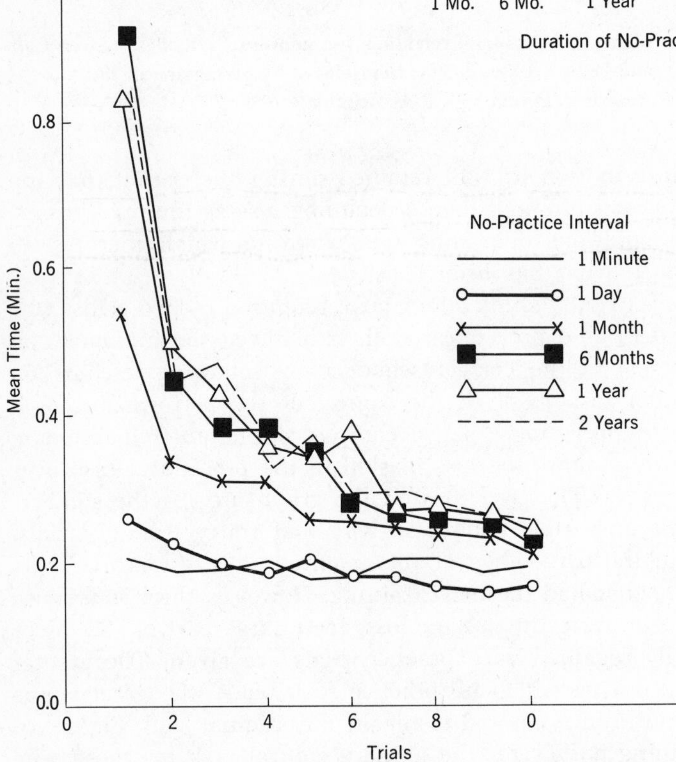

Figure 10. Graph showing the relearning curves on a sequential task for groups retrained after various intervals. (After Ammons, et al., 1958, p. 321. Reproduced by permission of the American Psychological Association.)

Reminiscence

The first discussion of reminiscence comes from a paper by Ballard (1913) which became famous. Ballard worked for the London County Council school system and visited classrooms as an inspector for the system. On one such occasion he observed the children in a class memorizing a poem he had assigned to them. At the end of the class period he asked them to write out as much of the poem as they could remember, and he then collected and scored the papers. What the children did not know was that he was to return to the same class on the following day, when he asked the same children to write out again all that they could recall of the poem. Much to his surprise, he found that the children remembered more of the poem on the following day than they had immediately after learning. The additional learning that apparently occurred after the end of the learning period was referred to as *reminiscence*. The same pattern of study was repeated with a variety of other materials, which ranged from nonsense syllables to meaningful material, and similar results were achieved. The curve of retention did not show a decline beginning immediately after learning, but rather, it first showed a rise before the typical fall began. For nearly half a century students of education were taught about the reminiscence phenomenon, until an experiment was undertaken that indicated that in all likelihood the phenomenon was nothing more than an artifact of the experimental situation. Perhaps one lesson to be learned from this is that the mere repetition of an experiment is not enough to demonstrate the soundness of the conclusions.

The demonstration that the phenomenon of reminiscence with verbal material is probably an artifact of experimentation and not a genuine phenomenon provides a worthwhile lesson in the problems of experimenting with learning. For this reason we may spend a little more time in discussing the matter than it would otherwise merit. Let us consider first the classical design that has been used in the supposed demonstration of reminiscence. In this design the following steps were taken:

1. A learning period
2. A test of retention
3. A period of unrelated activity
4. A test of retention

Ammons and Irion (1954) saw that there was a basic defect in this design. It is conceivable that the measurement of retention that occurs immediately after the learning period may function as an additional learning period and produce learning that does not show up until the next time retention is measured. Reminiscence may be nothing more than the learning produced by the situation in which learning is measured. What Ammons and Irion did was to test this hypothesis by the following experimental design, which used two groups rather than the one that had been typically used in previous experimentation:

Group A	Group B
1. A learning period	1. A learning period
2. A test of retention	2. A period of unrelated activity
3. A period of unrelated activity	3. A test of retention
4. A test of retention	

The only difference in the treatment of the two groups lies in the omission from Group B of the test of retention immediately after the learning period. The results of this experiment are interesting. What happens is that in Group A the final test of retention shows a rise in comparison with the test of retention given immediately after learning. However, Group B, on the final test of retention, shows a performance similar to that of Group A immediately after learning. In other words, Group B does not show the reminiscence phenomenon, though it should if the phenomenon is a genuine one. Only Group A shows the reminiscence phenomenon, and only Group A had the advantage of the test of retention immediately after learning and the possibility of benefiting from the practice that this test of retention may have provided. The data strongly suggest that the reminiscence effect with verbal material is due to the practice provided by the test of retention given immediately after learning.

The reminiscence phenomenon and the way in which it is produced reflect some of the difficulties that are encountered in collecting data for plotting a curve of retention. One cannot plot a curve of retention by the simple procedure of measuring from time to time the amount retained; for each time one does this, additional learning opportunities are afforded. What one generally has to do is train a large group to a given point of proficiency, then divide the large group into a number of subgroups which are then tested, each at a separate and distinct interval of time. Thus Subgroup 1 might be tested after one day, Subgroup 2 after two days, and so forth. Each person would be tested only once after the end of the learning period.

Although the Ballard type of reminiscence phenomenon appears to be an artifact of the experimental situation, there is a related phenomenon that is genuine. Reminiscence over a short period of time, of the order of several minutes, takes place with a task involving muscular coordination. This phenomenon has commonly been demonstrated with what are called *pursuit tasks*. In these tasks, the subject is required to turn or move levers in order to keep a movable sight on a moving target. The target moves and has to be followed by the sight through the appropriate manipulation of the levers or cranks. When practice is given on such a task, the level of skill continues to improve after practice has stopped. This has been shown by many research workers, including Bourne and Archer (1956), Ray (1959), and Eysenck (1956).

The interpretation generally given to this short-term type of reminiscence is that during the period of practice an inhibition process develops that has the effect of interfering with the performance of the skill. When the period of practice ends, then the state of inhibition slowly dissipates and the level of skill improves.

Meaningfulness and Retention

The opinion is commonly held that meaningful material is more easily retained than nonsense material. The early students of learning phenomena, such as Ebbinghaus, who conducted his classic experiments in the last century, were impressed with this difference in retainability, which appeared to be dramatized by the results of their experiments. However, the experimental results are not as clear-cut as they appear to be on the surface, for this happens to be a difficult area for experimentation.

Consider, for example, the problem of obtaining meaningful and meaningless material for the conduct of a study of retention. Suppose a poem is to be compared for retainability with a list of nonsense syllables. Immediately one is confronted with the problem that any poem is meaningful, because it has already entered into past learning. A child who is learning the lines

Listen my children and you shall hear
Of the midnight ride of Paul Revere

is not learning completely novel material. He is already familiar with the name of Paul Revere and the story associated with him. He has also learned something about the typical order in which words appear. When he encounters the word *you* in the first line, he knows that it is almost certainly followed by a verb. Thus many of the associations between words that the learning of the poem requires have already been to some extent made. Meaningful material, because it is meaningful, is material that has already entered into some learning. To conclude, then, that meaningful material is more easily retained than meaningless material would be merely to conclude the obvious—that the material already partially learned is the more readily retained.

Verbal Mediators in Learning Association

Experimenters have noted that when a person is asked to learn a paired-associate task (such as associating bus-house, bird-auto, lamb-china, and so forth), the subject often introduces words that link up the two terms to be associated. In the case of the pairs of words just cited he may say to himself, "The bus stops at the house," "The bird was killed by the auto," and "The lamb was made of china." The words introduced are verbal mediators, and the learner introduces them to facilitate retention. Similar mediators are commonly introduced in daily life, as when we say to ourselves, "Mr. Green is as young and green as his name denotes," thereby linking the name of Green to the person designated by it.

Montague, Adams, and Kiess (1966) have reviewed a number of studies showing that associations learned that involve verbal mediators are better recalled later than are associations that do not involve them. In their own study, the task used was a paired-associate task in which pairs of nonsense syllables were presented and in which the subject had to learn to give the second syllable when presented with the first. In learning such a task, subjects commonly use verbal mediators. A subject, in reading the pair of syllables *san-lub* may transform it into something like *santa-club,* or *santa is lubly.* These research workers found, when they tested the subjects twenty-four hours later, that retention was substantial for those pairs in which the subjects had reported using verbal mediators in learning, but negligible for those pairs of syllables on which no verbal mediators had been reported as being introduced. The evidence suggests that the use of verbal mediators makes it possible to transfer the information from short-term memory to long-term memory, but that in the absence of such mediators the information is more likely to be lost.

Why such mediators are effective in promoting attention is not at all clear. One suggestion has to do with the fact that the introduction of a mediator introduces an association that is already strongly established and that this helps to establish a link. In the case of the syllable *san-lub,* which the subject encounters for the first time, there is probably virtually no association. Then the subject introduces the mediator *santa-club,* representing a strong and well-established association. The strength of the latter association may transfer to the association between *san* and *lub.* This is very speculative. Another possibility is, of course, that it is not the mediating verbal behavior that produces the improvement. When there is verbal mediation, the subject may spend a longer time dwelling on the materials to be associated, and this, in turn, may produce more effective learning. This is generally a less attractive hypothesis than the one previously cited, in that there is substantial evidence that retention is closely associated with the fitting of the new incoming knowledge into the previously stored system of knowledge.

Another interesting finding of the Montague et al. study was that exposing the syllables for a longer time during learning resulted in the more frequent formation of verbal mediators and, hence, superior retention. This finding may well account partly for the fact that the amount of learning taking place is commonly related to the amount of time provided for each trial. In addition, these research workers also found that the more the syllables resembled meaningful words the more verbal mediators tended to be introduced and the more learning and retention took place.

This study, once again, brings out an important distinction between short-term and long-term memory. In the former, information is taken in as is, but in the latter there is a linking with previous knowledge. In the one system information is stored, much as books are stored higgledy-piggledy in a closet when they first arrive at a library, but in the long-term storage system ideas are stored within an ordered system, much as catalogued books are stored within an ordered system.

What is said here does not imply that information lacking a high degree of organization cannot enter the long-term memory system, for obviously it can. Children learn such isolated associations as capital cities and the states in which they are found, but such information is difficult and time-consuming to learn because there is only the weakest link between the knowledge involved and knowledge already acquired.

Overlearning and Retention

Material may be learned to the point where immediate recall is just possible, or it may be learned beyond this point. If practice occurs beyond the point where immediate and complete recall is first possible, then overlearning is said to have occurred. Typically in schools, learning is organized so that considerable overlearning is scheduled. There is little merit in a child's learning to spell only to the point where he can spell the particular words immediately after practice but is unable to recall the spelling at a later date. Teachers for centuries have been familiar with the fact that the best single way of preventing subsequent forgetting is to provide for overlearning.

Overlearning does not have to take the form of drill or rote learning. For example, once a child has acquired some minimal mastery of the number products used in multiplication, the utilization of these products in the solution of daily problems both within and outside the classroom will provide extensive overlearning, so that the skill is ultimately retained for a lifetime. Similar overlearning occurs in reading, though many of the illiterates identified at induction stations during World War II had once learned to read but had not retained the skill.

Many skills are characteristically learned to the point where they are retained for life through extensive overlearning. Few persons ever forget how to ride a bicycle once they have learned, for there is extensive opportunity for overlearning. Much the same applies to skating; people who have learned to skate may spend years away from the sport and yet return to it with little loss of skill. Secretaries who leave the office for marriage do not forget how to type. Later, if they have to return to an office job, they regain their old skill in a matter of hours. Overlearning is generally a sound investment of the pupil's time, particularly if it is coupled with a meaningful activity, as when the pupil overlearns his multiplication tables by solving mathematical problems of consequence to him.

One cannot always count on unplanned opportunity to provide the needed overlearning. An interesting example of this is found in the teaching of music, where the learner must acquire technique before he can perform a composition adequately. Simple pieces of music have been found to be of limited value in developing technique, because they do not provide opportunity to practice particular skills that must be mastered. For this reason the great teachers of music have developed exercises, commonly known as études, which provide such practice. In learning the violin, the student will work on études whatever the level of his development. In the earlier stages he may work on études that provide him with extensive practice in such matters as rhythm, scales, and so forth. Later he will work on études by Paganini, which provide some of the most difficult aspects of violin performance. In violin playing there is an exercise to provide practice for whatever aspect of technique the person may be deficient in. Such exercises are the products of great teachers who had an intuitive understanding of the problems of learning we are now considering. In other areas of learning there has been much less done to provide such specialized opportunities to learn specific aspects of the skill involved. Although many teachers have worked on this problem, few of them leave behind a record of their experience or of the techniques of learning they have used. Musicians, in contrast, have handed down their systematic teaching skills.

An interesting instance of overlearning is found in the case of a person who has spent time reading and rereading material in order to memorize it, then continues to repeat it to himself after he has put the printed version aside. These additional repetitions add to learning or overlearning. The case is of theoretical interest in that it appears to be a case of learning occurring without any identifiable reinforcement. While the reader has the material in front of him, one might postulate that he spends much of his time trying to repeat it without looking at the page, and then a glance at the page would indicate the part he has right, which in itself provides some kind of reinforcement. This is perhaps plausible, but when the learner repeats the material to himself, these kinds of reinforcements are absent.

Learning and Retention as a Function of the Time Schedule

Almost every educational program is planned so that it fits some kind of time schedule that is believed to be efficient for the purpose at hand. Often, of course, such time schedules have to fit into a system prescribed by the administration of an educational institution, as when particular courses at a university are planned to fit the quarter system. Most educators also acknowledge the fact that some schedules are more efficient than others for learning particular aspects of subject matter. Difficult mathematics courses are always spread out over a considerable time, never compressed into short periods of one or two weeks as are some language courses given by universities during the summer.

When learning is scheduled on a concentrated basis with a single long period of practice that is extended until the material to be learned has been learned, it is said that the practice is *massed.* When learning takes place in a number of learning periods separated either by other activities or by periods of rest, the practice is said to be *distributed* or *spaced.* The relative merits of spaced versus unspaced practice was one of the earliest problems studied by psychologists interested in the systematic investigation of problems of learning. Ebbinghaus (1885), who is commonly regarded as the father of modern learning psychology, published a classic work describing a series of experiments that he had conducted in the field of learning, and laying the foundation for the future experimental development of the scientific study of learning. In particular, he was the first to realize that the study of learning could not easily be undertaken through the learning of meaningful materials, because some people would come to these materials with more previous experience than would others. In order to eliminate this source of difficulty, Ebbinghaus asked his subjects to learn nonsense syllables, such as *gub, zac, ref, kes,* and so forth. These nonsense syllables have the advantage of being fairly unfamiliar, and hence all learners start at roughly the same point in their learning. But some initial differences may exist in familiarity with these materials, for at least some of them will be recognized as parts of words familiar to some of the subjects; and the person who is familiar with the greatest number of words is most likely to have the most familiarity with these syllables.

With such materials, Ebbinghaus was able to conduct experiments with massed and distributed practice. His conclusion, which has been well substantiated by other studies, is that distributed practice has a considerable advantage over massed practice—that is, it takes less time to learn material if learning is distributed over several spaced sessions than if all the work is done at a single session. At one time the advantage of distributed practice was ascribed to the effect of reminiscence, but this explanation does not hold today. A more likely explanation is that, with massed practice, inhibition builds up that interferes with learning. Spaced learning provides opportunity for the inhibition to dissipate. What is commonly referred to as mental fatigue is an inhibitory process similar to the one considered here.

Another possibility comes from the fact that the processes involved in retaining information continue after formal learning has ended. These processes involved in the consolidation of what has been learned may continue to take place for twenty or more minutes after the material to be learned has been put aside or the person ceases to practice. A pause after a learning trial may take advantage of this continuation of the learning process. Distributed practice takes advantage of this continuation of the learning process, which extends beyond the student's immediate efforts.

It would be useful if we could now state how long a learning period should be, and how far apart the periods of practice should be spaced. But, although there have been many studies undertaken of the relative efficiency of learning when the intervals between trials are varied, there is no consistency in the results they have produced. The results of such studies are conflicting because it probably makes a difference what kind of task is to be learned. For example, in an early study by Warden (1923), subjects were required to learn to find a path through a maze. Different groups were given practice at intervals of six hours, twelve hours, and one-, three-, and five-day intervals. In this study the twelve-hour interval produced the most efficient learning. In another study by Lorge (1930), rather different results were obtained. Lorge used three tasks, as follows:

1. Mirror drawing. In this task the subject was required to draw a line around a given pattern, being guided by what he could see in a mirror.
2. Mirror reading. The subject had to read printed material appearing in a mirror.
3. Code substitution. The subject was required to substitute letters in printed material with new letters, according to a code given him.

In the Lorge study, the tasks were learned under three conditions. One of these was massed practice; the second was distributed practice, with one-minute intervals between trials; the third was distributed practice, with twenty-four-hour intervals between trials. With every task, the subjects performed more efficiently when practice was distributed than when it was massed. Surprisingly small differences were found between the distributed practice with one-minute rest intervals and twenty-four-hour intervals.

What are the practical implications of the work on distributed versus massed practice? The most obvious one has already been put into effect —namely, that the work in school should be divided into rather short sessions covering particular areas of content. The fact that distributed practice is generally (but not always) more efficient than massed practice may raise some problems about the efficiency of a core curriculum as it is commonly run. The breaking down of subject-matter lines and the assignment of rather long blocks of time to combinations of subjects such as English and social studies, which are not then taught as separate subjects, may sometimes tend to make for massed practice, but this does not have to be so. The forced division of time into periods has certain advantages in this respect. It does require the teachers to change regularly the learning activities involved.

The place in which there is least application of the principle of distributed practice is probably when the pupil studies in his own home. Such study tends to represent massed learning, and is consequently much less efficient than it should be. The high-school pupil who has to learn a speech from Julius Caesar is likely to sit down and attempt to learn it at a single session; and this practice is indirectly encouraged by teachers who give occasional large assignments of this kind and ask that they be completed in too short a time (or too long a time, which results in procrastination, with similar effects). In such an assignment the pupil should probably start by reading through the speech to be learned a few times, concentrating on the meaning and looking up any words that he does not understand. He should then plan several short learning sessions distributed over several days. There are also some advantages in planning these sessions for just before going to bed, so that the learning period is not followed by any activity that could interfere with the learning of the speech.

The educational psychologist can never be content just to know that one method of learning requires a shorter total time in the capacity to repeat the material than does some other method. Quite as important as the matter of speed of learning is the extent to which material is retained. What would be the use of a speedy method of learning if it were found that retention was poor? Our immediate question is whether learning by distributed practice produces as satisfactory retention as does learning by massed practice. This is a question that numerous studies have been designed to answer with a great range of different materials.

Cain and Willey (1939), who compared retention curves of massed and distributed practice for meaningless material, found that after seven days those who had had distributed practice retained almost three times as much material as those who had had massed practice. Much the same results hold for meaningful material, although the results are not always quite so dramatic. The results hold for a variety of materials. In one relatively unique study by T. W. Cook (1936), the finding was that the solutions to puzzles were retained better over a considerable period when the problems had been solved by distributed-practice sessions than by massed-practice sessions. The nature of the materials learned is also a factor in determining what is retained.

Nearly all of the research on distributed versus massed practice has been undertaken with materials that do not much resemble the kinds used in schools, but a recent study by Leith, Biran, and Opollot (1970) used materials related to the teaching of physics in a classroom setting. They found a quite clear advantage of spaced practice over massed practice. The result is not only significant in terms of classroom practice, but it also shows how laboratory results can, sometimes at least, be generalized to the classroom situation.

Imagery and Memory

Many problems of memory are closely tied to problems concerning the nature of imagery. One cannot today discuss the one without bringing in the other. Images are inferred from verbal behavior, as when a person reports that he can see in his mind's eye a friend's face, or his living room, or the desk in his office. Such internal representations of the outside world are generally extremely sketchy and ghostlike representations of objects. Images can sometimes be extremely vivid, and yet the person knows that they do not represent perceptions of real events in the world. These are called hypnagogic images. The author remembers a hypnagogic image he had under circumstances typical of their occurrence. He had just crossed the Atlantic Ocean on a ship in which he had had a cabin where there was much engine vibration and also a great deal of noise from people walking on deck immediately above him. On the first night off the ship he settled down to sleep in a bed in a hotel and, as he began to doze, he began to feel the vibration of the ship's engines and to hear the sounds of footsteps on the deck above. While engaged in this experience, he realized that it was all illusory, and yet it was vivid and real. Such images are most likely to occur after the person has had some prolonged and unusual experience and they appear most commonly in the moments before sleep, though they may take place at other times. If a person has vivid images but does not realize they are just images, he is said to be having hallucinations.

Imagery can be studied experimentally in the laboratory. One can, for example, show a person a picture for a given amount of time, then remove the picture, and ask him to conjure up an image of the picture. One can then determine facts about the level of detail of the image, whether he can see it all at once, and so forth. The fact that images are internal phenomena does not mean that one cannot study them indirectly. Much of what the scientist investigates is studied indirectly. The fact that the concept of imagery is introduced into a discussion of memory does not mean that psychology is returning to an armchair approach in which the psychologist spends his time looking inside himself.

Some extraordinary feats of memory are associated with a form of imagery known as *eidetic* imagery. Those who have eidetic imagery are commonly referred to as *eidetekers.* The phenomenon of eidetic imagery is what is commonly called a photographic memory. It is a visual form of memory in which a person is exposed quite briefly to a complex visual display and is asked shortly afterward to report on the *details* of what he saw. Ordinary imagery that most people report lacks detail and is not likely to include items that were passed over unnoticed at the time of exposure. The eidetaker, on the other hand, is able to report at least some detail that he did not notice at the initial exposure. The limitations of our knowledge of this phenomenon, despite the fact that it has been studied for nearly a century, lie in the primitive methods that have been used and still are used to investigate it. How much detail is actually retained in the eidetic image is still a matter of speculation. One of the few well-established facts, which has not been disputed for half a century, is that the eidetic is always a child and that his ability to have eidetic images slowly dwindles as he grows up, disappearing by the time he reaches adulthood. Even in children, the frequency of eidetic imagery is quite low. Haber and Haber (1964), who studied the phenomenon, reported that only 8 per cent of the children in an elementary school showed eidetic imagery. These children were not just the better memorizers. They showed entirely different memory phenomena from the other children. They were different in the sense that children born with an extra toe are different. Technically, one says that the eidetekers are *discontinuous* with the rest of the children on the memory tasks presented. The Habers also found that the eidetic image does not last very long, perhaps only a minute or so, and that the eidetic children did not use the time to attempt to transfer the visual information provided by the pictures to permanent memory. The advantages of eidetic imagery are dubious. Indeed, some have even suggested that it is a phenomenon associated with brain damage. The controversial data related to this issue have been discussed by Richardson and Cant (1970).

Certain important facts about images have been discovered and have been brought together by Hebb (1968), who has also attempted to provide a theoretical interpretation for them. First is the fact already noted that visual images do not usually have the clarity of the original perception and lack detail. A second fact is that when a person is asked to conjure up an image of, say, his living room, he can shift his attention from one part of the image to another just as if he were looking at the actual room. The person asked to conjure up such an image says that he can see his entire living room, but when asked to tell what he can see in the region of the fireplace and then the region of the door, he finds that he has to shift his attention from the one to the other, much as he would shift his attention in viewing the actual living room. The reason for this can be understood by considering an experimental type of situation in which a person is asked to study a portrait and is then asked, later, to describe his visual image of the portrait. In examining the portrait, he will not take it in all at once. Indeed, if the portrait is about two feet from his eyes, clear precise vision (foveal vision) covers a part of the portrait only about as large as a fifty cent piece. For this reason, the viewer is likely to gaze first at the head, and then scan the upper portion of the body, and, finally, he might turn his attention to the background. The picture is taken in through the eyes fixating a point for a few seconds, then moving to another point, which is then briefly fixated, and then to another point, and so forth. The information from the picture is received through a sequence of "shots," much as a camera might take a number of separate shots of different parts of a scene in order to permit a technician to piece them together into a single image. Because the perception of a scene is laid down in a sequence of shots, it is hardly surprising that the image of the scene also cannot be examined as a whole but has to be examined piece by piece.

Hebb (1968) takes the position that some cell assemblies in the nervous system become active when a particular stimulus is presented, but once the stimulus is classified as belonging in a particular class (say the class of *circles*), then the cell assembly that resonates to that *class* of stimuli takes over the activity. Thus he proposes that there are cell assemblies that resonate in the presence of particular stimuli, and also cell assemblies that will resonate when any one of a particular class of stimuli is present. In the normal person, the cell assemblies indicating the presence of a particular circle stop resonating very shortly after the stimulus is removed, but the cell assemblies at a higher level continue to resonate for some time. Thus one knows he has seen a circle but the details of how large it was and how it was drawn escape him very quickly. The eidetic is believed by Hebb to show detailed imagery because the cell assemblies that record the particular features of the stimulus continue to function for a longer time than they do in the normal child. The vague images of the normal child are a result of activity of the second set of cell assemblies, which register major overall characteristics of what has been seen. This latter system of cell assemblies forms the basis of memory related to imagery.

Imagery has long been a neglected area of psychological inquiry and earlier psychologists often wrote off the area as one involving only trivial phenomena. In more recent times some psychologists have questioned this assumption and have begun to demonstrate interesting relationships between imagery and retention. Paivio (1969), in particular, has conducted a whole series of investigations. He finds that just as mediating verbal associations may help tie ideas together in memory, so too may images provide mediating processes that also facilitate memory.

Some of his research derives from the old parlor trick which starts with memorizing a list of numbers and concrete nouns such as *one-bun, two-glue, three-tree, four-door,* and so forth. The person first masters this list, which may include one hundred or more items. The person is then in a condition to master quickly another list of concrete nouns, which are read to him in a numbered list. If the first word in the new list is *car,* then he imagines a car inside a bun. If the second word is *ham,* he imagines a piece of ham covered with glue. At the end of the reading of the list, he is asked, for example, "What was the fourth word?" The fourth word was hamburger, and when that word was originally presented, he imagined a hamburger tacked to the door. In recalling the fourth word, he conjures up the image of the door and sees a hamburger tacked to it. In this way he can readily recall any word in the list by referring to the images he created when the word was presented. Such images appear to have the property of fixing information in memory and can be as powerful in this respect as verbal associations used for a similar purpose.

The findings suggest that groups of words that produce imagery should be more readily remembered than groups of abstract words. This is exactly what Paivio and Rowe (1970) found. Research of this kind tempts one to jump to the conclusion that, in the teaching of a foreign language, vocabulary should first be built with words that evoke images, for the new words can then be attached to the images and be readily learned. Such plausible applications of studies of imagery jump too far ahead of knowledge, however, for, as Palermo (1970) has pointed out, the facilitating effect of imagery is only for short-term memory. There is, as yet, no evidence that imagery facilitates long-term memory. Any effect it may have on long-term memory is probably very weak, if it exists at all, in comparison with its effect on immediate memory.

Memory Systems

Although the belief is commonly held that there is a single memory system, scientific evidence points to a number of distinct memory mechanisms, each one of which has special characteristics and unique functions. The evidence for this has been well reviewed by Adams (1967) and in Howe's very readable brief book (1970) on the subject. Psychologists have long suspected that most higher organisms are able to retain for a short time a trace of the signals they receive from their environments. This is represented in Hebb's (1968) system by the resonation of cell assemblies involved in the perception of particular pieces of information. Evidence for this transitory retention mechanism comes from a number of sources. One of these is the fact that one can readily condition an animal to salivate to the sound of a bell by exposing the animal to the sequence *bell-food* repeated a number of times, but conditioning does not take place if there is too long a delay between the sound of the bell and the presentation of the food. The experience of experimenters in this area is that if there is a delay much greater than about three seconds, the animal never learns to associate the sound of the bell with the presentation of food. In most such experiments, delays up to two or three seconds can take place and still permit conditioning to occur. The usual explanation of this is that what becomes hooked up, in the conditioning process, is an internal memory or trace of the bell and the appearance of the food. If the delay is prolonged much beyond about three seconds, the memory trace of the bell has faded to the point where it cannot be linked with the appearance of the new stimulus.

A similar kind of trace is also provided as an inherent part of the human memory system. Broadbent (1958) refers to this as a short-term memory system, although the latter term is now reserved by most writers for a memory system of longer duration. Broadbent has shown in a series of studies that the trace fades in a matter of a few seconds, and also that the trace has great significance for many common activities of everyday life. For example, a person reads a telephone number in the directory and remembers it just long enough to reach the telephone, then usually has to repeat it to himself before dialing. By repeating back the number to himself, he is able to put it back into the trace system. If he has to walk to another room before dialing the number, he may have to keep on repeating the number to himself as he goes for, if he does not, the trace is likely to have faded into oblivion before the telephone is reached. Broadbent's experiments are much more systematic than this discussion implies, but our purpose here is only to give the gist of his concept of a rapidly fading memory trace that characterizes all experience. The trace described by Broadbent is very similar to the trace discussed by those who have experimented with conditioning in animals.

The transitory trace is a memory mechanism particularly important for understanding human perception. Sperling (1960) has demonstrated experimentally the existence of a brief trace-memory system.

The second and third memory systems to be considered here are now widely referred to as the short-term memory system and the long-term memory system. In much of the current literature the abbreviations of STM and LTM are used. Of these two concepts the short-term memory is the one least well defined, although much of our knowledge about it comes from an area of rigorous experimentation, namely, the area of verbal learning. In typical verbal learning studies, the subject has to learn to associate together pairs of words or nonsense syllables. After learning such a series of paired associates the subject learns, for example, to respond with the syllable *wub* whenever the syllable *zer* is presented, or to respond with the syllable *jex* whenever the syllable *gur* is seen. A list of ten such paired associates may have to be run through ten or more times before the subject can respond correctly to each of the ten syllables presented as stimuli. Retention of such a task is generally rather short and within twenty or thirty minutes after the end of the experiment, the subject has forgotten the set of correct responses.

Long-term memory is a permanent memory system reserved for information that has high utility and, in particular, high future utility. The person's language that he acquires in childhood represents one of the sets of learnings that become placed in permanent memory.

There has long been a conflict of opinion between those who hold that the long-term memory system provides completely permanent retention and those who take the position that memories gradually become disrupted and fade. Those who hold that the memory system is absolutely permanent account for forgetting in terms of the development of difficulties in retrieving the information stored. Thus inability to remember is accounted for in terms of the stored information becoming less and less accessible.

The concept of a permanent memory of vast capacity has been claimed to find support in the work of Penfield (1951), a neurosurgeon who started out with an interest in the control of epilepsy by the surgical removal of parts of the brain. Penfield's technique involves the removal of part of the cranium and the exposure of large sections of the cortex, and this is done with the use of local anesthetics only. The patient experiences no pain and is fully conscious during the entire operation. Although the operation is performed for the purpose of removing a small section that seems to be the seat of the epilepsy problem, Penfield has also been able to explore with his patient the effect of stimulating electrically various portions of the exposed cortex. When Penfield stimulates a particular area of the cortex, the patient reports what he experiences. The so-called sensory projection areas, such as the visual cortex and the auditory cortex, do not produce meaningful experiences when stimulated, although they do produce experiences related to the particular sensory system involved. Stimulation of the visual cortex produces flashes of light of different colors, but never a picture, and stimulation of the auditory cortex produces ringing and other sounds, but never a melody. Other areas, when stimulated, do produce the most vivid images of past events and it is the study of these that are of the greatest interest in research on memory.

Several facts are significant about Penfield's observations. One is that the experiences reported when the temporal lobes are stimulated are not single static memories, such as might be represented by a single frame on a motion picture film, but rather, they are like sequences of events as they were originally experienced. The person being stimulated does not see the image of a friend, like a portrait, but rather the friend walking toward him and meeting him. Penfield claims that the experiences are so lifelike and vivid that the patient can pick out details which he did not notice at the original time. Often the material recalled represents events that the patient believed he had long forgotten. On the surface, the research gives the impression of providing evidence that whatever is experienced is recorded in memory in the greatest of detail, but there are certain weaknesses in the data that leave doubts about this conclusion.

The data are greatly limited by the fact that Penfield was an explorer rather than a systematic experimentalist. Penfield did not expose his patients to particular materials, such as a sheet of newspaper, and then try to revive an image of the experience through his surgical technique. If he had done this kind of thing, and could show that the patient could later report the content of printed sections of the sheet of newspaper not observed at the time of the original exposure, then he would have a strong case for claiming that memory is like a photographic process providing a permanent record of detail, regardless of whether such details were or were not noted at the time. Because Penfield was not an experimentalist in this sense, he caught what data he could, but the significance of the data is not clear. Suppose a patient has one of his temporal lobes stimulated and reports that he sees an old friend of twenty years ago walking toward him. He reports that the friend is wearing a blue pin-striped suit, has a red handkerchief protruding from his pocket, and that the suit is single-breasted, with two buttons on the front. Given such data, one cannot tell whether the "memory" genuinely represents what was originally seen, or whether it represents a plausible reconstruction, with perhaps the addition of details that were never really there. There is substantial evidence from the literature of experimental psychology that man has a great capacity for making constructions of what he believes happened, but these constructions may have little relationship to what actually happened. This is a major reason for conflicts of evidence in courts of law, when two witnesses provide entirely different accounts of what happened and each swears that his account is the correct one. The phenomena reported by Penfield may be artifacts of man's capacity to make constructions that he believes represent events in the past.

Another problem is also presented by the Penfield findings. Suppose that the stimulation of a particular area results in the patient's recalling and re-experiencing a dinner he had with a friend. Now if this area is surgically removed, the patient does not lose all memory of the dinner with the friend. Indeed, the particular memory is not likely to be disturbed at all, indicating that the site stimulated, which produces the particular memory, is not the site where the memory is stored. The site stimulated may represent an area of the brain where the visual memory is *reconstructed.*

Short-Term and Long-Term Memory—Two Systems or One?

There has long been controversy as to whether there really are distinct short-term and long-term memory systems or whether they are a part of a single system wherein information may be held for varying lengths of time. In a classic paper, Melton (1963) pointed out that the laws of memory for the two supposedly distinct memory systems were so similar that it seemed to him more reasonable to conclude that they both represented a single memory system. Others have taken issue with him, and a strong case on the other side has been prepared by Adams (1967) in his book on memory. Adams cites cases in which surgery on the hippocampus, a structure in the brain, has produced dramatic changes in memory functions, which throw light on this problem. He reports a case (from Penfield) in which, after such surgery, the patient was able to remember much of what he had learned prior to the operation, but was unable to learn anything new. If he were told where to find the lawnmower, he would retain that information long enough to be able to go to the location and find it, but next time he wanted to find the lawnmower he would be quite unable to recall where to go. Even after frequent use of the lawnmower, he still was unable to remember where the machine was kept. He remained familiar with the neighborhood where he had lived shortly before the operation, but found it impossible to learn to find his way back to the new house in which he now lived. He was also reported as reading the same magazines time and time again, as if he had never seen them before. A general interpretation of the patient's problem is that his short-term memory system is intact, for he can make immediate use of information and follow directions in locating objects. In addition, his long-term memory system is also intact, in that memories of preoperative events have not been disturbed. What is not functioning is his ability to transfer information from the short-term system to the long-term system. When he is told where to find the mower, he can retain this information in his short-term memory system long enough to find the mower, and then the information is lost. In normal humans, the information about the mower would be transferred from the short-term memory system to the long-term memory system, and the person would be able to remember next day where the mower was kept. The patient was unable to make this transfer from short-term to long-term memory, and was for this reason unable to use tomorrow the information given to him today. The case argues strongly for a distinct and separate short-term and long-term memory.

A second argument put forward by Adams is that the errors of recall in many kinds of experiment are different for short-term and long-term memory. There is a marked tendency for errors of short-term memory to be what are called acoustic errors. In such an error the person substitutes a similar sounding word for the correct word, as when the correct word to be recalled is *dark* and he recalls *bark*. On the other hand, in recalling information held in long-term memory, the tendency is to provide similar meanings. Again, if the word to be recalled was *dark*, the person might recall the word *night*. The fact that the errors of recall are different for short-term and long-term memory suggests that two separate systems are at work.

A third argument is that the short-term memory system appears to have a rather small capacity, whereas the capacity of the long-term memory system is relatively large.

There is a fourth argument pointing to the distinctiveness of the two memory systems. Some years ago Kleinsmith and Kaplan (1963) conducted a study of learning to associate together pairs of words. Such a learning situation is commonly studied in the laboratory, but these research workers introduced a novel element into the experiment. They measured what is known as the galvanic skin response to each pair of words. This response is a change in resistance across the skin of the hand which occurs when a person is presented with an emotion-arousing situation, and it is commonly taken to indicate the extent to which the person is aroused by the situation presented, in contrast to remaining passive and calm. Kleinsmith and Kaplan found that when a pair of words produced a strong galvanic skin response, indicating arousal, the retention of the association between the words was reduced for short-term memory but improved for long-term memory. If a condition that improves long-term memory depresses short-term memory, and if a condition that improves short-term memory depresses long-term memory, then the two memory systems would appear to be quite distinct.

Rehearsal and Memory

One of the time-honored procedures for committing material to memory is that of rehearsing it. Over half a century ago it was demonstrated that if a certain amount of time is available for learning verbal material, then more time should be spent on rehearsing the material than on reading it. The reasons why rehearsal plays a significant role in memorization are many. One is that rehearsal represents practice of the performance that the person hopes to acquire. His goal in learning is not to be able to read the material, but to be able to say it without the text in front of him. Therefore, he will learn best by saying the material, insofar as he can, without the material in front of him.

Another factor that has been investigated by Tulving (1967) is the fact that rehearsal provides opportunities for organizing the material. Whereas the older experiments on the effect of rehearsal involved the learning of material such as poetry, Tulving has introduced another technique. He uses lists of forty words; the words are presented one at a time to the learner, and, at the end of the list of words, the learner attempts to write out all the words he can remember. In the typical procedure, the learner's attempt to recall is then followed by a second presentation of the list, then a second attempt at recall, and so forth. Tulving introduced an interesting variation. After the subject had completed his attempt to recall, instead of being shown the list of words again, he was asked to once again recall the words. Tulving found that this second attempt to recall the list produced as much learning as a presentation of the list. In other words, the attempt to recall functioned like a learning trial without the actual material. The attempt to recall in the Tulving experiment appears essentially the same as the attempts to rehearse used in earlier experiments.

Tulving also found that one presentation of the list and four attempts to recall provided as effective learning in a given time as alternating the presentation of the list and the recall.

Tulving's explanation for this phenomenon is that the recall process provides opportunity for organizing the list of words into categories and this, in turn, facilitates learning. Presumably, in much the same way, rehearsing poetry to be learned results in all kinds of associative processes, which facilitate the learning of the poetry.

Capacity of the Memory Systems

Although there has been an enormous amount of reflective thinking and research concerning the capacities of the various memory systems, no clear-cut answers can be given on this matter. The initial trace appears to be in a large capacity system. The trace of a visual experience certainly contains a large amount of information, most of which cannot be retrieved for further use. The decay of the trace, during the few seconds of its existence, is so rapid that only a small fraction of the information present can be snatched for further use. What is snatched from a single brief exposure to the environment is a very limited amount of information. This amount is commonly referred to as the *span of attention* or *memory span,* and it is generally limited in quantity to about seven digits, seven letters, seven words, or seven chunks of information. This is not the capacity of the short-term memory system, however; it represents only the amount of information that can be obtained and used from a single brief viewing of the environment.

The capacity of the short-term memory system is controversial. Writers of a decade or more ago were inclined to view the system as having a quite small capacity, but a number of studies have suggested that the capacity may be much larger than was previously estimated. One such study is that by Shepard (1967). In the first part of the Shepard study two groups of 270 words each were selected, the one group representing common words and the other group rare words. These words were shown in random order, one after the other, to the subjects, who were then tested to determine whether they could remember the words they had seen. The test consisted of presenting the subjects with pairs of words, one of which belonged to the list they had seen and one of which was new. In the test, the subject had to identify the word he had seen. The new words that were paired with the words they had already seen had similar characteristics to the words in the original list, that is to say, they belonged to the same difficulty level and were derived from the same general source. The surprising finding of the study was that after the subjects had been through the list of 540 words once, they were able to identify with an 88.4 per cent accuracy the words they had seen. They were slightly better at identifying the rare words than the common words, but the difference was only a matter of a few percentage points. Shepard then went on to perform the same demonstration with approximately the same number of short sentences and, in a third study, he employed a procedure that used pictures. For sentences, the retention was about the same as for words, but the immediate retention rate for pictures went up to 96.7 per cent. In the case of the pictures, the test for retention was also given after seven days and then again after one hundred and twenty days. Different subjects were used for each of the delayed recognition conditions from those used for the immediate recognition condition. The surprising finding was that even after seven days the percentage recognition of pictures was 87.0 per cent. After one hundred and twenty days the percentage recognition was 57.7, but this is not as high as it may seem to be, in that, by guessing alone, the subject would be expected to achieve a score of 50 per cent.

These results are unexpected and quite puzzling, for it is as if a transitory contact with materials led to the transfer of these materials to long-term memory. The general conditions of the experiment are those used in the study of short-term memory and one would have expected that the evidence of the experience would have vanished within a few hours, at the most. Instead, the record of recognition even seven days later indicated that permanent memory had taken place. The fact that little evidence was left after one hundred and twenty days suggests only that subsequent exposure to words, sentences, and pictures may have interfered with the memory. Also, one commonly makes the assumption that when information is transferred to the long-term memory system it becomes organized in the process. The very large quantity of information to which subjects were exposed in the Shepard experiment appears to have left a record, but there is no indication that the information was in any way organized as it was taken in or after it was taken in. The experiment clearly brings out the fact that there is much we do not know about the human memory system.

The capacity of the long-term system has been a matter of controversy for many years. Many well-known scientists have believed that the human information storage system has a vast capacity. An argument commonly introduced to support the position of an almost limitless memory is the well-established fact that there are billions of nerve cells in the central nervous system. This argument is not as impressive as it might appear to be on the surface because nobody knows how many of these nerve cells are actually concerned with the storage of information. Many of the cells have other functions, including those of the conduction of information in and out of the system, the analysis of information, and the control of the general level of activity. The storage system may well involve only a small fraction of the total number of cells in the brain. Even if all the cells were involved in storage, there is doubt whether the system would be sufficient to record all the information provided by the sensory system at any given instant.

An entirely different view is presented by those who take the position that much evidence supports the position that the permanent memory system has a very limited capacity. First of all, it takes work to place an item in relatively permanent storage. We all know what a struggle it is to learn a foreign language, and this is because of the immense amount of work necessary to memorize the large vocabulary required for obtaining command of a new language. If information is slow to enter the long-term memory system, it surely is extremely probable that there is a very limited amount of information that can be placed there. Life would be too short to store, piece by piece, a *vast* quantity of information.

A second argument is that the human system appears to be designed so that a minimum of information is stored for long-term purposes. Both a perceptual trace and a short-term memory are available for holding information for brief periods, and much of our daily life is made possible by these systems that hold information long enough for it to be used, and then discarded. If an engineer were designing a memory system, he would introduce such short-term memory mechanisms in order to prevent the long-term memory from becoming cluttered with details that are of only transitory interest. The system for retaining information is designed *as if* the long-term system had to be protected from being overwhelmed with unnecessary detail.

Finally, there is an additional factor that will be discussed further in the section on the theory of forgetting, which has considerable implications for estimating the capacity of the memory system. This is the fact that every item of information introduced into the memory system tends to disrupt information that is already there. The addition of a new piece of information to the system does not produce that much gain in the information stored, for the amount added is partly balanced by a certain amount of information that is taken away from the system by the addition. This is the major reason why a review of what we know from time to time is important to strengthen the storage of it in the memory system. Review is necessary largely because the store of information is being constantly eroded as new information is stored. This, in itself, limits the amount of information that can be placed in the system.

Retention in Terms of Chunks

In free recall tasks, the number of units that can be presented and later recalled has little to do with whether the units are fairly large units or small units. For example, Bower (1969) undertook a study in which he compared performance in a free recall task in which subjects were either exposed to a list of nouns or a list of three-word expressions such as *fair-weather friend, good old days, Happy New Year,* and so forth. He found that the ability to retain and recall, in terms of the number of units involved, was the same for the single nouns as for the three-word expressions; that is to say, if the average recall performance was twelve nouns, then the average recall for three-word expressions would be twelve three-word expressions. The material is said to be learned in *chunks,* and the hypothesis tested in the Bower experiment is known as the *chunking hypothesis.*

A point to note in this connection is that the task of the student is not that of learning the nouns or expressions, for these are already familiar to him and all of them have been previously stored in his long-term memory system. What he is learning is, so to speak, to tag these nouns and expressions already in his permanent storage system as the particular ones now presented to him. The task is like pulling off a library shelf those books mentioned in a review. This is an entirely different task from placing the books on the shelf when they are first purchased. Thus the studies of chunking show that information, already stored, can be tagged as easily in large chunks as in small chunks. One is tempted to generalize and suggest that information in the long-term memory system is stored in chunks, but too much evidence points in another direction.

The External and Internal Storage of Information

There has long been a controversy among educators concerning the extent to which the pupil should be expected to store information internally and how far he should become dependent on the use of reference works, such as encyclopedias, for the storage of information. This is a complicated problem. In order to take sides on the issues one would have to know the storage capacity of the human and also something about the time it takes to store particular bodies of information. If the human has a limited-capacity storage system, then it is clear that he must learn to use reference sources, where information is stored external to himself, for he would have no other choice. On the other hand, if his storage capacity is very large, then there are advantages in storing internally as much information as possible—unless disproportionately large amounts of time are needed to acquire and store the information.

The practices that have evolved in our society place emphasis on systems of storing knowledge external to the individual. Thus a machinist operating a lathe must have available a handbook that stores all the information he needs for setting up the tool. He consults the handbook to determine the cutting speed he should use on a particular piece of metal. He does not have to store within his brain the equivalent of several pages of detailed specifications for cutting speeds; all he has to store is the knowledge that the information can be found in the handbook. If he were to commit the material to memory, he would have to spend many hours of study distributed over several weeks. Even after devoting this much effort to the task, he would still not be able to reproduce the data from memory with the same accuracy with which he could find it in the handbook.

The occupation of the machinist is not unique in this respect. Workers in almost every occupation use extensive bodies of information stored externally. Most professional people have at hand a library of important sources of information they can consult. Even a source of twenty or thirty books can contain large quantities of information. Salesmen do not have to remember the names of all of their customers; they have a file containing such information with the data placed in some order, such as alphabetical order, from which information can be readily retrieved. Modern civilization is highly dependent on the existence of information storage systems that vastly increase the human's capability of using available knowledge.

Although man has long used storage systems external to himself, in the form of scrolls and tablets and, later, books, no entirely satisfactory system has been devised for enabling him to obtain access to the information thus stored. The index to a book, the table of contents, the library catalogue, and related devices are all designed to assist the individual to gain access to stored knowledge; but none of these is completely satisfactory, as any user knows. Extensive research is now being undertaken on this problem, mainly by people involved in information science.

The assumption generally made is that whatever is learned in elementary school should be stored internally so that the performance of the skills involved can take place without referring to a book or other source of information. At the secondary-school level, there are clear advantages in being able to add and multiply without having to consult a table. The same can be said for the learning of a foreign language. Unless a person can store internally the vocabulary and general rules of syntax of a foreign language, it is of little practical use to him. On the other hand, the fine details of geography might as well remain stored in a book, though the pupil should undoubtedly retain a broad general knowledge of the subject. Perhaps it is important to know that Paris is in France, but it is much less important to know exactly where in that country the city is located or on what river it is to be found. However, the pupil should know just where to find these details.

What Is Retained in the Information System?

The chapter on the anatomy and physiology of the nervous system points out that we do not know precisely how information is retained in the nervous system or just where particular information is retained. The evidence points to the synapses as the most probable location of information retention, with the synapses working like on-off switches. The relationship of these on-off switches to behavior is undoubtedly extremely complex. One can say with confidence that there is no simple relationship. It is not that the memory for a particular word corresponds to a particular synapse. Also, information retained in the nervous system is probably retained in many different psychological forms. It is to this matter that we must now turn.

A basic form of information storage is in terms of simple response tendencies. One learns to put the foot down on the brake when a red light appears beside the road ahead. One automatically inserts the key in the lock on returning home. One moves from one part of the house to the other in the dark without having to think about the floor plan of the house. In such simple learned activities, it seems reasonable that what one stores are action tendencies. The activities are undertaken without the mediation of words or images. They are relatively automatic and are performed with high reliability. They are situation-specific, as is evident from the fact that what I have learned about moving around my house cannot be used when the problem is that of moving around somebody else's house. Action tendencies are a basic and primitive system of storage that must surely exist in all forms of life capable of learning.

A second category of information stored is that which represents directly the sensory information taken in from the environment. When Penfield stimulated the cortex of the exposed brain of his conscious patients, they experienced most vivid images of events they had previously experienced. The information necessary to conjure up such images had to be stored. The simplest explanation at the present time is that nerve cell assemblies correspond to such images and represent the means through which they are stored. In other words, this explanation says that one can conjure up a particular image of a past experience because the information about the past experience is stored in one or more cell assemblies. When these cell assemblies become active, an image is experienced. This is pure conjecture, but plausible. As has already been noted, storage in terms of images or in terms of the material that produces images is always storage of information lacking in detail, except in the case of those who have eidetic images.

Man's great capacity for storing information as compared with that of other living creatures is not represented by any greater tendency to store action tendencies or fleeting perceptions of the world. Rather, it must be attributed to the fact that man can code his experiences in terms of language. A person can meet his friend John in the street and can, perhaps, record the data needed for producing at a later date an image of the encounter. He can also say to himself, "There is John," and may later reproduce this verbal information when he says to his wife, "I met John today." Much of the information that comes to us through the sensory systems is coded internally in this way before it is stored and there is evidence that this kind of coding adds greatly to the accuracy of the information stored. Chan and Travers (1966) conducted an experiment in which semimeaningful shapes were shown to subjects who later had to identify those they had seen. If the shapes were labeled in suitable ways—as when a shape that looked like a can opener was labeled "can opener"—then the shapes were more readily remembered than when no labels were provided. Translating the visual information into verbal information, that is to say, coding the visual information verbally, facilitated retention. One suspects that most visual information has to be coded into verbal terms to be easily remembered. If someone looks at a cathedral and says to himself that it is Perpendicular Gothic, made of limestone, and contains traditional stained glass windows, he has coded a great amount of information and can reconstruct the main features of the cathedral from that description.

While memory related to imagery generally lacks precise detail, verbal memory provides an immense amount of detail. The amateur actor often marvels at the fact that the professional can commit to memory a part such as that of Hamlet, and reproduce it almost without error. That same person who marvels at the accomplishment of the Shakespearean actor could equally well marvel at the fact that he himself is probably able to define accurately as many as 50,000 words in his mother tongue and perhaps 10,000 in each of several foreign languages. Verbal memory has a capacity and precision not found in other memory systems. These achievements of memory are to be contrasted with the limited memory of the portrait artist, who might be expected to have as good a memory as can be found for visual information. Yet the fact is that such an artist finds his memory so unreliable that he will never depend on it in his work, always insisting that the subject of a portrait sit before him as much as possible. Only the most unimportant details are handled with the subject absent. It seems that the artist is quite unable to have a memory image of the subject of a portrait that can provide him with the detailed information he needs. This observation fits with the observation already made that images do not provide detailed information.

Underwood (1969) has suggested that what is stored in the memory system is primarily a set of attributes, that is to say, characteristics of experiences. In the chapter on perception, the point is made that recognition processes are possible because the person making the recognition can analyze whatever he experiences into its attributes, and from the attributes thus analyzed, is able to recognize what is before him. Underwood expands on this concept in describing the memory system. The memory for most common objects would, almost certainly, involve an immense number of different attributes as well as other components. For example, my memory of the car I drive involves the retention of many action systems related to driving it. When I enter the car, I perform a sequence of acts related to starting the car and leaving the garage, and these take place quite atuomatically. In addition, I have stored information related to the attributes of the car such as whiteness, year of model, the noise made by the engine, the sound of a bad rear bearing, and numerous other characteristics. Some of these attributes are probably stored in a form closely related to auditory language, but some, such as the sound of the rear bearing, have not been coded into words. It is the total sum of the retained attributes and action systems that form what might be called the memory of the particular car.

Organization of Memory

Philosophers and psychologists alike have long viewed the human memory as representing an organized system of storage. Nearly two hundred years ago, the great German philospher and educator Johann Friedrich Herbart described the memory system as one that could virtually hold only organized knowledge. Indeed, Herbart proposed that the key to effective learning was for the teacher to present knowledge in such a way that it could be tied in with knowledge previously learned. Herbart's concept of organizing teaching so that it provided this tie-in of new knowledge with previously acquired knowledge still remains a key concept in the planning of curricula. Little progress was made in the development of this concept of memory organization until relatively recent times, when new ideas began to emerge both from psychologists working on educational problems and from other psychologists conducting research in the area of verbal learning.

Among the work of psychologists studying educational problems in this field that of Ausubel (1963) must be regarded as having had major impact on educational thought. For Ausubel, information can be most readily stored in the information system if it is related to a pivotal idea, referred to as an *organizer*. An organizer is a key concept that may form a basis for understanding a great many happenings. One can point to concepts in physics, such as density, which are of crucial importance in organizing knowledge. The concept of density organizes such information as why ships float, why divers have to wear weights, why smoke rises in the atmosphere except on a hot and muggy day, and numerous other common events.

The problem of how memory is organized has also been attacked by experimental psychologists, using special materials developed for experimentation. An early experiment on the organizing functions of memorizing and retention is illustrated by a study conducted by Underwood (1964), who presented to his subjects lists of words that could be organized into groups. For example, one list consisted of four names of countries, four birds, four diseases, and four elements, and these were presented in a jumbled order so that words in the different categories were likely to be separated. Other lists presented sets of words that did not fall into obvious categories. At the end of the reading of each list, the subjects were asked to write down all the words they could remember. Although the lists containing groups of words had the individual words presented in random order, the words were recalled by the subjects in groups. That is to say, the learner tended, after hearing the words, to recall all the diseases together, and all the countries together, and all the birds together, and all the elements together. He didn't just remember the list as it was presented, but organized the list into categories. In addition, the lists that included categories of objects were remembered more easily than were lists that did not include obvious categories.

A series of related studies by W. A. Bousefield and his associates have also been conducted on the organization of material in the memory system. The technique adopted for the study of this problem is that of free recall. The learner is presented with a list of words, one at a time, and then, after the entire list has been read, must recall all the words he can remember. Shuell (1969) and Tulving (1969) have summarized the results of these studies. The recalled items do not generally appear in the order in which they were presented. If the experimenter has selected the words so that they are easily categorized, then the learner is likely to use the organization into which the words readily fit. However, if the words have been selected by the experimenter at random, then the learner imposes his own organization on the material. For example, if the list of words includes the items—*house, stamp, envelope, tree, street, office*—the subject might repeat back the words in two groups, (1) *house, tree, street,* and (2) *stamp, envelope, office*. He might also use other groupings, such as placing *office* and *street* together. The subjective organization imposed by the learner is not always apparent from examining the list of words in the order in which they are reproduced by the learner, but some organization is always there. Organization appears to be crucial in the transfer of information from the short-term to the long-term memory system. Indeed, one suspects that one of the major differences between the mentally handicapped individual and the normal individual lies in the incapacity of the former to organize information for transfer to the long-term memory system. The mentally handicapped often show excellent performance on short-term memory tasks, but it is on tasks that call for organized stored information that they experience difficulty. Shuell also cites evidence that young children show less capability to develop subjective organizations in free recall tasks than do adults, a fact that points up the conclusion that the strategies involved in organizing information are learned.

The reader can now see one reason why it is that well-organized material is better retained than poorly organized material. If the learner is left to organize material as it enters the short-term memory system, then some of the information is lost in the process. Organizing the material before it is presented to the learner saves him this step, and perhaps makes it possible for the information to enter directly into the long-term memory system.

The data suggests that a primary fact remembered is the category to which objects belonged. Thus a person reading the Underwood list remembers that there were four birds. In the case of the particular list, he would only have to remember that it included four *common* birds to have most of the answers in this category correct, but subjects also remembered enough about the specific birds mentioned to be able to identify them, for very few errors were made on recall. The fact that errors of memory of material stored in the long-term system tend to involve the recall of the wrong item in the right category suggests that items to be remembered are tagged with a category, and that one starts with the category when one wants to retrieve the item. The category is generally more readily retrieved than is the actual item itself. Thus we may recall having gone to a lecture some years previously on the topic of poetry, but we may not remember which particular poems were discussed.

Numerous experiments have been conducted showing that the more readily a list of words is structured, the easier it is for the learner to remember. However, Bower et al. (1969), who have reviewed these studies, point out that the gains produced by word lists including words that are readily organized have been what they describe as "disheartening." They then proceeded to conduct a study in which they were able to show that, under some conditions, organized material might be learned two or three times as quickly as the same material presented in a disorganized order. Bower et al. prepared a list of words that could be presented with varying degrees of structure. The material involved the following words and categories in which they belonged:

Minerals

METALS			STONES	
Rare	*Common*	*Alloys*	*Precious*	*Masonry*
Platinum	Aluminum	Bronze	Sapphire	Limestone
Silver	Copper	Steel	Emerald	Granite
Gold	Lead	Brass	Diamond	Marble
	Iron		Ruby	Slate

Such material can be presented in many different ways. Earlier experiments had generally compared the presentation of the words, one by one, either keeping together words in particular categories or arranging the words in random order. A comparison of the learning under these two conditions generally showed that the organized list was learned a little better than the random list.

Bowers et al. point out that the method of presenting words one by one does not help the subject utilize the organizational structure in the material. In one condition in their experiments they presented the entire body of material at the same time; either they showed the words within a structure, as in the case of the structure of minerals, or the words were assigned at random to groups and the set of groups of words was shown at one time. Under the former condition, the learner could make the most use of the structure of the words. He could see the various categories and learn the words as groups in terms of the categories to which they belonged. Under the random condition he would have to study the words and find some structure into which he could arrange them. Under these conditions, the categorized words were learned about three times as effectively as the randomly presented words.

Bowers et al. conducted a whole series of experiments related to this problem, and its explanation and their data are very consistent. The real problem is why the organized material is more readily learned than the random material. They conclude that if the learner can discover a simple rule that can be used to characterize and group the items in a list of words, then he uses that rule in carrying out a retrieval plan that permits him to reconstruct the list from memory. If he remembers, for example, that four of the words refer to the four commonest precious stones, then he can easily reconstruct the list of words that includes sapphire, emerald, diamond, and ruby. It is much easier to generate a set of words using a principle or rule than it is to recall a set of words unrelated to one another. For example, a person may not be able to remember the names of all the shops on Main Street, although he has seen the names many times, but it is easy to remember all the shop numbers if he knows that they start at 1 and go up to 218. Organized information calls upon the memory system to remember less information than when the information has no inherent organization. When one recalls a list of words by using a rule to generate the list, the errors that occur are what are called intrusion errors. They result from the rule failing to discriminate between the words that should be produced and other words. However, in applying a rule such as that the names of rare metals are to be given, a person may recognize a name of a metal as not belonging on the basis of the knowledge that he knows he has not seen that word in print recently. Words are tagged, so to speak, with a recency label. One knows whether he has or has not seen a particular word recently. The recency and time of an experience is recorded as a part of the memory of that experience.

A great amount of evidence suggests that the long-term memory system is organized in a hierarchical manner, from broad general categories to highly specific details. For reasons not understood, information stored at the broad category level is likely to have the greatest permanence. In recalling information, sometimes a person may be able to recover only very general information when he may wish to recover information at a much higher level of detail. For example, one meets an acquaintance and would like to recall his name, an operation that would involve the recall of considerable detail. However, all one can recall is that the acquaintance had a German name, or that he had a very long name, or a name difficult to pronounce. The better one's memory, the greater the amount of detail that can be recalled. Loss through forgetting appears to proceed generally in the order from fine detail to broad categories. In the case of the kind of school learning discussed by Ausubel, forgetting would occur from the least inclusive concept to the most inclusive. It would also appear that details have some chance of survival in the memory system only when they are closely tied to ideas at a higher level of generality.

The knowledge, reviewed up to this point, of the conditions that favor the transfer of information from the short-term memory system to the long-term system has some implications for understanding the learning problems of the slow learner. When slow learners and fast learners are given psychological tests, the two groups are likely to differ little on those tests that involve short-term memory and immediate recall. Other tests show that the slow learner has much less information stored in his long-term storage system than does the fast learner. The difficulty of the slow learner is, at least partly, as we have seen, that he has problems in transferring information from his short-term storage system to his long-term system. The slow learner probably has difficulty in organizing information in the short-term system so that it can be transferred to more permanent storage. The slow learner may perhaps also have difficulty in conceptualizing future uses of the information, which is an important condition for this transfer. Shuell and Keppel (1970) have shown that if material is learned equally well by both slow and rapid learners, it is remembered about equally well after twenty-four- and forty-eight-hour intervals, a finding which suggests that the differences in the two groups do not lie in their memory systems, once information is stored there.

The Retrieval System

The fact that a piece of information is stored within one's memory is no guarantee that one can obtain that information for use. We may know that we know the name of our congressman, but when it comes to writing him, we may suffer from a temporary block of memory. On such an occasion, we may know well that the congressman's name is tucked away somewhere at the back of our minds, and we know we would recognize the name if it were presented to us. We also know that, given enough time, we will be able to remember his name.

Obtaining a piece of information from our memory is termed retrieval. It is quite clear from what has just been said that the retrieval system is independent of the memory system, for we can know that we have a piece of information stored, but we may not be able to retrieve it. Older people have major difficulties with their retrieval systems. It is not so much that there is something wrong with the memory system of the older person, but rather that he has trouble with his retrieval system. Of course, there are some older people who also have difficulty in placing new information in their memory systems.

The retrieval system has several interesting features. One is that the person knows whether he does or does not have a particular piece of information stored, and whether it is worth spending time trying to recover it. I may not be able to give an immediate answer to the question, Who was President at the outbreak of World War I? But I do know that I have that piece of information and can recover it with a little thought. On the other hand, if you ask me the question, Who was the leader of the Zulus in the Zulu War? I can tell you immediately that I do not possess that information. The retrieval system functions as though it had a catalogue of the information stored and could tell from this catalogue, instantly, whether the information is or is not there.

An interesting approach to the study of the retrieval system is found in the study of what is called the tip-of-the-tongue phenomenon, in which one is attempting to recall a word but can recall only words similar in form or meaning. Brown and McNeill (1966) initiated work in this area and came up with some interesting findings. Their technique involved the preparation of the definitions of a list of rare words such as *ambergris, nepotism,* and *cloaca,* which occur less often than once in a million times in English written materials. Each definition was read to the subjects. After the definition was read, some subjects said they knew the word and others said they did not know it. These subjects indicated their knowledge or lack of knowledge on a sheet of paper and had nothing more to do. The others were those who felt that the answer was on the tip of their tongues but it would take them a little time to retrieve the word from their memory. These subjects were asked to indicate some of the characteristics of the word they were searching to find by indicating how many syllables they thought it was, what was its initial letter, what other words were similar in sound to it, and what words might be similar to it in meaning. The word sought is referred to as the target word.

A very significant finding from this study is that subjects in the tip-of-the-tongue state were able to identify significant aspects of the words they were trying to recall, even though they could not recall the actual words. They had considerable success in identifying the number of syllables in the target word, if the words were of one, two, or three syllables in length. Longer words tended to be identified as three-syllable words. In addition, subjects were able to guess with better than chance accuracy the first letter of the word sought and also the syllable that was stressed when the word was spoken. In the case of the words similar in sound that they wrote down, there was a tendency for the first and last letters to be matched correctly. There was also a tendency for subjects to be able to identify correctly suffixes involved in the target word.

Another finding is that the subject is able to judge which one of two target words most resembles the target word. This is also a familiar experience. When we are seeking to retrieve a person's name, one can often say "It is a name like Black and not like the name Cross you have suggested." Furthermore, when we are told the correct name, we know immediately that the name suggested is correct. Now in both of these cases we take in information and are able to compare it with information already stored. Somebody suggests that the missing name may be "Black" and we behave as if we were able to compare this suggestion with the name stored within us and say that it is close, but that it is not an exact match. When the name "Stack" is suggested, we know that we have found what we were looking for. Again, we behave as though we received the suggested name, compared it with the stored name, and concluded that there was an exact match. The odd thing about the entire process is that one can compare incoming information with information already stored while having no direct knowledge of the stored information.

Brown and McNeill have a more complicated explanation of the phenomenon, suggesting that we do not store whole words but perhaps only critical components. The critical components of the input are then checked against the critical components of the stored word. This does not explain how one can recognize that a word is not the correct one even when it varies in some quite minor way from the correct word that is stored. It is much simpler and probably as satisfactory to assume that the entire word is stored, perhaps in an auditory form, than to assume a cue storage.

The data considered here suggest that the retrieval mechanism is quite different from the memory mechanism. Failure to recall is not necessarily a memory failure, but may be a retrieval failure. In older people, who claim that their memory is failing them, the difficulty is generally with the retrieval mechanism rather than with the memory itself. In others, the retrieval system may work well, and the memory system may have a satisfactory record of much of the individual's past, but there is damage to the system that transfers new information to the memory system. Such persons cannot learn anything new, but knowledge acquired earlier may remain intact and be readily obtainable.

The extent to which retrieval can occur depends to some extent on the degree to which cues that can arouse the relevant responses are present. Many cues are provided in recognition tasks, but fewer cues are provided when the process involves recall. Furthermore, in some recall situations, adequate cues are provided; but in others, the cues may be so inadequate that incorrect responses are evoked. The poorly worded essay question may evoke an inappropriate response on the part of the examinee, who claims that he was misled by the question; and the well-worded question may evoke the appropriate response in every student who has profited from study. A related question is whether irrelevant cues present during learning should be present in the recall situation if recall is to be facilitated. If the student learns while the radio is tuned to his favorite music, does the absence of the sound of such music during the examination limit the student's recall of the material he has learned in its presence?

One of the few technical discussions of this problem is provided by Bugelski (1956). He points out that most studies of retention have attempted to keep the conditions of learning and the conditions of recall approximately the same. However, he points out that any serious change in these conditions is generally assumed to interfere with recall, and cites the common example of the child who in the privacy of his room learns a poem for recitation and then is quite unable to recall it when on the stage in front of an audience. Bugelski also points out that the one study that has some bearing in this kind of situation was designed to investigate a problem in retroactive inhibition. The study was conducted by Bilodeau and Schlosberg (1951). The task to be learned involved the memorization of pairs of adjectives. A part of the data of this research permits the comparison of material learned and recalled in one situation with material learned in one situation and recalled in another. The two situations involved differences in posture (standing versus sitting), differences in the room, and differences in the methods of presentation. The investigation showed that when the recall situation varied from the learning situation, there was much more serious interference with the recall process than when the conditions remained the same.

These findings have interesting implications for education. They suggest that what is learned in the classroom is most readily recalled under classroom conditions. Of course, the teacher hopes that what is learned in class will be most readily available in the situations of life outside the classroom to which it is to be applied. In order to make knowledge more readily available in different situations, the pupil should have experience in using it in those situations. Field trips involving the use of knowledge acquired in the classroom, special out-of-school assignments, and perhaps even homework may help to overcome the tendency for the retrieval of knowledge to be tied to the presence of particular cues.

Finally, a comment must be made on the school child's familiar system for helping his memory, namely, the mnemonic device. A child has difficulty in remembering the names of recent Presidents. His teacher points out that the first initials of Truman, Eisenhower, Kennedy, Johnson, and Nixon form a funny name, TEKJN. All the pupil has to do is to remember that name. This he does, and his difficulty of remembering the Presidents is solved. What this sort of device does is to provide a set of cues that can be used for retrieval of the information. The names of the Presidents are probably stored and the problem of the pupil is to be able to retrieve them and to retrieve them in the right order. The mnemonic device provides the cues necessary for initiating retrieval.

Very simple mnemonic devices involving diagrams, and not words, have been shown to be usable by children as young as three and a half years of age (see Ryan, Hegion, and Flavell, 1970). However, one doubts whether there would be much educational utility to such devices at such a young age.

Theories of Forgetting

Learning theories have characteristically maintained that what is learned is probably learned permanently, unless a specific activity is undertaken that in some way disposes of the response that has been learned. This viewpoint is in sharp contrast with that of the layman, who generally takes the position that once the active process of learning has ceased, forgetting rapidly sets in, until, after a time, whatever has been learned ceases to exist as a habit or a skill. The learning theorist accounts for most forgetting by some process other than that of fading. He has to account for forgetting, because forgetting is an incontrovertible fact. Let us consider at this point some of the processes that may account for forgetting.

Forgetting As a Decay Process. The theory of forgetting that is most widely held by the public at large is the theory that whatever is learned slowly fades, much as the pattern on a pair of draperies fades from prolonged exposure to the sun. This theory is derived from the common experience that, as time goes by, a memory becomes less and less accessible and the details become more and more obscure. One piece of evidence that is quite embarrassing to this theory is that memories that appear to have completely faded may sometimes return with remarkable vividness under special conditions such as hypnosis or clinical treatment. So striking is this phenomenon to the clinician that many have suggested the possibility that whatever is learned is never lost but merely becomes unavailable under most circumstances. This is an extreme point of view and represents a generalization that goes way beyond the facts. Few psychologists today, if any, would go along with such a position. Most would take the view that a theory of forgetting that is just a theory of decay through disuse is largely unacceptable. If this kind of a process occurs at all, then it is a minor one. Forgetting occurs mainly for other reasons.

Another piece of evidence that runs counter to the decay theory of forgetting is that material learned just before a period of sleep shows relatively little decay when retention is measured as the subject wakes up. There is some decay over time during sleep, but the decay could be attributed to the fact that the sleeping subject is not completely passive and that some activity may take place that disrupts the trace of what is learned.

The difficulty with the decay theory of memory is that there is no way of finding out whether decay does or does not take place. The disruption of memory can always be more readily accounted for in terms of the theory now to be considered. There is no clear and unambiguous way of demonstrating whether decay does or does not occur.

Interference Theories of Forgetting. Experimental studies have produced strong evidence supporting interference theories of forgetting. Interference effects fall into two categories. First, there are retroactive effects, that is to say, learning may have a depressing effect on the retention of material previously learned. Second, there is a proactive effect, which means that learning taking place at a particular time may have a depressing effect on the retention of material subsequently learned.

Most of the research undertaken to date has been on the retroaction effect which can be clearly demonstrated in the laboratory. The usual demonstration involves the learning of a set of paired associates, referred to as the *A-B* series, in which the learner has to learn to make a response with the word designated here as *B* whenever he sees the word designated as *A*. After learning this series, he is then required to learn a new paired associate series designated as the *A-C* series. In this series the stimulus words are the same as in the original series, but the responses learned to the stimulus words are different. Thus the first two words in the first list might be *chair-car*, and the first pair of words in the second list are *chair-box*. In doing this, the experimenter has taught the subject one habit, namely, to say *car* whenever the stimulus word *chair* is presented, and then the subject is taught a second and inconsistent habit, namely, that of responding to the same stimulus word *chair* with the word *box*. One can then demonstrate that the learning of the second of these associations disrupts the retention of the first set of associations. This is the retroactive inhibition phenomenon. It is a well-established phenomenon and is presumed to account for some of the forgetting that occurs in daily life. It is not specific to the learning of verbal associations but is also found in the retention of motor skills involving the manual manipulation of the environment (and other physical manipulations as well). It will be referred to again in the chapter on transfer of training, where it will be viewed as a case of negative transfer.

The second interference effect, known as proactive inhibition, has not been investigated to the same extent, but the effect is a clear one, and generally somewhat stronger than that of retroactive inhibition. The common procedure for demonstrating this effect is that of the subject learning, first, the paired associate list *A-B*. He then learns the list *A-C*, and it can be demonstrated that the previous acquisition of the list *A-B* interferes with the learning and retention of the list *A-C*. The proactive effect, as with the retroactive effect, occurs not only in the case of verbal learning, but also with motor skills.

There is much theoretical speculation about how retroactive and proactive inhibition exert their disruptive effects. One proposed explanation of the retroaction effect is that the learning of the one response tends to extinguish the other response that has been learned. Up to this time, no experiment has been designed that can clearly demonstrate whether the extinction hypothesis is an acceptable explanation. Regardless of the value of particular explanations, interference theory is still the most influential theory of forgetting.

Forgetting As a Repression Process. A very old theory of forgetting is that the stored information remains permanently stored but may become inaccessible when there is strong motivation *not* to recall. Thus a person forgets a dental appointment, but when a few hours later he remembers the missed appointment, it becomes clear that his problem was not one of the memory of it having become erased, but one of the record not being recalled at the appropriate time. In describing such instances of forgetting, Freud stated that information was repressed when the recall of the information might produce anxiety, and he would have explained the missed dental appointment by suggesting that even thinking about it might produce anxiety and hence the best way to avoid such anxiety would be to forget the whole matter.

Although the term repression, as used in this connection, is probably a misleading description of what happens, it is so well established that it is likely to be used for a long time to come. For this reason one finds research on the effect of anxiety on the "repression" of learned information. There is some evidence that anxiety associated with particular items of information may result in the information being "repressed." For example, in a study by Krugman (1958), a group of psychiatric patients and a group of normals were given a learning task, an interpolated activity, and then a task to measure retention. The interpolated task involved either failure or success, or was neutral with respect to such matters. The failure experience generally had a significant depressing effect on retention, which suggests that the anxiety involved may have resulted in some degree of repression of the learnings with which it had been associated. The psychotic patients showed a greater effect of the failure experience on retention than did the normal group.

Finally, a brief discussion must be introduced of what happens when one tells a person to forget something he has learned. Only recently has this problem come under experimental attack. Bjork (1970) carried out a pioneer study of this problem in which he presented a paired-associate learning task to subjects, but signaled that certain items were not to be remembered. He was able to show that to-be-forgotten items function as though they were forgotten and do not produce the kind of interference with the retention of other items that they would if they were remembered. The Bjork demonstration recalls the research by Nuttin and Greenwald (1968), which shows that items that the learner knows do not have use beyond the confines of the experiment are not remembered. Perhaps what Bjork is really investigating is the effect of intent to learn on subsequent retention. If a person has no intent to learn, this means that he will discard the information from his short-term memory system.

Summary

1. The progress of learning is commonly represented by a graph known as a learning curve. Such a curve represents only one aspect of learning. Each one of a number of separate curves may represent several distinct aspects of the learning involved in the acquisition of a complex skill.
2. Learning curves may have many different shapes, depending on the conditions of learning and the degree to which the skill or component skills have been previously mastered. Although the typical form of learning curve that has been presented in textbooks of educational psychology for the last fifty years shows a rapid early rise followed by a period of less rapid learning, such a curve is not necessarily found. Many learning curves are found that are shaped approximately like an S. Such curves are found in cases in which the skill is learned right from the beginning. They are found in both classical conditioning and in instrumental learning. Typical school learning may be considered to represent the upper portion of such a curve.
3. Families of curves produced in studies of learning sets may show progressive changes in the shape of the learning curve as the learner becomes more sophisticated. In the illustration given, the learning curves showed a progressive change from a S-shaped

curve to the typical learning curves that have long been given in textbooks.

4. Some curves representing learning show a flattened-out portion followed by a rise. Such a flattened-out portion is referred to as a plateau. The conditions under which such plateaus occur are obscure, and there is even some doubt whether they are genuine phenomena. There is the possibility that they may be produced by some uncontrolled factor in the learning situation, and would not occur if such a factor were controlled. If plateaus are genuine phenomena, many explanations may be offered for their existence.
5. The typical flattening-out of the learning curve represents a crude limit of learning. This is not the absolute limit of learning but the limit under the particular conditions operating. If conditions are changed, the learner may achieve higher levels of skill.
6. Attempts have been made to derive theoretical learning curves from assumptions about the nature of learning. This represents a new avenue to the study of the learning process, one that offers considerable promise.
7. The degree to which acquired skills are retained can be studied by many different techniques. Some are much more sensitive than others for indicating that some skill has been retained.
8. Methods for measuring retention differ in the extent to which they provide cues that can elicit the skill originally learned. The recall method provides the fewest cues; the recognition method provides a greater number. The most sensitive of all methods is the relearning, or saving, method, which may measure retention even when the recognition method fails to do so. The extinction method has been widely used. This latter method is used in typical experiments involving both classical and instrumental conditioning, particularly when simple skills are involved.
9. The curve representing retention generally shows a sharp decline after training ceases. This is followed by a much less marked decline as additional time passes by. The development of any theory of forgetting is handicapped by the lack of knowledge concerning the mechanism involved in the retention process.
10. The phenomenon of reminiscence has long been investigated and discussed in educational literature. The research at the time of writing indicates that reminiscence occurs over short periods in the case of motor skills, but that it is not a genuine phenomenon in the case of verbal learning. In the latter

case, what was considered to be the phenomenon of reminiscence is almost certainly an artifact resulting from the design of the experiments.

11. Overlearning is necessary if information is to be retained for a long time and is to resist being disrupted through the learning of new material.
12. In the learning of tasks of the paired-associate type, learners introduce new terms between those to be associated. These mediators appear to be effective in producing learning. The reason for their effectiveness is not well understood.
13. There has been a renewed interest in imagery in recent years because of the role it may play in the memory system. Imagery is typically lacking in detail and, at any one time, only a partial representation of the field of view. In some children an unusual type of imagery referred to as eidetic imagery occurs. The usefulness of eidetic imagery is doubtful and it may well represent a defect in the neural system. Hebb interprets imagery as the resonance of those cell assemblies that had previously resonated when the original scene was presented. The latter is a highly speculative explanation.
14. It has long been established that it is more effective to distribute practice over time than to attempt to undertake learning at a single session.
15. Several distinct memory systems exist in the human. First, there is a transitory trace that lasts for only a few seconds. Such a trace can be demonstrated in animals as well as in men. Second, there is a short-term memory. In view of the fact that it may take as long as thirty minutes to transfer information from a short-term memory to a long-term memory, the short-term memory system would appear to be necessary to hold information long enough to make the transfer possible. Third, there is a long-term memory system. Although short-term and long-term memory systems share many common properties they also have their own distinctive properties that make it necessary to consider that there are two distinct systems. Particularly compelling evidence is found in cases of individuals who, through brain damage, have good short-term memories but are unable to transfer the information to the long-term system. In addition, the two systems produce different errors of recall; also, a high level of arousal facilitates long-term memory but disrupts short-term memory.
16. The capacity of the memory systems is not known, but the evidence generally points to a long-term memory system that

does not have the vast capacity suggested by the number of nerve cells in the nervous system. The short-term memory system is of more limited capacity.

17. Information may be stored internally or externally to the human nervous system. External systems of storage, such as are represented by reference books, permit the individual to have at his fingertips very large quantities of information, without having to go through the tedious task of committing the material to memory. Much of education involves teaching the pupil to retrieve information from external storage systems, such as libraries.
18. Information is probably stored in many different forms in the nervous system. The simplest pieces of information are stored as action tendencies though, in a sense, all information stored has an action component attached to it. Some information appears to be stored in a crude form related to imagery. The latter storage does not provide detailed information, but has the capability of producing rather vague internal images. The most detailed and precise information is probably stored in a coded form related to words and other symbols. The superiority of man's memory system over that of subhuman creatures lies, almost certainly, in man's capability of coding information and storing the coded information.
19. The retrieval system is independent of the storage system. One can know what information one has stored in memory even though one cannot retrieve it. In such instances it is not 'memory' that is at fault, but the retrieval system. The retrieval system operates most effectively when retrieval is undertaken under conditions similar to those that occurred when learning took place. Quite small differences in the overall situation may make it difficult to retrieve particular items of information.
20. Theories of forgetting are the decay theory, interference theory, and repression theory. Decay cannot be effectively demonstrated. Interference theory has strong experimental support. Repression theory is concerned with forgetting, resulting from a failure of the retrieval system to retrieve.

CHAPTER FOUR

Transfer of Training

PREVIOUS CHAPTERS HAVE FOCUSED ON SOME OF THE CONDITIONS THAT may facilitate the learning of particular skills, but the teacher is also concerned with providing instruction so that the skills acquired can be applied by the learner to a broad range of new situations. The skills involved in the addition of numbers must be so learned that they can be applied with equal facility to the addition of sums of money, the addition of distances, and the addition of other quantities that might be encountered. If a child learned to add using sums of money, he would probably not be able, immediately, to add numbers representing distances. He would rapidly learn the new skill of adding distances, however, once he had learned to add sums of money. As he applied the rules of addition to many different situations, he would become more and more readily able to apply the skill in any novel situation he might encounter. Learning the skill of adding sums of money shows *positive transfer* to the acquisition of the new and related skill involving addition; that is to say, it would facilitate the learning of the new skill. Some new skills are easy to acquire because they are closely similar to previously learned skills and, when this is the case, one customarily says that there is positive transfer of training.

There is also another sense in which there may be positive transfer of training. The learning of a new skill may facilitate the retention of another previously acquired skill. For example, one may learn to skate on ice and then not skate for some years, after which he learns roller skating. The acquisition of skill in roller skating may facilitate the retention of the related skill of skating on ice. Thus the learning of one skill may facilitate the retention of previously acquired skills and it may also facilitate the acquisition of new skills.

When the effect of transfer is on subsequent learning, the term *proaction* is often applied or one refers to *proactive transfer*. When the effect of transfer is to enhance or depress the retention of some previous learning, then there is said to be *retroactive transfer*. Most of the research on transfer has to do with proactive effects. Indeed, relatively little is known about retroactive effects, though some of the research related to this problem is reviewed in the earlier chapter on memory, in which the retroactive effect was stated to represent a major cause of forgetting.

The acquisition of a skill may sometimes have a negative effect on the retention of previously learned skills or the acquisition of new skills. The author once gave French lessons to a child who had had two years of Spanish in school. A major difficulty in teaching this child French was that he persisted in reading French words with a pronunciation appropriate to Spanish. This is a case of negative transfer of training. One should note that some aspects of the skills involved in learning French transfer positively to the learning of Spanish, and that negative transfer is confined mainly to the matter of pronunciation.

The learning of a skill may also interfere with the retention of a previously acquired skill. A person who has a superficial knowledge of German spends a year in Holland, where he acquires a fluent speaking knowledge of Dutch. At the end of the year he is likely to find that when he tries to speak German, he imposes on it Dutch words and Dutch grammatical structure. The learning of Dutch has disrupted his memory of German.

Transfer is not limited to intellectual responses alone; many emotional responses demonstrate transfer phenomena. One transferable type of response is the anxiety response. A child who is made highly anxious by the treatment accorded him by a teacher may show similar anxiety responses in the presence of other teachers. The anxiety may then spread to the entire school situation and may even transfer to the doing of homework and to all activities related to the school.

During the acquisition of a skill, some events occur that are not learning phenomena as such, but that may affect the acquisition of subsequent skills. For example, sometimes fatigue may depress the further acquisition of learning; in such a case, one would not speak of negative transfer.

Another phenomenon that resembles transfer but is not a true learning phenomenon is that of the "warm-up period." When a person begins a new activity, he does not function at maximum efficiency until some time has elapsed; this may be a matter of seconds or minutes, depending on the activity. In many activities this is a recognized phenomenon. The pitcher always goes through a warm-up workout before he is sent to the mound. The musician, even when practicing in his own home, goes through a warm-up activity such as playing scales before he undertakes more complicated exercises. The concert artist may practice behind the scenes right up to the minute of going on to the platform. The lecturer may spend some time right before his lecture reviewing ideas in his mind before he starts speaking, and he may do this even when he is to give a lecture he has given many times before. These are practices that have been arrived at through practical experience with the daily problems of living.

To a limited extent, one may expect that one activity may serve as a warm-up for a related activity, and there is some evidence that this is so. There also appear to be individual differences in the length of the warm-up period necessary. Some persons require little; others require an extended period. This characteristic of behavior has some implications for the planning and scheduling of the periods in the school; but not enough is known about it to be able to predict with any confidence that one arrangement of classes is better than another. Individual differences suggest that no one schedule can be arranged that will be effective for all children. Here, as elsewhere, mass education requires some compromises; and even then some children may be placed on schedules that are not the best for them.

Stimulus Generalization, Response Generalization, and Transposition —Simple Cases of Transfer

Stimulus Generalization

Stimulus generalization was first demonstrated by Pavlov in experiments with dogs, but it has also been demonstrated with human subjects of all ages. Pavlov showed that, when a dog had been trained to raise its foot to the sound of a particular note, such as middle C, then the animal would almost certainly make the same response to the sound of other notes as much as an octave up and down the scale. The dog is demonstrating stimulus generalization, because it is responding to a range of stimuli other than the specific stimulus to which it was trained.

The range of stimuli to which the dog will respond by raising its foot can be reduced by providing the animal with discrimination learning training. If the animal is rewarded only when it responds to middle C, and is not rewarded when it responds to other notes, then it will slowly cease to respond to the other notes.

The dog in the Pavlovian experiment is demonstrating a simple form of transfer of training. It is trained to respond to a particular note, but later shows a capability of making the same response to a range of notes. What appears to be learned, in the first place, is a response to a class of notes, even though only a single note is used in training.

Much the same is true of the child who is learning to talk. He learns to call his own dog a "dog," and will not only call all other neighborhood dogs "dogs," but will use the same word to designate cats and perhaps even horses, cows, goats, and other animals. Here again generalization has occurred, and a range of stimuli are capable of eliciting the one response "dog." Here also, as in all generalization phenomena, the generalization may be limited. The child may not respond to very large animals, such as elephants, nor to very small ones, such as mice, with the word *dog*.

Objects most similar to that to which the response has been learned are more likely to elicit the response than those that are very different. Objects that are greatly different do not elicit the response. A child who has learned the appropriate verbal response to the printed word *boy* may make the same response to words that have similarity of form, such as *toy*, but will not so respond to a word that is greatly different in shape and contour, such as *house*.

The concept of stimulus generalization is closely related to the concept of *equivalent stimuli*. Stimuli are said to be equivalent for an organism if they generate a similar response. In a young child all moving and living creatures encountered may arouse the response "cat." The creatures represent equivalent stimuli for him, because he has not learned to discriminate one from the other. This child's lack of discrimination is a social disadvantage in attempting to tell others about his experiences. In other situations, advantage may be gained by responding to a set of stimuli as if they were equivalent. For the child to show an avoidance response to all moving objects on the street, regardless of their shape and size, even has survival value. Learning when to generalize and when not to generalize is an important part of education.

Without stimulus generalization, the living creature would learn to respond only to the specific situations in which learning occurred. If the child learned to say "boy" when the printed word *boy* was written on the blackboard, then, without stimulus generalization, he would not be able to make the same response if the word were written smaller or in different type. Stimulus generalization permits the learner to respond to a wide range of stimuli as though they were all the same. Thus, what is learned in one situation can be applied in other situations even though they may differ.

In order that a child may learn to respond by saying "boy" only to the printed word *boy*, it is necessary that he learns to discriminate the word *boy* from other words. In this period of discrimination learning, if it is well planned, the child will first learn to make easy discriminations among words and will be exposed to successively harder discriminations. Some generalization will still occur, particularly under circumstances in which the stimulus is exposed only briefly. The famous case is that of the errors the proofreader lets by. In such cases, he responds by the correct word even though the incorrect one is printed. Years of experience in proofreading will reduce this error of stimulus generalization, but probably never to the point where it does not occur at all.

Mednick and Freedman (1960) have pointed out that the concept of stimulus generalization is an experimentally demonstrated phenomenon and one does not know, as yet, how far it can be used as a basis for understanding various aspects of behavior. A child's tendency to use a new word in a broad range of situations and not to restrict its use to the limited situation to which it can be appropriately applied may be considered to be an illustration of stimulus generalization, but what other phenomena illustrate stimulus generalization is not always entirely clear. Mednick and Freedman point out that the concept has been used to account for phenomena in psychotherapy, the behavior of brain-damaged children, the behavior of schizophrenics, psychoanalytic displacement, and numerous other events in the universe of psychology. The legitimacy of using the concept for such a variety of purposes is quite questionable.

Semantic Generalization

The early work on stimulus generalization involved quite simple stimuli. Pavlov conditioned dogs to the sound of a tuning fork of a particular pitch and determined the generalization to tones of other pitch. Other studies were conducted in other laboratories to the intensity of sound, to the size of a simple figure such as a square or a circle, and other quite uncomplicated dimensions. Later studies of generalization involved much more elaborate stimuli. An area of particular significance to human learning that has been explored through the study of stimulus generalization is that known as *semantic generalization.* The essence of semantic generalization is that a response conditioned to a particular word will generalize to words similar in meaning and, to a lesser extent, to words similar in sound. The initial work in the latter area was a demonstration by a Russian, Ivanov Smolensky, that a human subject, conditioned to make a particular response in the presence of an object, would make the same response when confronted with the word representing the object. Later, near to midcentury, Gregory Razran conducted a whole series of experiments in which subjects were conditioned to respond to particular words, following which the generalization to other words was studied. In most of the Razran experiments the response conditioned was that of salivation. In one early study subjects were exposed to the words *style, urn, freeze,* and *surf,* while eating or chewing gum. Later, the salivary responses of the subjects were measured on exposure to other words, with interesting findings. Razran came up with the discovery that, for example, the conditioned response to the word *urn* generalized well to the word *vase* but not to the same extent to the similar sounding word *earn.* Razran concluded that subjects became conditioned more to the meaning of a word than to its visual or auditory form. There was some generalization to similar sounding and similar appearing words, but this effect was weak compared with the generalization to words similar in meaning.

A whole series of similar studies have been conducted over the years with similar findings. Despite the fact that many of these studies have serious experimental flaws, nobody has yet seriously disputed the general findings of Razran. Feather (1965), who reviewed the studies up to the time of his article, suggests that generalization may, perhaps, be attributed to the tendency for individuals to classify and categorize all inputs. One may take this argument one step further and propose that inputs are categorized prior to storage in memory and that perhaps the psychological location of a piece of stored information depends upon how it is classified in the first place. On hearing a word such as *urn,* one may classify it as belonging in the vase class, and one might also classify it in the class of things to do with funerals. Once classified, then it would have the same response-arousing features of all other words in that class.

Gradient of Generalization

If a response has been established to a stimulus S_1 then the response will occur with varying degrees of strength to stimuli S_2, S_3, S_4, and so forth, which resemble S_1 in varying degrees. The greater the degree to which the new stimulus resembles S_1, the greater is the likelihood that the response will occur or that it will occur in full strength. The relationship between the response R and the stimulus S, as S is varied from the original stimulus with which learning took place, is known as the *gradient of generalization.*

The phenomenon of the gradient of generalization was well illustrated in Pavlov's original work with salivation in dogs. A dog trained to salivate at the sound of a tone pitched at 440 vibrations per second will also salivate to a sound one octave lower (220 vibrations per second), but it will salivate to a lesser degree. Drop the pitch of the sound still lower and the dog will salivate even less. The closer the note is to the original note, the more the amount of salivation approximates that produced by the original note.

The gradient of generalization is known to occur in a great range of situations. It occurs not only in the case of positive responses that have been acquired, but also in the case of avoidance responses. A person who, through having been seriously injured by a power saw, develops a fear of power saws and withdraws from them may also show a similar but lesser withdrawal from other power tools. Although the whine of a power saw may produce in him intense fear and a need to escape from it, the noise of a power drill may merely give him the feeling that he does not want to touch the device. The drill induces an avoidance response, but it is milder than that induced by the saw.

An example of some data demonstrating a gradient of generalization is provided by a study made by Bahrick, Clark, and Bahrick (1967). The idea underlying this study is that when a person is shown an object and asked to remember the details, he will later identify not only the same object as the one he saw, but may also identify similar objects as the one seen. The response of identification generalizes to other similar objects.

In the case of the Bahrick study, black-and-white drawings were prepared of sixteen common objects. Each of these drawings was then taken in turn, and similar drawings which resembled the original in varying degrees were prepared. For instance, one of the pictures showed a cup, and drawings were therefore prepared of roughly similar cups which resembled the original in varying degrees. Special methods were used in the preparation of the materials to ensure that the drawings of cups in the final series of ten represented a carefully graded series of discrepancies from the original. Each subject was shown each of the sixteen original drawings, one at a time, for two seconds each. Then each subject was given the recognition test. In this test subjects were shown rows of pictures, one row at a time. One row, for example, consisted of the original picture of the cup they had seen and ten variations of this picture, with the eleven pictures arranged in random order. The subject had to pick out the original picture from the row of eleven pictures. He would do this for each one of the sixteen rows of pictures corresponding to the sixteen objects in the original set of drawings. The materials and circumstances of the experiment permitted the experimenter to vary the number of learning trials to which a subject was exposed and also the

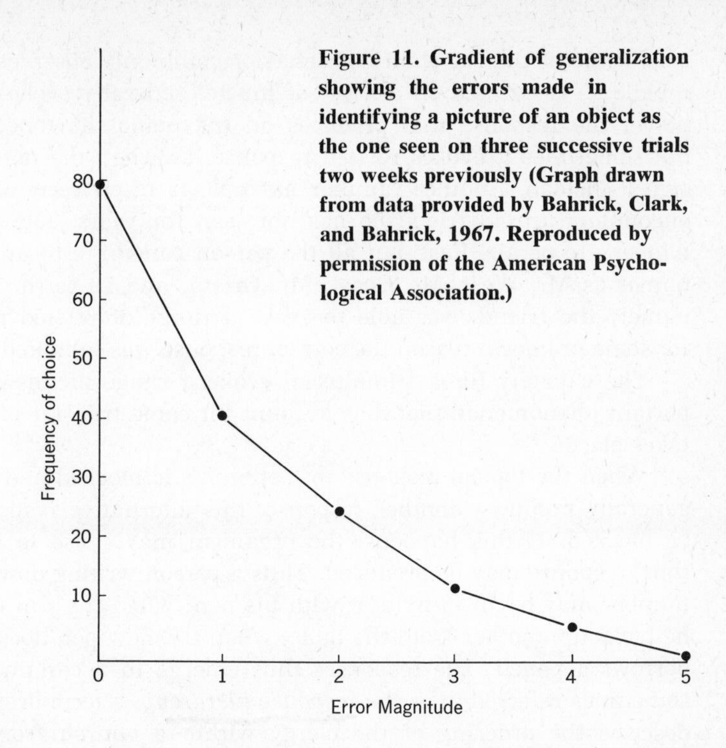

Figure 11. Gradient of generalization showing the errors made in identifying a picture of an object as the one seen on three successive trials two weeks previously (Graph drawn from data provided by Bahrick, Clark, and Bahrick, 1967. Reproduced by permission of the American Psychological Association.)

time elapsing between the training trials and the administration of the recognition test.

From the data of this experiment, curves can be drawn showing the gradient of generalization for each one of the conditions studied. For example, Figure 11 shows the gradient of generalization for the group who were given nine learning trials and tested two days later. This group was able to identify about half of the objects correctly, but when they made an error, they were much more likely to choose an object similar to the one previously observed than one that was very different.

The point to note is that the subjects respond to the incorrect figures as if they were the correct ones. This is the essence of stimulus generalization.

Response Generalization

Just as a living creature is capable of responding with the same response to a range of stimuli as though they were the same, so too does a single stimulus have the capacity of evoking a range of responses. The fact that a stimulus may evoke not only the response with which it has been characteristically associated, but other related responses as well, is referred to as *response generalization.* This phenomenon accounts for at least some of the variability of behavior commonly observed. The note of middle C, as printed on a sheet of music, generally evokes in the piano player the response that produces on the piano the tone of middle C, but sometimes it evokes related response, as when the notes B or D are struck instead. Another familiar example is often seen when a person encounters an old friend he has not seen for years. The friend's name happens to be Mr. East, but all the person can think of are such related names as Mr. West, Mr. Coast, Mr. Orient, and so forth. The stimulus, namely the friend, was able to evoke a range of related responses, but for some unknown reason the correct response was inhibited.

The capacity for a stimulus to evoke a range of answers is an important phenomenon that may account for some transfer of training that takes place.

When the typical response to a stimulus is blocked and the organism generally produces another response, this alternative response may also be blocked. If this happens, the organism may cease to respond, or a third response may be produced. Thus a person writing down a telephone number may begin to write it with his pen; when the pen does not work he picks up another from the table; when the new pen does not work, he borrows a pencil. The responses thus emerge in a certain order that is sometimes referred to as the *response hierarchy,* a term originally used to describe the ordering of the clergy within a church from the highest official to the lowliest. Responses in relation to any particular stimulus can be regarded as being ordered from those most likely to occur to those least likely.

Stimulus Generalization and Transposition: Unlearned Transfer Effects

Another special case of transfer of great interest is found in what are known as *transposition phenomena.* The demonstration of this transfer phenomenon takes many forms, but in the case of young children, a common form of the demonstration is as follows:

The subject of the experiment is confronted with two upside-down dishes; one, two inches in diameter, and the other, three inches. What has to be learned is that some desired object, food or a trinket, is under the larger three-inch dish. After learning this, the task is changed so that it now involves a three-inch and a four-inch dish, and the desired object is still under the larger of the two dishes. The subject invariably goes to the larger of the two dishes. The demonstration is important in that if the subject had simply learned to respond to the three-inch dish in the first task, then one would expect him to go immediately to the three-inch dish in the second task, but this is not what happens. What the subject *seems* to have learned from the first task was that the desired object was under the *larger* dish, and not that it was under the dish of a particular size. The transfer can be shown to occur in a wide range of living creatures. This transfer has long been used as a basis for arguing that animals react to relationships, in that they show a capability of learning to respond to the larger or the smaller of two objects. So long as the first task is mastered, the correct response occurs when the second task is presented, provided the experimenter has set the rule that the food is under the larger dish, or the smaller dish, and not that it is under the three-inch dish.

Transposition problems may assume various forms. Another common problem in this category is the intermediate stimulus problem. In such a problem, the subject learns that the correct choice is the middle-sized dish among three dishes that are respectively three inches, four inches, and five inches in diameter. Then he is presented with a new problem consisting of dishes that are four inches, five inches, and six inches in diameter, and chooses the five-inch dish.

The two-stimulus problem (responding to the larger of two stimuli) is generally easier than the intermediate stimulus problem. Indeed, in the intermediate stimulus problem some learners, both animal and human, learn to respond to the particular object rather than to the middle object, and then show no transposition.

Other forms of transposition occur at more complex levels, but are so familiar that they occur daily without one's taking any notice of them. One can hear a melody played in one key and readily recognize it when it is played in another key. Without transposition, one would not be able to do this. One can recognize the plan of his city regardless of the scale to which it is drawn. One can easily identify a human figure even when it is presented in the form of a small porcelain figurine. One can perform these tasks because the relations within the configuration remain the same when other characteristics are altered.

A book by Reese (1968) has summarized the hundreds of studies of transposition phenomena, but points out that no theory of transposition accounts for all the experimental results. The oldest theory was that the learner showing transposition, as in the two-stimulus problems, had learned to solve the problem by recognizing the *relationship* between the two stimuli and hence recognized the same relationship in the two new stimuli. This explanation is simple and quite plausible, but other explanations are also possible. The late Kenneth Spence was able to produce a rather complicated account of simple cases of transposition that did not require a learner to perceive relations at all. There are also some other quite simple proposed explanations which also do not assume that animals can perform the latter feat. One is that when a learner is first confronted with a three-inch and a four-inch dish and learns that a desired object is under the four-inch dish, he also learns a sense of familiarity with these two sizes of dish. When the same learner later is confronted with a four-inch and a five-inch dish, he is presented with a familiar dish, the four-inch dish, and an unfamiliar dish, the five-inch dish. Now animals and men tend to show approach behavior toward unfamiliar objects, and for this reason the learner approaches the five-inch dish rather than the familiar one. The explanation is highly plausible, but probably far from being a complete explanation of how transposition occurs. Reese takes the position that the phenomenon is probably complex and cannot be accounted for in terms of any single explanation.

Although transposition, like stimulus generalization, occurs without any identifiable training, numerous conditions influence the extent to which transposition is shown. The more effectively the first task is mastered, the more tranposition is likely to occur on the second kind of task. Increased incentives related to the first task also seem to improve transposition, probably because they result in greater attention on the part of the learner and the better utilization of information. Practice with transposition tasks also increases the amount of transposition. The fact that the phenomenon is found in subhuman animals shows that it is not dependent upon verbalization. It appears to be a quite primitive and predictable form of transfer of training.

Transfer of Training in Associative Learning

The early research on transfer of training was carried out in school-like contexts and with school-like materials. Such work did not yield scientific principles of the kind that researchers hoped were forthcoming and since about midcentury there has been a tendency to study problems of transfer of training in much simpler experimental situations. One of the most productive of these situations has been that of paired-associate learning. This technique, mentioned briefly in the previous chapter, must now be discussed in greater detail in relation to transfer of training.

The general format of the paired-associated learning task requires that the subject associate the words in a set of pairs. One pair of items in the list might be the words such as *book-car*. In such a case, the task of the subject is to learn to associate the words together so that when the word *book* appears in front of him, he will either say "car" or in some way show that he knows that the correct associate is *car*. Lists commonly involve about ten pairs of words or nonsense syllables. Custom is to call the first word in a pair the *stimulus* word and the second word the *response* word. Of course, both words are, in a sense, stimuli, and the learner has to respond to each. Many different procedures are used for presenting the pairs, and the choice often depends upon the purpose of the study. In what is termed the *recall procedure*, the pairs of words are presented for about two seconds for each pair. After the entire set of pairs has been run, the stimulus words alone are then presented in a scrambled order one by one and the learner must, when each is presented, either say, spell, or write the response word in each case. In the *anticipation procedure,* the stimulus word of each pair is presented first, generally for two seconds, and the learner must quickly guess the response word. Then both the stimulus word and the response word are presented together for the same length of time. On the first trial, the learner has no way of guessing what the response word is when he sees the stimulus word, but on the second trial and on subsequent trials he is expected to guess what the response word is just as soon as the stimulus word appears. As soon as he has guessed, both words appear before him and he can check on the accuracy of his guess. The pairs are presented in a different order on each trial so that the learner cannot just decide to learn the list of response words, in order, and fail to associate them with the stimulus words. It is common to introduce a pause of generally about two seconds between the presentation of the stimulus word and the complete pair of words. In addition, all kinds of different time schedules have been used.

Another important variation in the paired-associate technique is that of familiarizing the learner with the separate words or syllables before beginning the learning series. If one is using nonsense syllables such as *huk, fov,* and *kug,* a part of the difficulty of the learner's task may be due to the fact that he has to learn the syllables themselves before he can begin to associate the one syllable with the other. In order to make the task one of learning associations, and not one of learning individual syllables, a common procedure is to give the subject an initial period of familiarization training with the individual syllables. This is done by taking all the syllables and presenting them in random order. The individual is tested for his familiarity with the syllables by being given the complete list, but with one letter omitted from each. He has to fill in the missing letters. If he fails this test, he is then given further familiarization training until he shows that he is thoroughly acquainted with the individual syllables. The training is then begun on learning associations between pairs.

The value of the paired-associate task for exploring problems of verbal learning is evident from the fact that several books have appeared in recent years devoted entirely to results achieved with the technique. An excellent summary of research in this area is found in a volume by Goss and Nodine (1965).

Learning pairs of nonsense syllables may seem to be, at first sight, a long way from education, but it is not. When a child learns the names of common objects he is engaging in a task similar to the laboratory task of paired-associate learning. When a high-school student learns the vocabulary of a foreign language he learns either to associate the foreign words with objects or to associate the foreign words with the words in his native tongue. In both cases, he is engaged in paired-associate learning. Learning synonyms is also a similar task; so too is learning to label the parts of an animal, flower, machine, or other object. Educational activity abounds with such tasks. Maybe they are not the most crucial tasks in which the individual engages, but they are significant tasks.

The technique permits the study of a range of problems related to transfer of training. One can, for example, find the effect of transfer of training from the learning of one list to the learning of another list under a number of different conditions. One condition is the *A-B, A-C* condition. Under this condition a list is learned, and then a second list is learned in which the first word of each pair is the same as the corresponding word in the first list. One could describe the two tasks as being ones in which the stimulus element remains the same, but in which the response element is varied. Transfer under the latter condition, from the learning of the first list to the learning of the second list, can be studied. In another experiment one can study the reverse condition, in which the stimulus elements are changed but the response elements remain the same. The latter would be represented as an experiment involving *A-B* and *C-B* lists of words. In addition, there is the possibility of making two lists of words different in varying degrees. The word *house* in one list could be represented in the second list by the synonym *residence*, or by words that differed by some determined amount from the original word. Words such as *cottage, cave,* and *hat* represent a progressively more remote relationship to the original word, *house.* The technique of paired-associate learning is an extraordinarily flexible one for the study of transfer of training.

The early studies in which the stimulus similarity of two tasks were varied or the response similarity was varied were summarized several decades ago by Osgood (1949), who attempted to reduce the results to the form of a graph, which has become known as the transfer surface. The graph is shown in Figure 12. The two dimensions of the gray plane are stimulus similarity and response similarity in the two tasks. The point in the plane farthest away from the viewer represents a case of two tasks calling for the same responses but providing different stimuli. The point nearest the viewer represents two tasks involving similar stimuli but calling for opposite responses. Paired-associate learning rarely involves learning in task 2 the opposite of the responses learned in task 1. The responses may be dissimilar, but they are not generally opposite. However, in motor-skill learning opposite responses are often introduced in task 2, as when a person learns to push a lever when a blue light goes on in task 1 and then has to pull the lever to the same stimulus in task 2.

The graph is a three-dimensional one. Two of the dimensions have already been discussed. One of these represents the extent to which the stimuli in two tasks resemble one another. The second dimension represents the extent to which the responses called for by the two tasks are similar or different. Thus, any two tasks can be represented as a point on the gray plane shown in the figure. One such point is represented by the letter X. The latter point represents two tasks that provide similar stimuli and call for similar responses. An example of two such tasks outside the field of paired-associate learning would be those of driving a small Ford with an automatic shift and driving a Cadillac also with an automatic shift. The stimuli provided by the two tasks are very similar, but not identical, and the responses are similar. As anybody knows, if one learns one of these tasks, then much of what one has learned is transferred to the learning of the other task very quickly. Now if our figure correctly represents transfer, then it should show that there should be positive transfer.

In order to read from the figure the amount of expected transfer, we must first note that in addition to the stimulus similarity dimension and the response similarity dimension, there is a third dimension labeled "positive transfer-negative transfer." This third dimension permits one to draw in a curved surface, indicated on the figure with ruled lines. This surface represented by the ruled lines is called the transfer surface.

Now let us go back to the two tasks represented by the point X and consider the problem of determining whether positive or negative transfer is to be expected. Draw a vertical line up from the point X and note that it cuts the transfer surface in the portion marked "positive transfer." This means that positive transfer is expected. If the point X had been in the extreme left-hand corner, an even greater degree of positive transfer would have been expected.

Now work a problem for yourself. Look at the point on the gray plane surrounded by the letter O. How do the two tasks resemble each other? What transfer is expected from the one task to the other task? There is maximum negative transfer or interference when one learns a particular set of responses on one piece of equipment and then moves to another piece of equipment which requires the opposite set of responses. An example of the latter would be learning to fly in a plane in which the throttle was opened by pulling a lever and then changing to a plane in which the throttle was opened by pushing a lever. The latter situation produces the maximum interference of the old habit with the new. Many years ago, before the controls of planes were standardized, this kind of situation fairly often occurred and accidents were attributed to the habits learned in one plane interfering with the habits required by a new plane. Those who occasionally type on a foreign-made typewriter experience this interference in the use of the backspacer and margin release keys, which are on the opposite sides from where they are in American-made machines.

Osgood claimed that when he reviewed the literature, no exceptions could be found to his model, but some exceptions have been found since that time. The figure generally provides a good means of predicting whether one can expect positive or negative transfer and how this will be changed by modifying the tasks. Although the figure is based largely on data from paired-associate learning studies, it seems to provide a sound basis for predicting transfer from one skilled performance to another in activities commonly learned in schools or pursued in daily life.

Since Osgood developed the transfer surface that carries his name, extensive additional research has been done which generally confirms his conclusions. In later reviews of the problem by Matin (1965) and by Shea (1969), the main effort of investigators has been to attempt to identify more precisely the shape of the surface, with some studies investigating the boundaries and some the interior part of the surface.

The Osgood model appears to be based partly on the mechanism of stimulus generalization that may underlie transfer phenomena. If two tasks present similar stimuli and require the same responses, then what is learned in relation to the stimuli presented with one task will generalize to the related stimuli provided by the second task. Thus what is learned in relation to the one task is to some degree transferred to performance on the second task. This represents the operation of stimulus generalization. On the other hand, consider the case of two tasks that call for different responses to similar stimuli. The response learned on the first task interferes with the response to be learned on the second task, and hence negative transfer is produced.

The Osgood model takes advantage of the fact that the learning of one set of responses to stimuli can also strengthen related responses. Thus, the child studying French who learns to form the association *rue-road* also learns at the same time to associate *rue-street,* even though the latter association is never deliberately practiced. The association that is directly learned, in this case the association *rue-road,* will be strengthened more than other related responses that are strengthened by generalization. Thus, when a list of French words and their English equivalents have been learned, it is easy for the student to learn the same French words and the synonyms of the English words. However, the learning of the original list of French and English equivalents would not help the student to learn a new list in which the original French words had to be associated with nonsense syllables, as for example in the association *rue-tek.*

The learning and transfer that have been considered up to this point

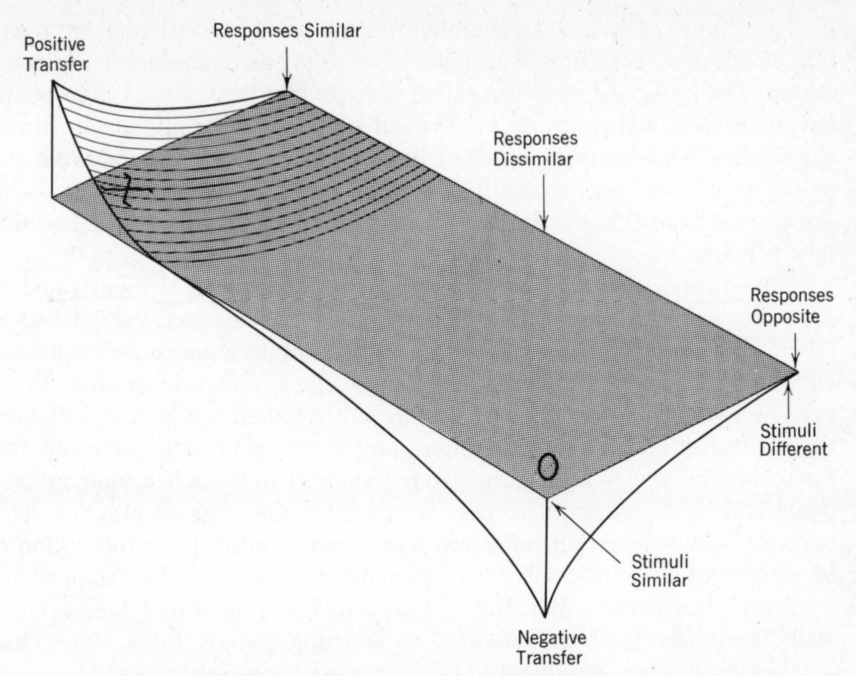

Figure 12. Diagram showing the relationship between response similarity and stimulus similarity of two tasks and the amount of transfer expected from one task to the other. The diagram is an attempt by Osgood (1949) to bring together the findings available at the time. (Reproduced by permission of the American Psychological Association.)

have involved quite simple processes. Such processes manifest themselves in the learning of some school subjects. For example, the learning of one foreign language may interfere with the learning of another language, but may assist the learning of still another. However, much of what is learned in school involves not the acquisition of simple habits but the acquisition of rules and strategies that have potential for subsequent problem solving, and it is the acquisition and transfer of such rules and strategies to which we must now turn.

The Transfer of Rules and Strategies

Learning How to Learn: Learning Sets

Transfer phenomena reviewed up to this point have been largely those considered to represent specific transfer. In the case of specific transfer, some quite identifiable characteristic of a situation or a response in a particular task has a subsequent effect on the acquisition or retention of another task. Not all transfer of training is of this kind, for some forms of transfer are what are called nonspecific. Postman (1969) points out that such nonspecific transfer effects do not result from simple similarities between tasks but that they involve a carry-over of skills and habits from one task to another. One of the best-explored examples of nonspecific transfer is found in the case of the phenomenon of learning how to learn.

That people can learn how to learn has long been demonstrated in experimental situations. This phenomenon has been well established in laboratory studies of the learning of meaningless nonsense syllables, chosen because such material is supposedly equally unfamiliar to all subjects. Ward (1937) showed that as subjects learned lists of syllables, their speed of learning became more and more rapid with each new list. Later, Melton and VonLackum (1941) showed that such a phenomenon could still be demonstrated after considerable amounts of practice. This learning-how-to-learn phenomenon represents a rather permanent kind of learning and is manifest for long periods after practice has stopped.

Somewhat earlier, Woodrow (1927) had demonstrated that even in such familiar classroom activities as learning poetry, facts, dates, and foreign vocabulary, pupils could be taught learning techniques that would improve their learning efficiency.

A similar phenomenon was demonstrated by Harlow (1949), who developed a program of research in this general area, first working with monkeys and later extending the studies to human subjects. In the typical Harlow type of experiment, a monkey is trained on simple discrimination problems. The monkey may be presented with two objects, a cube and a solid triangle; under one of them there is a raisin. Soon, the monkey learns that the raisin is under the cube and not under the triangle. Having mastered this problem, he is presented with the next one. This time the two objects are both cubes, but one is black and one is white. He must learn a new discrimination, and it takes time to master this problem. When the monkey has mastered it, another new problem is presented, and so forth. After a long series of such problems, the monkey is able to master new problems with great speed and requires very few trials compared with the trials that were required to master the first problems. It is said that the monkey has learned how to solve problems of this kind. He has learned, so to speak, what to look for. He also has learned to switch as soon as the rules are switched. He has learned how to learn new problems. Harlow, in referring to this phenomenon, states that the monkey has acquired a *learning set* for solving the problems. A similar phenomenon has been shown to occur with young children. As problems of a particular class are solved, new problems in the same class are solved with increasing speed and facility.

A learning sequence that produces the development of a learning set generally consists of a long series of problems that are presented to the subject. It is not uncommon in this work for there to be several hundred problems in a single sequence designed to build a learning set. These problems are generally distributed over many sessions, which take place on successive days. The formation of learning sets has been demonstrated in the case of young children with materials very similar to those used in studies with subhuman primates. The same phenomenon has also been demonstrated with adults solving anagram problems in a study by Di Vesta and Walls (1968). If individuals are put through one series after another of anagram problems, they develop a great facility in looking for new rules to solve the problems and also a repertoire of rules that can be applied.

The development of learning sets would seem to involve the acquisition of at least two aspects of skill. One aspect is the learning of problem-solving strategies. Another is learning that when a strategy does not work then it should be dropped quickly and another strategy should be adopted. The rules or strategies may involve verbal skills, as they do in the case of human learning, but they may be at a nonverbal level. Postman (1969) has attempted to identify through research some of the strategies involved in paired-associate learning. These strategies, which have transfer value, are very numerous and varied. Postman also points out that the learner may acquire not only rules that simplify the task of acquisition, but he may also invent ways of prompting recall. The student who has to learn a list of words, such as names of plants, may note that the first letters of the terms spell *firebol*. When this mnemonic device is memorized, it can be used to cue recall.

Internal verbalization or related thinking processes may greatly facilitate the ability to shift strategies, as is evident from a line of research involving what are called reversal shifts and nonreversal shifts.

The technique for studying reversal and nonreversal shifts, as described by Kendler and Kendler (1962), involves the presentation of pairs of stimuli such as squares and circles which may be either white or black. The subject must decide which one of the two is "right." The experimenter arranges that only one of the dimensions (either the black-white or the circle-square) is to be the relevant one in the training series, and, perhaps, he decides that a black figure is to be considered "right" and a white figure "wrong." Then, after the subject has learned to choose the black figure, the rules are changed. The change can be made in either of two ways:

1. The experimenter can reverse the rules. In this case, the white figure is now the right one and the black figure is wrong. Learning the new rule involves what is called a reversal shift.

2. The experimenter may shift to the other dimension and call the

square "right" and the circle "wrong." The learning of this new rule involves a nonreversal shift. (In later studies this has been referred to as an *extradimensional* shift.)

In this technique, all of the subjects are first trained to respond to one particular characteristic, such as the black figure; that is to say, they learn to discriminate on the dimension of brightness. Then half of the subjects have the rule changed so as to involve a reversal shift, and the other half have the rule changed by introducing a nonreversal shift.

The Kendlers report that older children and adults perform a reversal shift more readily than a nonreversal shift, but for very young children and subhuman animals the opposite is true. This is an interesting finding, for one would expect, in terms of the Osgood transfer surface, that strong negative transfer would take place in the reversal shift situation (the stimuli are the same but the responses are opposite). The fact that with older children and adults this does not occur is inconsistent with the model and suggests that the model holds only when complex mediating responses do not occur. (The data supporting the Osgood model generally involves situations in which one does not have to assume that complex mediating responses are occurring.) The Kendlers suggest that in older children and in adults a mediational mechanism is operating that permits a rapid change in response to occur in the reversal-shift situation. The Kendlers propose that the mediational mechanism is a language system, for such a system distinguishes the younger children from the older.

In a later experiment, Kendler (1964) attempted to find some more direct evidence that the mediational process involved in children is verbal. What she did was to force the children to verbalize what they were doing during the task and related this to what happened when the rules were changed. She believed that the evidence derived from the experiment supported the position that appropriate verbalization facilitated the reversal shift.

Transfer of Organizing Skills in the Memory System

The chapter on memory and retention emphasized the point that the transfer of information from the short-term memory system to the long-term memory system takes place with the greatest efficiency if the information is organized. If disorganized material is put into the short-term memory system, it tends to be organized, as is evident from the fact that lists of words given to the individual in random order tend to be repeated back in a form that shows some degree of structure. Organizing skills are learned and, in fact, courses that claim to improve memory achieve this goal mainly by teaching the individual how to organize information in such a way that it becomes readily transferred to the long-term memory system.

Although this aspect of transfer has long been used in practical memory training courses, it is a phenomenon that can also be verified experimentally. A study by DeRosa, Doane, and Russell (1970) was able to show very clearly that by merely presenting learners with a list of words that had some organization, they were able to profit from the organization provided and apply the same system of organization to the learning of a second list. Some of the skills related to organizing materials for transfer to the long-term memory system are already taught in schools. One procedure that accomplishes that end is outlining material to be memorized. The function of outlining is that of drawing the attention of the learner to the inherent structure of what is to be learned, around which the details can be clustered.

Transfer of Principles

The studies by Kendler and Kendler drive home the importance of verbal mediating processes in the transfer of what has been learned to the solution of novel problems. Ausubel and Robinson (1969) in their review of the relevant literature come to very much the same opinion. Although they might take the position that the transfer surface developed by Osgood provides good predictions of transfer in relatively simple situations that have clearly identifiable stimuli and well-defined responses, the transfer surface cannot be applied to predicting transfer in most of the complex learning situations that occur in schools. In these situations, the crucial factor is not so much the characteristics of the stimuli and responses as it is the internal verbalizations that take place.

One of the simpler tasks in the education of the child, which has value only insofar as transfer of training results, is the concept-learning task. If a child learns the concepts of an oak, a maple, and an elm by studying the trees on the school grounds, one would hope that the same child would be able to classify other trees in other parts of town into these categories, even though these trees might be smaller or larger than the ones used for teaching. The concepts of an oak, a maple, and an elm would have been taught in the hope that transfer of training would take place. Concepts are always learned in anticipation that the classification systems they involve will be applicable to the classification of new and significantly different instances in the future. Although concepts are taught in anticipation that such transfer will take place, the conditions of transfer have not been extensively studied by research workers. A single study of this problem by Stones and Heslop (1968) throws some light on what is involved.

The Stones and Heslop study used a technique invented many years ago by a Russian named L. S. Vigotsky. The materials used in this technique involve twenty-two small wooden blocks of five different colors, six different shapes of cross section, two different heights, and two different cross-sectional areas. The problem is to classify the blocks into four groups. The four groups of blocks are named LAG, BIK, MUR, and CEV, and these names are printed underneath the block on the side on which the block rests. The LAG blocks are tall and fat, the BIK blocks are small and fat, the CEV blocks small and thin, and the MUR blocks are tall and thin. Thus, two attributes are used in the classification of the blocks. A very interesting feature of the classification task is that once the system has been learned it can be applied to the classification of other objects. In the case of the Stones and Heslop study, the children who attempted to learn the classification system eventually had to apply it to the grouping of pictures of buildings, plasticine models of men, and pictures of trees. It is fairly easy to see how the classification system could be transferred to the grouping of various objects other than the blocks on which it was learned.

The children included in the study varied in age from 6.5 years to 11.5 years. The youngest children were virtually unable to solve the concept-learning problem and, of course, had no knowledge to apply to the transfer problems. On the other hand, a considerable number of the older children were able to solve the problem, and some were able to describe what the solution involved. Between a third and a half of those children who solved the problem with the blocks were able to solve the transfer problems using different objects. A particularly striking finding is that of those children who solved the block problem, and those most likely to solve the transfer problems were the ones who were able to verbalize the solution. They were able to say what attributes of the blocks made them fit into one category rather than another. The data hint that a person who is able to solve the block problem at an intuitive level may not be able to transfer the solution easily to other problems. What is meant here by the solution of the problem at the intuitive level is solving the problem but being unable to state what the essence of the solution really is. At several other places in this volume the point has been made that words give man an extraordinary power over his actions, and it is hardly surprising that knowledge that is verbalized can be more extensively applied to new situations than can knowledge that is understood only at an intuitive level.

In the case of the transfer of concepts, the Osgood surface has little relevance in predicting whether transfer will or will not occur, but the presence or absence of verbal mediating responses is of great importance. The role of verbal processes becomes even more central in the learning of rules and principles for solving problems. Consider, for example, the case of a student who learns Archimedes' principle through a demonstration involving the change in weight of a piece of lead when it is immersed in water. His understanding of the principle is then tested in a situation in which he has to explain why smoke rises in a chimney. Some students will be able to transfer the knowledge gained by studying the loss of weight of an object when immersed in water to the chimney problem. Some positive transfer will occur, but surely not because of any simple similarity between the task elements involved or the overt responses involved. What the pupil must do is recognize that a solid body immersed in water has an upward force exerted on it by the water and that a body of hot gas also has an upward force exerted on it by the surrounding air. Both situations have to be coded as situations involving an upward thrust on a body exerted by a surrounding medium. In order for the pupil to be able to do this he must have learned in the first place not just that a body immersed in water loses weight, but that this is an example of a class of situations in which a body is surrounded by gaseous or liquid substances. He has to learn to code such situations as belonging to a class. It is through learning to code situations as presenting or not presenting the essential features of Archimedes' principle that transfer becomes possible. The application of a principle to different situations demands that the situations have some similarity, but the similarity may be at an abstract level, as it was in the case just examined.

A point to be noted is that when a student learns Archimedes' principle by observing the loss of weight of a piece of lead as it is immersed in water and then applies his knowledge to understanding why smoke rises in a chimney, any positive transfer that occurs can hardly be interpreted in terms of any simple concept of stimulus similarity. A body immersed in water and smoke rising in a chimney do not have stimulus similarity in any simple sense of the term. However, the physicist who examines the two situations can *abstract* certain similarities. He sees that water provides a certain buoyancy for the lead, and that the air around the chimney provides a buoyancy for the smoke in the chimney, sufficient in each case to make it rise. Transfer from the one situation to the other occurs because the individual is able to *code* the information from the two situations in the same way. If a person were not able to code the information in the two situations in the same way, involving coding categories such as *buoyancy,* transfer would probably not occur.

Two studies by Overing and Travers (1966, 1967) throw some light on some of the conditions that facilitate the transfer of knowledge of a principle to a new situation. These studies are quite complex and only their essence can be presented here. The situation used in these studies was one that has been used several times previously in related research. The situation involved the teaching of the principle of refraction and the measurement of the extent to which the learner can apply what he has learned to the solution of a novel problem. The problem to which the knowledge of refraction has to be transferred is that of shooting at a target placed under water. As most people know, if one wants to shoot at an object under water, say from the bank of a river, one must not shoot directly at where the object appears to be. Direct aim at where the object appears to be will result in a miss. This is because the light from the object is bent (refracted) as it leaves the surface of the water. In the Overing and Travers studies, the task of shooting at the object under water was simplified so that the subjects did not actually fire the gun but merely had to indicate at what spot on the surface of the water they were aiming the gun. Thus a pupil participating in the experiment might say that he was aiming the gun at the line numbered 6, or the line numbered 4.

In the first of the two experiments children in the upper elementary grades were given instruction in the principle of the refraction of light by means of one of the following four methods:

Method 1. The children were given a lecture through a tape recorder. The information on this tape became the basis for the information given in all other instructional procedures in which any verbal information was also transmitted through a tape.

Method 2. The information was given through a tape, but simple line diagrams were also used to clarify the presentation.

Method 3. A realistic demonstration of the refraction of light was given by showing a light beam bend as it entered the surface of the water in a fish tank. A commentary on this demonstration was also presented by means of a tape.

Method 4. This was the same as Method 2 except for the fact that the presentation was preceded by a brief anecdote about a hunter who was trying to shoot a crocodile from the bank of the river. The crocodile was deep in the water. The anecdote pointed out that the hunter would not hit his game if he were to shoot directly at the place where he saw the crocodile, but that he would have to aim at a point directly below the crocodile.

The interesting finding with respect to the matter of transfer is not that the realistic condition produced more effective learning and transfer to the problem than did the use of diagrams, but that almost as good results were achieved with the use of the simple line diagrams, provided that their use was accompanied by the anecdote about the hunter and the crocodile. The use of the tank along with the other features of the realistic demonstration and the use of diagrams preceded by the anecdote were about equally effective teaching procedures, and more effective than the other two teaching situations. What these two effective teaching approaches have in common appears to be that both involve linking up the knowledge to be acquired with facts and situations that are already familiar. Books on pedagogy have long suggested the importance of the latter for learning, but have failed to indicate its significance for transfer.

Another finding of the study pertains to the value of verbalizing a principle. Half of the subjects at the end of the period of instruction on the principle of refraction were required to take a written test that did not add to the information they had learned, but that required them to verbalize the information. The results of the transfer of training tests showed that the pupils who were required to verbalize their knowledge, through taking the test, performed rather better than those who were not required to verbalize the principle, although the difference is small and cannot be presented with substantial confidence.

The second study explored whether principles taught in the presence of either much or little irrelevant information could be most successfully generalized to other situations. In this experiment two training conditions were used, both involving the use of a tank of water and a beam of light. In one training condition the tank was presented in a darkened room and little could be seen except the beam of light bending as it entered the water. In the other training condition, many irrelevant cues could be seen, including the sides of the tank, the bottom of the tank, the equipment producing the beam of light, and so forth. Two testing conditions were also provided. In both testing conditions the pupils had to aim at a target under water. In the one case, the testing involved a very simple target, but in the other case, the target was embellished with a design. The finding was that the pupils trained under conditions involving a minimum number of irrelevant cues performed well on the tests that also involved a minimum of cues, but relatively poorly on the tests that involved a considerable number of irrevelant features. On the other hand, those trained in the presence of many irrelevant cues were equally successful at the testing problems regardless of the extent to which they included irrevelant cues.

The findings of the second study suggest that one of the factors involved in learning a principle is that of learning to discriminate relevant from irrelevant features of the situation. A principle taught in a rarefied environment that eliminates all irrelevancies does not prepare the individual to handle problems in a world filled with irrelevancies.

An interesting possibility has been raised by Logan and Wodtke

(1968), who suggest that the application of a principle may sometimes be interfered with because the person falls back on some rule of thumb. Teachers of technical skills have long noted this kind of phenomenon with students who have been trained in effective methods of trouble shooting, but who tend to fall back on more primitive procedures. For example, a student is confronted with an engine that does not start. Instead of undertaking a systematic diagnosis of the cause of the difficulty, he arbitrarily decides that the problem is probably in the fuel pump, which he changes. In this case, the principles involved in trouble shooting are scrapped and a rule of thumb is instituted. In the Logan and Wodtke study, students learned how to identify the number of significant figures in the product of two measurements. For example, a rectangle has sides measuring 9.53 and 8.67 centimeters; how many significant figures are there in the product which provides a measure of the area of the rectangle? The answer to this problem can be found by the application of principles that can be used to show that the answer with the correct number of significant figures is 82.6. There is also another rule-of-thumb way of arriving at the number of significant figures, which in most cases comes up with the correct answer. This simple rule is to take the same number of significant figures in the answer as there are in the factor with the fewest significant figures. Although the rule of thumb generally comes out with the right answer, it is sometimes misleading. The results of the study indicated that the giving of the rule of thumb, even with the warning that it might occasionally give incorrect results, interfered with the transfer of the principles that were also learned. It seems that problem solvers are willing to take a small risk that they may not be able to solve the problem if a simple procedure permits obtaining an answer quickly with a fairly high chance that it will be correct.

Transfer by Extension of a Rule

In most transfer studies a rule is learned and the subject is then confronted with a situation in which he is expected to apply this rule to provide the solution to a new problem. Another aspect of transfer is where a rule is learned and then extended to cover new phenomena, or the rule is broadened to make it a more comprehensive one. Much of the development of science is of this character. Isaac Newton, for example, saw that the laws of falling bodies were specific examples of other laws of much greater generality. Few individuals are able to generalize specific rules so that they become significant general laws, but the tendency of at least some high-school pupils to do this was demonstrated in a study by Scandura and Durnin (1968). One may well suspect that this is a very difficult feat to perform.

Level of Learning of the First Task in Relation to the Amount of Transfer

The relationship of level of learning on one task to the amount of transfer to a second task is clearly an important and practical problem. If increased learning on the first task produces an increase in the amount of transfer, then there is strong argument in favor of thorough learning of whatever is learned in school, for much of such learning is offered because of its supposed transfer value.

Underwood (1951) found that with a verbal learning task the amount of transfer depended on the degree of learning of the initial task. This is to be expected where transfer is positive and where it depends on the generalization of the response involved. Atwater (1953) found a similar effect. Another and quite complex investigation by Mandler (1954) in general confirmed these results, but also indicated that the relation between the level of learning on the first task and the amount of transfer to the second task is not a simple one.

The results of these studies generally indicate that the amount of transfer is likely to increase with increases in practice on the first task. An outstanding fact in the whole of the literature on transfer indicates that thorough learning is a desirable condition for efficient transfer. This fits well with many common observations made on behavior. The pupil who learns to speak a halting French in the classroom becomes unable to deliver a word of the language when faced by a visitor from France. The person who has recently learned to drive a car has the greatest difficulty in switching to a new car; the driver with many years of experience has no difficulty in switching to any new model that comes off the line. The experienced musician can switch from his customary instrument to another similar one with little difficulty, but the novice is upset by any change in his equipment.

Knowledge of this aspect of transfer suggests the tremendous importance of thorough learning of whatever is learned. This in turn suggests that learning should be so planned and scheduled that overlearning is the rule. Hasty and superficial treatment of subject matter in schools would appear to be a waste of time.

Task Difficulty and Transfer

An interesting problem of some educational significance is whether transfer occurs more readily from an easy task to a complex task or from a complex task to an easy one. A few years ago psychologists were inclined to take the position that transfer would take place more readily from the complex to the simple. The argument was that the complex task would include all the elements involved in the simple task, though including also some additional elements; but when the reverse procedure was adopted the simple task would not include all the elements involved in the complex task and hence much less transfer could occur. This is a persuasive argument, and a few early studies seemed to provide supporting evidence. However, when Holding (1962) reviewed all the studies he could locate, he found as many studies reporting more transfer in the easy-to-difficult situation as those reporting more transfer in the difficult-to-easy situation.

Holding showed in an experiment of his own that, with a simple task, optimum transfer occurred from the easier to the more difficult problem; but with more complex tasks, optimum transfer occurred from the more difficult to the easier problems. His experiments indicate that there is a complex relationship between task difficulty and amount of transfer.

Transfer Across Sense Modality

Another important problem for all educational planning is the extent to which material learned through one sense modality, such as hearing, transfers to learning through another sense modality, such as vision. For example, suppose a child learns to say French words, corresponding to common English nouns, as they are spoken by his teacher. When he has reached the point of being able to give the French equivalent of an English word that he *hears,* will he be equally proficient at giving the French word when he sees the *printed* English word? A further problem is the extent to which learning involving spoken words will transfer to situations involving the actual objects named. The transfer from the printed word to the spoken word, or the reverse, is a problem of particular interest in the field of foreign language instruction.

An extensive study of this problem has been undertaken by Asher (1964), who provided different groups of undergraduates with training in vocabulary in Spanish, Japanese, Turkish, Persian, and Russian. None of the students had had any previous experience with the language in which they were given training. Asher's general procedure was to provide vocabulary training in one of these languages through one sense modality (hearing or vision) and then, later, he asked the same students to relearn the lists of words in the other modality. The experimenter could then determine the extent to which learning the list through one sense modality facilitated learning through the other. Because the study covered many facets of language learning, a comparison of the transfer from vision to hearing and from hearing to vision can be made only with respect to Spanish, Japanese, and Russian. In the case of Spanish and Japanese, the sequence of learning through vision and later relearning through hearing was found to be superior to the reverse; but there was no significant difference between the orders of sequences of learning for Russian. It should be noted that the Japanese was presented in the Romanized alphabet (similar to that used here), but the Russian was presented in Russian script.

Asher suggests that the problem of transfer is one of what he calls *phonetic fit*. What he means is that there will be good transfer of learning from hearing to seeing, or the reverse, in a language in which there is a close relationship between the spelling of words and the way they are pronounced. English is an example of a language with a poor phonetic fit. When the phonetic fit is poor, the transfer is reduced from the one modality to the other. Thus the study indicates that the extent to which there is transfer from spoken instruction in a foreign language to printed instruction, or the reverse, depends on the extent to which there is a straightforward and simple relationship between print and speech.

An interesting finding was that when intensive training in oral Russian was given first, then exposure to printed Russian produced *pronunciation shock*, characterized by a decrease in the quality of spoken Russian. However, the reverse effect was found with Japanese, in which the introduction of printed material improved the quality of pronunciation.

The Asher study was concerned with the transmission of only verbal material, either through the visual or auditory modalities; but an interesting problem is given by associating an English word with a foreign word, when the learner on a later task has to name visually presented objects. One might expect that there would be less transfer across modalities when the transfer was from a task involving words to a task involving objects than when the transfer is between two verbal tasks. A direct study of this problem does not appear to have been undertaken.

A study by Kale, Grosslight, and McIntyre (1953) examined the related problem of the value of pictures, either still or in motion, in the teaching of Russian vocabulary. They found some evidence that the use of pictures, particularly motion pictures, appeared to facilitate learning. They also found that the simultaneous auditory presentation of the words displayed on the screen seemed to interfere with rather than facilitate learning.

Implications of Knowledge of Transfer for Classroom Practice

Most of the research on transfer reviewed in this chapter has been of relatively recent vintage. Research conducted by Thorndike early in the century is now so well known in education that the details were not discussed here. However, in reviewing the implications for education of the research that has been done on transfer, one cannot avoid pointing out that the studies of transfer of training, undertaken nearly three quarters of a century ago, probably had more impact on education than any other studies that psychologists have ever undertaken. Thorndike believed his studies and the studies of his contemporaries showed that one could not expect any broad benefits from study in a limited area, as many educators of the day believed. Thorndike emphasized that the learning of a particular skill was likely to facilitate the learning of another skill only insofar as the two skills had common elements. In contrast, educators in the early part of the century generally believed that the study of such subjects as mathematics and Latin had a general disciplining effect upon the mind—a theory that took the position that the learning of a particular skill provided very broad training in a wide range of thinking skills. Thorndike's work on transfer of training provided an entirely new basis for curriculum planning. No longer could subjects be included in the curriculum because of a belief that they were generally beneficial as devices for training the mind; a school subject had to be justified because of the *specific* skills, knowledge, and understanding it provided. The early research on transfer of training provided a revolutionary new basis for selecting subjects for inclusion in the curriculum.

Later research on transfer of training had other contributions to make, but none have had such sweeping effects on education as had the early research, the conclusions from which have generally proved to be valid.

The early research on transfer placed emphasis on what not to do in the field of education, such as not to teach Latin in the hope that it would generally discipline the mind. More recent research has suggested some of the things that teachers *should* do. The research suggests that a high degree of mastery is important if transfer is to occur, and hence the teacher should ensure that learning be pursued with thoroughness. This may sometimes mean that the pupil will have to develop a level of skill beyond that with which he feels satisfied.

If transfer is to take place, there is considerable data to support the point of view that the pupil should have experience with a wide range of problems that differ somewhat from one another. This provides experience in dealing with the slightly unusual, and develops an expectation that each problem will have to be solved in a way that is somewhat different from that used in the solution of previous problems. In a sense, this may be called training for flexibility; but it is one of the keys to transfer of training.

The teacher should emphasize principles and their application. Many teachers make the error of citing numerous facts without indicating that each is an example of the same underlying principle. But the statement of a principle is not enough. Pupils must also have the opportunity of practicing the use of the principle in a variety of problem situations.

If a principle has been learned, then the pupil should learn to apply it in situations in which there are many distracting and irrelevant elements. Unless he does this, he may have difficulty in learning to discriminate between the relevant and the irrelevant features of situations and may not see the applicability of a principle simply because he is distracted by an overwhelming mass of trivial detail. For example, applications of principles of physics in very complex situations can be discussed and explored in the classroom and on excursions outside the school, and pupils can be given practice in attempting to tease out the relevant elements in very complex situations. For example, what happens when a tornado forms is a problem that illustrates several different physics principles operating in a very complicated situation. Various aspects of the tornado have to be dissected intellectually in order to understand the principles that are operating. The pupil also has to be able to put aside irrelevant aspects of the tornado, such as the darkness that often accompanies it.

Another point to note is that acquired knowledge tends to be most readily available to the person who has learned it in the situation in which it was acquired. This means that opportunities should be provided for the pupil to learn and use knowledge in a variety of situations. Field trips and homework assignments can help to prevent knowledge and its uses from becoming tied to particular situations.

A final point needs to be emphasized. Teachers of today, like teachers at the start of the century, are much too optimistic in their hopes that transfer will occur. After educators ceased to believe that the difficult subjects such as Latin and mathematics had special powers for disciplining the mind, educators came up with other formulae for achieving the same goal. During the 1930's the belief was widely held that if Latin and mathematics would not do the trick, then, perhaps, exercises in critical thinking would. Analyses were made of the nature of critical thinking, and exercises were developed that were designed to develop the component skills involved. The hope was that the skills developed through such exercises would become very general skills. The effectiveness of curricula related to critical thinking was probably never as broad as educators hoped it would be. Later research has indicated that thinking skills do not show as much generalization as most earlier educators expected. Critical thinking, learned in the context of political discussion, may not generalize to the critical thinking involved in the design of an experiment, and vice versa. The skilled politician, shrewd in the analysis of political situations, may show himself to be completely naive in the design of a simple experiment. The sophisticated physicist may think like a child in the area of political issues. Thinking skills tend to be tied to particular areas of knowledge, and especially to those in which they have been learned.

In more recent times, interest has shifted to the development of creative thinking skills. Once again the thought has been that such skills developed in a limited context will also appear in other contexts. Creative skills *may* be readily transferred to new situations, but what we know of transfer of training would lead us to expect that they would be tightly bound to the situations in which they have been learned.

Summary

1. Learning in one area may facilitate or interfere with subsequent learning in other areas. It may also facilitate or interfere with previous learning. These are the phenomena of transfer of training. When the acquisition of one skill facilitates the learning or retention of another skill, the term positive transfer is used. When there is interference, the term negative transfer is applied. Transfer effects may be either proactive or retroactive. Transfer is commonly distinguished from the related phenomenon of warm-up.
2. Stimulus generalization is a basic form of transfer. The essential nature of stimulus generalization is that a response that comes to be elicited by a particular stimulus can also then be elicited by a range of similar stimuli. There is a gradient of stimulus generalization in that the closer the resemblance of the new stimulus to the stimulus to which the response was originally learned, the greater is the likelihood that it will elicit the particular response.
3. Generalization takes place from learned responses to objects, to responses to the words that denote the objects. Generalization also takes place across words when responses are conditioned to words used as stimuli. In the latter case, generalization is to words of similar meaning rather than to words of similar sound or to words similar in graphic form. This is referred to as semantic generalization, to indicate that generalization is along a dimension of meaning. Generalization may be due to a tendency to classify all inputs into categories, and responses are then learned to the categories and not to the specific stimuli.
4. Response generalization also constitutes another basic transfer mechanism in which the learning of a response to a particular stimulus also strengthens all related responses.

5. An additional basic transfer mechanism is that demonstrated by transposition. Although transposition has been extensively studied, the nature of the learning involved is not really understood.
6. In recent times, the study of transfer has been undertaken through research involving simple and well-defined forms of behavior. The paired-associate learning task has been found to be particularly useful for this purpose. In such tasks it is possible to find the effect of varying the stimulus element or the response element.
7. Research on transfer involving fairly simple situations using the proaction design have been quite well summarized by Osgood through a graph known as the transfer surface. This graph represents the fact that maximum positive transfer occurs when the two tasks present similar stimuli and call for similar responses, and that maximum negative transfer occurs when two tasks provide the same stimuli but call for opposite responses. The graph provides good predictions of the transfer to be expected between two tasks involving motor skills.
8. An important case of transfer related to problem solving is the acquisition of what have been termed learning sets. These are facilities in solving problems of a particular class. They appear to involve the learning of strategies and also flexibility in attempting different solutions. They do not necessarily involve the verbalization of the rules applied, as is evident from the fact that learning sets can be demonstrated in animals other than man. Out of this work have emerged studies of the factors that facilitate the shifting of strategies and rules for solving problems. Older children show a great capacity to make such shifts, although young children and other primates are slow. The difference between the older children and the young children and other primates is suspected to be attributable to the ability of the older children to use language in the solution of problems.
9. Although the Osgood transfer surface may provide a good description of the transfer to be expected in simple situations, it probably has little relevance when complex verbal learnings are involved. Some data suggest that being able to verbalize the solution to a concept-learning problem is important for being able to transfer the knowledge acquired to the solution of new problems. The extent to which transfer will occur in the case of human learning appears to depend much more on whether the problem is understood at a verbal level than whether it is intuitively understood, that is to say, understood but without the understanding being coded into words.

10. Studies of the learning of principles show that the conditions under which they are learned may facilitate or interfere with transfer. Transfer of a principle is facilitated if the situation in which it is learned involves many irrelevant cues and if it is to be transferred to other situations involving also many, but different, irrelevant cues. The application of a principle may also be disrupted because the individual involved falls back on some rule of thumb.
11. A significant case of transfer involves the extension of a rule to produce a more comprehensive generalization. This is probably a rare form of transfer, but it does take place even with children.
12. The degree of learning of the first task appears to be related to the amount of transfer that occurs. The data also suggest that if there is to be expected negative transfer from Task 1 to Task 2, then the amount of such negative transfer will decline as Task 1 is more and more adequately learned.
13. The relationship of transfer to the relative difficulty of Task 1 as compared to Task 2 has not been clearly identified by research. The results of studies lack consistency and lead to no firm conclusion.
14. Transfer across sense modality is an important educational problem. Transfer from auditory training to visual training in a verbally taught foreign language will take place effectively if the written and spoken forms of the language display phonetic fit.
15. Research on transfer of training has long had an important impact on education. The early research of Thorndike destroyed the doctrine of formal discipline and suggested that school subjects had to be justified because of their intrinsic nature. Later research has placed emphasis on the importance of the pupil's achieving thorough mastery, if transfer is to be achieved. In addition, research on the learning of principles has shown that transfer is most likely to take place if the pupil is given extensive practice in the application of the principles in a variety of situations.

PART TWO

SOME SPECIALIZED ASPECTS OF LEARNING

CHAPTER FIVE

Acquisition of Motor Skills

TASKS THAT INVOLVE COMPLEX MUSCULAR RESPONSES, AND PARTICULARLY those that involve the use of equipment, are said to call upon the subject to perform what are termed *motor skills*. Driving a car involves a motor skill and so too does using a hammer, or engaging in the pole vault, or sewing by hand or by machine, or tight-rope walking, or flying a plane. All such activities require that complex responses be made in keeping with the requirements of the task and the nature of the equipment involved. The term motor skill is also used rather loosely to refer to some complex responses that do not involve equipment. For example, sometimes it is said that speech is partly a motor skill, in that it involves the precise control of musculature. On the other hand, nobody would be likely to refer to a handshake as a motor skill. Where the cutoff between simple muscular responses and motor skills should be made is a matter for judgment at this time.

Motor skills are sometimes referred to as psychomotor skills, rather than as motor skills, to indicate that more is involved than just movement and that the performance calls for complex psychological processes. Another term commonly used is that of perceptual-motor skills, a term taken to indicate that motor skills involve perceptual processes from which they cannot be readily separated. No uniform term or set of terms has emerged, so in this chapter reference will be made to motor skills rather than to the more elaborate terms that have evolved.

A motor skill, as defined here, is one in which a major component is muscular activity that has some direct impact on the environment. Driving a car clearly meets this requirement, for the mechanical manipulation of the controls has direct physical effect on the motion of the automobile. Most athletic activities fall into the motor skill category. Crafts and trades of a century ago would have involved mainly motor skills, but today the use of machine tools has largely eliminated the importance of fine muscular adjustments in their pursuit. Although Stradivarius shaped each piece of his violins by hand and the precision of the craftsmanship depended on his steadiness and control, only a few of the modern violinmakers follow the same procedure. Most manufacturers of violins today produce the parts through the use of jigs that guide the cutting tools, and motor skills play only a very minor part in the production of the instruments. Modern manufacturing operations require little skill or practiced motor control.

Motor skills can be regarded in many different ways. One of the modern ways is to view the human and what he is doing as a system having a certain input and a certain output. In driving a car, there are inputs through the eyes and the ears concerning the location of the car in relation to the road and other objects, and there are outputs of the human operator which result in the car being driven properly through traffic. Much of the study of motor skills involves a study of the relationship of the inputs to the outputs. If the driver of a car doesn't manage to maintain a proper relationship between the inputs and the outputs, he is likely to land in the ditch. The inputs may be very simple, as they are when a car is driven along a monotonous interstate highway, or they may be very complex, as when a person is driving in heavy traffic through a city bedecked with numerous traffic signs and traffic lights, and with many lines of traffic entering and leaving the main flow. Outputs on motor tasks may also be simple or complex. The driver of a streetcar produces simpler outputs than the driver of a vehicle that has to be guided. Still more complex is the output of the operator of a space vehicle, who has to guide the craft in three dimensions, rather than the two dimensions used by the driver of a ground vehicle.

Stages in Learning Perceptual–Motor Skills

Fitts and Posner (1967) have attempted to describe the course of learning of motor skills in general terms. Their analysis provides a good introduction and a basis for more detailed discussion of some of the problems involved in motor-skill training. They suggest that motor-skill learning can be conveniently divided into three phases.

In the first phase, which Fitts and Posner describe as the early or cognitive phase, the emphasis is on learning to recognize the important cues that have to be attended to. This might be referred to as the perceptual phase of learning. In learning to operate a typewriter, the novice must first learn to recognize what the various controls will do, such as what key to press to write a particular letter, to back-space, and so forth. All motor tasks involve this phase of learning, although in some it is undertaken under informal conditions. In the case of learning to drive a car, much of the perceptual phase of learning is undertaken through casual observation long before the young person ever sits in the driver's seat. By the time he is old enough to learn the skill, he knows where all the controls are and how they are operated. To a lesser extent this is true in the case of typing, but in the case of some skills the cognitive phase is learned through formal instruction. For example, most of those who learn to fly a plane are thoroughly unfamiliar with the arrangement of the controls in the cockpit and have to begin by acquiring knowledge of the location of the controls and what they do. In addition, the novice has to learn about the various instruments in the cockpit and what their dials show. There is much to be learned about the task of flying long before the novice ever takes to the air. Perceptual familiarity with the controls and gadgetry in the cockpit is essential for learning to fly the plane.

In the cognitive stage, the pupil learns what responses can be made but he does not yet learn to make the responses on appropriate occasions. In learning to typewrite, he will know at the end of this phase where the various keys and controls are. In a sense, he has all the responses necessary for typing, but this is not enough to make him a skilled typist.

In the second phase of learning a perceptual-motor skill, the responses become tied to the appropriate stimuli. This may be much more complex than it seems. In learning to type the word *man*, the student must not only see each one of the letters and type the appropriate letter, but the striking of each key must become the trigger that initiates the striking of the next key. This stage in the learning is not too different from a corresponding stage in many verbal tasks. For example, in learning a poem the student will begin by familiarizing himself with the general content of the piece of verse. Then, in this second stage, he must learn to say the various phrases in proper order, and the completion of one must trigger the initiation of saying the next.

In the second stage, wrong habits that are brought to the skill from past experience must be eliminated. The pilot must learn that one does not turn the plane by manipulating the hand controls, but through the foot pedals. As a car driver he has learned to steer with his hands, but he must learn to abandon this habit as soon as he climbs into a plane. He must also learn not to feel for the gas pedal on the floor, for planes do not have such a pedal. In this phase, such inconsistent habits have to be extinguished.

In the final stage, the skill becomes more and more automatically performed as control is taken over by the lower centers of the brain. This is the stage where performance becomes so smooth and automatic that the person can engage in the skill while thinking about other things. Thus the automobile driver, after years of practice, can easily hold a conversation with a passenger while driving down the road.

The Retention of Motor Skills As the Retention of a Program

When a child first learns to tie his shoelaces, he tediously performs each component act step by step. After he has performed the first small part of the task, he is likely to stop and inspect what he has done and, from the results, figure out what the next step should be. Each step is guided by his visual inspection of the previous step. What a contrast the early performance of this skill is with the smooth, efficient, and quick performance of the older child!

The evidence now seems clear that the early performance of a complex motor skill is quite different from a mature performance. In the early stages of learning a complicated motor skill, the components are executed one at a time. The feedback provided by the accomplishments of one stage is used to trigger the next stage. If a stage has not been successfully completed, then the next stage does not take place. In contrast, in the case of the well-practiced and expert performance, there is no clear division between the various stages, for behavior flows smoothly. Although the learner divides the execution of the skill into stages, the skilled performer shows a continuous flow of behavior until the goal is reached.

Keele (1969) points out that there is substantial evidence to show that although a motor skill may be learned, in the first place, component by component, the more advanced stages of the acquisition of the skill involve the development of an internal program that permits the complete performance to run off with very little feedback. The concept of a *program* is derived from the area of computers. A computer program involves a complete set of directions for performing a sequence of mathematical operations. One can, for example, have a computer program for working out the square root of a number. Once the program is set to work, it will carry through the entire process of deriving a square root.

The square-root program is a relatively short program, but some programs may involve many hundreds of steps.

Now consider how the analogy of the computer program applies to our understanding of the performance of a well-practiced motor skill. Just as the computer may store a program containing all the operations necessary to perform a particular computation, and may produce the operations one by one, so too may the brain store the entire program necessary for performing a complex motor skill, and then send out the correct sequence of commands to the muscles to execute the skill. In the case of the program in the nervous system that controls a motor skill, the commands to the muscles go out in sequence, and with very little monitoring of the behavior involved. For example, the series of acts involved in bowling is run off as a smooth sequence. If one of the movements is not quite correctly performed in the later stages of the bowling act, the bowler may not be able to stop the sequence in time and may throw a bad ball. He knows that the ball will be a bad one before it even leaves his hand, but the entire sequence of activities has been triggered and, in order to halt the action, the bowler must not only make the decision to stop it, but he must also take the necessary action to do so. This may take perhaps a half second and, during that time, the last step may have been taken and the ball thrown.

In the case of highly practiced skills, the program in the nervous system may run off with very little monitoring by the perceptual system. Thus one may open the door of the car, enter, sit down, put the key in the ignition, and start the car while thinking about other matters. Intervention in the sequence is likely to occur if something goes wrong, such as the lock of the car sticking in winter, but otherwise the program runs off quite automatically.

The learning of a motor skill, beyond the initial clumsy stages, involves the laying down of a program for the performance of the skill within the central nervous system. This program, when triggered, runs off smoothly and with each step in proper sequence. One presumes that the cerebellum has the function of assembling and coordinating such a program.

Analysis of Typewriting

One of the few analyses of a motor skill that have any deep significance for the educator is found in West's volume (1969) on the analysis of typewriting skill. West's analysis is based upon the broad understanding that psychologists have already achieved of the nature of motor-skill learning as well as on research on the learning of typing. West begins his analysis with the very first stages of typing, at which time the learner has had only the common familiarity with the typewriter as it is seen by the nonuser. The learner knows that keys have to be struck in order to produce writing but that is about all, and his task is to strike keys denoted by the letters on the page of copy placed beside the machine. West points out that in the first phase of instruction (Fitts and Posner's second stage) the learner is involved in a long chain of internal activities that partly account for the slow pace of the skill during the initial stages. The chain of internal events involves (1) the perception of the letter to be copied and the vocalization of the letter, (2) the location of the key to be pressed, (3) the selection of the finger to be used in striking the key, (4) the vocalization again of the letter, and (5) the striking of the key. An important point to be noted is that the internal activity which triggers the striking of the key is that of the person saying to himself the letter in stage (4) of the sequence. After the letter is struck, the typed letter provides the feedback necessary for the learner to know whether his response has been correct. In the second phase, acquisition of speed in the performance of the skill involves first a reduction in the internal processes involved. When the learner has achieved a speed of about fifteen to twenty words per minute, he has reached the stage where he perceives a letter, and then says it to himself, and immediately strikes the right key. In addition, at this stage he has learned to take cognizance of the sensations in his muscles so that a stroke either feels right or feels wrong. As his level of skill is increased, he becomes more and more dependent upon the information coming from the muscles within his body, which tells him where his fingers are and what they are doing. As the latter happens, he becomes less and less dependent upon looking at what he has typed in order to check the accuracy of his work.

In a still later stage of learning the skill, the typist no longer has to vocalize each letter, but the stroke occurs in response to the perception of the letter. Then the perceptual-muscular behavioral unit ceases to be focused on individual letters; instead, groups of letters are read and the entire group typed as a unit. Although West implies that the typing of one letter produces sensations that become the stimuli for initiating the next letter, and thus a chain of behavior is established, it seems more likely that groups of letters are run off through sequences of messages being sent to the muscles from the brain. Indeed, the speed of typing at the level of the expert is such that no credence can be given to the theory that the sensations accompanying each stroke are the stimuli for initiating the next stroke. If this theory were correct, the maximum possible level of performance of the typist would be extremely slow. At a fast typing rate there is just not enough time for the stimuli produced by each stroke to initiate the next stroke.

The analysis of the learning of typing skill leads West to propose training methods that are in direct conflict with those that have been emphasized in the past. He points out that, in the early stages of learning, the student should be concerned with learning the locations of the letters. In order to do this, he should use a typewriter that has the letters printed on the keys, and not the blank keyboard that has been preferred by teachers of the past. In order that the student may not have to shift his eyes back and forth from the copy to the keyboard, the teacher may read the letters to be typed. Later, of course, the habit of watching the keyboard has to be eliminated. As the student learns to type material presented beside the typewriter, and begins to strive for speed, he is forced into glancing at the keyboard less and less. Perhaps this is one of the reasons why the emphasis on speed rather than on accuracy produces the best learning condition during the early stages of acquiring the skill. The research evidence seems to be overwhelming that emphasis on speed rather than accuracy is extremely important for the effective acquisition of this particular skill. The fact that this generalization emerges from research on typewriting does not mean that it is applicable to other motor skills. For example, it is extremely probable that the person studying a musical instrument should strive for accuracy rather than speed. It is the consensus of teachers of music that speed comes naturally if the pupil will just concentrate on accuracy but, unfortunately, most pupils want to strive for speed. Teachers of music could be wrong, as teachers in other fields have been demonstrated to be wrong, but the evidence still has to be collected.

Probably no generalizations can be made at this time in the matter of deciding whether speed or accuracy should be stressed in the learning of particular motor tasks, except in cases, such as typing, in which the matter has been closely studied. The problem is really quite complex. Striving for speed can give the learner the feeling of accomplishing something, even if he makes errors, but slow, deliberate, accurate typing may at first be at such a slow speed that the learner may give up, simply because he feels he can never master the task. On the other hand, emphasis on speed means that many errors will be practiced, and the practice of error always interferes with the learning of any task. In the case of typing, the advantages of speed seem to outweigh the negative effect of the increased practice of error. In the case of learning a musical instrument, the practice of errors probably has an overwhelmingly bad effect on ultimate level of performance.

Important Facts About the Study of Perceptual–Motor Skills Derived from the Study of Tracking Tasks

Motor skills have been studied in the laboratory in situations that resemble tasks commonly encountered during life but generally involve much greater simplicity. For example, driving a car along a winding road involves keeping the car in a fixed position with respect to the edge of the road or the center line, if there is one. The latter task is very much like many tasks, known as tracking tasks, that are used in the laboratory study of motor skills. In tracking tasks there has to be what is referred to as a target, which is simply a mark such as a spot of light on a screen. The movement of the target is controlled by the experimental equipment. In addition, there is also a marker, which may be another spot of light, but this is controlled by the subject in the experiment. The task of the subject is to watch the target and, when it moves, to move the marker to keep it directly over the target. The subject moves the marker by pushing or pulling a lever, by turning a crank, by pressing a brake pedal, or by some other mechanical device. The target may move in a regular pattern, or with complete irregularity, depending upon the particular experiment. The rate of movement can also be fast or slow. Many common motor-skill tasks are tracking tasks. For example, learning to write in the first grade by copying letters and words written on the chalkboard or elsewhere is essentially a form of tracking behavior, and in performing this task the child is learning a form of motor skill.

The kind of laboratory tracking task considered up to this point is referred to as a *pursuit tracking task,* but other tracking tasks have also been invented. Another is compensatory track in which the target is fixed but the marker tends to drift away from the target, and the subject must bring it back onto the target through moving the controls.

Other devices that have been used for the study of motor skills include simulations of the cockpit of a plane equipped with both a joystick and pedals for rudder control. With these devices the flight pattern of a miniature plane in front of the cockpit can be controlled. Another simple device is the track-tracing apparatus in which the subject must move a metal stylus along a path without touching the boundaries of the path. Designed to study other aspects of motor skill is the apparatus for measuring steadiness, in which a stylus must be held in a small hole without the stylus touching the sides of the hole. Other equipment has long been used for the study of speed of reaction.

Of all the various techniques used for the study of motor skills in the laboratory, probably none has been used more widely, nor produced more information, than tracking tasks. These tasks seem to be peculiarly well suited to providing knowledge about motor behavior.

An excellent review of the literature on tracking behavior has been prepared by Poulton (1966). The literature is not readily summarized because tracking behavior may be very simple, as when the target moves at a uniform speed along a line, or very complex, as when the target moves in three dimensions in a pattern that never repeats itself. In addition, the target may move at a uniform speed or accelerate or decelerate. Thus tracking tasks may vary from very simple ones that involve a single control to complex ones involving three or more controls. The conclusions that can be drawn about learning simple tracking tasks cannot always be applied to the complex tasks.

Most of those who have ever undertaken a tracking task have the impression that it involves a continuous adjustment on the part of the operator of the equipment. The driver moving his car along a winding road has the impression that he keeps the car moving smoothly around the curves. In actual fact, he does not do this at all. What he does is to turn the steering wheel in a number a short and discrete adjustments. Each is a separate and distinct movement followed by a pause when he takes stock of the results of the previous adjustment. If the driving is difficult, he may make perhaps two adjustments of the steering wheel in a second, but normally he does not make more than one adjustment per second.

The Poulton article points out that there is considerable evidence that tracking behavior involves a series of decision-action sequences. The person performing a tracking task makes a decision to move in a certain direction and, once the move has been initiated, the direction cannot be readily altered. It is estimated that it takes about a third of a second to make a new decision and to change the direction of action. Thus there is a delay of about a third of a second between the arrival of information at the performer's eyes and the initiation of action and then, if new information arrives, it may take about another third of a second to change the direction of action again. These kinds of delays may be serious to a person landing a jet plane under conditions of poor visibility, when the plane may move one hundred feet before a pilot can change from the initiation of an incorrect decision to the making of a correct decision. However, in many tracking tasks, the lag in behavior is not serious in that the person can anticipate, in advance, what he has to do. Thus the driver of a car can watch the road as it winds into the distance and make decisions well in advance of the actions that have to be taken. It is under conditions where the equipment operator cannot anticipate what is going to happen that lags in decision-action sequences become of real importance.

Thus, in tracking tasks, the equipment operator does not make continuous adjustments; rather, he makes a jumpy set of adjustments. He makes one adjustment and then remains stationary, and then he makes another adjustment. The task is continuous, but the adjustments of the operator are discontinuous. Furthermore, the operator can make only about two adjustments every second, at the most. This fact has important implications for equipment design. If a piece of equipment, involving a tracking task, requires the operator to make more than about two adjustments a minute, then it may be impossible for the operator to keep on target. Of course, if the adjustments can be anticipated, then the tracking task is greatly simplified, and more than three adjustments per second can be made.

A key to training persons to perform in many tracking situations is to teach them to *anticipate* changes in the direction of the track. A person learning to drive a car often begins by concentrating on the immediate state of affairs and, in turning a corner, he may fail to begin to turn the wheel in time. As a result, he overshoots the turn and swings far out from the side of the road where he should be. Learning to run and catch a baseball is largely a problem of learning to anticipate where the ball will be after a particular interval of time.

Performance on most tracking tasks can be improved if the person is given supplementary feedback concerning the size of his errors. For example, in a laboratory tracking task a buzzer may sound whenever the performer has been particularly accurate in keeping the marker on the target. An alternative procedure is for the buzzer to sound whenever a particularly large error has been made. Both of these procedures lead to more accurate performance than is otherwise achieved. One presumes that similar feedback would also be of value in learning to drive a car. Although the driver knows well whether he is, or is not, roughly in the correct position on the highway, the instructor will probably facilitate learning by indicating when he is doing particularly well or particularly poorly. Such supplementary information probably has quite complex functions, in that it serves to provide a standard by which the driver can judge whether he is doing well enough or whether he is not meeting the standards that society expects of him.

One of the problems that has been studied using tracking tasks is whether the learning of a motor skill is best undertaken through learning the components, piece by piece, before the total skill is attempted, or whether it is best to go about learning by attacking the total task in its entirety from the beginning. This kind of problem is encountered in planning training on any complex piece of equipment that requires the simultaneous operation of several controls, such as, for example, a bulldozer, fork-lift truck, or a crane. The question is whether practice should be given on each of the component control systems separately before the total task in its entirety is attempted. The answer to this problem cannot be stated in simple terms. If the controls really operate completely independently of each other, then there seems to be some virtue in practicing the component skills first; but when, as is generally the case, there is some interaction between what is done with one control and what is done with the other, then the complete skill should be practiced as an entirety. An example of where the component skills interact is found in the case of the operation of a stick-shift car. The clutch is one control and the foot brake another, but the two interact in that when the person wants to stop he must know that he depresses the brake first and then depresses the clutch slightly later. The brake and clutch skills have to be practiced together because they interact.

The most important single factor that has been identified in relation to the training of individuals in motor skills is the rate at which the initial task is increased in difficulty. There is some agreement that in the case of those skills where the task can be slowed down, as it can be in tracking tasks, initial training should be given at a slow rate. The rate should then be increased as rapidly as the learner can adapt to the new rate. Indeed, without such an increment in rate, the learner's performance may decline, for he seems to need the incentive of an increased rate from time to time in order to provide some challenge. If a training device is built to teach a particular skill as, for example, in the case of flying light aircraft, then the trainer can be designed so that the difficulty of the task is always adjusted to the level of skill of the learner.

Some understanding of the reason for the need to adjust the task difficulty to the level of performance of the learner is found in the work of Fitts and Peterson (1964), who take the position that a crucial factor in the learning of a motor skill is the information capacity of the learner. When a task is adjusted so that it involves excessive speed, the learner has difficulty in coping with it because he cannot handle the information required to perform the task effectively. This conception of the main source of difficulty in the learning of motor skills interprets well the common experience of learning to ride a bicycle. The novice who first attempts this task finds himself confronted with an array of controls and a mass of visual, kinesthetic, and other sources of information that he does not yet know how to use effectively. He is clumsy, partly because he is flooded with all kinds of information which he cannot relate effectively to what he can do to maintain his balance. If the task can be slowed down, in the sense that he has less information to handle at any time, then this will facilitate learning. In the case of learning to ride a bicycle, one can attach training wheels so that at first the learner need only attend to the problem of pedaling and steering. Once he has learned to handle these automatically, he can turn to the problem of balance.

The training wheels can then be slowly raised so that the learner becomes more and more dependent upon his own skill for the maintenance of balance.

Performance on tracking tasks is characterized by a quite rapid decline in performance, due, presumably, to the building up of inhibitions. In popular language, one might say that the learner of the motor skill quickly becomes tense, with a resulting decrement in performance. For this reason, during the acquisition of a motor skill rather short sessions, interspersed with rest periods, are likely to provide a learning situation in which there is continuous improvement. There is some evidence that, even though performance on a motor skill that is being learned shows a rapid decline during a particular learning session, learning still continues to occur. It is just that the learning is not manifest in immediate performance, although it may be evident in the level of performance at the next training session. A similar decrement in performance in a motor skill does not appear to happen when the skill is highly practiced. A skilled typist may show a small decline over the course of a morning, but it is a very small decline compared with that found in the learner.

When the level of performance on a motor skill has shown a decline towards the end of a training session, even a short rest period is likely to produce a remarkable increase in performance. This rise in performance is due to the dissipation of the inhibitory effects that had built up during practice.

Indirect Methods of Teaching Motor Skills: Mental Practice and Observation

Instructors in physical education sometimes assume that improvement in a motor skill will take place through an internal rehearsal entitled mental practice, and through observation of a demonstration. The effectiveness of these techniques needs to be studied experimentally, more than it has been, but some evidence is available at this time.

Some rather weak evidence was found by Hammer and Natale (1964) that the initial stages of touch typing could be learned with greater accuracy, though not with increased speed, by a procedure involving mental practice rather than by a traditional procedure. Whether mental practice is or is not effective probably depends upon the nature of the skill and the extent to which it involves high-level cognitive processes. If this is correct, then one would not expect much effect from mental practice in the case of a skill in which cognitive processes did not play an essential role but in which the person had to learn to use cues from his own muscles. Thus, in the studies by Start (1964a, 1964b) on the effect of mental practice on performance of the single-leg upstart on the high bar, one would not expect much effect, because what has to be learned is probably dependent upon the lower centers of the nervous system and particularly on the cerebellum. Start could not find any effect of mental practice. However, in a rather similar study by Jones (1965) an effect was found. A much earlier study by Harby (1952) showed a slight but statistically significant effect of mental practice on the development of skill in the basketball free-throw. The greatest improvement was shown by the group that combined mental practice and physical practice.

An additional eleven studies on the effect of mental practice on the development of a motor skill have been reviewed by Richardson (1968). These studies involved such varied skills as the tennis forehand and backhand drive, dart throwing, muscular endurance, card sorting, and juggling. The overall evidence from these studies is difficult to interpret, often because no tests of significance were applied. Richardson concludes that the trend of the studies is to show that mental practice is associated with improved performance. As one would expect, a combination of both mental and physical practice generally gives the maximum improvement. Richardson points out that one of the crucial factors in determining the efficacy of mental practice is the familiarity of the learner with the task. A person can hardly be expected to undertake mental practice on a task he has not yet performed on any single occasion with any degree of success, for under such conditions all he can do is rehearse his inadequate performance. The studies reviewed by Richardson also produced some unexpected and perhaps inexplicable results. One of these is the tendency for mental practice to produce an improvement in tasks involving simply muscular endurance! Richardson also points out that at least two of the studies stress the difficulties that subjects experience in undertaking mental practice and that, if it is used at all, then the periods of practice should be short. Indeed, there is even the suggestion that periods of mental practice that exceed only a few minutes may result in either boredom or frustration and lead to a lowered performance.

Delay in Knowledge of Results

Irion (1966) has reviewed the literature on the effect of delay in feedback or delay in knowledge of results on the acquisition and performance of motor skills. Much depends upon the nature of the task. If it involves some continuous activity, as in tracking tasks or driving a car, the immediate knowledge of results is important for the guidance of behavior. On the other hand, if the motor skill involves discrete acts, as in drawing freehand a line of specified length or in throwing a ball over the shoulder at a target, the feedback on a particular trial may be delayed seconds, minutes, days, or even weeks, without its losing its effectiveness. In such tasks a person may be able to use information about his performance, given after a long interval, to just the same extent as information given immediately after the act. This concept is used in the training of professional athletes in many fields, when their performance is filmed during contests or during practice and then the films are shown later for the purpose of correcting errors. In training programs of the latter kind, more time may be spent in the classroom studying films of practice than in the actual sessions themselves.

In the case of the question of the efficacy of teaching motor skills by demonstration, the problem is not whether they can or cannot be taught by this method, for obviously demonstration often has to play an important part. If one is training a person to tie a particular knot, a common problem in training Navy men, some kind of direct demonstration of what is involved is necessary. In the case of the knot-tying task, the minimum that the learner has to be given is an example of the knot as it is finally tied, but this final product is generally not a sufficient basis for learning. Additional information can be provided by showing the knot at various stages of being tied. A more complete version of the task can be provided through a film that presents the complete process of tying the knot. Whether the motion picture is superior as a teaching aid to the set of partly completed knots is a matter of conjecture. The advantage of the set of incomplete knots is that the learner can move both forward and backward and, when he has difficulty at a particular stage, he can examine the corresponding stage as long as he wishes. On the other hand, the film is not so readily stopped and held, and generally cannot be slowed up at a particular stage to help a particular learner. A finding of Rimland (1955), which has not been pursued further despite its intrinsic interest, is that a film demonstrating knot tying was most effective when it was shown twice without intervening practice, suggesting that practice is not effective until the learner's knowledge has developed beyond a certain critical point. Still earlier studies have also shown that in order for a demonstration to provide a useful, immediate guide to practice, the demonstration must proceed rather slowly (see, for example, the 1949 study of Roschal, or the 1950 study of Jaspen, or the 1953 study of Ash and Jaspen). It seems that the learner becomes overloaded with information rather easily in the early stages of learning a motor skill and that when this happens learning may cease. For this reason, teachers would probably do well first to provide a complete and slow demonstration of the motor skill before permitting the learner to attempt to reproduce it. A difficulty in following this advice is that many motor skills often cannot be slowed up for the purposes of demonstration. The high jump, in its entirety, cannot be performed in slow motion and neither can the long pass in football.

The Limits of Skill

Very little can be said about the limits of the improvability of motor skills. Much depends upon the incentives provided for improvement and the amount of time devoted to practice. Fitts and Posner (1967) have summarized some interesting findings concerning the improvement of skills that are practiced over extended durations. Several studies are presented in which the improvement in the performance of a motor skill continued over long periods. In such studies the patience of the experimenter often became exhausted before the subjects showed any decline in daily gains. Much more extended practice is found in some industrial studies in which the recorded performance of workers has been available over periods of years. In a well-known study by Crossman (1959) the production of cigar makers with varying amounts of experience was recorded. The data seemed to indicate that improvement in production occurred for at least the first four years and perhaps even longer. The data in the area suggest that improvement in motor skills takes place over long periods and that the achievement of any limit on the level of skill requires an immense amount of practice to attain. The graph, showing the improvement in the skill of cigar makers, is reproduced as Figure 13,

Figure 13. Graph showing relationship between time required to make a cigar and years of experience. (Reproduced by permission of "Ergonomics.")

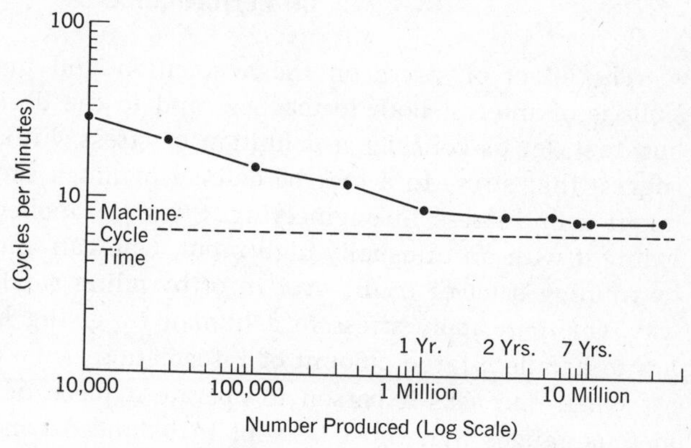

which needs some explanation. The units on the vertical coordinate are centiminutes, that is to say, one-hundredth parts of a minute. The latter unit is much more convenient for scientific purposes than the units of the minute-second system. The task of making a cigar involves the use of a machine that helps form the cigar. This machine takes a certain amount of time to go through one cycle, about seven hundredths of a minute, and this is the fastest rate at which it is possible to make cigars. During the first year employees produce, on the average, one million (1 M) cigars each. After the first few days, when they learn the job, they take about twelve hundreths of a minute to make a cigar. After a year, the time taken to make a cigar has declined to about ten hundreths. After two years the time is about nine hundreths. A slow increment in speed is still apparent after four years. One suspects also that, if added incentives had been provided, additional gains in speed would have been made.

There is much evidence from the area of athletics to suggest that once a maximum level is achieved, massive amounts of practice are necessary in order to maintain that level of skill. Professional bowlers find it necessary to have their own private bowling alley in order to put in the practice required for maintaining their maximum level of skill, and they may bowl twenty or more games a day. Musicians may have to practice eight or more hours a day to stay at their professional peaks. The professional pool player has to practice almost continuously to stay in championship form. Years of practice seem to be required to reach a peak of performance, but to stay at that peak requires the same kind of practice that made it possible for the peak to be reached initially.

The Effect of Stress on Performance

The effect of stress on the acquisition and maintenance of motor skills is of interest both to teachers and to the designers of equipment, but, first, let us consider a definition of stress. Fitts and Posner (1967) suggest that stress in a task be defined in much the same way that one might define stress in engineering. Stress is applied to a beam by providing it with an unusually high input. One can apply stress to a bridge by running a lot of traffic over it, or by piling sandbags along the roadway. One can apply stress to a human by giving him a task where he has to handle a large amount of information.

When one asks a person to operate a piece of equipment with numerous gauges that must be kept in balanced conditions and with numerous controls that have to be adjusted, and when the task is such that it is far more complex than the skilled operator can handle, the person is unlikely to adopt the attitude that he can perform only part of the task and neglect the other part. He will, almost certainly, attempt the entire task and produce a confused and disorganized performance. An excessive input of information to the operator, a condition of high stress, produces poor performance. Now let us consider a situation in which there is very low stress, that is to say, a situation in which there is a low input of information. Such a situation is provided by tasks similar to those undertaken by operators of radar equipment, who must watch radarscopes for the appearance of small bright spots indicating the presence of an unknown flying object. Such tasks are known as vigilance tasks. They all involve watching for rare signals, and the information input to the human operator is at a very low level. These are, by definition, very low stress tasks. When an individual is faced with a very low stress task, he also becomes very ineffective. After he has performed a vigilance task for less than thirty minutes he begins to miss signals. His problem is that the input of information is so low that he finds it impossible to concentrate on the task. A certain amount of input is necessary in order for the operator to remain effective.

The picture resulting from such data is that performance on a perceptual-motor task is most likely to be effective when the conditions are somewhere between those of very low and very high stress. A moderate information input is necessary in order to keep the individual operating efficiently, but this level must not be raised beyond a certain level or behavior will become disorganized. This generalization holds true, not just for motor tasks, but also for many verbal tasks. When speech is speeded up to three hundred, four hundred, and five hundred words per minute, the point is soon reached where the person ceases to understand anything, despite the fact that the individual words are still intelligible. If speech is slow enough, say forty words per minute, the thread of each sentence may be lost before it is finished, and behavior is also inefficient.

Retention of Motor Skills

Common experience tells us that the retention of motor skills is excellent over long periods. A person may not skate for a ten-year period, and then when he takes to the ice he finds that he can skate almost as well as when he left off. Psychologists have found similar data in the laboratory. Studies of the long-term retention of motor skills have been undertaken by numerous research workers over the past half century and all with closely similar results. A study by Fleishman and Parker (1962) will be discussed briefly as a basis for opening up an understanding of the reasons for the lack of forgetting on such tasks.

Fleishman and Parker used a task that resembled, in some superficial respects, the manipulation of the controls on a plane. A joystick was held by the subject and could be moved forward or backward or to either side. The stick provided two dimensions of movement. The feet were used to control a rudder bar that could be moved like a seesaw about an axis. The stick had to be manipulated so that it maintained a dot of light on a cathode-ray tube in a central position. The dot tended to drift away from the central position and the stick could be used to return it to a central position. The foot-controlled rudder bar was used to adjust a voltmeter placed just below the cathode-ray tube. Whenever the needle on the voltmeter strayed from the central position, the subject had to recenter it by moving the rudder bar with the feet. Thus the task was complex, involving both the observation of a dot of light and the observation of a needle on a voltmeter. The subject then had to adjust the position of the dot and the needle by manipulating the stick and the rudder with hands and feet. The task was not readily learned and required fifty practice sessions, each of six minutes' duration, in order for the subjects to achieve a level of learning which showed no improvement. The practice sessions were spread over seventeen days. So much for the training part of the experiment. Then Parker and Fleishman tested their subjects for the retention of the skill, with one third of the subjects being retested after nine months, one third after twelve months, and one third after twenty-four months. The nine-month and the twelve-month group showed virtually no loss of the skill. The twenty-four month group showed a slight loss that was almost completely recovered after three six-minute practice sessions. In other words, the data showed a high degree of retention over a two-year period and the findings were consistent with everyday experience. Now let us consider why there is so little loss of motor skill, compared with a corresponding loss in verbal knowledge, over such a long period. One cannot be certain of the validity of the answers given here, but those answers are highly plausible and consistent with what is known.

Consider first one part of the task performed in the Fleishman and Parker study, namely, the adjustment of the voltmeter needle with the foot bar. This is essentially a highly repetitive task, for the subject must, again and again, bring back the needle to center by moving the foot bar. After three hundred minutes of doing this, the subject must be considered to have had an extraordinarily large amount of practice. Perhaps a comparable task in the verbal field might be one in which the subject had to say "X" immediately, every time the experimenter said "P". Three hours of practice on such a task would bring it to the point where the response would be made immediately and without hesitation. The simplicity of the response and the extended amount of practice would almost certainly ensure that the learning would be highly permanent, for the reason that overlearned responses are less easily lost than are responses that have had little practice. The superior retention of most motor responses studied may be attributable not to the fact that they are motor responses but to the fact that they are highly overlearned and rather simple in character.

Second, there is the fact that such tasks are continuous tasks. If one were to design motor tasks so that they involved a number of separate and distinct responses, then they might not be so well retained. The latter kind of tasks involve more distinct components than a simple tracking task, such as the Fleishman and Parker task, and in this respect might be more comparable to verbal tasks. Complex motor tasks involving discrete responses generally involve, like a game of checkers, a number of distinct moves that have to be made. These may each involve the throwing of a correct switch or the moving of an appropriate lever. Generally, some kind of complex signal is given, such as the turning on of a combination of lights. The signal indicates the switch to be pushed or the lever to be positioned. Once the subject has responded, the lights go off and the machine is reset for the next stimulus and the next response. On such tasks forgetting is extremely rapid and closely comparable to that found in verbal learning tasks.

A third factor that may help to account for the superiority of the retention of motor skills has to do with the fact that the laboratory tasks used are not similar to those used in daily life and, for this reason, the learned skill is not disrupted by subsequent activities with related motor skills. The retention of a verbal task is probably readily disrupted by similar verbal behavior undertaken day-in and day-out, for the laboratory task involves just the same elements as are undertaken in daily life. This argument is not particularly strong, in that we have no way of determining the extent to which laboratory motor tasks are similar or dissimilar to tasks involved in daily life.

There is still the possibility that motor skills are actually more readily retained than are verbal skills and verbal information. Motor skills are highly dependent for their retention on the cerebellum and lower brain centers, which have the capability of taking them over and making them quite automatic. These centers may have a greater capability of retaining the traces necessary for their performance than have the parts of the brain concerned with the retention of other skills and information.

Aptitudes for Motor Skill Learning

Psychologists have long been interested in the identification of those persons most likely to be capable of learning motor skills successfully. The problem is one of great practical significance, for training in some motor skills can be an extremely expensive venture, as it is in the case of learning to fly a light airplane. In order to develop a successful means of identifying persons who learn motor skills easily, one has to know whether there is just a general motor ability that some individuals have more of and some less, or whether there are a number of separate and distinct aptitudes involved. For example, does a watchmaker who successfully dismantles, cleans, and reassembles watches have the same aptitudes as a person who uses his motor skills to assemble a frame building successfully? If different aptitudes are involved, then one would choose people for training as watchmakers on a different basis from that one would use for selecting trainees who are to learn how to put together frame buildings. One should note that the one activity involves fine manipulations of the fingers while the other involves gross movements of the limbs.

Tests of motor skills have had a long history, and their development preceded the developments of tests of intellectual skills. Some of the earliest were developed by Galton a century ago, who administered his battery to many thousands of subjects of all ages. By the turn of the century, American psychologists had become interested in the area; and most of the work undertaken was prompted by the idea that tests of simple motor skills could be used to predict performance in complex activities that involved these skills. Thus it might be assumed that tests of hand steadiness might predict rifle marksmanship, because steadiness is a component in the total skill of rifle marksmanship. Another example is the possibility that finger dexterity might be used to predict success in watch-repair work. Here again, the skill that is measured, finger dexterity, is a component of the total skill involved in repairing watches. Sometimes such predictions were found to work out rather well; sometimes, for unaccountable reasons, the expected relationships did not materialize.

The advancement of knowledge in this area has been handicapped greatly by the difficulties of undertaking research. Tests of motor skills generally require apparatus, which is expensive to build and maintain. Unlike most paper-and-pencil tests of intellectual skills, students taking the tests show great improvement with practice; and the question has to be raised whether the most useful measure is a person's initial performance or his performance after he has had some practice. All these problems have added greatly to the difficulty of the task faced by the research worker interested in the area. Some meager knowledge is, however, available concerning the number of different motor skills that may be involved in complex tasks, and this must now be considered.

At the present time there appear to be a limited number of distinct abilities in the motor area. Measurement of these abilities may be used at a future time for the purpose of predicting the ability of individuals to learn skills that involve these motor abilities. The abilities as identified by Fleishman (1956) are as follows:

Reaction time. This is the speed with which an individual can make a response to a stimulus he is expecting. One measure of this ability is that of raising a finger at a predetermined signal, such as a click, or when a light is turned on.

Tapping ability. This skill is the speed with which an individual can perform a rapid movement, such as tapping a table top.

Psychomotor coordination. This ability is represented by such skills as require the coordination of the eye and the hand. It is involved in both fine and gross movements.

Manual dexterity. This skill is a popular term with a technical meaning. It refers to the ability to make skillful, controlled arm or hand movements at a rapid rate. In one test of this ability, the subject must turn over blocks as rapidly as possible.

Finger dexterity. This skill involves the rapid manipulation of objects with the fingers. It does not include arm motion, as does manual dexterity. In one test of this ability, the subject is required to manipulate small pegs with tweezers.

Psychomotor precision. This ability, although very little is known about it, appears to involve speed as well as precision. It is similar to finger dexterity, but seems to involve more eye-hand coordination.

Steadiness. Steadiness is measured by tests in which a steady hand yields a high test score.

Motor kinesthesis. This skill is measured by placing the individual in some unstable piece of equipment, such as the simulated cockpit of a plane. The cockpit is so arranged that it may tip to one side or the other, but can be righted by the movement of a rudder. The person must maintain the cockpit in an upright position by the control of the rudder.

Aiming or psychomotor speed. This is skill in performing at a high speed a simple task such as making dots in circles or making marks on standard answer sheets.

Ambidexterity. This skill is measured by asking right-handed subjects to perform simple tests, such as tapping tests, with the left hand and vice versa.

Many of these abilities require equipment for their measurement, although some of the others can be measured through paper-and-pencil tests. There is little possibility that reaction time can be measured through a paper-and-pencil test, but such tests have been devised to measure tapping and aiming. The abilities identified by Fleishman are quite distinct one from another. A person who scores high on one of these does not necessarily score high on any of the others. The abilities are highly independent one from the other.

The motor skills that we have considered here do not represent, so far as is known, stable and enduring traits, and should not be used, at least not at this time, for making any long-term predictions concerning what trade or skill a person can or cannot learn.

Summary

1. Perceptual-motor skills are complex outputs of behavior involved in performing specified tasks. The performance of these skills generally require that the individual take in information through his sense organs, and the motor skill represents adjustments to the intake of information.
2. Much of the study of motor skills involves the study of the relationship of human inputs to human outputs.
3. Several stages have been identified in the acquisition of motor skills. In the first phase the learner has to recognize the cues he will later use to guide his behavior, and the general characteristic of the equipment used in the performance of the motor skill. Thus the initial phase is a perceptual phase. The second phase is an action phase in which responses come to be triggered by certain cues. Responses have to become tied, not only to whatever external stimuli trigger them (as when one types a letter of the alphabet after seeing the letter on the printed page), but the responses also have to become coordinated to some extent by the responses that preceded them. In the final stage, the responses become almost automatic and

are taken over by the lower centers of the brain, and probably particularly those in the cerebellum.

4. In the learning of many skills, a major task of the learner is to overcome the influence of previously learned skills.
5. One of the few motor skills taught in an educational setting that has been extensively studied is typewriting. The early phase of learning this skill takes place largely informally. Instruction usually begins in what Fitts and Posner refer to as the second stage. This stage, in the case of typing, is more complicated than that described by these scientists, in that it involves also verbal behavior which forms an important part of the skill in the early stages of learning. In other words, the learner says to himself the letter he is going to type before he types it. At a later stage, the internal verbal behavior drops out. In the final stage, the typing of sequences of letters takes place immediately and unhesitatingly in response to the perception of the copy being typed. The typist probably runs off sequences of letters, emitting the proper behavior in sequence. It is doubtful, however, whether the response to one letter becomes the stimulus for the response to the next letter.
6. West proposes that typing should be taught with the use of typewriters on which the letters are printed on the keys, although this has not been done in the past. He also suggests that the emphasis should be on speed rather than on accuracy.
7. The laboratory tasks most commonly used for the study of motor skills are tracking tasks. Many of these tasks bear a considerable resemblance to tasks undertaken in daily life, such as driving a car, or copying written material. Tracking tasks may be either pursuit tasks or compensatory tasks. These tasks may be varied systematically in difficulty, often by varying the number of dimensions involved and the number of controls that have to be manipulated. Tracking behavior involves a sequence of decisions followed by actions. In a task involving keeping a pointer in line with a moving dot, the subject will wait until the pointer and the dot become out of alignment and then make a movement to adjust the pointer. The dot and the pointer are kept approximately in line by such sequences of inactivity followed by an adjustive movement. About three such movements per second are commonly made in fast-moving tracking tasks. Tracking behavior is undertaken in small jumps and not in a smooth continuous movement. Supplementary feedback may improve tracking behavior.
8. Perceptual motor skills should be learned in terms of the component skills only when the components do not interact. If

the components interact, as they usually do, then the task should be learned as a whole.

9. Performance on most perceptual-motor skills shows a decline after some practice has been undertaken, because of the build-up of inhibitions.
10. The most important single factor with respect to the planning of training in motor skills is control of the rate at which the task is increased in difficulty. The central factor in determining the difficulty of a perceptual-motor task is the rate at which the task provides perceptual information that has to be utilized to perform the task.
11. Some motor skills can be learned, to some degree, through what has been termed mental practice. The extent to which a motor skill can be learned in this way depends upon the extent to which it involves mediating processes. If mental practice is used at all, it should be for very short periods.
12. In the learning of some perceptual-motor skills, knowledge of results or feedback may be delayed for considerable periods, even days, without there being any loss in the resulting learning. Demonstration has some utility in the learning of some skills. The rate at which demonstrations are given is crucial in determining their success.
13. Skills may improve over long periods and there are instances where there have been increments of skill over several years. Even when the person has reached what he believes is his limit of skill, frequent practice is necessary in order for the person to stay at his peak.
14. Stress on the performer is defined as the extent to which he is loaded with, or overloaded with, information from the task itself. Excessive inputs of information to the operator of a piece of equipment produce stress and generally also produce inefficiency. Very low inputs of information also produce inefficiency. Examples of the latter kinds of tasks are vigilance tasks. Perceptual-motor tasks are performed at the peak of efficiency, when the task provides neither a very low nor a very high input of information, but an input at the intermediate level.
15. Motor skills involving continuous tasks are retained, almost without loss, over a period of many years. Discontinuous tasks are less readily retained, perhaps because they contain more information than continuous tasks, and do not involve as much overlearning.
16. Psychologists have long been interested in the aptitudes involved in the learning of motor skills. Motor ability appears to be fairly complex and involves a number of distinct components. Those

that have been identified have been named as reaction time, tapping ability, psychomotor coordination, manual dexterity, finger dexterity, psychomotor precision, steadiness, motor kinesthesis, aiming, and ambidexterity.

CHAPTER SIX

Perception and Perceptual Learning

THE PSYCHOLOGY OF LEARNING HAS LONG FOCUSED ON RESPONSES, because responses are readily observable and tangible events, but only a very limited knowledge of behavior can be derived from such observation alone. Those psychologists of the past who adopted the language of physiology recognized that responses were not enough to constitute a science and stimulus events also had to be considered. However, the concept of a stimulus in psychology has always been a little vague.

For the most part, stimuli have significance because they are interpreted in a particular way. In a sense, an organism is always responding to the particular interpretation it makes of stimuli. The frog whips out its tongue and catches a small flying insect because it has a mechanism, built into its nervous system, that permits it to discriminate between small objects to be caught and small objects to be disregarded. If the frog's information system classifies the object in its field of view as one to be whipped into the mouth, then the correct reaction ensues, for frogs are built that way. The frog probably has first to analyze information about objects to which it does not respond with its tongue as well as those objects to which it does respond in order to classify objects into those to be responded to and those not to be responded to.

Although psychology has long been influenced by the language of physiology, there are many who take the position that such a language has very little utility for developing a science of behavior. In recent times, some psychologists have taken the position that more is achieved by viewing the human, not as an organism making stimulus-related responses, but as a system concerned with the handling of information. One can view the human as a creature living in an information-filled environment, from which some information is taken in and utilized in one or more of a number of different ways.

In this chapter we are concerned with human information analysis and reception. Some of the knowledge possessed about this process has been derived from the physiological study of the nervous system, and will be reviewed in a later chapter on this subject. The knowledge presented in this chapter has been derived from studies of how man handles the information presented to him. The general plan of these studies is to present subjects with some source of information, that is to say, to provide some inputs of information and then to study some outputs, along with the processes through which information is utilized, transformed into different forms, and utilized. Discrepancies between inputs and outputs provide knowledge of how the information has been handled.

The Collectors of Information

The nervous system collects information both from sources in the external environment and from sources within the body. The basic collectors of information, the sense organs, are extensions of the nervous system that are particularly sensitive to changes in their surroundings. This statement can be better understood by knowing that, in the developing human embryo, the eye begins as a bud that grows out of the primitive nervous system and consists at first of cells that are much like any other nerve cells. As the eye grows, and as the cells multiply within it, they become progressively more specialized in the function they perform, but they still are essentially a part of the brain structure. Much the same story can be told about the other systems of sensitive cells that handle the reception of information.

The sensitive cells that receive information are organized into five main systems, as Gibson (1966) has pointed out. Within any one of the systems, many different kinds of sensitive cells may be involved. The sensitive cells, called receptors, are not arranged so that one kind of cell, and only one kind of cell, is found in only one of the systems. Generations of thinkers since the time of Aristotle have become involved in arguments about how many different senses there are, and in recent times much of this argument has revolved around the question of how many different sense cells there are. The question is not an important one and it diverts attention away from the fact that the receptors are only components of information-gathering systems. Indeed, it is not too meaningful to talk of the senses, for a much more meaningful concept is that of an information system or a perceptual system, as some prefer to say.

Gibson takes the position that there are five major information systems related to the human's orientation to his external environment. These systems are the visual, the auditory, the haptic, the taste-smell, and the basic orienting system. Each of these five systems consists of far more than a collection of receptors that wait passively to receive information from the environment. They are active systems for the collection of information.

Let us consider further the concept that each one of the five systems is an active information-gathering system. The visual system, for example, is not just a retina on which a picture of the outside world imprints itself. It is an extremely active system, for the eyes are designed to rotate in their sockets and continuously scan the world, first in one direction and then in the other. Watch the eyes of a person walking down the street. They are not fixed in a position looking directly ahead of him; they scan fairly large sections of the environment. When the eyes are viewing a newspaper, they stop at various points across a page, and sometimes they move along a line, stopping at perhaps two or three points. The eyes form a part of a scanning system. The scanning of the environment by the visual system is also aided by the fact that the head and body can turn so that more can be taken in than would be possible if the system were static. The eyes do not just wait for information to arrive; they are involved in an active search for information. Thus the visual system must be considered to include not only a set of light-sensitive cells in the retina and the general structure of the eye, but also a very complex muscular component and the nervous network that coordinates the muscles.

The auditory system has much less capacity for scanning the environment for information than has the visual system, and this capacity is notably less in man than in other higher animals. A dog has the capacity of turning its ears and will typically move them in order to pick up particular sounds. Man has negligible capacity for orienting his ears, but he does turn his head in order to adjust the strength of incoming signals.

The haptic system is a highly complex and active exploratory system involving touch receptors in the skin and also an extensive system of receptors in the joints and muscles. This system has related to it a musculature that makes it possible for the person to actively explore the world through the touch system. Watch a person in a department store pick up a china ornament that he wishes to explore further. He will handle it, run his fingers over its general contour, and gently feel the texture of its highly polished surface. The examination of the object is an active, not a passive process. The exploratory process involves much more than the mere stimulation of the receptors in the skin by the surface of the object handled. Movement is involved, which provides information about shape, and this information is picked up by the receptors in the muscles and joints through which the movement is executed. The adult learns to acquire a great amount of information about shape and texture by the visual inspection of objects, but the need to explore through the haptic system still remains strong, a fact which is evident from the "Please do not touch" signs so prevalent in department stores, museums, zoos, art collections, and flower shows. Man has considerable difficulty in controlling the natural exploratory activity of his haptic system.

The taste-smell system represents a single basic system relatively underdeveloped in man. The receptors are cells that are highly sensitive to certain chemical substances and, indeed, as a detection system, the taste-smell system is often comparable in sensitivity to many microchemical techniques. The system permits a limited amount of exploration when substances are placed in the mouth. Watch a young child who is given a new food. He will roll the food around in his mouth to bring it into contact with the various sensitive membranes. He may also fill his mouth until it is stuffed, as if to stimulate as many taste buds as possible. Exploration by the taste-smell system is also facilitated through the hand, which, in the case of the young child, tends to bring to the mouth every object grasped as if to explore it more fully. Although the muscles of the tongue are those that form the essential component of the taste-smell system, the muscles of the arm and hand, and other muscles too, may function as components of the system. Objects must be brought to the mouth before they can be explored by the mouth.

The main organs of the basic orienting system are two sets of three canals, one on each side of the head in the inner ear. These organs are not a part of the hearing mechanism, although they are located close to it. The main function of these organs is to respond to sudden movements of rotation, such as occur when there is a loss of balance. The information provided by this system brings into play righting reflexes, which then keep the individual right side up to the world and restore his balance. The orienting system has relatively little relevance to the topics discussed in this volume.

Most of our concern here is with the first three of the perceptual systems considered here, for they are the systems through which most teaching and organized learning occur. One can refer to these and the other two systems as the perceptual systems or, if one prefers, as the information systems. Through them arrives all the information used in learning and in adjusting to the environment.

The amount of information available to the perceptual systems is always very large. Indeed, it has been said that all the information that can be provided by a single glance at a scene of the countryside is so large that it could not be recorded by the human memory system or in any artificial memory system so far developed. Such a scene would include an immense amount of detail about the exact position of each leaf on each tree, the location of each blade of grass, as well as the gross features of the scene. The quantity of information at the detailed level presented each instant to the visual system is enormous. It is not only quite clear that the amount of information available to the visual system is vast, but it is also clear that only a very small quantity of this information is ever used. A parallel situation exists in the case of the auditory system. There is a very large amount of auditory information available to the perceptual system that is never used. A person listening to the conversation of another is unlikely to be able to record the precise intonation of each word, the syllables that were slurred over, the pitch of the speaker's voice, the breathing noises that accompany speech, the numerous other sources of sound that occur in almost any environment, and so forth. The perceptual systems are almost continuously flooded with information. What the systems have to do is to abstract essential information from the mass of detail, and then interpret that information. The perceptual systems are continuously engaged in information analysis, a process that must now be considered.

Information Analysis at the Sense Organ Level

Perception is taken so much for granted that it is difficult for the layman to understand that there is any problem to be investigated in the matter of how persons acquire the information they do acquire. This becomes more apparent if one considers the problem of designing a machine that will undertake some kind of perceptual task, such as that of recognizing a word printed on a piece of paper. This is a relatively straightforward perceptual task that one might design a machine to do, particularly if there are spaces between the letters. The machine would have to be able to discriminate black from white, identify the spatial location of the various sections of the black marks, and it might be designed to recognize each letter by comparing the shape of each of the printed letters with some stored shapes. The machine would have to be quite complicated even though the perceptual task involved is really quite simple. Indeed, the design of such a machine might well tax the ingenuity even of competent engineers. If the task set for the machine were the more complicated one of recognizing a particular portrait, the design of the information-processing equipment involved might well be beyond the capability of modern engineers. Yet this same recognition task is undertaken readily by creatures at a much simpler level than man. Pets recognize their owners, though perhaps not through the contours of the human features. Pigeons are able to perform the enormously complicated task of distinguishing between pictures that include the form of a human and those that do not (see Herrenstein and Loveland, 1964). Such a task is performed by the perceptual system of the pigeon, although the total weight of the pigeon's brain is less than an ounce. How the perceptual system or systems take in the information available, sort out that which is necessary for the solution of the problem at hand, and analyze the information in order to arrive at some decision is the very difficult problem we must now consider. Some knowledge is available concerning how this is accomplished, but our information about this is far from complete.

The analysis of information begins at the sense-organ level. The eye, for example, has a capability of analyzing incoming light into different colors. The retina can also locate the position of particular points of light. When one is looking straight ahead, a point of light from a source to the right will strike a different part of the retina from a point of light coming from the left. The arrangement of light sources in front of us corresponds to the arrangement of light in the corresponding image on the retina.

The ear is a mechanical analyzer of sound. The sound-sensitive receptors are motivated by vibrations of a membrane known as the basilar membrane, but different parts of this membrane vibrate most vigorously to sounds of particular pitch. The basilar membrane can take a sound to bits and analyze it in terms of its components, much as the retina takes light apart and analyzes it into color components.

The haptic system also has a complex system of analyzers. The system can analyze various aspects of touch into such components as temperature, roughness, shape, and so forth. One knows that an object is both hot and rough because, when it is touched, heat-sensitive cells in the skin are activated in it and so also are touch-sensitive cells, intermittently activated to indicate roughness. All the details of how the information provided by an object in contact with the skin is analyzed are not yet clear, but there is no doubt that the receptor system does undertake an extensive analysis of the incoming information that is then passed on to the higher centers of the nervous system.

Other analyzing mechanisms occur in both the taste-smell system and in the basic orienting system, but we will not consider these at this time.

The kinds of analyzer mechanisms mentioned here are characteristic of the human, but other analyzer mechanisms exist at the level of the sense organs in other living creatures. In the chapter on the nervous system, it is pointed out that the retina and optic nerve of the frog have analyzer mechanisms that permit it to identify certain kinds of objects having food value. The human probably does not have such mechanisms at the sense organ level.

Coding at the Receptors

Information arrives from the environment at the receptors as light waves, sound waves, mechanical pressure, and in various other forms. The receptors function as devices that engineers call transducers, that is to say, devices that change energy from one form into another form. The energies from the outside world, if they have sufficient impact on the receptors, result in the production of nerve impulses that then travel up the sensory nerves towards the central nervous system. The change in the form of energy that occurs at the receptors is also sometimes referred to as a coding process, for the pattern of nerve impulses produced represents, in some way, the pattern of impact of the energies of the outside world on the receptors. As the reader will find in the chapter on the nervous system, the nerve impulses are generally all or none and, along any nerve fiber, are of uniform strength.

Nerve impulses cannot vary in size in any particular nerve, they can only vary in frequency. In the case of most receptors, the stronger the stimulation, the greater is the frequency of the impulses that pass up the nerve fiber leading from it. In other words, the intensity of a stimulus is coded into frequency of nerve impulse. The exception to this general rule is found in the case of the auditory nerve in which the intensity of the stimulus does not produce any change in the frequency of impulses along the particular fiber that leads from a particular receptor. A stronger sound stimulates more nerve fibers.

This is not the entire story of the coding of information by the receptors. Indeed, physiological coding is much more complicated, and several factors of great psychological importance have been identified. One is that the higher centers of the brain can depress the sensitivity of the receptors. Thus a receptor may not react and code information because it has been inhibited from doing so by the higher centers.

Other kinds of coding also take place. One of these is known as lateral inhibition, and probably takes place both at the sense organ level and within major sensory nerves. Lateral inhibition is a tendency for activity in one nerve to inhibit activity in neighboring nerves, or for activity in one receptor cell to inhibit activity in neighboring receptor cells. This may not seem to be a particularly important feature of the operation of the nervous system, but in the case of the visual system it has very significant consequences. One of these is that it tends to produce a great accentuation of boundaries and edges in the visual field. This accentuation of edges and boundaries is very important for ordinary behavior. The success of one's negotiations around the environment are highly dependent on being able to determine the boundaries of objects. It would be difficult to find one's way through a door without paying close attention to the boundaries of the door frame. One could not pick up an apple on the table with smoothness and ease were it not for the fact of knowing precisely the location of the boundaries of the apple. Our negotiations with the environment are enormously dependent on our ability to locate the boundaries of objects.

Although this effect of the accentuation of boundaries of objects has been discussed here as a physiological effect produced by lateral inhibition, it does have its psychological parallel. Visual materials developed for instruction are commonly produced in such a way that they present only boundaries. The typical black and white sketches used for illustrating textbooks are of this character. They too accentuate boundaries. They are highly informative because they accentuate the characteristics of objects that are the most significant, namely, the edges and boundaries.

Psychological Coding of Sensory Information

Information undergoes a complicated process of physiological coding as it is received by the receptors and is conducted to higher levels of the nervous system. In the higher levels of the nervous system very complicated kinds of coding take place, which can be described in psychological terms. A form of coding in which there is the greatest interest at the present time is that which involves the reduction of perceptual information into words. In simple terms, if I look at a dog and say to myself, "That's a fine Doberman!", I have coded the visual information into words. Much of the information received through the perceptual systems is coded into a word form. The information is converted into something like inner speech and is probably often stored in that kind of form.

There is considerable controversy concerning the nature of the inner verbal activity into which information is often converted (see Wickelgren, 1969). The words may not be actually articulated. That is to say, verbal coding may not involve actual muscle movements of the vocal cords and related structures, and it may involve only activity strictly within the nervous system. It does appear to be more closely related to speech as heard than to verbal material as seen. Also, the information thus coded appears to be retained in its verbal form rather than in any other form. Thus, if I meet Jones in the street, and say to myself, "There's Jones!," I am likely to retain that piece of verbal information, and relate it later to my wife, rather than retain the actual visual information. Verbal coding is a kind of shorthand for the recording of memories. The process of verbal coding is of the greatest significance in understanding man's extraordinary intellectual capacities.

Figure and Ground

Although a vast amount of information arrives at the perceptual system and is picked up by the receptor system, only a small part of that information becomes available for use. Sperling (1960) has stated this fact in an interesting way by saying that we recognize only a small part of what we see. Much the same fact was presented in entirely different words half a century ago by the Gestalt psychologists who said that the perceptual field was always separated into a figure and ground. The part of the perceptual field called the figure was a part that appeared highly structured and which the person recognized as the object of his attention, and the ground was the undifferentiated background of vague detail against which the figure was contrasted. In viewing a particular object, one sees it as standing out against an undifferentiated and quite amorphous background.

What is structured in the visual field changes from time to time. One looks at one object and then looks at another. The visual environment is continuously scanned and different objects become figure against the ground.

The structuring and recognition of some object as figure in the perceptual field is sometimes referred to as the development of a percept. It is not an instantaneous process at all, even though in the case of familiar objects, the structuring is rapid. This statement might suggest that a brief viewing of some object, say for one tenth of a second, would not permit a full perception of the object to occur, but it actually does. A brief glance at a scene for one tenth of a second permits one to recognize many objects, even though object recognition may sometimes take as long as half a second. This perception and recognition is possible because, although the sensory impression is brief, it leaves behind a trace from which information can be read. Evidence for the existence of such a trace is discussed in the chapter on memory. In a sense, the trace is a very short term memory that holds information for not more than about two seconds. The existence of such a sensory trace has long been recognized by psychologists and has to be introduced for understanding many phenomena related to perception.

Some structuring takes place without learning, but the structuring is primitive and is almost devoid of meaning. This was demonstrated a long time ago by the German ophthalmologist von Senden (1960), who became interested in the psychological problems of patients who gained vision, for the first time, as adults, as a result of a corneal graft. These patients all had had opacities in the cornea virtually since birth and gained vision when their own opaque cornea was replaced by that of another human eye. Von Senden was particularly impressed with the fact that when these patients recovered from surgery, with optically perfect eyes, they were still unable to use vision. Indeed, some of them never did, but continued to live as if they were blind people. Others found the impact of the visual world so bewildering and frightening that they would avoid opening their eyes when the scene was complex, as it is on a crowded street, but would venture to use visual information only in the security of their own homes. From the point of view of the present discussion, a very important point brought out by von Senden was that one of the few positive things the recovered patient could do was to be able to say that there was an object in front of him. He could be shown a simple object, such as a piece of board cut into a square, and the patient could say that he saw an object in front of him, but he could not say that it was a square. The data indicate that the visual world can be structured in some kind of way even before the individual has learned to identify the details of what he sees. Newborn infants show some evidence of being able to structure their visual world, even though they clearly cannot respond to the details or discriminate shapes. For example, an infant as young as a few days will fixate a bright source of light but it could not discriminate a square source of light from a round source.

The structuring of particular objects as figures takes place so rapidly that only in the last fifty years have psychologists come to recognize that a process is involved and that the process takes time. Several different techniques have been developed to order to slow up the process of perceptual structuring and make it amenable to study. One procedure developed has been to show a person an object or scene for a very short time and ask him what he sees. Then the object or scene is shown again and he is again asked what he sees. This is done again and again until a clear perception is achieved. In this way the development of a percept can be studied. The technique is not quite as straightforward as it may seem, for even after a person has had a brief glimpse of an object he still retains a representation of it in what we call his mind's eye. Conditions have to be arranged so that the effect of this delayed internal representation of the object is minimal. The device used for making such short presentations is called a tachistoscope. Such devices are generally designed to provide very short presentations of material of the order of one thousandth of a second or less.

An illustration of research on the development of perception utilizing this device is found in the work of Haber (1969), who exposed words, one word at a time, for a duration of only a few milliseconds. The subjects were told that a single word would appear for a very short interval, that they were to try and see the word and all the letters of which it consisted. On the first exposure the viewers would generally report that they saw nothing. Then the same word was flashed on the screen again, and then again repeatedly. After a few repetitions, the subjects would report seeing parts of letters. Then one or more complete letters might be seen. Oddly enough, a person might report seeing a particular letter, clearly and unequivocally, on one exposure, and yet on the next exposure the letter could not be seen at all. Finally, the entire word would be seen. In that final stage the subjects would report that they could see the entire word very clearly together with all the letters. If all the exposure times are added together to the point where the word is clearly seen, the total exposure time is only about fifty milliseconds. Presumably, the recognition of common and familiar objects takes place at about this speed, which gives the perceiver the impression that perception is instantaneous. However, the data of Haber indicate that perception takes place through a piece-by-piece analysis of whatever is presented to the senses.

Another and older method for slowing up the perception is to provide material that is difficult to structure, such as an ink blot, and then study the slow emergence of the percept or percepts that gradually emerge. Allport (1955), who has made a classic review of the historical literature on the subject, and more recent writers too, all take the position that the structuring of all inputs to the perceptual systems is preceded and accompanied by a state of expectancy. Solley and Murphy (1960) have elaborated on this idea. Each individual is characterized by a host of expectancies of what he is going to perceive at a particular place and a particular time. We awake in the morning and expect the alarm clock to go off, we expect that the sun will be just above the horizon, we expect to hear the sounds of breakfast being prepared, and we expect to hear a chatter of voices from the family preparing themselves for the day. The ordinary control of behavior involves matching expectancies with actual inputs to the perceptual systems. If we awoke and the sun was shining, but a deathly silence devoid of the rumble of traffic met our ears, we would be immediately aroused into action to determine why there was a discrepancy between expectancy and perception. This continuous matching of expectancies with inputs is only one function of expectancy, for expectancy also determines to some degree how the perceptual inputs are structured. One tends to see what one expects to see rather than the unexpected. Indeed, when highly unexpected events occur, one may comment afterward, "I did not believe my eyes." What this means is that the percept had a certain unreality about it because it did not conform to expectation. Also, under such circumstances, the percept may have been difficult to structure. A percept is more readily structured in terms of expectancies and may be very difficult to structure otherwise. A midwestern American may have to look several times, and give several long looks, before he will actually see the escaped tiger in his back yard. He has no expectancy of seeing a tiger under such conditions, and has difficulty in structuring the information that his visual perceptual system presents.

The perceptual systems do not necessarily structure the incoming information in a way that provides correct information about the environment. When the incoming information is structured in such a way that it leads to adaptive behavior, one says that the percepts are veridical, a word that implies that the perceptions have a certain truthfulness to them. Under conditions when the expectancies do not correspond to the inputs of the perceptual systems, there is difficulty in achieving veridical perceptions. The midwesterner into whose back yard an escaped tiger has wandered may perceive it first as a patch of brown in the flower bed, or even as a pile of fabric. Only after every attempt has been made unsuccessfully to perceive it as a common and expected object will a veridical percept be achieved, and he will see it as a tiger. Similar situations can be simulated in the laboratory in which words are flashed on a screen. The situation is arranged so that the viewer expects to see certain words, such as state capitals. Under such conditions he sees ATBAUY as ALBANY, and insists that he has seen the word ALBANY. Only after several brief exposures to the word is he able to read it for what it is.

There is considerable evidence that children's perceptions are less veridical than those of adults. One reason for this is that children have had much less experience than adults on which to build their expectancies and, in the absence of a useful system of expectancies, nonveridical perceptions are most likely to occur. Children also have difficulty in distinguishing between what happens inside them and what happens outside them. In addition, children lack sophistication in checking on the percepts they form, to determine whether these percepts are veridical or should be restructured to provide a more realistic perception of the world.

At least in the relatively mature individual, the formation of a percept is commonly followed by some kind of check on its veridicality. The hunter thinks he sees a deer, but is not sure. He waits until the brown object moves so that he can see more of it. As he sees more of it, it begins to look less deerlike. For one thing, it is too large, and when he has realized this, it no longer looks as much like a deer as it did. It begins to look like a cow, but then its head appears above the brush and it is seen for what it is, an elk. At least some perceptions involve a sequence of the formation of a percept, the checking of the percept against further information, the formation of a new percept, and perhaps then a further check. This is particularly likely to occur when the information available is fragmentary or in some way partially obscured.

In the case of perception in common situations, such a process of arriving at a final veridical perception by trial and error probably does not occur. In reading a page of print, perceptions of sections of the printed material are rapidly perceived and recognized, with considerable help from the fact that what has already been read provides expectations of what is going to be read and these expectations guide the perceptual process efficiently and smoothly. Sometimes the expectations lead one astray and cause one to perceive words other than those that are there. This is shown in proofreader's errors, in which the proofreader sees the correct word in print and not the incorrect word that is actually printed.

When there are virtually no expectations concerning what one is going to perceive, the process of developing a structured percept is slow. This happens when a person is shown an ink blot and is asked what he sees in it. The person viewing such a blot may look at it for several seconds before he says that he sees it as a butterfly or as some other object, but he does slowly manage to find some structure there, a structure that he virtually imposes on it. In order for an ink blot to be seen as a butterfly, it is necessary that the individual structure his perception with minimum help from the blot itself. This is the reason why a person's perceptions of such an unstructured visual display may throw light on other aspects of his behavior, for it reflects propensities to structure sensory information in particular ways.

A person viewing one of the ink blots develops a perception slowly, but does not typically arrive at the development of a stable percept. He tends to produce one perceptual hypothesis after another, first seeing this object, and then that object, and then still another object in the blot. The unstructured nature of the blot makes it impossible for him to achieve a final stable and veridical perception of what is there.

Although some primitive structuring occurs without learning, most structuring of perception is almost certainly learned. That such learning is necessary can be made evident by pointing to some common experiences. Listen to a completely unfamiliar language, such as Mandarin Chinese, which few Americans have heard spoken. When one first hears this language, it seems to be nothing but a jumble of noise. If one wishes to learn the language, then he must begin by familiarizing himself with some of the commonly recurring sounds and groups of sounds. When one has had some experience at recognizing the common sound components, that is to say, the phonemes, then he can begin to pick these out from the flow of sound produced by the speaker of Mandarin. At this stage, one has acquired the ability to structure perceptually some of the sound components of the spoken language, but they may as yet have little meaning. One may be able, then, to copy a sound pattern that has been spoken, an act that he could not do at first because of not being able to structure perceptually the vocalizations of speakers.

When the information provided by the environment is clear and unambiguous, veridical perceptions are most likely to occur, but when the cues are not clear, then distortions in perception are common. The perceptual process manifests a characteristic tendency to supply missing details, so that the perceiver reports that he sees a complete object even though the entire object is not presented to his senses. A simple demonstration of this is to present a small circle with a broken boundary through a tachistoscope thus ◯. The presentation has to be for a very short exposure, perhaps no more than a few hundredths of a second. Under such conditions, the person perceives not a circle with a break in the contour, but a complete circle. At a more complex level, the brief presentation of a display such as *Wxshxxxton, D. C.*, will almost certainly be read as "Washington, D.C." and the person will insist that that is what he saw. These kinds of phenomena demonstrate that perception is not just an interpretation process but an active process of constructing a representation of the environment.

One of the most important and elemental tasks in acquiring perceptual skill is that of learning to identify those aspects of form and structure that have constancy in the world in which we live. Let us now turn to that aspect of perceptual learning.

Learning the Perceptual Constancies

A child raised in a particular environment has to learn the perceptual constancies in his environment. These are the features of his environment that are of significance in his life. They are also features to which he must give a uniform interpretation regardless of the condition under which they are perceived. He must learn, for example, that the dish from which he eats must be recognized as a dish and be perceived as the same dish regardless of whether the dish is near or far away, or whether it is seen from above so that it projects a circular image on the retina, or whether it is seen obliquely and projects an eliptical image. The child has to learn to see the dish as the round dish it is, regardless of the size or shape of the image that it projects. He must learn that, despite variation in the sensory input, the meaning must always be the same. Constancies related to size and shape are of the greatest importance for transacting his business with the world around him, but there are many other constancies that he has to master. One of these pertains to the matter of the whiteness of a surface. A piece of black cloth placed in the sun is, in terms of the amount of light reflected, whiter than a piece of white paper placed in the shade, but even a preschool child will call the piece of cloth in the sun black and the other piece white. He has learned that the whiteness of an object has to be judged in terms of circumstances and the amount of light reflected by other objects in the surroundings.

The constancies of speech have to be understood before spoken language can be interpreted. The child has to learn that it is not the pitch of the sound that matters in order to understand a word, but the inflections and changes in pitch as the word is enunciated. Once he has mastered this feature of interpreting speech, he has some potentiality for differentiating words. He must also understand that the loudness of a sound is not usually a critical element in speech interpretation.

Although emphasis has been placed here on the learning of the environmental constancies, all may not be learned. Bower (1966) has undertaken an interesting experiment with infants in which he was able to show that these infants did not respond to a cardboard square, held at a distance, as though it was a smaller square than one of the same size held near to the infant but interpreted its size correctly. On the surface this evidence may be taken to imply that size constancy is not learned, for the infants were in their first year of life and had had little opportunity to respond to the size of square objects. However, the infants had had other experiences that may have taught them size constancy. One very significant experience in this connection is that they had seen their mother at varying distances and may have learned that the mother continued to have the same properties regardless of the distance. The feeding bottle had also been seen at various distances and size constancy might have been learned in relation to that object.

Another phenomenon suggesting that there may be important innate factors related to distance recognition and the resulting size constancies is the visual-cliff phenomenon, which has now been demonstrated in a wide range of living creatures including the turtle and man. The visual-cliff phenomenon is manifested in very young creatures who will avoid a steep drop such as is provided at the edge of a table. The young creature will not go over the cliff but backs away from it or goes around it if he can find a way around. Learning does not seem to be involved in the avoidance phenomenon, which depends upon some primitive judgment of depth.

Perception and Memory

Gibson (1966) has long emphasized that perception and memory are intimately connected. This is demonstrated by the fact that perception is highly dependent upon a system of anticipations, called expectancies, and these expectancies are residues of past experience and can exist only in so far as a memory system exists. Another illustration of how the perceptual and the memory systems are intimately related is that the little bit of the world we see in front of us is assumed to be a part of a total visual world that includes also everything we cannot see at any particular instant, including the world behind our backs. The immediate perception of the world has a continuity with the rest of the world and also a continuity with the past, which one cannot know in the immediate present except through one's memory. The memory systems and the perceptual systems are not two distinct sets of systems, but are highly dependent one upon the other.

The intimate interrelationship of the perceptual and the memory systems helps to account for the perceptual limitations of the young infant, who begins with no expectancies to guide his perceptions and no memories into which experiences can be fitted. This makes it difficult to imagine the nature of the perceptions of the newborn infant. Jean Piaget has speculated on this point and has come up with the suggestion that there are inborn mechanisms that integrate and give meaning to elemental experience. These he calls schema. He proposes, for example, that there is a schema related to sucking behavior that gives some kind of meaning and organization to the perceptual experiences related to sucking. Other schema are related to the other natural activities of the infant. These primitive schema are slowly added to and built upon and form primitive memory organizations.

The Identification of the Structured Figure

Let us consider the basic problem of how an object perceived as figure against a ground may be identified as a meaningful object. The various theories of how objects that have been perceptually structured can be identified have been reviewed by Neisser (1967), who points out that the oldest theory is what he calls the template matching theory. According to this theory, one may structure a tree as a figure against the background of its surroundings and then attempt to identify it by trying to match it with other representations of trees stored in memory. The representations of trees stored in memory are the templates, and if a reasonable match with one of these is achieved, then the object is identified as a tree.

Template matching theories sometime make the assumption that each previous experience is stored separately, and that the new experience is matched with the record of previous experience that best fits. This is very implausible, because it assumes that the capacity of the nervous system to store information is vast. Most evidence suggests that the nervous system does not have a vast capacity for information storage. There is, however, another brand of template matching theory that does not make such extraordinary demands upon the nervous system. The alternative template matching theory is that the traces of previous experience are not stored separately, but are somehow consolidated into a composite trace. An analogy to this is the composite photograph. The latter is produced, in the case of a composite photograph of a group of people, by photographing each person separately, and then making a print by exposing the photographic paper to each one of the negatives separately for a short time. Such composite photographs bring out differences in appearance between groups of people, such as Northerners and Southerners, vegetarians and meat eaters, and so forth. There is a possibility that an analogous kind of consolidation may take place in memory and may result in the formation of a limited number of templates. This form of template theory has plausibility and has appealed to many psychologists including Bartlett (1932), who made use of this concept in his theory of memory. This form of template theory places much less strain on the memory than would the alternative, which involves storing each experience separately, but there are difficulties associated with it. One major difficulty, which virtually eliminates it as a plausible hypothesis, is that perception takes place too rapidly to permit a process of rummaging through a large inventory of templates to determine which one matched best the immediate input. Recognition of an object is described by the human observer as being almost immediate. Although the nervous system functions with great rapidity, it could not function rapidly enough to make this form of template theory tenable. Although this may not be the common way in which recognition takes place, there is still the possibility that perception may *sometimes* involve this kind of a matching process.

A second theory, which is by far the most plausible theory of recognition, is that an object is recognized by a two-step process. The first step involves the identification of the distinctive features of the object to be recognized, and the second step requires that the particular combination of the features is used to identify the object. At first sight, this theory would appear to involve as much time as would the template theory, but this is not the case. Devices have been developed that will do this at very high speeds. For example, a device has been developed to enable blind people to read printed material, which does just this. The device makes an analysis of the features of each printed letter, and feeds the information into an analyzer, which immediately triggers a device that says the letter aloud. The entire process takes place at very high speeds. Also, the device does not have to store vast quantities of information, for only some of the information about each letter has to be stored. This theory of recognition is supported by a great amount of experimental evidence. We know, for example, that children learning to read recognize particular words by identifying such distinctive features as double letters, particular letters in particular locations, and features such as the length of a word. An animal seen in a fleeting glimpse in a forest may be identified only by its color and size, to name one common experience of recognition and identification by feature analysis. The laboratory provides much more solid evidence that recognition takes place by this kind of process. One can briefly expose pictures by means of a tachistoscope and study how the recognition of an object slowly develops. Show a child a picture of an elephant in this way for one tenth of a second. He is likely to say after this single short exposure that it must be an animal because he saw four legs. After a second exposure, he may say it has to be an elephant because it not only has four legs but it also has tusks. Thus the attributes of the object are identified and, once this has been accomplished, the nature of the object can be guessed or readily identified.

If this analysis of recognition is correct, one can readily understand how misinterpretations occur. One sees a distant figure on a street and recognizes it as that of a friend one is meeting. All one sees is an upright oblong object, but the few features identified are sufficient to reach the conclusion that it is the friend and not anyone else. Recognition is a conclusion drawn from limited fact, but the perceiver generally manages to glean enough information from the situation confronting him to jump to right conclusions. Occasionally he does not, and then he experiences a misperception. Such misperceptions are most likely to occur when only fleeting glimpses of a situation are obtained. The glimpses of an automobile accident that one catches in the fraction of a second that the accident takes to happen are typical of a situation that results in misperception. That is why witnesses so often disagree about what happened in an accident, even though they were present. They just did not pick up enough information to reach a sound conclusion, and correct perception is a matter of reaching a sound conclusion on the basis of fragmentary information. There are some cases of misperception that are not so easily handled by this theory of recognition, which will be discussed in relation to a third theory of recognition still to be considered.

The chapter on the nervous system provides important additional evidence supporting the attribute analysis theory of recognition. In that chapter substantial evidence is cited showing that many creatures have built-in mechanisms for recognizing particular features of the environment.

An interesting question is whether the mechanisms that analyze the features of an object all operate simultaneously or whether they work one after another in a step-wise fashion. Perceptual recognition would be a very slow process in the case of recognizing objects where many attributes had to be identified, if recognition took place through attributes being identified one at a time. However, it also seems unlikely that all analyzing mechanisms operate simultaneously. Work by Dick and Dick (1970), for example, has provided evidence that in a task involving letter recogntion, the position of a letter in the visual field is recognized before the features of the letter related to its identity are analyzed. This does not mean that all the analyzing mechanisms operate one after the other, but only that some operate sequentially in this way. The total data suggest that some of the analyzers operate simultaneously, but that some operate one after another.

A third theory of recognition, which is really two theories, is referred to as the analysis-by-synthesis theory. This theory was evolved originally by scientists working on problems of speech, where some attractive evidence can be found to support it. The essential nature of the theory is that, when the perceptual system is confronted with some problem of recognition, an attempt is made to build, inside the nervous system, a representation similar to the image of the object presented by the perceptual system. Thus, if one heard a word, then recognition of the word would be achieved through an internal attempt to build a word to be matched with the word presented. This may seem to be a roundabout way of recognizing the objects of the real world, but not entirely as unrealistic a suggestion as it may seem. Neisser (1967), who finds the suggestion to be a very plausible explanation of recognition, points out that this is exactly the kind of process used by a machine developed by the U.S. Post Office to recognize the written name of the state to which letters are addressed. The device attempts to synthesize a written address until it comes up with one that closely matches the one written on the envelope. In the case of the Post Office machine, this procedure for recognizing addresses seems to be more feasible than that of feature or attribute analysis, or template matching. The computer that performs this process of matching does it at tremendous speeds, far in excess of those of which the nervous system is capable.

There are two theories of speech recognition through analysis by synthesis. These have been referred to as the active model and the passive model. The active model proposes that speech is recognized through the listener actively synthesizing speech with his vocal cords. The synthesized speech must match the trace of the speech coming from the outside. This theory, like motor theories of thinking, does not fit the facts very well. Speech recognition takes place much too rapidly for it to have to depend upon silent speech of the listener. Also, speech recognition takes place quite well when the vocal cords are fully occupied by translating the heard speech into a different language, as in the case of United Nations interpreters, who hear in one language and speak in another at the same time. But perhaps one should not be too quick in discarding such a theory, for young children often repeat back a sentence immediately after hearing it, as if the saying of it was necessary for comprehension. Recognition and understanding may perhaps sometimes assume this form, but adults almost certainly do not use vocal or subvocal echoes of what they hear as a basis for understanding.

The latter theory of recognition through analysis by synthesis is known as the Haskins model because it was developed at the Haskins laboratories. It is to be contrasted with the Halle and Stevens model (1962), which is sometimes called the passive model. An essential difference between the two models is that in the Haskins model muscular activity is essential for recognition, but in the Halle and Stevens model the attempts to synthesize what is heard take place entirely within the nervous system. The Halle and Stevens model is much more complicated than is implied here and suggests very specific mechanisms of analysis and synthesis.

Analysis-by-synthesis theories of recognition find support in one very interesting phenomenon known as the verbal transformation effect. Warren (1968) has summarized the research on this effect. A typical way of demonstrating it is by playing the same word again and again on a loop of tape. The listener first hears the word correctly, but then suddenly he begins to hear a different word and, in a few minutes, he may report that he has heard several different words played back to him. When the word *tress* was played over and over again in one study, the listener reported hearing a variety of words such as *stress, dress, Jewish, Joyce, florist,* and *purse*. It is not that the word presented sounds like the various words reported. The words reported are heard and are like vivid hallucinations that the person cannot differentiate from reality. The transformation effect does suggest that, under some circumstances, the person does synthesize internally a representation of what he hears, but this does not necessarily imply that all recognition involves a synthesis process.

Stimulus Sampling

Visual perception appears to involve what is referred to as *stimulus sampling*. The general conception of stimulus sampling, as presented by Neimark and Estes (1967), is that all situations can be regarded as being comprised of a large number of stimulus elements, which are collectively called a population of stimulus elements. The person responding to the situation does not respond to all of the stimulus elements simultaneously, but only to a sample of them. Some research workers have speculated that the person viewing a situation samples the stimulus elements at random, while others have preferred to assume that each stimulus element has a certain probability of its own of being included in the sample. Certainly, one responds much more readily to some elements in the environment than to others, and the latter position seems to be the more justifiable. Stimulus sampling theory always makes the legitimate assumption that the perceptual system is a limited capacity system that can take in and process only a limited amount of the information provided by the environment. It is assumed that the perceptual system draws a sample from the information available. If the sample does not provide a basis for action, then another sample is drawn.

Stimulus sampling theory helps one to explain some common experiences that teachers encounter. A teacher shows a travelogue type of film to children, giving them a rapid tour of Stockholm. After presenting the film, the teacher asks the children what the town hall was like. A brief glimpse of the building had been included in the film. One child says the town hall had high brick walls. What else did he see? Well, he didn't see much else. Another child then says he noticed that the town hall had battlements on top. Did the building have any windows? He didn't notice that, but another child noticed that the building had tall and narrow windows. Different children sampled the information differently. Some obtained a sample that included information about the brick walls, and other students obtained other information. As the teacher goes over the film, it becomes perfectly apparent that each child obtained a rather different sample of information from every other child. That is one of the reasons why it is desirable to discuss, in advance of showing a film, the features that should be noticed. The discussion exercises some control over the sample of information that the children are going to obtain from the film. The procedure does not provide complete control over the sample of information that each child will obtain, but it provides some control. Also, some children will obtain a larger sample of information from a film presentation than will others.

There is evidence beyond question that the development of a perception of a complex scene requires successive stimulus sampling. If a picture of a common scene is presented by means of a tachistoscope, so that it can be seen for only a short interval of one fourth second at a time, the individual will see little the first time the scene is exposed. On the second exposure, he will pick up a few more features and, after perhaps ten brief exposures, will have a good idea of what the picture presents. What is shown in this demonstration is that on each successive exposure the individual is able to obtain an additional sample of information. The total sample needed to provide a comprehensive description of the picture cannot be obtained in any one brief viewing of the picture.

Travers (1969) undertook a study using the technique described with children aged four to twelve and found some interesting differences in the way in which the children of different ages sampled information. The older children behaved very much in the way already described. In contrast, the younger children failed to obtain new samples of information on successive exposures of the picture, but tended to report the same items on each successive exposure. It would seem that the young children had not yet learned to obtain new samples of information from each successive exposure to a scene. The children would have recognized most of the elements in most of the pictures at all of the ages studied, so it was not just that the younger children latched onto the few objects they recognized. They simply failed to sample widely the information presented. The study also led the investigator to suspect that even the more mature individuals, in the group of children studied, often failed to sample information effectively, suggesting that training in sampling skills might possibly have value.

Trabasco and Bower (1968) have provided some interesting data that show how stimulus sampling is related to learning. In their studies they have used a learning task of the type in which the subject has to learn to put diagrams including red circles into class A and those that include a blue square into class B. Now the point to note is that subjects can learn this task in a number of different ways. They may learn to classify in terms of shape (square or triangle), or in terms of color (red or blue), or in terms of both shape and color. It is also conceivable, but probably rare, that a person might put those with triangles in one category and those that were blue in another. It seems that subjects generally either sample for shape or sample for color. An outcome of considerable interest is that those who solve the problem on the basis of shape rarely note that color could also be used to solve the problem, and that those who solve it in terms of color do not notice that shape could also be used to solve the problem. When a sample of information is found to be successful, other samples of information are not sought. No particular differences could be found between learners who used just one cue and learners who used both.

Stimulus sampling theories have almost nothing to say about what the stimulus elements are that are sampled. The position of the theory is very similar to that of the theory of recognition known as attribute analysis, insofar as neither theory specifies what are the primary stimulus elements that are identified. For example, would an outlined square figure be a single element, or would it consist of a set of elements? If it consists of a set of elements, are these elements lines or angles or dots? The basic components may be different for different individuals, depending upon the training to which he was exposed early in life. That some stimulus sampling occurs seems clear, but what is sampled is very obscure.

Attention

Teachers have long believed that the key to learning involves gaining what is called the attention of the student. Although psychologists have been intrigued with attention as a concept in learning, they have had difficulty in coming to grips with the concept, for it does not suggest any direct means through which it can be studied. Indeed, considerable difficulty has been experienced in the identification of the events that take place when a person attends to some particular source of information. Russian psychologists have long been interested in some of the immediate reactions of the human being to stimuli that carry information of significance to him. The initial response is either one known as the *startle response* or one known as the *orienting response*. These two responses are very different in terms of the physiological reactions accompanying them. The initial stages of what is commonly referred to by American psychologists as attention can be described in terms of the orienting response—a response that is accompanied by dilation of the blood vessels in the head, the disappearance of the alpha waves in the brain, the dilation of the pupils of the eye, a temporary arrest of the breathing mechanism, and other reactions. The orientating response should be regarded as a preparatory response that prepares the individual to become the recipient of information. One presumes that a component of the response is a clearing away of whatever information is being held in the trace system. If the trace were not cleared, there would be a confusion between the information held in the trace system and the new information that the orienting response is preparing him to receive.

The term *attention,* as it is commonly used, implies that there is a selective process of taking the information into the perceptual system.

Many of the factors that result in the entry of information into the perceptual system are known, and are used by teachers to ensure entry. Some of the more important ones are less well recognized. The intensity of stimulus is one factor that influences whether a stimulus is or is not received in the perceptual system as information, and this is why teachers often shout in order to gain the attention of the child. Strong stimuli, whatever their content, cannot generally be blocked from entering the perceptual system. More subtle stimulus characteristics, which determine the priority of information, are those of novelty and complexity, both of which can be utilized by the teacher to gain the attention of pupils.

Novelty, as a factor in attention, can be regarded as having several components. A stimulus can be novel, in that it has not been present recently. Stimuli that have not been presented for some time have priority over those that have been more recently presented. A stimulus can have novelty attributable to the fact that it appears in an unfamiliar context. Another way of saying this is that if there a low probability of stimulus being present, and the stimulus appears, then the stimulus may be said to be novel. The appearance of a horse and buggy on a busy street has novelty today because there is a very low expectancy of such an event. An object can also have novelty, to the extent that it has never before been presented to the individual involved. In most of the literature on the effect of novelty on behavior, all of these meanings are used quite interchangeably.

In the case of all higher organisms, an object that has novelty attracts attention. That is to say, it produces an orienting response followed by behavior that can be described in general terms as behavior involving watchfulness. If the novelty is not extreme, then the attending response is also accompanied by approach behavior, particularly in those species that have become domesticated.

There is survival value in a tendency to give priority of attention to that which is novel. An animal that had a different assignment of priorities would not survive very long, for it is the novel that is most likely to bring disaster. The novel is always a potential threat, if not a real one. Wild animals tend to show a watchfulness of novel objects at a safe distance, but domesticated species are more likely to show cautious approach behavior.

The complexity factor, as a basis for attracting attention, is of both practical and theoretical significance. Travers (1970) has reviewed elsewhere the related research. There seems fairly clear evidence that, even at the very youngest ages, babies show a preference for viewing materials that have a certain degree of complexity to them. When diagrams are displayed above the head of an infant (Thomas, 1965), the babies spend different amounts of time fixating with their eyes the different diagrams. Very simple ones are viewed the least, but there is probably an optimum amount of complexity and this optimum increases with age. A similar kind of phenomenon is also evident in studies of eye movements in which the fixation time on particular parts of a visual display can be studied. Yarbus (1967), who has brought together the numerous studies made of eye movements, finds firm evidence that when the eye scans a complex display, such as that presented by a map, the tendency is for the eye to dwell mostly on those parts that are the more complex. This finding can be interpreted in another way, by saying that the eye dwells longest on those aspects of the display that present the greatest amount of information, and least time on those that contain the least information. If a display consists of a map of an island, a part of which has a smooth coastline and a part of which is quite jagged, then the eye will dwell longest on the jagged coastline and least on the smooth part. If the interior of the island is represented by a blank space, with no markings, then the eye will spend almost no time on the vacant area. Yarbus brings out in considering this matter that, in contemplating a human face, the viewer spends more time directing his gaze toward the eyes and the mouth than toward any other part. Oddly enough, the same is true even when an animal's face is involved. The eyes and the mouth appear to be a source of more information than is any other part. Attention, and processes related to information intake, are regulated to some degree by the amount of available information. In this kind of observing behavior, there is a very clear tendency for perception to be directed in such a way that it provides a continuous input of new information.

An interesting effect related to complexity has been explored by Wohlwill (1968), who prepared two sets of slides, one set showing a number of pieces of modern art and the other set showing scenes from different geographic environments. Each series of slides was scaled in terms of level of complexity. College students were given the slides and each student was allowed to view each slide as often as he chose. The study showed that the more complex the slide, the more frequently the student was likely to view it. This is what one would expect, for the more complex the presentation the more information is available and the longer time it takes for the viewer to become saturated with that information. However, Wohlwill also found that the individual's preference for a particular slide was not related in a simple way to complexity. As the complexity increased, the preference for the slide increased up to a maximum. From that point on, an increase in complexity resulted in a decline in the expressed preference for the slide. The data suggest that individuals choose to view slides not just in terms of what they like or do not like, but in terms of the amount of information present.

Studies of eye movements have produced some interesting findings related to perception. One of these is that some movement of the eye is necessary for the perception of an object. The eye does fixate objects and, in reading, the eye will appear to stop at places along the line of print. Nevertheless, these fixations of the eye are not motionless stops, for the eye continues to make slight movements called saccadic movements. These are almost like slight vibrations, and are necessary for perception. Under some experimental conditions, one can arrange conditions so that the image remains motionless on the retina. When this is done, the object producing the image disappears from view within a few seconds. The continued perception of an object requires the continued motion of the eyes. Perception is a very dynamic process and the so-called fixation of the eye is only a state of relative motionlessness.

Two aspects of attention of considerable practical interest are those involved in the two operations known as scanning and vigilance. These are referred to as detection tasks. In scanning tasks, an individual has to locate a particular item of information among a large quantity of irrelevant information. Such tasks in the laboratory may involve the identification of particular letters of the alphabet in long strings of random letters or in pages of meaningful printed prose. Pupils in schools are often involved in scanning tasks when they leaf through books searching for information on particular topics. Skill in scanning is, obviously, a very important one and research on scanning has considerable potential value for educational practice.

Much of the work on scanning behavior, up to 1970, has been summarized by Travers (1970). The research shows that scanning is a highly trainable skill. A second important finding is that it is much more efficient to scan material searching for two or more items at the same time than it is to scan for a single item. The workers in newspaper-cutting services demonstrate this phenomenon, for they are able to scan newspapers, at high speed, searching for information on a large number of different topics simultaneously. At least one study has shown that young adults can scan for ten different items of information as rapidly as they can scan for a single item. Even among children of elementary-school age, research has shown that they can scan for two items of information as rapidly as for one, and it is possible that they might be able to scan for many more items simultaneously and with equal speed and efficiency. These findings should, perhaps, be applied with caution in that they have been derived from research using rather simple types of material. Scanning a book for information about some broad topic, such as the behavior of birds, may be a somewhat different task from that involved in scanning a page of type and identifying all the letters *e*. Indeed, the task of looking for the letter *e* in a string of random letters is different from that of looking for the same letter in prose. In the latter case, the silent *e* tends to be missed.

Scanning tasks can take place at enormous speeds. Many persons looking through printed material for particular categories of information may cover material at several thousand words per minute. How this is accomplished is far from clear, although some information is available. In order to discuss some of the explanatory concepts involved, let us introduce two technical terms used by research workers in the field. The item that is searched for during a scanning operation is referred to as the target item. The material that the target item is embedded in is referred to as consisting of nontarget items. Thus if a person is searching for references to the word *reflex,* then the latter word is referred to as the target word and all other words are referred to as non-target words. One can show that a person conducting a search has to examine, to some degree, both the target materials and the nontarget materials. This can be demonstrated by giving the individual practice in picking up certain targets. Then the nontarget materials are changed. When this is done, the task of locating the target items immediately becomes more difficult, thus providing evidence that responses to the nontarget items influence the difficulty of the task. However, a logical analysis of the task of scanning shows that this has to be the case, for how could a person ever identify target items if he were not able also to identify nontarget items? The identification of target items requires that each item be identified either as a target or a nontarget item. It is probable that the nontarget items may not be analyzed at the same level of detail as the target items.

Scanning tasks are commonly referred to as signal detection tasks. The targets are the signals to be detected. Another type of signal detection task, which also throws some light on the attention process, is that known as a vigilance task. The latter type of activity involves the detection of rare and typically faint signals. A common laboratory task of this kind exposes the subject to a continuous tone, but from time to time the pitch of the tone is raised slightly for perhaps a quarter of a second. A corresponding visual task involves occasional slight changes in a spot of light. The number of different tasks used for the study of vigilance behavior is legion, but there are also many tasks involved in some occupations that also call for a similar ability to detect rare signals that are not readily detected.

Studies of vigilance behavior (see Sanders, 1967) demonstrate a number of significant aspects of behavior related to attention. The human requires a continuous input of information in order for the higher levels of the nervous system to function effectively. When the input of information is reduced, as it is in the performance of vigilance tasks such as that of watching a scope to detect a faint and rare "blip" to appear on it, the individual begins to search for other sources of input. In other words, his perceptual systems are likely to become directed away from the vigilance task and toward other parts of the environment that have greater potential for providing greater inputs of information. This is why attention directed toward the vigilance task cannot be maintained for more than a short time. The evidence also shows that the level of motivation of the person engaged in vigilance behavior is highly related to his level of performance. Presumably the same would be true for most rather boring tasks. Another interesting finding is that there are great individual differences in the ability to perform vigilance tasks. Some individuals have an extraordinary ability to engage in tasks involving a very low input of information and are able to maintain their performance at quite a high level, but others cannot. Some evidence has also been found that some individuals are better on visual vigilance tasks and some on auditory tasks, though the overall performance of a group may be the same on two types of task.

Studies of vigilance bring out very clearly the fact that the maintenance of an attentive posture is highly dependent on the amount of information that is being received, the level of motivation of the person involved, and also dispositions related to the maintenance of an attending response, which are not fully understood at this time. The missing of signals that occurs in vigilance tasks with increasing frequency as time goes by is commonly explained in terms of stimulus sampling. If a signal is not included in the particular sample of stimuli taken at the instant when the signal occurs, then the signal is missed. Because the sampling is least from those aspects of the environment that provide the least information, the display tends to be sampled less and less with the passage of time. Sampling theories of perception have value in explaining all kinds of perceptual failures (see the paper by Wolford, Wessel, and Estes, 1968).

Incidental Learning

The concept of attention implies that the perceptual systems can be set to take in information from a narrow region of the environment. Does this mean that no other information can be derived at the same time from other regions of the evironment? This problem is known as the problem of incidental learning. The earlier writers in the field contrasted *incidental* learning with *intentional* learning. They argued that learners undertake tasks with intent to learn and, while learning what they intend to learn, they also acquire and retain other information about other aspects of the situation. This other information acquired is referred to as the material incidentally learned.

This definition turned out to be far from satisfactory. One difficulty was that of determining just what the individual originally intended to learn, for during learning his intentions may change. If the material is verbal printed material, he may begin by intending to remember the words, but then he may become bored with this task and begin to note the characteristics of the printing and type face. When he does the latter, he would be considered by some psychologists as engaging in an intent to learn the characteristics of printing, but others would classify the resulting learning as incidental rather than as intentional. The word *intentional* is far from being clear and fails to provide a proper distinction between incidental and nonincidental learning.

An attempt to clarify this situation has been made by psychologists of more recent vintage who, instead of using the term intentional learning, define incidental learning as that which occurs outside the assigned task. This defines the two categories of learning in terms of the instructions given to the subjects. The procedure has a certain objectivity to it, but instructions are never entirely clear. What if a person interprets the instructions to learn a list of words as including instructions to learn about the characteristics of their printing?

Numerous different techniques have been developed for the study of incidental learning. In one of these a list of words is read to the subject, who is either instructed to remember as many words as possible, or is told that he is to listen because he is going to have to rate the speaker on various speech characteristics. If he is instructed to learn the words, then this is the assigned task. If he is instructed to be the speaker, then the words he learns represent incidental learning. In another technique, subjects are required to match words and designs. The intentional learners are told to remember the matches they make and the incidental learners are simply instructed to make the matches as best they can. In still another technique, subjects are paired and in each pair one subject is told to read the list to the second subject, who is told to learn the words. For the reader of the list, the words learned represent incidental learning. For the listener, the same learning is intentional. In all of these experimental techniques, incidental learning and intentional learning are defined in terms of the instructions given the subjects. However, subjects do not always follow instructions. Indeed, many investigators have discovered to their chagrin that subjects told only to read lists of words become so bored that they set themselves the more interesting and challenging task of committing the material to memory. Postman (1964) has discussed the difficulties involved in the development of experimental techniques in this area, but an even more critical review by McLaughlin (1968) has also summarized the findings.

The main finding conforms with expectation, namely, that in the kinds of experimental tasks used, more is learned by intentional learning than by incidental learning. This may be due to the nature of the tasks. Some psychologists, such as Berlyne (1960), have suggested that the latter finding is almost certainly an artifact of the experimental situation and suggest that, in ordinary life, the reverse may be true and more may be learned by incidental means. There seems some rather unclear evidence that most incidental learning takes place early in most tasks. Presumably, the learner begins by scanning the materials presented to him and picks up sundry pieces of incidental information. However, if the task is prolonged long enough, so that the materials have to be learned far beyond the point where they can be repeated back, then substantial incidental learning also takes place in the later stages of learning. One suspects that when a learner is forced to repeat again and again a task he has mastered, he begins to explore other aspects of the material.

There are wide differences in the amount of incidental learning manifested by different subjects, an observation that ties in closely with the common observation that some individuals pick up a great amount of information about the world around them, while others limit their information gathering to the particular tasks that they have to undertake. These individual differences do not seem to be related to measures of intelligence. Incidental learning occurs both among the gifted and among retardates.

Some of the clearest and most consistent findings with respect to incidental learning are found in the areas of motivation. As drive level or motivation is increased, there is a tendency for the amount of incidental learning to decline. Just how this effect is produced is not clear at this time and much more experimental evidence must be collected before an acceptable explanation can be advanced. It is, of course, easy to say that, under high motivation, attention is restricted to the main task, but this does not mean much. A more meaningful and testable hypothesis is that the visual perceptual system naturally engages in scanning activity, but that instructions to respond to certain characteristics of whatever is presented cut down the scanning activity, and the amount that it is cut down depends upon the drive level. Experiments could be undertaken to test such a hypothesis.

Perhaps one conclusion more than any other emerges from research on this problem. It is a conclusion originally reached by Postman (1964), namely, that no rigid line can be drawn between intentional and incidental learning. They are both part of a unified single process of information reception and short-term storage.

Perceptual Learning

The clarification of what is meant by perceptual learning has occupied the time of many psychologists over the last half century, but in recent times the main positive outcomes of such explorations must be attributed to the work of E. J. Gibson, who has devoted a lifetime to the investigation of the problem. In an article in 1953, Gibson reviewed a great quantity of research which demonstrated that in many perceptual discrimination tasks improvement seemed to occur merely through the individual's attempts to make the discrimination. If a person is given pairs of objects and is asked to judge which one of each pair is heaviest, he will slowly improve his performance even though he is never told whether he is right or wrong. The mere practice of an unfamiliar perceptual discrimination task results in improved performance. Similar improvements occur when other sensory systems are involved. The person who is given practice in reading letters at a greater distance than that at which they can be clearly read shows a remarkable improvement in his performance through the effect of practice alone. Many schemes for producing better vision without glasses depend upon this improvement effect. One should note that although improvement in such sensory tasks takes place without any kind of feedback or reinforcement, improvement occurs more rapidly when the person knows after each trial whether he is right or wrong. The important point, however, is that even though improvement may be accelerated by feedback, feedback is not essential to learning in such tasks. This learning effect is to be contrasted with the learning of motor skills, in which some form of feedback is of more crucial significance.

A second example of perceptual learning is found in exposing subjects to particular objects and events early in life, and determining the extent to which later discriminations with respect to those objects and events are facilitated by the exposure. Many psychologists have suggested that stimulation of appropriate kinds early in life results in superior cognitive development. Those who maintain this position propose that the environment of the infant in the first few months of life should contain a great variety of forms, sounds, and tactile experiences. Indeed, those who argue for such an environment have generally taken the position that the worst possible type of environment is that of foundling institutions, in which the infant sees little more than a uniform white field. The suggestion has been made that the later intellectual inadequacies of many such children may be due to their early environment.

Although the problem is one of vast significance in education, research related to it has been minimal, largely because of experimental difficulties. Experiments with humans can be conducted with children in foundling homes, but advantage has been taken only recently of such opportunities. The earlier studies conducted on animals have been reviewed by Epstein (1966).

A distinction must be made between studies of general stimulus deprivation and studies where the effect of exposure to particular stimuli is studied. The chapter on development in the Epstein book pointed out the existence of overwhelming evidence that exposure to a bleak and uniform environment, early in life, generally produced an animal with extraordinary learning disabilities. The narrower question of whether exposure to *particular* stimuli produces a later facilitation in solving problems related to those stimuli is a more significant problem to investigate, and it is to that problem that our attention must now turn.

In the typical animal experiment, an experimental group of rats is raised in cages on the walls of which forms are suspended. The forms usually consist of such simple objects as equilateral triangles, circles, or squares. In a typical experiment, just two different forms are used. Half the rats from each litter used are raised in cages with the forms suspended on the walls, and the other half of each litter are raised in cages without such objects. Some months later, after the rats have reached an age at which they are capable of being used in form-discrimination studies, their ability to discriminate the two different shapes is tested. The studies show some consistency in findings. The evidence seems fairly clear that mere exposure to the forms results in later superior ability in discriminating between the particular shapes involved or closely related shapes. It is not clear whether there are, or are not, any general benefits in shape discrimination produced by exposure to particular shapes. The evidence does suggest that exposure to one particular shape alone facilitates the subsequent discrimination between that shape and other shapes to which the animal has not been exposed.

Just what is learned during the exposure to the forms is not clear at this time. It could be that the animal learns some familiarity with the shapes, but one does not have to assume that such learning takes place at all. There is a possibility that animals brought up in an environment that is visually complex learn to use vision more than rats brought up in a simpler and more barren environment. Rats do not favor the use of visual cues when other cues can be used.

The experiments reviewed by Epstein are also important for another reason. They add to the slowly accumulating body of knowledge that reinforcement is *not* an essential condition for learning. Many psychologists already make this assumption. For example, those concerned with the study of paired-associate learning commonly assume that if the two words of each pair enter the perceptual system, then they will become associated. Those who take this position would view reinforcement as determining the kinds of tasks in which the person or animal engages, but would not view it as a condition of learning. Thus reinforcements may be responsible for a child's choosing to read a book, but they may not determine what he learns from the book. What he learns may be determined mainly by what material from the book enters his perceptual system.

Gibson and Gibson (1955) have formulated a definition of perceptual learning, which they define as *an increased ability to obtain information from the environment.* This 1955 article provided an interesting demonstration of perceptual learning, in which some of the conditions favorable to such learning were identified. In this demonstration, the material used consisted of a set of visual nonsense items. Just as one can construct nonsense items out of letters of the alphabet, so too can one construct nonsense items out of other materials. The Gibsons used small pencil scribbles for their material. A subject was shown a small scribble printed on a card and was told that some of the items in a pack of cards had the same scribble printed on them. The standard scribble was then removed and the subject was shown the scribble on each card and had to decide whether it was the same or different from the standard one he had just inspected. After going through the pack, he was shown the standard scribble again for five seconds and then went through the pack of cards again. The procedure was continued until the individual could go through the pack, correctly identifying the standard whenever it occurred. At no time was the subject told whether he was right or wrong in his judgments, but learning took place and, after a few trials, the standard was readily identified in the pack.

Gibson and Gibson were also able to show that when the standard differed from the scribble to be judged in only one respect, differentiation was difficult to accomplish, but if the two differed in many respects, then differentiation was quite easy.

The learning that occurred cannot be understood in terms of a theory of reinforcement or feedback. The subject was able to extract slowly the information necessary for making the differentiation, and this is the core and essence of perceptual learning. In a later work (1969) Gibson explored further the nature of this process of learning to extract information from the inputs of sensory data provided by the environment.

The Gibson theory of perceptual learning is what is termed a perceptual differentiation theory. The essence of this theory is that the environment has potential for supplying a vast amount of information, and the task of the perceiver is to learn to respond to certain distinctive features of this mass of information. In the case of the experiment in which individuals slowly came to recognize the difference between the standard scribble and other scribbles, learning involved a recognition of the distinctive features of the scribbles that made such differentiation possible. It is hardly surprising that the greater were the number of distinctive features that differentiated the standard from another scribble, the greater was the opportunity for discovering distinctive features that differentiated the two, and the greater were the chances of making a successful discrimination. As the scribbles were examined on successive trials, the learner became progressively more aware of the features of the scribbles that made them different from the standard scribbles.

Gibson (1969) examines a number of other situations in which exposure results in differentiation. She points out, for example, that the basic sounds of speech, referred to as phonemes, have distinctive features that makes it possible for the very young child to slowly differentiate one from another. Presumably, when the infant first hears speech, the component sounds are not at first discriminated, any more than a set of scribbles, viewed by an adult, are at first discriminated. Repeated exposure to the sounds of speech slowly permits the infant to make discriminations among the sounds. Ultimately, the phonemes can be sufficiently well discriminated that the child can recognize the distinctive situation in which specific combinations of them are used.

One can point to many common experiences that demonstrate the gradual recognition of distinctive features. For example, listen to a fairly complicated melody for the first time. The first time it is played, the distinctive features of the melody that give it a unique quality may not be recognized at all. The second time the melody is played, it may begin to be less a jumble of notes and more an organization of sounds. After a few repetitions, the melody is recognized as a sequence of notes that is completely distinctive and different from all other melodies.

Gibson offers a number of principles that account for perceptual learning. These principles have some application to the management of human learning, particularly in the case of young children, and have relevance to the task of teaching. The first three of these principles have to do with discrimination learning.

1. In the learning of perceptual discriminations, the learner discovers the differences that distinguish the sets of stimuli presented. This is a statement of the principle of differentiation already presented. A child learns to discriminate his printed name from other printed names by learning to respond to the distinguishing features. He may be able to do this long before he can learn to read the letters involved. If he goes by the name of "Lou," he may be able to learn to pick out his name from the other names merely because it is shorter than that of any of his classmates. If he is transferred to another kindergarten, in which there are other children who also have three-letter names, he may then have difficulty in picking out his name, but even though he may make mistakes, he will probably do better than he would by chance. Learning is related to the characteristics of the way his name is written. Learning related to the characteristics of an object, in contrast to learning that pertains to discriminating that object from other objects, is referred to as prototype perceptual learning. Perceptual experience results in learning dimensions of difference and also in prototype learning.

2. Discrimination learning is facilitated by emphasizing the distinctive features to be used in making the discrimination. Teachers have long used this principle. A teacher attempting to give students an understanding of what is meant by Romanesque architecture would not be content

to show the students a few examples, but would almost certainly point out the distinctive features of the style. The teacher would bring to the attention of the students the round arch, the use of heavy piers, the profuse ornamentation, and so forth. By bringing these features to the attention of the students, the concept of Romanesque architecture would be developed more rapidly than if the students merely viewed many examples of it. The students might learn to discriminate Romanesque architecture from other forms of architecture if instruction consisted only of exposure to many examples of Romanesque architecture in which the student himself could slowly identify the common features, but instruction would be much more efficient if it called the distinctive features to the attention of the student.

3. Discrimination learning is facilitated by providing first examples showing marked contrasts. Much of the research on which this principle is based comes from the study of species other than the human. Pavlov noted long ago that in teaching an animal to respond differently to a standard note, say middle C, and other notes, then training should begin with two notes that were very different indeed. After learning the coarse discrimination, then training could proceed using notes that were more nearly the same. One presumes that the same principle should be applied in human learning, although evidence to support that contention could not be located. If a teacher is trying to explain what is meant by good composition in painting, he might do better to present the student with one piece showing good composition and one piece that is, beyond any question, poorly composed. The contrast should be so marked that the students can appreciate the difference and recognize that good composition has features that give a persisting unity whereas poor composition results in a disorganized appearance. The preliminary exercise in the sequence might begin with the student identifying the distinctive features that make a difference. Later, paintings can be studied in which there are finer differences and more subtle points. Discrimination learning, if well planned, should certainly begin with high-contrast situations.

Gibson also points out other techniques that may be used to facilitate discrimination learning. One of these is to exaggerate the distinctive features to be used in the discrimination. A number of experiments have been conducted that involve the use of cartoon techniques. The essential feature of a cartoon technique is that it exaggerates the distinctive features of a face or other object. The evidence suggests that the use of such techniques in teaching may have advantages. The studies in this area are somewhat remote from teaching, and one is left wondering whether children would learn to identify famous historical characters if they first viewed cartoons of them rather than lifelike portraits. The evidence suggests that the use of cartoons would facilitate the recognition of the faces, but it is quite remote evidence.

Gibson makes a distinction between learning the features of an object and learning to use the features to differentiate that object from other objects. If a discrimination task involves both learning the features and learning to use the features to discriminate it from other objects, then the task is much more difficult than when the features are already known. For this reason, one may have great difficulty in discriminating unfamiliar objects. One may also have great difficulty in discriminating between unfamiliar foreign languages. I have difficulty in discriminating between Italian, Spanish, and Portuguese, because I have no knowledge of these languages and cannot discriminate any of the words spoken. But I do know enough French and German to have no difficulty in discriminating between them, even though they are no more distinctive than Spanish and Portuguese. Once one has picked up a few of the common words in a foreign language, one has no difficulty from that point on in discriminating it from other languages.

The role of reinforcement in perceptual learning remains controversial. Certainly, the Gibson (1969) experiments provide indisputable evidence that perceptual learning can take place without reinforcement. Gibson takes the firm position that reinforcement is quite irrelevant to perceptual learning as she defines the phenomenon. She also points out that evidence supporting the role of reinforcement in perceptual learning is derived from studies in which rather weak results were found and these results have been difficult to replicate. However, authorities do not agree on this issue and Epstein (1966) takes the opposite position.

The fact that one can point to instances of perceptual learning in which reinforcement plays no role is not a sufficient basis for denying the direct effect of reinforcement in other forms of learning. Two words may well become associated together merely because they enter the perceptual system at nearly the same time, but the events involved are very different from those involved in the acquisition of a motor skill or a problem-solving skill, in which the development of skill is highly dependent upon the consequences of performance. Indeed, even in the area of perceptual learning one can identify cases where reinforcements have an intimate relationship to learning.

The problem of the effect of reinforcement on perception is usually studied through the use of materials that can be perceptually structured in two different ways. An example of such material is shown in figure 14. The two components B and C can be fitted together to form figure A. The two components can each be seen as a separate distinct face, but the one looks towards the left while the other looks toward the right. When A is viewed, it can be seen either as face B or face C, but it cannot be seen at the same instant as both faces. One can arrange an experiment so that whenever the one face appears, the subject who sees it is rewarded, but when the other appears there is no reward. After training by

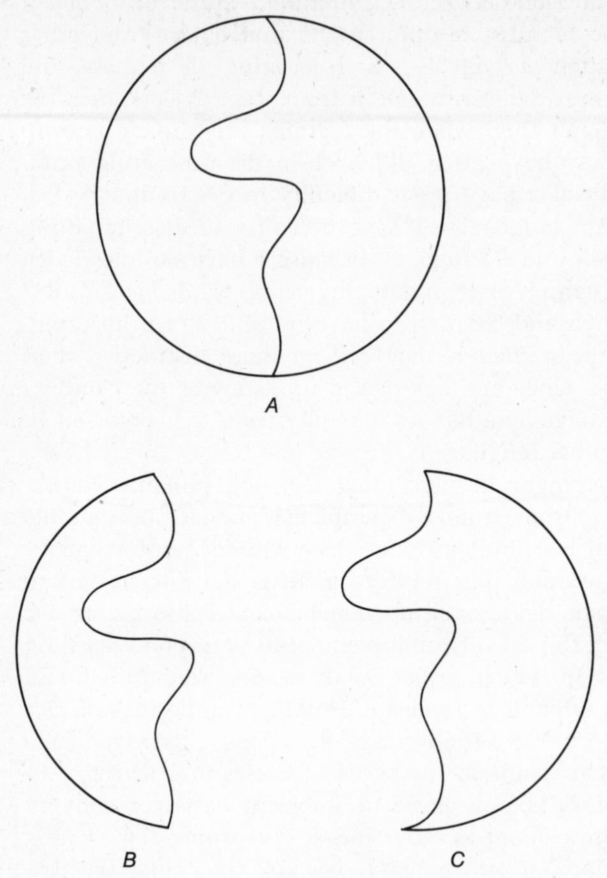

Figure 14. Either one of two profiles can be seen in A. The two profiles are seen separately in B and C.

this procedure, the subject is then shown the two faces combined (A in the figure). If reward has an effect on the way in which perception is structured, then the person viewing the combined pair of faces would be expected to see the face that has been accompanied by reward rather than the nonrewarded face. Epstein (1966) has reviewed the research on this topic, noting that the results are not entirely consistent. Some studies have shown an effect of reward on the way in which the combined figure is structured, but others have not. Epstein makes out a strong case for the proposition that the differences in the results can be accounted for in terms of the value of the rewards given. Monetary rewards of a few cents in the early 1940's appear to have been effective with college students, but by the 1950's such rewards seemed to be ineffective, probably because a combination of inflation and a new affluence of students rendered such rewards trivial. If one accepts Epstein's interpretation, one would conclude that if there are alternative ways of structuring incoming information, then the information is most likely to be structured in the way that has been followed by reward.

Epstein rightly points out that the results related to punishment are much less consistent, on the surface, than those related to reward. Many years earlier, however, Solley and Murphy (1960) were able to bring order into the studies that had been done up to that time and their conclusions still seem to be valid. The difficulty of interpreting the data stems from the fact that aversive events may sometimes sensitize the individual to the presence of particular stimuli and makes the individuals more receptive, but sometimes punishment makes them less sensitive, even to the point of ignoring the events. The crucial factor involved is whether the perception of a particular event does or does not provide a warning that the person can use in order to turn off the source of punishment. If the experimental situation is such that the perception of a particular stimulus is a signal for punishment, a punishment that cannot be avoided, then sensitivity to the particular stimulus is reduced. On the other hand, if the perception of a particular stimulus is understood to be a warning that permits the individual to take action to prevent the otherwise anticipated punishment, then sensitivity for the particular stimulus is heightened. This kind of phenomenon is also seen in the two-faces experiment, in which the appearance of one face is followed by electric shock. When the combined faces are shown, then the shock-related face is less likely to be seen than the other face, provided that there is no way of avoiding shock. If, on the other hand, the appearance of the one face was a warning permitting the individual to press a key to turn off the electric shock, then the punished face is more likely to be seen.

Summary

1. Earlier chapters treated learning from its traditional standpoint, discussing learning in terms of a vocabulary derived from physiology. This chapter discusses learning in terms of a different vocabulary derived from the field of information processing.
2. The collectors of information, the sense organs, are components of what Gibson refers to as the perceptual systems. These are complex systems, including muscular components, that engage in the active collection of information. The perceptual systems are not passive mechanical arrangements that wait for information to arrive. They engage in a search for information.
3. The amount of information available to the perceptual systems

is always very large, much larger, in fact, than the amount that the higher levels of the nervous system can use. The perceptual systems are selective in the information they use and interpret.

4. A primitive type of information analysis takes place at the sense-organ level where the incoming information is first coded. Some subhuman creatures have quite complex information analysis systems in the sense organs and peripheral nerves. Presumably, information analysis takes place at all levels of the nervous system, and each level has particular functions to perform in this respect. Information analysis at the lower levels is complicated by the fact that sensory activity can be depressed or enhanced by activity in the higher centers. Processes such as lateral inhibition also play a part.
5. Only a small part of the information available is generally structured and recognized. The part that is structured is sometimes referred to as the figure and the remainder of the information is referred to as the ground. Structuring appears to involve two stages in its development. Some primitive structuring takes place without learning. Von Senden's corneal graft patients could see objects, but they could not identify the objects. They were able to provide some structure to their visual world, but they had to learn to give meaning to the structure. At more advanced stages of development, structuring and recognition are intimately related.
6. The structuring of information involves a process of trial and check and, where necessary, repeated attempts to structure are made until the structure arrived at checks out with other data. One sees a friend standing on the street corner but, as one approaches, certain features do not check out with what one knows about this friend, so the person is then perceived as a stranger.
7. The structuring of perception is generally studied under conditions that slow up the entire process. One way of doing this is to present the subject with an unfamiliar and quite unstructured object, such as an ink blot. Another is to present the material to be viewed and structured under unfavorable conditions, such as exist when they are presented for a very short time or under low illumination. Through such experimental techniques, one can demonstrate that perception is influenced by expectancies. One can also demonstrate that, when the information provided is difficult to structure, the person may try first one way of structuring the information and then another, until a structure is found that fits most satisfactorily. A perception that leads to effective behavior is said to be veridical.

8. Much of the learning that takes place early in life involves identifying the perceptual constancies necessary for effective living. There is considerable controversy concerning which constancies are learned.
9. The perceptual systems and the memory system are intimately interrelated. Meaningful perceptions are possible only because the memory has a record of past experience in terms of which new sensory inputs are interpreted.
10. A core process in perception is the recognition of whatever is perceptually structured. Three main theories of recognition have been developed. These are referred to as template matching, attribute or feature analysis, and analysis by synthesis. Template theory has long been the most widely accepted theory, but it is vague and there are difficulties in visualizing how such a theory would work. There is also little evidence to support it. On the other hand, there is substantial evidence that there do exist mechanisms in some creatures that undertake feature analysis. The visual analysis system of the frog provides an example of how visual information may be analyzed. Nevertheless, the issue is far from settled, for there is some evidence providing strong support for the analysis-by-synthesis theory of recognition. The possibility must still be considered that recognition may take place by more than one process, depending upon the conditions involved.
11. Considerable evidence has been accumulated showing that perception involves the sampling of the information in the environment. Successive exposure to the same environment may result in different samples of information being drawn. This phenomenon can be observed when a picture is shown briefly to the same person again and again. On each exposure, he is likely to obtain new information and thus slowly build up an overall comprehension of what the picture presents.
12. The complex response known as attending has long intrigued psychologists. An important component of the attending response is the orienting response, which has been studied largely by Russian psychologists. The orienting response is a preparatory response that prepares the respondent for receiving new information. Two important environmental factors, related to the attending response, are those of novelty and complexity. Novel stimuli have priority over other stimuli in commanding attention. In addition, there is a certain amount of preference for inputs of information that have some degree of complexity, though there is a preferred optimum level of complexity. Studies of eye movements show that the eye also tends to be directed most toward those aspects

of a visual display having the greatest complexity and containing the greatest amount of information.

13. Two signal detection tasks have been extensively studied, namely, those of scanning and vigilance. Scanning tasks are of particular interest to those involved in education, in view of the importance of scanning reference works for particular items of information. A finding of significance is that material can be scanned for more than one item of information as rapidly as for a single item. Studies of vigilance behavior show clearly how the maintenance of attention requires a continuing input of information. Tasks that provide a low input of information cannot be attended to for very long.
14. Some psychologists have suggested that more useful information may be learned by incidental learning than by intentional learning, but this would be a difficult hypothesis to test. Experimentation in the area has been difficult to pursue because of the problems involved in defining what is meant by intentional and incidental. A significant finding in this area is that a high level of motivation to perform the central task is accompanied by a low level of incidental learning. However, no rigid line can be drawn between intentional and incidental learning.
15. Studies of learning in the past half century have tended to emphasize learning in which emphasis has been on the acquisition of muscular control. The study of learning intimately related to perceptual processes is more difficult to undertake. There is now overwhelming evidence that mere exposure to inputs of information can, under some conditions, produce learning. Although reinforcement is clearly related to learning in many tasks that have been studied, there are equally clearly some tasks where this relationship to reinforcement does not exist.

CHAPTER SEVEN

Problem Solving

IN THE EVERYDAY LANGUAGE OF THE CLASSROOM, ANY QUESTION THAT IS asked of a child is called a problem, and so, too, is any other set of circumstances where he has to come up with an answer. The psychologist generally uses the term *problem* with a more restricted meaning. For the psychologist, a human being is said to be confronted with a problem when faced with a situation in which (1) there is a goal to be achieved and (2) the individual does not have in his repertoire of behavior any readily available response that will permit him to achieve the goal. This definition can be applied to human behavior because one can identify whether the human does or does not have a goal to achieve, for one can ask him what he is trying to accomplish. The same definition cannot be applied to animals for obvious reasons. Hence, a more widely applicable definition of a problem would state that it is a situation in which an organism is in a state of disequilibrium (hungry, thirsty, sex-deprived, etc.) and has no readily available response that will restore equilibrium. Many other variations of these definitions have been reviewed by Berlyne (1965).

After a problem has been successfully solved, one can say that a response to the situation has been learned. When the same situation is encountered the next time, the appropriate response will be produced almost immediately, or at least more rapidly than on the first encounter. In terms of the definition given here, the situation is no longer a problem.

The solution to a problem is the response that leads to the goal. Let us illustrate this with a simple example.

Many children in the first grade if asked "How much is 2 and 2 and 2?" will say immediately "Six." This is not problem-solving behavior because the child has been asked this question many times before and has the answer. He can produce the answer immediately after he is asked the question. This is not problem solving because he knows the answer. On the other hand, one can ask the same child, "If I had six pieces of candy and wanted to divide them among three children, how many pieces of candy will each child get?" The child will probably have no ready-made answer to this question, which he may not have encountered before. Even if he knows what three twos make, this latter piece of knowledge may not help him, for children of that age cannot see that the new problem is the reverse of the familiar problem. When the child is asked to divide six pieces of candy among three children, without being given pieces of candy with which to do it, he is likely to make a wild guess or to say he does not know. He has no ready-made response available, even though he knows what has to be done. In such a situation he is said to be confronted with a problem.

If the child faced with the problem is given some encouragement, he may manage to concoct a solution, that is to say, manufacture a response that he did not have in the first place. The production of this new response is called problem solving.

Problem solving may involve behavior that can be observed by others or it may involve behavior that is internal. The child, given the problem of dividing six imaginary pieces of candy among three children, may attempt to find a solution by asking for six pieces of candy that he can then divide among three imaginary children. The child may even be able to find the solution through using six slips of paper that are viewed as make-believe candy. A few children in the first grade may solve the problem without manipulating any real or imaginary candy. They do this through performing internal operations commonly referred to as thinking, but which are technically referred to as mediating processes. Problems are typically solved in daily life through a combination of internal thinking operations and actual manipulations of things and objects.

After a person has solved several similar problems, he may discover general procedures for solving problems of that particular kind. These procedures for solving classes of problems are referred to as problem-solving strategies. Different individuals may acquire different strategies for solving problems as they pass through life and hence may show different approaches to solving the same problem.

From the definition of problem solving and problems given here, it follows that what is a problem to one child may not be a problem to another. A first grader may have to pursue a problem-solving procedure in order to find out how to divide up six pieces of candy among three children, but the second-grade child can give the answer immediately. The second grader has learned the answer and for him the situation no longer presents a problem.

The Classification of Problems

Theories of education of the last century held out the hope that education could develop general problem-solving skills through exercises involving the "hard" subjects, such as Latin and mathematics. In the present century, considerable skepticism has been expressed about the latter viewpoint and instruction in problem solving has generally been given within each subject matter area separately. Training in scientific problem solving is generally given separately from training in social studies problem solving. Psycholoigsts have been interested in finding some more fundamental classification system in terms of which problems may be grouped, and have evolved classifications of problems which do not depend upon subject-matter field. One of these psychological systems of classification that has had considerable impact on education is one advanced by Guilford (1959). Guilford takes the position that the intellect manifests itself in problem solving and that an understanding of the intellect requires an understanding of the nature of problems and a classification of problems. Guilford has a three-dimensional classification of problems. He states that problems can be classified in terms of the content of the problem, and he considers such categories of content as are involved in the use of figures, or symbols, or words and word meaning, and not subject-matter categories. He also states that problems can be classified in terms of the operations performed by the problem solver. Such operations include those of memorizing, making evaluations, recognizing, identifying, and knowing, and also what he considers convergent and divergent operations. He also has a classification of problems in terms of their outcomes. The outcome of solving a problem may be a number, as in the case of an arithmetical problem, or perhaps the production of a complicated system, as in designing an electronic circuit. Guilford tries to squeeze all problem solutions into six categories. The Guilford classification system thus involves four categories of content, five categories of operations, and six categories of products. As every problem-solving task can be classified in terms of content, operations, and product, there are altogether 4 x 5 x 6 categories of problems, that is to say, 120 categories. A detailed discussion of Guilford's classification system and some of the implications it has for education is found in Meeker's book (1969).

The system for classifying problems has appeal, but it has not brought to problem-solving research the order that one might have hoped it would bring. There are questions whether it has been derived on a sound basis, and many would say that not enough is yet known to produce a comprehensive set of categories. Nevertheless, the system has had impact on education at one important point by including within its scope the categories of convergent and divergent thinking. Convergent thinking refers to thinking in relation to problems that have one fixed solution. Divergent thinking refers to thinking in the case of open-ended problems, that is to say, problems that have no fixed solution and where many new and original solutions are possible. This classification of problems into those involving convergent thinking and those involving divergent thinking has long had appeal to those engaged in problem-solving research. These categories have also appealed to the interests of educators, who have also long been interested in creative problem solving and who have taken the view that divergent problem solving is a creative activity. There is some evidence that the abilities involved in divergent thinking are different from those involved in convergent thinking and perhaps require separate training. Many educators have taken the position that problems involving convergent thinking call for noncreative thinking, but that problems in the divergent category involve creative thinking. Such a view is hardly reasonable. Consider, for example, the case of Isaac Newton pondering the problem of what kept the planets in their orbits. Eventually, Newton arrived at the principle of universal gravitation as the underlying explanation. The problem is a convergent one, in that there is only one possible solution, and yet most historians of science would view Newton's solution as a highly creative one. Again, if only divergent problem solving is viewed as creative, then Einstein's development of the theory of relativity would have to be classified as a noncreative act, for it is a unique solution to a problem. Such a conclusion is nonsense. Convergent and divergent thinking may call for different abilities, but the categories cannot be identified with those of creative and noncreative thinking.

A few of Guilford's problem categories have been a source of considerable research, as has been the case with the convergent and divergent categories, but most research programs related to problem solving have shown little influence of his classification scheme. Much of the research of recent years has been focused on two classes of problem. The one class is that commonly referred to as concept learning. Although concepts do not have to be learned through a problem-solving procedure, many are, both in the laboratory and in educational situations. The second class of problem is that of the anagram, a class that has less obvious relevance to education than has concept learning, but the study of anagram problem solving has provided a means of studying how problem-solving strategies are acquired. The research in these two areas has provided some clues concerning the conditions that facilitate the kind of learning referred to as problem solving.

Concept Learning

A basic form of problem solving, and often one of the elements in more complex problem solving, is concept learning. In common language, the term *concept* is used to designate what is ordinarily described as an idea, but the technical use of the term requires a more precise definition.

Systematic research on concept learning has been closely tied to the observation that living creatures behave as though they classified the objects in their environment into categories. A dog behaves as though it had classified people into those toward whom it shows friendly behavior and those toward whom it barks. The same dog classifies other objects into those to be eaten and those to be avoided. It also responds to other animals either as those to be chased or those to be played with. The very complex environment is thus simplified by being treated as though it included just a few basic categories of objects and events. All other living creatures show the same tendency to categorize their encounters with their surroundings. A child learns that certain objects are all to be included in the category *dog*, other objects are all to be included in the category *flower*, and still other objects are to be included in the category of objects that are *hot*. Each category represents a concept. Learning to place objects and events in categories is sometimes referred to as categorizing behavior.

Great advantages accrue from learning to place objects in categories. Once a child has learned that certain objects fall in the category *hot*, then he can learn how one behaves towards all objects that fall in that category. He learns, for example, to approach such objects with caution, to place the hand near them for a few moments before deciding to touch them, to move into their vicinity if he is cold, and so forth. He learns a single set of responses to these objects that will permit him to handle effectively the entire category. He does not have to learn one set of responses to guide him in dealing with hot chocolate and another in dealing with hot porridge. A basic category of responses is learned to cope with all objects placed in the category *hot*. If the child did not place all such objects in the same category, then he would have to learn a separate response to each of the objects, and life would be vastly more complex than it is. Classifying objects in the environment into categories, so that the objects in any one category are all equivalent stimuli, has the effect of simplifying transactions with a complex environment. Categorizing behavior is simplifying behavior.

A concept is a category within which objects or events are treated as equivalent. Animals develop concepts as do humans. Pigeons can be trained to discriminate between pictures that include human figures and those that do not. In terms of the definition given here, the pigeon thus trained can be said to have a concept of a picture containing a human in the sense that it can correctly classify such pictures. In the case of the human learner, the acquisition is closely related to the acquisition of language, although language is not necessary for concept learning.

Many words denote concepts. The word *house* does not refer to any particular instance of a house alone, but it refers to the category into which all houses are classified by the user of the term. One might say that the word *house* refers to one's idea of a house, which is another way of saying that it refers to a category. The word *move* also refers to a concept involving objects that have changes in space displacement with respect to time. However, not all words refer to concepts as they are defined here. The term *point* as it is used in Euclidean geometry refers to a position in space that has zero size and, hence, cannot be seen. One can show a person a dot but one cannot show a person a geometrical point. There is no possible physical representation of a point as defined by Euclid, and so there is nothing to place in the category of *points* that can be distinguished from *nonpoints*. Anything of visible size that can be classified is, by definition, not a point, but a dot. In a popular sense we have a concept of a point, but in terms of our present definition, we do not.

Learning a concept is a form of problem solving. A child faced with the problem of what is to be classified and what is not to be classified within the concept of a *snake*, has the problem of finding out why worms are not snakes and neither are eels. Discovering the meaning of most concepts involves problem solving. At a more advanced level, a student of botany may be confronted with the problem of classifying a plant. If he has learned the concepts involved in the botanical classification system, then he has the key to the solution to his problem. If he has not learned these concepts, then he has to learn the concepts, and the learning of each involves learning the solution to a classification problem.

The idea of a concept considered here was originally developed by Clark L. Hull as a part of his doctoral dissertation. Later, pioneer research was undertaken by Jerome S. Bruner that laid much of the groundwork for present research. On the contemporary scene, a substantial fraction of the research in the area is being produced by Lyle

E. Bourne, who has also provided an excellent summary of research up to the mid-sixties (see Bourne, 1966). A slightly later summary is that of Byers (1967). The research in this area is significant to educators in that it provides some information concerning the conditions that facilitate concept learning and the conditions that interfere with it. First, however, it is necessary to introduce some further terms in order to be able to understand the research and the findings.

The Basis of a Category

Objects and events are categorized on the basis of their attributes or characteristics. Squares form a category because all instances have four equal sides and four equal internal angles. Objects that do not meet these two conditions are not squares. Most objects that fall into a particular category designated by a word must have many particular attributes to be so classified. An object that is classified as an orange must be round, derived from a citrus tree, of a particular color, cellular in structure, and so forth. Generally, in classifying an object into a particular concept category, one does not check on all the necessary attributes. If I see round objects that are orange in color in the fruit store, I will classify them as oranges and neglect the possibility that they may be manufactured of plastic or that they may be some rare fruit that is quite different from an orange. The attributes of a fruit are quite simple to identify in contrast with the attributes of, say, a dog. As dogs come in all kinds of sizes, shapes, and textures, the attributes that identify a dog, as a dog, are subtle and difficult to pin down, and probably very large in number. Despite the fact that most of us cannot identify these attributes with any accuracy, we can make a flawless classification of animals into those that are dogs and those that are not dogs.

In order to experiment with concept learning, psychologists have devised simple learning tasks in which the attributes involved can be clearly identified. In one such simple task, the objects to be classified consist of triangles and squares of two sizes that are colored either red or blue. As there are two different shapes, two sizes, and two colors, the total number of objects that can be made by combining these is $2 \times 2 \times 2 = 8$. A more complex set might involve four different shapes, three different sizes, and five different colors, providing a total number of sixty different objects. In most experiments, one of these objects is drawn on each card and the cards are shown to the learner in succession. He is told that some of the objects are "right" and some are "wrong." His task is to find out what makes a "right" object right. At first he can only guess, but he is told whether his guess is correct or incorrect. Ultimately, he will solve the problem and be able to indicate immediately whether an object belongs in the "right" or "wrong" category. He has learned what makes an object "right."

In such an experiment, the experimenter decides upon the attributes that are to make an object right. He may decide, arbitrarily, that all the objects that are blue are the "right" objects, or he may adopt a more complex rule and decide that only objects that are both blue and square are to be regarded as "right."

Two kinds of problems may be involved in such concept-learning tasks. One problem of the learner may be that of identifying what the relevant attributes are that have to be used in identifying a card as right or wrong. In such a task he is told, for example, that two particular attributes have to be present to make an object *right* and he must find out what they are. After several trials, he may conclude that, in the particular experiment, color has nothing to do with the classification, but that size and shape have, and that all "right" objects involve large triangles. In another experiment he might conclude that both color and shape were the basis of classification, but that the size of the objects had nothing to do with it. In such a case, color and shape would be referred to as the *relevant* attributes, and size would be called an *irrelevant* attribute. In a second type of problem, the learner may be told what the relevant attributes are, and his task is that of finding out the relationship of the attributes to the designation of an object as "right" or "wrong." He may have to find out, for example, that "right" objects are either blue and triangular or red and square. When he discovers this rule, he has solved the problem, which is said to involve rule learning.

Any one of the following rules might be the key to the solution of a concept-learning problem, but his task is to find the rule that makes it possible for him to classify the objects correctly on every occasion:

All right objects and only right objects are both blue and red.

Only blue *or* red objects, or objects both blue and red, are right.

Many rules can be devised. One rule is referred to as the conjunctive rule, when both attributes have to be present. The first of the rules listed above is the conjunctive rule. Another rule is referred to as the disjunctive rule, and involves an *either or both* kind of statement. The second rule listed is the disjunctive rule.

Many common concepts illustrate these rules. For example, consider the concept denoted by the word *wine*. Essential attributes of wine are that it is liquid, that it is derived from a fruit juice, and that it contains alcohol. If any of these characteristics are not present, then the substance is not wine. The attributes follow the conjunctive rule. The legal system has numerous examples of concepts that involve disjunctive rules. The concept *contempt of court* is defined by many different behaviors, including that of failing to show proper respect to the judge, refusing to answer questions while under oath, and refusing to obey the court. Any one of these attributes on the part of a witness may result in his being convicted of contempt of court.

When the rule that relates attributes is the conjunctive rule, then one commonly refers to the concept as a conjunctive concept. When the disjunctive rule applies, then one is dealing with disjunctive concepts. The conjunctive rule and the disjunctive rule are two common rules that have to be discovered in concept learning, but there are other rules also that may have to be discovered.

In some concept-learning experiments the materials used have resembled more closely the kinds of materials used in the classroom. In one set of experiments, the materials used were cards presenting flower-like objects. The sketches of flowers were especially prepared so that the flowers were characterized by attributes such as the number and shape of the petals, the position of the flower on the stem, size of flower, and other rather obvious attributes. In the experiments, the experimenter decided, in advance, the characteristics of "right" flowers.

In the case of our experiment with sixty objects drawn on cards, in which the learner has to discover the basis for calling an object "right," all the cards in the "right" category represent what are called *positive instances* of the concept, and all cards in the "wrong" category are referred to as *negative instances*. Some writers refer to positive and negative *exemplars*, which means exactly the same thing. In the case of teaching a child to identify oak leaves, one might show him a number of leaves, some of which would be positive instances, that is to say, oak leaves, and some negative instances, that is to say, leaves from other trees.

Some concept-learning problems provide redundant information. If "right" instances are always both red and blue, and if neither red nor blue is found in negative instances, then these colors can be said to provide *redundant* information. If the learner notices that red is a crucial attribute, he can solve the problem even though he does not notice that blue is also a crucial attribute. The problem can be solved by noting the one attribute or the other attribute or both attributes.

Just as one can increase the number of relevant attributes, so too can one design problems that will increase the number of irrelevant attributes. This has the opposite effect, namely, that of making the problem potentially more difficult. One can readily understand why this is so. The more features one has to examine in order to solve a concept-learning problem, the more time it takes, and also the more information one has to remember.

It now becomes evident that, at least in real life although not always in the laboratory, concept learning involves attribute learning, and rule learning. First, the learner must identify what relevant attributes are related to the acquisition of the concept. Then he must find the rule that has to be applied in using the attributes. This is not quite the clear two-stage affair it is made out to be here, for rule learning can go along with attribute identification. In conducting experiments in the laboratory, the two kinds of learning involved are generally kept separate. At the beginning of an experiment confined to attribute learning, the experimenter may tell the learner that he has to identify the two charatceristics that have to be present for an object to be classified as right, and that both characteristics have to be present. On the other hand, at the beginning of an experiment on rule learning, the person may be told that red and blue are the significant characteristics that will enable him to distinguish right instances from wrong instances, but he has to find the rule to apply so that all instances can be properly classified. The latter is a rule-learning experiment.

Applications of Concept-Learning Research

Although research on the identification of small blue squares as "right" objects may seem to be remote from anything that one recognizes a student as doing, the relationship is not as remote as first appears. In the concept-learning studies, the person involved must slowly identify the attributes that place a design in a particular class. The solution of a concept-learning problem is slow and deliberate and involves a great amount of internal activity which the learner is quite unaware of undertaking. What happens is not too different from what is believed to happen in perception, when one recognizes an object, such as a leaf from a tree. In the chapter on perception, the point is made that the recognition of an object probably requires that the brain undertake a very rapid analysis of the attributes involved and then a determination of what object could be represented by that particular combination of attributes. The latter takes place in a time perhaps less than a tenth of a second, but in the case of concept learning, the analysis of the attributes and a decision to classify the object as "right" or "wrong" require several seconds. Despite the great differences in speed, the two processes have essential elements in common. They both involve the identification of attributes and a classification of whatever is being examined. The similarity of the processes involved in laboratory studies of concept learning and ordinary recognition processes, also involving stimulus classification, suggests that laboratory research is along the right lines, and will ultimately provide information useful in teaching.

Numerous researches have been undertaken on the conditions that influence the acquisition of concepts. Many of these have been summarized by Clark (1971), Bourne (1965), and Byers (1967), who also suggest that some caution be exercised in applying the conclusions of the research in the area because it involves simplified laboratory situations and not the complex situations of daily life through which concepts are typically acquired. Nevertheless, the conclusions drawn by these reviewers from research do appear to have implications for teaching concepts to children, in view of the fact that they are highly plausible as suggestions for teaching. Some of the major conclusions are summarized as follows, after the summary provided by Clark, together with illustrations given by the present writer:

1. Concepts are most easily learned when positive and negative instances are clearly distinct and where positive instances are very uniform. For example, the concept of *good taste in dress* is difficult to teach because examples of good taste in dress vary in numerous different ways and also because there is no clear demarcation between good taste and bad taste in this respect. On the other hand, the concept of a *square* is easy to teach because the attributes of objects that are square can be readily identified and precisely defined, and a square can be easily distinguished from other geometric figures.

2. Research has shown that problems in which there is redundancy of positive attributes are easier to solve than problems in which there is no redundancy. This simply means that the more cues provided for the solution of a problem, the more likely it is to be solved.

3. A question that has some significance for teaching is the relative extent to which the learner can be expected to benefit from positive or negative instances. Bourne has outlined the history of this problem in research involving studies of learning conjunctive rules. He concludes that learners, when first brought into the laboratory, tend to derive more information from positive instances than from negative instances, even when these are so arranged that each can provide an equal amount of information about the solution to the problem. This effect seems to be due to the fact that in daily life learning is more typically accomplished by seeing positive instances. We learn what a French Provincial chair is like by studying a French Provincial chair, and comparing it with chairs of other kinds we have seen in the past. However, although the human guinea pig tends at first to learn more from positive than negative instances, this tendency disappears after he has been trained on a large number of problems in which negative instances contribute to the solution of the problem. Bourne (1968) was able to show that, on rule learning, subjects performed consistently better when there was a mixture of negative and positive instances, suggesting that the best learning situation requires a judicious combination of both types of instances.

What has been said here about the relative value to the learner of positive and negative instances does not seem to apply to the learning of disjunctive concepts.

In the case of concepts involving disjunctive rules, the learner has to attend carefully to negative instances in order to identify the attributes and rules necessary for making correct classifications and hence he is forced into using positive and negative instances. Probably, any concept that is difficult to acquire forces the learner into using all the information available, and he cannot afford to concentrate solely on the positive instances. Concepts involving disjunctive rules are generally more difficult to learn than those involving conjunctive rules.

4. Most studies show that concepts are made easier to learn by reducing the number of irrelevant attributes. However, findings in this area are not as clear as one might wish. A study by Byers and Davidson (1968) compared the effect of adding relevant information and irrelevant information to a concept-learning problem. The addition of relevant information facilitated the solution of the problem, but the addition of irrelevant information had virtually no effect. Simplified drawings may help in the teaching of concepts because they cut out all the irrelevancies which may distract the student from noticing the attributes that the teacher may want him to notice. Sometimes, verbal descriptions may help in the learning of a concept, because these descriptions also cut out most information except the relevant information.

5. Concept-learning skill increases with age. Younger children appear to attend most readily to the physical characteristics of objects, such as form and color, and this limits the concepts they can learn, but older children attend to the functional aspects of objects, namely, what they are used for.

6. Anxiety is related to concept learning. In the case of simple concepts, an increase in anxiety results in an increased ease with which the concept can be learned. However, if the concepts are complex, then anxiety has a disruptive effect on learning. These findings are closely related to the Yerkes-Dodson law (see the chapter on motivation).

7. Concept learning is facilitated if directions are given that focus attention on the relevant attributes. Thus, if a child is learning to distinguish oak trees from elms, the teacher should point out the features that distinguish the two species of trees.

8. For maximum ease of concept learning, positive and negative instances should be presented side by side. An elm leaf and a maple leaf presented alongside each other are more likely to help the student distinguish between the two than is the procedure of first viewing one leaf and then viewing another.

9. Sometimes it appears to be of advantage to present several positive instances at the same time. For example, in teaching very young

children the concept of a triangle, several triangles might be shown simultaneously so that the children can abstract from them the critical attributes of triangularity. Clark views the evidence as suggesting that four instances of a concept is about as many as should be presented simultaneously, because more instances may overwhelm the learner.

10. There is considerable evidence that concepts are better learned and are more readily applied to new situations if the learner verbalizes to himself the relevant attributes. He also gains by verbalizing the irrelevant attributes. For example, this suggests that he does not learn very efficiently the concept of African mahogany, as a wood, by merely looking at it, but he does learn effectively when he says to himself, "The wood is open-grained and a brown rust color. It is very hard and is well marked." He is also helped in remembering the concept if he says to himself the concept name "*mahogany*."

11. At least under some conditions, concept learning is enhanced if the learner can actually handle and manipulate the instances rather than if he is only allowed to view them. One would expect that this would be particularly important in teaching young children the names of classes of objects.

12. The more complete the feedback, the better the learning. A pupil gains by knowing why he is wrong as well as why he is right. Information given the pupil should be precise and complete. Any ambiguity in the information given, or any misinformation, interferes with the learning of a concept.

13. The greatest transfer to new and novel instances is most likely to occur when the original concept has been thoroughly learned through the study of many instances showing great variety.

14. Concepts should not be taught in isolation (Ausubel, 1969). The basic notion is that a pupil must be prepared for learning a new concept by providing him with a framework into which he can build it. The argument is that learning a concept in isolation limits the value of the learning.

15. Mixed methods of teaching concepts should be used. Most studies on the teaching of concepts have used highly artificial laboratory tasks, but a single study by Johnson and Stratton (1966) used methods of teaching concepts similar to those used in the classroom. The teaching methods used were (1) using a brief definition, (2) embedding the concept in a sentence, (3) showing by means of short sentences the objects or events to be included in the concept, and (4) giving synonyms for the concept. In addition, a fifth procedure involved a mixture of the four procedures, but the length of the instruction involved was the same as that in the others. Students who participated in the experiment were exposed to only one of the teaching procedures, but they took the tests designed around all five teaching procedures. The findings

were that the first four teaching procedures were virtually identical in the learning produced, but the fifth mixed method showed itself to be superior. One suspects that the reason for this is that any teacher who varies the teaching procedure and who does not get stuck in a groove is going to hold the attention of students better than one who is rigid.

One of the most interesting features of the Johnson and Stratton experiment was that there was excellent transfer from one particular learning situation across all of the testing situations. For example, a student who learned a concept through a definition was as able to identify the concept when it was embedded in a sentence as when it was identified through a synonym. It seems that concepts learned in a verbal setting are readily transferred to other verbal settings.

16. In concept-learning tasks, the learner must be provided sufficient time to assimilate the information he is given. A series of studies have now well established that a critical factor in solving a concept-learning problem, under the conditions provided by most laboratory experiments, is the post-informative feedback interval. This is the time allowed after the learner has made a guess and has been told whether he is correct or incorrect. The procedure may involve the immediate presentation of the next card with the next object, or an interval may be provided during which the subject may continue to look at the card about which he has made some judgment, and about which he has been provided with information by the experimenter. The length of the post-informative feedback interval was shown first by Bourne and Bunderson (1963) to be quite critical, because it is a period during which the subject has an opportunity to examine the object presented and try and find out why his guess was right or wrong. It is a period that permits the learner to make good use of the information provided. Rownton and Davis (1968) have shown that when the problem is difficult, the length of the post-informative feedback interval becomes more critical than when the problem is easy.

The research related to this particular problem shows the importance of providing sufficient time for the utilization of information in learning tasks. The findings carry with them the suggestion that learning cannot be speeded up beyond a certain point because the limiting factor is the amount of information that can be assimilated in a given time. Attempts to provide more information in a given time than the amount that can be successfully assimilated are likely to result in confusion of the learner rather than in increased efficiency.

17. Finally, something must be said about a matter that still remains as a controversial issue. Should the learner be presented with a selected series of positive and negative instances, or should he select the instances that he is to judge? One would expect that giving the learner freedom to select his own instances would facilitate learning, for the

person could then select instances for checking out particular hypotheses. Although this is plausible, the single study that could be located (Huttenlocher, 1962) that throws any light upon the problem came up with the conclusion that in the case of the seventh-grade children studied, the learner selecting his own instances was not as efficient as the learner who was presented with a set of instances through which he had to learn the concept. This is a matter that needs further investigation.

Strategies of Learning Concepts and the Learning of Concepts Outside the Laboratory

In a classic work on the topic of concept learning, Bruner, Goodnow, and Austin (1956) proposed that individuals go about solving concept-acquisition tasks in different ways called strategies. In a laboratory situation, a learner is presented with a complicated colored geometric pattern, and he guesses that it is a "right" pattern and the experimenter confirms the correctness of his guess. The learner then says to himself, "I have a hunch that it is the presence of a large blue square that makes it right." This is a hypothesis and represents a strategy for solving the problem. His statement to himself includes three different dimensions (size, color, and shape), and he is guessing about several different things at once. He could have approached the matter more cautiously and said, "Whether a figure is right or wrong has something to do with the color blue." The latter would have been a much simpler hypothesis than the former, and he might have been content to check out this simple hypothesis and then slowly test out the relevancy of other attributes one by one. These two approaches represent different strategies of solving concept-learning problems.

One can say at this time that, in laboratory tasks, individuals do differ in the strategies they show, but that the same person may often switch from one to another. Relatively little research has been done on strategies and their relative effectiveness, despite the fact that this might represent a teachable element in problem solving. One factor that determines strategy is the ability of the learner to retain information derived from each trial. If one is in a museum and sets oneself the task of learning the concept *Chippendale furniture*, one can approach this task in a number of ways. One might seize upon the opportunity of looking at many different pieces of furniture, subsequently checking in the catalogue whether the piece was or was not Chippendale. This procedure still leaves open many strategies, one of which is to check out one feature at a time. In the pursuit of the latter strategy, one might hypothesize that such furniture generally had ball-claw feet. One could find out whether this is a critical factor in identifying Chippendale furniture by selecting several pieces that had ball-claw feet and then looking them up in the catalogue. One could then go on to check out other features one by one. This would be a slow way of discovering how to identify a Chippendale style. A more efficient way might be that of checking out several features at once. One might hypothesize that such furniture was characterized by straight molded legs terminating in either ball-claw or Marlborough feet, serpentine or bowed fronts on chests, and delicate backs on chairs. One would then select items of furniture having these characteristics and check out the hypothesis. If the hypothesis did not check out, then a new hypothesis might be set up, including perhaps some of the same features but also including some new features, and then this new hypothesis would be tested. The difficulty with this procedure is that it is hard for the learner to keep track of all the information provided by each trial. In other words, the procedure places strain on the memory system, or, as others prefer to say, it produces cognitive strain. In the case of complex concepts, it may achieve results sooner than the one-attribute-at-a-time method, but only if the person can keep track of the information he receives.

Concepts as Organizers of Learning

Up to this point, concepts have been regarded as largely a means of reducing a complex environment to a relatively few categories and have been so defined. But this is a limited view of how concepts operate and influence behavior for, clearly, some words refer to ideas that are very much like concepts as these have been defined here save that they are at a highly abstract level and do not represent anything that can be directly experienced. There is no way of experiencing what a physicist means by a vacuum. Such ideas are referred to as *abstract concepts,* and they play a crucial role in the sciences. They also often play a very significant role in learning organizers, a topic to which we must now return.

The notion that certain concepts may function as organizers of learning has been developed almost entirely by Ausubel. This idea is extensively discussed in Ausubel and Robinson (1969), who have summarized some of the rather sketchy research on the topic. The thesis proposed is that in order to master almost any given fragment of subject matter efficiently, the learner should first be exposed to certain anchoring ideas around which the new knowledge can be organized. The position is that unless such anchoring ideas, organizers, or advanced organizers, as they are variously called, are learned prior to particular subject-matter assignments, learning cannot be well organized.

Organizers are concepts around which new knowledge is built. Many teachers have long used this approach to introducing new subject matter. Audiovisual specialists have also taken the position that the effective use of any instructional film requires that it be properly introduced by the teacher. The common suggestion for teaching from films is that the pupil be introduced to the topic and know, in advance, just what he is to look for. This is another way of saying that the teacher provides the student with a useful set of organizers so that he can learn effectively from the film presentation.

Organizers are generally at a more abstract level than the subject matter that becomes organized around them. They are also ideas representing a broader range of knowledge than the knowledge to be acquired. In introducing a new topic, the first statements presented are generally those that have to do with the general nature of the subject to be discussed. Ausubel makes the point that sometimes a good beginning in teaching a new concept may be to explain how the concept is different from related concepts with which it may be confused. In teaching American students the nature of an Oriental religion such as Buddhism, it may be important to point out the differences that exist between Buddhism and the religions with which the student is familiar, so that he is prepared to organize his knowledge around new concepts rather than mold it in terms of his own religious concepts.

Some subject matter is extremely well structured in terms of organizing concepts. The better developed sciences such as physics and chemistry are this way. Organizers are the key terms and the powerful ideas in a discipline, and it is hardly surprising that it is in the most fully developed disciplines that there is consensus concerning what these terms are and when they should be introduced to the student. In less developed and less completely structured areas, such as the social studies, there is considerable debate concerning what the key ideas are and when the student can encounter them to greatest advantage. In the well-developed disciplines the teacher does not have to worry about when to introduce the organizing ideas, for experimentation by several generations of teachers has produced a sequence of subject matter that provides a good organization for the student and leads to the acquisition of structured knowledge in his memory system.

The earlier chapter on memory pointed out that the evidence suggests that the memory system stores information in an ordered hierarchy. The theory that learning takes place best if it is planned around organizing ideas is another way of expressing the same idea. If memory is organized in a hierarchy, then learning should be planned so that it permits the student to lay down in his memory a hierarchy of ideas. The difficulty of implementing this approach in practice is that one knows little about how concepts should best be organized for instructional purposes. There is not even a good system for classifying concepts to be learned.

Harré has pointed out (1966) that the search for a classification of concepts is one of the oldest problems in philosophy. Aristotle was intrigued by the question and proposed a classification that included the classes of relational, substance, quantity, and quality. The latter two categories are still widely used today, and subject matter in the sciences is typically taught first by introducing qualitative concepts and then quantitative concepts. A student learns the qualitative idea of gravity before he learns how the gravitational constant is measured. He learns that the blood picks up oxygen before he measures in the laboratory how much oxygen can be carried by the blood. Harré points out that Aristotle's classification of concepts was based largely on the kinds of questions that Aristotle was interested in asking, and that it is a classification of convenience rather than one based on any theory of the nature of knowledge.

Harré states that a second important approach to the classification of concepts is to order them in terms of the degree to which they have explanatory value. The concept of *universal gravitation* explains such varied phenomena as the path of a planet, the trajectory of a missile, and the behavior of a free-falling body. On the other hand, the concept of *distance,* a concept that enters into the understanding of the effects of universal gravitation, does not explain anything at all, but is one of the givens in experience. At least some concepts can thus be arranged in a hierarchy, with those concepts that explain little at the base, and those that have the greatest explanatory value at the top. On the surface this sounds like a good way of arranging concepts for teaching and, in a few limited cases, it may be. In most subject-matter areas, teaching could not proceed along such lines. In the teaching of history, for instance, the concept of power and status conflict has far more explanatory value than that of the geographical circumstances of historical personages, or their hereditary standing, but one would not delay using the concept of power and status conflict until concepts with less explanatory power had been learned. The ordering of concepts in terms of explanatory power may have value in the teaching of physics, but is probably useless as a basis for teaching in most other areas.

Other approaches to the classification of concepts are illustrated in such writings as those of Gagné (1970) and Woodruff (1964), who take the firm position that concepts to be learned within formal schooling can be arranged in an optimum order. The examples commonly cited in this connection are derived from mathematics, where agreement can be reached on how concepts should be ordered.

Most of those who write in education about the ordering of concepts have not stated explicitly what the basis of the ordering should be. Some seem to believe the very unlikely proposition that the concepts in most subject-matter fields can be organized in a logical structure, much as are the concepts of mathematics. Others imply that they are following the classical tradition of ordering concepts in terms of explanatory power. Still another possibility for ordering concepts is in terms of the difficulties involved in understanding them. A concept such as the physicist's concept of mass is much more difficult to understand than the ordinary conception of weight. Any of these different attempts to arrange concepts rely heavily on intuitive judgment, and the classifications provided are of very dubious validity.

The Role of Verbal Associative Learning in Problem Solving

Although concepts can be learned without the help of verbal processes, the labeling of the attributes by means of words can facilitate the process of concept learning. Furthermore, the utilization of concepts may be facilitated when the concept itself is given a verbal label, and thus concept learning is intimately associated with the development of language and effective thinking.

Only the very youngest of human beings use words singly, as when a child says "cookie" or "No." Groups of words appear in two distinctly different forms. First, there are groups of words that appear in the form of natural language, generally in the form of complete utterances. Second, words may be said in groups without any clear structure, as when a person attempting to solve a crossword puzzle encounters the clue *sailboat.* He is likely to run through words that are related, such as *yacht, schooner, brig, sloop, ketch, clipper,* and so forth. In many search tasks, one runs off lists of words that are not fitted into any sentence. The latter are referred to as associative processes and they not only represent some of the best studied processes in the area of verbal learning, but also play a very significant role in problem solving.

Verbal associations may sometimes show impact on problem-solving behavior. An interesting example of this is found in a study by Judson, Cofer, and Gelfand (1956). The central task for subjects that forms the focus of this study is known as the Maier two-string problem. In the original version of this problem, the subject is presented with two strings suspended from the ceiling of a room. The room is empty except for a pair of pliers, which appear to have been carelessly left on the floor. The subject is instructed that his task is to tie together the ends of the two pieces of string, a task that appears to be deceptively simple. Most subjects go about attempting to solve this problem in a direct fashion. They take hold of the end of one piece of string and then reach over to take hold of the other. They find that the two pieces of string are sufficiently far apart to make this impossible. They are long enough to be tied together, but the two ends are so far apart that it is impossible to reach one piece while holding the other. One solution to the problem is to use the pair of pliers lying on the floor. What the subject must do is to attach the pliers to one of the strings, which can then be swung as a pendulum. Once the string is swinging, it can be caught while the subject holds onto the other string, and the problem is solved. This is a rather difficult problem; not more than 50 percent of college students can be expected to solve it.

In the Judson et al. study, subjects were asked during class hours on four consecutive days to learn word lists. One of these word lists included the sequence *rope, swing, pendulum;* this word list was administered to only one group. None of the other word lists included this sequence of words. On the fifth day all groups were given the Maier string problem and asked to solve it. The important result was that the group that had learned the word list containing the "rope-swing-pendulum" sequence were significantly more successful than the other groups in solving the problem. It may be noted that in this test the Maier problem was administered in a paper-and-pencil form, with an illustration of how the strings were suspended and the sketch of a person trying to reach one while holding the other.

This study clearly illustrates the way in which past associations between words or ideas can influence and facilitate problem-solving behavior. Many times, in solving some kind of novel problem, the solution appears to come out of the blue. What probably happens in such cases is that some association built in the past suddenly influences behavior.

The research on the famous two-string problem brings out a very well-known problem solving phenomenon known as *functional fixedness*. The essence of this phenomenon is that objects are not readily used for new purposes. Pliers are not used in ordinary daily life as a pendulum bob. They are used for grasping, bending, straightening, and related uses, and they are viewed as a tool for performing those activities. In order for a problem solver to use them as a pendulum bob, he must break away from the concept of how pliers should be used. This he finds difficult to do because he views pliers as having a fixed function.

Previously learned associations are not the only factor triggering novel ideas in a problem-solving situation. Glucksberg and Danks (1967) performed an ingenious experiment showing how other relationships between words may also generate solutions. Glucksberg and Danks devised an experiment in which subjects were confronted with the problem of completing a simple circuit, for which an insufficient amount of wire was provided. Subjects were provided a tool for loosening and tightening the posts to which the wires had to be attached, and the solution to the problem involved using the tool as a metallic conductor to make up for the lack of wire. For one group, the tool was referred to as a *wrench*. For a second group, the tool was called a *channel-lock-pliers*, and for the third group it was referred to as a *pliers*. The point to note is that the terms *wires* and *pliers* rhyme. The data turned up the interesting finding that those performing best on the problem, by a considerable margin, and those who most readily used the tool as a substitute for a wire, were the ones in the group for whom the tool was referred to as a pliers. The study suggests that associations along an acoustic dimension take place in such a situation and that, in the case of the study, this led to the finding of a solution. The results of this study are not quite as clear as they might be, in that the word *pliers* and the word *wires* often appear together in the same statement, as when a person says, "I cut the wires with the pliers." Such an association might account for the results of the experiment, except it is hard to understand why, when the tool was referred to as channel-lock-pliers, the facilitating effect did not appear.

There is evidence that, at least on certain kinds of problems, the finding of the solution is facilitated when the problem solver can allow himself to associate freely while looking for promising ideas. This ability has been called *fluency* by those who work in the psychological measurement area. There is also evidence that a person's score on a test of fluency of ideas is related to his ability to solve certain classes of problems. This suggests that training in free association of ideas might result in an improvement in the ability to solve such problems. Numerous studies have been undertaken in an attempt to determine whether such training will result in improved problem-solving ability. Some of these have been laboratory studies, but others have involved courses designed to improve creativity. A long sequence of such studies by Irving Maltzman, conducted in the late 1950's, and many subsequent studies all reported the positive effects of training in free association. The data were highly plausible and fitted expectation well, but many of them involved a serious research flaw which was not brought out until a study was undertaken by Gerlach et al. (1964). In most of the studies of the effect of free-association training on problem solving, performance was measured on tests of fluency before and after training. Such tests, in themselves, call for a free-association activity as, for example, the Unusual Uses Test, which asks the person to list all the uses he can think of for common objects such as ashtrays, tiles, cardboard boxes, etc. Performance on such tests shows improvement with training, but Gerlach and his associates showed that a similar improvement could be demonstrated by expanding the directions on the test so that the subject was encouraged to give associations freely and understood that speed would help him to obtain a better score. Such a small change in the directions produced a very substantial gain in score. The implications of the study are that what the subjects learned in training was what to do when faced with a test involving fluency.

There can be little doubt that the mere urging of subjects to produce more solutions to problems, or more associations, does increase production. Some interesting data related to this problem have been produced by Johnson, Parrott, and Stratton (1968). In the latter investigation, the problems used included that of writing as many titles as possible to a paragraph describing a plot, or writing titles for a table presenting agricultural data. The group urged to write as many solutions as possible produced more superior solutions, although the average quality was then poorer. The subjects in this experiment were able to improve their judgment of the quality of the solutions they produced and hence were eventually able to exercise some control over both the quality and quantity of the solutions produced.

Not all the findings of research on the effect of free association training can be explained in this way. For example, Freedman (1965) found positive results of free-association training, but the problem-solving test used was not one in which the subject's orientation to take it in a certain way would appear to be of any consequence.

Research on the Anagram Problem

One of the few partly standardized techniques that has evolved for the study of problem solving is that involving the use of anagrams. Although anagram problem solving represents a specialized activity, the study of it has yielded some results of quite broad significance. Much of the research on anagrams has been reviewed by Johnson (1966). In the typical anagram, the problem consists of several letters that have to be rearranged to form a word. The form of the problem has many advantages in that various characteristics of it can be modified and the effect of the modification on the difficulty of the problem can be studied. Some of the more obvious characteristics of the problem that might be likely to influence problem solving are the number of letters involved in the word, and the rareness or commonness of the word that constitutes the solution. In addition, the letters can be presented in different orders. Numerous different orders can be used, from those that retain some of the letters in the same order as that of the original word to orders in which the syllables presented are different from those that have to be produced. The letters may also be presented in an order that spells a word different from that which the problem solver has to produce. The number of anagram problems that can be produced is immensely large, because there are numerous words in the dictionary and a great many ways in which the letters in each can be presented. This is perhaps the reason why the anagram problem has not been completely standardized, for each investigator tends to choose words that meet his particular specifications. It is this lack of standardization that makes it difficult to compare the results of any two studies. Conflicting results of research in this area may sometimes be attributable to differences in the anagrams used. Skill in solving anagram problems is generally measured in terms of the time taken to solve the problems, but sometimes problems are given with a time limit and performance is scored on a pass-fail basis. Procedures may also involve the subject's talking aloud or working out his solution on a piece of paper. There are also an almost infinite number of different ways in which the directions may be stated.

The Johnson summary brings out very clearly that one of the most important factors in solving this kind of problem is what is termed *set* —a factor that has been well identified in many other problem-solving situations. A problem-solving set can be established by giving such instructions as that the letters spell the name of a city, or the name of an animal. Similar sets can also be established by providing a long series of problems to solve in which all the solutions involve, say, names of cities. The evidence is overwhelming that the establishment of such sets facilitates the production of solutions in the case of problems in which the set is appropriate. How such sets operate is a matter of conjecture. Presumably, the task of constructing a word in a certain category involves the search of one's memory for words having the same number of letters as the number of letters presented. A set may restrict the amount of searching that has to be done. The situation is analogous to that of finding a book with certain characteristics in a library. If one knows the section of the library in which the book is to be located, the search time is much shorter than if one does not have that particular item of information to use as a guide.

Set may also operate in a different way. If a series of problems are solved by adopting a particular procedure, then there is a tendency established to adopt that same procedure in the solution of future problems. This is what has been called the *einstellungen effect,* which is nothing more than the operation of the principle of reinforcement. The operation of this effect comes out quite clearly in the solution of anagrams. If the subject first solves a large number of anagram problems by starting with the last consonant given and using it as the first letter in the solution, then the problem solver is likely to adopt this procedure on future problems. Such habits established through a series of successes probably influence all problem solvers. Television repairmen tend to look for bad rectifier tubes, because defective rectifier tubes are very commonly a major source of difficulty. Problem solvers appear to store large quantities of information about the probabilities of particular procedures being successful.

Many sets probably operate in any particular problem-solving situation. Complex sets can be shown to operate in the solution of anagram problems. In the solution of a particular problem, the solver may bring to the problem the set that the word to be found is the name of a bird and that it consists of two syllables. Compound sets have a stronger effect than simple sets.

Johnson also cites many studies showing that anagrams are more easily solved when the word involved is common than when the word is relatively rare. It is as if the responses that could be considered to represent a solution to the problem were arranged in a hierarchy and are produced in a particular order with the most commonly occurring words being the most available. Frequency of previous experience also has another interesting effect on procedures for solving anagram problems. When a person is given an anagram to solve, he is likely to start by arranging the letters into pairs, but he does not arrange them in pairs at random. The pairs chosen tend to be commonly occurring pairs of letters. If the given letters are G T I N H, the problem solver is likely to choose pairs such as I N and T H, which he often sees in print, and avoid a rare pair such as T G or H T. One would like to be able to generalize from these findings and state that the early stages of problem solving are characterized by familiar actions and attempts to apply commonplace solutions. However, one cannot go as far as this, for there is no substantial data derived from the study of other kinds of problems to give any support.

One of the more surprising findings of the review is that the mere performance of anagram problems, with feedback concerning the correctness of the solution, does not seem to produce any marked improvement. This suggests that the problem solver himself, when confronted with a series of anagrams, is not able to identify the elements in the situation that make for the speedy discovery of a solution. In other words, the solution of anagram problems does not help the problem solver to evolve new strategies. This finding raises the interesting question of the extent to which one can expect practice with problems to produce superior problem-solving ability. One does know that practice is effective in some cases. An example is the oddity problem, in which a person has to identify which one of three objects does not belong in the group. Both children and primates show substantial and rapid practice effects on this type of problem, but one would like to be able to formulate a general statement concerning where practice in problem solving will be effective and where it will not be effective.

Computer Simulation Approaches to Problem Solving

An entirely new approach to many scientific problems has been developed in recent years through the availability of high-speed computers. The chemist can now hypothesize the nature of the mechanism underlying a particular chemical process and can then set up a computer to calculate the experimental results to be expected if the mechanism actually operates. The "data" produced by the computer can then be checked against real data collected in actual experiments. The comparison permits an evaluation of the reasonableness of the hypothesized underlying mechanism. Much of the time, computers, when they are used by physical scientists, "generate" data that are later compared with actual data.

The psychologist has learned to perform similar kinds of operations with computers. Everybody today knows that computers perform many operations that resemble thinking activities. Indeed, computers are often called giant brains and the storage units they contain are called memory units. Speculative articles on building thinking machines and on using computers to perform thinking operations have been written for at least a century. It was not until an article appeared by Newell, Shaw, and Simon (1958) that any real specifications were set out concerning how this could be accomplished.

Before further discussion of this problem, the student should know that for a computer to perform the operations considered here it must be provided with (1) information to be used in solving the problems, and (2) a program, or set of procedures, that tells the computer how to behave. The program may instruct the machine to look for certain elements in a problem, make comparisons, and so forth. In the study of thinking and problem-solving processes, the program includes operations that the human thinker or problem solver is believed to perform.

The basic idea presented by Newell et. al. is that problem solving involves the manipulation of statements according to certain rules of logic in order to reach a particular conclusion that is sought. Consider, for example, the following very simple arithmetic problem stated in the form of two propositions that constitute the basic data and a third incomplete proposition that specifies the conclusion sought:

Board A is 6 feet long.
Board B is ⅔ the length of board A.
The length of board B is ______.

In order to find the solution, the problem solver must build a new statement that says, "The length of B is equal to 6 × ⅔." To do this, he has to know (or be programmed in) the rules of setting up propositions from data. Just as human problem solvers can learn to make proper deductions from data and then set up new statements or propositions that represent these deductions, so too can computers be designed to store propositions and then derive new propositions from those stored. The computer has to be programmed so that it will perform only operations that are logically correct. An example at a more complex level would be that of starting with the axioms of Euclidian geometry and logically deducing certain conclusions, such as that two straight lines can cross at only one point. By producing new propositions on the basis of the axioms, the computer can eventually arrive at the proposition it is desired to produce as a deduction from the original axioms.

The argument of Newell and his associates was that a machine could be programmed to solve certain classes of problems and then the program could be adjusted until it solved problems in humanlike ways. The anticipation was that the research worker could produce, on the computer, humanlike problem solving and that, in this way, a model of human problem solving could be evolved.

Simulation of problem solving on the computer does require the psychologist to specify precisely what the elements are in a problem and exactly what operations have to be performed to produce a solution. It is an excellent exercise in precise thinking about problem solving, but it can be undertaken only when one knows precisely what the problem is. Much of the time in real life our difficulties stem from the fact that we do not know exactly what the problem is that we are trying to solve.

At this time, it is difficult to evaluate just what has been accomplished by this approach to the study of problem solving. Computers have been programmed in such a way that they have undertaken quite complicated reasoning problems. The most notable demonstrations of this kind have involved utilizing computers to generate proofs of Euclidean theorems. A computer thus programmed can not only generate proofs of theorems, it has not been "taught," but it can then store the new theorems and use them in the development of subsequent proofs. In doing such work, the computer performs in quite human like ways as, for example, in attempting to develop a new proof by substituting terms in another theorem already stored in memory. The computer may also attempt to work backwards from the proposition it is desired to prove, or it may break down the problem into components, each one of which is handled separately. What this demonstrates is that computers can undertake humanlike activities, but this is a long way from demonstrating that the operations performed by a computer in solving a reasoning problem are the kinds of operations performed by the human problem solver.

More recently, Paige and Simon (1966) have attempted to simulate on a computer the operations performed by children in reading arithmetic problems and then arriving at a solution. Paige and Simon point out that the steps involved in the solution of arithmetical problems have been outlined in books on arithmetic for generations. The first step generally involves reading the problem and finding the statements in it that are crucial. These statements then have to be converted into numbers or symbols that are then fitted into an equation. The equation is then solved and the solution is checked back against the conditions in the original statement of the problem. In solving the problem about the boards, the child would probably be faced, first, with a statement of the problem in narrative form such as the following:

> *A carpenter had two boards. One was 6 feet long and the other was ⅔ of that length. How long was the second board?*

In solving such a problem, the computer and the child have to recognize that the problem involves the length of two boards, one of which is specified directly, whereas the length of the other is only implied and has to be found. The one unknown quantity has to be expressed as a function of the known quantity. The basic problem is that of coding the information provided. This turns out to be one of the most difficult operations to program the computer to perform. It is also the major difficulty encountered by the child.

Up to this time, the main contribution of this approach to the study of problem solving has been to demonstrate that computers can solve certain classes of problems in much the same way that humans are taught to solve them. The hope is that, in time, the method will evolve a sophisticated theory of problem solving.

The simulation of logical problem solving on a computer has had other important outcomes that must be mentioned briefly. The spark behind such research has often been the hope that the study of the problem-solving capabilities of computers would ultimately lead to the development of an artificial intelligence, that is to say, an intelligence that is nonhuman in character, that might be able to solve problems far more complex than that which the human intelligence can solve. The broad goal of such work has been to produce a general problem-solving machine, and perhaps even a machine that would redesign itself. Strangely enough, the work undertaken up to this point suggests that it may be much easier to build a general problem-solving artificial intelligence than it may be to build a device that will successfully simulate the way human intelligence works. Machines can be made to behave in strictly rational ways, but human behavior is filled with arbitrary and unexpected elements.

Theories of Problem Solving

Psychologists have long hoped that they would be able to find a simple set of principles of behavior that could be used for understanding even the most complex of behavioral events. Pavlov regarded the principles of learning discovered in his laboratory as the key to the understanding of the so-called higher mental processes. This theme was later developed in the writings of the American John B. Watson, who saw Pavlovian principles of psychology, discovered in the context of simple laboratory settings, as a basis for understanding all of man's behavior. The lack of success achieved by these early workers in throwing any light on complex behavior, such as problem solving, discouraged a whole generation of psychologists from following a similar path. The success of explaining the complex in terms of the simple has been so successful in physics that psychologists have never been willing to give up a similar quest in the behavioral sciences for very long. Indeed, it was only twenty years after Watson's attempt to do this began to lose popularity that a new attempt appeared on the horizon. This attempt was focused on B. F. Skinner's work and used what have been called the principles of operant conditioning as the basic elements in terms of which complex behaviors were to be described. A volume edited by Kleinmuntz (1966) contains three papers on problem solving by three eminent psychologists, Israel Goldiamond, B. F. Skinner, and Arthur W. Staats, who attempt to explain problem-solving behavior in terms of the simple processes of conditioning.

The operant-conditioning model of problem solving has generally used concept learning as an example of problem solving. Concept learning *may* involve very difficult problem solving, as when one tries to discover why certain pictures in an art show are considered by the critics as great art but other pictures are not so classified. Most concepts are, of course, acquired without the learner undertaking any problem solving at all, as when he acquires the concept *brass* by being told exactly what brass is and how it is identified.

Consider a simple concept-learning task in which a child is shown pairs of objects and has to press the button beneath the one he thinks is correct. If he is right, he receives an M & M, and then the next problem is presented. If he is wrong, the next problem appears immediately. Eventually, he solves the problem by discovering that if he always presses the button beneath the blue object, then he is always right. In terms of operant conditioning, one would say that blue is the *discriminative stimulus* and that as the problem was solved, the behavior of the child came more and more under the control of the blue stimulus. If the problem had been a very complex one, such as that of discriminating art described by the experts as "good" from art described by the experts as "bad," then numerous different aspects of the stimuli would have had to become a part of a complex of discriminative stimuli. This description of the solution of this problem in terms of the language of operant conditioning really accomplishes nothing except to translate a common language description of problem solving into a different language. It does not explain in the sense in which scientists attempt to explain. It just states what we know already, but in a slightly different way. It tells us nothing new about how to predict or control problem-solving behavior and nothing about how to arrange conditions so that problems in the particular class are more readily solved.

Skinner brings out in his discussion of problem solving the well-established fact that words and language play an important role in remembering the discriminative stimuli that have significance in the solution of a particular problem. Skinner (1957) states that words are (p. 231) "descriptive stimuli which improve the chances of success." The implication of this is that when the child sees the blue object and says to himself, "It is blue and blue objects are right," he is increasing the chances of making a correct response. The latter appears to be a very dubious assumption, although the coding of information into words may help memory.

The Staats approach (1966) in the third chapter in the Kleinmuntz volume is also written to a great extent in the language of operant conditioning, but it also introduces classical conditioning concepts. In this article, as in his later book (1968), Staats makes an effort to integrate concepts of operant conditioning with concepts from more traditional stimulus-response theory. He also tries to integrate these with what has been learned from studies of verbal learning. The entire enterprise is an immensely ambitious attempt to bring together a great diversity of knowledge. Ambition on this scale is certainly doomed to failure in our present state of limited understanding. Short words and sentences are learned, Staats claims, by operant conditioning. The derivation of a proof of a theorem he regards as the generation of a series of statements in which each statement in the proof becomes the stimulus for the next statement. Staats tries to illustrate this with the proof of Thales' theorem which states that when straight lines intersect, the opposite angles are equal. In commenting on the Staats paper, as Kleinmuntz (1966) says (p. 4), "The resulting argument is so totally unconvincing and unreasonable that it implicitly demonstrates the need for something else." If the Staats account of problem solving were correct, then the person trying to find a proof of a theorem would start to build the proof at the beginning and slowly work through to the end. In fact, we know that this is not at all what the problem solver does. He is quite likely to start with the statement he wants to prove and work backwards for a time. When that is not too successful, he may then start working forwards again. Then he may later switch around and try working the problem backwards. Problem solvers just do not do what Staats suggests they do.

Some day it may be possible to demonstrate how very simply psychological processes can account for complex behavior such as problem solving. This cannot be done in any convincing way at the present time, but this does not mean that a science of problem solving cannot be developed. There is no rule in the universe that says that complex phenomena have to be reduced to simple component phenomena if they are to be understood. Thermodynamics, for example, is the science of how big energy systems behave and interact. An understanding of such systems and their interactions does not require that one understand anything about the laws of the interaction of the atoms involved in the systems. A parallel situation may exist in the development of a science of problem solving. It may well be possible to develop a scientific understanding of problem solving that deals with problem solving at the level of gross behavior. Such a science of problem solving may well permit the prediction of the conditions that facilitate and interfere with problem solving and the factors in background experience and training that contribute to the skill. Such knowledge may permit the prediction and control of problem-solving behavior, and prediction and control is the essence of what the scientist accomplishes.

Attempts to produce theories of problem solving of the type considered up to this point have all taken the position that the problem solver has a repertoire of responses that are triggered by appropriate stimuli. In this sense, the role of the problem solver is passive and controlled by immediate circumstances. Not all problem-solving theories are of this type. Most of those who have attempted to simulate problem solving on a computer have held the view that the role of the problem solver is active and that he engages in an active search for a solution. In the programming of a computer to prove a theorem in geometry, the computer is equipped with certain active strategies for undertaking this task. It will be programmed to search its memory for theorems that have similar elements. If that procedure does not work, it may break down the theorem to be proved into sections and then search for stored theorems that resemble the components. The computer engages in an active search for a solution.

Many believe that a satisfactory theory of problem solving will have to be one in which the problem solver is viewed as an active searcher for a solution. Such a position is taken, for example, by Piaget (see the account of Piaget in this respect given by Flavell, 1963, and Phillips, 1969). Even the young child is not a passive agent that must wait for some appropriate set of circumstances to release particular responses from his repertoire. On the contrary, the young child is an active explorer of his environment and, given any problem, goes about exploring the problem situation. At an early age, the child's behavior is highly bound to the manipulations of the concrete world, but these manipulations reflect a basic tendency to explore, manipulate, and act on the environment.

The Piaget view of the development of problem solving stresses the slow development of the child's ability to engage in internal thinking independent of immediate circumstances. Development along these lines is very gradual and is believed to be highly dependent upon maturation. Even at the elementary-school age, the capacity for thought independent of the immediate situation is limited, but by the first grade identifiable changes have already taken place in this respect (see Kendler and Kendler, 1962, and Kendler, 1964).

At each stage, the child is limited in the internal operations related to problem solving that he can perform. Piaget has attempted to reduce these to logical operations and has conducted research on the age at which particular logical operations can be performed. The chapter on development provides examples of internal thought operations that a child cannot perform until he reaches a particular level of development.

In the final stage of intellectual development, during the teens, thought achieves real independence from the immediate situation and the child becomes capable of formal logical operations such as are involved in long trains of reasoning. An example of an operation that plays a crucial role in much problem-solving behavior is what is called reversibility. Let us consider an illustration of reversibility. If the adult is told that $A + B = C$, he can easily figure that to find B all one has to do is subtract A from C. In the same way, if the adult knows that a bottle can be filled by adding the contents of a 10 oz. cup and an 8 oz. cup, he can figure that if the bottle is full, he can leave 10 oz. in it by taking out 8 oz. Reversibility in logic is being able to start at the end of the argument and then work back. Children can work through an argument forwards and understand what it is about, but they have difficulty in then starting at the end and working backwards. A person who cannot show reversibility in his reasoning has difficulty in solving many problems that have to be solved by taking what appears to be a solution and then working back. If one is presented with a relatively simple problem, such as that of measuring out 17 oz. of water using three jars that hold, respectively, 3, 7, and 8 oz., one will almost certainly start at the end. One is likely to say to oneself that 17 can be divided into a number of quantities such as $7 + 8 + 2$, and see whether one can produce those quantities from the measures available. Thus one goes back and forth from the final end point of the problem to the materials given to start with, and then one is likely to move forward again. Thus the problem solver will move backwards and forwards until a solution is found. The child in the lower elementary school grades will probably move only in the forward direction. He will experiment with combinations of the quantities provided by the jars, but he will not be able to go to the end of the problem and then move backward in an attempt to find a solution. Such a child's thinking does not manifest reversibility.

This section of the chapter has been included to provide the student with some taste of the theorizing taking place in the area of problem solving. Although research workers have managed to discover a wide range of important findings, theorizing is still at quite a primitive level. The field of problem-solving research probably has not yet reached a level of knowledge that permits successful theory building. If the present writer had to make a guess concerning the kind of theorizing most likely to be successful over the next decade, he would probably choose either the kind of theorizing that emerges from the computer simulation of problem solving or the kind of model that Piaget and his associates have been working upon, but that is just a personal choice.

Problem Solving and Intelligence

The literature of psychology has long identified problem-solving ability with intelligence, treating the one term as a synonym for the other. The measurement of intelligence has always involved the presentation of a series of problems from which some measure of performance is derived. Early psychologists, including Binet, dreamed that a suitable series of problems could be developed so that skill in solving them would be highly independent of the person's background and experience and thus measure something described as innate ability. Early studies encouraged psychologists in thinking that devices could be built that would measure an inborn ceiling of intellectual ability. These early studies gave encouragement because they indicated that intelligence, as it was commonly measured through devices that produced an intelligence quotient, showed very stable intelligence quotients over periods of several years. What was not recognized was that the intelligence quotients remained stable because the cultural conditions to which each child was exposed also remained stable. During the first half of the present century, data that did not fit this pattern tended to be disregarded or disbelieved. The fact that Madame Montessori, before the turn of the century, had been able to take what were believed to be ineducable slum children and bring them to the point where they passed the regular school exams with distinction was viewed as incredulous. The work of Beth Wellman, who presented data showing quite large increments in intelligence-test scores of children exposed to a kindergarten program, was viewed as some kind of artifact of the data. Such findings could not be brushed aside forever, because they kept coming from different sources. In addition, scientists working on problems of perception began to produce data showing that deprivations in early experience could produce dramatic effects on problem solving in a great range of living creatures.

The fact that problem-solving ability responds well to the kind of environment provided by middle-class homes and middle-class schooling does not mean that any immediate dramatic growth in intellectual development can be achieved by taking a child from culturally impoverished surroundings and placing him in the kind of environment in which the intellect thrives. The beneficial effects, in this respect, are not likely to become evident in weeks or even months, but will manifest themselves over periods of years. If one measures problem-solving ability through a test such as the Wechsler Intelligence Scale for Children, one might expect that a dramatic improvement in the environment might produce a change of perhaps one or two points a year on the intelligence quotient scale. Such changes appear small, but over the twelve grades of schooling they are sufficient to make the difference between a person very unlikely to succeed in any college and one who could obtain a bachelor's degree in a good institution.

What has been said does not mean that there are no differences between individuals in the height to which the intellect can develop. Given optimum circumstances for development, some individuals would probably develop a higher level of problem-solving skills than would others, but intelligence test scores probably do not indicate who would be at the top or bottom of the order under those circumstances. Such tests tell us something about who is at the top and who is at the bottom of our present society in terms of opportunities to acquire problem-solving skills.

A second important question is whether there is a single central problem-solving ability called intelligence or whether there are distinct aptitudes for solving particular classes of problems. Here again, the original hope of psychologists was that by some means there could be discovered a set of innate components of intelligence, but such hopes were not, and probably could not be, realized. What has been demonstrated is that, by high-school age, intelligence does appear to show a number of distinct components, each one of which can be measured. The following table illustrates items from the components that are commonly measured. These components are measured because they have been shown to have predictive value, particularly in academic learning situations.

No claims can be made that these components are related in some way to the genetic code through which characteristics are inherited, though earlier psychologists, including L. L. Thurstone, hoped that they would be. On the other hand, little is known about the extent to which such specialized abilities are trainable. Despite this ignorance, the measurement of these specialized abilities is useful as a part of the guidance procedure, for they indicate present levels of functioning of these abilities. Changes in the level of any one of them may be brought about, but change is likely to be a very slow process. The level of ability shown in any one of the areas given in the table must be regarded as the result of many years of exposure to conditions ranging from rich experience to deprivation.

Some of the Aptitude Factors Commonly Measured by Tests Included in Aptitude Test Batteries

Illustration of test problem	*Name given to factor measured*	*Predictions commonly made with this type of test*
What is the meaning of the word "ascend"? 1. go up 2. lift 3. elevate 4. rain	*Verbal factor*	Predicts grades in academic work, particularly in those fields where the content is largely verbal. Sometimes used for diagnosing difficulties in reading if the difficulty is believed to be due to a deficiency in knowledge of the meaning of words.
Multiply the numbers as indicated. 46 × 6 39 × 4	*Numerical computation*	Used for the prediction in the learning of skills which require numerical operations of a simple character, as, for example, many trades and skills such as those of the machinist and the bookkeeper.
What is the next number in the series? 2 4 8 16 ____	*Numerical reasoning*	Used for predicting grades in academic work involving reasoning with numbers. Physics is an example of such academic work, and so too would be work in engineering. Tests of this kind are used for predicting success in such areas at the college level.
Which object can be made by folding the paper along the dotted lines?	*Space-relations factor or perceptual factor. (There are several perceptual factors.)*	Used for predicting the ability to learn engineering drawing, sheetmetal work, and other skills involving space relations.
In the following list of pairs of names, place a check in the parentheses after a pair if the two names are identical. Chamberlin Chamberlin ( ) Jeremiah Jeremiah ( ) Gleason Gleeson ( ) Learned Learned ( )	*Perceptual-speed factor*	Has had a long history of predicting success in simple clerical jobs.
Which jug of water is most likely to tip over?	*Mechanical-aptitude factor*	Predicts learning of a great range of mechanical skills.

Some of the Aptitude Factors Commonly Measured by Tests Included in Aptitude Test Batteries (Continued)

Illustration of test problem	*Name given to factor measured*	*Predictions commonly made with this type of test*
Place a check mark in the parentheses after each word which is correctly spelled. Perscription ( ) Opportunity ( ) Fundermental ( ) Demonstrate ( ) *In the following sentence choose the correct version.* Each one of the students were / was / are allowed to correct his own examination.	*Language usage*	Used for predicting performance in learning higher-level clerical tasks such as involve stenographic and secretarial skills.

Problem Solving and Teaching

Those concerned with the practical business of teaching have long been intrigued with the idea that the most careful education may well be provided by problem-solving situations in which the student derives from his own experience the truths that constitute the major outcomes of his studies. This conception of education has generally been stated in the form that the student should *discover* the truths that are to be learned or that he should engage in *discovery learning*. The assumption is that he will benefit more from knowledge acquired through problem solving and discovery than from the same knowledge presented to him on the page of a textbook or presented to him by the teacher through a lecture. This has long been an attractive proposition that has intrigued generations of teachers. The fascination for this concept has not waned, as is evident from the support it has received in recent years from such persons as Jerome Bruner and J. R. Suchman. The latter prefers to use the term *inquiry training* rather than the more conventional terms of *discovery learning* or *discovery teaching*. Teaching by the discovery method is contrasted with what is called *expository teaching*, which amounts to a teaching technique of presenting to the student the information he is to acquire. The issue is of particular interest in connection with the topic under discussion, in that a major claim for discovery teaching has been that it leads to greater transfer of training than teaching involving the direct memorization of subject matter.

It was not until after World War II that the problem was studied experimentally. Worthen (1968), who has reviewed many of the studies made of this problem, points out that the main outcome has been a set of conflicting results. Some studies purportedly gave results that supported discovery teaching, while others, often supposedly attacking the same problem, led to completely opposite results. Worthen concludes that the apparent conflict among the findings is due to the fact that no clear meaning has been assigned to such terms as discovery learning, guided discovery learning, and expository teaching. Indeed, the confusion is so great that what one person refers to as guided discovery learning another may label as expository teaching. Another excellent review of the problem by Wittrock (1966) emphasizes the point that one of the basic weaknesses of research in the area is that most research workers have not specified just what is to be discovered by the student.

The difficulties of deriving generalizations from research on discovery learning that can be applied to teaching can be most readily explored by considering an example. Let us suppose that the pupil is concerned with understanding the conditions under which a beam can be balanced by placing weights on it on opposite sides of the fulcrum. The student might be started on this exploration by being given two weights and a beam marked off in inches from the center. He might be given the beam balanced on a knife edge and be left to place the weights on the beam in such a way that they balanced. This would represent a very unstructured situation in which he would have few cues provided that would help him to arrive at a solution. Given the two weights, the beam, and the balancing edge, few pupils in the elementary school would be likely to discover the principle involved. Most teachers would want to provide more cues so that the pupil would have a greater chance of discovering the principle involved. One way of doing this would be to present the pupil with the balanced beam, as shown in Figure 15, and to ask him to state the rule of how the weights are to be placed on the beam if they are to balance. At this point he could be left to manipulate the two weights, or he could be shown other examples, such as are shown in Figure 15B and Figure 15C. He may be given unlimited time to solve this problem or he may be given additional cues. One helpful cue that might be given might involve the statement, "Now look at A. The beam is balanced when an 8-pound weight is placed 2 inches from the balance point and when the 2-pound weight is placed 8 inches from the balance point. Write down these numbers: 8 at 2 and 2 at 8. What do you notice about them?" If the pupil still does not see the relationship, tell him to write down the corresponding numbers from B which would read 6 at 3 and 2 at 9. If, by that time, he has not multiplied 6 × 3 and 2 × 9, then he can be given the additional prompt of being told to multiply each weight by its distance from the point of balance. As the number of cues increases, the procedure becomes more and more closely similar to expository teaching.

In few discovery learning situations is the pupil left with almost no

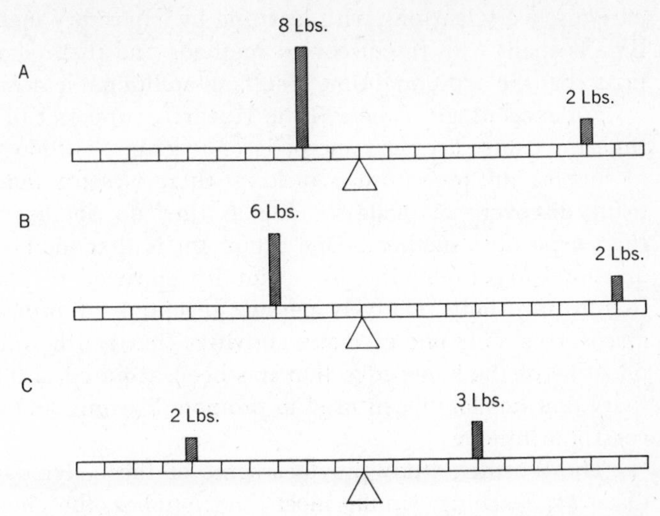

Figure 15. Example of task used in discovery learning procedures.

cues to discover a simple principle. Indeed, he would have to have the intellect of a Newton to find a principle under such circumstances. The pupil generally has to be provided with extensive cues in order to arrive at the principle he is to discover. Under such circumstances, there is likely to be very little discovery involved in the student's work. Studies of discovery learning rarely state the degree to which cues are provided. Some of the apparent inconsistency of findings can be attributed to differences in this respect.

Another source of inconsistency across studies of discovery learning is that in some, the effect of learning is appraised through a measure of the pupil's ability to recall what has been learned, while others have used a measure of the ability to transfer what has been learned to the solution of new problems. The previously cited study by Worthen shows that conditions that favor the recall of what is learned may not be the most favorable for transfer. One can easily see how this might happen. If the goal is to parrot back information, then rote learning may be efficient, but the acquisition of understanding may lead to effective transfer even though it may interfere with giving quick answers to short questions.

Mention must also be made of a very important condition, not discussed in most studies of discovery learning. This is the matter of the amount of time spent on learning. Discovery learning procedures are generally much more time-consuming than those involving expository teaching. When more time is spent in learning, more learning is likely to take place. Indeed, learning is generally limited by the time factor rather than by any other. One suspects that in many studies that compare discovery learning with learning by expository methods, much more time is spent with the discovery methods and there should be small surprise that the additional time results in additional learning.

For reasons given here, little research support can be found at this time for using discovery methods of teaching. Although direct evidence to support the procedure is lacking, there is some indirect evidence for using discovery methods so long as they do not use much more time than expository methods. One argument is that methods of learning requiring learner activity are generally superior to learning conditions that require only relatively passive reception of information. However, discovery is only one of many activities that can be introduced. The application of the knowledge that has been acquired also represents an activity that has long been used to promote learning and is probably a successful technique.

The Worthen study provides some of the better data in the area of discovery learning. Unlike most other studies, the characteristics of expository and discovery teaching were quite well defined and the pupils were exposed to sufficiently large doses of these two kinds of pedagogy that any notable difference should have shown up. Worthen was also able to collect data on what the teachers did in the classroom and was able to provide some evidence that teachers assigned to the different methods actually did behave differently. In addition, instruction by each method involved the same amount of time. The children were tested for the knowledge and skill acquired from instruction in mathematics by expository and discovery methods at the end of the six-week period of instruction, and also five weeks and eleven weeks later. The tests involved both measures of the ability to use the knowledge directly and the ability to transfer the knowledge to the solution of novel problems. The results showed very small differences in the learning of the pupils exposed to the different teaching procedures. On the immediate measure of retention there seemed to be a very slight superiority among the pupils exposed to the expository teaching. On the delayed measures of retention there was a very slight superiority for the pupils exposed to the discovery methods. In the case of the tests of transfer of training to new situations, differences were of negligible magnitude. The chief weakness of the study is that the account of it does not specify precisely just what the students discovered nor what was presented to them in the expository teaching, perhaps because scientific accounts have to be brief and often cannot give all the details that the reader would like to know.

The results of the Worthen study follow closely a much earlier study of Wittrock (1963), in which pupils worked problems involving the deciphering of a code. In the Wittrock study the pupils could learn, either by discovery or by expository teaching, the rule needed to solve each problem and the answer to each problem. The only really clear results of this study were that on the test of immediate retention the expository method, which involved the giving of both the rule and the answer, produced superior results. However, when the test was delayed or when a test for transfer of training was involved, then a mixture of the expository and discovery methods showed slight superiority. The mixture involved giving the rule but not giving the answer to the problem.

An interesting hypothesis has been injected into the controversy concerning the relative virtues of expository and discovery methods of learning through a study by Roughead and Scandura (1968). These research workers have taken the position that whatever is learned by a discovery method can be learned by an expository method. They argue, for example, that if the use of a discovery method teaches children how to discover principles, then there must surely be rules that guide behavior in the discovery of principles and these rules can surely be learned by expository methods. The difficulty in teaching such rules by expository methods is that they have not yet been adequately identified, but there is also another difficulty involved, even when the rules are known. In expository teaching, because the children do not have to derive the rules and understand the rationale for them, there is little incentive for acquiring insight into the derivation of the rule. For this reason, they may never discover why a rule is sound. For example, the child taught the rule for multiplying simple fractions may not be interested in knowing the reason why, for a knowledge of the rule alone enables him to get the right answers. On the other hand, the discovery method forces him to go through the procedure of inventing the rule and this he cannot do without understanding how the rule is derived.

Summary

1. In the case of human behavior, problem solving is defined as a situation in which there is a goal to be achieved but no previously learned response that permits the direct achievement of the goal. A broader definition is customarily used when the behavior of other living creatures is involved. In the latter case, a problem is a state of disequilibrium for which there is no previously learned response for the restoration of equilibrium.
2. Problem-solving behavior often involves extensive internal activity that results in the production of a solution, if a solution is achieved. This internal behavior may be accompanied by manipulations of the environment.
3. Although many attempts have been made to find a classification of problems that would have scientific utility, no satisfactory

classification has been evolved. The Guilford classification has had some small impact in encouraging research in the areas of convergent and divergent thinking, but in other areas the impact has been slight.

4. One of the basic areas of research on problem solving has been that referred to as concept learning. A concept is commonly defined as a category into which experiences may be classified. A word, such as *house*, represents a category into which certain objects in the environment may be classified and thus represents a concept in terms of this definition. This is a much narrower definition of a concept than is commonly used, and it does not include abstract concepts, which do not refer to directly observable events of the real world.
5. Objects and events are categorized on the basis of their attributes. Perception is basically a process of analyzing sensory experiences into their attributes so that objects can be identified. Attributes that define a category may be few and easily identified, or they may be many and subtle.
6. Concept-learning tasks may involve attribute identification, rule identification, or both of these. In rule identification tasks, the learner is told what the attributes are and he must discover the rule that relates the attributes. In attribute learning he is given the rule and must identify the attributes.
7. In the experimental study of concept learning, as well as in the study of concept learning in real-life situations, positive instances and negative instances of the concept may be provided. These instances are often referred to as exemplars. Some evidence suggests that learning of concepts is best achieved through a carefully chosen combination of positive and negative instances.
8. Some concept-learning tasks involve redundant information, that is to say, not all of the relevant attributes have to be identified in order to learn the concept. An increase in the number of relevant attributes makes a concept easier to learn.
9. Most concept-learning tasks in ordinary life involve many irrelevant attributes.
10. Concepts are most easily learned when negative and positive instances are quite distinct and when the positive instances are very uniform.
11. The effect of irrelevant attributes on the acquisition of concepts is not clear. Increasing the number of irrelevant attributes does not seem to have the same clear effect as does an increase in the number of relevant attributes.
12. Concept learning skill increases with age. Anxiety has a disrup-

tive effect on the learning of concepts only if the concepts are complex or difficult to learn.

13. Concept learning is highly tied, in the case of the human learner, to the use of language, which becomes a means of labeling concepts. There is some evidence that if the learner verbalizes what he is doing in solving a concept-learning problem, he will learn it more easily than if he does not verbalize the problem.
14. Advantages may accrue from permitting the learner to select his own instances and handle and manipulate them.
15. Thorough learning is important if the concept is to be used later. Concepts should also be learned, if at all possible, within a framework of previously acquired concepts. Teaching techniques should probably provide variety if the teaching is to be efficient.
16. Many different strategies may be used in learning the same concept. Some strategies place more strain on memory than do others, but those that produce least strain on the memory system are likely to be the most time consuming. Strain on the memory system is sometimes referred to as cognitive strain.
17. Although concepts in some fields of subject matter may not readily form a structure, they are likely to be structured by the person learning them because the human memory system naturally organizes information into a structure.
18. Verbal associative learning has been demonstrated to play an important role in problem solving. Many problems are solved if useful associations can be made between the names of the objects available for solving a problem and the functions these objects may have in the solution. The two-string problem used in many demonstrations of this phenomenon can also be used to demonstrate what has been termed functional fixedness.
19. A very substantial body of research on problem solving has used the anagram problem—a problem that permits the control of many important conditions. The anagram problem clearly demonstrates the role of *set*. Research on the anagram problem has produced the quite surprising finding that practice with anagrams does not produce any marked improvement in the skill. Training in strategies for solving anagrams, however, might well produce an increase in skill. The finding in the case of anagram research is to be contrasted with other findings, using other problem-solving situations, which have suggested that practice with feedback may result in improvement.
20. A modern approach to the study of problem solving has been that of attempting to simulate on a computer the behavior that humans undertake in solving problems. The approach is interest-

ing and novel, but it has run into many difficulties that are difficult to overcome. Scientists have been able to demonstrate that computers can be programmed to perform very much like humans, but the approach has not yet produced any fundamentally new ideas in the area.

21. Attempts to develop theories of problem solving have not met with any particular success. The main theoretical approach of American psychologists has been that of attempting to reduce problem-solving behavior to simple components such as classically conditioned or instrumentally conditioned responses, but this approach cannot be said to have achieved any notable success. A somewhat more successful approach finds its origins in the work of Piaget, who regards mental development as being largely a matter of the development of problem-solving skills. Piaget's work provides numerous hypotheses concerning the development of problem-solving skill and the sequence in which various problem-solving operations can appear during development.
22. Problem-solving skill has long been considered to represent the core of intelligence and has been the main skill measured by intelligence tests. The idea that the intelligence quotient is a quantity established by heredity has long been abandoned. Although there may well be a limit to intellectual development fixed by heredity, and individuals may differ in what that limit may be, very large changes in intellectual level can be produced by the environment. The change that can be produced in intellectual level through improved environmental conditions takes place very slowly but, over a period of many years, may be very substantial.
23. Some educators have taken the position that the best education is one that focuses on problem solving. Such an approach to education is commonly referred to as involving discovery learning or inquiry training. Research on the merits of discovery learning has been difficult to undertake in that the term does not have any single well-accepted meaning. Any differences between discovery learning procedures and procedures involving expository teaching have generally been found to be small.

CHAPTER EIGHT

The Learning of Attitudes

MUCH OF THE BOOK UP TO THIS POINT HAS BEEN CONCERNED WITH problems related to the acquisition of skills and cognitive learning, but another large class of learnings have hardly been touched upon. These are learnings related to approach and avoidance tendencies, which are first seen in early childhood when certain objects become attractive and are approached and other objects initiate withdrawal. Approach and avoidance tendencies, which are so clearly seen in the observable behavior of the child, later become a part of his internal behavior and he comes to place a positive or negative value on objects, events, and ideas. Some of these internal tendencies to accept or reject are referred to as attitudes, others as interests, and still others as values. Distinctions among these terms are not clear. Sometimes it is said that interests refer to preferences for activities; and attitudes refer to a positive approach or negative avoidance of ideas and objects. Both interest and attitude involve the concept of rejection or acceptance, and both involve some kind of affective (feeling) response to the object involved. Attitudes and interests have much more specific objects of reference than do values as they are technically defined. The latter relate to broad goals, such as the achievement of wealth or power or social status, but attitudes and interests are related to narrow channels into which activity is funneled—either toward or away from an object or idea. Interests and attitudes may determine the choice of means through which the value system and the goals implied by it may be achieved. A person's life may be dominated by religious values and religious goals, but he may have positive and negative attitudes to various religious practices and to the means of achieving religious ends.

Although the origin of attitudes is seen in simple responses of approach or withdrawal, in their more mature form attitudes represent highly complex aspects of behavior. Psychologists have slowly managed to tease out some of the components attitudes involve. An attempt to do this by Katz and Stotland (1960) suggests that attitudes include the following components:

Affective Components. These consist of positive or negative affects (feelings). Attitudes may differ in the extent to which they involve such affective components. Some attitudes are quite irrational and involve little except this affective component. Political attitudes, in their most primitive form, may be primarily of this character. The person who likes one set of political ideas and dislikes another, but cannot tell why, reflects an attitude that has a major affective component but very little else. Many attitudes are of this nature.

Cognitive Components. Attitudes differ in the extent to which they involve knowledge and beliefs. Some attitudes are highly intellectualized. A person may take a particular position on a certain political issue because he has thought through the problem and, after considering all the available evidence, has decided that the position he takes is the most acceptable one. Sometimes attitudes are based on a large store of incorrect information and false beliefs. These are cognitive elements, even though they do not represent true knowledge. The cognitive basis for many attitudes may be misinformation. A person may hold an attitude and have no strong feelings about the matter—that is, the affective component may be minor. On the other hand, his attitudes may not only be highly intellectualized, but may also have a strong affective component. The intellectual component and the affective component work hand in hand, but they are still independent components. The intellectual component of attitude discussed here is sometimes referred to as the cognitive component. The word *cognitive* implies knowing. Hence, the cognitive component of an attitude is that aspect which is based on beliefs or knowledge.

Action Components. Every student of the psychology of attitudes is impressed with the fact that many expressed attitudes bear little relation to behavior. A person may express strong religious attitudes, and yet his membership in his church involves little more than paying a pledge. In such a case the religious attitudes lack any substantial action component. The fact that the action component can be independent of the other components is important for planning education. Much of what goes on in the name of attitude education is the education of the affective and the cognitive components of attitudes, and these components may never be carried over into action systems. Thus one finds that the American public, probably the best-informed public in the world, has a deplorably poor record at the polls; the percentage of the population voting is small compared with that of most other democratically run countries. The positive attitudes toward democratic institutions often lack appropriate action components. How relationships are established between the cognitive components of attitudes and action systems is not clear at this time. This is really a problem of transfer of training. Although there is some evidence that transfer can take place from cognitive systems to action systems, the conditions that make this possible have not yet been established. Clearly, teachers cannot remain content with educating only the cognitive aspects of attitudes, for education must involve something more than preparation for an armchair approach to life.

Although the writer finds this analysis convenient as a basis for thinking about related educational problems, the reader should not be left with the impression that psychologists are agreed on what they mean by attitudes, for obviously this is not the case. McGuire (1968), who has reviewed numerous definitions of attitudes, concludes that these definitions differ in almost every conceivable important way. Some psychologists define attitudes as inner states, but a few refer to attitudes as consisting of groups of responses. Some define attitudes as a disposition to respond, but others consider the response as representing the attitude. Some regard an attitude as having a unity, but others regard it as having a set of distinct components, as do Katz and Stotland. Some distinguish between attitudes and knowledge, but others regard both as unified cognitive components. Numerous broad and important differences arise among those who use the term *attitude*. These differences reflect the fact that knowledge in the area has not yet attained a well-organized state. Despite the fact that the area has not yet reached the point where psychologists have concluded that they have identified clear and unambiguous phenomena of unquestioned importance, it is nevertheless an area of vigorous research activity and some of the findings appear to have implications for educational practice.

Function of Attitudes

The function of skills is generally so obvious that one does not even have to discuss the matter in a chapter of a book on skill learning. One learns to type to earn a living, or to handle personal correspondence more efficiently for some other well-identified purpose, but why does one learn an attitude? The functions of attitudes are as varied as are the functions of skills, but these functions are much less easily identified. Indeed, a whole research literature has developed around the functions of attitudes. McGuire (1969) has attempted to bring together this literature and to identify a number of different categories of function. The different classes of function he proposes are the following:

Adaptive Functions. Some attitudes serve highly utilitarian purposes. Consider, for example, a withdrawal response that a child learns from touching a hot object that has burned him. The withdrawal response that occurs on subsequent occasions, whenever the object is seen, represents a primitive attitude that serves the purpose of protecting the individual from physical harm. At a more complicated and sophisticated level of attitude development, a person may develop an attitude because it enables him to become accepted by his group. A young man in business may adopt "establishment" attitudes for he views these as aiding his advancement. The development of attitudes of convenience is a widespread phenomenon that social psychologists have studied intensively. The phenomenon can be of enormous social significance, as it was in Nazi Germany where millions adopted anti-Semitic attitudes for the purpose of surviving in a Hitlerian culture; yet when Germany was later occupied by the Allies, anti-Semitism hardly seemed to exist—or to have existed.

Cognitive Functions. Another section of this book on concept learning makes the point that concepts permit the classification of the endlessly varied phenomena of the world into a limited number of categories, and that in this way the environment is simplified so that interactions with it can be more readily handled. We perceive an object and classify it as a table and, once we have done this, we do not have to bother about the wealth of detail that the particular table involves. Having thus classified the object as a table, we are in a position to respond to it as we respond to all objects in that particular class, by making such responses as putting things on it, eating off it, and placing chairs around it. These responses are related to the *class* of objects denoted by the word *table* rather than to particular instances of tables. Attitudes also have a similar simplifying function. They result in generalizations that are gross oversimplifications of an overwhelmingly complex universe. The Russian who takes the position that all capitalists are a menace to an egalitarian society, or the American who takes the position that the only good Communist is a dead Communist, are both expressing attitudes that oversimplify, to an appalling degree, the real world. Although living creatures can adapt to the world only if they are able to treat it as though it were much simpler than it actually is, sometimes oversimplification can also produce problems, as is evident in the case of the illustration just discussed.

Need Gratification Functions. The title of this category is a little confusing in that all attitudes must, in some way, serve the individual who possesses them. The functions included here are those that involve the very direct gratifications of needs. Men have positive attitudes to women and women toward men. We have positive attitudes toward good food, friendly company, and a warm and dry environment. Attitudes are also related to some of the more subtle needs.

Ego-Defense Functions. Some attitudes are held in order to bolster the individual's own evaluations of himself. An extreme example is found in the Nazis' belief that they belonged to the master race; in order to maintain this belief, they had to accept at the same time the belief that other identifiable outgroups such as Jews, Negroes, Frenchmen, Communists, and so forth, were grossly inferior to them. In the case of the Nazis, the picture is also complicated by an idealized conception of a father figure, in the form of a Führer, against whom no hostility can be felt without arousing feelings of extreme guilt. In such a situation, pent-up hostilities become directed toward outgroups against whom extreme cruelty can be exerted without arousing any feelings of guilt whatsoever. A familiar example from our own culture of an attitude functioning as an ego-defense mechanism is found in the case of political figures with a limited education who insist on referring to professors as *stupid intellectuals.* Such politicians feel enormously threatened by the academic intellectual, but the threat can be reduced by calling the intellectual stupid.

Theories of Attitude Change

Social psychologists, vigorously engaged in programs of research and producing a great harvest of experimental results, have readily jumped into the task of theory building. Two large volumes have appeared summarizing, and criticizing, various theoretical positions (Abelson et al., 1968, Insko, 1967). Thus we find in the literature several reinforcement theories of attitude formation and change: classical conditioning theories, cognitive consistency theories, type theories, adaptation-level theories, and at least a dozen other theories with established names. It would be useless, even futile, to plunge the reader into this morass of theorizing.

What seems to be profitable is to consider first the two theories that are most closely linked to traditional views of learning. These are the theories that view the acquisition and modification of attitudes as examples of either operant conditioning or classical conditioning. These theoretical positions are obviously closely tied to much that has been included in this book, but they cannot be considered to the exclusion of all others, in view of the fact that their contribution has been extremely limited. For this reason, a third theory, cognitive dissonance theory, has also been included, because this theory is probably the most influential of all theories in the area at the present time. This third type of theory comes from a family of theories known as cognitive consistency theories, which have been summarized in a massive handbook edited by Abelson, et al. (1968).

Reinforcement in Attitude Acquisition and Change

One position with respect to attitude acquisition and change comes from those interested in operant conditioning. According to this view, attitudes are groups of behaviors that can be established in the first place, or modified, through reinforcement procedures. In other words, the assumption is made that attitudes are learned in exactly the same way as are skills. This viewpoint is to be contrasted with the more conventional one that assumes that attitudes are internal conditions influencing behavior and that although attitudes may manifest themselves through behavior, they are not just groups of behaviors. Thus the psychologist who views all learning as operant conditioning considers attitudes to be observable events, whereas most psychologists would view attitudes as internal and not directly observable.

The position that attitudes change according to the principles of reinforcement is one that has prompted a considerable body of research. The operant conditioning approach to attitude change suggests that the way to modify attitudes is to wait for some slight change in the desired direction to occur, and then reinforce the changed attitude. Thus a Republican who wishes to change the political attitudes of his Democratic friend might wait until the friend expressed some favorable opinion about the Republican party, and then he would reinforce the behavior of his friend. Another approach might be for the Republican to arrange a situation in which his friend was likely to express a favorable comment toward the Republican party and then apply reinforcement. He might do this by arranging for his friend to meet a particularly likable Republican and hope that this situation might elicit attitudes that he might want to reinforce.

Laboratory techniques have been developed for testing this theory that attitudes are learned and changed through reinforcement. These techniques have been well summarized by Insko (1967), together with the experimental results. One technique involves asking students to prepare short speeches to be presented in debating an issue. Some of the participants in the experiment are asked to support in their speeches a position opposite to or very different from their own position. This procedure requires the individuals involved to express attitudes different from those which they ordinarily express. The psychologist can then determine whether the reinforcement of these new attitudes results in their becoming established. The person who presents the speech can either win or lose the debate, and the experimenter generally rigs the experiment so that certain designated persons are declared winners, regardless of how they perform, and others are declared losers. This is one way of reinforcing the expressed attitude. An alternative is to provide cash prizes for certain performers in the debate, who are thus designated as outstanding.

Another technique for studying attitude change through reinforcement involves inducing a person to make a statement contrary to his opinion. Festinger and Carlsmith (1959) exposed subjects to a series of boring tasks and the subjects were then paid to tell other subjects that the experience had been interesting and enjoyable. Later, the participants thus paid were asked to rate truthfully how much they had enjoyed or been bored with the tasks. Still another technique requires students to write essays on an issue presenting a particular position. Students can be assigned positions to write about that differ in a specified degree from their own position. Here again, rewards may follow the performance or they may not.

In most studies, but not in all, the mere expression of an opinion different from that initially held results in a negligible amount of shift of attitude, but when these expressions of attitude are coupled with a strong reinforcer, such as money or praise, substantial changes in attitude occur.

It is easy to adopt a simplistic position and say that the reinforcement produces attitude change in the experiments just described, but a sufficient amount is known about the problem to be able to provide a more sophisticated explanation. In most of the studies one cannot state very clearly what is being reinforced, which is perhaps the reason why the results are not always entirely consistent from study to study. If a person is given a prize for presenting a speech that takes a position opposite to the one he holds, the prize may tell him that he has done a good job of presenting a thesis with which he does not agree. In such a case his skill in acting is what is being reinforced. On the other hand, if he is told at the time he is given the prize that his ideas were very well organized and well presented, then what is reinforced is his skill in organizing ideas. Reinforcement theory would also have to concede that what is being reinforced is his ability to make statements presenting a particular position. A study by Wallace (1966) throws some light on this problem.

Wallace used the typical experimental design, beginning by measuring the attitudes of the subjects, and then asking each to give a talk presenting a position different from that which the individual subject held. The topic was capital punishment and those not in favor of capital punishment presented speeches in favor of it. The speeches were presented in front of an audience of stooges. Although the design of the experiment was complex, the essential feature for the present discussion was that two kinds of reinforcement were given. Each member of one group at the end of the presented speech was told that the content presented was given a high rating by the audience but that the manner in which it had been presented was average. Each member of another group was told that the manner of presenting the speech was good but that the content was average. The interesting finding was that those reinforced for their ideas showed little attitude change but very substantial changes were shown by those told that their manner was excellent even though their ideas were average.

Now these results do not fit ideas commonly expressed about operant conditioning. Indeed, in terms of the latter ideas, one would have expected that those reinforced for the content of their speeches would have shown the greatest changes, but the opposite occurred. Those reinforced for their manner made the greatest changes. Wallace has an explanation.

Wallace suggests that when a subject is told that he had an excellent manner in presenting his material, this means that he has been viewed by the audience as presenting an exemplary role of one who holds the particular position given in the speech. A person who is in favor of capital punishment, when placed in such a position, would suddenly discover that he is seen by the audience as having a sincere commitment *against* capital punishment. This produces strong internal conflict, in that the subject knows himself to be in favor of capital punishment, but he also suddenly sees himself as a convincing opponent of this form of punishment. One way to resolve this conflict is to change his internal attitude and he can say to himself that he never really was completely in favor of capital punishment and that he just favored it under some circumstances. In this way he can harmonize his beliefs with his action.

The very small change in attitude that occurred when the quality of the content of the speech was rewarded also needs explanation. The simplest view in this respect would be that the subjects who were told that the content was good were not troubled in any way with the lack of harmony between what they had said in their speeches and what they believed. They recognized that there was discord, but the discord would be only temporary for they had been engaging in some kind of intellectual exercise that called for such discord. At the end of the discord they could forget about the content of the speech they had made and return to their original position. They did not have to resolve the perception of themselves as a sincere and committed believer in a new position with the position they had long previously taken on the issue. Thus the one group was highly motivated to change its attitude, but the other group was not.

Classical Conditioning Theories of Attitude Learning

An entirely different approach to attitude learning has been developed by Staats (1968), who describes his approach as a classical conditioning theory. The theory assumes that the development of attitudes is highly dependent on the use and learning of language, and it also assumes that attitudes are a reflection of the way in which emotional responses are tied to words. Consider the word *democracy,* for example. Although this word has a definite meaning in terms of the institutions to which one can point as examples of this particular form of government, it also conveys meaning in terms of emotional expression. The word elicits outgoing, warm, and supportive behavior, when it is used in certain contexts, as when the President appeals for a democratic approach to the solution of contemporary problems. The word has the capability of eliciting various approach and withdrawal tendencies under various conditions. Staats has conducted research to show what he believes to be the general laws under which such emotional meanings are acquired, and he identifies these emotional meanings with the term *attitude.* Although Staats has initiated experiments in this area, the basic idea is not new and has been outlined in a general theory of meaning developed by Osgood (1963), which in many ways is more satisfactory than that of Staats.

Staats demonstrated in an early experiment how words can have new emotional responses tied to them. He read to his subjects a list of common words that do not ordinarily elicit any strong emotional responses such as *radio, these, chair, lake, box, large, five,* etc. The words were read in random order and each word was repeated several times. In the case of the word *large,* the enunciation of the word was followed by either a strong unpleasant noise, or an electric shock of uncomfortable strength. The word *large* was presented altogether fourteen times and after nine of these presentations one or other of the two noxious stimuli were presented. Staats was able to show that, following this experience, the word *large,* when presented alone, had the property of eliciting emotional responses that could be measured in terms of physiological changes (galvanic skin response.) Furthermore, the experiment was able to demonstrate that, after the experimental treatment, subjects found that the word *large* tended to have an unpleasant connotation that it had not had prior to the experiment.

The experiment fits well the classical conditioning model of learning, in that the electric shock and the loud, unpleasant sound both have the property of eliciting a number of bodily responses, including the galvanic skin response. These responses to shock or loud sounds are not presumed to be learned responses. When these same stimuli are paired with the word *large,* then that word also becomes capable of eliciting these same responses. There is still a stretch of the imagination involved in believing that the word acquires an unpleasant connotation by this same classical conditioning procedure, because one cannot identify any particular bodily activity that is the bodily component of the experience of unpleasantness. Staats writes in a very convincing way that the responses attached to words, which give them their fullness of meaning, are acquired by classical conditioning, but his convincing style should not be confused with convincing data.

Up to this point the Staats demonstration follows closely the procedures involved in classical conditioning in animals and men, but the procedure is not sufficient to account for attitude development. One does not acquire a favorable attitude toward democracy by having good things happen when the word is used. Our positive feelings about the word are not derived by any simple conditioning in schools and Staats agrees that something more complicated is involved. His argument is that words such as *democracy* acquire positive meaning because they are associated with other words that have strong emotional components in their meaning. Perhaps the concept of *dictatorship* can be used to illustrate the point. The word is learned early in social studies lessons by pointing to examples, but these examples are taken to show that dictatorship *harms* or *hurts* people. Now the words *harm* and *hurt* acquired deep emotional meaning early in life when, perhaps, the parent accidentally steps on the child's hand as he plays on the floor. The upset parent probably protests, "I didn't mean to *harm* you," or "I didn't mean to *hurt* you." Through such situations the words acquire emotional components to their meaning. Later, when the word *dictator* is discussed as denoting a person who is likely to *harm* or *hurt* people, these same emotional components tend to become attached to the word *dictator*. Staats accounts for this learning also in terms of classical conditioning, but through what is known as higher order conditioning.

An example of higher order conditioning is found in the case in which a dog learns to salivate when a light flashes by pairing the flash of the light with a bell that has already become a conditioned stimulus for salivation. The initial procedure involves the pairing of the food and the bell in a simple classical conditioning situation. Once the bell has been firmly established as a stimulus that will elicit salivation, the bell can then be paired with a light which flashes on whenever the bell sounds. After a number of pairings of the light and the bell, the bell then acquires the property of eliciting the salivation response. The latter is a case of higher order conditioning. Staats claims that when a word such as *hurt* is paired with a word such as *dictator,* then the emotional responses produced by the word *hurt* come to be produced by the word *dictator,* just as the light comes to trigger the emotional responses that were triggered in the dog at the beginning of the experiment by the bell.

The argument is highly plausible, and Staats has developed some laboratory demonstrations of this phenomenon. He describes (1968) a number of experiments that do just this. His experimental technique involves taking nonsense syllables, such as *xeh, laj, yof,* and *wuh,* which are relatively neutral in any emotion they may arouse, and then presenting them to subjects in situations in which they are paired with words that have emotion-arousing properties. In one study, some syllables were paired with such words as *beauty, win, gift, sweet, honest, smart, rich,* and so forth, and other nonsense words were paired with such words as *thief, bitter, ugly, sad,* and *worthless.* Later, the nonsense syllables were rated for the extent to which they were regarded as pleasant or unpleasant words. Those paired with words having pleasant associations were rated as more pleasant than those that had been paired with words carrying a disagreeable meaning.

Although the Staats theory of attitude change has considerable plausibility, it has not met with general acceptance. Several reasons account for the fact that it has had little impact. One is that it is generally viewed as a gross oversimplification of what probably happens. There already exist much more sophisticated theories of how words acquire meaning. One such theory developed by Osgood (1963) had already taken the position that simple classical conditioning is not enough to explain how words acquire meaning. Osgood points out that when a word is heard, it is first identified as belonging to a class. Thus, the word *house* is identified as belonging to the same general category that includes *building, cottage, habitation, dwelling,* and so forth. Any conditioning that takes place is to the class of words taken as a whole. In doing this, Osgood has introduced a mediating process into the perception of the meaning of words, but he then goes on to point out that the theory is still too simple to account for the acquisition of word meaning. He then proposes an even more elaborate theory. The highly simplified theory of Staats is probably quite inadequate to account for the linking of emotional responses to particular words.

A second fact that accounts for the lack of support found for the Staats theory of how attitudes are acquired and changed is that it has not helped scientists to make useful and interesting predictions. On the other hand, the next kind of theory to be considered, dissonance theory, has provided a basis for predicting whether attitude change will or will not occur in particular situations. Dissonance theories of attitude change have also stimulated an enormous body of important research. The stimulation of research is one of the very important functions of a good theory.

Dissonance Theories of Attitude Change

Although a simple concept of attitude change through reinforcement or through classical conditioning finds support in much of the data that have been discussed, more complicated explanations have to be introduced in order to understand the results of some studies. For example, Rosenberg (1960) conducted a study in which subjects were hypnotized and then given a post-hypnotic suggestion to become very favorable in their attitude toward such matters as blacks moving into white neighborhoods, comprehensive federal medical insurance, and other widely discussed issues. In other words, the subjects were commanded to feel differently from the way they had felt prior to hypnosis, but they were not reinforced for manifesting particular behaviors. The interesting result was that although the subjects did express different feelings toward the various issues under post-hypnotic suggestion, they also showed a tendency to change their actual beliefs with respect to these issues in a manner that tended to make them consistent with their newly acquired way of feeling. Rosenberg's position was that attitudes tend to change in a direction that makes the person involved more consistent internally. If one wishes to produce attitude change, then one must arrange for inconsistency in the individual's feelings and beliefs, for only under such a condition will attitude change occur.

The data derived from the Rosenberg study, like that from many other studies, does not fit the reinforcement model of learning. In order to understand such data, the concept is usually introduced that man cannot tolerate any inconsistencies that he perceives in himself, and also that he will change in a direction that tends to reduce internal inconsistency. Thus a person who believes in an isolationist position on foreign policy and who feels strongly and positively about the isolationist position has almost certainly a system of beliefs consistent with the way he feels. He will tend to acquire further information consistent with the way he feels and consistent with the information previously acquired. He is likely to forget information presented to him that does not support his beliefs and feelings.

This concept of man that emphasizes striving toward unity has had a long history and a substantial impact on education. The great Prussian educator Froebel was one of the first to view man in this light, although he derived this conception from the theological doctrine that the soul is characterized by unity. Psychologists later came to observe that people do not readily tolerate inconsistency within themselves and that many psychological mechanisms have the function of minimizing inconsistency in what the individual perceives in himself. Freud long ago observed that people commonly fail to recognize in themselves those characteristics that do not fit their own self-concept. A wealthy man, who regards himself as a philanthropist, may fail to recognize a streak of stinginess in his day-to-day dealings. A man of generally kindly disposition may fail to recognize the numerous small hostile acts he directs toward his mother-in-law. Later research workers noted that a reader tends to assimilate information consistent with his own personal viewpoint much more readily than information that is inconsistent.

Such observations, backed up in recent times by a substantial body of research, have led psychologists to develop theories of cognitive consistency summarized in the handbook on the subject by Abelson et al. (1968). Such theories deal with a variety of phenomena, from an apparent tendency to remember only those facts that are consistent with previously acquired knowledge to problems related to attitude acquisition and change. One of the most influential of such theories of attitude change is that which Festinger has developed. The original theory was presented in Festinger's book (1957) but it has since received elaboration at the hands of various research workers. Festinger, unlike many other research workers in the field of attitudes, has presented a theory that emphasizes cognitive elements in attitude change, that is to say, elements involving knowledge. He is broad in defining what he means by these cognitive elements, in that information held that is incorrect is also thought of as a cognitive element. These elements are called cognitions. Festinger does not make a distinction in formulating his theory between knowledges, beliefs, and opinions, because, so long as they are a part of the individual's psychological make-up, they function in a very similar way.

Although the theme of Festinger's book is that man strives to remove inconsistency, he prefers to use the term *dissonance* rather than *inconsistency*. The entire book is concerned with four propositions. First, the presence of dissonance is "psychologically uncomfortable" (p. 3), hence, dissonance motivates the person to reduce it. Second, the person actively avoids situations likely to increase any dissonance already present. Third, an inconsistent environment tends to continuously produce dissonance within the individual. Fourth, individuals differ in the extent to which they will tolerate dissonance within themselves. Festinger also suggests a number of mechanisms that commonly come into play when dissonance occurs. Some of these can be illustrated by an example. Suppose that a person, strongly opposed to the United States' program of foreign aid, were exposed to a lecture in which the arguments in favor of foreign aid were clearly presented and evidence was given to support the arguments. Such a lecture presents a situation producing dissonance in our listener. He may reduce this dissonance in a number of different ways. First, he may pass off the arguments and evidence as "nonsense" and forget about the whole affair. Second, he may retain the information provided in the lecture but take the stand that it involves assumptions he does not accept. Third, he may change his attitude toward the foreign aid issue. He is most likely to do this when the arguments are only moderately different from his present position. If the arguments are highly inconsistent with his present position, then he is more likely to behave in terms of the first two alternatives.

Festinger describes four conditions to which dissonance may be attributed. These four conditions bring out quite clearly the role that cognitions, that is to say, beliefs about the world, play in his theory. The first source of dissonance is logical inconsistency. Consider the following two statements:

1. Cigarette smoke damages the lungs.
2. Cigarette smoking will not hurt me.

If a smoker, like many smokers, makes both statements to himself, he will be in a state of dissonance. The one is logically inconsistent with the other.

A second source of dissonance is inconsistency with cultural mores. The writer can remember in 1965, when there were still few anti-Vietnam demonstrations, joining a small band of people protesting the war. The group of about thirty individuals marched through town under the eyes of a hostile police force, and a mob of swearing and unruly citizens. Such a situation produces dissonance, for the behavior involved was highly inconsistent with the need to be accepted by others. The dissonance provides a situation highly favorable for attitude change, but in the case of the situation described the high morale and the mutually supportive behavior of the members of the small group of marchers probably counteracted the dissonance effect.

A third source of dissonance is where there is inconsistency between a particular behavior and the general trend in behavior, or, as Festinger says, between one cognition and a more general cognitive state. A cautious and well-trained automobile driver who takes liberties with the speed limits because he is in a hurry experiences such dissonance.

A fourth source is probably the most common. Whenever an event does not fit our past experience, dissonance is produced. If an old friend is suddenly rude to us, or if the car that has always started does not start, or if the voice we expect to greet us at the door is not heard: in all of these situations dissonance occurs.

Another important aspect of Festinger's theory is that he deals with situations in which decisions have to be made. It is in such situations that dissonance is most likely to occur and attitudes are most likely to be changed. Because in the making of decisions rewards are generally at stake, the magnitude of the reward is also a factor in determining the degree of dissonance that the decision and the resulting state of affairs produces. Suppose an honest politician has to choose between (1) backing a corrupt candidate he does not like, but with the understanding that if he does so he will receive a large party contribution toward his own election, or (2) choosing somebody he likes and not obtaining party funds. Under such conditions, if he backs the corrupt candidate, his action is dissonant with his own standard of ethics, but the extent he experiences dissonance will depend upon the size of the party's reward in contributing campaign funds. If the reward is small, the resulting dissonance will be large, but if the financial contribution is large, then the amount of dissonance will be relatively low. The dissonance is small when the reward is large because, under that set of circumstances, he can say to himself that the large sum of money makes it all worthwhile and that the money will support a good cause, and that the good accomplished outweighs the bad. Under such circumstances dissonance is resolved.

The presence of dissonance is believed to be necessary for attitude change. Consider the case of the person who for some reason chooses to attend a lecture presenting an opinion with which he disagrees. If he finds the speaker extremely likable, even though the views of the speaker are different from his own, he will experience little dissonance in the situation. The latter situation is like that of having a large reward built into the situation. However, if the speaker is a disagreeable fellow, much more dissonance will be produced and the amount of attitude change is likely to be larger. Dissonance theory has produced some predictions, like this one, that seem unlikely, in terms of popular psychological ideas, but that have been verified experimentally to some degree. This relationship between speaker attractiveness and change in attitude is not found when the listener is *forced* to listen to a presentation (see Jones and Brehm, 1967), but only when attendance is voluntary.

A different approach to the study of the effect of dissonance on attitude change is found in a series of studies reviewed by Aronson (1968). In these studies, dissonance was produced by paying subjects to take a position contrary to their beliefs. The amount of money paid was varied. In such experiments, the typical situation has been one in which a person's beliefs are first identified, and then he must present to the experimenter, or to an audience that includes the experimenter, a defense for a counterposition, that is to say, a position that is opposite to that of his beliefs. Later, his beliefs are again determined to find evidence of change. The conclusions from such experiments are surprisingly consistent, namely, that when the reward offered for the presentation of the counterattitude is small, then the change in attitude is larger than when the reward offered is greater. The proponents of dissonance theory interpret this by saying that when the reward is small, then subjects have to find a reason for saying the things they are saying. The easiest reason to find is that what they are saying really has some truth to it. On the other hand, when the reward is large, the person admits to himself that he is being bribed, and this is justification for expressing beliefs with which he does not agree. Aronson also points out that there are a few studies in which this effect was not found, but they are all studies in which the subjects did not have to face an audience when they were presenting ideas inconsistent with their own beliefs. In the latter situations they typically wrote essays. In such situations there is an entirely different relationship between reward and change than there is in the face-to-face situations previously considered. While in the latter situations the greatest change occurs when the reward is smallest, in those situations that do not involve face-to-face relationships the largest reward produces the greatest attitude. There is apparently a real and important difference between facing an audience and presenting ideas in which one does not believe and doing this in a more secluded situation. Aronson suggests that the psychological difference between these two situations is a difference in what he calls the commitment involved.

The relationship of reward to attitude change in the class of experiment just discussed is different from what one would expect in terms of reinforcement theory. In these experiments, increasing the size of the reward has a negative effect on the learning one is interested in bringing about. Dissonance theory, in this situation, makes better predictions than those made from reinforcement concepts. However, it must be noted that dissonance theory makes good predictions only when there is commitment on the part of the subject, in the sense in which the term commitment is used by Aronson.

One of the very interesting events predicted by dissonance theory is that a mild threat is more likely to make a person desist from an activity he likes to engage in than a strong threat. Aronson (1968) has been largely responsible for developing and testing this hypothesis and has reviewed the studies related to it. He argues that if a child is threatened with severe punishment for performing an activity that he likes to perform, then he will continue to like the activity but perhaps temporarily stop performing it. The threat is sufficient justification for not performing it but he will return to the activity later if the threat is removed. However, if the threat is mild, the threat and the activity are dissonant, and dissonance can be reduced by the child's telling himself that he really does not like the activity. As a result, his tendency to perform the activity is reduced. Aronson reports a series of experiments in which children were threatened with either mild or severe punishment for playing with a desired toy. Those threatened with mild punishment showed a reduced liking for the toy, but those threatened with severe punishment continued to show a liking for the toy at the same level as previously.

Another prediction made also by Aronson and his associates (1968) was that individuals who went through a disagreeable initiation ceremony in order to enter a group would be more likely to value highly the activities of the group than those who were not required to go through an initiation or who went through a bland and innocuous initiation. In this experiment, women students in a psychology class were divided into three groups. In order to become a member of a discussion group on the psychology of sex, the members of one group were each required to read aloud, to a male instructor, a list of taboo words, that is to say, words not ordinarily used in social life. Another group had a mild initiation involving no socially prohibited words, and the third group had no initiation ceremony. All groups then heard a recording of a discussion of the psychology of sex. They did not know that it was a taped recording but believed that what they heard through the earphones was an ongoing, live discussion. The discussion had been made deliberately boring. At the end of the session the subjects had to make an evaluation of the discussion. Those who had been subjected to the severe initiation evaluated the discussion with more praise than those who had had either a mild initiation or who had had no initiation. The dissonance produced by reciting the list of taboo words was reduced by taking the position that it was a price worth paying for gaining access to an interesting discussion.

The findings of the initiation-ceremony experiment have been confirmed rather strikingly in studies in which the severe initiation was replaced by a series of electric shocks (Gerard and Mathewson, 1966). Once again it was found that following electric shock, the discussion that subjects listened to was rated higher.

Cognitive dissonance theory in its various forms has been immensely successful as a stimulus for research, as is evident from the large number of studies that have been produced that are related to the ideas that flow from it. Some of these experiments have also had considerable significance to the whole field of psychology, in that they have pointed out some of the limitations of the predictions that can be made from a simple reinforcement theory. The reader should not think there is an issue of whether cognitive consistency theories are nearer or farther from the truth than reinforcement theories, for this is not a real issue. In some situations cognitive dissonance theories provide the best predictions, but there are other situations in which reinforcement concepts are the most serviceable. The immediate scientific problem is to identfy the conditions under which each can be most effectively applied, much as physicists have discovered the conditions under which the wave theory of light and quantum theory can each be most effectively applied to the making of predictions. Whether the wave theory of light and quantum theory can be fully resolved still remains to be seen. Reinforcement and dissonance theory may also have a long history of mutual coexistence.

The chief limitation on dissonance theory, for which it has been widely criticized, is the vagueness of the term dissonance. Festinger originally described two elements as being dissonant if the "obverse of one element would follow from the other" (1967, p. 13). The word *obverse* is highly ambiguous and is used by Festinger as a synonym for opposite, but this is not really what obverse means at all in logic, where it is widely used. Perhaps the word *opposite* would have been a more appropriate one to use, but even that is not a very clear term. The term *inconsistency* is also widely used as a synonym for dissonance. Aronson (1968) suggests that when it is said that two cognitions are dissonant it means that, given the one cognition, then the expectancy of the other cognition is very low. If I buy a car for eight thousand dollars and it refuses to start, there is dissonance for, having paid a high price for a car, I expect it to go. If I believe in capital punishment and find myself in a situation in which I am arguing against capital punishment, there is dissonance because, given the fact that I believe in capital punishment, I do not expect to find myself advocating its abolition. Dissonance seems to be quite well defined in terms of conflicts between cognitions and expectancies, but the measurement of expectancies is not always easily undertaken.

Katz (1968) points out that another source of evidence that runs against dissonance theory is the very evident fact that people do not resolve many, or perhaps even most, of the dissonances within themselves. If they did, then each would end up with nice tidy views of the world devoid of any inconsistencies. Many individuals are not at all concerned about the fact that the views they proclaim on Sunday about brotherly love are quite inconsistent with the ways in which they behave during the rest of the week. They also make no attempt to resolve these inconsistencies and, indeed, commonly do not even recognize them in their behavior. Such observations suggest that one aspect of dissonance theory that has to be developed is the identification of the conditions under which inconsistency becomes a motivating force that energizes behavior in the direction of resolving the inconsistency.

Despite these limitations, dissonance theory has proven itself to be one of the most stimulating innovative ideas in social psychology and has been the initiator of research in a whole area of learning where straightforward reinforcement concepts have had only the most limited value. The theory has also done more than stimulate research, for it has also been effective in making predictions in situations in which predictions have not been effectively made from alternative formulations. This does not mean that dissonance theory can be viewed as a general substitute for reinforcement concepts. Both systems provide limited capabilities for predicting behavior in limited situations. Finally, the point must be made that dissonance theory is offered as a contribution to theory of motivation, in that the motive to reduce dissonance is offered as a source of motivation. There is no suggestion that this is the only motive operating, but it is one motive of considerable importance.

Attitude Learning: The Impact of the Different Theoretical Positions

The three theoretical positions related to the acquisition or change in attitudes presented here do not constitute a comprehensive review of the different theoretical positions found in the literature, but they represent the main positions. Insko (1967) has reviewed eleven different theoretical positions, and still others could probably be culled from the research literature. The three that have been chosen represent classes of theory of which the others represent variations. The three also represent positions around which research has been organized. The positions represented by these theories are immensely different—indeed, they could not be more different—but competing theories in a scientific area may often be completely incompatible one with the other. All the theories have shown a limited capacity to provide a basis for making predictions, but they have all also provided notable failures in this respect. Scientific theories have to be able to make predictions in order to be able to survive, and all three positions have shown a limited ability to survive in this respect. Scientific theories can also be evaluated in terms of the extent to which they have been able to stimulate research. The three positions differ considerably in the extent to which they have been able to provoke scientists to undertake research. The most effective of the three has been dissonance theory, in that it has resulted in the development of a prolific research literature. Some of the findings from research have been extraordinarily supportive of dissonance theory, which has shown a capability of making verifiable predictions that neither the operant position nor the classical conditioning theory would have made. Nobody would take the position that dissonance theory, which is basically a perceptual theory of learning, has been verified and established by research. It has shown itself capable of making some kinds of predictions and it has been an unusual source of stimulation of research. That is probably about as much as one can expect from a psychological theory at this time.

Communications that Change Attitudes

Up to this point in the chapter we have undertaken a rather brief exploration of major positions that have been used to account for attitude change. This review has highlighted the difficulty of making predictions of the conditions under which attitude change can be most readily produced. In educational settings, the setting most likely to be used to bring about attitude change involves written or spoken communication. A considerable amount is known at this time about the particular conditions occurring during a communication that make for effective attitude changes, and it is to these conditions that consideration must now be given.

Many hundreds of studies on the effectiveness of communications in producing attitude changes have been reviewed by Berscheid and Walster (1969). This excellent review divides the problem into three components: (1) the characteristics of an effective communicator, (2) the characteristics of an effective communication, and (3) the characteristics of the receivers of communications, for some receivers are much more likely than others to react to a communication. This section of the chapter is addressed to the problem of attitude changes and is not concerned with the problem of the effectiveness of communications for imparting information. Following the structure provided by Berscheid and Walster, let us consider each one of these aspects of communication separately.

The Characteristics of the Effective Communicator. The best explored of these characteristics are expertness and trustworthiness. The sources of some communications represent a higher level of expertness than do others and the assumption has long been made that the more expert the source, the greater will be the influence on attitudes. Research on this issue is complicated by the fact that the immediate effect is often different from the long-term effect. The more expert or credible the source of a communication, the greater is the immediate effect on attitudes. However, when the effect of a highly expert source was compared with a less expert source, the difference in the change in attitudes produced declines with time. Berscheid and Walster suggest that memory for the characteristics of a communicator fades much more rapidly than does the content of the message itself. Thus any influence that the communicator may have on the attitudes of the person receiving the message also declines rapidly with the passage of time.

The relationship of the person who hears a communication to the source of the communication can vary in so many different ways that the effect of each one of these relationships on attitude change has not yet been fully investigated. Most studies have varied simultaneously several of the factors involved without making it possible to separate in the data the effects involved. The listener may be a part of a captive audience, just as most children in school are captive audiences and cannot walk out on the source of communications. The listener may be noncaptive and happen to overhear a communication. The communicator may hold a very different opinion from that of the listener, or his opinion may be rather close to that of the listener. The communicator may announce that his intention is to change the attitude of the listener, or he may blandly declare that he is not interested in changing anybody's beliefs but is merely engaged in passing on information. The effect of each of these variables cannot be clearly and concisely determined at this time from the research findings to date.

There is some trend in the findings of studies to suggest that communications overheard, as if by accident, produce greater attitude change than those directed to the listener. Much seems to depend on whether the overheard communication has, or does not have, relevance for the listener. If I am overweight and eavesdrop on a discussion of the importance of weight reduction, the discussion is likely to have no influence on my attitude toward the problem unless I am one of those who wants to reduce, even though I am one of those who has not found a way to do it.

The effect of the size of the discrepancy between the communicator's attitude and that of the listener has been studied and with some suggestion that the greater the discrepancy between the listener and the speaker, the greater will be the attitude change. If such a finding can be solidly established, it will strike a strong blow in favor of dissonance theory. The larger the discrepancy the greater the dissonance, and the greater the dissonance the greater the need to resolve it.

Communicator characteristics that have little relevance to the communication may have an influence as well as relevant characteristics on the degree to which a particular communication influences a listener's attitudes. Indeed, these so-called irrelevant characteristics may often have more influence than relevant characteristics. The attractiveness of the speaker has long been a subject for research, but the results are not as clear-cut as one would like them to be. Earlier, mention was made of the fact that when a person voluntarily listens to a presentation, then a speaker rated as somewhat disagreeable may produce greater attitude change than a speaker who is personally more attractive. An example of an effect of this kind was obtained by Zimbardo et al., (1965) in a study in which an effort was made to persuade Army recruits and students to eat a highly objectionable food, namely, fried grasshoppers. The audience for this experiment was a captive audience, but each was free to decide whether he would or would not choose to taste fried grasshoppers. An important feature of this experiment would appear to be this freedom of choice. Some of the subjects were exposed to a communicator who was considerate, pleasant, and calm, and who was described as the positive communicator. Other subjects were exposed to a negative communicator who was disagreeable, irritable, and cantankerous. Both communicators were well organized and credible in their presentations. Before and after the experimental procedure, the attitude of subjects toward eating grasshoppers was measured by a paper-and-pencil device prepared for the purpose. The interesting finding of this study was that those who were confronted with the negative communicator and who tasted the grasshoppers showed a more favorable change in attitude than those who tasted them and who were exposed to a positive communicator. Those who did not taste the grasshoppers showed a boomerang effect regardless of the communicator and ended up with an even greater aversion for fried grasshoppers than that with which they started.

Such findings give support for dissonance theory. There is dissonance between the action of eating grasshoppers and the initial attitude toward doing it. This dissonance is increased by the presence of a disagreeable communicator and, it is presumed, increases the tendency for attitudes to change. A positive communicator, on the other hand, reduces the dissonance, for the listeners justify listening to the speech by saying to themselves that he is a nice fellow and that one should treat him courteously.

The relationships that have been discussed between the attractiveness of the speaker and change in attitude are found only under certain conditions, namely, those under which the listener chooses to listen or chooses whether or not to engage in certain activities. In the typical research in which the subjects are captive and are required to listen to a speech on some topic, the opposite findings are more typical. Under the latter conditions, the attractiveness of a speaker is positively related to the extent to which attitudes are changed as a result of the presentation.

Finally, a review by Simons, Berkowitz, and Moyer (1970) brings out some other characteristics that generally make for a more persuasive communicator. The latter is generally more competent than the other members of his peer group. He is better informed. He is gregarious. He tends to belong to the top crust of the social class with which he is identified. He is also, in a peculiar way, what is called super-representative of his group: that is to say, although he stands apart, he embodies in a vivid way the group characteristics. He is also viewed as an instrument for achieving goals important to the group members.

Characteristics of the Communication. It is quite evident that the characteristics of the communication influence its persuasive properties, and some of these characteristics are so obvious that nobody has even bothered to study them. One such characteristic is whether the ideas are clearly presented. In many areas, a clear presentation of the facts would appear to be important for changing attitudes, particularly when the attitudes to be changed are founded on misinformation. For example, many individuals on the American continent have long held that the mixing of the blood of different racial groups has disastrous biological effects on the offspring. This belief has led to the adoption in many states of laws that forbid the intermarriage of different racial groups. A change in the attitudes related to such a belief has been highly dependent upon presenting facts to show that the alleged biological disasters do not occur when members of different races intermarry.

Differences among communications in the information or misinformation they present are easily recognized and can be directly measured. Communications may also differ with respect to much more subtle characteristics. One such property of communications is the emotional tone they convey. Some communications are coldly intellectual, some humorous and charming, some are hostile or threatening, and some attempt to coax the reader into new ways of thinking. There is also an additional vast range of different overtones that may be carried by the main theme of a communication. Educators need to know much more about the significance of these intangible aspects of the communicator's skill, but little is known as yet about their effect upon the receiver of a message. Most research up to this time has been involved with much more tangible aspects of persuasive communications.

One of the oldest controversies in the field of attitude change is whether a communication designed for such a purpose should be one-sided or two-sided. Although these terms have long been used, there is considerable ambiguity concerning what really constitutes a one-sided argument, which is generally defined as one in which only positive support is given for the position the writer or speaker wants to sustain. One could conceivably design a one-sided argument in which only a particular view was presented, along with a rebuttal for all the opposing arguments. Equally, two-sided arguments that have been used for study in research are not really two-sided. Such arguments provide positive support for the position it is desired to support but they also give opposing arguments, along with a rebuttal of each of these arguments. In a sense, the arguments are really still one-sided, even though they mention both sides of the issue. Other variations are also possible. The positive side may be presented either first or last. Arguments may be presented so that they draw a firm conclusion or they may be presented in such a way that the listener or reader has to draw his own conclusions. So many different variations are possible that a generation of graduate students looking for problems for master's theses will not exhaust all the possibilities.

Berscheid and Walster (1969) have attempted to fit together the results of research on this problem, and so has McGuire (1969). Both of these reviewers agree that when the overall effects of a one-sided argument are compared with the results of a two-sided argument (as a two-sided argument is defined here), there is very little difference in the amount of attitude change produced, but much depends on the circumstances of the experiment. If the subjects are relatively intelligent, then they are more likely to be influenced by a two-sided argument than a one-sided argument, but the reverse seems to be true if the subjects are relatively dull. The research suggests that the relatively dull subjects are confused by the two-sided argument.

The Characteristics of Receivers of Communications and Attitude Change. Inquiries into the ability and personality traits that characterize persuasible people have long been investigated, but the problem has shown itself to be much more complex than any of the early research workers had expected it to be.

The nature of a message is highly important in determining whether it does, or does not, attract attention and hence permit the possibility of having impact. Psychologists have always been attracted to the hypothesis that individuals will readily listen to messages with which they agree, but may turn away to other things when confronted with a message with which they do not agree. This has sometimes been termed a cognitive consistency theory of selective attention, and the evidence for it has been summarized in the sourcebook on the subject edited by Abelson et al. (1968). A briefer summary has been provided by Berscheid and Walster (1969) in an article that brings together some of the more important research findings. Berscheid and Walster point out there is quite substantial evidence showing that, in daily life, people do actually listen to and read a preponderance of messages with which they agree and fail to attend to the majority of available messages in their environment with which they disagree. The evidence shows, for example, that Republicans tend to listen to talks by Republican candidates, and Democrats listen to Democrats. Such a trend is found, not only with respect to the major issues of life, but also with respect to the lesser issues. For example, those who have given blood through the Red Cross are more likely to attend a film urging people to donate blood than are nondonors. The evidence seems to be incontrovertible that when audiences consist of members who choose to attend a speech, most speakers find themselves addressing people with whose opinions they already agree.

The basis for this trend in behavior is still not properly understood. One simple plausible explanation runs along these lines. A Republican is a Republican because he has been reinforced throughout his childhood for listening to Republican points of view. Such reinforcements would have led to a habit of attending to Republican messages, which manifests itself in the studies undertaken. Also, because a Republican has not developed a habit of attending to Democrat messages, he is unlikely to attend to such messages. Such habits undoubtedly play a part in these attention phenomena, but they are probably not the entire story. An alternative explanation is found in what has been termed cognitive consistency theory, which, in its simplest form, states that individuals will assimilate information consistent with the information they have already stored and will tend to reject information that is inconsistent.

Psychologists have attempted to design experiments to tease out the different factors involved. In the kind of research we have just been considering, clear tendencies were shown for people to go to certain sources of information rather than to others. Similar kinds of studies can be undertaken under laboratory conditions, where, for example, one can measure the attitude of individuals toward established religions and then offer them the titles of various articles, one or more of which they must choose to read. The titles show clearly that some of the articles are favorable toward established religions and others are unfavorable. The researcher can then test the hypothesis whether individuals tend to choose articles supportive of their own particular position. Sears (1968) has reviewed the numerous laboratory studies conducted in this area and finds that, unlike studies based on everyday behavior, there is no clear-cut tendency for people to seek supportive information and avoid non-supportive information. The discrepancy between laboratory studies and the common life situations needs to be explained. One reason may well be that many of the subjects for the laboratory studies were college students who have been trained to seek out information that conflicts with their opinion. This explanation is plausible, but one may well doubt whether education is as successful as this theory suggests it to be. The conclusion of Berscheid and Walster with respect to this matter is that when individuals have confidence in their knowledge and their positions with respect to particular issues that they are more likely and willing to read communications with which they almost certainly differ. Unwillingness to do this reflects insecurity.

Not all individuals can have their attitudes changed with equal readiness. Most experiments in this area show very large individual differences in this respect and some individuals are highly resistant to all efforts to change their attitudes. McGuire summarizes the findings on the influenceability of attitudes by pointing out that one of the most significant variables is age. He concludes that suggestibility increases through early childhood until about the age of nine. From that age on, there is a decline in suggestibility until adolescence, and then this tendency levels off. The picture is complicated by the fact that this age effect is not the same for all techniques of attitude change. For example, the effect of prestige on attitude change is different at different age levels from the effect of suggestions.

Berscheid and Walster (1969) point out that enough is now known to say that no simple relationship can be expected between intelligence, or educational level achieved, and persuasibility. They go on to note that, if a complex argument is presented to promote a point of view, then the less intelligent may not be moved by it because they do not understand it. The intelligent may be persuaded because they see points they had not seen before. But this does not mean that the more intelligent are always the more persuasible, for they are not. The less intelligent are often more readily persuaded to change their attitudes by a quite naive argument, which may antagonize those who have the capability of seeing through it. Thus, sometimes the more intelligent and sometimes the less intelligent are the more persuasible, depending upon the nature of the communication.

One of the more influential sources of individual differences in influenceability is sex. A long history of research in this area comes up with the unassailable conclusion that women's attitudes are more readily influenced than are those of men. An explanation of this is much more difficult to deliver than the fact itself. On the surface this seems to suggest that women are just more suggestible than are men, but McGuire comes up with an alternative explanation, probably closer to the facts and one that is much less insulting to women and less flattering to men. McGuire musters evidence to support the proposition that the effect is largely due to the fact that women are better listeners than men and that in almost any teaching situation women learn rather more than do men. Certainly among youth of school age this is true, and the girls tend to be a little ahead of boys in what they learn. The essence of the theory of the greater influenceability of women is that because women are likely to absorb more of messages designed to influence their attitudes than are men, they are also more likely to have their attitudes influenced. The relative lack of influence on men is attributable to their inability to listen.

There are also greater individual differences in men than in women in influenceability. This is hardly surprising in that men show greater differences among themselves than do women in practically all abilities and this effect is particularly marked in the case of personality traits and measures of interests. The source of this greater uniformity among women than among men is usually attributed to the fact that girls are expected to conform more than are boys. Also, boys are given much more freedom than are girls and are therefore able to expose themselves to a greater variety of experiences.

Another variable that offers some promise as a correlate of persuasibility is vaguely defined as self-esteem. Although research workers generally shy away from such concepts, because of the difficulty of defining them, this one can be defined in quite specific terms. This has been done in experiments in which a deliberate effort has been made to lower or raise self-esteem by administering a test to the subjects and, then telling some subjects, regardless of how they performed, that they did very poorly, and telling others, also regardless of how they performed, that they had done well. Such an experience of being told that one has done poorly, or well, does have the effect of changing a person's behavior during at least the few hours that follow the experience. Whatever is changed by such a procedure is referred to as self-esteem.

Another technique is to administer a questionnaire that attempts to measure self-esteem. This technique could be regarded as one that attempts to explore the individual's self-concept by finding out what the individual says to himself about himself. One would expect rather different effects from those studies in which an attempt is made to raise or lower esteem than from those that compared a high and a low self-esteem.

The findings derived from the study of this problem seem to be somewhat inconsistent and difficult to fit together. Berscheid and Walster (1969) conclude that attempts to raise or lower self-esteem indicate that, when it is lowered, there tends to be increased influenceability, but when self-esteem is directly measured by means of a questionnaire, no such simple effect is found. McGuire (1968) suggests that a high degree of modifiability of attitudes is associated with either a very high or a very low level of self-esteem. Those who are in the middle range on this variable are the most unchangeable.

An entirely different but insightful approach to the problem comes from research on the characteristics of so-called dogmatic or authoritarian people. This research came into the limelight with the development of a number of testing devices, produced for the purpose of measuring personal dogmatism. The best known of these devices are the California *F* Scale and the Rokeach Dogmatism Scale. These devices have had some success in identifying persons who are commonly described as dogmatic, closed-minded, closed to new ideas, authoritarian, and inflexible. There seems clear evidence that the dogmatic style of personality exists and can be identified, as is evident in a review of the related research by Vacchiano, Strauss, and Hochman (1969). The latter reviewers find the high-dogmatism individual to be psychologically immature in addition to being stereotyped in his thinking and defensive. In addition, such an individual has been shown to be intolerant, impulsive, and poorly adjusted. On the other hand, the low-dogmatism individual has been found to be enterprising, calm, mature, forceful and efficient. One is tempted to speculate that high-dogmatism individuals would also be those whose attitudes would be most difficult to change. One can certainly say that such a hypothesis is attractive. Miller and Rokeach (1968) have reviewed research related to these problems and have come up with the answer that here, just as in other areas of attitude research, simple hypotheses are attractive but misleading. The early research in this area produced the finding in some studies that the highly rigid person, thus defined, was not one whose attitudes and beliefs were readily changed, but in a few studies such individuals were shown to be highly susceptible to being changed. Some insight has now been achieved with respect to these inconsistent findings, which are not really inconsistent at all. Miller and Rokeach point out, as a basis for understanding the early findings, that the person who scores high on dogmatism scales is a person who prevents himself from being exposed to views inconsistent with those that the individual holds. He also avoids information inconsistent with his views and, when he encounters it, is more likely than the nondogmatic person to forget it. Thus he protects himself from any external influence that might produce change in him. He cannot tolerate information or beliefs that are inconsistent with his own. On the other hand, the person who scores at the other end of the dogmatism scale has less difficulty memorizing inconsistent information, and is much less bothered by expressed beliefs different from his own. The difficulty encountered by the highly dogmatic or authoritarian personality is that he cannot tolerate inconsistency or, in terms of theory of attitudes, he has a very low tolerance for dissonance and therefore avoids encounters that might produce dissonance.

But what happens to the high-dogmatism individuals when they cannot avoid being exposed to information inconsistent with their beliefs? This condition can occur in experiments in which students are required to participate in order to fulfill course requirements, and it can also occur in daily life. One interesting situation of the latter kind identified by Miller and Rokeach was derived from a study, undertaken for another purpose, in relation to the Eisenhower-Stevenson presidential contest. This study by Paul (1956) involved identifying a group of voters as either authoritarian or equalitarian. Some people in each one of these categories voted for Eisenhower and some voted for Stevenson. Eisenhower, of course, won the election and hence those who voted for Stevenson would have experienced dissonance through their nonfavorite candidate winning the election. The dissonance thus produced could be reduced by taking a more favorable view of Eisenhower. However, the authoritarian individuals should experience more dissonance because of their inability to tolerate any inconsistency. If they experienced more dissonance, then there should be greater incentive for them to change their view of Eisenhower. This Paul actually found. When the highly dogmatic group was appraised later of their view of Eisenhower, they were found to have changed more in a favorable direction than the equalitarian group.

Miller and Rokeach also cite a number of convincing experimental studies to show that the same kind of phenomenon revealed in connection with the study of the Eisenhower-Stevenson election can be produced in the laboratory. Perhaps the most impressive of these is an unpublished study by Hunt and Miller, for which quite complete data are given by Miller and Rokeach. In the latter study, the technique was adopted of requiring subjects to write statements of belief related to the topic of disarmament. One group wrote statements that they believed, a second group wrote irrelevant statements, and a third group wrote statements contrary to their beliefs. The subjects were also so selected for the experiment that they were either high-dogmatic or low-dogmatic. The attitudes of the subjects toward disarmament were measured before the experimental procedure was undertaken, and also afterward. The one group that showed a substantial change in attitude was the high-dogmatic group that wrote statements at odds with their own belief. This is the group that could tolerate least the inconsistency between their own belief and what they were writing.

The overall evidence from such studies shows that whatever is measured by scales of dogmatism and authoritarianism is a powerful variable related to the individual's ability to tolerate that which is inconsistent with his own characteristics. The same individual may respond to such inconsistencies either by ignoring the incompatible element or by making changes in himself that will tend to remove the inconsistency. Which one he will do will depend upon the particular circumstances involved. One suspects that the first response is that of ignoring the newly presented inconsistent element. Only when this action is not possible will the individual make changes in himself to reduce the inconsistency.

The results of research, on the relationship between measures of dogmatism and persuasibility should not lead the reader to assume that the high-dogmatism person is any less likely to benefit from traditional schooling than is the low-dogmatism individual. Ehrlich and Lee (1969) have reviewed studies relating dogmatism scores to school performance and found that most of these studies showed no relationship between these variables. They did manage to uncover some interesting evidence of a case (Costin, 1968), in which students were learning to discard their misconceptions about behavior in a basic course in psychology. The high-dogmatism students had a significantly greater difficulty in discarding their misconceptions than did the low-dogmatism students. The latter is an example of the way in which this characteristic, dogmatism, may interfere with becoming educated.

Delayed Effects of Conditions That Produce Attitude Change

McGuire (1969) has summarized the literature related to the permanence of changes in attitudes produced by the various techniques discussed here. If an experiment is designed to produce attitude change, and if the attitude is measured after various different times have elapsed, there is likely to be for some time after exposure to the experimental materials designed to change attitudes a steady change in attitude. This phenomenon is quite marked and sometimes may cover a period as long as several months. In a World War II study cited by McGuire, troops were exposed to a film on the Battle of Britain, which was designed to develop in them highly positive attitudes toward the cause for which they were fighting. Eleven weeks after the showing, the impact of the film was still continuing to have an effect. This so-called *sleeper effect* is not understood at this time, although there are a number of theories concerning how it might operate. One difficulty in arriving at an explanation is that one cannot control what happens to the subjects after the end of the main experimental procedures, and what happens may account for at least some of the subsequent attitude change. The men in the World War II study may have discussed the film among themselves during the eleven-week period, and the discussion may have been instrumental in producing further changes in viewpoint. There is also evidence from a number of sources that psychological processes related to beliefs and knowledge, that is to say, cognitive processes, may undergo a very slow organizing and consolidating process during the time that follows an experience that introduces new cognitive elements into the picture. This slow consolidation may well be the cause of the sleeper effect. Presumably, this consolidation effect may sometimes involve verbal processes, as when a person thinks through what he has recently heard and draws conclusions that he did not draw at the time when he first encountered the particular communication.

The slow increased change that follows an attempt to change attitudes ultimately levels off. There then follows a change in the reverse direction and the position of the attitude tends to slip slowly back to the position taken before the attempt to change it was made. The slippage of the attitude back to its previous position is very much like forgetting, and is regarded by McGuire as a forgetting phenomenon. He suggests that the attitude tends to slip back because the individual tends to forget slowly those arguments and points that originally resulted in opinion change. McGuire has been able to demonstrate, by measuring both attitude and knowledge retained of the message that produced an initial attitude change, that as the memory for the message declines so does the attitude tend to slip back.

Strengthening Attitudinal Positions So That They Are Resistant to Attack

Most teachers, and particularly religious teachers, have long been interested in whether attitudes can be bolstered by defenses in such a way that they become highly resistant to change. Many of the ways in which this has been done in our society have not represented techniques with which experiments can be readily undertaken. One social technique is that of associating deep guilt feelings with holding any deviant opinions. Most religions do this by developing in the young the belief that any deviation from the teachings of the particular religious institution is grievously sinful or will lead to eternal damnation. The technique seems to be moderately successful, although some individuals do grow up to master their guilt feelings and do change their attitudes, beliefs, and opinions. A second technique, widely used by religious groups, is that of denying the individual access to either printed material or discourse that might produce a change. Some religious groups place on a censored list certain books to which the faithful are prohibited from having access, and some adopt the related technique of prohibiting their members from mixing with or attending meetings of other religious groups. I once lived in a neighborhood where the predominant religion was X, and the children, the little *x*'s, were forbidden to play with the little *y*'s. The technique of denying access to other ideas is obviously successful as long as it lasts, but children cannot be kept forever from mixing with those of other faiths and, when they do, a boomerang effect may well occur.

A third technique of making attitudes resistant to change is what has been termed the anchoring technique. A prejudice may be given stability by tying it to strongly held beliefs. The traditional prejudice of the Anglo-Saxon toward those with darker skins has been anchored to a set of beliefs such as that those with other shades of skin are stupid and unmotivated and immoral, and so forth. Such beliefs, accepted as if they represented knowledge, keep the prejudice from being shaken.

A fourth technique involves producing in the individual what is termed commitment. The latter is a difficult term to pin down, but it generally means a commitment to some form of action. A young man who decides to become a priest has a commitment in life, and this commitment in itself is likely to prevent the related attitudes and beliefs from being changed. The mere making public of one's position on an issue results in a commitment that makes the underlying attitudes extremely resistant to change. For this reason, many religious groups encourage the public pronouncement of their beliefs by the faithful. Public testimony seems to be an effective way of fixing beliefs.

Experiments in strengthening attitudes to make them resistant to change have generally taken an intellectual approach to the problem.

There are several quite obvious ways of attempting to bolster a person's attitudinal structure against attack. One of these is to warn him that his attitude will be attacked. It seems reasonable to assume that in the psychological field, as in the physical, to be forewarned is to be forearmed. Another technique is to provide him with supportive arguments for his point of view. If he is raised to believe in marriage as an institution, then he may learn to argue that the institution protects children, that it provides some order and stability on a society, and so forth. A third approach involves learning how to rebut arguments presented to change the person's attitudes. The religious person learns many such arguments during his upbringing and thus when he is told that there is no visible evidence for the existence of a God he can make the comeback that many realities, such as subatomic particles, also cannot be observed directly.

The problem considered here has been commonly described as that of *psychological immunization.* Common observation and excellent experimentation support one another in the conclusion that such immunization is possible and probably generally effective. Indeed, the extraordinary stability of beliefs of individuals during early adult life reflects, to some extent, the effectiveness of the immunization that takes place during childhood and adolescence. Such a conclusion is, of course, speculative in that one does not know the extent to which individuals are exposed to propaganda designed to change their attitudes. Only experimentation can provide direct evidence of the effectiveness of immunization procedures. Such evidence has found clear-cut results indicating that immunization procedures are effective in producing stability of attitudes (see McGuire, 1968). Even the simple technique of forewarning a person that one of his cherished beliefs is going to be attacked may increase his resistance to changing his attitudes. Just why forewarning has this effect is not clear. The evidence seems to suggest that forewarning, particularly when it provides some information concerning the nature of the attack to be encountered, activates appropriate defense mechanisms that require a warm-up before they can operate effectively.

Evidence from experimentation also supports the conclusion that the learning of either supporting or rebutting arguments protects attitudes from being changed, but that the rebutting arguments are more effective in this respect than are the supporting arguments. This is hardly surprising. Suppose that I am a firm believer in a free enterprise system and have to debate with a socialist. All the arguments I can muster to support free enterprise may not dispose of my opponent's arguments, for perhaps I am not as smart as he is. My supportive arguments may make me feel better under attack, but my opponent's counterarguments still lurk in the background of my mind because they have not been disposed of. On the other hand, if I were able to provide a complete rebuttal of my opponent's arguments, then I could dispose of them and they would not haunt me as threats to my position.

The most substantial work in this area is found in a series of studies by W. J. McGuire and his associates carried out over almost a decade. These studies and their conclusions have been summarized by Kiesler, Collins, and Miller (1969) in their book on attitude change. The findings of this series of studies may be summarized as follows:

1. The most effective immunization of a belief against attack is to provide both supportive arguments for the belief and exercises involving the presentation of arguments against the belief followed by counter-arguments.

2. The immunization produced by the presentation of arguments against the belief, followed by refutations of those arguments, derives its effect from giving the person practice in mustering his defenses. This is shown by the fact that, after such immunization, he also shows an improved capability of refuting novel arguments against his beliefs that he has not heard before.

3. A condition of threat, introduced by telling the subject that the experiment is a test of their persuasibility, enhances the effect of immunization. A related finding is that telling the subjects that others accept the particular beliefs as true beyond question reduced the effect of immunization. It would seem that, in the latter case, the subjects were lulled into a state of apathy where they were not willing to muster counterarguments when faced with an attack on their beliefs.

4. The effect of immunization first increases for a short period at the end of the immunization training period, and then declines. The decline is to be expected in view of the fact that memory is involved and the information contained in the counterarguments will slowly become less and less readily available.

Finally, a limitation is placed on the generality of the conclusions that can be drawn from most immunization studies, in that they have typically used a single category of belief for study. Most of the studies have been focussed on the stability of common beliefs when these come under attack. Examples of such beliefs are represented by such statements as that one should brush one's teeth after every meal, or that mental illness is not contagious. The results of such studies need to be confirmed with a range of materials before they can be considered to have general application.

In addition to the studies designed to investigate the intellectual manipulation of beliefs, McGuire (1969) has located a number of studies that collectively support the thesis that commitment provides stability for attitudes. The typical study in the latter connection is one in which the stability of attitudes are compared for individuals who have publicly proclaimed their attitudes and those whose attitudes remain private.

Such studies provide a rather frightening view of the politician who, because he has publicly committed himself to a certain position, may be locked into a position from which he cannot readily escape. Even more frightening are the results of unpublished studies also cited by McGuire indicating that those who have to publicly defend their opinions show even more resistance to change than those who simply proclaim their attitudes.

Summary

1. Attitudes emerge in a primitive form in the early years of life, manifesting themselves as tendencies to approach or withdraw from particular classes of objects. The terms attitude, interest, values, and approach and withdrawal tendencies cannot be clearly differentiated. Custom prescribes that the term interest be used to refer to the person's relationship to particular activities, and the term attitude refers to behavioral tendencies related to particular objects and ideas. The term value generally refers to a broad goal.
2. Attitudes are generally considered to be complex and such a view has led to productive research. The view that attitudes are simply particular responses has been held by psychologists interested in operant conditioning, and although it has stimulated some research, it has not represented an especially productive approach to problems of attitude learning and change.
3. Those who view attitudes as complex have commonly taken the position that all attitudes have a number of components. A major component is the cognitive component, that is to say, the mass of beliefs, some true and some false, on which an attitude is based. A second component is the affective component, that is to say, the tendency of the attitude to be represented by positive and negative feelings. This is the component of attitude that is commonly measured by attitude scales. Why this component has become the focus of attitude research is hard to say, but the main reason may well be that devices for measuring this component have been readily available. Most psychologists deplore the lack of research in the third component of attitudes, namely, the action component, but such research has not been extensively undertaken largely because it is difficult to carry out. Attitude research has been largely limited to studies of what people say about themselves.

4. Attempts have been made to identify the functions of attitudes, but these functions are numerous, and perhaps not too well identified. Attitudes may serve highly utilitarian purposes, as when a person adopts the attitudes of a particular political group because he belongs to that group's constituency. More subtle are the cognitive functions of attitudes. Attitudes function very much like concepts, in that they help to simplify transactions with a very complex world. Attitudes may also provide a very direct gratification of needs. In addition, attitudes may bolster the individual's conception of himself and may help to defend him against psychological attack.
5. Research on attitude acquisition and attitude change has been rich in the production of theory. Although some of the theorizing has been closely linked to traditional theories of learning, such as operant and classical conditioning, some of the newer developments represent new departures in theory construction. Dissonance theory of attitude acquisition and change has played a very important role in the development of social psychology and is probably the newest and most vigorous of the three theoretical positions considered.
6. Considerable research has been undertaken on the basis of the belief that attitudes are particular categories of behavior and that reinforcement procedures, such as those advocated in operant conditioning, are the key to attitude acquisition and change. Some of the experiments on attitude change, undertaken near to midcentury, appeared to give support to this position. Later work has thrown considerable doubt on the usefulness of operant conditioning for understanding the mechanism involved in attitude change.
7. A second theoretical position is that attitudes are learned through classical conditioning. This view has been developed almost entirely by A. W. Staats, but it has not received widespread support, perhaps because it is based on questionable inferences. The fact that words can have negative and positive values attached to them through being associated with other words bears only a remote resemblance to classical conditioning.
8. The third major theoretical position is that of dissonance theory, a branch of cognitive consistency theory. Cognitive dissonance theory takes the position that individuals cannot easily tolerate inconsistent elements in their cognitive system, that is to say, the system that includes knowledge, beliefs, opinions, images, and so forth. Much of the development of dissonance theory owes its origins to the appearance of a work by Festinger (1957). The central thesis of dissonance theory of attitude change is that

dissonance is a condition that individuals seek either to avoid or remove. A person who encounters new information inconsistent with his attitudes may reduce the dissonance involved by ignoring the new information, or by taking the position that it really is not relevant or that it involves assumptions he does not accept, or he may change his attitude to make it consistent with the new information. Dissonance may be derived from either logical inconsistency, or inconsistency with cultural mores, or inconsistency with the general trend in behavior, or inconsistency with past experience.

9. Dissonance theory has much to say about decision situations because it is often through such situations that attitudes are changed. It also incorporates statements about the effect of rewards. The effects of rewards predicted by dissonance theory are different from those predicted on the basis of operant conditioning theory, and the former theory has provided more accurate predictions in some situations. A finding of considerable significance derived from dissonance studies is that mild threats are more likely to exert a lasting effect upon the behavior of children than are severe threats.
10. The major limitation placed on dissonance theory comes from the fact that the terms used to state the theory lack the precision that they need to have. Clarification of these terms will be achieved ultimately and some progress has already been made. The proposal that dissonance can be defined in terms of conflicting expectancies is one suggested improvement that may help to clarify some of the issues.
11. Dissonance theory has stimulated a large number of studies related to communication and how to make communication effective in changing opinion. The most intensively studied characteristics of the communicator are those of trustworthiness and expertness. These characteristics have immediate impact in producing attitude change, but they do not seem to have a lasting effect. Those who are exposed to a communication by an expert are influenced by the fact that he is an expert. A communication overheard is more likely to be of influence than a communication that is known to be directed toward the communicator. However, an overheard communication is likely to have little influence unless the hearer has some intent to change. Sometimes irrelevant characteristics of the communicator, that is to say, characteristics that have no bearing on the worth of a communication, may have considerable impact on the effect of a communication. At least under some conditions, a negative communicator may have more impact than a positive communicator.

12. The characteristics of communications that are persuasive have been intensively studied, but much of the research has been directed towards the study of the rather unclear issue of whether one-sided or two-sided arguments are the more persuasive. Such studies, considered collectively, show little difference between these two approaches. Much depends upon the ability of the individuals involved. Two-sided arguments may confuse relatively dull listeners or readers. Relatively bright listeners are more receptive to the so-called two-sided argument than to the one-sided.
13. Individuals differ in persuasibility. The persuasibility of children seems to increase to a maximum at about the age of nine. The relationship of intelligence to persuasibility is obviously complex. A communication that is highly persuasible for one level of intelligence may be quite ineffective for other levels. Women's attitudes are more readily influenced than those of men, perhaps because men are poorer listeners. Self-esteem is also another characteristic that appears to have some effect on whether subjects are readily influenced.
14. One of the most productive approaches to the problem of identifying the characteristics of the persuasible individual comes from research on the dogmatic or authoritarian personality. The dogmatic individual tends to avoid information inconsistent with that which he possesses, but when exposed, he is more readily changed in attitude than is the less dogmatic individual.
15. Changes produced in attitudes tend to disappear as time goes by, partly because there is some forgetting of the factual information involved. In addition, there is a tendency for a change produced in attitudes to be enhanced for a short period after the impact of some event that produces change. It takes time for the event to have full impact.
16. Several techniques designed for preventing attitudes from being changed have been studied. The most effective of these is to arm the individual with arguments that are supportive of his beliefs and arguments that could be used against any counterarguments that the individual might encounter. Mere security in knowing that one's beliefs are shared by others has little effect except that of lulling the individual into a state of false security. An important condition that produces stability of attitudes is what is referred to as commitment.

PART THREE

CONDITIONS RELATED TO LEARNING

CHAPTER NINE

Development and Learning

CONCEPTIONS OF HUMAN LEARNING ARE CLOSELY RELATED TO CONCEPTIONS of development. The intellectual and personality characteristics of the adult are assumed to be at least to some extent a product of the individual's history and of the learning in which he has been engaged during his lifetime. Any effective attempt to describe learning must provide a description that could be used for accounting for the manner in which man's personality and intellect are shaped during any period of development. Two rather different kinds of theorizing are evident on the current scene with respect to how learning and development interact. One of these is based on the assumption that a few fundamental learning processes evident in both animals and humans account for the developmental process insofar as it is controlled by learning. Those associated with the ideas of B. F. Skinner generally take this position and assume that a few basic processes, such as positive reinforcement, negative reinforcement, generalization, and extinction can account for learning at all age levels and under all conditions. Those who assume that learning can be described in such simple terms also assume that learning is controlled largely, if not entirely, by events in the environment. In line with this concept of learning, attempts have been made to describe such aspects of development as the acquisition of language and the development of social behavior.

In contrast with those who view human learning as always illustrating a few basic simple processes, evident in the learning of all living creatures, are those who take the position that as human behavior develops, the acquisition of skill in the use and manipulation of symbols introduces processes quite different from those evident in animal behavior. The latter position is exemplified by Piaget and by others, who represent what are called cognitive approaches to the development of learning in children. Psychologists who take a similar position generally assume that learning and development take place in stages and that learning at a more advanced stage cannot be understood completely in terms of the processes operating at an earlier stage. A new stage generally involves new processes. Some psychologists make the assumption that the new processes that appear as a new stage of development is reached are mainly a result of the growth of new structures in the nervous system, and some emphasize that the new processes represent a building on previous learnings. The role of the sheer growth of the nervous system in the appearance of new processes has long been considered in relation to the role of what is called *maturation*.

The Concept of Maturation

The essence of the concept of maturation is that the growth of the structure of the nervous system is set at conception by the genetic code and that the code includes a schedule that determines the time at which particular structures will emerge. The concept of maturation also includes the idea that as the growing nervous system acquires new structures, it also acquires the potential for new behaviors. Conversely, until the structures in the nervous system necessary for developing particular behaviors have been acquired, no amount of training will make it possible for those behaviors to be learned. Thus it is claimed that what can be learned depends upon the stage of growth of the nervous system.

The concept of maturation is derived largely from anatomy and embryology, which show clearly that the nervous system has a systematic pattern of development and that some structures do develop before others. However, the evidence from these sciences is derived largely from the study of embryos and prenatal organisms and does not settle the issue whether, in the case of the human child, new structures in the nervous system continue to emerge after birth. Some early studies of the development of motor skills in children sought to provide evidence on the latter issue and provided data which has since become recognized as highly controversial. The typical pattern for such studies involves a procedure known as co-twin control. In this procedure, the study is conducted on a set of identical twins. One twin is prevented from displaying the particular skill and the other is given special training. In the classic study by Myrtle McGraw (1943), the skill involved was stair climbing, and it was found that the child given special training did not perform at a younger age nor with more skill than the child who was deprived of the opportunity to practice the skill. A similar study in training in toilet habits also produced similar results. The general results of such studies of thirty or more years ago were taken to support the maturationist position in education, that is to say, that training should not begin until the nervous system had developed to the point where the necessary mechanisms had developed. In actual fact, such studies had nothing to contribute to problems of education, for all they showed was that, in the case of certain motor skills, learning plays very little role at all. The studies can also be criticized on the grounds that the untrained twin generally was not deprived of all situations that involved training related to the skill studied. For example, in the case of stair climbing, the children who were not given special training still had the experience of climbing up on chairs and on other low objects, a task that may involve all of the skills required in stair climbing.

These early studies were often interpreted by people in education as indicating that teaching should not be attempted until the child's nervous system had developed to the point where learning could be undertaken efficiently. On this basis, the proposal was made that the teaching of reading should be postponed until early in the second grade. The argument was that not only was the nervous system of the first grader insufficiently mature for the easy learning of reading, but it was alleged that the eye and related structures also lacked the necessary maturity. The argument was far-fetched, unrelated to any data on maturation, and probably quite wrong.

Although the argument is probably sound that some motor skills do not emerge, and cannot be made to emerge by special training until the nervous system has reached an appropriate stage of development, the same is probably not true for most factual learning about the world around us and it is probably not true even of most motor skills. The concept of maturation, with its emphasis on the importance of waiting for physiological readiness before instruction is begun, probably has little relevance to education. Indeed, the evidence suggests that the age at which particular learnings are undertaken is set by such factors as tradition and convenience rather than by level of maturation. The learning of a particular skill at a younger age than has been customary has often been successful and has produced no noticeable damage. One of the major deathblows to the doctrine of maturation as a basis for educational planning appeared in an article by Fowler (1962) on cognitive learning in infancy and early childhood. In this article, Fowler reviewed the many studies undertaken up to that time in which an attempt had been made to start instruction at a much earlier age than was customary. For example, there are several well-documented reports of children taught to read before the age of two, with no evidence of later damage to their personalities. There is also at least one study in which children four years of age and of average ability were successfully taught to read. Much of the evidence related to the effects of teaching children at a very young age to do the kinds of tasks typically mastered in the elementary grades comes from parents who began instruction often as early as the first year. Although such children were often superior in terms of the characteristics they inherited, they did show extraordinary mastery of skills and concepts at a very early age, and some similar results have been derived from studies involving children who clearly did not have the same superior background. In certain areas, such as music, the evidence suggests that a very early beginning of instruction is very important for a high level of performance later on. It may be too late to wait until the elementary-school years for providing instruction in musicianship.

The evidence suggests that concept learning can be begun at a much younger age than it has been typically undertaken and sometimes with advantage. The limiting factor is not the level of maturation of the nervous system, but the kinds of learning to which it has already been exposed. In order to read, a child must be able to discriminate visual form and such visual discriminations are learned through exposure to tasks that involve them. One of the most difficult and complex tasks that any person ever has to master is learning to understand and produce speech, yet considerable skill is acquired in this area before the age of three. In many ways the task of learning to read is a simpler task than that of learning to understand speech, in that words are printed clearly while spoken words are often slurred and poorly enunciated. The child learns speech under conditions that are extraordinarily unfavorable—yet he learns. The reader should not leave this discussion with the view that anything can be taught to any child at any age, for there is at least some persuasive evidence that the child may have to pass through at least some of the intellectual stages described by Piaget and in the order described.

Closely related to the concept of maturation have been attempts to describe development in terms of age scales. The traditional measure of mental age was an attempt to provide a measure that would indicate the maturational level of the child. Some research workers, about midcentury, went so far as to suggest that all aspects of maturation tended to go hand in hand. Olson (1959) suggested that when a child was inadequately developed in the carpal bones of the wrist, or in height or in weight, that the child also tended to be underdeveloped not only in other bodily functions, but in intellectual performance and achievement. Olson proposed that a general measure of level of development, referred to as the organismic age, be used to describe the child's level of development or level of maturation. The proposal was that all bodily and behavioral functions grow together and that any retardation in one of these is accompanied by a retardation in all others. According to this theory, all bodily and behavioral functions represent a unity, and one aspect cannot be impaired without other aspects becoming impaired too. The argument is attractive, for even common experience shows that even a minor ill of the body may interfere with a person's performance on unrelated tasks. However, studies undertaken to explore this problem have not supported the position that all functions, behavioral and physiological, develop hand in hand. Indeed, there can be a considerable amount of specificity about development. The child with the brilliant intellect may be backward in the development of the teeth. The well-built child may have difficulty reading. The conclusion at this time is that the findings of Olson, which were quite convincing in terms of his data, may have been a result of some peculiarities in the data themselves.

Many psychologists have suggested that different learning processes appear at different stages of development, and these descriptions make varied use of the concept of maturation. Three such views will be considered here, namely those of Donald Hebb, Jean Piaget, and Robert Gagné. All attempt to describe human learning in terms of stages. Perhaps what the stages described by these psychologists have most in common is that they are all having an impact on education. However, there is little within any one of these conceptualizations of learning that is grossly similar to, or inconsistent with, what is found in the other two. Probably none of the three provides a complete picture of the role of learning in development; rather, they are concerned with different aspects of learning in relation to development. One contrasting difference between the three is that Hebb and Piaget present their positions as a part of a theory of development; Gagné does not, and he writes more as a learning theorist, but he has nevertheless written one article (1968) in which he points out the advantages of his classification over that of Piaget.

Hebb's Two-Stage Learning Model

Hebb (1949, 1966) presents evidence to indicate that perceptual learning, when considered over the life span, is a two-stage process. The first stage, referred to as early learning, involves certain fundamental processes that must be mastered before more complex learnings can be undertaken.

The concept of early learning is easily misunderstood; the layman thinks of the first steps in learning as consisting of such processes as the learning of words and certain manipulative skills that are involved in feeding, washing, playing with toys, and so forth. However, from the point of view of the psychologist, these are quite complex skills, and presuppose that still earlier learning has taken place. The first steps in learning may involve such processes as recognizing two sounds as different, recognizing a line as a line and perhaps also recognizing the meeting of two lines to form a corner as a corner, and recognizing tactile sensations of roughness, smoothness, etc. Such recognitions and discriminations are taken so much for granted that it is hard to realize that they require any learning at all. As a matter of fact, some psychologists of the past have even supposed that complex shapes can be recognized and complex discriminations made without any learning. One group of psychologists, who became known as the Gestalt psychologists, took the view that the capacity to see simple shapes is inborn and requires no learning; but this does not seem to be the case.

Research on the influence of early perceptual learning began with informal studies involving case histories of animal behavior, but research has recently become more systematic with more adequate control over relevant conditions.

Hebb (1949) was the first to realize the importance of von Senden's (tr. 1960) work showing that adult patients who gained vision might not be able to use it. He pointed out that the adult who gains vision for the first time has to undertake a tedious early learning process which, unlike later and more complex learning, is very slow indeed. The adult learning to use vision is similar to the infant slowly learning the simplest discriminations.

Certainly, the learning of the adult who gains vision is hard to understand unless one introduces the concept of an early stage of learning that is very slow. Such a position has important implications for child rearing, for the period of infancy then comes to be regarded as a period when crucially important learning is taking place. If this is so, then experiences in infancy may be expected to have important bearing on learning that takes place later.

In all of the cases in which there had been a deprivation of early learning experiences, the result was a certain stupidity of behavior that is not easily overcome. Prolonged learning is necessary if this deficiency is to be removed, and this fact suggests that the slowness with which the very young child learns may reflect the slowness with which early learning takes place. The term *early learning* refers to the learning of the fundamental ability to discriminate and identify stimuli; the evidence indicates that these learnings must precede more complex learnings. We do not know at this time whether deficiencies in early learning can ever be entirely made up later in life. This matter requires systematic investigation. A few pieces of evidence suggest that some of the deficiencies produced by a lack of early learning may be rather permanent.

Piaget's Theory of Learning and Development

Hebb's conception of a two-stage learning process is consistent with Piaget's description of learning and development, but Piaget's model is vastly more complex and difficult to describe. Only the haziest outline can be given within the scope of a few pages. Piaget's contribution to knowledge has appeared in articles, monographs, and books, which he has been publishing since 1921 in a steady stream. An academician could well make a career of studying and understanding Piaget, as some have and as some will do for many generations to come. On the contemporary scene, J. McV. Hunt (1961) and Flavell (1963) have provided the most complete concise accounts of Piaget's conception of learning and development. A brief account is also provided by Phillips (1969). This short section, designed to provide the student with an introduction to Piaget, owes much to the writings of these other authors, whose works it is hoped the student will explore further after his intellectual appetite for understanding Piaget has been whetted.

Piaget, like Hebb, has throughout his work the orientation of both the philosopher and the biologist. Central to his theoretical system is the concept of adaptation, but it is far from the crude all-inclusive concept that it has been in the past. For Piaget, the concept of adaptation has two components, referred to as *assimilation* and *accommodation*. An understanding of the psychological significance of these terms is most easily achieved by considering their physiological counterparts. Living creatures maintain an adaptive relationship with their environment by foraging and eating. In doing so, animals utilize and synthesize into their own structures chemical substances from their environment. This is assimilation at the physiological level. Piaget postulates what is essentially the same relationship between the inner psychological organization and the outer environment. Contacts with the environment result in information about the environment becoming incorporated in the inner psychological organization—a process that parallels the intake of substances in the form of food and the incorporation of these substances, or materials synthesized from them, into the tissues of the body.

Some substances are not just assimilated in this way. Small doses of pollen that penetrate the membranes of the nose may produce a strong reaction known as hay fever. By carefully controlling the doses of pollen, the chemistry of the body may be changed so that it can handle such foreign substances without strong tissue reactions. This is physiological accommodation. The foreign substances are not assimilated, but there has been accommodation to them.

Piaget views all development as involving accommodation and assimilation at the psychological level. An illustration from the area of perception may help to clarify this important distinction at the psychological level. If one reads a statement in the paper, one may interpret it in such a way that it fits one's previous ideas about the topic. This is adaptation through assimilation, and it can be regarded as analogous to that of digesting foods in order to obtain the molecules that fit our established chemical requirements. There is also another way in which a reader can respond to a printed statement. He may modify his own ideas in order to fit more closely those represented by the statement. This is adaptation through accommodation.

Another example of assimilation and accommodation is presented by a four-year-old child who sees adults refer to the parts of an object cut in two as halves. He assimilates this information and learns to refer to one of two parts of an object as a half. Later, in kindergarten, the teacher explains that the two parts of an object are halves only when they are the same. In order to acquire this new piece of information, he must accommodate his concept of a half. In other words, the learning of the new information from his kindergarten teacher requires him to modify his concept of a half.

In the context of learning, the concepts of assimilation and accomodation imply that there is a something within the learner to which new information can be assimilated, and that there is a something that the learner can change to accommodate to new information. The something is referred to by Piaget as a *schema.* American psychologists do not have any familiar concept that quite parallels Piaget's concept of a schema, although terms such as organization of knowledge or cognitive structure come fairly close. Some British psychologists have used the term schema in a sense closely similar to Piaget's usage of the term. For Piaget, the term refers to some internal organization of experience in a limited area and the control systems related to activity in that area of experience. Thus, at the infant level, there are schemata related to sucking, to grasping, and to seeing. Unlike the British psychologists who use the term schema to refer to an organized record of events in memory, the schemata of Piaget have strong action components and some innate components.

In the development of the intellect according to the model proposed by Piaget, it is the schemata that are centrally involved in the process of adaptation. A particular experience may result in a schema being added to in some way, as when a new piece of information is fitted into what we already know. Another experience may present information that cannot be fitted into the corresponding schema and the schema may be modified to accomodate the new information received.

The learner is not a passive agent in his intellectual development; rather, he reaches out to the environment, seeking experiences that may result in the development of schema. Higher organisms are experience-seeking creatures, and exploration whets the appetite for further exploration.

The very primitive schemata of the first few months of life are referred to by Hunt (1961) as sensorimotor organizations to indicate that they involve both the material for interpreting sensory experiences and elements that result in relevant action. The schema related to grasping behavior organizes the incoming sensory information about objects that might be grasped and generates the behavior of grasping. The child comes into the world endowed with some primitive schemata, as, for example, that related to sucking behavior, and some may emerge through the unfolding of the pattern of development.

Piaget provides an extremely detailed account of intellectual development. Flavell summarizes the detailed analysis by saying that there are three major stages of development which Piaget divides into many smaller steps that are not always distinct phases but overlapping stages of development. The broad phases of development are roughly from birth to about one and a half to two years of age, from two until about 11, and from 11 until some level of maturity is reached. The first of these, commonly called the sensorimotor period, involves development from an initial level in which little more than reflex behavior is manifested to a stage where behavior shows well-developed organizations of sensorimotor behavior. The newborn shows such reflexes as sucking when any part of the face is stimulated, gripping reflexes of the hand, eyelid reflexes, and so forth, but by the age of a year the child can perform such complex acts as fixating his eyes on an object held in front of him and then grasping the object and bringing it to his mouth while following it most of the way with his eyes. Development at this stage involves the acquisition of perceptual skill in utilizing information about the outside world and motor skill in manipulating the environment. At this stage, learning has to do with the development of very simple contacts with the environment, and the expanded organization of the basic schemata of perception and action. The sensorimotor stage corresponds to Hebb's stage of early learning, in which basic perceptual elements are learned.

The second stage of development covers the gap between the age of one and a half to two, at which crude sensorimotor development has been achieved, and the stage where reflective intelligence typical of the educated mature person has been developed. A point to note is that Piaget has confined his studies to children in the experimental school of the Rousseau Institute. These children come from middle-class homes and have every opportunity for intellectual development. It may well be that less educated groups never reach even the end of this second stage of development.

The dominant feature of this second stage is the development of symbolic forms of behavior. Piaget makes a distinction between the use of language as a means of symbolizing events and objects in the environment and other preconceptual developments of ability. He suggests that images may first begin to function as representations of things in the environment but, when language begins to develop, symbols become substitutes for the primitive imagery. The development of language permits the appearance of what are called concrete operations. The latter include such activities as (1) classifying, as is involved in the grouping of objects, (2) identifying relations, as when a child recognizes that one stick is longer than another, and (3) utilizing number concepts. Coupled with these developments are the ever increasing scope of the schemata that organize both perception and behavior, but throughout development the key invariants are the processes of accommodation and assimilation.

This second stage of development can be broadly divided into two phases. The first lasts until about the sixth or seventh year and the second covers roughly the elementary-school years. During the first of these two phases, the child has very limited capacity for rational problem solving, but once the second phase is reached, the child can perform many important logical operations, provided they are tied to concrete events. For this reason, the age of about six to twelve years is described as the period of concrete operations. The operations that the child becomes capable of performing include those of grouping and classifying objects in terms of particular attributes, and the mathematical operations such as addition, subtraction, multiplication and so forth. Piaget is partial to identifying the operations the child can perform in terms of the language of mathematics and logic. The pattern of development is assumed to be uniform for all children, except that some children may move from one stage to the next at a younger age, or at an older age, than other children.

From this point on, the pattern of cognitive development described by Piaget is highly tied to concepts of logic and mathematics which would first have to be understood if the system were to be outlined in a sketchy fashion. In the final stage of intellectual development the person is able to cut some of the ties to the world of immediate experience and to think in terms of propositions that can pertain to an abstract world or a world that may not even exist. This is the stage of formal operations.

The concepts of formal logic play an unusual role in Piaget's attempt to describe the development and nature of intelligence. He implies that the knowledge of logic developed by academicians is a reflection of the mode of operation of man's intellect. Man did not discover logic and then put it to use in improving his own thinking, but logic is the system that nature has built into man to permit him to handle his environment effectively.

This conception of learning and development has emerged to a great extent from Piaget's own particular manner of collecting data. Although he writes of his work as being experimental, it is not experimental in the tradition of American experimental psychology. Piaget observes children solving problems that have slowly been evolved for the purpose of probing intellectual life. During the solution of the problem the child may be asked questions about what he is doing and how changes in the situation might change his actions. This procedure has been undertaken with children as young as four years of age, but inquiry into intellectual development below that level has to be studied by observation of behavior alone, without interrogation. The procedures require great skill and what they have achieved must be attributed largely to the genius of Piaget and his associates.

It is easy to jump to the wrong conclusions that the stages of development described are separate and discrete stages, but they are not, and are not so described by Piaget. A mature adult, capable of undertaking all the logical operations of the fully developed individual, may still behave at the level of concrete operations. Such an adult, confronted with a television that does not work, may strike the cabinet in the hope of getting results. He could have checked the plug, the lead to the antenna, and undertaken a few other rational operations in an attempt to solve his problem, but his approach was at the concrete operations level. There are also some problems that can be solved only in terms of concrete operations. All levels of behavior in the developmental pattern are found in the adult who, on occasion, manifests even very primitive responses, such as pencil sucking.

Because American psychologists regard Piaget's entire procedure for obtaining knowledge as highly unconventional, it was not until some time after midcentury that his ideas became discussed in the United States. Since that time his ideas have become the focus of rather extensive experimentation, much of it designed to test the validity of his theorizing by conventional experimental procedures. Much of this experimentation in more recent years has been directed toward determining whether training can speed up some facets of intellectual development.

Gagné's Analytic Approach to the Identification of Stages in Learning

Gagné (1965, 1970) has proposed a classification of learning phenomena which he considers to have similar significance to those just described (see Gagné, 1968). The classification system has had extensive impact on the writings of educators. Gagné's proposed categories of learning also represent an attempt to describe stages through which learning must proceed if complex skills are to be acquired. The stages are such that the necessary learning involved in one stage has to take place before learning at the next stage can occur. The categories presented are the following: (1) signal learning, (2) stimulus-response learning, (3) the acquisition of chains of behavior, (4) verbal association learning, (5) multiple discrimination learning, (6) concept learning, (7) principle learning, and (8) problem solving. This classification of learning, unlike that proposed by either Hebb or Piaget, is not derived from experimentation, but is based on an intuitive analysis of what is involved in complex learning. For example, in order to learn a principle such as that friction produces heat, the student must supposedly be already familiar with the concepts of heat and friction. In order to be able to acquire the concepts of friction and heat, and to give them names, the person must have learned how to discriminate one word from another, among other complex discriminations. Thus learning can allegedly be traced back to simpler and simpler components until basic learning is found in signal learning. The argument presented by Gagné is quite convincing, but it depends entirely on a logical analysis of the components of complex learning. The sequence of learning categories suggested by Gagné may well represent a useful system for organizing learning rather than a necessary sequence in the learning of complex behaviors.

The intuitive approach to the development of sequences of learning, supposedly involved in the development of complex learning and complex behavior, must necessarily remain suspect of being a figment of the imagination until it is backed up by experimental evidence. The system of categories has not, as yet, stimulated a large body of research, as has the sequential learning system proposed by Piaget. In time, it may stimulate such research, but at present research workers interested in the Gagné system seem to have difficulty in beginning any program of systematic research related to it. Many applications can be pointed out, but none of these have to do with the verification of the system.

At this point a comment should be made on the dangers of armchair analysis in the solution of educational problems and the design of learning and teaching situations. One of the better examples of the disastrous consequences that can ensue is seen in the traditional analysis of what is involved in the teaching of reading. The early curriculum workers in the field concluded from their examination of the reading task that, in order to read groups of words, the learner had to be able to read single words, one at a time. The curriculum workers also agreed that, in order to be able to read individual words, the reader had to be able to read letters, and hence the task of reading was begun by teaching the child to identify letters. What was not recognized in the analysis of the reading task was that children can learn to identify and discriminate words without first learning the alphabet, and that children can acquire such a recognition vocabulary rather quickly and thus can learn to read simple books rapidly. The analysis of the curriculum makers was wrong. A person does not have to be able to read letters before he can read words.

Indeed, what the early curriculum workers failed to understand was that mature readers do not read material letter by letter or even word by word. One can start learning to read by learning directly to do what the mature reader does, namely, identify particular words by particular cues. Later, one can learn word analysis so that new words can be uncoded. The analysis of reading undertaken by the early curriculum workers was pure fiction. The Gagné type of analysis may be equally faulty, but we do not really know at this time. Sometimes an armchair analysis turns out to have a certain utility, but most of the time it produces a plausible system of doubtful value.

A Comparison of the Three Conceptions of Stages of Learning

The three conceptions have certain common emphases. One of these is that a great amount of learning has to occur before formal learning, of the kind that takes place in school, can be successfully undertaken. The typical human is completely unaware of much of this learning. There is not complete agreement about what is learned at these very fundamental stages of the emergence of the human intellect, although there is some agreement. Both Piaget and Hebb emphasize the learner's identification of simple elements in the world he perceives and the fitting of these into systems. For Piaget, the systems into which the new elements in the perceptual world are fitted are basically innate organizations such as that related to sucking behavior, but for Hebb the organizations are not implied to be a part of the child's native equipment. The basic learning, described by Gagné as learning to respond to signals, probably has much less relevance for understanding the development of the intellect than do the early learnings described by either Hebb or Piaget.

The emphasis that all theoreticians have placed on the prime importance of a very basic class of learnings as a foundation for all further learning has done much to stimulate, on the one hand, the development of a large volume of research on the effect of early environmental conditions on subsequent learning and, on the other, a basis for an understanding of the inadequate intellectual development of the less privileged members of our own society. Past generations of psychologists were prone to attribute the relatively unintelligent behavior of the less privileged members of our society to lack of native intellect, but the more recent writings of psychologists have tended to take the position that the underprivileged show intellectual inadequacies because they never had the opportunity to undertake the basic learnings on which all further intellectual achievement has to be based.

Learning is also viewed by all the developmental systems as a cumulative process. Each primitive learning opens the way to learning at a more complex level, but in Piaget's system this phenomenon is also coupled with a motivational factor, in that learning stimulates the quest for more learning. Piaget also is able to account more satisfactorily than the others for the way in which knowledge of the environment is built, in that he describes memory mechanisms as well as learning mechanisms.

Another contrast within the three systems must also be brought out. Both Hebb and Gagné have developed their systems in the tradition of American psychology, with the organism viewed as being inactive until the stimuli of the outside world initiate responses. Piaget, on the contrary, views the child as a creature who actively seeks contact with the environment and, the more that contact is made, the greater is the tendency to seek further contact. For this reason, the views of Piaget have generally been preferred by professional educators to those of typical American psychologists.

The Effect of Deprivation Early in Life

Studies of the effect of various forms of deprivation early in life have long been considered to provide an important key to the understanding of the nature of human intelligence. Prior to midcentury, such an approach to the understanding of the development of intelligent behavior was hardly considered by American psychologists, partly because of a common belief that intelligence depended heavily on inherited characteristics and that variations in the human environment within the American continent were not sufficient to produce large variations in the level of intelligent behavior. This assumption was not only wrong but it ran counter to a considerable amount of evidence that has long been available.

Studies of deprivation during the growing period have had to be undertaken to a great extent with animals, in that experiments that involve deprivation in children can be carried on with only mild deprivations and for only short periods of time. Some human studies have been undertaken on children who have suffered various forms of deprivation because of the circumstances of their birth, and these have sometimes involved extensive deprivation. Animal and human studies can be conveniently classified into the categories of those involving reduced stimulation, those involving an enriched versus an impoverished environment, those in which a creature is isolated socially from its own species, and those involving confinement. An excellent summary of the research is found in a volume edited by Zubek (1969).

Extensive research has been undertaken on the effect of depriving animals of the use of a particular sensory system. Deprivation of vision has most commonly been used because of the ease with which an animal can be raised in the dark, although other means of preventing the use of vision have also been used. Such studies also make it possible to study what happens when the animal is later given the opportunity to use vision, and physiological studies can be undertaken to determine whether deprivation of the use of a sensory system results in deterioration of that system. The evidence indicates that sensory deprivation, if extreme and if prolonged enough, may produce permanent damage to the sensory system. However, when von Senden (1960) studied his patients who acquired vision in adulthood through corneal grafts, he found that after prolonged training most of them, but not all, managed to learn to use the visual system. It may well be that physiological deterioration did not occur in the case of the von Senden patients because all of them had eyes that were exposed during the day to light. Light stimulation, even when filtered through a clouded cornea, may be sufficient to prevent physiological deterioration from taking place. In subhuman subjects deterioration has generally been noted in the optic tracts of animals that have been confined in total darkness during the period of growth. In summary, one can say that sensory deprivation can result in permanent damage, but this kind of deprivation is rare in humans, except for the occasional child raised in a darkened or semi-darkened environment. Such children are generally illegitimate and have been hidden away because the mother is ashamed of having given birth to the child. Of much greater relevance to the study of human development are those studies in which the effect of a psychologically enriched versus an impoverished environment has been studied. Enrichment may involve introducing any element of variation and change. In the case of animals, this has often involved no more than handling the animals occasionally in contrast with leaving them in a cage.

In the area of enrichment, one of the earliest and longest series of studies has been undertaken with a procedure involving what is called gentling. In the application of this procedure the animal involved is handled daily by being picked up and stroked from head to tail. Such a procedure, when undertaken daily during the growing period, produced adult animals that reacted better to stress conditions than those raised without this additional stimulation. The early investigators interpreted the results as indicating the importance of tender loving care during infancy, but such an interpretation was later shown to be wrong when research workers also demonstrated that animals given periodical electric shocks during infancy also tended to have a higher ability to handle stress. The critical factor seemed to be quantity of stimulation and not the character of the stimulation. Animals given unusual forms of stimulation also showed superior performance in handling the kinds of learning tasks typically given such creatures. Almost any type of stimulation will have this effect, as is evident from the studies in which animals were stimulated by being tossed in the air or exposed to heat.

The reader may be unwilling to think of gentling or shocking rats as involving an enrichment of their environment but, like all forms of enrichment, the condition involves altering an environment from a state where it provides great uniformity of stimulation to one in which there is some variety. Generally, enrichment of the environment involves increasing the variety of the inputs to the perceptual systems.

Studies of enrichment have sometimes involved introducing large numbers of manipulable stimuli and new objects into the environment of an animal, as in the classic studies undertaken at McGill University, in which some puppies were raised in the house of an experimenter while litter mates were raised in cages in which they had minimal contact with humans or with manipulable objects. The home-reared puppies were generally superior in their ability to solve problems and also showed marked personality differences compared with those raised in the caged situation. One difference of interest was the social spontaneity toward visitors shown by the pups raised in cages. The pups raised in the home were sophisticated enough to know that visitors to the laboratory were just not worth paying attention to. Particularly interesting is the behavior of dogs in the McGill laboratory, who were raised under circumstances that deprived them from experiencing pain through contact with hard or pointed objects or from falling off high places. Such animals showed an extraordinary inability to respond effectively to pain when released to more normal circumstances. One such animal repeatedly knocked its head on a low pipe and, although it behaved like an animal that had hurt itself, showed almost no ability to learn to avoid the object (Hebb, 1966).

Data related to the problem, based on human subjects, is voluminous but far less precise in what it says. Most of it involves cases of environmental deprivation caused by circumstances of accident rather than circumstances carefully produced by an experimenter. Considerable work has been reported on the lack of intellectual development of those who spend the first year of life in a foundling home. However, the question has always been raised whether the intellectual inadequacies of such children could perhaps be accounted for in terms of characteristics inherited from the parents, because the mothers of such children are often wayward girls who became involved in trouble partly because of their own intellectual inadequacies.

The classic work of Hunt (1961) provides an excellent summary of the work up to about 1960 on the influence of the environment on altitude of intellectual development. Most of the work had basic flaws in research design and, as often happens, dramatic studies that showed virtually nothing because of intrinsic flaws often had widespread impact on thinking in the field. Particularly notable in the latter respect were the studies by R. A. Spitz, a psychiatrist concerned with what he believed to be the intellectual deterioration that took place in the foundling home. As often happens, Spitz was a keen observer and his intuition was probably right concerning the effects of the impoverished environment of the foundling institution on the infant's development, even though his data did not show what he claimed they showed. Spitz described a collection of symptoms shown by these children, which he referred to as *hospitalism*.

More recent reviews include that by Deutsch (1965), which places special emphasis on the studies related to the language problems of the disadvantaged. She cites a number of studies showing that the disadvantaged not only have a poorer vocabulary than more typical children but that their internal verbal processes are also less adequate. Because thinking is highly dependent upon internal verbal processes, the implication of this finding is obvious. In addition, the fact that long-term human memory is highly dependent upon information being coded into words, lack of verbal skill can have far-reaching effects. An analysis of the cause of this problem of language deficit by Raph (1965) suggests that this difficulty is caused by a combination of lack of vocal stimulation during infancy, a lack of conversation with adults during childhood, and a lack of opportunity to handle intellectual problems that call for linguistic skills.

Another review by Hunt (1966) has focused on the problem of the effect of cultural deprivation on adolescence, and points out the mounting belief that the effects of deprivation may be largely irreversible. Although educators should not give up all hope that the culturally deprived child has been damaged beyond repair, the chances at this time are not good that educational intervention can make up for an inadequate background.

More dramatic evidence of the effects of impoverished or enriched environments on human intellectual development comes from much earlier studies undertaken on identical twins raised apart. Identical twins are rarities—roughly one in three hundred births at the time when the studies were taken, but they occur more frequently today. Even more rare are those identical twins who are raised separately in different environments, and still more rare are those that are raised in fundamentally different environments in terms of the enrichment-impoverishment dimension. Nevertheless, Newman, Freeman, and Holzinger (1937) were able to find nineteen pairs of twins reared separately and, in the case of a few of these pairs, the environments are about as different as one might expect to find in the United States. In the case of such twins reared apart, the maximum difference in the intelligence quotients of the twins thus separated was twenty-four points—the difference between a person of limited educability and a person of average intelligence. Such a difference is large.

The nineteen pairs of twins reared apart were classified according to the differences in the education to which each member of a pair had been exposed. The most pronounced differences were seen in three pairs in which members of a pair differed on an Intelligence Quotient Scale by 24, 19, and 12 points, respectively. The greatest of these three differences was between a pair of twins known as Gladys and Helen. Gladys had received only three years of grade school, while Helen had received a college degree and had become a teacher. The intelligence quotients of these two youngsters were 92 and 116, respectively. The pair whose intelligence quotients differed by 19 points were James and Reece, whose measured intelligence quotients were 96 and 77, respectively. James had lived with a good small-town family and had completed high school; Reece had lived with a primitive mountain family and had gone to school part-time through the eighth grade. The third pair, Eleanore and Georgiana, had intelligence quotients of 66 and 78. Eleanore had gone through five grades of schooling; her sister had received a full high-school education and an additional three years of normal school.

Much of the more recent evidence of the effect of cultural conditions on the development of the intellect comes from studies other than those involving identical twins. Stein and Susser (1970) have reviewed data from numerous different sources that all point in the same direction. For example, they show that the socially disadvantaged tend to manifest a decline in intelligence quotient as they grow older. Children in institutional settings have depressed intelligence quotients, which tend to be raised after they are moved into homes. Enduring gains and losses appear to follow marked changes in the social and economic environment. There is even some evidence that a decline in the frequency of mental retardation accompanies improved social and educational conditions. Stein and Susser also point out that the level of the intelligence quotient is not determined solely by social and economic conditions, but there is a mounting body of data showing that it is also related to quality of schooling.

The data lead to the conclusion that if the environment is impoverished in terms of the kinds of stimulation it provides, the effect can be quite disastrous on the development of the intellect. The least adequate environments in the United States might be expected to produce an intelligence level of the children raised in them perhaps as much as 30 IQ points below that of similar children raised in a good middle-class environment.

One must point out, in passing, that current literature commonly takes the position that the culturally deprived child *lacks* stimulation. This is a misconception of what is happening, as Bosco has noted (1970). Such children are raised in an environment that is noisy, buzzing with unorganized activity, overcrowded, and far from being unstimulating. What these infants lack is stimulation they can structure, to which they can give meaning, and to which they can acquire some organized response. They need stimulation, but with events that are repeated and represent quite simple inputs. What they do receive are large quantities of very disorganized inputs.

Now that research has begun to determine the intellectual importance of early learning, attempts may be made to develop learning programs that reach right down into infancy. Although educators have long recognized the importance of early childhood in the development of a well-adjusted personality, a new appreciation of the importance of this period for intellectual development also suggests that the early years should be years of planned learning. At present, these years are little influenced by planning.

Many attempts have been made to train underprivileged parents to improve the psychological environment to which their children are exposed. One of the first of these studies, by Gordon (1969), illustrates some of the techniques involved, the problems encountered, and the kinds of results that can be achieved. The Gordon project was directed primarily toward the task of changing the behavior of disadvantaged mothers in poor rural communities in Florida so that they might provide a better environment for their infants during the first two years of life. The project aimed at helping these mothers to understand what they could do to provide a more stimulating environment for their babies and give them tasks that they could undertake in relation to their children. These tasks generally involved providing the baby with forms of stimulation that he would not otherwise receive and opportunities to perform various activities within his capabilities.

An important feature of the Gordon study was that the education of the indigent mothers took place, not through visits from members of the middle-class professional community, but through visits from persons of similar social class who had been trained in the techniques that the mothers were learning to apply. These parent educators were black, as were the indigent mothers to whom they gave training. The parent educators were generally better educated than were the mothers, but they were still culturally nearer to the mothers than were the psychologists and educators running the project.

The success of the training of the mothers was determined by testing the infants, when they were two years old, on a series of tasks calling for perceptual skills and motor coordination. The group of infants whose mothers had received instruction during the two-year period were superior in their performance to that of a group of control infants who had not had the program of enriched stimulation. However, infants on whom the program was carried out only during the first year of life did not show any superiority.

Although the study was focused on the development of the infants, there were other benefits derived from training the mothers. The latter found that the help of the parent educators gave them a feeling of having greater control over the rearing of their infants.

The study represents a pioneer demonstration of the great importance of events early in life to the development of competencies. What must be found out ultimately is whether early deprivation produces inadequacies for which later training cannot compensate. These are very difficult problems to study, because our species is one on which only the most limited experiments can be undertaken.

Critical Periods and Stages of Development

Psychologists have long toyed with the possibility that certain skills or behaviors can be learned only at certain periods of development and also that certain skills cannot be learned until a certain stage of development has been reached. Scott (1968) has summarized much of the research related to the first of these problems. Scott reports a series of experiments in which dogs from the same litter were raised in isolation from human contact. Every few weeks a pup was taken from the litter and an attempt made to train it by means of typical dog-training procedures. In some breeds of dogs the finding was that the dogs raised in isolation for more than a certain number of weeks became extremely difficult to train or were virtually untrainable. The problem seemed to be that such dogs, reared in isolation from human contact, did not seem able to form a relationship to man of a kind that made training easy to undertake. Scott argues that there is a critical period in the formation of this attachment and, once this critical period is passed, the attachment cannot be formed. Training can occur without the dog forming an attachment, but it is difficult to accomplish. In the case of the dog, the attachment formed to man is generally interpreted as a displaced attachment to the dog's own mother.

A similar phenomenon has been found in the Wisconsin Primate Laboratory, where it has been shown that primate infants, deprived of warm soft contacts with their natural mother or with objects with the same warm soft properties, show severe handicaps in their social development, which do not appear to be remediable. Other related findings are that primate infants deprived of contacts with other primate infants also develop social difficulties that psychologists have not been able to remedy.

The concept of a critical period related to particular learnings sounds attractive and plausible, but it may well be an artifact of experimentation. Consider the young puppy raised in isolation, and let us assume that it is highly trainable at eight weeks but seems quite untrainable at sixteen weeks. The untrainability of the older pup may be partly a function of size of the animal. A larger animal is much less controllable than a small one. Perhaps less explainable is the behavior of the young primates deprived of either contact with their mothers or contact with their peers. It may well be, for example, that the young primate interacting with another young primate engages in biting behavior, and this in turn produces a response in the animal bitten. The animal thus learns that it can produce a response in another creature, and the response of the other creature may reinforce biting and other playful behavior. However, in the older animal in which teething is completed, there may be no tendency to bite other objects and animals, and this simple basis for interaction does not exist. For this reason social behavior may not develop because of the lack of a biting response—a response that is peculiar to the teething period. The critical event in the critical period might well be something as simple as a teething response.

In a sense, then, one can say that in certain species there are critical periods during which circumstances make it particularly easy to form certain habits. Later, circumstances change, and the learning of the same habits becomes much more difficult. Whether critical periods, in this sense of the term, also apply to human development is controversial. Certainly, at least some of von Senden's cases learned to use their vision, although they had to undertake the kind of learning, with respect to the visual sense, that the infant has to undertake. Some never learned, but the problem of those who failed seemed to be more a matter of lack of motivation than lack of ability. A person who can live successfully as a blind person may find no reason for learning to use vision. In the case of a person who has been deprived of learning what is ordinarily learned at a particular age, and who is later given the opportunity to learn, explanation can be given concerning the advantages of acquiring the skill. He may thus be motivated in a way in which it would be impossible to motivate an animal.

Development and Conditions in the Home

Intellectual Development. All three theories we have reviewed of the stages involved in learning place great emphasis on the sequence of the learning as representing the acquisition of what is commonly called intelligence. If the components of intelligence are acquired in proper sequence, then an intelligent person emerges, but a person deprived of critical opportunities to learn may never develop effective ways of handling his environment. Thus, in the case of Hebb's description of the course of development, a person deprived of the opportunity to use his eyes, cannot use vision effectively when sight is restored and shows extraordinarily stupid behavior when confronted with visual tasks. In the complex system of intellectual development described by Piaget, restricted opportunities to explore a rich and varied environment not only limit what is learned but also limit exploratory behavior. In addition, Piaget assumes that certain kinds of thinking tied to the concrete world have to take place before complex abstract thinking can take place. For both Hebb and Piaget the central factor in the development of intelligence is learning, and little is said about the possibility that intelligence may be to some degree inherited. The past generation of psychologists concerned with the growth of intelligence tended to emphasize inherited factors. The present trend is to emphasize learning, but this does not mean that the effect of inheritance is denied. It may be much more important from a practical point of view for us to understand how intelligence may be enhanced by providing a suitable environment than to determine the limits placed upon it by heredity.

A very large crop of studies is now appearing designed to discover the relationship between specific aspects of the early childhood environment and subsequent mental competence. A review of research up to 1967 is provided by Freeberg and Payne (1967).

This review takes the position that much of the work has made its major contribution by clarifying what is meant by an enriched or an impoverished home environment. If a similar clarification had taken place in defining the attributes of an enriched curriculum, what progress might have been made! As a result of this analysis, quite specific aspects of the parent-child interaction have been identified and the evidence indicates that some of these are important for child development. One of the critical elements in the interaction is the pattern of communication, which consists largely of verbal interaction. The verbal environment of the child includes not only the speech he hears and with which he interacts, but also the books read to him, and the daily interaction he sees among other members of the family. The major distinction between the environment of children in different social classes is in the nature of the verbal interaction in the home. An effective verbal environment in the home is highly important for the development of intelligence.

The importance of the pattern of communication in the home has been made very clear through studies of the disadvantaged child, who often comes from a home in which there is almost no communication except admonitions from the parents. Such a child may never have held a conversation with an adult and may not know how to. He has been shouted at and told what to do, but he has never discovered that one can learn by asking an adult a question. This he may slowly have to learn when he comes to school, and by that time he may see the adult only as a punishing figure and be unable to develop a different kind of relationship.

A second important class of variables is in the extent to which the adults in the home are permissive or restrictive. An interesting matter brought out in this connection is an observation made by Freeberg and Payne that a similar variable has been stressed as important in research on teaching. One of the few consistent results of research in the latter area is that the permissive teacher tends to produce higher achievement than the highly controlling and restrictive teacher. Permissiveness in the home coupled with concern for achievement appears to develop the motivation to achieve.

Since the time of publication of the Freeberg and Payne review, a number of new studies have appeared that add substantially to the findings. One of the richest new sources of information in this area comes from a thirty-year follow-up of children born in Berkeley, California, in 1928 and 1929. The original sample was first identified and studied by Jean W. Macfarlane but many other research workers have participated in following up the group and in undertaking studies with the resulting data. Of the original sample of one hundred and twenty-four children, only fifty-eight could still be studied at the age of thirty. The others had either died or were lost track of during the intervening years. The individuals participating in the study were systematically tested on well-known tests of intellectual ability at intervals over the thirty-year span. A study by Honzik (1967) reports the relationships found between intellectual development at the age of thirty and conditions existing in the home at the age of twenty-one months.

The study found the usual relationship between the educational level of the parents and the intellectual development of the children, taken at a particular age. This relationship is not particularly interesting in view of the fact that it is highly contaminated by the tendency for intellectual abilities to be, to some degree, inherited. Much more interesting are the relationships between intellectual development and such conditions as socioeconomic condition of the home, parental social adjustment, parental conflict, parental characteristics, parental attitudes and concerns, and family affectional relationships.

Relationships between these variables and the intellectual development of the children show an interesting pattern. The relationship generally increases with age. Thus, family income shows no relationship to intellectual development at the two- and three-year-old level, but from four years of age onward there is a considerable relationship, both for boys and for girls. When a relationship exists between a condition in the home and measures of intellectual development, the relationship tends to increase with age. The reasons for this are probably twofold. One is that measures of intellectual development, for the younger age groups, are very inadequate. Another is that the longer a home can exert an influence, the more it is likely to have some effect on the child.

The extent to which play facilities were superior was found to be related to mental development, but this relationship does not appear until the age of three in girls and not until the age of ten in boys. The latter results fit a substantial amount of evidence that the home facilities have more relevance for the development of daughters than sons, perhaps because the boys are likely to have more freedom in finding experiences outside the home.

The extent to which there was conflict between the parents in matters of religion, finance, cultural standards, and recreation was related to a slight degree to the girls' intellectual development, but no relationship could be discerned in the case of the boys. One suspects that this characteristic of the home environment is more closely related to aspects of development other than the intellectual.

Many relationships were found that could not have been readily predicted. Mothers who were worrisome, tense, and unstable had sons who showed superior mental development. One of the most striking relationships was found between the mother's level of energy and the children's mental test scores. Honzik points out that this finding suggests that the energetic mothers are those who stimulate their children early in infancy and that such stimulation has been found in subhuman species to foster the development of the higher levels of the nervous system. In contrast, the father's energy level was negatively related to the intellectual level in the case of both boys and girls. Perhaps fathers may tend to direct their energies to activities outside the home, from which the children do not directly benefit. Mothers who worry and are concerned are also probably those who stimulate their children intellectually through frequent attention to them.

Unrelated to the boys' intellectual development are such factors as the father's irritability, his reaction to conflict, and his energy level. The father probably does not have sufficient contact with his children for his energy level to have the same effect as that of the mother. Daughters are affected little intellectually by the father's energy level, and they are also unaffected by the father's stability, worrisomeness, and self-confidence.

A particularly important finding is that the mother's concern for educational achievement is considerably related to the intelligence test scores of both boys and girls and particularly the boys. Of interest is the fact that concern for achievement on the part of the parent of the opposite sex is of greater importance than the concern of the parent of the same sex. The parent-child relationship expressed by these findings is probably complex. Other evidence, reviewed in the chapter on motivation, suggests that it has to do with the acquisition of motives. The father's satisfaction with his work situation seems to have some effect on the test scores of his son. This is also probably a motivating effect. The father who feels he is getting nowhere may well have a son who believes that striving to achieve is hardly worthwhile.

Relationships involving affection within the home are correlated with intelligence test scores, and, in fact, provide some of the highest correlations found in the entire study. The closeness of the mother to the son is of particular importance and has a striking effect on the development of verbal intelligence. This finding fits well with data derived from earlier studies. The girl's mental development does not seem to be influenced in the same way and seems to be more related to the extent to which the parents have a compatible relationship. Close mother-daughter relationships, over the long haul of the growing period, make for a lowered rather than a raised level of intellectual development.

Honzik has reviewed earlier studies in connection with the one reported here and attempts to put together a picture of the environment that produces the most favorable condition for intellectual and academic achievement. Her conclusion is that it is of paramount importance for the boy to have a warm and close relationship with the mother and then, later, opportunity to identify with a father who is both successful and concerned about his son's success. In the case of the girl, optimum conditions are found when the father has a friendly relationship with his daughter and a compatible relationship to the mother. Parental agreement and lack of conflict about discipline and cultural standards is also important. The early environmental conditions that accelerate development are less clear in the case of girls than they are in the case of boys.

The findings of studies concerned with the development of intelligence cannot be readily translated into what is known about learning. In the case of boys, the effect of vigorous and concerned interaction of the mother in the early years of life may be to provide many reinforcements for the child's attempts to master his environment, but this is unlikely to be the whole story. At least as important a factor is that this interaction constantly brings the child into contact with new aspects of his environment, and this interaction can have two effects. One effect is the development of the perceptual system, as Hebb has postulated in his theory of early learning. Hebb implies that mere frequent exposure to numerous aspects of the environment will result in the development of mechanisms in the child's brain that permit accurate perception of his environment. Stimulation also has another consequence. It has an energizing effect on behavior. There is certainly much evidence that children raised in bleak environments, with little to stimulate them, show retarded development. The mother who is concerned with the achievement of her child and who interacts warmly with him provides just the reverse kind of environment.

The Honzik study is of particular interest because it is concerned with intellectual development as it is measured by the broad objective measures provided by intelligence tests. There are also other behaviors that can be considered to represent competencies in dealing with the environment. Some of these were studied in a research by Baumrind and Black (1967). Examples of such characteristics are independence, assertiveness, cooperativeness, and friendliness. Baumrind and Black studied the relationship of the characteristics of the family to the development of these and other characteristics in one hundred seven preschool children. Because the average age of these children was only forty-seven months, and because relationships between children's characteristics and parental characteristics have not fully emerged by that age, it is quite surprising that some relationships were found.

Warmth was not found to be an important factor in predicting the aspects of competence studied, although there was a weak relationship between the warmth of the parental behavior and the degree of independence shown by the boys. This fits with the data provided by Honzik. An interesting finding is that punitiveness on the part of the parents was not found to be associated with fearful and compliant behavior. Oddly enough, punitive behavior on the part of the father was associated with domineering behavior in the girls. In the case of the boys, punitive behavior of the parents was associated with the child's being described as unlikable.

Baumrind and Black found that consistent paternal discipline was associated with independence and assertiveness in boys and with affiliativeness in girls. When the children were studied in a school setting, consistent discipline in the home was associated with what they describe as "constructive nonconformity" in the case of the boys and with "well-socialized, friendly, and dependable" behavior in the girls. Parental willingness to be reasonable and to listen to the child was also associated with independence on the part of the boys and stability in the case of the girls.

Finally, the study showed that restrictiveness on the part of the parent and an inability to permit independent behavior was accompanied by lack of imaginative behavior in the child and also a tendency to be stereotyped in thinking.

This study, like the Honzik study, brings out the fact that intellectual skills are developed or restricted by the characteristics of the home in which the child is raised. Even in the homes of above average middle-class children, the characteristics of the home can make very large differences in the extent to which children develop competence in handling the problems of their environment.

Personality development. In the last decade some information has been accumulated concerning the relationship of child-rearing practices and certain aspects of social learning. The outstanding study in this area is one conducted by Sears, Maccoby, and Levin (1957), which involved the child-rearing practices of 379 mothers. Child-rearing practices are defined as dimensions of maternal behavior.

In the Sears et al. study, the group of mothers carefully studied came from two suburban towns in a large metropolitan area of New England. The group was derived from a complete range of social classes, and in this respect must be considered highly representative of a New England population of mothers. The median age of the group was 33.6 years. Both ends of the education continuum were well represented, with 22 per cent having completed college and 14 per cent never having completed high school. The group also represented a wide range of income.

Data were collected concerning the child-rearing practices of this group of mothers by means of extended interviews that had been carefully planned. The aspects of the mothers' behavior studied were those considered to be most influential with respect to the child. For this reason, careful inquiries were made into such matters as disciplinary measures, permissiveness, severity of training, temperamental qualities of the mother, and attempts to develop more mature behavior. Much of the study is descriptive and provides a record of the child-rearing practices of a group of New England mothers at midcentury. Studies of child-rearing practices conducted fifty years from now will undoubtedly compare the data with that collected by Sears et al. The strictly descriptive aspects of this study are not related to the topic at hand, and therefore will not be reviewed here. What we are concerned with here are the ways in which these characteristics group themselves and the relationship of these groups of behavior to aspects of the learning process.

Sears et al. subjected their data to a factor analysis in order to determine the way in which the characteristics of child-rearing practices grouped themselves. Five major groupings were found, which are described as follows:

Permissiveness-strictness. This characteristic emerged from the study as the most all-pervasive of the ones studied. At one end of the scale are mothers who imposed strong restrictions on children with respect to play in the house and showed high demands for good table manners, quietness, orderliness, and neatness, low permissiveness with respect to aggression toward parents, siblings, and other children, as well as low permissiveness with respect to sex behavior. The relationship of this aspect of parental behavior to the behavior of the child brings out the interesting finding that permissiveness concerning aggression results in a high level of aggressive behavior on the part of the child. The implication is that such behavior is not learned by reinforcement but has to be controlled by some degree of suppression. This fits well the findings of Lebo and Lebo (1957), who found that children who expressed most aggression in their classrooms also expressed the most in a free-play situation conducted by a therapist. They did *not* find that those who failed to express aggression in daily life tended to show aggression in play therapy. Aggression, it appears, can be either generally expressed or generally absent. The same effect is not evidenced in the case of dependency relationships. A permissive attitude toward dependency does not seem to encourage dependency.

General family adjustment. This characteristic is the extent to which the mother manifested such attributes as high esteem for herself and her spouse, was happy about becoming pregnant, enjoyed interaction with her baby, and was satisfied with her present life situation. Although this has commonly been considered to represent one of the most important conditions related to the development of desirable attributes of personality, the study provides virtually no data concerning its relationship to the later characteristics of the child.

Warmth of mother-child relationship. The name for this characteristic provides a good description of the behavior to which it refers. This characteristic appeared to have an all-pervasive effect on the behavior of the child. Maternal coldness was associated with difficulties related to the negative functions such as feeding and bladder control, and emotional difficulties related to these functions. In addition, maternal coldness was associated with slowness in the development of a conscience. The authors of the study suggest that the warm mother offers more reinforcements than the cold mother, and hence provides a more favorable condition for many of the learnings that must take place in the first few years of childhood.

Responsible child-training orientation. The high end of this scale describes a mother who takes her child-rearing duties with great seriousness and feels the weight of her responsibilities. Little information is given concerning the relationship of this factor to child behavior.

Aggressiveness and punitiveness. The mother who is high in this dimension expects the child to be aggressive toward other children, but administers severe punishment if the child should show aggression against the parent. The high end of this scale identifies a mother who has a high level of aggression, but who will not tolerate aggression toward herself. The researchers concluded that a high level of punitiveness is quite ineffective in child training, a conclusion that is consistent with data reported in other parts of this book. They also point out that their data support the position that punishment does little to eliminate undesirable behavior. Severe physical punishment was associated with feeding problems and with aggression in the home. Nevertheless, some caution is necessary in drawing conclusions from this aspect of the study. Sears and his associates conclude that under certain conditions punishment may be effective, but the nature of these conditions has not yet been determined.

A follow-up of the Sears et al. study was conducted years later by Sears (1970), who administered a series of self-concept scales to eighty-four girls and seventy-five boys whose mothers had been interviewed. Good self-concepts were found to be associated with both maternal and paternal warmth. Also those with the most desirable self-concepts came from the smaller families and tended to have an early position in the order of birth. Some differences were found between the relationships of boys and girls to their home background. In the case of boys *only*, a good self-concept was associated with low father dominance in the father-mother relationship.

Other cultures provide different contrasts in child-rearing practices that may add to an understanding of the relationship of early training conditions to adult personality. A particularly striking contrast is presented in Israel, where the child-rearing practices with children raised in the kibbutz can be contrasted with those of the more typical family situation. Rabin (1965) compared the behavior of children and young adults who had been raised in each of these two situations.

Each kibbutz is a voluntary organization of individuals who have come together to pool their energies and resources, to live in a state of economic collectivism, and to delegate to the group as a whole the main responsibilities of child-rearing. In such a collective, the mother has continuous contact with the infant only during the first four months; after that, the contacts are steadily reduced until daily contacts between parent and child are resricted to one or two hours, when the parents visit the child-raising houses and interact with the child. The typical child-rearing practices of the parents are taken over by the *metapelet,* a term that is translated as "one who takes care of." Thus, in infancy and early childhood, those raised in the kibbutz come into contact with many adults who are responsible for their welfare, including the biological mother, the metapelet, the people who relieve the metapelet at various times during the day, the night watchwoman, and perhaps others too; and the child must compete with many other children of similar age for the services and attention of these adults. The kibbutz child-rearing situation appears to provide a socially more complex environment than does the typical family situation; and, in the early years, the kibbutz situation may be intellectually more deprived. There are also lessened opportunities for intense identification with single adult figures.

The complexity of the early environment in the kibbutz appears to have a retarding effect during the first few years. The children are not only less intellectually developed than are the family-reared children, but they also show a greater frequency of emotional problems such as are reflected in tantrums. Nevertheless, such problems are short-lived, for the difficulties of early life are soon overcome and a benign educational environment produces effective educational development. The kibbutz child with his relationships to many adults shows few strong attachments and also fewer conflicts with adult figures, particularly during adolescence. The conflicts of the teen-age period are largely absent because the youngster does not have to struggle for independence and for personal identity—he has already gained these at a much earlier age.

The study suggests that early emotional problems do not necessarily forewarn of subsequent emotional problems at a later age. Apparently, they do not represent learned patterns of responding, but rather they reflect states of disorganization, which are replaced later by more adequate patterns of responding. The data also suggest that an intellectually barren infancy does not do irreparable damage that a stimulating environment in the later years cannot remedy.

A striking feature of the outcome of the child-rearing practices of the kibbutz is that the children develop almost no intellectual aspirations. Few ever go on to college, although such a possibility is open to them. Indeed, the kibbutz may often have to bring in from the outside some of the technical skills needed because their own youth have no interest in higher education. The kibbutz-reared child may fail to develop any drive to achieve because he lacks a close relationship to a mother deeply concerned about her child's achievement, or a relationship to a father who is enjoying success. The lack of such relationships removes from the kibbutz child's environment some of the most important sources of achievement motivation. Thus the children develop in a manner that makes for good social adjustment in a static and nonprogressive society.

Language Development

Although language development seems to lie at the very heart of the growth of intelligence, surprisingly little is known about how language is acquired by children. It is not that there has been a lack of research, for the number of studies involved is vast and several thousand have appeared in the last few decades. Most of these studies have provided descriptions of development that throw little light on what the crucial matters related to language development really are. Two main positions have emerged that attempt to describe language development. One of these is associated with the name of B. F. Skinner and the other with the name of Noam Chomsky. Neither is strictly experimental in origin, in that the positions were formulated originally on the basis of an analysis of what the learning of a language appears to involve. Some would refer to this as an armchair analysis. However, the work of Chomsky has stimulated an enormous amount of research, most of which has been supportive of his position.

The views and speculations of Skinner (1957) will be considered first. Skinner writes on the subject with both conviction and charm, which has persuaded others to accept his interpretation of the psychology of language, but his position is much at variance with what is known today about language development. The essential position of Skinner is that speech is an instrumental form of behavior, that is to say, a form of behavior that is used as an instrument for achieving goals and manipulating the environment. Behaviors that are instrumental in achieving goals are referred to as operants. Verbal behaviors of this kind are referred to as verbal operants. Having taken this position, Skinner (1957) then attempts to describe the development of language in the same terms as he describes the development of any other skill.

Skinner's interpretation of verbal behavior is that it is a form of instrumental behavior that results in the manipulation of the environment. It is shaped, he claims, by the same laws of learning that shape all other forms of instrumental behavior. The child who learns to say "please" to obtain a cookie has learned an instrumental act that has been promptly reinforced in the past by his being given the desired cookie. Skinner does not introduce the notion that the word *please* has meaning for the child; rather, it is an effective form of goal-directed behavior. The word *please*, then, is a verbal operant. A thirsty two-year-old who says "water" expects that this word will produce the desired substance and, according to Skinner, is functioning in much the same way as a rat that presses a lever in order to obtain food. That the environment is rich in the reinforcements it provides for the linguistic efforts of the child cannot be denied. Within limits, a reinforcement concept of the development of language has high plausibility, particularly in the early stages.

Skinner classifies usage of speech not in terms of categories used by grammarians, such as nouns, adjectives, and so forth, but into categories representing the behavioral function that the particular usage serves. A brief discussion of two of the major categories of speech introduced by Skinner will serve to illustrate the kind of analysis of language he is attempting to make. These two categories he names the *mand* and the *tact*.

The term *mand* is derived from such words as *demand* or *command* and represents a form of speech designed to produce a change in the environment. A young child who says to his mother, "Come," is using a mand that may have the effect of bringing his mother closer to him. *Give it to me*, *Take it away*, and *Put that down* are all mands. Sometimes the mand may be quite subtle in the way in which it manipulates the behavior of others. The student who comes to the counselor and says,

"I am just no good at anything," is probably fishing for the answer, "But that is not true; you are good at quite a few things." In this case the behavior of the student would be wrongly interpreted if the bare meanings of the words were taken at their face value. The student is almost certainly not attempting to inform the counselor of his incompetence. His statement is, rather, a verbal operant likely to produce a reassuring response from the counselor.

The *tact* is another major category of behavior within Skinner's classification system. The tact is a verbal behavior that directs attention toward an object in the environment. *What is this? What is happening here? I wonder how this works? Could this be fixed if this part were replaced?* are all tacts. The term *tact* is derived from the word *contact* and refers to a contact with the environment.

More complex forms of verbal behavior can be explained within the system by the proposal that the child can also be taught, through reinforcement, to copy behavior and to echo the speech of the adult. Such imitative verbal behavior is called *echoic* behavior. Children may thus learn to produce complex chains of words.

Skinner also assumes that there are a number of classes of subvocal behavior that are controlled by external stimuli. He assumes, for example, that a person reading a book makes subvocal responses that correspond to the words of the text. Skinner refers to these as *textual responses*. He makes a similar assumption about the behavior of the person who is listening to a lecture, and implies that there is some internal echo of the words that are heard. Some readers do make such subvocal responses, but the evidence is clear that such responses are quite unnecessary for understanding either printed or spoken verbal material. Also, the evidence suggests that the muscular responses involved in reading silently are quite different from those involved in talking aloud.

Skinner's book on verbal behavior is filled with delightful anecdotes told in a style that reflects his own habits of thinking. He has done little to follow up on any of his speculations with research, although a little work has been undertaken by others.

A very similar, but more recent, attempt to describe the learning of language in terms similar to those of Skinner is found in a book by Staats (1968). Although this appeared more than a decade after the Skinner book, it adds no evidence to back up the speculative analysis. The Staats version also does not have the persuasive charm that characterizes the writings of Skinner and it offers an utterly unconvincing attempt to describe the development of language in terms of instrumental and classical conditioning.

Experimentation on language change and language development from the Skinner point of view has not been forthcoming except in a very limited area. One approach to the testing of his position has been to determine whether language habits can be changed by means of reinforcements. If, for example, an individual is reinforced for beginning his sentences with "I," does he then slowly increase his usage of the word *I*? A considerable experimental literature has developed related to this problem, but with results that are not entirely clear. A grunt of approval from a listener whenever a person uses the singular personal pronoun has, in most such studies, produced an increase in frequency in its use, but not all studies show such an increase. The effect is generally a rather weak one, which partly accounts for the fact that it sometimes appears and sometimes does not. Those mainly interested in such studies have been clinical psychologists who, through such research, have been alerted to the fact that their grunts, smiles, and other gestures may be reinforcing aspects of the way in which the client talks about himself. An extensive research literature has developed around the problem of whether it makes a difference whether the person whose behavior is being modified is or is not aware of the significance of the reinforcing events, the ambiguities of which have been pointed out by Rosenfeld and Baer (1969). Such research has not yielded very useful results, in that research workers have encountered difficulties in identifying and defining what is meant by a subject's being aware of a reinforcer.

The Skinner position on the development of language lacked any direct experimental foundation and, since the time when it was first published, it has gathered little additional support. Indeed, much of the evidence that has accumulated in recent years has led psycholinguists to take the position that instrumental conditioning and classical conditioning have almost nothing to offer in the matter of understanding the nature of behavior involving language. The alternative position, influencing most research in progress at the present time, is that of Chomsky (1967, 1969). The reader interested in acquiring more information about the Chomsky position is advised to start by reading a simplified presentation of the position, such as that provided by Deese (1970). A more comprehensive account of psycholinguistics can be found in Herriot (1970).

The basic position of the psycholinguists is that the development of language does not conform to the description provided by the instrumental conditioning model at all. Language behavior does not show random emission of sounds that are slowly shaped through reinforcement and extinction into words. In the next stage the child does not slowly learn adult grammar and gradually produce closer and closer approximations to what the adult considers to be grammatically correct statements. The first step in the development of all linguistic skills is that of learning to recognize, as separate and distinct, some of the basic sounds of the language. Those concerned with the psychology of perception, such as Gibson (1969), have long recognized this. Just as Piaget has to assume that the nervous system has innate organizing schemata that permit the organizing of experience related to biological functions such as eating, so does it seem necessary to assume that the nervous system has basic mechanisms that permit the child to recognize and differentiate particular speech sounds. This point is more easily understood if one reflects that a computer could not possibly recognize speech sounds unless it had built into it a special mechanism for handling that kind of data. Recognition and differentiation always require that some information is already stored about the phenomenon to be recognized or differentiated from other phenomenon. Deese (1970), like most other research workers in the psycholinguistic area, argues for some kind of innate mechanism that permits the child to learn to recognize the basic sounds of speech. Psycholinguists argue that just as the frog has an innate mechanism that permits it to recognize and respond to small flying insects, so does man have innate mechanisms related to the perception of speech.

The argument of the psycholinguists goes further in the matter of innate mechanisms. They have mustered evidence to show that there are also innate mechanisms related to the production of utterances. Their position is that the child is not a passive receiver of speech sounds and that his speech is not slowly and passively molded by external circumstances. On the contrary, the child is an active experimenter with speech and has an innate capacity to devise and use rules related to the putting together of words into utterances.

A term that is quite crucial for understanding the psycholinguist's position on the development of speech is the term *generative grammar*. A grammar is a set of rules that determine what sentences can be produced and what sentences cannot be produced. A three-year-old child will produce certain kinds of sentences but not other kinds of sentences. Presumably, his behavior is controlled by certain underlying rules the child has generated. A child who is protesting his mother's efforts to undress him may say, "No go bed." This is a very typical grammatical form for a child of three although it is not found in adult speech. The three-year-old has produced rules of speech that result in the production of such utterances. He has not learned these rules from the adult world which simply does not use the same speech form. Indeed, young children develop their own grammars, which are quite characteristic of the children in the particular culture. The proposal is that the human intelligence has a built-in mechanism that has a capability of producing some order in the speech to which the young child is exposed and to generate rules that will enable that child to produce speech.

A great amount of evidence has been brought together by Lenneberg, showing that the general pattern of speech development is highly uniform across cultures and it is also surprisingly little affected in its early stages by gross deprivations. The speech development of children of deaf parents who do not speak, for example, is surprisingly similar to that of children raised under more normal circumstances. Lenneberg also points out that children in an institution in which their main exposure to speech was a television set that was on all day showed, again, a typical pattern of development. Lenneberg argues that it is mere exposure to the language rather than the reinforcements provided by the adult world that stimulates the early stages of speech development. The language the children are exposed to determines the language they will speak, but he argues that they are endowed with a nervous system that permits them to analyze the language they hear, to find structures in it, and to experiment with structures of their own.

A generative grammar underlying speech is not much like the traditional grammar that has been taught in schools for generations. It is also not a set of rules taught to the child, but a set of rules he invents. He does not know the rules in the sense in which an adult knows the rules of the highway and can describe them to a foreigner. They are rules that govern the behavior of the child and represent lawfulness of his behavior. A sentence that is perfectly correct from the point of view of traditional English grammar may be quite unacceptable in terms of the underlying generative grammar. Chomsky (1969, p. 410) cites such a sentence: "For him to understand this sentence is difficult." The nature of the underlying generative grammar has not been worked out at this time, though many of its characteristics at different stages of development have been determined.

Deese states there is some evidence that the simple rules generated by the child in his early attempts to produce speech are very similar for different languages. One speech activity common in English-speaking young children and in children exposed to other languages is for the child to take what is called a pivot word such as *tree* and to make utterances such as "tree-boy," "tree-good," "tree-fall," "tree-eat," "tree-go," and so forth in a long stream. Such an activity involves a playful combination of words, but it also involves a primitive grammar, for some words are pivot words and other words are those attached to pivot words (see Brown and Fraser, 1963). In such an activity, a child shows evidence of being an experimenter with language. The child is neither emitting words at random nor is he emitting short phrases that have been previously reinforced. Any attempt to understand such behavior in terms of an operant conditioning theory of learning appears to be so much nonsense.

The grammar implicit in the language of the child, which the child himself invents, is different from adult grammar in many respects. For one thing, it is simpler and permits very few things to be said. It involves utterances that can be understood only when the situation in which they are made is comprehended. A child who says "egg gone" is not saying clearly whether the egg has fallen on the floor or whether he has eaten it all up. The utterance is highly ambiguous, largely because of its brevity and simplicity. The parent can understand this utterance because he sees the child make it in a particular situation. Adult utterances are longer and more complex and are less ambiguous. They involve an underlying grammar that includes far more rules for generating sentences and a grammar that is much more complex.

The difference in sentence length at different ages is of interest. An important factor in limiting the length of a sentence is the span of attention. Young children cannot generate very long utterances because they would not have the capacity of remembering the first part of the utterance while speaking the last part. For this reason, the utterance of the two-year-old generally involves only one or two words. Adults also limit the length of their utterances. One could build a perfectly grammatical sentence that involved 1,000 words, but it would be quite unintelligible. One simply cannot keep track of the information in such a long utterance. Before all the dependent clauses have been said, the listener or speaker has forgotten what they were dependent upon. For this reason, intelligible speech generally involves quite short sentences.

The theory of generative grammar takes the position that the growing child discovers rules in adult speech that permit him to produce statements that conform more and more closely to those of the adult world. It is not that the child is just reinforced for correct English, although such a process may play a part. The idea that the nervous system is a mechanism for discovering order is not unique to the area of knowledge developed by the psycholinguists, for a similar assumption is commonly made by those engaged in research on perception.

The increasing complexity of rules used to generate utterances as language develops is also accompanied by another change in language, in which Piaget has been particularly interested. This is the change from the use of language to refer to highly concrete and immediate situations to the use of language for referring to situations not immediately present or to abstract situations. Deese points out that language does not always show the complete development from the simple descriptive language of the young child to the complex abstract statements of the adult. Deese points to evidence indicating that those brought up in underprivileged conditions may continue, throughout their lives, to speak a dialect resembling more the language of the child than that of the educated adult. This failure for language to develop to the full limits that a mature generative grammar may permit places the person from an underprivileged environment at a serious disadvantage. It means that such a person is limited in the things that he can say and can speak.

Chomsky implies that before a sentence is enunciated, a complete program for its production is internally formulated. A sentence is not produced by each word being the stimulus for the next word, as traditional learning theorists would want us to believe. A sentence is produced much as a complex motor skill act is produced, as a whole, and not as a chain of elements with each element in the act triggering the next element. The theories of Skinner and Staats on how a sentence is produced by a speaker are so implausible that they contribute nothing to our understanding of language.

The main issues of controversy related to the development of language are also the central issues in other areas of psychology. They pertain to the nature of man. The major question to be answered, which creates these issues, is the extent to which man is to be regarded as a passive creature whose behavior is molded by circumstances in his environment and the extent to which he is an active organizer of the information that the environment provides and an experimenter in the use of that information. Man is probably, to some extent, both of these, but psychologists of the past have almost certainly grossly underestimated the extent to which man is an active organizing agent.

Summary

1. Conceptions of learning are closely related to conceptions of human development. Most contemporary psychologists assume that the ability to learn and behave intelligently is highly related to the individual's history.
2. The concept of maturation has long had a significant impact on educational practice, for the assumption has been made that the nervous system has to develop to a particular point before particular learnings can be undertaken. Although some aspects of motor learning may require particular levels of maturation, the child is probably capable of undertaking many tasks, including reading, at a much earlier age than was formerly considered possible. Nevertheless, intellectual development may have to take place in a certain order, of the kind that Piaget describes. The learning of certain skills, such as those involved in conservation tasks, may not be possible before a certain age, because other prerequisite learnings may have to take place first. Several attempts have been made to describe stages in the development of the intellect. Those having particular impact at the present time are the outcomes of the work of Piaget, Hebb, and Gagné. The descriptions of the stages in learning provided by Hebb and Piaget are derived from experimental data. That of Gagné is derived analytically and intuitively.
3. Hebb proposes that there are two main stages in learning. First,

there is a stage in which the individual learns to identify certain highly significant stimuli and to differentiate them from other stimuli. The second stage involves complex perceptions. The first stage is extremely slow and tedious, but, in the second stage, learning takes place with rapidity.

4. What Hebb has to say about stages in learning is not in any way inconsistent with the highly detailed account of development provided by Piaget. For Piaget, the keys to development are found in two concepts derived from biology, namely, assimilation and accommodation. The one involves the incorporation of some input, or piece of information, into already existing psychological organizations. The other involves the modification of existing structures so that they can incorporate within them some new element. Piaget sees the child as reaching out to the environment rather than as a passive recipient of whatever the environment may bring. He provides a detailed account of how the child's development proceeds from a stage of simple interactions with a complex world to a stage in which much behavior involves the internal manipulation of symbols and the performance of logical operations with those symbols. Within Piaget's system, as with the much simpler system of Hebb, what can be learned at each stage depends upon what has been learned at an earlier stage.
5. Gagné's analysis of learning, unlike the two considered, is not based on experimental data but on a logical analysis of the way in which learning tasks can be ordered. Until much more is known about the system, through experimentation, it will have to be regarded as only an interesting set of conjectures.
6. Theories of development assume that the individual deprived of particular learning experiences early in life may be blocked from learning at more complex levels. Studies in which animals and humans have been deprived of particular opportunities to learn have considerable theoretical and practical significance. Deprivation of opportunity to use a sensory system may have the effect not only of limiting the ability to use that sense department but may also, in extreme cases, result in actual damage to the sensory system. Probably few humans are ever so completely deprived of stimulation of a sensory system that the system undergoes deterioration.
7. Studies of the effect of enriching the environment involve introducing some source of stimulus variation. In the case of animals, the introduction of rather limited amounts of stimulation during the growing period has been shown to result in superior development. Animals raised in enriched environments, in contrast with

those raised in impoverished environments, show superior ability at solving problems when full growth is reached and also rather different personality characteristics. Well-designed researches involving human subjects in which the effect of either an enriched or an impoverished environment is studied are few, but there is an increasing amount of evidence that intellectual development is highly dependent upon the stimulation provided by the environment.

8. The issue of whether there are critical periods during development when particular skills have to be learned, if the skills are to be learned at all, is a matter about which there is considerable controversy. What is not known is whether the animal ceases to be able to learn the particular skill once the natural age for learning it is passed, or whether other circumstances make learning difficult. No real evidence is available to suggest that there are critical periods in the case of human learning and development, but it is conceivable that these may still be found.
9. Of crucial importance to the development of intelligence are conditions in the home during childhood. An effective pattern of communication in the home is of the utmost importance to the development of intelligence. A second significant class of variables is the extent to which the parents are restrictive or permissive. Just as highly controlling teachers tend to be less effective than more permissive teachers, so too are highly controlling parents less effective in developing the intellects of their children. However, permissiveness on the part of the parent is not enough. It has to be coupled with a concern for the achievement of the child. Play facilities, as might be expected, are related to intellectual development. The energy level of the mother is also a factor, perhaps because it determines the amount of stimulation provided. The affection in the home also plays a role, but this role is not well understood at the present time.
10. An interesting finding is that the effect of the various conditions in the home becomes more marked as the child grows older. The prolonged exposure to these conditions over the years is what produces the effect. For this reason, school programs of short duration may not be expected to remedy the consequences of psychological deprivation.
11. Studies of general personality development have generally yielded less than studies of intellectual competence, largely because of the difficulties encountered in measuring nonintellectual attributes. A particularly significant finding is that permissiveness with respect to aggression in children tends to increase the level of aggression. In contrast, if the child is encouraged to be de-

pendent on the parent, the child does not grow progressively more dependent.

12. Studies of child rearing practices in different cultures also help to throw light on the relationship between these practices and the developing child. Studies of the kibbutz suggest some of the factors that may contribute to the development of achievement motivation or the lack of it.
13. Central to the development of effective human learning is the development of skill in the use of language. Although an immense amount of effort has been directed toward understanding language development, most of the crucial issues have not yet been resolved. The most important unresolved issue is the extent to which language development can or cannot be understood in terms of a simple reinforcement conception of learning. There are at least some language phenomena that are not well accounted for by a reinforcement theory. Evidence derived from the reinforcement of verbal behavior in the adult provides only weak support for the Skinner position.
14. An alternative interpretation of language development has been provided by Chomsky and other psycholinguists. This alternative position emphasizes the active role played by the child in language acquisition and his innate capacity for assuming that role. Mere exposure to language is emphasized as the essential condition for language learning and the part played by reinforcement is considered to be quite trivial. Children are considered to have the capacity for assimilating some of the information that the structure of language provides. They also have the capacity for generating rules for producing verbal utterances.

CHAPTER TEN

Motivation and Learning

Traditional Approaches to the Problem of Motivation

Trainers of animals have long recognized that an essential condition for training is that the animal must be active or, as it is commonly said, energized. Sleepy, lethargic animals are virtually untrainable until their behavior is in some way activated. The trainer will see a part of his task as that of arranging conditions so that he is working with a vigorous and energetic animal and not with a sluggish creature. This is a part of the problem of motivating the animal he wishes to train. Another aspect of motivating behavior is that of arranging conditions so that the animal's behavior becomes directed toward the performance the trainer wishes to produce. If a trainer wishes to teach a lion to climb on a stool at a given command, then he must arrange conditions so that the lion moves in the direction of climbing on the stool rather than in any other direction. Thus, there are two components of the problem of motivation. The one involves the energizing of behavior. The other involves the direction of behavior. Let us consider first the problem of energizing behavior as it has been traditionally treated in psychological literature.

The traditional approach to the study of motivation in animals has been to assume that behavior is energized through strong stimuli that may be internal or external. The jockey applies a whip to the rear of his mount in order to provide a strong stimulus, which will, in turn, energize the horse. Such a strong stimulus that produces action is called a drive stimulus. Sometimes drive stimuli are internal and are produced by states of deprivation. Deprive an animal of food for twenty-four hours, and the body chemistry will be upset sufficiently to produce strong internal stimuli that have much the same effect on energizing behavior as does the external stimulus provided by the whip of the jockey. Hunger pangs represent a part of these strong stimuli. Any deprivation of the necessities of life, such as food or water or oxygen or an adequate temperature of the surroundings, produces a bodily imbalance, which in turn activates behavior. Behavior remains active until the animal finds food or water or oxygen and the balance of chemicals in the body is restored. This is commonly referred to as a homeostatic theory of behavior. Such a theory assumes that the basic source of activity is some kind of imbalance in the chemistry of the body.

A drive state produces activity that continues until some action of the organism reduces the drive state. An example of such an action might be a thirsty and active animal drinking water. A psychologist wishing to study learning in the rat will want to experiment with an active rat, so he will probably starve the animal to be studied for twenty-four hours. Such a hungry animal is then placed in the starting box of the maze, if maze learning is the area of research. The activity of the animal takes it through the various corridors of the maze until it reaches the goal box, where it finds a small quantity of food. The amount of food provided is generally so small that it does not influence the drive level of the rat. The rat is then placed back in the starting box, and the performance is repeated.

The object in the goal box that has potential for reducing the drive is commonly referred to as the incentive, but it is also referred to as the reinforcement. The evidence is clear that the food in the goal box, like all objects related to drives, has important effects on behavior. Although it is quite obvious that there would be little learning if there were no food in the goal box, the presence of the food also has another effect, namely, an effect upon the drive itself. This is shown by the fact that relatively large amounts of food in the goal box result, for a few trials at least, in a much more vigorous performance than small amounts of food. Of course, over many trials, large amounts of food also produce a food-satiated rat likely to go to sleep in the maze. Over the short haul, however, incentive adds to the drive state produced by deprivation from food.

Although one is likely to think of deprivation from food and the resulting drive state as an example of an inborn and relatively simple drive state, quite uncontaminated by learning, such an interpretation is probably a gross oversimplification. One can show, for example, that quite young animals may have learned cravings for particular kinds of foods if they have been fed large quantities of these foods. Indeed, the craving may be such that it results in an unbalanced diet and an early death. Human behavior in relation to food in civilized countries is more like a craving than behavior that restores a chemical balance in the body, for the civilized human eats at specified times regardless of whether he is or is not hungry. Eating behavior, and its relation to a hunger drive, is certainly a complex matter.

Directional Properties of Drives

Although most people assume that an animal can discriminate whether it is hungry or whether it is thirsty, experimental findings do not support this commonsense belief. In one of the earlier studies of the capability of an animal to discriminate hunger from thirst, Hull (1943) had considerable difficulty in teaching animals to make such a discrimination. The animals did eventually learn, but only after a prolonged series of learning trials that must have involved both a frustrated experimenter and frustrated animal. This is hardly surprising when even the simpler sources of drive are not readily identified.

The mechanism involved in the raised level of activity that accompanies food deprivation is complex. Although the older theories took the position that the contractions of the stomach that accompany hunger were the main sources of the activity, possibly through the contractions producing pain-like sensations, Cofer and Appley (1964) cite evidence that there are at least two centers in the brain that respond to deprivation of food and satiation following feeding. The mechanism is undoubtedly complex.

The fact that animals cannot discriminate the sources of drive states, except after prolonged training, does not mean that man cannot ordinarily make the discrimination. Man has plenty of opportunity to learn to distinguish between, say, hunger and thirst, and may well learn such a discrimination. However, all of us have had the experience of becoming restless during the night and of tossing and turning in a drowsy state for hours wondering what the cause may be. In such a state one may ask oneself whether one is hungry, or perhaps not quite warm enough, or thirsty, and not be able to pinpoint what the cause of the increased level of activity may be. Indeed, one may have to experiment with pulling up another blanket, drinking some water, or eating some food, before the situation is brought under control. Under such conditions one is not able to determine the source of the drive state, perhaps because drowsiness prevents one from making fine discriminations.

Little purpose would be served by reviewing here in detail the extensive research that has been undertaken on motivation in subhuman subjects involving the deprivation of the animal from food and water. It is sufficient to have mentioned some of the important ideas that have emerged from this research. At this point, we must turn to some of the experimentation that has been undertaken on human motivation. Experimental approaches to the study of human motivation are new in that they have emerged largely since the end of World War II, but they are beginning to produce ideas of considerable importance.

Human Motivation

Although imbalances due to deprivation of food, water, sex, suitable temperatures in the environment, and so forth, play some small role in human behavior in a civilized society, it is also quite obvious that man's behavior is energized in other and much more important ways. Pyschologists have long discussed the issue of whether man is *endowed* with sources of motivation that animals do not possess, or whether he starts life with the same basic drives as all other higher creatures and slowly builds on these a set of acquired drives or motives.

The basic concept involved in the acquisition of new drives is that a stimulus present when a drive is aroused comes to acquire drive-arousing properties of its own. If a maze is a place where a rat is placed when it is hungry and active, then the maze comes to acquire, on its own, the property of producing activity in the rat even though the rat may not be hungry or thirsty. By a similar mechanism, objects that do not originally have incentive value can acquire incentive value if paired with incentives or, stated in another way, objects that do not have reinforcing value initially can acquire reinforcing value by being paired with objects that are reinforcers. Thus, although a buzzer has no incentive value or reinforcing value for a rat, it can be made to acquire these properties by pairing the buzzer with the delivery of food. The theory has some experimental evidence to support it, but must nevertheless be regarded as simplistic. The fact is that even though much is known about how complex motivations are related to human behavior, psychologists cannot provide a satisfactory account of how these motives are derived.

Those who have taken the latter position consider all drives as either primary or secondary, in terms of whether they are part of the individual's native equipment or are learned. The difficulty with this position is that no agreement can be reached on what drives should be included in the list of secondary or acquired drives. For example, all higher organisms show what is termed exploratory behavior, that is to say, when placed in a strange environment after a period of confinement, they move around and undertake a kind of inspection of their new surroundings. They do this even though they are well fed and have had all their bodily needs taken care of. Monkeys will grasp and inspect unusual objects placed in their cages and under conditions where they are not looking for food, water, sex objects, and so forth. The question that has been asked is whether the drive underlying this behavior can be considered to be a primary or a learned, or secondary, drive. Those who argue that the drive is learned suggest that hungry animals become active and the activity brings them into contact with new parts of their environment. In this way, the presence of novel surroundings becomes associated with a drive state and, in time, comes to trigger that drive state. Those who take the position that the drive underlying exploratory behavior is unlearned take the view that the exploration of new surroundings is so significant an activity for animals that the drive must surely be inborn. An animal that did not have a high drive to cautiously explore new surroundings would probably starve to death, and also the hazards of the new environment would never be discovered. Exploratory behavior has survival value and is as basic to the perpetuation of a species as is eating or drinking or sex behavior. The issue of whether an exploratory drive is innate cannot be settled at this time and the same is true for many other drive states, hence there is no way of drawing up an agreed-upon list of primary drives.

Relationship of Motivation and Learning

The study of simple drives in lower animals has been suggestive of what may be the relationship between motivation and learning in higher organisms, including man. There is, for example, some evidence that as drive level increases, learning also increases, until the drive reaches an optimum level. If the drive is increased further, then performance deteriorates. The evidence generally points in this direction although there is some conflicting evidence. An elaboration of this relationship between motivation and performance is found in what is known as the Yerkes-Dodson law, which states that as tasks are increased in difficulty, the optimum level of motivation declines. This means that on complex tasks the optimum level of motivation is lower than on simple tasks. As all of us well know, if we are faced with a complex task, we had better take our time. If we are highly motivated to complete it in short order, we may well make many errors. The level of motivation has to be an optimum for the task. This kind of relationship has been found with a wide range of species, although the writer could not find a study on which it had been tested with human subjects, largely because of the difficulty of systematically varying the level of motivation in the human. One is nevertheless very much tempted to believe that this relationship does apply. Common experience suggests that individuals can be too highly motivated and spoil their performance because they wanted too much to succeed. The overmotivated person can be as ineffective as the undermotivated. Indeed, there does seem to be an optimum level of motivation. Also, when the problem faced is difficult, one needs to be calm and to take one's time, and this is the picture of the moderately motivated person. On the other hand, when the task is very simple, as in running a quarter of a mile, then the optimum level of motivation is very high. Indeed, there is a question whether a person undertaking such an intellectually simple task *could* be overmotivated.

In addition, as the drive level is increased, there is a tendency for behavior to become more vigorous physically. This may be a great advantage in a sporting event, but of very dubious utility if the task is an intellectual one. Physical vigor may make the writer strike the keys of the typewriter harder, but it probably does little for the quality of the manuscript.

The central problem related to human motivation is the identification of the particular conditions that energize human behavior. An understanding of what these conditions are would permit the control of human motivation. A substantial beginning has been made in this respect in recent years with the acquisition of extensive knowledge about achievement motivation, to which we must now turn.

Goal Objects, Incentives, and Motives

Objects and events that were earlier described as reinforcers have been described by other psychologists as representing motivating conditions or incentives. The chapter on reinforcement discussed this issue briefly, and it is appropriate to raise it once more and to point out the role of such objects and events in motivating the individual. Suppose that a ten-year-old is given a piece of paper with a problem printed on it and is asked to solve the problem. Let us also suppose that the child is not particularly intrigued by the problem for, after reading it, he says he doesn't even want to try to solve it. At this point he is told that he will be given a dollar for solving it. Immediately his behavior is energized and he begins to attack the problem with energy. Eventually he solves it. Next day he is presented with a second problem, but without being told whether or not he is going to receive a dollar, and he immediately sets about attempting to solve it. Those psychologists who talk the language of operant conditioning would say that the dollar provided a reinforcement for problem-solving behavior, for persistence in finding a solution, and for using the skills involved, and hence, although the child was reluctant to attempt to solve the first problem, the dollar reinforcement strengthened these behaviors so that they were more likely to appear on the second occasion. An alternative account of what happened is that, on the first occasion, the behavior of the child is energized or triggered into a drive state by the demand for the goal object and it is this same demand for the goal object that energizes behavior when the second problem is presented on the next day. The explanation is plausible, indeed, so plausible that various forms of it have been given extensive support by such notable psychologists as K. W. Spence, O. H. Mowrer, E. C. Tolman, and C. L. Hull. In addition, the area of research known as *achievement motivation,* discussed in the next section, has been powerfully influenced by the significance given to the role of what has been termed here a *demand for a goal object,* an expression originally coined by Tolman.

This account of motivation is so attractive, simple, and in keeping with personal experience that one may wonder why it has not achieved wide acceptance by psychologists. The reasons have to do with the reluctance of psychologists to build theories around terms that cannot be precisely defined. The theory of motivation being considered here involves such terms as the *anticipation* of a goal or the *expectancy* of a goal being reached, or the *demand* for a goal. These terms are rather vague and cannot be easily defined in terms of behavior that can be readily identified and observed. Some psychologists who have attempted to develop this kind of theory of motivation have suggested ways in which words such as expectancy can be tied to quite observable forms of behavior. Hull (1943) tried to do this by suggesting that the responses associated with the achievement of a goal become classically conditioned to stimuli in the situation that leads to the goal. Thus, parts of a rat's eating response become classically conditioned to the stimuli provided by the maze. Thus, after a few maze running trials, when the rat is placed in the maze it immediately shows components of the eating response such as salivation, licking the lips, and so forth. These, in themselves, raise the general activity level of which they are a part. In the same way, a child put in a situation that he knows can lead to his getting money shows the same kind of excitement as when he is actually confronted with money he can obtain. This kind of theorizing, involving components of the goal responses known as fractional anticipatory goal responses, has some plausibility to it. The chief difficulty with the theory is that it has not led to very promising lines of research and evidence that might verify it has been scarce or altogether lacking.

Despite the technical difficulties involved in defining the terms of a theory of motivation that focuses on expectancy, or anticipatory responses, or on demand for a goal, many psychologists continue to do research related to this concept. An interesting line of research involving many different studies is that which investigates the extent to which delayed rewards are effective in comparison with immediate rewards in energizing behavior. The general finding is that for a delayed reward to be as effective as an immediate reward, it has to be larger (see Mischel and Staub, 1965). A finding of contemporary interest presented in a study by Walls and Smith (1970) is that disadvantaged children show a greater preference than nondisadvantaged children for immediate rewards. Walls and Smith propose that learning is required in order for a person to be able to respond to and be energized by delayed rewards, and disadvantaged children probably have few experiences that permit them to learn in this way. Walls and Smith also cite a number of studies that support this contention.

This discussion of the influence of a goal as an energizing agent leads at this point to the discussion of achievement motivation, a concept of motivation that has been much influenced by the idea that demand for a goal is an important factor in motivation.

Achievement Motivation

One of the most significant experimental programs in the area of human motivation is that connected with the development of the concept of achievement motivation. Research related to this concept has had a long history, beginning in the mid-thirties and continuing today as a vigorous area of inquiry. The history of the development of this concept shows well the fact that useful scientific concepts in the behavioral sciences cannot be developed overnight, but are a product of long and persistent struggle. The early researches in this area were initiated by H. A. Murray and were summarized by him in a well-known volume (1938). Murray proposed that human needs fall into categories, the viscerogenic and the psychogenic. The viscerogenic needs were a part of man's inherited constitution and consisted of needs related to such bodily events as lack of water and food, distension of the bladder and bowel, and so forth. Murray's viscerogenic needs are very similar to what other psychologists have referred to as primary drives. Psychogenic needs, on the other hand, according to Murray, are learned. His list of psychogenic needs is broad in coverage and includes such diverse items as a need to gain possession of something, a need to be orderly, a need to display oneself, a need for autonomy, a need to show aggression, and a need to take care of others and help them. Some of the needs included in the list are relatively rare in occurrence, as is a need to be rejected. Few individuals manifest a need to be rejected, and a need to exhibit oneself is seen primarily in women. Murray's list includes common psychological needs as well as the rarer ones within its twenty-eight items. Not all persons are presumed to manifest all needs. Indeed, the lives of some individuals may be dominated by a high level of one particular need, and negligible influence from any of the other needs in the list.

The research of Murray stimulated research on the measurement of needs but, like all research programs, only a very small fraction of it ever bore fruit. By far the most productive line of research has been that related to the measurement and study of achievement motivation.

The work of Murray lay dormant as a scientific enterprise during the war years of the forties, although attempts were made to give it some practical applications, and it was not until peace came that further scientific initiative was shown in the development of his theory of motivation. This development was brought about, first by one of Murray's original associates David McClelland, and later by a whole school of followers scattered across the world. Most of the work of this school of research workers became concentrated on the study of achievement motivation, but some of it became directed towards the investigation of affiliation motivation, the need to be accepted by others and to feel that one belongs. Of these two enterprises, the study of achievement motivation has been the most successful.

The literature in this area of motivation research is substantial. Summaries of much of the more significant earlier work is found in Cofer and Appley (1964). Somewhat later summaries of research are found in Atkinson and Feather (1966) and in Heckhausen (1967). The fact that each one of these works refers to several hundred different researches indicates the general vigor of the research enterprise involved. A volume edited by Smith (1969) is restricted to studies of achievement motivation in children.

The significance of the research into achievement motivation lies largely in the experimental findings, which are intertwined with theorizing that has been much less successful. Only theory at a relatively crude level is needed in order to understand the general nature of the findings. A need is a disposition that may be quiescent and latent and show no effect on behavior unless it is aroused. A person may have a high need for achievement, but if no situation arises that may challenge his need, then he will not show it. Needs have to be aroused in order to be manifested. The pupils in a class may appear bored and listless, but this does not mean that they do not have potential for showing achievement motivation. Perhaps their needs are not being aroused. Attempts to measure needs under conditions under which they are not aroused produce useless measures. Needs are aroused by some stimulus related to its satisfaction. Achievement motivation is aroused by any task that challenges the individual. A listless school child, given a new and interesting problem, may suddenly become a dynamo of energy. His achievement motivation has been aroused. A motive may also be aroused by deprivation. After a prolonged and boring situation, almost any situation may arouse the achievement motivation of a person in whom this can be aroused to a high degree. Given sufficient boredom, almost anything may become a challenge and arouse achievement motivation. There are stories, for example, of Einstein sitting at tedious meetings and being seen playing tic-tac-toe with his neighbor—perhaps not the greatest challenge for one so great, but a small avenue through which his achievement motivation could find some avenue for releasing pent-up energies.

The theory discussed here is presented at a crude level compared with the sophisticated versions found in the literature on the subject. A very sophisticated presentation of this aspect and other aspects of motivation theory is found in a volume by Madsen (1961), and another sophisticated attempt to present a theory of achievement motivation has been made in the volume by Atkinson and Feather (1966).

Early attempts to measure achievement motivation by means of questionnaires proved fruitless, partly because it is not sufficient just to probe for a disposition to manifest achievement need. What has to be done is to arouse that disposition, and then to determine the strength that it shows under the aroused conditions. The essential core of achievement motivation is that of a need to achieve some standard of excellence. A person is not showing the results of a need for achievement if he just wants to complete a particular job, for he may want to complete it to obtain money, or to please a superior, or to gain status. He has to want to complete the job *well*, because it is worthwhile to do the task well, and not for other reasons. This is what distinguishes the person showing achievement motivation. How he performs makes him a success or failure in his own eyes—if he is motivated by achievement need.

The preferred method of measuring achievement motivation has become that of providing the person in whom it is to be measured with a situation in which he produces fantasies related to achievement. These fantasies are then scored. One good situation for producing fantasies is that in which the person is provided with a picture and is asked to tell a story about it. The pictures may be selected so that they arouse achievement need rather than other needs. For example, a picture of a boy poring over a book late at night is more likely to arouse achievement need than it is to arouse need for affiliation. In the typical procedure used for measuring achievement motivation, the subject is asked to organize his fantasies by answering the following four questions as he looks at each of a set of pictures:

1. What is happening?
2. What has led up to the situation?
3. What are the people thinking or feeling?
4. What will be the outcome?

The fantasies reported are all recorded and are later scored. In order to accomplish this, the records are scored in each of a number of categories for what is referred to as achievement-need imagery, that is to say, indicating in some way a striving after a standard of excellence. The story as a whole is first scored for the extent to which it shows achievement orientation. For example, the subject who looks at the picture of the youth studying and says, "The boy wants to do well in the examination tomorrow," is scored positive for achievement imagery. On the other hand, if the subject said, "The boy seems to be reading a book," he would be showing an absence of achievement imagery. The statement is neutral and does not even suggest a motive for why the boy is reading at all. The technique is designed so that the subject projects his own motives into the people in the picture.

Two important categories of achievement motivation are those of expectation of success and fear of failure. Contrast the two following responses given to the same picture:

> "The boy is studying because he wants to do well on the examination he has to take tomorrow."
>
> "The boy is studying because he is afraid he might fail the examination he has to take tomorrow."

The first of these statements is success-oriented and the second is failure-oriented. The one represents the *approach* of a goal because of the intrinsic value inherent in the goal itself, but the other represents the *avoidance* of the consequences of failure rather than the pursuit of the goal of achievement for the sake of achievement. The approach response reflects, in the subject's past history, the effects of positive reinforcement, and the avoidance tendency, the effects of negative reinforcement.

In obtaining an overall score for achievement motivation, through the use of a picture interpretation test, the various component scores are added together and, from the total score, there is no way of telling whether the person is primarily motivated by an approach or an avoidance tendency or by a mixture of both. For some purposes, it is important to keep these two components separate, for they make rather different predictions concerning how behavior will occur in some situations.

Fear of Failure and Expectation of Success. The area in which these two aspects of achievement motivation have a distinctive role is in what is called *risk-taking behavior* (see Heckhausen, 1967). In a risk-taking situation, a person is faced with a goal to be achieved that has a designated level of attractiveness. He also knows the odds that he will not be able to achieve the goal, that is to say, the risk of failure. Whether he will decide to go ahead and try to achieve the goal or whether he will abandon the goal in such a situation depends to a considerable extent upon whether he is primarily motivated by expection of success or fear of failure. If he is motivated primarily by fear of failure, he will accept the risk if the odds of success are either very good or very poor, but he will abandon the goal if the odds are in the moderate range. Thus the fear-of-failure-oriented student will be willing to attempt courses that are either known to be very hard or very easy, but will tend to avoid the run-of-the-mill course. The reason for this is that, for such a person, the price of genuine failure is painful to pay, and that is why he chooses, on the one hand, situations in which he has a high expectation of success. The reason he also chooses the very risky situations is that he does not have to blame himself for failing in them, for he can always say to himself, "The task was so hard that anybody might have failed." In doing this he is saying that nonattainment of the goal cannot be considered as failure, for nobody could really be expected to succeed.

The success-oriented person, on the other hand, tends to choose situations in which the chances of success are in the middle range of those ordinarily encountered, and he avoids either very high-risk or very low-risk situations. The moderate-risk situation provides him with sufficient challenge to satisfy his achievement need and he also has reasonably good chances of success. The very easy, no-risk situation is avoided, for it too offers little challenge and does not arouse the achievement need. The very difficult, high-risk situation is also avoided, because it supplies only very poor opportunities for satisfying the need for achievement, which is not satisfied by failure.

The risk taking discussed here does not refer to situations involving games of chance, but risk taking where success or failure is dependent upon the person's own skill and initiative. For the adult, games of chance do not arouse the achievement motive, for success or failure cannot be attributed to the individual's own capability. On the other hand, children below the age of ten have considerable difficulty in discriminating between a situation in which they succeed because of their own skill and situations in which success is dependent upon circumstances outside of their own control. When a young child wins at a game of chance, he is likely to give himself credit for winning, as if the situation were mystically under his control. The adult is more modest about his accomplishments. For this reason, the choice of risk-taking situations involving games of chance do not bear the same relationship to fear of failure and expectation of success as they do when the situations involve a genuine accomplishment.

A final point still has to be made about the two aspects of achievement motivation under consideration, namely, that a person can have both fear of failure and hope of success in relation to the same situation. When this happens, he may have great difficulty in deciding whether to pursue the situation through to the goal it involves or to remove himself from the situation and set himself some other goal. Fear of failure tends to make him want to withdraw, but hope of success urges him to become involved in the situation. The approach and avoidance aspects of the motivating mechanism come into conflict. When there is this kind of conflict, the person involved tends to show vacillating behavior. He first tells himself he will go ahead, but as he draws nearer to the task his fear of failure builds up and he changes his mind and withdraws. As he withdraws, the possibility of failure begins to seem more remote and he decides that perhaps he should go ahead with the task, and so he vacillates back and forth. He may resolve this conflict in many ways. One is to decide, at some point, that the task is not worth the trouble anyway. This is usually rationalization for escaping. Another is to take the position that, if he fails, it is not really going to be his fault because the task is really beyond him. Thus he provides himself with a built-in excuse for failing, in the event he should fail.

Research in the area of fear of failure and hope of success is in many ways an outgrowth of an earlier series of studies on what was termed level of aspiration. This concept refers to the level of performance on a particular task that a person expects to achieve. Kurt Lewin developed this concept and many of his students went on to undertake research on it, but the research did not turn out to be productive. The level of aspiration which individuals set for themselves did not turn out to provide useful measures of motivation, perhaps because the level did not take into account whether the task involved was, or was not, a challenge to the person setting his level of aspiration. Success does tend to raise the level of aspiration, but the effects of failure are quite variable.

The Development of Achievement Motivation. Some important facts have slowly emerged concerning the development of this motivation, although the entire picture is far from clear. Though most writers take the position that achievement motivation is acquired through learning, there may well be components that are inherent in human nature. Observers of child behavior, including Karl Bühler and Jean Piaget, have noted infant behaviors that have some marks of achievement-oriented behavior, and particularly the wanting-to-do-it-alone reaction that becomes particularly marked in the third year. This last response is most likely to occur in the case of newly learned skills that the child can perform with some adequacy. This response does differ from most achievement-need-motivated responses in that it occurs in the case of tasks that offer relatively little challenge, that is to say, the tasks are relatively easy and have been already quite well mastered. Heckhausen (1967) points out that in order for achievement motivation to function, the learner has to be able to perceive himself in relation to the situation and in relation to the outcomes, and that children in the first three or four years of life are not yet capable of doing this. He suggests that the wanting-to-do-it-alone reaction is a pleasure-oriented reaction of a primitive kind and has little relationship to achievement motivation.

Heckhausen and Smith (1969) suggest that the numerous studies of the development of achievement motivation collectively suggest that the motive can be first detected around the age of five and that it develops through the elementary-school years. One of the most noticeable features of its development in the American culture is that it comes to characterize boys much more than girls, and that the adult American woman does not show it developed to the same degree as does the male.

Particularly important in the development of achievement motivation are conditions in the home, and a middle-class home provides the most favorable environment in this respect. The children in whom it develops to the greatest extent are those who come from homes in which responsible freedom of action on the part of the child has been encouraged. Children who have been allowed to go downtown by themselves at an early age tend to show a higher level of achievement motivation than those whose parents are more protective. Independence is not enough, for the poor sections of our community permit their children great independence, and this does not result in achievement motivation. Indeed, apathy toward achievement is the usual outcome. The middle-class parent, on the other hand, combines a permissive attitude toward his children with a demand that the child also achieve mastery of the skills he attacks. The freedom such a child has enables him to achieve competence in important areas of living. There is some conflict in the evidence of whether the relationship of the child to his parents should be warm or cool, but there seems no question that it should not be hostile.

Heckhausen has summarized a great number of studies related to conditions that are favorable or unfavorable to the development of achievement motivation. Several studies have been made that have compared achievement motivation in different countries of the world. Heckhausen reports that Japanese mothers give their children more opportunities for independence at an earlier age than do American mothers, but this does not seem to raise achievement motivation, perhaps because it is ballanced by a greater emphasis on conformity in the Japanese culture. Heckhausen suggests that lack of insistence on conformity may be of more significance than merely giving the child independence. He also points out that upper-class Brazilian children show a lower level of achievement motivation than do their counterparts in the United States. He suggests that this may be because the parents express great hopes for the future of their children but nevertheless demand little of them. The result is an adult who has an excessively grandiose concept of himself, but waits for the world to bring its bounties to him. This reflects the heritage of an aristocratic culture.

The cross-cultural studies bring out clearly the crucial role played by parent-child relationships in the development of achievement motivation, and other sources of evidence also support this. Fatherless families tend to produce children low in achievement motivation. Different religious groups also differ in the extent to which they produce achievement-oriented children. The Catholic home appears to provide a relatively unfavorable milieu for the development of this kind of motivation, perhaps because of the pressures exerted toward conformity in ideas. The latter finding is also consistent with the finding that in Western civilization Protestants have a rather better record for creative activity than do Catholics. The crucial factor, again, seems to be whether the religious training in the home involves an insistence on a broad spectrum of conformity or whether it encourages individual thinking. There are, of course, homes in all religious groups where conditions favorable to the development of achievement need occur.

Certain cultures and certain periods of history are characterized by different levels of achievement motivation. McClelland (1961) has attempted to show that one can determine the strength of achievement motivation in a society of the past by studying the documents it produced and identifying the frequency of occurrence of statements reflecting achievement need in those documents. He has also attempted to show that periods in which such statements commonly occur are followed by periods of great cultural and economic growth. The research is ingenious, but there are technical difficulties involved with its development that make it in some ways questionable. One should not jump to the conclusion that a simple way to produce progress in a society is to arrange conditions for the development of achievement motivation in the growing generation.

Numerous studies have been conducted on the matter of whether measures of achievement motivation predict performance in learning situations. On the surface they should, but superficial analyses of this kind are often wrong. The many studies conducted on the relationship of measures of achievement motivation to grades show very variable results. Perhaps as many as half of those conducted at the college level have shown a moderate correlation between achievement-need scores and grades, of the order of 0.2 to 0.3, but why this relationship sometimes appears and sometimes does not is an important question. In laboratory situations, where much can be controlled, a relationship is found between achievement need and performance on a task, if the task presents a challenge to the subject. If the task presents no challenge, then no relationship is found. For example, subjects can be given a rather tedious task such as that of crossing out on a page of print all those words that have both a *c* and an *a* in them. Performance on such a task is unlikely to be related to the measured achievement need of the subjects. However, if the task is presented as one involving a challenge, as when the subjects are told, for example, that it is a task that measures an extremely critical ability in personal competence, then performance on the task is likely to be related to measured achievement need. The absence of correlations between achievement need and grades in some research may indicate that the grades were in courses that provided little challenge, even for the most achievement-oriented student. In such courses one would not expect grades to be related to achievement motivation.

An important additional point is mentioned by McKeachie and his associates (1968) as a reason for the lack of prediction found in their study and in other studies involving college grades. They point out that college students are highly motivated to obtain good grades for many reasons—some because it will lead to a good job, some because they want to please their parents, and some, perhaps, because of a generalized tendency to pour energy into whatever they do. If the students are highly motivated to work hard, and do well for reasons other than that of achieving a standard of excellence, then the presence or absence of achievement motivation may make little difference. Indeed, the addition of a source of motivation to a student who is already well motivated may interfere with rather than facilitate his performance.

Achievement Motivation—Evaluation of the Present Status of the Concept. The identification of this important variable in human motivation must be considered to be one of the more important breakthroughs of recent years in the area of human learning. Indeed, up to this point there have been few measurable variables related to human motivation that have offered even the vaguest promise of providing successful predictions. The variable offers some promise of providing a basis for predicting where human accomplishment is most likely to occur. Insofar as it may be possible to control the degree of the development of achievement need by controlling various aspects of parental behavior, some hope is offered that man may now be able to have, or not to have, a progressive, dynamic society at his own choosing.

There are many important unanswered problems related to the development of achievement need for which answers must be found if effective educational planning is to be undertaken. One question is whether the elementary-school teacher can develop achievement need in a child in whom it has not been developed through his relationship to his parent. One suspects that one of the major deficiencies of the underprivileged child is that he has not developed need for achievement to any degree, and, in fact, there is some evidence to support that point of view, reviewed by Smith (1959). Can the teacher develop a relationship to the child that involves both independence and a demand that skills be mastered? Progressive educational practices of the kind that were developed between the two world wars came close to providing such conditions. The more recent trend toward more rigid classroom procedures would seem to be a move in the wrong direction insofar as the underprivileged child is concerned.

Although those who have developed the concept of achievement motivation have stressed the learned nature of this motive, some questions have been raised in recent times about the possibility that some aspects of achievement motivation may be innate. Piaget's position has long remained unnoticed in this respect, for he, more than any other psychologist, has tended to take the position that there is an innate drive to derive information from the environment. Zigler (1970) has pointed out that achievement motivation seems to grow upon the foundation of a basic need to explore and that infants do show marked individual differences in their activity level, which must be regarded as the basis of exploratory behavior. Zigler suggests that the strong individual differences in level of activity, seen from the moment a child enters the world, may produce differences in achievement motivation. This is a problem that is going to be extremely difficult to investigate, but it is a very significant one.

Other Attempts to Measure Motives Within the Murray Framework. No area has been so carefully explored as has achievement motivation, but some research has also been undertaken on other motives within Murray's conceptual system. In no case has a variable with as great potential significance as achievement need been identified and measured. Measures of other needs have tended to be less reliable and have provided less consistent predictions. The concentration of research on achievement need has probably occurred because of the promise offered by the early researches. Research workers tend to migrate toward successful developments.

The area receiving the next most attention is that of affiliation need, the need to feel accepted by others and to belong to a group. This need has been measured through the same kind of exploration of the subject's fantasy as was discussed earlier. Interest in affiliation need in relation to learning stems from the fact that it is a likely candidate as a source of motivation related to the acquisition of conforming behavior. Marlowe and Gregen (1969), who have reviewed the literature in this connection, come to the conclusion that it is those in the middle of the range of affiliation-need scores who are the most conforming. Studies of affiliation need bring out another interesting finding, namely, that those in whom the need is most developed show an unusually frequent use of the telephone for making local telephone calls. They also are great letter writers and visit more frequently than others do relatives and friends who are living at a distance. A number of devices designed to measure related motives have also been developed, as, for example, Crowne and Marlowe's (1964) measure of what they term the approval motive.

Earlier research workers had often commented on the fact that a need for approval commonly interfered with the precise measurement of personality characteristics. They noted that, when subjects were given questionnaires to fill in concerning their habits, views, likes and dislikes, and so forth, answers were commonly colored by a need of the subject to present himself in a favorable light. Subjects tend to present themselves as more honest, better adjusted, socially more adept, and generally more adequate and worthy than they really are. This effect is so marked that many psychologists have been inclined to the view that the typical personality inventory may measure nothing else than the individual's need to present himself to others in a favorable light. The designers of personality measures have made considerable efforts to eliminate this contaminating effect from their measures, but even in the best designed instrument it is likely to show through.

Crowne and Marlowe developed an inventory designed specifically to measure the extent to which individuals are motivated by the need for approval. Unlike other designers of inventories they were concerned with maximizing the effect of this variable, rather than with its elimination. The questionnaire thus produced provides a measure that has been shown, in subsequent studies, to have interesting relationships to other kinds of behavior. Crowne and Marlowe went on to study differences in the behavior of persons with high and low scores on this and related devices in a number of different experimental situations. The first experiment they undertook was to expose subjects to a dull repetitive task of fitting a dozen spools into a box, then emptying the box and starting over again. Individuals with a high need for approval described the task as being more enjoyable than did subjects with a low need for approval. Presumably, the former group was afraid of offending the experimenter by making derogatory comments about the experiment, and acted accordingly.

A second experiment involved typical verbal conditioning tasks. In this task subjects were required to just say words without putting them into sentences. The subject thus sat and said disconnected words one after the other. Whenever the subjects said plural nouns, they were either positively reinforced by the experimenter mumbling "Mm-hmm," or they were negatively reinforced by the experimenter saying "Uh-uh." This is a typical verbal conditioning experiment. In addition, two other verbal conditioning situations involving more common types of situations were used. One was a personal interview. In these verbal conditioning situations, the high-approval-need subjects were found to be more readily conditioned by reinforcement. Such subjects seem to be more aware of what is going on in such a social situation and more responsive to the reinforcements provided. In order to win approval, a high degree of sensitivity to what is happening in such a social situation would appear to be necessary.

Crowne and Marlowe also found evidence that individuals with high approval need tended to show more conforming behavior and, on a word association task, tended to give common associations rather than any associations that might be considered to be either original or unusual.

Crowne and Marlowe also undertook a number of studies on what has been termed the defensiveness of subjects. One of their approaches was to flash on a screen for a very short time words that were either common words or words in a class that they termed taboo words. In such a task, performance depends to a marked degree on how the subject perceives the task. If he sees the task as merely a task requiring speed of perception, then his need for approval will move him in the direction of performing well. However, if he perceives it as a task in which his sensitivity to dirty words is at stake, then he may show delay in reporting such words if he has a high need for approval. The person with high need for approval is defensive, as is also evident in studies of high- and low-approval-need people who are undergoing therapy. The high-approval-need people are more likely to drop out of therapy than are the low-approval-need people.

Studies in this area seem to have identified a quite important variable that may significantly modify behavior as it occurs in the classroom. The course of the development of this motive still needs to be explored.

The Self-concept and the Energizing of Behavior

While some psychologists have been investigating achievement motivation, others have been performing a closely allied line of research, which uses a different language for describing findings. The latter program of research is conducted by those engaged in exploring what has been termed the *self-concept*. The latter term is defined in many different ways, which often involve complicated and lengthy definitions (see Diggory, 1966 and Kabiriec, 1970). A simple form of definition is implied in most research undertaken by psychologists interested in the area, for these investigations generally use measures of the self-concept derived from the kinds of statements that the individual makes about himself. A person would be described as having a positive self-concept if he makes positive statements about himself, about what he can accomplish, about the extent to which he regards himself as a successful person, and about his expectations of being able to handle the future. A negative self-concept is indicated when a person makes statements about himself that are derogatory, that describe his performance as inadequate, and that reflect a withdrawal from challenges.

Psychologists have long believed that the self-concept is acquired through the child's listening to the statements that the adults make about him. A child hears his mother say day-in and day-out, "You're a bad little boy." The child is believed after some time to begin to make the statement about himself and to say to himself, "I'm a bad little boy."

Thomas et al. (1969), in reviewing the history of the term *self-concept,* point out that psychologists and sociologists have also taken the position that the self-concept is derived in childhood, not from statements of *any* adult but from the statements of what are referred to as *significant adults*. These are adults who play a crucial role in the life of the child, such as those who provide for all of his physical needs during infancy. The evaluations of the child made by the "significant others" are listened to by the child and become his own self-evaluations.

The belief has been widely held that a positive self-concept has an energizing effect on behavior and results in a vigorous pursuit of goals that the individual believes are worthwhile. This concept is very much like the idea that a person with a high level of achievement motivation is energized by tasks that challenge him. The two concepts are closely related even though they are not quite parallel. The implication has been with respect to the self-concept that a positive self-concept has energizing properties and that successful achievement is partly a result of a positive self-concept. The difficulty with this point of view is that although measures of self-concept are correlated with achievement, there is the possibility that a good positive self-concept is a product of high achievement, and not that a positive self-concept *produces* high achievement. A high level of achievement might just as plausibly produce a strongly positive self-concept as a strongly positive self-concept might lead to high achievement. Which way the relationship works is a matter that can be settled only by experimentation, but experimental attempts to change the self-concept are difficult to undertake. One such study was undertaken by Thomas et al. (1969).

In this study a systematic attempt was made to change the self-concepts of ninth-grade children by means of an intervention through their parents. The procedure involved arranging meetings between the research staff and the parents of a group of low achievers. The object of the meetings was to help the parents understand what they could do to help their children improve their schoolwork. Emphasis was placed on helping the pupil to develop a more positive concept of what he could accomplish in a school setting and to develop a recognition of the pupil's responsibility for his own accomplishments. An explanation was given of the effect of a person's self-concept on what he could accomplish. Quite specific advice was given on how the parent could help the pupil in this respect. Finally, individual conferences were held with the parents to help them work out particular problems. Two control groups were used. In the case of one control group, called the placebo group, the parents were also invited to participate in conferences, but these were focused on the general problems faced by the adolescent. A second control group of pupils involved no parent intervention.

The attempts to work with the parents took place in the months of November, December, and January. Measures were made on the pupils before the work of influencing the parents began in November, then again in the following June, and finally in the following January. The findings were that the group of pupils in whom an effort was made through the parents to change the self-concept showed a much more substantial improvement in grade-point average than either one of the control groups. The members of the control groups also showed an improvement, which was due to an unavoidable artifact of the experimental design. The data also provided some additional information of even greater significance.

One important fact that emerges is that the main change in the self-concept occurred during the period of November to June, but the main change in *achievement* occurred in the subsequent period of June to January. The data suggest that the change in the self-concept of the student had to occur first before any change could take place in his achievement. This study fits well with the results of other studies suggesting that the individual's expectations of how he will perform on a particular task are more important than his general level of optimism about how he will perform in general. A pupil's expectation of how he will succeed in mathematics seems to be much more significant for mathematics achievement than his vague expectations of how he will succeed in general.

The Thomas et al. study provides strong evidence that the self-concept does influence achievement and that parents can influence the achievement of their children through influencing the self-concept of the children. Such an influence involves changing their expectation of success in a positive direction.

The findings are not entirely consistent with what has been said about achievement motivation. The reader will recall that the person characterized by fear of failure may be one showing high achievement motivation. Yet a person who has high fear of failure would be described as a person having a negative or poor self-concept and, in terms of self-concept theory, might be expected to be poorly motivated. There is an inconsistency here that further research will have to resolve.

The Generalized Drive Concept of Motivation

One of the oldest concepts in the area of human motivation is the concept of a generalized drive. The concept derives from the fact that behavior shows variation in the level of activity both from time to time in the same individual, and also from individual to individual. Sigmund Freud postulated that behavior was energized by what he termed a source of libidinal energy, and thus he identified the energizing of behavior with basic sexual functions in a doctrine which had much mysticism surrounding it. Later writers and thinkers have tended to retain the concept of a generalized drive in the development of motivation theory, but have discarded unnecessary elements of mysticism. Woodworth (1958), for example, has taken the position that it is of the nature of higher organisms to *act upon* their environments so long as they are in the waking state. Harry Harlow has also come to a similar conclusion after observing the fact that even after the basic needs of a primate have been well satisfied, the animal continues to act on its environment by manipulating any objects it can find, engaging in climbing and swinging activity, as well as activities such as throwing and breaking small objects. Such animals are not just reacting to their environment. They are acting *on* the environment. The play of children falls into this category of activity, in that the child will act on his environment through any means that he has available. Another version of this same concept is found in B. F. Skinner's concept that organisms emit behavior and do not have to wait for the appearance of particular stimuli in order for behavior to be emitted.

The fact that one cannot readily identify any stimuli related to the energizing of behavior does not mean that they do not exist. An old and significant experiment by Campbell and Sheffield (1953) brings out this point clearly. These two investigators starved rats for three days and, during the period of starvation, kept them in a soundproof room which was equipped with a masking noise to overshadow any sound that might leak into the room. The box was so arranged that a record could be made of any movement of the rat. Under such circumstances the rats did not become progressively more active, as starved rats are generally supposed to become. The only time they showed any increase in activity was once a day when the masking sound was turned off and the light was turned on. Hungry rats do not become more active as hunger increases, but they do become more responsive to stimuli and any new stimulus produces activity. Hunger and other imbalances in the internal chemistry do not energize behavior directly, but they make the organism more responsive to the environment.

A very hungry animal is highly sensitive to new stimuli, but all sensory inputs have some activating properties in themselves. In the chapter on the nervous system, the point will be made that sensory inputs provide information, which goes to the sensory cortex of the brain by a quite direct route. In addition, the sensory inputs also are channeled to the reticular formation, where they produce activity which, in turn, has an activating effect on the entire cortex of the brain. Generalized drive can be conceived of as the degree to which the reticular activating mechanism is producing an arousal effect in the higher centers of the nervous system. When the reticular formation is least active, as it is during sleep, then behavior is least energized. A large amount of sensory input may produce a state of considerable excitement, indeed, a far higher level of excitement and arousal than is needed for effective behavior. Many primitive native dances slowly work the participants into a frenzy of excitement through a large volume of input including auditory inputs of loud music, visual inputs involving the movement of dancing figures in brightly colored costumes, and inputs from the muscles and the haptic system produced by the individual's own participation in the dance. Many night clubs, in a very similar way, try and produce high arousal in a clientele that would otherwise fall into a state of somnolence.

One difference one might expect between the quiet, subdued, and highly organized classroom and the noisier classroom of the more modern program, filled with highly interesting exhibits that are changed from day to day, is the level of arousal of the pupils. The traditional classroom probably produced conditions that did not raise the arousal level of the pupils to a sufficient extent, though some modern classrooms may do the reverse, at least for some pupils who may become overexcited.

The relationship between level of arousal and learning is almost certainly complex. Much of what is known is summarized in the famous Yerkes-Dodson law, mentioned at other points in this volume, which states that there is an optimum level of arousal for learning a particular task, but that the optimum for simple tasks is higher than for complex tasks. One result of this complex relationship is that when a straightforward comparison is made between the level of arousal of pupils, measured in some way, and learning, little relationship is usually found. Also, some pupils may be able to learn effectively at a higher level of arousal than others. An additional word of caution must also be added here. Some research workers have pointed out that the Yerkes-Dodson law is best established in the case of aversive sources of arousal, and virtually not established in the case of arousal produced by other means (see Fantino, Kasdon and Stringer, 1970).

Much needs to be done to identify the conditions that raise or lower the arousal level of pupils. The amount of praise and criticism offered pupils may do this, as Spear (1970) has shown. How praise or criticism is given must also determine whether it produces heightened or lowered arousal. One suspects that the teacher who automatically praises every child may not be raising the level of arousal by so doing. What is effective under one set of conditions in raising the arousal level may not be effective under other conditions (see Berlyne, 1969).

Another approach to the identification of major components of what has been termed generalized drive has been to consider it as closely akin to what is commonly called anxiety. This approach was largely developed by Janet Taylor Spence, who developed a questionnaire known as the Manifest Anxiety Scale, in order to measure this component of drive in human subjects. In terms of this scale, high anxiety would be identified as a high-drive state. Some early experiments in this area produced promising results. These experiments involved mainly simple classical conditioning tasks such as are involved in conditioning the eye-blink reflex to a sound. The eye-blink reflex is naturally triggered by a slight puff of air on the eyeball and this response can be readily conditioned to a bell, a click, or a flash of light. Those subjects who obtain high scores on the Manifest Anxiety Scale are more easily conditioned than are those who obtain low scores on the scale. However, when the task is made more complex, the reverse occurs. A slightly more complex task would be a choice-reaction task in which the subject has to learn to press a key when one of two lights goes on, but to avoid pressing the key when the other light goes on. On such tasks, the high-anxiety subjects do less well than the low-anxiety subjects. The explanation commonly given for this is that high motivation makes more responses available and these compete to take over. The competition among responses reduces the effectiveness of the subject in such a situation. The finding does fit well with other findings such as the Yerkes-Dodson law which proposes that high motivation interferes with performance on complex tasks, except for the fact that the choice reaction task is really not a very complex task.

A series of studies in the early sixties showed that on problem-solving tasks, the low-anxiety subjects tended to do less well than did the high-anxiety subjects. This is in accordance with the predictions derived from the early studies in the field, but this is not the whole story. Denny (1966) undertook an experiment in which subjects were either of high or low intelligence as defined by the test given by the College Entrance Examination Board. The subjects were given a fairly complex concept-learning task. Denny found that among the most intelligent subjects, the high-anxiety subjects performed better than the low-anxiety subjects, but among the least intelligent of the subjects the reverse occurred and the least anxious subjects performed the best. The data were as if, for the most intelligent students, the problems were simple problems, for it is the simple problem on which the most anxious have generally been able to perform at their best. Under the right conditions anxiety has a facilitating effect, but its interaction with other variables is such that teachers probably are not in a position to predict when it will and when it will not facilitate learning.

Another point must be stressed in connection with anxiety as a source of motivation. The Manifest Anxiety Scale developed by Taylor measures the general level of anxiety typical of the individual. It also emphasizes physical symptoms of anxiety, such as sweating of the palms and forehead, pounding of the heart, trembling, and so forth. Whether anxiety as thus measured functions in the same way as anxiety induced by threats is an open question. When anxiety is manipulated through threats, and some pupils are made extremely anxious, these anxious pupils may not behave in a way similar to the normally anxious pupils who have not been threatened. Even if the teacher were to know that a task is best learned by pupils who are normally anxious, this is not reason for inducing anxiety in the normally nonanxious pupils.

Although the studies have been undertaken on college students, rather similar findings have been reported in experiments with elementary-school children. Casteneda, McCandless, and Palmero (1956) developed a form of the Taylor Manifest Anxiety Scale for administration to children. High-anxious and low-anxious children were selected on the basis of the scale and then given a series of problems in which the child had to find the combination of buttons to press to turn off a particular combination of lights. They found that the high-anxious group performed better than the low-anxious group on the easy combinations, but that the high-anxious group performed more poorly on the more difficult combinations.

Grimes and Allinsmith (1961) investigated the relationship of achievement to anxiety in children learning to read by two different methods. The children in twelve classrooms were taught by a phonetic method in which the teaching situation was considered to be highly structured. Children in another twelve classrooms in a different school system were taught by a look-and-say method that involved much less structured teaching and far more informal activity. They found that, in the unstructured setting, high anxiety was related to poor performance in reading, but that in the structured setting there was no relationship between anxiety and reading achievement.

As the reader has worked his way through this section of the chapter, he must have begun to wonder whether there is a difference between the component of achievement need called *fear of failure* and the variable referred to by others as *test anxiety*, that is to say, anxiety measured by some kind of paper-and-pencil test. The volume by Smith (1969) suggests that fear of failure and anxiety, as measured by tests, are both very complex variables that show some similarity, but each has some distinctive properties of its own.

Curiosity and Exploratory Drive

A discussion of human motivation inevitably brings in the topic of exploratory behavior and curiosity. This is an area in which substantial research has now been undertaken, and a number of interesting phenomena have been identified, but it is an area in which ideas still lack organization. The fact is that not enough is yet known about the phenomena to arrange them together in an organized picture.

A basic concept in this area is that behavior shows variability. If an animal is placed at the starting end of a T-maze, it will move down the straight alley and, at the place where the crosspiece joins the straight alley, will make the decision to go either to the left or the right. Suppose that on the first trial the animal goes to the left. On the second trial it is most likely to go to the right and to enter the alley that it did not enter before. In general terms one can say that whatever response an animal makes on the first trial in a two-choice situation, it is most likely to make the alternative response on the second occasion. This is known as alternation behavior, and it is characteristic of human behavior as well as that of animals. If a human subject is required to say any number from one to five after each word said by the experimenter, and no numbers are right or wrong, the subject will tend to vary the number given on each trial. If on one trial he says "two", he is least likely to say "two" on the next trial. This phenomenon is known as *alternation of behavior*. It has at least two important components.

On the one hand, there is a perceptual component, that is to say, there is a tendency to avoid places that have been recently visited. This tendency can be demonstrated in T-mazes, using animals such as rats. At the beginning of the experiment, one of the arms of the T-maze to the right is painted black and the other one is painted white. The animal runs down the alley and chooses, say, to enter the white alley. Next time it is placed at the starting point it enters the black alley. One does not know from such an experiment whether the animal switched from a left turn to a right turn, or from choosing a white alley to choosing a black alley. In order to obtain more information on this point the experiment has to be rerun, but in the case of some of the rats, after trial 1, the black and the white alleys are reversed. Under such conditions, the animal that turned left on the first trial into the white alley, on trial 2 has to choose between turning left into what is now the black alley or turning right. If it turns left, it is avoiding entering the same alley with the same appearance on the second occasion. If it turns right, it is avoiding making the same motor response. What the rat typically does is to avoid the place that has the same *appearance* as the place it last visited. An inhibition is built up resulting in an avoidance response toward whatever was recently seen. This might be referred to as a perceptual inhibition. The basic studies in this area have been reviewed by Travers, Reid, and Van Wagenen (1963).

Variability in behavior is also produced by response inhibition, that is to say, by the tendency for the last response that was made to be inhibited. This phenomenon has already been referred to as reactive inhibition. Such a phenomenon prevents responses from being frequently repeated and hence produces variability in behavior.

One aspect of exploratory behavior is, then, a tendency to avoid places recently inspected and another is a tendency to make responses different from those that have been recently made, but this does not account for all of it. This aspect represents avoidance behavior, in that the subject involved either *avoids* places and objects recently viewed or *avoids* responses recently made. But avoidance is only one aspect of this complex phenomenon. Another aspect is approach behavior, which will have to be considered a little later.

The general exploratory behavior that we have considered is probably of enormous biological value. An animal that continued to explore the same little part of its environment again and again would probably die of starvation as it consumed all of the edibles, but a built-in tendency to move on to new places leads to new supplies of food. Species that do not mate for life are dependent upon such exploratory tendencies for meeting a mate. The effect of this tendency is always dampened to some extent by the fact that, for example, in the case of predatory animals, the creature will also tend to return to those locations where success has been achieved in the killing of game. The exploratory tendencies of children are mellowed by the tendency to return to the one place where most of the reinforcements for living are distributed, namely, the home. Nevertheless, even well-reinforced responses may be modified through such exploratory tendencies, as Edward Tolman showed many years ago. In the famous Tolman demonstration, hungry rats learned to run a maze by the shortest path to the goal box. The running of the maze was consistently reinforced for taking this particular path. However, after a rat had run the same path on many successive trials it would suddenly switch to a longer path and continue to run that path for a number of successive trials. The latter type of behavior cannot be understood in terms of a simple reinforcement theory of behavior, although some of the concepts introduced in this chapter help to make it understandable.

The kind of behavior under consideration cannot be understood completely in terms of place avoidance and response avoidance. Fowler has summarized (1965) some of the studies that suggest that other mechanisms are also at work. A type of experiment that illustrates the operation of alternative mechanisms involves the confinement of an animal to a restricted space. The animal is then released and is free to "explore" a large open space, and the amount of its movement around that space is then measured. Confinement does increase the amount of so-called exploratory behavior in such open-space situations. Nonconfined rats show very little exploratory behavior, but rats that have been confined in a box only slightly larger than the rat itself show considerable activity in the free situation. One interpretation of this finding is that when the animal is deprived of opportunities to explore, an exploratory drive builds up in strength, much as depriving an animal of food builds up a drive related to food deprivation. This explanation introduces the concept of a drive that is built up through deprivation, just like any other drive. Some researchers, such as Fowler, prefer to refer to the drive as a *boredom* drive rather than as an exploratory drive, in that it is boredom that builds up during the period of deprivation rather than an exploratory tendency as such. All one can really say is that the tendency to activity builds up through confinement and that this *can* be interpreted as the build-up of a drive.

At this point a distinction must be made between general exploratory behavior, of the kind that has been considered, and the tendency to approach and observe specific objects in the environment. The former type of behavior is not aroused by particular objects, but the latter is. The condition necessary for the manifestation of the one form of behavior is merely space in which movement can occur. The condition necessary for the other form of behavior is the presence of a particular object that has particular properties. The one form of behavior is commonly called general exploratory behavior, but the latter is more commonly referred to as curiosity or curiosity behavior.

Jean Piaget has long noted the fact that young children show positive approach tendencies towards novel objects in their environment. He has also noted that the more a child is encouraged to explore particular objects, the more likely the child is to engage in further exploration of other objects. He has pointed out that engaging in such behavior whets the appetite for exploration. Children encouraged to explore may develop an insatiable appetite for exploration.

Some of the basic facts related to curiosity behavior are also summarized by Fowler in his essay on *Curiosity and Exploratory Behavior* (1965). A crucial factor determining whether an animal or human will or will not show curiosity behavior is the extent to which the object presented is different from objects recently examined. The greatest amount of such behavior is shown when the new object is entirely different from objects previously encountered. The behavior can also be controlled, to some degree, through deprivation procedures. Such behavior has been studied in primates through an apparatus known as a Butler box. The animal is placed in such a box and learns that by pressing a lever it can see through a window, for a short time, either a novel object or a motion picture of some novel event. The longer the animal is deprived of any novel stimuli, the more likely it is to press the lever and expose itself to the novel experience. Novel stimuli that are highly dynamic have very high incentive value for pressing the lever.

In one set of experiments, the display that the primate would work hardest to see was a motion picture of a train passing by.

Animals engaged in the exploration of unfamiliar objects presented in the form of puzzles may learn to solve them even though no reinforcements are provided by the experimenter for so doing. Primates will learn quite complex disassembly tasks in which they have to take apart wire puzzles, and what is learned transfers to the solution of new problems with similar characteristics. There are also species differences and age differences in responses to novel stimuli. Harry Harlow has pointed out important facts in this respect from observing the development of young macaque monkeys in his University of Wisconsin laboratory. When the monkey is just a few months old, it will show some approach tendencies toward novel objects, but the behavior is characterized by much conflict. This is shown in the fact that the young monkey will leave its mother to approach new objects placed in the cage, but before reaching the object it is likely to withdraw to the security of the mother. The mother provides a base from which sorties toward unusual objects are made. The older the young monkey, the more it will show approach behavior and the less there will be a tendency to retreat to the security provided by contact with the mother. The mature monkey, raised with a natural mother and provided with the security that the mother can give, ultimately learns to show positive approach tendencies toward unusual objects and events in the environment (see Schrier, Harlow, and Stollnitz, 1965).

The effect of the presence of the mother on the exploratory behavior of the infant was first observed in subhuman primates, but, of course, psychologists then became interested in whether a similar phenomenon would occur in the case of human mothers and human infants. Ainsworth and Bell (1970) studied the exploratory behavior of infants aged forty-nine to fifty-one weeks of age in the presence and absence of their mother. The main conclusion from their study was that the presence of the human mother generally increased the amount of exploratory behavior of her infant, and that the phenomenon was very similar to that observed in other primates. An additional interesting finding was that when the mother was removed from the situation for a short time and then brought back, the infant then tended to show a heightened degree of attachment behavior for a short time, and a depression in the amount of exploratory behavior.

Species vary greatly in the extent to which they show positive approach tendencies toward novel objects and events in the environment. There are often dramatic differences between domesticated and wild strains of the same species. The familiar, domesticated, laboratory rat tends to show approach behavior toward novel objects introduced into its cage, but the wild Norwegian rat shows entirely different behavior.

The latter animal is likely to be extremely attentive to any strange object, but shows little approach behavior. The posture is one of attentiveness, maintained at a distance. Indeed, the animal is not likely to approach the novel object even when highly motivated to do so. For example, a starving rat placed in a cage in which there is food in some form other than that which the rat has previously encountered, will not approach the new food. Indeed, it may virtually starve to death rather than approach or partake of the novel food. Such behavior partly accounts for the extraordinary ability of the rat to survive, despite worldwide attempts to exterminate the animal. Indeed, the rat is one of the few species that has multiplied in numbers despite man's deliberate attempt to exterminate it.

Devices have been developed for the study of curiosity in man. One such device is reported by Day (1968), who adapted it from some materials developed by Berlyne (1963). The device consisted of twenty-eight abstract designs that varied in complexity from very simple to quite elaborate. These designs were shown for five seconds each to pupils in the seventh and eighth grades, and the pupils were asked to rate each for "interestingness." A score for curiosity was derived for each pupil from the extent to which the designs were rated as interesting. A fascinating finding of this study was that this score correlated significantly with the teacher's ratings of the pupils on a curiosity scale. The study suggests that there is such a trait as general curiosity and that it can be measured through behavior in particular situations. The measure of curiosity correlated to a small and inconsistent extent with school grades. Why the highest correlation with school grades should have been in the area of spelling is something of a mystery. Could it be that the pupil who learns to spell is one who has the curiosity to look words up in the dictionary? Such speculation is fun but not too useful. More understandable are the correlations between measured curiosity and industrial arts grades and English composition. Whatever is measured by intelligence tests is a much more significant correlate of school achievement than is a measure of curiosity. This is really hardly surprising. The mastery of most school subjects is not dependent upon the pupil's curiosity, for the materials are brought to him and he does not have to seek them out. Whatever curiosity he has may actually sidetrack him from the tasks he is required to do in order to achieve the set objectives.

Finally, in accordance with expectation, Penney (1965) found a negative relationship between a measure of curiosity and the score on the Castaneda children's version of the Manifest Anxiety Scale. This fits well with what might be expected. The children filled with curiosity might be expected to display more approach behavior when confronted with the new and unusual. Anxiety would function as an inhibitor of approach behavior in such situations and be more consistent with avoidance responses.

The fact that curiosity can be measured with a promising device represents just a beginning. The danger of teachers using such a device is that they are likely to conclude that some children have high curiosity and others low and, from then on, only the high-curiosity children are given the opportunities to explore interesting new objects brought into the classroom. The assumption is made that the low-curiosity children are just lacking in curiosity and nothing can be done about it. What one needs to know about curiosity is how it is developed and how its development can be controlled in the school. Other questions also have to be answered, such as whether there are disadvantages as well as advantages in having a high level of curiosity, and whether the child has to learn to be discriminating in deciding when he will exercise curiosity and when he should look the other way.

Frustrative Nonreward as Motivation Arousing

Most positive reinforcers are thought of as providing incentives and, hence, as tending to energize behavior. There is a very important exception to all this, which is found in a phenomenon known as *frustrative nonreward.*

The phenomenon, like many others that are of significance to human behavior, was first established through experimentation with animals. There are many ways in which it can be demonstrated. One way is to arrange a situation in which a food-deprived rat learns to run down an alley to a goal box where it receives a pellet of food. A door then opens that gives it access to a second alley and, on running the second alley, it also receives a pellet of food. This routine can be continued as long as the rat is hungry, but an interesting variation can be introduced. Experimenters have asked the question, "What happens when, after the initial acquisition trials, no food is given after the first runway?" The answer is that the animal runs the second alley with increased vigor and increased speed. The situation is described as one of frustrative nonreward, that is to say as one in which an anticipated reward in terms of previous experience is not received. The result is increased vigor of behavior. Nonreward functions as though it raised the level of motivation. Another technique of demonstrating the frustrative nonreward effect is the double-alley technique. Rats are run in two distinctively different alleys. In the one alley they are reinforced on 100 per cent of the trials, but in the other they are reinforced on only a proportion of the trials. The finding is that in the alley on which there is less than 100 per cent reinforcement, running is faster and more vigorous. The frustrative nonreward effect has been found in numerous experiments with animals, in which it has shown itself to be a consistent and substantial effect.

Although the frustrative nonreward effect has long been demonstrated on animals, attempts to demonstrate it on human subjects are of much more recent vintage. Ryan and Watson (1968) have reviewed the literature covering the first ten years of research. They point out that the phenomenon was, at first, not readily demonstrated on young children, suggesting that it is perhaps a weaker effect in the human than in the rat, where it is readily apparent. The technique used to demonstrate it on humans involves a simple task of pulling one lever when one light goes on and another lever when another light is turned on. The pulling of a lever may release a marble. In order to demonstrate the nonreward frustration effect, one lever is set to provide a 100 per cent delivery of marbles (100 per cent reinforcement) while the other is set for delivery of marbles on 50 per cent or fewer occasions. What is found through the use of such equipment is that children tend to push the lever associated with occasional nonreward with greater vigor and speed than the lever associated with 100 per cent reinforcement. However, when very low rates of reinforcements are used, which approach 0 per cent, the effect is reversed and slow rates of responding occur. Thus if all levels of reinforcement are used, from 100 per cent to 0 per cent, the vigor of the response can be represented by a U-shaped curve, with the most vigorous responses in the middle range and the least vigorous at the 100 per cent and 0 per cent levels.

In these experiments, the children involved could not regard their performance under any of the conditions as a failure, in that they must have recognized that whether they received or did not receive the reinforcement depended upon the equipment and not on their own ability. A few children may have regarded the situation as one that they might be able to control if they could only find the right formula, but the research workers involved do not report such cases. The effect of frustrative nonreward occurs in situations in which the subject does not regard his performance as one of success or failure. In situations in which there is genuine failure and in which the person recognizes that, because of his own inadequacies, he has failed to reach a goal, then the effect of failure is that of lowering motivation and reducing the vigor of response.

There is some evidence that nonreward is more frustrating for older subjects than for the young preschool child. Older children have firmer expectations for reward, whereas the young child often finds that engaging in a task is rewarding in itself. A related kind of effect is found when the strength of the nonreward frustration effect is compared for retarded and normal children. The retarded generally show much less of the effect than do the normals. The retarded do not expect reward, for their lives have not been filled with rewards, as have the lives of the normals.

Nobody knows at this time whether nonreward frustration theory can be applied to the problem of raising the level of motivation in children. One can only speculate that the condition in which the child is praised for everything he does may not produce a pupil whose behavior is energized to a full degree. Appropriate withholding of praise on some occasions may be as important as providing appropriate praise.

Problems of Classroom Management Related to Motivation

The research reviewed in this chapter does not provide a complete and unified picture of how human behavior becomes energized or how the energized behavior becomes directed into particular channels. Research to this point touches on problems of motivation only at key points, with most of the picture remaining a blank canvas. Three conclusions emerge. One is that we cannot expect any simple relationship between measures of motivation and achievement, and that there is no likelihood that a simple instrument can be prepared to measure the extent to which a pupil's behavior in the classroom can be expected to be energized in the directions prescribed by the school. Second, some of the conditions related to motivation, as is the case with achievement motivation, are related to the preschool experiences in the home. A third conclusion is that behavior can be energized by controlling the sensory inputs. In many respects, it is this third conclusion that has the most implications for teaching. Let us consider this conclusion a little further.

Traditional methods of teaching were commonly based upon the assumption that if the classroom contained little material to distract the pupil, he would attend to the work assignment placed before him. Motivation was presumed to be derived either from the assignment itself or from a moral commitment on the part of the pupil to do his best at his work. The drab classroom that resulted from such a theory of behavior failed to function in the way it was supposed to. Such classrooms were filled with problems of discipline. Many children failed to learn, not only because the conditions of learning failed to motivate the pupils, but also because the lockstep design of the curriculum meant that many children found themselves trying to keep afloat in intellectual depths long before they had mastered the necessary skills. The progressive education movement, beginning with the work and writings of Horace Mann, recognized that much was wrong with traditional classrooms and the theory of motivation and learning on which they were based, and began to propose alternatives to remedy some of the central deficiencies.

The progressive education movement, particularly in the period between the two world wars, sought to remedy what were seen to be the basic deficiencies of the traditional classroom, and much of what was proposed had to do with the motivation of the pupil. Classrooms were converted from situations in which the only social interactions were between the teachers and individual pupils to situations in which pupils also interacted with pupils. The environment was restructured so that the pupil was confronted with a classroom filled with interesting materials as well as stimulating conversations. The program of the movement had a very deliberate policy of increasing the quantity of input to the pupil with the intention of invigorating his behavior. Two assumptions seem to have been involved. One was that a classroom that was richly furnished with various displays might lead the pupil to investigate many matters that he would not otherwise have investigated, and that this would lead to learning. The other assumption seems to have been that an environment that provided a great range of novel stimuli might result in a more vigorous pursuit of the particular assignment on which the pupil happened to be working. Both of these assumptions seem reasonable in terms of what is known about motivation. At least they led to classrooms in which the pupils were never half asleep and in which tasks were energetically pursued. The notion that increasing the inputs would add to the drive level was a basically sound idea.

However, an increase in the activity level of pupils is no guarantee that the energy thus released will be directed into productive lines. Children may become busy and active, and perhaps even engage in considerable learning through contact with the objects and displays that are stimulating them, but this does not mean that the child will also engage in the systematic organization of the knowledge acquired, which seems necessary for mastering basic skills and disciplines. Whether or not energy is directed into these channels seems to be dependent more on aspects of motivation outside of the control of the teacher. Pressure in the home from an early age to achieve mastery of whatever skills are attempted is apparently important, although desire to please the parents may also have its effects. So far, there is no recipe that can be given to the teacher for handling those children who have not been exposed to these conditions in the home.

Summary

1. Much of the early experimental research undertaken on motivation was pursued in a biological tradition and with the manipulation of hunger and thirst as the main means of varying motivation. Deprivation produces an increase in activity, unless the animal is in an environment free from stray sounds and free from

visual stimulation. The data suggest that deprivation produces an increase in responsiveness to stimuli.

2. In such animal experiments, the incentive provided by food or water in the goal box adds to the drive state produced through deprivation. This is evident from the fact that larger amounts of food and water may produce more vigorous behavior in running the maze.
3. Even what appear to be simple unlearned drives become at an early age interwoven with learned elements, as is shown by the fact that animals, including man, may develop cravings for diets and drugs that are harmful to them. Indeed, the behavior of the adult toward food is much more like that of an addict than like that of a creature consuming naturally the material that is necessary to restore homeostatic balance.
4. Although animals can be trained to discriminate between hunger and thirst, the task is a difficult one for rats and other species to achieve. This suggests that drive states should generally be regarded as activated states rather than as states that give direction to behavior. Man may well be more discriminating in this respect and the common experiences of living may provide him with the basis for discriminating the experiences associated with different drive sources.
5. Basic research with animals has provided little information about motivation that has significant implications for the control of motivation in educational situations. Such animal research has used the classification of drives into those that are native to the organism and those that are learned. The difficulty in using this classification scheme is that many drive states cannot be clearly classified in the one or the other category. Indeed, one does not know, at this time, which should be considered as mainly innate, even though there may be some learned component.
6. As motivation is increased, performance tends to show a corresponding increment in vigor until a maximum is reached. Further increments in motivation produce a decline in performance. The level of motivation that produces optimum performance varies with the nature of the task. With complex tasks, the optimum level of motivation is lower than with simple tasks. This is known as the Yerkes-Dodson law.
7. A human motive on which research has made some progress is that of achievement motivation or achievement need. The concept was originally derived from a theory of motivation developed by H. A. Murray, in which achievement need was one of the learned motives in the system. According to this system, needs

are aroused by some stimulus related to its satisfaction. In the case of achievement need, the stimulus is a situation that provides the individual with an opportunity to achieve some standard of excellence. Just wanting to complete a task does not reflect achievement need. To reflect this need, the person must be striving to achieve some standard of excellence that he has set for himself.

8. Achievement need is measured most readily, at this time, through projective tests in which the person taking the test is shown a picture, selected because it has potential for arousing achievement need, and is asked to tell a story about what led up to the scene depicted, what is happening, and what is going to happen. The stories told can then be scored for the extent to which they reflect achievement need.
9. Achievement motivation manifests itself in two forms. One is hope of success, and the other is fear of failure. Many individuals taking a projective test show both hope of success and fear of failure, although their behavior may show a predominance of the one or a predominance of the other. A tendency for behavior to be dominated by the one or the other influences the kind of risks that are taken. The fear-of-failure-oriented person tends to take risks that are very high or very low. If he fails at the high-risk task, then he can blame the task, but if he succeeds, then it is very much to his credit. The success-oriented person is, perhaps, more realistic in his choice, in that he selects tasks that are both a challenge to him and on which he can succeed. Thus achievement need has a subtle relationship to what Kurt Lewin referred to as level of aspiration.
10. Although achievement need is discussed as though it were an acquired need, components of it may be native. The need to do it oneself may well be an inborn disposition, on the basis of which achievement need may grow. Achievement need, as it is defined here, is first detected around the age of five. It is more characteristic of boys than of girls, and is particularly evident in the middle class. The home conditions most likely to foster its development are those which provide the child with independence and freedom, yet which demand that independence and freedom be enjoyed with responsibility. Independence alone is not sufficient but must be accompanied by a demand on the part of the parents that the child master skills related to his independence. Parent-child relationships are crucial for the development of achievement motivation. The religious affiliation of the parents also influences the extent to which the child develops achievement motivation.

11. Straightforward relationships between measures of achievement need and performance in academic studies are not to be expected, for the student may be motivated to do well in school for many reasons other than a need to achieve a standard of excellence. Relationships do appear between performances on tasks that the student can view as a challenge and achievement-need measures.
12. None of the other attempts to measure motives within the framework provided by Murray has been as successful as that involving achievement need, but some success has accompanied attempts to measure affiliation need and approval need.
13. An important and very old concept in the area of motivation is that of a generalized drive. In the case of human motivation, one component of such a drive has been considered to be anxiety. Studies involving relationships between anxiety and performance have produced relationships that are similar to those described by the Yerkes-Dodson law.
14. Complex living creatures show a marked tendency to avoid making responses that they have recently made and also to visit those parts of the environment that have been most recently visited. These behaviors form two components of what has been referred to as an exploratory drive. Higher organisms also have a tendency to attend to any novel aspect of their environment and may show behavior toward such objects that may vary from watchful waiting to approach behavior. Exploratory and investigatory tendencies have many properties similar to those of drives. An animal confined to a small space shows a heightened tendency to exhibit exploratory behavior when it is released, much as a food-deprived animal shows heightened activity after being deprived of food. The tendency to explore and to approach novel objects is heightened in children when the child is encouraged to engage in this activity and has opportunities to do so. Primates do learn when the major drive operating is that described here as an exploratory drive. Attempts to measure curiosity in children offer some promise, for there seems to be a tendency to be generally curious or noncurious. What needs to be known is how curiosity can be increased and controlled through educational experience.
15. A condition related to motivation that has potential applications to teaching is the condition known as frustrative nonreward. In this condition an expected reward is not delivered and the result is an increased vigor or response. It is a strong and well-established response in subhuman animals, which is still quite detectable in human behavior. Frustrative nonreward suggests that the

withholding of rewards may be sometimes as important as the giving of a reward.

16. Although research on motivation may provide the teacher with some understanding of the nature of human motivation, it does not, as yet, provide the kind of knowledge necessary for controlling the motivation of pupils. What has been accomplished to date suggests that the time may come when the teacher may be able to take steps to remedy gross deficiencies in the motivation of young children in relation to their work in school.

CHAPTER ELEVEN

Social Factors Influencing Learning

A CHAPTER ON SOCIAL FACTORS RELATED TO LEARNING CANNOT GIVE coverage of a topic that is commonly discussed in book-sized treatises. The wealth of material is evident when one contemplates the fact that the current edition of *The Handbook of Social Psychology* includes five massive volumes. Although it is true that not all of social psychology is involved with conditions related to learning, much of it is, and one could make out a strong case for the proposition that teachers should receive far more training in that field than they now receive.

In this chapter an attempt has been made to select a very few topics from the field of social psychology that appear to have particularly significant implications for the teacher. Most learning still takes place in a social setting and social factors play an important role in determining what is learned and also how efficiently it is learned. The social setting of learning is there, because society has decreed that one or more adults and a large number of children shall occupy the same area of a school. Some attempts have been made by educational technologists to reduce or eliminate much of the social context of learning by proposing, and sometimes introducing, teaching machines at which the pupil may work in an isolated booth, but the effect of social isolation produced by such an instructional setting is not known at this time. Despite this trend much of human learning will continue to occur in a social context, and social conditions will continue to have an impact on what is learned and how it is learned.

Most adults in most civilized communities have long held the belief that some of the more important aspects of behavior are learned through children observing the behavior of adults. More recently, emphasis has been given to the fact that children also learn from the example set by other children. Learning by example is agreed to be a matter of crucial importance in the education of children and it is to this topic that we will first turn in the discussion of social factors in learning.

Imitative Behavior

The social context of learning is such that imitation represents one of the most significant educational processes that can be commonly observed. A demonstration provided by the teacher is generally followed by an attempted imitation of the demonstration by the students. The value of a demonstration is generally highly dependent upon the ability of the student to imitate. But the usefulness of imitation is generally considered to go beyond the intellectual field and to represent the main avenue through which personality characteristics are also acquired. Imitation is taken so much for granted as a common learning procedure that it hardly attracted the attention of psychologists until World War II. The assumption before that time seems to have been that imitation takes place easily and naturally and that there is little to be gained by studying it. Furthermore, in the field of animal psychology, research on imitation had proven to be a rather barren venture. Although most animal psychologists had not been successful in producing imitative behavior in laboratory animals below the level of primates, Miller and Dollard (1941) conducted experiments in which they were able to *teach* such animals to imitate, by reinforcing them for manifesting imitative behavior. These same research workers were also able to demonstrate, in the case of children, that tendencies to imitate could be strengthened. Implied in this approach was the idea that most imitation, if not all, is a learned phenomenon.

Miller and Dollard also made many interesting observations on imitative behavior that have not yet been fully followed up by subsequent research workers. One is that, among humans, there is often a tendency for a person to match his behavior to that of another person with whom he associates, but without his making any deliberate effort to make such a match. This they referred to as *matched dependent behavior,* and contrasted it with *copying behavior.* Copying behavior is a deliberate attempt to reproduce the actions of another. The teacher who shows the pupils how to write the number 2 expects copying behavior on the part of the pupils. In order to do this successfully, the pupil must be able to discriminate differences and similarities between his performance and that of the teacher. In a sense, copying behavior is intelligent behavior, but matched dependent behavior is stupid. The distinction is a useful one in education, although it is not one that subsequent research workers have, as yet, noted to any extent.

Before discussing some of the more recent research literature, let us introduce a few terms. The person whose behavior is imitated is, today, referred to as the *model*. The person who does the imitating is referred to as the *observer*, or as the *learner*. When the model is reinforced and the observer watches the reinforcement, then one commonly speaks of the observer as being *reinforced vicariously*.

In recent years, psychologists have been able to demonstrate imitative behavior in subhuman species, although earlier psychologists were largely unsuccessful in such an undertaking. In Aronfreed's review of research on imitation in animals (1969), he points out that there is overwhelming evidence that primates learn to perform a simple task more easily if they first have the opportunity of observing members of their own species perform it, but what this form of imitation involves is not clear. The findings suggest that when a chimpanzee observes another chimpanzee perform a task, the observer's attention is drawn to certain cues in the situation to which it would not be drawn otherwise. One wonders whether the chimpanzee would learn if it observed a task performed by a machine. Perhaps not, because chimpanzees have a natural tendency to observe other chimpanzees (In contrast to rats who do not spend much time observing other rats). When the chimpanzee directs his attention to another chimpanzee, the stage is set for taking in information about what the other chimpanzee is doing. Such observational learning is not restricted to primates but has been recorded also as far down the evolutionary scale as the cat. In addition, birds seem to require exposure to the song of their species in order to present the vocalization typical of their species. The latter is commonly believed to represent, not so much the imitation of an observed act, but the release of an innate mechanism that will produce the song once the bird has been exposed to it.

Aronfreed's review came out at about the same time as another review by Flanders (1968), undertaken for a rather different purpose. Flanders points out that research shows that animals as far down the evolutionary scale as the rat can learn to imitate through the use of reinforcement. However, the review shows a surprising lack of studies in which animals with a strong innate tendency to imitate particular behaviors have been examined. Here, as in many other areas of inquiry, the tendency has been to study animals whose behavior fits a particular behavior theory. The research review by Flanders could easily lead the unwary to conclude that reinforcement of imitative behavior is the key to imitation, but this might be a false conclusion.

There are immense difficulties encountered in separating the innate and the acquired components of imitative behavior, for they intermingle in an inseparable way. For example, a well-trained bitch that is let out to have a bowel movement along with her young puppy will go some distance from the house. The puppy follows its mother and also goes far from the house. The puppy may have a bowel movement or a bladder evacuation while the mother is doing likewise and this may happen by chance or be triggered by the smell of the mother's stool or urine. If this happens, then the bladder or bowel evacuation may reinforce the tendency for the puppy to go far from the house when it is let out to perform its biological functions.

Nevertheless, even the most cautious interpretation of the data reviewed by Flanders leads to the conclusion that many creatures do profit from being exposed to models, and that this phenomenon is particularly evident in the case of primates. What is not clear at all is whether this imitative behavior has developed through animals learning that there is likely to be a payoff if they imitate other members of their species. There may well be subtle reinforcers operating, which produce a learned tendency to imitate.

In the case of the young human, no way has been found for establishing whether there is or is not an innate tendency to imitate. Many studies have reported that quite young children do sometimes show imitative behavior even though the experimenter provides no reinforcer, but the child may already have learned to imitate through the operation of reinforcers on other occasions. There is no particular reason for believing that the child either has or has not an innate tendency to imitate, for some species do and some do not have this tendency. One can say that whether such a tendency exists or not, the use of reinforcers can strengthen any tendency that may exist in this respect.

The learning of imitative acts may be facilitated through two different conditions of reinforcement. Under one condition, the behavior of the observer is reinforced for performing the imitated act. Under the other condition, the behavior of the model is reinforced. Reinforcement for imitation does, of course, increase the tendency to imitate, but in many studies it is often difficult to distinguish between reinforcing an attempt to perform an act and the imitation of the act itself. If the model and the observer sit opposite one another, and the observer is to pick up a ball of the same color that the model picks up, the experimenter is not only reinforcing a tendency to imitate the model, but he is also reinforcing a tendency to pick up a ball. The fact that he reinforces a tendency to pick up balls will also increase error behavior, because the observer will also tend to pick up balls when the model has not done so. The findings of studies show that reinforcing the behavior of the model increases the probability that imitation will occur. Also, the more frequently the behavior of the model is reinforced, the greater will be the tendency for the observer to imitate.

A number of fairly obvious factors control the amount of imitation shown. Children show an increased tendency to imitate the model when they are instructed to do so, and probably the optimum conditions for imitation would include directions to imitate coupled with positive reinforcement of the observer's behavior as well as that of the model.

A particularly interesting feature of the review by Flanders is the extensive research he was able to find on the relative effect of filmed models versus live models and cartoon models. The typical finding in such studies is that a cartoon model is just as effective in producing corresponding behavior in the observer as is either a live model or a filmed model of a live person. A little evidence points in the direction of suggesting that the effect of the live model may be somewhat more durable, but this finding still needs to be checked. The evidence suggests that children identify with cartoon characters in much the same way as they identify with the adults with whom they come into contact. The studies of aggression involving the imitation of models, still to be considered, are of particular contemporary interest when one considers that perhaps most of the models to which a child is exposed are in cartoon form.

The results considered to this point are of interest, but do little to provide any understanding of what is involved in imitative behavior. Two necessary conditions for imitative behavior to occur are the attention of the observer and the acquisition by the observer of enough knowledge about the model's act to be able to replicate it. The attention is controlled in a favorable direction in the modeling situation by the fact that children choose to watch other children, much as any primate chooses to watch other primates. Another factor that influences the attention factor is the novelty of the behavior of the model. Studies have shown that observers learn to imitate models more readily if the behavior to be modeled has novel features. This statement probably needs some qualification, for there is obviously little tendency for normal individuals to imitate the behavior of psychotics, which is highly novel behavior. Novel behavior will be imitated only when it is in some way related to the observer's needs.

Many patterns of behavior of models cannot be readily imitated because the observer cannot easily obtain by observation the information necessary for replicating the act. One does not learn to hit a baseball with a bat by observing others perform the act, and, even when excellent incentives are provided for learning, the amount of learning that takes place by watching a model is negligible. A major reason for this lack of learning is that the stroke of the batter as the ball approaches takes place with great rapidity. It is a complex act in itself, and when the entire stroke takes place in less than a tenth of a second, there just isn't time for the observer to gather and retain the information needed for making some semblance of a replication of the act. Too much information arrives too quickly to provide usable knowledge for later use.

A third condition related to imitation, which would appear to be necessary for it to occur, is some disposition to reproduce the behavior of the model. An innate tendency is not ruled out, but most human modeling behavior takes place for immediate utilitarian purposes.

A fourth condition appears to have a unique role in the case of human imitation, namely, self-esteem. A review by Bourdon (1970) brings together some scattered research on this matter. Various scales have been developed that measure self-esteem, which can be described in broad terms as the extent to which the individual thinks well of himself. Such measures of self-esteem are related to the tendency to imitate or to match the behavior of another. Those whose self-esteem is highest show least tendency to imitate. One presumes that such individuals, who feel adequate, have a repertoire of behaviors of their own to call upon to handle situations that arise, but those who feel less adequate perhaps have a lesser repertoire and have a greater need to borrow behaviors from others.

The Acquisition of Standards of Conduct

Society requires that, in a certain area, value judgments and the decisions related to them must have a certain uniformity in all of their constituent members. This area is commonly referred to as that of morals and the behavior related to moral issues is referred to as conduct. The learning involved in the acquisition of moral behavior is social in two different senses. First, one can speak of behavior as being either moral or immoral only when it occurs in a social context. A man living alone on a desert island cannot be considered to behave in ways that are either moral or immoral, for such behavior can occur only in relation to other human beings. Thus the question of the morality of behavior can be raised only in a social context. Second, standards of conduct are learned in a social context and are intimately related to the rewards and punishments administered to the developing individual by other members of the community.

The development of the child's ideas concerning the nature of moral standards was first studied systematically by Piaget and appeared in one of his early book-length studies (1932). Later work by Kohlberg (1969) has produced very similar findings. There seems to be considerable agreement that very young children judge the seriousness of offenses in terms of the observable damage done and not at all in terms of any of the more subtle criteria used by adults. Punishment is regarded as something that just happens when a particular act is undertaken and it is not viewed as an attempt to control the behavior. The greater the damage done by some misbehavior, the greater the punishment to be expected. Punishment has a certain inevitability to it, from the young child's point of view, as if it were just the kind of way in which the world operates. At a later stage of development children learn that there are rules of conduct, but these are viewed as rigid and immutable and not the kinds of matters that one could have a debate about changing. This childhood view of rules of conduct found in the early grades is also quite typical of the adult who has had little education and who opposes every step in reform of the law. Considerable education is required before the child can be expected to view rules and laws as representing conveniences that can be changed. At a more advanced stage of development, the child may learn that rules of conduct are derived from principles that are much more general in their application and much more abstract.

The fact that the young preschool child views acts as wrong because of their consequences means that each act is judged on an independent basis from any other act. A result of this is a lack of any coherence in the young child's moral judgments. This was brought out long ago in one of the oldest and most classic studies in the area, conducted by Hartshorne and May (1929), who showed that even children of school age showed a considerable lack of consistency in their behavior in activities involving honesty. Consistency would have hardly been expected except perhaps by a moralist armed with the prejudice that children have a unifying conscience—which they do not have.

Even the behavior of the adult may show considerable inconsistency within an area of conduct. A person who is scrupulously honest in his dealings with his fellow employees may still think it is acceptable to cheat the management, or the public transportation company, or other agencies remote from his life. Verbalized rules of conduct, even when they have been well-formulated, may still have only limited influence on behavior, much as cognitive aspects of attitudes are often only loosely tied to action systems.

What is not known at this time is the role that education plays in this pattern of development and whether more appropriate educational experiences could speed the emergence of a more mature basis for conduct. One suspects that children go through a stage of believing that the prescribed rules of conduct are fixed parts of the world, because they hear the rules proclaimed by adults as if they were of this nature. Only much later do they glean any information at all that might indicate that the rules of conduct have not been fixed throughout all ages and all times. The very large individual differences in the age at which the different concepts of the basis of conduct emerge suggests that differences in conduct may be related to differences in the experiences provided. Certainly, homes differ markedly in the education provided in relation to the acquisition of principles of conduct.

Aronfreed (1969) has not only undertaken extensive research in this area, but has also developed a comprehensive review of research on the problem. In this review he points out that many different psychologists have proposed that the child goes through stages in the development of moral patterns of behavior, but there is no substantial agreement on what those stages are or whether there are clearly defined stages at all. A central theme in Aronfreed's book is that the control of behavior related to conduct is, in its early stages, controlled by external events, but that development may proceed until, ultimately, internal controls become substituted for external controls. In the very young child, immediate rewards and immediate punishments may be the main conditions controlling behavior, but in the mature adult such immediate consequences of behavior may cease to be the controlling factors. For this reason, many young men during the Vietnam conflict refused to allow themselves to be drafted into the armed forces, despite the fact that they faced long terms of prison for so refusing. In such individuals behavior was not controlled by the immediate conditions of reward or punishment at all, but was controlled by an internal system. Such cases show dramatically the power that such internal controls may have, but the reader must also recognize that effective internal controls do not generally bring the individual into conflict with the society in which he lives. The mature adult may refrain from stealing, return money to a person who has unknowingly dropped it, and give to his church anonymously, for reasons internal to himself and not because of any rewards or punishments that these acts may bring.

There is some difficulty in defining what are meant by internal controls, but Aronfreed (p. 18) suggests that one can speak of internal controls when behavior has become independent of observable outcomes. This probably goes too far, for behavior is never completely independent of external outcomes. Those who resisted induction during the Vietnam conflict did so despite the knowledge that they would have to serve quite long prison terms, but if the penalty had been death, then many would have chosen other courses of action, such as fleeing the country. Although the choice would be, in a sense, under internal controls, it is not independent of external circumstances. Complete independence of external circumstances and complete internal control are found mostly in the psychotic.

Internalization, in its most primitive method, involves no more than the development of a rigid response system that is called into play regardless of the outcomes. At more complex levels of behavior, internal control of behavior is achieved through having an internal representation of the world which, in itself, may be quite abstract. Once a child has achieved some internal representation of the world, he can manipulate it, experiment with it, and view the consequences, and without being influenced by immediate circumstances. This kind of internalization has long been stressed by psychologists with many different approaches and notably by Piaget (see Phillips, 1969). The internal construction of a representation of the outside world does not, in itself, provide a control system, just as the storage system of a computer does not, when considered alone, provide any control over what is done with it. Computers have to have a separate executive unit that makes decisions concerning the programs to be performed on data at particular decision points. The human would appear to have to develop an analogous executive control system, but the nature of such a control system must be considered at this time to be largely a mystery.

What has been said cannot be taken to imply that most individuals in our society ultimately reach a state in which control over their behavior is exercised to a maximum extent by internal processes. A contemporary event brings this out clearly. In 1969 in Montreal, the police went on strike and did not appear for work during a twenty-four-hour period. The result was chaos: fourteen banks were held up, numerous stores were robbed, and there was a wave of almost every kind of crime. In the context of the present discussion, this turn of events would be described as the effect of removing external controls over behavior. The incident shows clearly that the police department ordinarily exerted considerable control over the behavior of many citizens who remained law-abiding because of it, but the removal of the police meant that a major source of behavior restraint was removed. Many individuals were then free to engage in the immediate gratification of their need for money and other possessions.

Aronfreed assembles considerable research findings to show that the development of internal control is more characteristic of the middle class than the lower class and more characteristic of the educated than the uneducated. He points out that during the entire life of most middle-class people they have great freedom to make their own decisions. The professional person is often so free of controls that he may be able to decide when he will work and when he will not work. In contrast, the working-class individual must appear for work at the command of a factory whistle and perform exactly the work to which he is assigned. The life of the middle-class person requires that his behavior be internally controlled while the life of the working-class individual, provided his needs are satisfied, moves along on the basis of external controls.

In addition, Aronfreed points out that in the American culture considerable evidence supports the position that men show relatively stronger tendencies for behavior to be internally controlled and women show relatively stronger tendencies to be externally controlled. This difference is almost certainly due to the fact, already brought out in the chapter on development, that girls, far more than boys, are trained to conform. This training results in behavior that is controlled by immediate circumstances. Boys are allowed to be much more adventuresome in almost all aspects of behavior. Even in such a matter as the use of four-letter words, boys are less likely to be censored than are girls. Aronfreed points out that in cultures where boys and girls are brought up on an equalitarian basis, as they are in the kibbutzim in Israel, this kind of a sex difference does not appear in adult life.

Much of the research on moral development reviewed by Aronfreed has been concerned with the effect of reinforcements on the development of conduct. Such research has considerable difficulty in coming to grips with the problem of how controls over behavior become internalized. One step in the process occurs when the child arranges for his own reinforcing contingencies, as when he tells himself that he has done the right thing or comments that he has been good. The internalization of conduct involves much more than the acquisition of such habits, but these habits may represent the beginnings of internalization.

An important situation for the acquisition of moral behavior is that presented by modeling situations, that is to say, situations in which learning occurs by example. Most studies of the effect of the behavior of a model on an observer have investigated the effect of aggressive behavior of the model on the subsequent aggressive behavior of the observer. A few studies have been concerned with the acquisition of moral standards. An illustration of a study involving the acquisition of moral behavior through the behavior of a model is one conducted by Hartup and Coates (1967). In this study the model (a child trained for the purpose) obtained trinkets for performing a maze task with a pencil, but of the six trinkets he received, he placed five in a dish designated for another child he did not know. Those children who watched this performance showed a considerably increased tendency *not* to keep the trinkets, but to place them in the dish for the "other" child when they performed a similar task under similar conditions. This same study also incorporated another interesting feature. The children selected as models were identified, in advance, either as children who tended to reward their peers or children who did not do so. These were called rewarding or nonrewarding models. The observers were classified also, either as children who received much reinforcement from their peers or who received little. Those children who had been the recipients of many rewards from their peers tended to imitate most the rewarding models. The latter is not surprising, but what is most surprising is that the children with a history of receiving few reinforcements from their peers tended to imitate most the nonrewarding models.

Altruistic and Helping Behavior

An aspect of behavior of great significance related to problems of conduct is that referred to as altruistic or helping behavior. Although this area has long been of interest to psychologists, research on problems related to it has suddenly mushroomed during the last decade, perhaps because of the wide recognition for developing a society in which such behaviors are more common. The reviews of research by Bryan and London (1970) and Krebs (1970) together list several hundred references. In addition, a symposium on the subject, edited by Macaulay and Berkowitz (1970), presents many interesting lines along which research is developing.

Altruistic behavior has been difficult to define, but recent attempts to define it have begun to sharpen the concept. The person who behaves altruistically performs in a way that has high cost to him and *apparently* low immediate payoff. The word *apparently* is advisedly used because there are payoffs to altruistic acts that are not all evident to observers. A person who gives away a fortune may later confide to another that he felt good about the act of giving. The statement suggests that his act of generosity resulted in some kind of internal payoff. Philosophers have long been interested in internal payoffs labeled by such words as pleasure, happiness, and satisfaction, and a whole school of philosophers, the hedonists, have argued that these payoffs determine much, if not all, of human behavior. The role of such internal payoffs has been difficult to study. Aronfreed (1969) has argued that young children are first reinforced by adults telling them that they are good, or kind, or in some way virtuous, and that children learn to make these same utterances to themselves and, in this way, provide events that have reinforcing properties. The latter position is really no stronger than that of the philosophers, for it is based mainly on speculation.

Because the identification of the payoff of altruistic or helping behavior has so far been a quite fruitless pursuit, research workers have become more concerned with the conditions in the social milieu that lead to altruistic or helping behavior. Bryan and London present evidence to show that altruistic behavior is most likely to be observed in children who come from homes where such behavior is common. Altruistic behavior is least likely to be seen in children who come from homes where a competitive spirit is encouraged, as it is among some of the well-to-do, or from homes where poverty virtually excludes generosity. A family that stresses status needs also provides a poor environment for the development of generosity. The learning of this behavior in the home appears to occur in the first decade of life, for altruistic behavior reaches its peak toward the end of that decade. Krebs (1970) adds to this conclusion by saying that research also demonstrates that people give to those who are similar to themselves, and also to those whom they consider prestigious or from whom they stand to gain.

The phenomenon of altruistic behavior is obviously extremely complex, as both the Krebs and the Bryan and London reviews bring out. One factor that complicates research on the problem is that altruistic behavior or helping behavior is elicited much more in some situations than in others. Dependency is an important condition eliciting such behavior, especially in females. Males often feel threatened when another person becomes highly dependent upon them, and the threat tends to suppress altruistic behavior that might otherwise occur. After reviewing such facts, Krebs points out that although man may appear to act altruistically, he may not be genuinely altruistic by nature, that is to say, he may not be acting out of genuine concern for the other person.

This area of knowledge, like all rapidly developing areas, yields endless interesting facts that do not all fit together very well. For this reason let us cite here just a few of such facts provided by the Macaulay and Berkowitz symposium (1970). The symposium has an interesting paper on why bystanders in crowds do not intervene and offer helping behavior in emergencies. The suggestion is that each bystander looks at the other bystanders and tends to interpret lack of action as lack of feeling. The person who interprets the behavior of others as not indicating real feeling for the emergency is likely to respond by suppressing his own feelings and doing nothing. The bystander's interpretation of the lack of feeling on the part of others is probably wrong, but it leads to inactivity. Another series of studies reported in the symposium provide evidence that merely observing the behavior of a model engaged in altruistic behavior does not necessarily produce altruism, for the consequences of altruism are important, including the extent to which the altruistic person seems to experience pleasure from the act. Mere talk on the part of a model about being generous has little effect on the behavior of children who are listening. The actions of models are of far greater influence than anything the models may say. A special case of altruistic behavior is found in those who give body organs, such as one of their kidneys, to help another. In such a case of altruism, the act itself may have dramatic effects on the future behavior of the donor. Significant acts of self-sacrifice may be landmarks in life that lead to periods of great change. The early findings from research on altruistic behavior are so fascinating that they are likely to attract able research workers to make further explorations, and the time may not be distant when the environment of the child can be planned to produce a more altruistic generation. Not enough is known as yet to be able to do this with any confidence.

Learning and the Control of Human Aggression

There is little debate that the human race must face and solve two problems of immense consequence if it is to survive on this planet. One problem is the control of the pollution of the environment, and the other is the control of the murderous assaults that some members of mankind perpetrate on other members. Up to this point the human race has shown little desire to identify and apply a solution to either of these problems, even though the solutions may not be far away. The problems of pollution are likely to be solved through a combination of technical advances and responsible legislation, but the problem of controlling human aggression is not likely to be so easily handled. The psychologist has learned something about the nature of human aggression and the problem of controlling it, and it is to some of this knowledge that we must now turn.

Richardson (1960) has estimated that during the period 1820 to 1945 59 million individuals lost their lives in what he terms deadly quarrels, a category that includes wars, individual murders, massacres, mistreatment in prisons, and civilians "accidentally" killed in wars. Richardson's book is probably an underestimate because of the immense number of murderous attacks that take place without leaving any record, and the numbers of people quietly murdered during wartime when armies occupy foreign territory. Although 59 million may seem a large number, even in terms of a modern world population, its magnitude can be appreciated only if one recognizes that most of these deadly assaults occurred during a period when the world population was only a small fraction of what it is today. If the killing continues at the same rate, and does not show an acceleration upward, one might well expect that perhaps half a billion people will be exterminated by their fellow men during the next century. The problem of controlling this self-extermination of the human species has to be seen as one of immense importance to the future of the species—if there is to be a future at all. The topic deserves a volume to itself, because of its significance. All that can be accomplished here is to indicate that our knowledge of the problem suggests that educators have an important role to play in the control of human aggression.

Extremely aggressive behavior in the human is puzzling because it is far in excess of anything ever observed in other creatures, who do not destroy their own species in a natural state although they may do this in captivity. Historians sometimes speak of men falling to the level of animals in the acts of cruelty that they perpetrate on other human beings, but the fact is that no other species inflicts on its own kind the suffering that humans have inflicted on other humans. Also other living creatures do not destroy other life on a massive scale for no other purpose than to enjoy killing other living things. Although a person, today, may condemn the slaughter of 50 million buffalo, most of which were shot for what is called "sport," those same individuals will, without thought, allow their young sons to spend a Saturday afternoon shooting a dozen or more birds, just for the fun of killing birds. Man has reached a point in his history where he is likely to exterminate all other life, except for the few domesticated species that he breeds for food. Man's destructiveness toward his own species is matched only by his destructiveness towards all other living creatures. How man evolved into such a dangerous species is a matter for speculation, but we *have* to find a solution to the problem of controlling that aspect of his behavior so likely to result in the elimination of all living creatures, including man himself, from the planet.

Although under conditions of captivity, many animals will destroy other members of their own species, similar destruction does not take place under natural conditions, where fighting is largely ritualistic. A species that engaged in self-destruction would not survive in the process of evolution. A well-known example of ritualistic fighting is found in the case of deer, the antlers of which have so evolved that they are not effective as lethal weapons. If deer had straight horns that could readily pierce the flank of other deer, combat among the bucks would have become lethal and the species would not have survived. Surviving species of animals that have potentially deadly straight and tapered horns, such as the old-time longhorn of Texas, simply do not engage in intraspecies combat. If they had become thus engaged, they would have exterminated themselves, long before man exterminated them.

Other primates are not as destructive as man either of other species or of their own species. Subhuman primates are typically forest-living and tree-living animals, vegetarian in diet, and the larger varieties are often quite timid. Man's ancestors at one time lived this kind of carefree life, attacking none and attacked by few. Then perhaps as long ago as 10 million years, there came into being a primitive manlike creature, a hominid, who showed strikingly different characteristics from those of his tree-loving ancestors. Freeman (1966), the anthropologist, has discussed the characteristics of this new Australopithecene hominid, in relation to the problem of the development of an aggressive primate species. He points out that this new primate lived on grassy plains and had become a carnivore. Although he had a small brain, about a third the size of modern man's, he had invented lethal weapons for use in preying upon other living creatures which he was poorly adapted for killing with his own hands and jaws. Unlike any other primate, man became a hunter. He was no longer the timid animal, although he could retreat to the tree tops when endangered. He was now the attacker. Man did not long remain merely content to kill and devour other species, for the evidence seems clear that Pithecanthropus man, who lived slightly later, devoured the brains of his fellow men, for this seems to be the only explanation of the peculiar holes cut in the backs of so many of the skulls found. Cannibalism came quite early in man's history and was probably a common form of behavior. But there was probably no organized warfare until much later—perhaps as late as the Neolithic period of only ten thousand years ago.

The early hominid was not an aggressive, attacking creature merely because he was carnivorous, for there are many carnivorous animals that kill only for food. Unlike other carnivorous animals he was a weapon maker, which gave him unlimited power over other living creatures. Perhaps because he was so dependent upon killing for survival, and because he had the specialized tools for destroying other forms of life, he became nature's prime killer. The tools were man's own creation, but the invention of the tools did not carry with them any inborn inhibitions about the tools of destruction being used only to satisfy nutritional needs. Other carnivorous animals have a built-in mechanism that limits the utilization of their killing power, but man does not.

Aggression appears to be related to a problem raised by Hebb and Thompson (1968), who suggest that primates are basically more emotional than simpler creatures in the evolutionary scale. Dogs may show sulking behavior and the baring of teeth and raising of hair, either when they are attacking or are attacked, but these are transitory states. In contrast, man may show prolonged anger, during which he may attack all kinds of objects, either living or inanimate. Nobody ever saw a dog bite a tree in anger, but it is common to see a man strike the top of a desk with his fist when some subordinate has transgressed. Anger behavior and other forms of extreme emotionality appear to be related to what we term aggressive acts. However, this is obviously not the only condition that triggers aggressive acts. Some of the most appalling acts of cruelty in history have been committed, in cold blood, by men who showed no observable signs of emotion.

Most animals have behavioral mechanisms built into them that limit the extent to which they will use their destructive capabilities. A dog will sometimes attack a dog, but if the attacked animal has had enough, it will turn its head and expose its neck, the most vulnerable part of its anatomy. When the attacked animal performs in this way, the attacker will immediately desist from the attack and the attacking animal will withdraw. Through the operation of such a mechanism dogs may attack dogs, but never to the point where they are in danger of exterminating their own species. Other species of animal have other signs that indicate "I have had enough." Indeed, man seems to be the only species that has not developed such a sign to an attacker from his own species that will be honored. Signals to desist appear to be universal outside the human species.

Although other predatory animals do not attack their own species when they are living in their natural surroundings, man very commonly does. This is not to say that there is necessarily any inborn tendency to do this. Humans do provoke other humans as other animals provoke one another, and such provocation often involves the loss of life, for there is no mechanism built into man that will inhibit him from doing this. For this reason, a most crucial problem of education is that of teaching the young human to inhibit his behavior when situations arise that would typically produce violent behavior. In other words, education has to produce through learning, an inhibition with which other species probably are naturally endowed. In order to provide such an educational program, knowledge is needed concerning ways in which human aggression can be controlled. Much of the knowledge needed to solve this problem is coming from laboratory studies undertaken with both men and animals.

One of the most productive of laboratory techniques in the present connection is that which studies the effect of the behavior of a model on the aggressive behavior of an observer. This type of experimentation has done much to explore the effect of personal example on this form of behavior, but it cannot solve all the problems of human aggression.

Studies of modeling aggressive behavior have used numerous different situations. Preference has been to show the behavior to be modeled on film, for the identical behavior can then be shown to different children at different times, and considerable evidence is available to support the contention that film performance and live performance have almost identical results on the observer children. In some studies of aggression, the model is shown as handling roughly, or even hitting, a doll. In other studies one adult is shown taking over the possessions of another adult either forcibly or accompanied by aggressive verbal behavior. Sometimes the models manifest very mild aggressive behavior, as when they rebuke or insult another person for no good reason. There is almost no limit to the variation in the aggressive behavior that has been used in studies of the effect of models on behavior. In addition, studies vary enormously in what happens after the model behaves aggressively. The model may be punished or rewarded. The model may reprimand himself or show that he is pleased with what he has done. The situations in which the observer may be placed following his observation of the model are many and diverse. An observer who has seen a doll abused, may be given an identical doll and the experimenter may record how he behaves toward it. On the other hand, the child who watches the model behave aggressively toward the doll may be observed in a situation in which his interactions with another child become the focus of interest.

The early research on the effect of observing an aggressive model on subsequent aggressive behavior was summarized by Bandura and Walters

(1963), who were largely responsible for the development of research in the area. Later reviews of research are provided by Bandura (1969) and also Aronfreed (1968), as well as several articles, notably that of Hartup and Coates (1967). The results are difficult to interpret. The observation of a model that is either rewarded for showing aggressive behavior, or who is not rewarded, produces more aggressive behavior in an observer than does the observation of a model punished for manifesting such behavior. Although a rewarded model may have more effect than a nonrewarded model, the difference is small. The important point to note is that aggressive behavior tends to be imitated whether it is or is not rewarded. On the other hand, the observation of an aggressor who is punished has a definite inhibiting effect on aggressive behavior. In some studies the rewarding of a model seems to play a crucial role, but sometimes imitation seems to have little to do with whether the model's behavior is or is not rewarded (provided it is not punished.) Aronfreed (p. 135) suggests that the difference among these studies may lie in whether the act of aggression is, or is not, one that the observer enjoys performing. If a child enjoys hitting a rag doll with a stick, then this behavior can be easily initiated by observing a model, and whether the model is or is not rewarded is inconsequential. On the other hand, if a child does not really like taking things away from other children, then this behavior is not triggered easily by observing another perform it, but if the model is highly rewarded for such a transgression of custom, then the reward provided can make the activity attractive to perform.

In the context of a social situation, the effects of a model on behavior are enormously complicated by many factors. It may make a difference, for example, whether the model is liked or rejected by the observer. A related factor that has been extensively studied is whether the model has been previously involved in the distribution of rewards to the observer (see Hartup and Coates, 1967). The weight of the evidence shows that models that have been identified as the source of reinforcements generally evoke more imitative behavior than those that are not so identified. Caution must be exercised in the interpretation of the latter finding because other sources of data show that if the relationship of the model to the observer has been one of punishment, then more imitation is also to be expected. The crucial factor would appear to be not reinforcement as such, but the fact that the model was capable of attracting the attention of the observer through having been either rewarded or punished.

Although the results reported here are both dramatic and interesting, there are certain differences between the laboratory situations and situations that occur in daily life. For this reason, one should exercise some caution in generalizing from the laboratory to events in the real world. Laboratory situations are typically brief and often the behavior of the model may involve only a few seconds of action followed by a few words of praise or criticism representing reward or punishment. Life situations that are commonly believed to provide models of influence may present sequences of action lasting for hours, as they do in full-length movies, and the reinforcement for the actions observed in the movies may involve a brief terminal event such as winning a bride, or exoneration for wrongdoing. Rosenkrans (1967) used a film showing how to play a particular game. Although the length of the film is not specified in the paper, the indications are that it lasted several minutes. Under such conditions the rewarding or the punishment of the model presented in the movie made relatively little difference in the amount of imitation. The suggested explanation was that the reward or punishment came at the end of a long sequence and probably had a reinforcing effect on the modeling of behaviors near to the end of the sequence. Perhaps the child who watches the lengthy transgressions of the crook, sees him eventually give himself up and confess, and then sees him shot by a trigger-happy sheriff, is likely to learn only that *confession* results in punishment.

A superficial view of the studies of the effect of the behavior of a model on the behavior of an observer child might take the line that these studies demonstrate that aggression may be learned by example. However, the meaning of the studies is much less clear as is shown in an excellent analysis of them by Aronfreed (1969), who points out that most studies of modeling behavior do not demonstrate learning at all. Consider the case of a child who views a movie of an adult hitting an inflated plastic doll and who shortly thereafter spends time himself hitting a similar doll. Did the model induce the observer to perform a new form of behavior? Almost certainly not! The child probably had already indulged in a similar behavior on previous occasions, and the effect of the model was to release this behavior. Nothing new was probably learned. Most studies of modeling behavior have not included an attempt to determine the extent to which the behavior manifested by the model is already a part of the repertoire of the observer, so the extent to which learning of aggressive behavior occurred is not known. Aronfreed also points out that in most studies involving the modeling of aggressive behavior, the observer children show little precise imitation of the model and very often there is a very general display of aggression toward a wide array of objects. The data suggest that exposure to the model results in the release of a general aggressive tendency.

The failure of children to reproduce with any precision the behavior of a model is not necessarily accounted for in terms of a lack of incentive to do so. Some light is thrown on this matter by the finding that the verbal behavior of the model is more likely to be imitated than the gross actions in which the model is engaged. The general activity of the model may be observed but, because the behavior is not readily coded into words, perhaps cannot be easily retained. The verbal behavior of the model, on the other hand, is readily retained, for the memory system seems highly capable of retaining large quantities of verbal information at a high level of precision. The imitation of action may be limited because the memory system of the observer does not permit him to retain the information needed for precise reproduction of the activity.

Knowledge derived from the study of modeling suggests not only that society should refrain from exposing children to models that show aggressive behavior, and particularly aggressive behavior that is rewarded; it also suggests that the teaching of history should avoid stressing reinforced aggressive models. Because most nations teach their children that the wars in which their nation has engaged were just wars and that the leaders of those wars were good leaders, history is to some extent taught as a sequence of aggressive, reinforced models. History would have to be interpreted differently if it is to function in some way other than as a releaser of aggressive behavior. Education will also have to work systematically on the problem of developing in children mechanisms that will actively inhibit aggressive behavior. Deep convictions that such behavior is wrong will have to be developed. Another approach, which needs further study, is that of converting human-against-human aggression into ritualized forms, much as animals have done. The Olympic Games represent one step in that direction.

Finally, a word must be said about the possibility of controlling aggression through punishment, that is to say, controlling aggression through aggression. The effect of punishment on a response, under these conditions, is somewhat different from the effect of punishment in most simple laboratory situations. Parke (1970) has conducted studies in this area and comes up with the conclusion that punishment may increase the response that it has been introduced to block. Punishment designed to reduce aggressive behavior, in fact, may actually increase it.

Social Facilitation of Learning

Some learning in natural settings occurs in group structures and some occurs in isolation. In many of the early experimental studies in the area of social psychology, the results showed that performance in group settings was superior to that in the isolated situation. Similar results were found when the individual involved was asked to learn some task rather than to perform a familiar task. Another aspect of the social setting has been studied in situations in which the individual has learned either in the presence of an observer or alone. The latter type of studies are generally referred to as studies of the effect of an audience. Ganzer (1968) has reviewed previous audience studies and has conducted a study of his own for the purpose of accounting for some of the inconsistencies in findings. He points out that many of the inconsistencies can be explained if one distinguishes between the performance of a well-practiced act and the acquisition of a new act. The presence of an audience appears to facilitate the performance of a well-practiced act but is detrimental to the learning of new skills. This does not account for all of the apparent inconsistencies, but the study of Ganzer makes a further contribution.

Ganzer selected the subjects for his study from the upper, middle, and lower thirds on the Taylor Manifest Anxiety Scale. They were then given the task of learning a set of nonsense syllables either after being told that there was an observer behind a one-way glass screen, or with the one-way screen covered and no mention being made of an observer. When the learning of the observed and the nonobserved groups were compared, the observed group did less well. However, when the groups were also divided into high-, middle-, and low-anxious, the finding was that the high- and middle-anxious did less well under the observed condition, but that the low-anxious group was unaffected by the announcement that an observer would be present.

The effect of an observer wears off rapidly. Indeed, in most studies in social psychology involving an observer, effects are found to disappear rather rapidly as the subject of the experiment becomes used to his or her presence (see Mills, 1969). In the case of the Ganzer study, the effect was no longer observable when a second session of the experiment was conducted a day later.

Studies of Pupils as Teachers

The history of education shows many examples of schools in which pupils have not only been the learners, but in which they have also been the teachers. Some modern institutions have attempted to adopt a similar system through assigning some pupils big-brother roles in relation to other pupils. The procedure adopted in state universities of teaching the beginning student through graduate student instructors is an example in the field of higher education of pupil teaching pupil. The original idea that pupils should participate in the actual instruction finds its roots in periods of history when teachers were few and pupils many. The first documented record of pupils assuming teaching roles was provided by a missionary, Andrew Bell, who founded a school in Madras, India. The only way in which many pupils could receive extensive instruction in Bell's school was for Bell to teach a few pupils, who would then each teach a limited group of other pupils. His school and its remarkable system might never have had any impact on the future of education had he not written a pamphlet about it—a pamphlet which an English educational pioneer, Joseph Lancaster, was able to obtain and read. Lancaster was enormously impressed with the potentialities of Bell's system for teaching very large numbers of pupils with very few teachers. He opened a school in the poor East End of London, and with only himself as the organizer was able to offer instruction to as many as one thousand pupils. The pupils were assigned to small groups, each one of which was instructed by a monitor—a pupil at a more advanced level.

Whatever educational limitation the system may have had, the economy it afforded in providing education at a low cost made it immediately attractive to educational leaders throughout the world. Many of the monitors trained in Lancaster's original school became the central teachers in other Lancastrian schools that were later established. The movement became worldwide, with Lancastrian schools becoming established throughout the eastern part of the North American continent from Quebec to Washington, D.C. Simón Bolívar became interested in the system and invited Lancaster to Bolivia, where he established schools following his pattern of instruction.

As there has been relatively little interest in the present century in using pupils to teach pupils, problems related to the system have not been the subject of intensive inquiry. Presumably, when this procedure is used, the teacher-pupil may learn while teaching the one designated as the learner-pupil. The extent to which the teacher-pupil may learn will, of course, depend upon the nature of the task. In the case of the Lancastrian system, the teacher-pupil, who read well and who taught less advanced pupils to read, probably had few opportunities of learning much during the teaching sessions, except perhaps how to teach. In two studies by Myers, Travers, and Sanford (1965), and by Travers and Myers (1966), the learning of teacher-pupils was studied under conditions in which considerable opportunity was provided for the teacher-pupil to learn. In these studies, pupils in grades four, five, and six learned the English equivalent of sixty German nouns divided into three batches of twenty. In the case of pupils working in pairs, the teacher-pupil held up a card on which was printed a German word and two English words, one of which was the equivalent of the German word. The learner-pupil read the four English words and then guessed the right answer. Then the teacher-pupil would read aloud the correct answer from the back of the card after saying, "The correct answer is———." The next card was then presented. After going through a batch of twenty cards, the teacher-pupil would take the learner through the same batch two more times. The second and third batches of cards were used on the second and third days.

The point to be noticed about this task is that both the pupil in the teacher role and the pupil in the learner role have equal opportunity to learn. The data showed that both learned, but the learner pupil showed a consistently higher level of achievement than the teacher pupil. Also, over the three-day period, the learner pupil showed some decline in performance on each successive day, perhaps because of a decline in interest in the task, but the decrement in learning was much greater for the teacher-pupil than for the pupil he was instructing. Teachers motivate pupils, but in our experimental situation there was nobody to motivate the teacher to do anything except teach. Related to this latter point is another finding of some significance. Another group of pupils was assigned the same task, but in a self-instructional situation in which they were given the deck of cards on which the instructional materials were printed, and they worked through the materials by themselves. This self-taught group achieved more than any other group on the first day by a substantial margin, but its performance rapidly declined until, on the third day, it had fallen far below the achievement of the pupils working with others functioning as instructors. At this particular educational level, the teaching materials were not able to maintain learning behavior. An additional analysis was made in which the amount of time involved in learning a syllable was analyzed. Thus if the pupil learned twenty syllables and spent forty minutes doing so, the amount of time per syllable would be 40/20, or two minutes. On this basis the pupils working alone learned almost twice as much per minute of time used as the pupils working with another functioning as an instructor. In addition, the efficiency of learning showed a substantial increase from grade four to grade six, but the main increase in efficiency was for the pupils working alone, reflecting their increased ability for self-sustained activity.

Group Problem Solving

Group problem solving has long been used as an instructional technique in schools. One can commonly observe in schools groups of children working on a problem. The technique is often adopted in teaching the sciences because there is insufficient apparatus for each child to conduct his own inquiry, but other virtues are often attributed to the procedure. The claim is often made that group problem solving procedures are particularly effective and that group activities in the classroom provide training in group solving skills. The argument is persuasive in terms of common experience but, whenever a person says that a practice can be justified in terms of personal experience, he should be particularly on his guard.

Experiments that compare the effectiveness of group and individual problem solving have long been conducted and with numerous variations. One type of situation widely used is that in which novel ideas are sought, involving anything from finding a title for a play to finding a slogan for advertising a new product. Other types of situations are those that require the individual to solve some kind of complex problem or that involve high-level logical reasoning, or administrative skills, or the organization of data, or a host of other features. The results of the many hundreds of studies conducted do not come out with a clear answer to the problem under consideration, for sometimes the individual approach produces the most effective problem solving, and sometimes the group approach. Much depends upon particular circumstances. In only one area can one speak with any certainty. It now seems clear that in finding novel ideas to solve a particular problem, such as finding a good advertising slogan, individuals perform rather better on this task when they work separately rather than as a part of an assembled group. The notion that brainstorming by a group is an effective way to function does not receive support. The free flow of ideas can take place better on an individual basis and with some economy of the time involved.

In the case of other forms of problem, the comparison of group and individual performance has not provided such clear-cut results. Maier (1967, 1970) has been able to bring together what appear, on the surface, to be contradictory experimental findings, and has been able to make some sense out of them. Maier points out that the conditions operating in groups are sometimes favorable toward problem solving and sometimes adverse. Let us consider the conditions that favor the group situation that Maier has been able to tease out of the research literature.

First, he points out that a group generally has collectively more knowledge than any of its individuals. This is generally true, though sometimes a very knowledgeable person may have more knowledge than any other member of the group and, in such a case, he has as much knowledge as the total group of which he is a part.

Second, a group is less likely to fall into a rut than is an individual. Maier points out the overwhelming evidence that the human problem solver tends to let his thinking fall into a rut and has difficulty in extricating himself from the rut. The diversity of viewpoints found within a group act as an antidote to this tendency.

Third, if the group solving the problem is the group that is going to have to live with the solution, then the group problem-solving situation leads to better acceptance of whatever solution is decided upon. Apart from the fact that individuals feel more favorably inclined toward solutions arrived at by a group in which they have participated, they also have better understanding of the solution.

Maier lists several disadvantages of the group situation for problem solving. Individuals in a group situation tend to show conformity. The resulting acquiescence to what appears to be a majority position may squelch some potential contributions. Maier quotes one of his own studies to support the position that in some kinds of groups, especially leaderless groups, minority views and ideas may fail to have any impact. He also makes the interesting point that in leaderless groups, the members often view majority solutions to problems as if they were correct solutions.

Solutions to problems in leaderless group situations tend to be accepted when a given number of supporting points have been supplied. A vocal minority can rapidly build support by rapidly enumerating points in favor of a particular solution. Also, the points do not have to be good and relevant points to throw their weight. Members of groups are often influenced by positively stated points that have little relevance to the issue at hand. In leaderless groups, and sometimes in groups with leaders too, the proceedings may become dominated by one person or by a small minority.

Finally, in the advanced stages of problem solving, after some of the options have been identified, the proceedings of the group may turn into attempts by one faction to persuade another faction to join them in a particular solution. When this happens, rational considerations are often casualties.

A particularly significant part of Maier's analysis comes in later sections of his paper in which he points out various factors that may be liabilities or assets, depending upon the leadership, or lack of leadership that may exist. In a leaderless group, disagreement may lead to the development of competing factions, but an effective leader can sometimes resolve disagreement, or sometimes show that, when there is disagreement about a solution, the different solutions offered are really solutions to different problems. The leader can often make his major contribution by making a clear analysis of what the problem is. He can also contribute by preventing factions from overwhelming the less dominant and ensure that the entire fund of relevant knowledge of the group is used effectively. He can also prevent a group from becoming preoccupied with consensus rather than with the task of finding a correct solution or a best solution.

The presence of a leader does not necessarily have a favorable effect on group performance. He may suppress the views of minorities, he may exert a dominant role that has an oppressive effect on the members, and he may play off members against each other.

Maier likens the role of the leader of a group engaged in an intellectual task to the coordinating function played by the nerve ring in the starfish. The five legs of this animal can function separately and independently and to some extent effectively even when a nerve ring coordinating them has been severed. This coordination can occur because when one leg moves the animal forward, the other legs are brushed against the ground and the resulting stimulation produces a walking movement. However, under some conditions, without the action of the coordinating ring, the legs may pull in opposite directions and destroy the animal. Groups show some coordination of behavior without the presence of a leader, but a leader can improve vastly the effectiveness of the group *if he recognizes his coordinating function.* Maier says that if the leader does not recognize this function, but just behaves as one of the group, then his main utility is lost. If he has information that the group needs, then it is appropriate for him to supply the information, but if the information implies a particular solution to the problem at hand, he should not supply the solution but let the group derive the solution from the information provided. The leader must direct his efforts toward utilizing all the relevant information of all the members and try and ensure that the group seeks a correct solution rather than just a popular solution.

The implication of the Maier attempt to integrate the findings of research on group problem solving is that group problem solving is effective when there is a leader or chairman who has the skills necessary for undertaking certain special tasks that make for effective group decision making. These skills are only in the process of being identified, but the time is not far off when enough will be known to provide training in these skills even at the high-school level. Leaderless groups are typically found among pupils who are assembled to engage in some kind of problem-solving project. These pupils may profit from engaging in this kind of project, but they may not represent a very effective problem-solving team.

Some Research on Control and Leadership with Implications for Teaching

A central issue in the conflict among the advocates of different teaching methods is the matter of the leadership pattern considered to be most effective in promoting learning. Some laboratory research has been undertaken in this area, and includes a study that has probably had more widespread influence on educational thought than any other experimental study ever undertaken. For this reason, it has to be mentioned in a chapter on social factors in learning, even though it leaves much to be desired by modern research standards. The reference here is to the famous study by Lewin, Lippitt, and White (1939), entitled "Patterns of Aggressive Behavior in Experimentally Created 'Social Climates.'" As the title indicates, the focus of the study was not on leadership in relation to learning, but leadership in relation to the incidence of aggressive behavior, but the implications drawn are generally related to learning.

In the study of Lewin, Lippitt, and White, boys aged ten and eleven were assigned to three types of groups, each type having a characteristic leadership that distinguished it from the other types. The three leadership patterns were (1) an authoritarian leader who directed the group in what to do, (2) a democratic leader who encouraged group-decision processes and who functioned as a member of the group, and (3) laissez-faire leadership that left the children to their own devices. The activities involved were those that would be considered hobbies: the building of model boats and planes, painting, and other manual arts and crafts. The incidence of aggressive behavior showed marked differences in relation to the three types of leadership involved. Laissez-faire leadership was accompanied by the highest incidence of aggressive behavior, and somewhat lower was the democratically led group. The groups with the authoritarian leaders showed either a very high incidence of aggressive behavior or a very low one. Although these results are of interest in connection with problems of discipline, so many of which are problems of aggression, they do not throw any direct light on problems of learning except insofar as aggressive behavior may interfere with learning. However the research workers involved in this study also collected some additional data concerning the amount of time spent in work under the three leadership situations, and these results have more direct bearing on the problem of learning. Output of work was related to type of leadership. As long as the authoritarian leader was present, there tended to be a high output of work; but the output declined rapidly when this type of leader left the room. In the groups exposed to democratic leadership, there was less output in the presence of the democratic leader, but the output of work continued in the absence of the leader. Under laissez-faire leadership, the presence of the leader seemed to be a disadvantage to the work of the group.

The results of this study have been widely applied to the planning of leadership roles for teachers, but many psychologists would doubt whether such application is justified. Rarely are the results of a single psychological experiment so sound and so secure that one can be certain they would be reproduced in other experiments. As far as this writer can determine, there has been no real attempt in America to replicate the experiment, a first step that should be taken before any extensive applications of the results are made. Similar experiments have been conducted by Japanese psychologists working with Japanese children. White and Lippitt (1960) report two studies conducted by Misumi and his colleagues, and cite the following conclusions:

> *. . . the group morale was higher in the democratic groups than in the other two. They frequently exchanged friendly remarks and showed more concern and satisfaction with the work and more willingness to continue it. . . . As to the quantity of work, the democratic groups obtained the highest rating; the autocratic groups the next, and the laissez-faire groups last. As to the quality, the*

autocratic groups did the best work, the democratic groups were next, and the laissez-faire groups last.

In a second experiment by Misumi and his colleagues (see White and Lippitt, 1960) some complicating results were found. On the more interesting of two tasks, the work done in the democratic group was superior; in the less interesting task, the autocratic groups performed best.

Anyone tempted to apply the results of the studies of Lippitt, White, Lewin, and others to a classroom situation should also read a study by Guetzkow et al. (1954) which virtually tried to apply the findings at the college level. The latter investigators were in charge of a seminar for graduate teaching assistants, the members of which decided to study the effects of different teaching methods in a course in general psychology. The teaching methods involved (a) a *recitation-drill* method, which was run on strictly authoritarian lines with the instructor each day giving a short lecture and asking the class prepared questions, (b) a *group-discussion* method, in which interactions with the instructor at meetings of the class were initiated largely by the students themselves and where the instructor played the role of chairman of the session, and, (c) a *tutorial-study* method, in which the instructor was available for helping the students find answers to the questions that came up in their independent study. These methods were selected because they represent different degrees of self-directed versus teacher-directed work, and because they also permitted a contrast between an emphasis on group work and an emphasis on individual work. The learning of the students was evaluated on the basis of a number of tests and other devices at the end of the course. The performance of the three groups in terms of measures in the course was strikingly similar; the only significant differences were on those measures on which the recitation-drill group did best—namely, the final examination, and the choice to go on and take more work in psychology. In terms of the usual measures of academic success, the classes run along authoritarian lines appeared to be the most successful.

Some of the data more recently published about the original experiment by White and Lippitt (1960) suggests that the autocratic leadership may have been so contaminated by an unpleasant social atmosphere that the results produced were quite inevitable. White and Lippitt state that the autocratic leaders gave disrupting commands in 11 per cent of their verbal behavior; that of the democratic leader was only 1 per cent. Twenty-four per cent of the verbal behavior of the democratic leaders represented guiding suggestions; but only 6 per cent of that of the autocratic leaders did. Little praise was given in any of the leader roles; but the autocratic leaders devoted 5 per cent of their remarks to praise and the democratic leaders 2 per cent, a slight margin in favor of the practices of the autocratic leaders. The general trend of the evidence indicates to this writer that autocratic leadership was accompanied by certain irrelevant and unpleasant elements that may have seriously stacked the deck. An experimenter who had read Machiavelli's *The Prince* might have designed a style of autocratic leadership that produced quite different outcomes. The writer is not arguing in favor of autocratic leadership in education; he is merely curious about the relationships that really exist between leadership and the performance of those led.

One is tempted to speculate at this point that the main difference between judicious autocratic leadership and judicious democratic leadership in a classroom may not be found in the quality or the quantity of learning produced, but in other factors. Learning under democratic conditions may be more pleasant. In addition, democratic practices may encourage decision making and other activities that can have important later consequences. In addition, of course, democratic practices in teaching may well contribute to the development of democratic values.

Further light on the relationship between classroom leadership and productivity and morale has been shed through a study by Meade (1967) undertaken in a Hindu culture in India. The plan of the study was very much like that of the original study in this area, but included only the so-called democratic and authoritarian leaders. In this study both morale and productivity were found to be superior under the authoritarian leader. Morale was measured in terms of the amount of absenteeism, the wish to continue the activities, and the expressed desire to remain under the particular leader. Meade suggests that the Hindu children had been raised in an authoritarian culture, which includes living in a communal family ruled over in an autocratic style by the senior woman in the group. With such a background, adaptation to a group run by a democratic leader is difficult, and the situation is sufficiently strange to interfere with effective work. Meade states, but without supporting data, that the Hindu children showed a greater number of acts of aggression under the democratic than under authoritarian leadership.

An overall view of the data suggests that the responses of children to different types of leadership in learning situations depends more on their cultural background than on the leadership as such. In both the United States and in Japan, children are raised in a quite permissive environment in which the parents give guidance rather than orders. Such children adapt well to similar conditions in the classroom. Hindu children, raised in a highly authoritarian society, also adapt best to school conditions similar to those in which they have been raised, namely, authoritarian conditions.

The problem discussed here is a part of the general problem of what constitutes effective human leadership. Perhaps one of the reasons why research on styles of leadership in teaching situations has not flourished is that it is generally considered to be a special case of leadership that has not been attractive to research workers. Research on leadership in other situations has flourished, but it has tended to avoid such broad categories as the democratic and the authoritarian. Indeed, the trend in research has been to analyze leadership into more basic components of behavior in particular situations. The studies cited elsewhere in this chapter on the conditions under which a leader can be effective in helping a group to solve a problem reflect the trend in research. The result has been the identification of some specific activities in which leaders can be trained. A review of leadership research by Hollander and Julian (1969) also brings out the fact that there has been a declining interest in the personal qualities of leaders and a tendency to focus on the situations in which leadership can make a contribution and the nature of the contribution that can be made. The evidence seems clear that there is little meaning in talking of individuals as leaders, as if they were a special group of individuals capable of exercising leadership in all situations. Probably few have the skills required to perform effectively in all the leadership situations that can be devised. However, a very large number of individuals include in their repertoire of behavior some items that may provide effective leadership in some situations. We are only just beginning to identify the skills required for effective leadership in the classroom.

T-Group Training

The lack of success that traditional teaching practices have had in the development of social skills have led to attempts to devise novel techniques that will hopefully result in the acquisition of these skills. In the early part of the century, optimism was expressed that the key to the solution of social problems was to be found in more effective communication. This was the theme of the prolific writings of Stuart Chase during the depression years and it is also evident in Dale Carnegie's books on personality development. Dale Carnegie came from the field of speech and one cannot be surprised by the fact that he saw effective speech as the cure for many problems of social interaction. The case that can be made for such an attack on problems of social development is quite convincing, but it is obviously not a complete answer. A communication may be clear but fall on deaf ears, because the listener blocks the reception of the message. Those who communicate need to be sensitive to the make-up and receptiveness of the persons who are to receive the communications. This is a problem that has received considerable attention in recent years by those concerned with what has been termed sensitivity training, a procedure that emerged from the research of Kurt Lewin on group dynamics of more than a quarter of a century ago.

The central technique of sensitivity training is the T-group, a term representing an abbreviation for training group. The training group consists of an assemblage of usually six to ten people and a person designated as a trainer. The latter is a graduate of previous T-group sessions and has also had some theoretical background in the theory of the procedure. What the group does during the training sessions is not structured in advance and does not have a rigid structure imposed upon it by either the trainer or its members. For example, it would be out of order for the group to draw up a rigid agenda at the first meeting and adopt Roberts' Rules of Order. The content of the meetings of the group is likely to involve the devotion of much time to the open discussion of the motives of members of the group, the particular characteristics of members that interfere with interactions, and the problems that the group as a whole encounters. The trainer may spend time observing the group and interact only at crucial points where his insights may pave the way for developing social sensitivity. This description is, of course, a gross oversimplification of a very complicated training technique that all agree produces deep emotional involvement in the group situation. This short paragraph does not do justice to the sophistication of some of those who write about the technique.

Thousands of individuals have been exposed to sensitivity training for many different purposes and for different lengths of time. Weekend sessions, involving one or two days, have been provided all over the country under the auspices of the National Training Laboratories, an affiliate of the National Education Association. The same organization has also provided summer training programs at Bethel, Maine, where the sessions may last as long as several weeks. In the earlier years of the program the main participants were business executives seeking to become more proficient in their work but, more recently, school administrators and teachers have shown an increasing interest in the approach. The involvement of school personnel involves similar motivations to those of businessmen, but some school systems have attempted to persuade teachers and administrators to become thus involved in the hope that this kind of training will facilitate the introduction of innovations. The argument is that a major difficulty of introducing innovations in school is the resistance and inertia of the school personnel. Sensitivity training, it is hoped, will make school personnel more aware of factors within themselves that result in the rejection of new ideas. In addition, it is assumed that administrators exposed to sensitivity training will be more aware of the blocks in others that result in opposition to change and may find ways of circumventing these blocks. T-group programs have existed largely on faith, not because of any lack of enthusiasm for research on the subject but because of the very serious difficulties involved in the undertaking of research.

Research on the effects of T-group training has turned out to be particularly difficult to undertake. Campbell and Dunnette (1968) made a comprehensive review of research in the area, emphasizing studies that might have some implications for management. They could find virtually no studies that could be taken to demonstrate that such training resulted in improved skills in handling people in typical management situations. The sheer difficulty of measuring any changes in behavior that might have been produced in a job situation has been found to be almost insuperable. For this reason, most of those who have undertaken research on T-group outcomes have abandoned any hope of evaluating training in terms of on-the-job performance and have attempted to use other criteria. Some have given paper-and-pencil tests of various kinds before and after training in an effort to detect personality changes, others have handed out management problems of various kinds to solve, and occasionally research workers have tried to concoct situations with the help of stooges that will permit the trainee to show his skills. The sum total of the evidence derived from such artificial situations is that training does produce changes, but a clear and consistent picture cannot be put together from the data. Examples of this kind of evidence are found in a number of studies in which the effect of T-group training of teachers has been estimated by administering the Minnesota Teacher Attitude Inventory. The results generally show that those trained exhibit a favorable change on this device, as compared with an untrained group, but this does not mean that behavior in the classroom will show a corresponding improvement. Also, one does not know whether the changes produced are relatively permanent. They may well be quite transitory.

Summary

1. Because most learning in schools takes place in a social context, an understanding of conditions that affect learning in schools has to include an understanding of social factors. In addition, much of education is also concerned with the development of social skills and attitudes where social factors have great impact on learning.
2. Imitative behavior has commonly been considered to be the key to the success of much of education. Research on imitative

behavior attracted few research workers until quite recently. Early research workers viewed imitative behavior as being learned, largely because no evidence could be found for any innate basis for imitation. The studies of Miller and Dollard were largely demonstrations of the fact that imitative tendencies can be learned. They also made the important distinction between matched dependent behavior and copying behavior.

3. In studies of imitative behavior, the person or animal whose performance is set up experimentally as a source to be imitated is referred to as the model. The subject exposed to the model is referred to as the observer.
4. Substantial evidence has now been provided that, in many species, the exposure of a member of the species to another already trained to perform a task results in a facilitation in the performance of the observer on the same task. The underlying mechanism is not understood, but those who have studied such phenomena generally assume that the effect of the model is to draw the observer's attention to elements in the task. In some cases the effect of the model may be that of releasing an innate mechanism.
5. There are serious difficulties involved in attempting to separate the innate and the acquired components of imitation, but there appear to be great species differences. Research workers would also like to be able to distinguish between situations in which the model releases a behavior mechanism latent in the observer and situations in which new behaviors are acquired by the observer.
6. Flanders found in his review that, in the case of human subjects, exposure to filmed models had about the same effect as exposure to the live model.
7. Two conditions necessary for imitative behavior to occur are the attention of the observer and the ability of the observer to acquire and store enough information from the model to guide behavior at a later time. Many behaviors in educational situations cannot be modeled because the act performed takes place too quickly for the observer to record what has happened.
8. A significant area of social learning is that which involves the acquisition of standards of conduct. Although there is much debate about whether there are, or are not, different stages of moral development, the evidence seems clear that there is a gradual transition from behavior that is externally controlled to internally controlled behavior. Great individual differences exist in the extent to which the internalization of control actually

occurs. Behavior is said to be internally controlled when it has the appearance of independence from observable outcomes. The development of internal controls appears to be dependent upon the existence of an internal representation of the world that permits the individual to experiment with different actions and imagine their consequences. Highly developed internal controls are most developed in the educated middle class. This may be linked to the fact that job requirements of the middle class often call for a high degree of internal control and such controls are necessary for success within this social class. Men show a greater degree of internal control than do women.

9. A major problem to which education can contribute a solution is that of the control of the aggression of the human toward his own species. Indeed, education is perhaps the last untried solution to this greatest of all problems. Australopithecene man or perhaps even earlier man evolved from tree-living ancestors who were largely vegetarian. His ancestors may have learned to use simple tools, as some primates do today, but this early hominid was a hunter on the plains and developed deadly weapons for use in his predatory activities. He did not evolve any mechanism in his personality that might inhibit him from using the same tools for the destruction of his own species. A major task of education is that of producing such inhibitory mechanisms.

10. Studies of modeling behavior generally demonstrate that the observation of the aggressive behavior of a model results in the subsequent release of aggressive behavior in the observer. The effect can be enhanced when the model is rewarded and reduced when the model is punished. Whether one can reasonably say that, under such conditions, the observer learns to be aggressive is questionable. Most psychologists would prefer to say that the effect of the model is to release aggressive behavior, because the aggression that appears in most experiments is typical of what has been previously manifested by the same person. There is some evidence that when a model is reinforced, the effect of the reinforcement may be related in the observer only to the behavior that preceded the reinforcement, and not to the entire sequence of behavior. Although the study of modeling throws some light on one of the conditions that releases aggressive behavior, it tells little about the development of such aggressive trends in the first place.

11. A social context is favorable to the performance of a

well-practiced act, but it is detrimental to the learning of new activities. Highly anxious individuals are particularly subject to the latter effect.

12. At the higher levels of education, advanced students are often used as instructors, but a similar practice was at one time used at the elementary-school level. Evidence indicates that pupils may learn while they are functioning as teachers, but less than when they assume a pupil role. When pupils work in pairs, the work may progress rather more slowly than when the pupil works in isolation, but his motivation seems to be better maintained.
13. Group problem solving is a common learning situation as well as a common management strategy. When group problem solving is compared with individual problem solving in terms of effectiveness, it may be better or worse depending upon circumstances. The advantages of the group situation include the fact that groups generally have more knowledge than any of the component individuals, they are less likely to fall into a rut in their thinking, and they can bring an understanding of the solution to more individuals. On the negative side is the fact that individuals in groups tend to show group conformity, and they also tend to be swayed unduly by a particularly vocal minority or by a dominant leader. Groups also often mistake majority opinion for a correct solution. The leader in a group can perform the important function of protecting less dominant factions, ensure that the knowledge of the group is properly used, and he may also prevent the group from becoming preoccupied with obtaining consensus. Group problem solving can be effective, particularly when there is a leader who has the skills necessary for helping the group arrive at an effective decision.
14. The classical studies of types of leadership in group learning situations involving children still continue to have impact on educational practice, though they have not stimulated much productive research. The extent to which authoritarian or democratic leadership roles of adults have good or poor influences on the work of children exposed to them is probably highly dependent upon the cultural background of the children. In the American setting, the advantages of a democratic type of leadership in educational settings would appear to far outweigh the disadvantages.
15. Considerable interest has been shown in education in the development of social skills through sensitivity training. The central technique for this is the training group in which there occurs a leaderless, unstructured, activity. Although such training has been widely given to teachers and administrators, there is little

evidence that it has accomplished the goals claimed for it. Some of the goals may be achieved, but there are great difficulties in obtaining evidence for this. Studies have shown that, on paper-and-pencil tests, T-group training does produce changes in those exposed to it, but whether these changes would influence on-the-job performance is another question.

CHAPTER TWELVE

The Nervous System and Learning

IN THE LAST QUARTER OF A CENTURY AN INTIMATE RELATIONSHIP HAS developed between those interested in developing a science of behavior and those concerned with the discovery of how the nervous system is built and how it controls behavior. Learning psychologists have often been able to suggest to the neurologist what he might look for in the nervous system and the neurophysiologist has been able to suggest to the psychologist some of the factors he should take into account in attempting to identify the conditions that are related to learning. The healthy relationship between these two groups has produced many important ideas. The purpose of this chapter is to review some of these ideas, but first let us take a look at the structure of the nervous system.

The classic work on the anatomy of the nervous system is that by Ranson, which has been revised by Clark (1959). A shorter and more readily understood text is that by Gardner (1968). Several works are now available that discuss the function of the system in relation to behavior. One of the most understandable is that by Woodburne (1967). A compact summary of structure of the nervous system in relation to psychological function can be found in a work by Riklan and Levita (1969), which is mainly concerned with an evaluation of the effects of surgical treatment of Parkinson's disease. However, the book is also an excellent elementary treatise on neural functioning.

The Microcomponents of the Nervous System

Like all other tissues of the body, the nervous system is made up of cells. These cells take on many forms, but they generally have a long fiberlike structure which extends from one end, called the axon, as shown in Figure 16. It is mainly along this fiber, sometimes as long as several feet, that nerve impulses travel from one part of the system to another. The nerve impulse is different from a current traveling down a wire, but it is still electrical in character. The sense organs consist of specialized nerve cells that respond mainly to particular stimuli. Those in the retina of the eye, for example, respond to light, and they also respond to mechanical impact, as is evident from the experience one has when struck a blow in the eye. The nerve fibers coming from the sense organs are gathered together into white glistening bundles that enter the spinal cord, at regular intervals, through spaces between the bony vertebrae that provide a protective casing for the spinal cord. The sensory nerves come from the surface of the body and also from the interior of the body and provide a communication system through which the individual is able to know what is happening both in the outside world and in the interior of his body. The optic nerve, the auditory nerve, and the nerves associated with the sensory systems at the head end of the body enter the enlarged upper portion of the spinal cord known as the brain stem.

Nerve cells do not connect directly to other nerve cells, for each cell

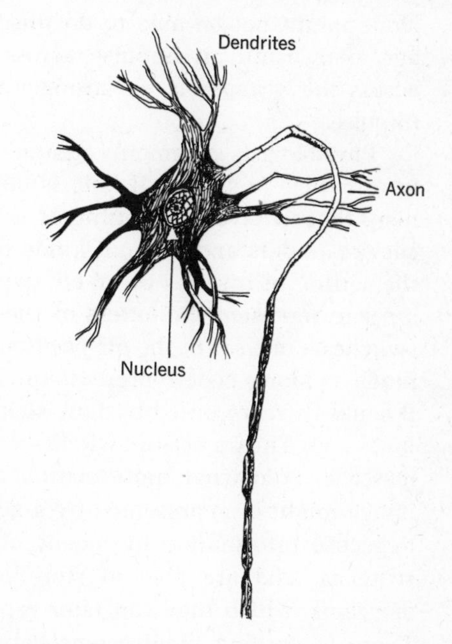

Figure 16. Drawing of a common type of nerve cell.

is completely enclosed by a membrane that separates it from all other tissues. There are places where the axon of a cell comes into close contact with either the cell body of another cell or with fine fiberlike structures that extend from the body of the other cell, called dendrites. A nerve impulse traveling down an axon can, at its terminal, cause chemical changes in the surrounding fluid, and these chemical changes may, in turn, initiate a response in the dendrites of a neighboring cell. In this way impulses may travel from one cell to another. The space between the termination of the axon and the dendrites or body of the other cell is referred to as the synapse, which behaves much like an on-off switch. If it is in the on position the impulse passes; if it is in the off position, then the impulse is blocked from transfer to the new cell.

Impulses in the cell body and axon are all or none phenomena, that is to say, the nerve cell fires an impulse or it is in a resting state. If it fires an impulse, then the impulse is always of the same size. The same is true of the function of the synapse, which either passes an impulse to another nerve cell or fails to pass the impulse. It never passes an impulse in a weakened form, and it never passes a part of an impulse.

A very important fact about synapses is that they can show variation in their ability to transmit impulses across them. Impulses may be blocked at a synapse or they may be readily transmitted. If two impulses, along two different axons, arrive simultaneously at a synapse, or in rapid succession, they may be able together to initiate activity in the synapse and produce a new impulse in another nerve cell, even though either alone might not be able to do this. When two impulses, together, manage to transmit an impulse across a synapse, the impulse transmitted across the synapse is no stronger than if it were initiated by a single impulse.

Physiologists commonly assume that the synapse is the place where information is stored. If this is so, information is stored by a mechanism that involves the setting of a large number of on-off switches. It is easy to understand how all kinds of information can be represented by the setting of a series of on-off switches. For example, we can use such a set to represent the letters of the alphabet, with A represented by two switches—one set to the off position, and the other set to the on position, much as Morse code represents the letter A by the symbol - —. The letter B could be represented by four switches set in the on-off-off-off positions (— - - -). Thus a set of switches could be used to represent any written message. Somewhat more complicated is the problem of how a visual image might be represented by a set of switches, but computers are able to record information by means of what are essentially a set of on-off switches, and are able to store information about visually presented diagrams, which they can later reproduce, from memory, onto a screen. There is nothing inconsistent between the idea that memory involves the storage of information through the setting of large numbers of on-off switches and that memory sometimes involves the storage of visual information in the form of images.

The number of synapses, which we have referred to here as on-off switches, is very large indeed and may well be in the billions. This number is far in excess of the number of corresponding on-off mechanisms found in the most advanced computer or in any computer that is contemplated. Indeed, the number in a single human nervous system may well be larger than the number in all the computers of the world combined, and is perhaps of the order of 10 billion.

The nervous system also contains a large number of cells of unknown function called glial cells. There are, in fact, more glial cells than there are nerve cells, and some neurophysiologists have suggested that these cells may be involved in the storage of information. Just how such a system of cells could provide an information storage system is difficult to see at this time, for they do not have any clear relationship to the input and analysis of information.

The Gross Structure and Function of the Human Nervous System

The human nervous system is basically a system that handles all the information provided by the sense organs, stores information, and has components that initiate and control the responses that are made. Much of it consists of bundles of nerve fibers carrying information into the system from the sense organs, called the afferent nerves, and bundles of nerve fibers through which impulses travel and initiate responses in both the muscles and glands, called the efferent nerves. The nerves from the sense organs enter the trunk line of the nervous system, the spinal cord, through bundles that join it at intervals along its length. The nerves that produce responses also have corresponding exits. The spinal cord itself is encased within the bony segments collectively called in common language the backbone. The spinal cord is thickened at its upper extremity to form what is known as the medulla. The medulla leads to a number of complex structures tucked well beneath the cerebral hemispheres, the large masses of nervous tissue that are commonly regarded as the brain.

Everyone knows that the nervous system is immensely complicated, and it is. This is why a simple exposition of its functions is difficult to undertake. Detailed anatomical drawings and photographs are confusing except to the highly sophisticated, so let us begin with a grossly oversimplified diagram of the main structures. Such a diagram is shown in Figure 17. In this diagram, the spinal cord is shown at the extreme and is not represented for its entire length, and neither are the nerves

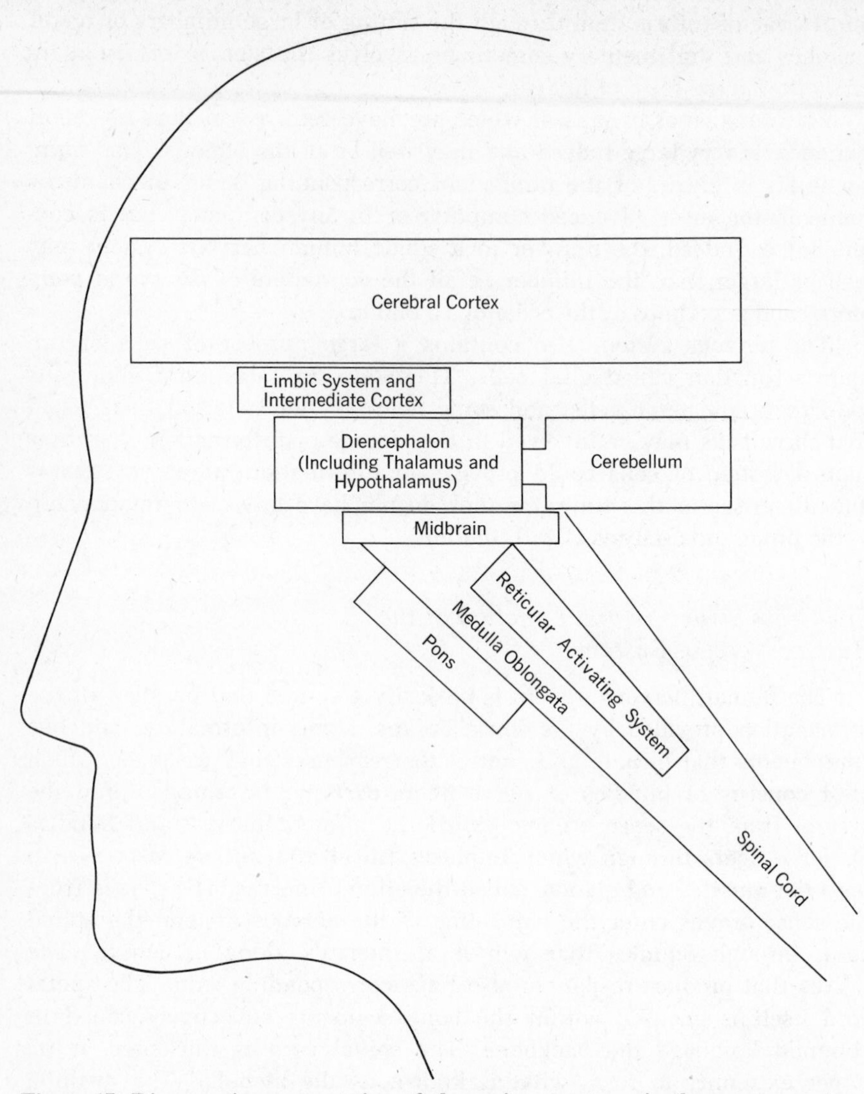

Figure 17. Diagramatic representation of the major structures in the nervous system.

entering or leaving it shown. The spinal cord as it approaches the brain itself is enlarged to form the medulla and includes a highly important structure known as the reticular activating system. There is also a thickening caused by a broad band of fibers that circle the brain stem, part way, and that have the major function of providing connections between the two cerebral hemispheres. These fibers form what is called the pons, a word meaning a bridge, because it forms a bridge between the two sides of the brain. In ascending the system, the next massive structures are the thalamus and hypothalamus. The connection between the thalamic structures and the cerebral cortex is through the diencephalon, which also contains the important structure known as the limbic system. Then come the cerebral hemispheres, which are responsible for the most complex analyses of sensory information and produce the most complex behavior. The cerebral hemispheres hide most of the other structures from inspection, although the pons is readily seen on the underside. The cerebellum is a bulb of nervous tissue that nestles underneath the cerebral hemispheres at the rear.

The actual appearance of the brain is much more like the sketch shown in Figure 18, with the cerebral hemispheres shown as the dominant structures. Even fine drawings prepared by a medical artist do not readily present the relative positions of the interrelated structures, partly because the drawings are flat and the structures exist in three dimensions. In this figure large cavities are shown in the interior, which are the ventricles of the brain. The important nerve centers that surround these cannot be identified in the picture, which can only show the surface of the cavities. However, it may be pointed out that the thalamus and hypothalamus would be represented in tissues that surround the third ventricle. Numerous structures are deeply embedded within the surface of the ventricles shown in the illustration.

Functions of nervous tissues can be conveniently divided into those referred to as specific and those referred to as nonspecific. Let us con-

Figure 18. View of the brain cut through the midsection to show the main structures.

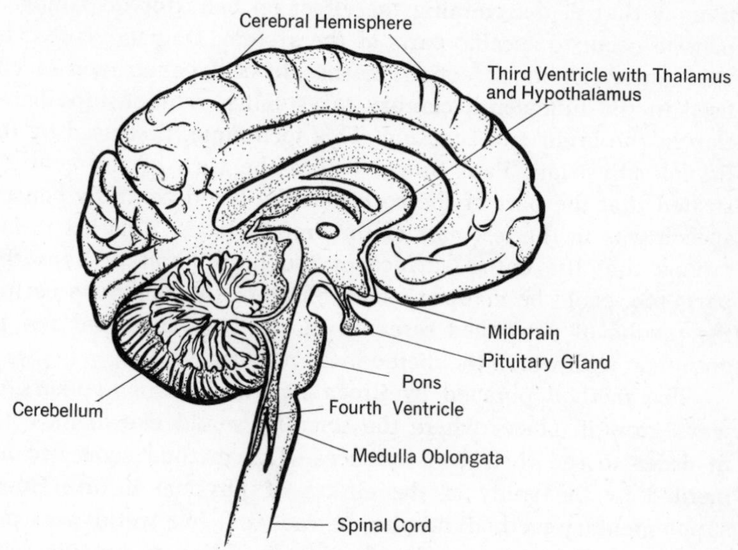

sider first the specific functions, that is to say, functions related to particular aspects of behavior. The spinal cord conducts upward impulses from the receptors associated with the sense of touch, pain, tension in the muscles, and deep pressure. The nerves from the eye, ear, taste-smell system, and sensory equipment at the head end enter the brain stem at a higher level. The spinal cord also contains major bundles of fibers that transmit impulses to the muscles and produce action. The spinal cord also includes fibers that interconnect various parts of the cord. When the cord is severed, there is complete loss of control of movement, that is to say, paralysis, but reflexes below the level of the cut remain and these would require the presence of many interconnecting fibers. A reflex is a simple form of behavior, but it involves complex nervous structures.

Specific and Nonspecific Neural Systems

The traditional approach to the study of the nervous system has been to attempt to identify the specific function of each particular anatomical component. This looks like a reasonable procedure, and is feasible up to a point. This is how an engineer would go about studying a strange piece of equipment, say, a piece captured from an enemy in wartime. The neurophysiologist has many techniques through which he can hope to discover whatever specific functions exist in particular locations in the nervous system, and these he has applied with some success over the last half century.

The oldest technique for establishing the location of specific functions is that of determining the effect on behavior of damage that happens to occur to specific parts of the system. Damage caused by tumors, vascular accidents, infection, or the physical penetration of objects was used in the nineteenth century to establish relationships between location in the brain and function. This technique, first used by the famous French physician, Paul Broca, before the turn of the century, demonstrated that the part of the cortex of the brain centrally concerned with speech was in the left part of the frontal lobes. This led to high expectations that the entire surface of the brain, and perhaps the interior parts too, could be mapped out in terms of the functions performed, but the results of prolonged research along these lines did not justify the optimism with which the method was pursued.

The method pursued by Broca had limitations. Tumors do not always grow in places where the scientist would like to have them grow in order to see their consequences. The method soon became supplemented by the study of the effects of physical injury. However, this supplementary method, despite the fact that two world wars provided an almost inexhaustible supply of subjects, failed to provide much useful data. One problem is that damage produced by the penetration of a piece of shrapnel or any fragment of metal does extensive damage through the wave produced by the impact. A bullet through the brain produces the same kind of extensive splash as would be produced by a bullet fired into a bucket of water. Few objects that have enough impact to penetrate the skull leave damage in a small, specific, and identifiable area. The damage is diffuse and typically fatal. In the case of animals, the technique can be used in a refined form by producing damage surgically. The damage can then be controlled precisely to a particular region of the brain and the precise extent of the damage can be determined later through the post-mortem study of the brain.

An additional technique involves the electrical stimulation of an exposed area of the brain. The muscular response of the person or animal stimulated can then be observed. In the case of human subjects, the experiences that accompany the stimulation can be noted. The technique can be used in the case of human subjects, because some surgical procedures require that sections of the skull be removed, exposing the brain. The removal of portions of the skull can take place with only a local anesthetic, and the actual stimulation of the surface of the brain is painless. An example of what happens is that when a certain area on the side of the cerebral hemispheres is stimulated, a person may say that he is experiencing a vivid visual memory of an event that happened many years ago. Stimulation of other areas may produce a twitch of a toe or the movement of an arm.

The technique can be further extended when subjects other than human are used, and electrodes can be implanted deep in the brain. The stimulation of the part of the brain in which they are implanted can be undertaken by passing a small current between the electrodes. The effect of this stimulation can then be studied.

Still another technique has evolved as biochemists have come to identify various substances used by various parts of the brain in performing their functions. For example, it is known that the part of the nervous system that has to do with reinforcement releases norepinephrine when it is active. Norepinephrine can be made to fluoresce, and thus after an animal has engaged in a particular activity and been killed, sections of the brain will show, through such fluorescence, the areas that have been active in producing norepinephrine. In addition, there are substances, such as reserpine, that deplete the brain of norepinephrine, and thus permit the study of what happens when those areas that use norepinephrine are deprived of it. In addition, very small quantities of norepinephrine can be traced and followed by supplying the brain with radioactive norepinephrine, which can be then detected in minute traces.

The result of research using this diversity of techniques is to show that some systems in the nervous system have highly specific functions such as that of producing speech, or transmitting information from a particular sense organ to a particular higher center, or controlling movement in a particular set of muscles, or controlling the temperature of the body, or controlling respiration. Other parts of the nervous system have what are called nonspecific functions, that is to say, they perform such tasks as keeping the higher centers in a general state of arousal or they may exercise some general control over the prevailing emotional states.

Now let us turn to a discussion of some of the discoveries made through these techniques concerning the specific functions of different components of the brain. The midbrain contains centers that control, in particular, the righting reflexes that occur when the body is thrown off balance. It is also the center that controls eye movements and the reflexes associated with the eyes. Of more extensive importance in the control of body movement and position is the cerebellum, a mass of tissue as large as a person's first, that lies at the back of the brain stem. This important nerve center receives nerve impulses from all the sensory mechanisms involved in the adjustment of the position of the body and the orientation of the body in space. Thus it receives information from the vestibular organs of the middle ear, and also from the joints, tendons, and muscles. There are also inputs from the organs of vision, touch, and hearing, which common experience suggests play an important role in keeping a man right side up to the world. Damage to the cerebellum produces difficulties in coordinating muscular activity and problems of maintaining balance. The cerebellum also sends impulses to both sensory and motor areas of the higher centers.

The diencephalon consists largely of two major structures, the thalamus and the hypothalamus. The thalamus is most noted as a sensory relay station. In addition, the thalamus receives information from the eyes, ears, and the smell-taste system. The sensory information coming up the spinal cord is relayed at the thalamus to the higher centers of the brain. Rather than saying that the thalamus sends the information up to the specialized areas of the cortex that handle this information, the neurophysiologist says that the sensory inputs are "projected" onto the sensory areas of the cortex of the brain.

The relatively crude information coming from the lower parts of the body may well undergo analysis at the level of the thalamus, and only the analyzed information may be passed on to the higher centers. There is much speculation at this time concerning the extent to which the thalamus is an analyzer of information rather than just a relay station. Some have also suggested that the thalamus may be the center of the awareness of pain.

The hypothalamus has important functions related to hunger, thirst, and sexual excitation, and also seems to have much to do with the control of emotional states. Some have described it as the seat of the emotions. The hypothalamus contains centers that maintain a homeostatic balance, that is to say, a balance in the internal chemistry of the organism. If the nucleus that controls water balance is disturbed through a growth or through injury, the person excretes enormous quantities of fluid and has to take in large quantities of water to keep from becoming dehydrated. A parallel phenomenon also occurs when the working of the hunger center in the hypothalamus is upset and animals will ingest large quantities of food and become obese. The center for hunger should not be thought of as a single nucleus, for it consists of a set of separate nuclei controlling appetite, initiating feeding, and the cessation of feeding on satiation. An interesting finding is that animals that have had a part of this area destroyed not only show disturbances in their eating habits, but they also behave in a peculiarly savage way. There are also centers concerned with the maintenance of body temperature and the control of such temperature-regulating functions as those of sweating, the dilation of the blood vessels in the skin, and panting. The neural mechanisms involved in cooling oneself in a hot environment are different from those involved in raising the temperature in cool surroundings. The one mechanism can go wrong while the other continues to operate. Other centers in the hypothalamus exert control over blood pressure and heart rate. The reader should take note that the description of the hypothalamus given here is certainly a gross simplification (see Valenstein, Cox, and Kakolewski, 1970).

A generation ago Walter B. Cannon discovered that the hypothalamus also has functions connected with what has been termed the rage reaction. This reaction in the cat is shown by hissing, arching of the back, the erection of hairs on the skin, the flattening of the ears, and the tightening of the muscles of the legs in a crouching position that makes it possible for the animal to rapidly attack or withdraw. Cannon showed that when connections of the hypothalamus to the cortex of the brain are severed the animal will go into the rage condition under the slightest provocation. Merely petting the animal may precipitate this response. Ordinarily, the cortex of the brain inhibits this response and prevents it from occurring, but the removal of this inhibiting influence makes the response more easily aroused.

The cortex of the brain itself shows some specialization of function in particular areas, as shown in Figure 19, but there are large areas that are quite nonspecific in what they do. A broad band down the middle is involved in muscular control and has to do with the initiation of movement. Just posterior to this region is another band of tissue, which has to do with general bodily sensibility. At the rear is an area that handles visual information analysis, and a specialized area that handles motor

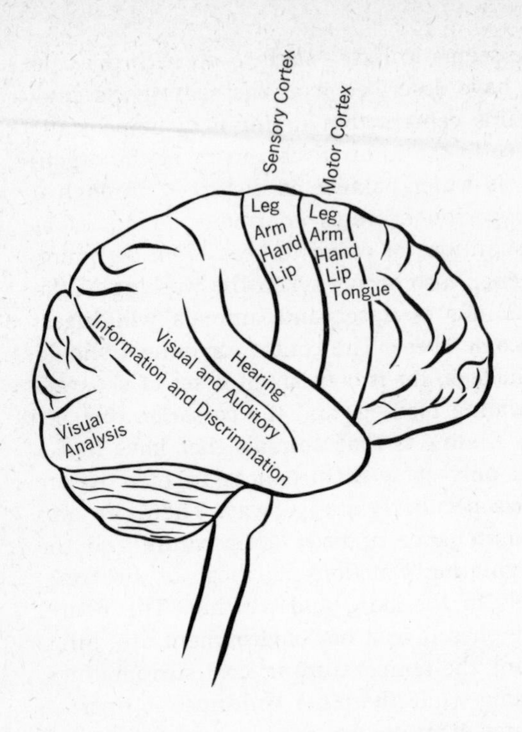

Figure 19. Some specialized functions located in the human cortex.

aspects of speech. An area on the right side of the brain handles auditory information analysis. The areas related to vision and hearing are not the areas in which information is stored. If these areas are stimulated electrically in a surgical patient on the operating table, the patient does not report any meaningful experience. However, there are other areas of the cortex, which do not have analysis functions, that can be stimulated electrically and that will produce vivid memories that are almost like hallucinations in the detail with which they are seen or heard. The meaning of this is probably that the specific sensory areas are involved in the analysis of information, and not the storage of information. For this reason, attempts to excite them do not arouse memories. Storage takes place in parts of the cortex other than those in which the incoming information is analyzed.

The little evidence available that comes from the study of the visual cortex of the cat is suggestive of how the specific sensory areas of the cortex handle information. Hubel (1963) has been able to show that the visual area of the cortex of the cat is arranged in a set of layers each of which identifies lines having a particular slope. What this means is that a visual presentation is analyzed in terms of a number of distinct attributes, each one of which is identified by a particular mechanism in the sensory cortex. The visual cortex can probably analyze many of the cues or all of the cues simultaneously. The sensory area in the cortex probably does not use all the information available in a particular display, but takes a sample of cues, which are then analyzed and provide the data necessary for identification. A small object moving rapidly across the floor is probably identified as a mouse solely on the basis of its small size and speed of movement. No other cues are necessary. An object lying on the floor can be identified as a coin merely from the size and metallic brightness. The sensory areas in the brain are probably mechanisms that pick up such relevant cues and thus permit identification of the object involved.

This sketch of the specific functions served by particular portions of the brain stem and cortex is, at best, fragmentary and is far from presenting all that is known at this time. The information that has been provided is sufficient, however, for understanding materials presented elsewhere in this book.

One cannot leave the discussion of the main body of the nervous system after a brief discussion of the specific functions, for some of the nonspecific functions are at least of equal importance for the understanding of learning. Let us begin the study of these by starting at the medulla. Deeply embedded in the medulla and extending up toward the brain is a mass of cells known as the reticular formation or the reticular activating system. This mass of cells receives impulses from the sensory nerves and, in turn, sends out impulses to large areas of the cortex of the brain. The impulses that it sends to the higher centers have the ability to produce activity in them. Indeed, if the higher centers were to cease to be bombarded, the higher centers would fall into a sleeplike state. Effective action on the part of the higher centers requires that they receive this bombardment at an appropriate level. If they are not sufficiently bombarded, then a state of torpor results. If they are bombarded to an excessive degree, then a state of great excitement ensues. On the basis of this fact one can understand why the reticular system is also called the reticular activating system. It is sometimes referred to as a part of the arousal system. A diagram of the system is shown in Figure 20.

The extent to which the reticular system bombards the higher centers with impulses depends upon the inputs it receives from the sensory nerves. If the input is low, then the output of the reticular system is also low, and vice versa. When a person relaxes, in order to fall asleep, he begins by shutting his eyes and lying very still. As he lies there, the sense organs in his skin and muscles becomes less and less active, sending fewer and fewer impulses up the spinal cord. As the number of impulses in the main sensory tracts decrease, so too do the number of impulses going into the reticular system. This decreases the output to the higher centers, which slowly fall into a state of sleep. Some drugs also have the effect of reducing the activity level of the reticular system and

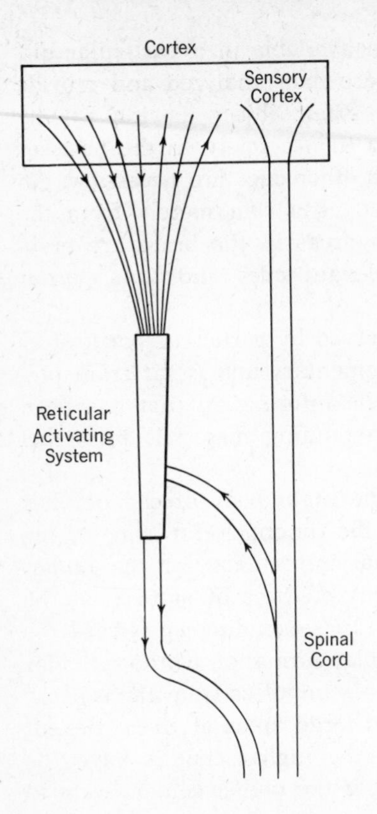

Figure 20. Diagram of some of the connections of the reticular activating system.

these also produce a state of drowsiness or sleep. A crucial factor in producing sleep is the control of the inputs to the nervous system.

Certain other features of the reticular activating system need to be noted. One is that the higher centers also send impulses down to the reticular system and have an effect of activating it. While the reticular system excites the cortex, the cortex also excites the reticular system. In addition, the system also sends impulses down the spinal cord and these also have activating functions. The effects produced by the reticular system are extensive and distributed almost over the entire central nervous system. Figure 20 shows some of the connections of the reticular activating system. The diagram also shows the inputs from the sensory tracts in the spinal cord, and the inputs to it from the higher centers.

The reticular activating system has no power, in itself, to increase wakefulness, but is dependent upon inputs of impulses for it to function as the activating system. If any of the channels through which its output of impulses is distributed is destroyed, the animal is likely to fall into a drowsy state. The system also has one other function, which is far from being fully understood at this time. It is believed to exert an influence on sensory inputs and can, at times, suppress these inputs.

The reticular activating system extends upward through the midbrain into the thalamus. The part in the thalamus is referred to as the thalamic activating system and it has rather different functions from those of the reticular activating system. The reticular system is very diffuse in its effects and activates very large areas of the cortex. In contrast, the thalamic activating system seems to activate rather more limited areas of the cortex at any one time. It probably has functions related to attention, alertness, and perhaps even to the orienting response. It also has functions in relation to the production of electrical rhythms at the level of the cortex.

An additional system that has general rather than specific functions, is the limbic system, the mass of tissue that lies beneath the cortex between the thalamus and hypothalamus on the one hand and the cortex on the other. The functions of the limbic system are varied and are still far from being thoroughly explored. The limbic system probably should not be described as a single system, and it is given a single name only because it is anatomically located in one particular location in relation to the cortex and the lower part of the brain stem.

The limbic system contains three main systems that have been intensively studied. The first system is primarily connected with and serves functions related to the sense of smell. The second system is referred to anatomically as the hippocampus. The third consists of the amygdaloid nuclei.

The hippocampus is primarily a part of the arousal system. The difference between the activating function of the reticular system and the limbic system is that the reticular system is very general in the activation it produces, but the limbic activating system seems to function on more specific parts of the cortex. There is some evidence that the hippocampus has to do with the laying down of permanent memory traces. It is not the seat of memory, but the hippocampus makes it possible for the cortex to retain permanently the information that it would otherwise retain for only a matter of minutes. There is also some possibility that proper functioning of the hippocampus may be necessary for recall.

The amygdaloid nuclei, or the amygdala as they are commonly called, have been studied by observing the effects of stimulating them electrically and by damaging them through surgery. The effect of stimulation depends on where it is applied. It may produce withdrawal or flight reactions, on the one hand, or it may produce extreme aggression on the other. Surgical damage also produces the expected corresponding effects. A particularly interesting series of studies has been undertaken over the years, in which electrodes have been placed, permanently, in the septal region of the limbic system in an anaesthetized animal. The animal can then be placed in a box in which the animal can press a bar, and when it does this, a small electric current is applied to the electrodes. This electrical stimulation of the limbic system has very strong reinforcing properties. The animal presses the lever and obtains electrical stimulation of its own brain. It will then continue to press the lever persistently and frequently. Indeed, when the animal is hungry and has a choice between pressing a lever that will deliver food and the lever that delivers stimulation to the brain, it is likely to choose stimulation to the brain. The opportunity to press the lever providing self-stimulation can be used as a reinforcement that will shape behavior in particular directions.

What this means is that direct electrical stimulation of appropriate areas of the limbic region functions in very much the same way as does positive reinforcement. Some evidence reported by Valenstein (see Riklan and Levita, 1969) suggests that stimulation over quite a wide region produces this effect and that this is also the region that has to do with the regulation of drives. That there can be a close relationship between reinforcement and drives cannot be disputed, but just what the relationship is has not yet been adequately explored.

At the level of the cortex of the brain, some areas have specific functions, while others seem to be engaged in more general memory functions. Some of the large areas that remain unmapped in Figure 19 are those primarily concerned with retention of information. Presumably, they function both to provide a short-term memory, as when a person retains a telephone number long enough to dial it, and also long-term memory. In the case of the adult, there can be considerable damage to these nonspecific areas without any loss of particular memories. This fact suggests that particular items of remembered information are not stored in particular localities, but may be stored simultaneously in different locations. Indeed, a tumor may destroy very substantial parts of the cerebral cortex without there being any corresponding loss of memories of the past. Just what kind of a structure or structures are modified when one memorizes the name of, say, a new neighbor, is not known, but it is not just the modification of a particular synapse.

The Cerebellum

A beginning has been made in achieving some understanding of the large mass of nervous tissue situated to the rear of the cerebral hemispheres known as the cerebellum. Eccles, Ito, and Szentágothai (1967) have referred to this mass of tissue as being like a computer. The theme of the book is that the cerebellum receives vast amounts of data both from the higher centers of the brain and from the muscles and skin, coordinates this information, and uses it in helping to provide a smooth flow of motor behavior. The outputs of the cerebellum are all related to motor activity and the organ brings together all the information needed to ensure that the flow of motor activity will be smooth and coordinated. The cerebellum is described by Eccles et al. as always being in a state of poise with the information at its disposal always available, so that movements can be made taking into account that information. The cerebellum does not just take in and store information related to the position and state of each limb and muscle in the body; the information is stored in an organized state for immediate use. The incoming information appears to be widely distributed through the system and, like the other major brain structures, the cerebellum does not store particular pieces of information in particular locations. The physiological function of the cerebellum is such that it does not manifest sustained neural activity of the kind associated with thought. Eccles et al. point out that within 0.03 of a second after an input, activity in the cortex of the cerebellum comes to an abrupt halt and the organ is in a state of readiness to use the input and to produce the output to the motor system.

Just how the cerebellum performs its functions is far from clear. It does not initiate action, for the initiation of a sequence of movements seems to take place in the cerebral cortex. Arbib, Franklin, and Nilsson (1968) suggest that the cerebellum could perform very much like a piece of computer equipment called a compiler, which assembles a computer program. One can tell a compiler, for example, that one wants a program to calculate a square root and the compiler will list all of the detailed operations necessary for doing this. If one's cerebral cortex were to tell the cerebellum to plan a series of movements to take one to the mail box, then a program of movements might be assembled such as those of getting up from the chair, going to the door, taking hold of the door knob, opening the door, going through the door, taking hold of the door knob, closing the door, and so forth. Then the program might run off fairly automatically, and one's thought processes would not have to intervene, unless something went wrong such as the door sticking and not opening. Arbib et al. point out that the decision to perform a series of actions and the execution of those actions appear to require rather different machinery, and probably quite independent machinery.

The Autonomic Nervous System

An important division of the nervous system is a complex of nerves and ganglia that constitutes what is known as the *autonomic,* or *sympathetic,* nervous system. Because many significant aspects of behavior are associated with the activity of this system, some consideration to its function in relation to behavior must be given here.

The most recognizable components of this system are two cordlike structures that extend through the length of the body cavity. These are known as the sympathetic trunks. Each one of these has a number of bulges along its length consisting of masses of nerve cells. From the trunks, nerves can be seen to go to the viscera. It is also known that this system has nerves connected to all the smooth muscles of the body, which are the muscles that are both slow-acting and not under voluntary control. The system also can activate certain glands, such as the adrenal glands.

The system derives its name from the fact that most of the functions it serves are not under voluntary control, and the system gives the superficial appearance of being an independent one, functioning on its own. The appearance here is deceptive, because it has been established that there are centers in the central nervous system that can induce activity in the autonomic system. The relationship to the central nervous system is highly complex.

The autonomic nervous system has built into it a complex series of reflex mechanisms. The pupil of the eye contracts automatically in the presence of bright light. Peristalsis occurs in the intestines when they are stretched by the presence of food, and by this means food is moved along the length of the tract.

The autonomic nervous system can be properly considered a part of the effector mechanism—that is, the efferent system that results in activity. That it does produce action is beyond question, but the action it produces is highly generalized and is not confined to specific muscles, as it is when an efferent nerve from the spinal cord is involved.

The autonomic nervous system also shows the effects of learning, and many visceral and other responses are acquired through a learning process that has not been clearly described as yet. The person who develops severe migraine headaches whenever he is placed in a stressful situation is manifesting an acquired response of the autonomic nervous system. The headaches are due to the activity of the small smooth muscles found in the walls of the blood vessels that supply the brain. A person's digestive system may not function properly in many situations that have been associated with stress. The blushing mechanism, in the case of a particular individual, may be triggered by numerous stimuli that do not ordinarily set it into action. Some of these learnings are relatively harmless, but others could conceivably have serious consequences and proceed to the point where the health of a person is damaged. Psychosomatic medicine is that branch of medicine that attempts to help people whose natural reflexes of the autonomic nervous system have been modified so that they are fired by inappropriate stimuli. One is tempted to suggest that the mechanism of classical conditioning might well account for disturbances of behavior occurring through the activity of the autonomic nervous system, but convincing evidence will have to be presented to prove that this is so. What can be demonstrated at the present time is that some of the reflexes associated with the autonomic nervous system can be conditioned, but there is a long step from such a demonstration to the position that psychosomatic disorders are a result of a process similar to classical conditioning.

The Location of Learning

A basic problem related to the structure of the nervous system is the matter of where learning is located in terms of gross structures. The point has already been made that the synapse is commonly suggested to be the structure in which learning is located, although this has not been definitely established. There are synapses, in billions, throughout the nervous system, so even if one were to accept the synapse as the seat of learning, this would not enable one to locate the gross structures involved mainly in learning. In addition, many synapses are involved in functions other than learning, such as the temporary holding of information, the blocking or facilitation of the transmittal of information to higher centers, the redistribution of information, and so forth.

It is quite obvious that learning is highly dependent upon the functioning of the cerebral cortex and animals that have had the cortex removed through surgery lose their capability to learn most of the complex skills they need to be capable of learning. Studies of patients who have suffered damage to various parts of the cerebral cortex show that no particular part can be associated with learning. A parallel finding is that, in the adult, damage to a specific area does not result in the loss of the memory for a particular piece of information. Siegel (1970) points out that the site of learning is even more elusive than this statement makes it out to be, for the complete surgical removal of the cortex does not eliminate completely the capacity to learn. At least in subhuman primates, and almost certainly in man, learning can take place at the midbrain level, but here again the site of learning is elusive and different areas can be destroyed without the complete loss of learning. Because learning through midbrain functioning, in the absence of the cerebral cortex, has been quite well demonstrated at this time, one is left wondering whether learning can also take place at an even lower level, say at the level of the spinal cord. The latter has turned out to be a much more difficult problem to study than has the matter of learning at the midbrain level, despite the fact that the microanatomy of the spinal cord is much better understood than is that of the higher centers. The typical procedure involved in attempting to demonstrate learning at the spinal cord level is to work with an animal in whom the spinal cord has been severed. In such an animal a reflexive contraction of a hind limb can be produced by applying a strong electric shock to the foot. An attempt can then be made to condition this response to a stimulus provided to the other foot. The evidence suggests that conditioning does take place, under these circumstances, but nobody can as yet be quite sure that it does because alternative explanations, other than conditioning, can be called upon to account for the experimental results. A best guess at this time would probably be that learning functions are very widely distributed throughout the nervous system and cannot be assumed to be the functions of only the higher centers.

Much the same controversy exists about the location of information-analysis functions. Although some areas of the cortex have been identified as specializing in the analysis of information, other areas also have information-analysis functions in addition to other functions. The cerebellum, for example, is a very complex information analysis and collating system. Some evidence suggests that the midbrain has such functions, some of which are coupled with regulatory functions related to basic body processes. There is also the possibility that even some of the masses of nerve cells that lie outside the central nervous system may be involved in information analysis.

The picture of the nervous system presented here indicates that information analysis and storage are quite different functions, dependent on different brain structures. What needs to be settled is the extent to which information from the sense organs is analyzed at successive levels of detail at the different levels of the nervous system or whether all information analysis occurs in the cortex of the brain. The very large amount of the brain that deals with the handling of the incoming information gives support to the view that learning is, to a great extent, a matter of learning to handle and utilize the incoming information. The view of learning as involving nothing more than the strengthening of a response is probably a vast oversimplification of what is known about learning, and what is known about the nervous structures on which learning depends.

An additional point that emerges from the study of the nervous system is that an extraordinarily large amount of tissue is involved in what are called the activating systems. Learning is highly dependent on the extent to which these systems are, or are not, maintaining an appropriate level of activity in the higher centers. The data also suggest that the level of arousal can be externally controlled, because the inputs to the reticular activating system from the sensory systems are important for initiating activity in the arousal system. However, an excessive level of activity produced by the arousal system may interfere with learning.

A final very important discovery is that information is not stored in single localities. The advantages of multiple storage are many. One advantage is the physiological one, for multiple storage means that slight damage to one part of the brain does not involve the immediate loss of what might be quite crucial items of information. In terms of behavior, the storage of information in multiple localities might permit that information to be related more easily to many other different items of information. As the neurophysiologist discovers how information is stored in the central nervous system, useful suggestions will be provided concerning how man organizes the information he derives from his senses.

Holding Mechanisms and Short-Term Memory

A complete account of the nervous system will have to explain the fact that while some information is stored permanently, other information is stored for only a short time. Indeed, most of the information that is acquired through the senses in the daily routines of life is stored only briefly. As one goes down the street and notes a puddle of water, one retains the information just long enough to avoid the puddle. One does not retain the experience for the rest of one's life. If one did, then the brain would become cluttered with useless trivia. The problem of envisioning a nervous mechanism that will hold information for a matter of a few minutes and then erase the information is not entirely easy. Inputs of nervous impulses from the sense organs are quite transitory bursts of activity and cannot maintain their own activity. An impulse continues until it reaches a synapse, and there it either dies or arouses enough chemical activity to start a new impulse in another nerve cell. Hebb (1966) has a suggestion of how one can retain a piece of information only long enough to use it. In the case of the puddle down the street that we see, recognize, and continue to remember, until we get past it, the suggestion is that the puddle arouses activity in loops of cells that have to do with memories of puddles. Two such loops of cells are shown in Figure 21. An impulse starting in one of the loops might travel around it, but, by the time it came back to the starting point, the synapse might not yet have recovered, so this time the impulse passes around the second loop. An impulse could continue to pass around such loops and provide the continued memory of the puddle to be kept in mind, until the person passed the puddle. In order to stop the impulses from traveling in circles indefinitely, one also has to propose that one or more inhibitory impulses can arrive on the scene to block the continued activity of the impulse. Nobody has seen a set of loops of this kind, but one can demonstrate that once an impulse has been started in certain parts of the cerebral cortex the resulting activity may continue for an hour or more.

What one can say about short-term holding mechanisms is highly

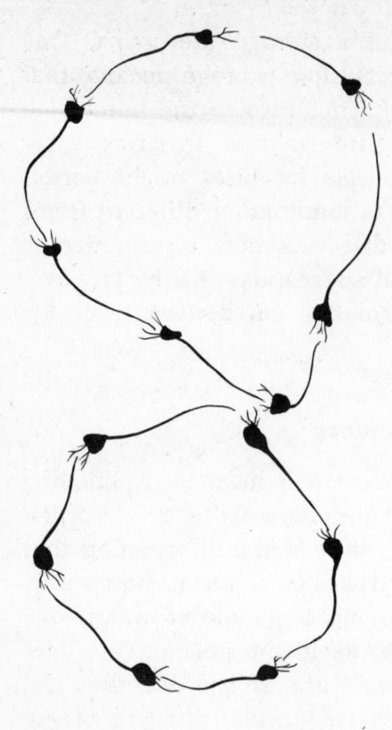

Figure 21. Schematic diagram of a part of a cell assembly that may permit continued activity within the nervous system after the stimulus initiating activity has ceased to operate.

speculative, for nobody has been able to demonstrate that the kind of holding mechanism proposed by Hebb actually exists. Even if it does exist, the possibility of demonstrating it is slim. Within the brain there is almost no possibility of dissecting out particular loops of cells, for each cell may, by itself, be an enormously complicated structure and have hundreds of synapses relating it to other cells.

Brain Damage and Learning

Of great significance to the educator are the effects of brain damage on learning. Although half a century ago little recognition was given to the fact that children might suffer brain damage, the evidence is now overwhelming that a large number of children start life with some damage to the nervous system through events that happen at birth. In the early part of the present century, the lack of recognition of the effect of brain damage on development was due to the fact that the assumption was made that brain damage had to be caused either by the penetration of a sharp object or through severe impact. Neurologists have now come to recognize that a much more frequent form of brain damage results from the brain being deprived of oxygen at birth. Indeed, the evidence indicates that pressure on the brain at birth has very slight effects compared with the very damaging effects that may occur when the baby is deprived of oxygen through the umbilical cord's becoming entangled or compressed. Damage due to lack of oxygen may have devastating effects on brain tissues and produce both widespread and permanent damage.

Children who have severe brain damage are identified at a quite early age and are much more likely to have their problems appropriately managed than those who have much less damage and whose difficulties are not recognized until a teacher reports learning difficulties. A relatively common severe outcome of brain damage is cerebral palsy. The victim of such a complaint is typically characterized by difficulties in controlling the muscles of the body. The complaint may be so severe that the child is unable to walk, feed himself, or speak, but it may also be so slight that it is evident only in some slight speech impairment. Sometimes the damage is not confined to the strictly motor components of behavior, and there may also be losses in sensory functions and in thinking abilities. However, the child with cerebral palsy is recognized today to be much better off intellectually than he was previously thought to be. A child who is unable to use his muscles to express himself, through movement or speech, has difficulty in demonstrating his capacity for thought and understanding. Such children may have intellectually high potential, although they are not able to show it until they have been given special training and means are found to assist them in controlling their movements. Although it was believed at one time that most cerebral palsy cases were beyond help, today a very large percentage of them are rehabilitated to the point where they can profit from education and become to some degree self-supporting. A part of the problem of the rehabilitation of those afflicted with cerebral palsy is the bad attitude of the public toward them. Such cases are often quite unprepossessing in appearance and the public often does not understand that one cannot judge a person from his appearance.

Another dramatic form of behavior that *may* find its origins in brain injury is broadly described as the epileptic seizure. The epileptic seizure shows a quite typical pattern of electrical activity in the brain, which can be recorded through an electroencephalograph. The record during a seizure shows a disruption of the typical electrical rhythms and very large electrical pulsations produced by many cells firing together synchronously.

Of much greater significance to the teacher are the relatively large number of cases that fall into the category of minimal brain dysfunction. The U.S. Office of Education reports on *Minimal Brain Dysfunction in Children* (1966, 1969) accept as a definition of such children (p. 53, 1969) those

> *of near average, average, or above average general intelligence with certain learning and/or behavioral disabilities ranging from mild to*

severe, which are associated with deviations of function of the central nervous system. These deviations may manifest themselves by various combinations of impairment in perception, conceptualization, language, memory, and control of attention, impulse, or motor function. These aberrations may arise from genetic variations, biochemical irregularities, perinatal brain insults or injuries sustained during the years which are critical for the development and maturation of the central nervous system, or from other unknown organic causes.

The definition is global and comprehensive and takes in such a wide range of cases that it does little more than alert the teacher to the fact that some children, most of whose behavior falls within the normal range, may still suffer from specific learning disabilities that are quite damaging to educational progress. For example, a child may have difficulties in the area of visual perception that make it very difficult for him to learn to read. Many of these dysfunctions may be subtle and not very evident to the teacher who has only limited contact with each child. A common characteristic of many children with minimal brain dysfunction is hyperactivity. This hyperactivity is not the typical busy goal-directed activity of the normal child, but an unorganized activity characterized by an inability to stay with a task until completed and a high degree of distractibility. Such children are potentially effective learners, but the unorganized hyperactivity makes it difficult for them under ordinary classroom circumstances to stay long enough with any task to permit learning. The hyperactivity is also often accompanied by visual perceptual difficulties manifested in an inability to copy quite simple forms. Many such cases are believed to be a result of damage due to lack of oxygen at birth.

The problems of the hyperactive child have been handled in two ways. One way is to place him in an environment in which there are minimal sources of stimulation. A classroom thus designed for the hyperactive child might have a table and chair for one child, no windows, the walls a uniform neutral tone, and no equipment and materials except those with which the pupil is working. Under such circumstances, the activity of the child is greatly reduced and the conditions may favor learning. An alternative approach is to attempt to control the surplus activity by means of drugs, many of which have been used for this purpose, including phenobarbitol, reserpine, and chlorpromazine. Such agents reduce anxiety, aggressiveness, and concomitant hyperactivity, and are known as tranquilizers. They do help to produce pupils who are much less troublesome to the teacher. Whether the learning is improved through the use of such drugs is an unresolved question. Much probably depends upon the dose required. There is some evidence to show that quite large doses of these drugs have a depressing effect on learning in animals. Through the use of such drugs, there is real danger of producing a classroom that is congenial to teachers but not particularly conducive to learning. The use of such drugs appears to have preceded the development of adequate knowledge concerning their usefulness in facilitating learning. Also, much needs to be learned concerning the long-term effect of the use of these drugs on the pattern of intellectual development. The mere fact that reserpine can be used for long periods of time with adults without harmful effects does not mean that the same applies to a young, developing child.

The main bases for differentiating normal children from those with minimal brain dysfunction are the results of psychological tests, which in themselves are far from being as valid as one might wish them to be. Thorough neurological examinations are also sometimes conducted, but the most developed neurological diagnostic techniques are focused on the lower centers of the nervous system, and those directed at the higher centers are still crude and primitive. One may hope that, ultimately, the neurologist may develop diagnostic devices that will permit the very early identification of children who have minimal brain dysfunction so that steps can be taken at an early age to correct or rehabilitate each child.

Summary

1. The nervous system consists of cells with specialized functions that transmit information into the central system and action-producing impulses to the muscles and glands. The sensitive cells in the sense organs represent nerve cells that have special functions. Nerve cells do not connect directly to other nerve cells, but are separated by gaps known as synapses. Impulses can be transmitted across the synapses through chemical changes.
2. The evidence points in the general direction of suggesting that information is stored at the synapses which function as a set of on-off switches. Storage at the synapses probably takes place through chemical changes that may well be highly stable once they have taken place.
3. That part of the nervous system that transmits information into it is called the afferent system, in contrast to the efferent system, which conducts impulses from the centers that initiate action to the muscles and glands that produce action. Afferent nerves enter the spinal cords at various locations along its length and efferent nerves leave through nearby locations. The spinal cord

represents a complex transmission system between the brain and the periphery and also provides some coordination of activity at very simple levels.

4. The structures that form what is commonly known as the brain are, in origin, enlargements of the upper regions of the spinal cord. In the mature nervous system the spinal cord shows some thickening as it approaches the brain. This thickening is known as the medulla. The upper part of the brain stem is also covered by the pons, a broad band of fibers that connects the two cerebral hemispheres. The largest structures in the entire system are the cerebral hemispheres, which include those structures having to do with the most detailed analysis of information, the storage of information, higher functions such as decision making, and the initiation of much action.
5. Although physiologists originally hoped that some precise function could be found for each location in the nervous system, the conception of nervous system function that this implied turned out to have only limited validity. Although some parts do have quite specific functions, much of the system involves what are called nonspecific functions. However, it is somewhat difficult to separate what is meant by a specific function from what is meant by a nonspecific function. For example, a part of the nervous system has to do with drives and the initiation of behavior through the operation of basic drives. This part is commonly said to have nonspecific functions, in that drives have a general effect on behavior. In a sense, though, this is quite a specific function and much more specific than the function of much of the cortex of the brain.
6. Brain function can be explored through a number of techniques, including those of studying the effects of lesions and mechanical injury to the brain, the effect of stimulating particular parts of the brain either through electrode implants or through the direct stimulation of the exposed brain, or through tracing chemical substances involved in particular kinds of neural activity.
7. The cerebellum receives information from all the sensory mechanisms involved in keeping the organism right side up to the world and also controls the righting reflexes that maintain posture. The thalamus is mainly noted as a relay station and some information analysis may take place at that level. The thalamus may also be involved in awareness of pain. The hypothalamus has functions closely related to the regulation of behavior related to such basic drives as hunger, thirst, temperature regulation, and sex. The control of these functions is complex and each drive state appears to involve several different

centers. The cortex of the brain shows some specialization of function. Some areas are concerned with the analysis of information coming from the senses. A large central area has to do with the initiation of movements, and an area on the left side has to do with the control of speech.

8. A major nonspecific function is focused on the reticular activating system in the medulla. Sensory inputs activate this body, which in turn activates widely distributed areas of the cortex. There is also a descending effect, for the cortex, in turn, sends impulses down to the activating mechanism and can increase activity in the reticular system. The extent to which a person is in a state of wakefulness or sleep depends in some degree on the state of the reticular activating mechanism. The limbic system, higher up in the nervous system, also has functions related to arousal and wakefulness. In addition, the limbic system has functions related to experiencing pleasure and its opposite. The limbic system also seems to have functions related to the laying down of permanent memory traces in the cortex of the brain. The phenomenon known as self-stimulation has also been shown to occur when electrodes are placed within the amygdaloid nuclei and the animal has the opportunity of pressing a bar that will deliver a small electric current to the electrodes. The animal is likely to engage in pressing the bar under these conditions. Much of the cortex of the cerebral hemispheres has nonspecific functions. Although the cortex must be considered to be the primary seat of memory, particular pieces of information do not seem to be stored in particular places. Damage in a particular location does not generally eradicate a particular memory.
9. The nervous system obviously includes mechanisms that make it possible to hold information from the senses for short periods of time. In addition, the nervous system has mechanisms for inhibiting various responses as well as for facilitating behavior.
10. A complex network of nerves scattered through the body constitutes the autonomic nervous system. The functions it serves are not under direct voluntary control. The functions of the autonomic nervous system are closely related to behavior under stress conditions.
11. The site of learning within the nervous system is highly elusive. Some evidence suggests that learning may take place at perhaps even all levels. Beyond any question, information analysis takes place in many different localities, from the sense-organ level to the highest levels of the entire system. Although most physiologists believe that the synapse is the place where information

is stored, critical experiments to support or reject this view have not yet been designed. A few physiologists have proposed that it is the glial cells that store information through some complex chemical process.

12. The effect of brain injury on behavior is of considerable interest to the teacher, in view of the fact that there are many children who show minimal brain dysfunction. Often these children not only present learning difficulties but are quite disruptive to the learning of others through their hyperactivity. Although the latter form of behavior can be controlled by drugs, the long-term results of such treatment are not known. Such children often also suffer from perceptual difficulties, which interfere with learning and particularly with the acquisition of reading skill.

PART FOUR

LABORATORY RESEARCH AND TEACHING

CHAPTER THIRTEEN

Some Points of Impact of the Laboratory on Teaching

EARLY IN THE BOOK THE POINT WAS MADE THAT A SCIENCE OF LEARNING influences education by providing broad principles in terms of which educational programs can be planned and built. This influence of behavioral science on education parallels the influence of physics on engineering. The engineer was first provided with a scientific guide to his work when Isaac Newton first published his famous *Principia,* outlining the principles on which all modern engineering practice is founded. Education today is being influenced by important bodies of knowledge derived from the behavioral sciences, much as engineering was influenced by the development of physics. If one views the field of education as a whole, and attempts to discern the influences that have been and are being exerted by the behavioral sciences, one cannot help being impressed with the impact that significant bodies of knowledge are having upon practice.

Two main bodies of knowledge and sources of influence are evident. The one body of knowledge stems from the approach to the psychology of learning typically taken by American psychologists, which is typically behavioristic. The other body of knowledge is more European in origin and emphasizes that man is characterized by behavior showing exploration, the extraction of information from the environment, the organizing of information, and the development of cognitive structures. Of course, psychologists from both continents have contributed to each of these conceptions of man, and research has been conducted on both continents within each of these frameworks.

In this chapter a brief review will be presented of a sample of the impacts that each one of these bodies of knowledge has had on educational practice. Such impact has been substantial. This review will omit the minor impact that pieces of isolated research, designed to solve particular educational problems, may have had, for the author believes that the major impact does not lie in such isolated contributions to knowledge. The two major aspects of the educational enterprise where impact will be briefly discussed will be those of the design of materials and the role of the teacher.

The Design of Materials

Perhaps the research studies that have had most impact on the materials to be included in curricula are the studies on transfer of training undertaken at the turn of the century. These studies showed that no special virtue could be ascribed to materials because they were difficult or because they taxed the mind. The studies demonstrated that no particular subject-matter field had special powers to train the mind, as the nineteenth-century educators had believed, and that each piece of subject matter should be included only because it had some worth of its own. The early studies of transfer undertaken by psychologists produced a revolution in curriculum design, and modern curricula show the impact of this revolution.

The sweeping effect on curriculum design produced by research on the transfer of training is unmatched in impact by other psychological research on learning. The design of books and reading materials would probably come second as an area in which research had influenced practice.

The first real source of impact of psychological research on the design of reading materials came through the basic research of E. L. Thorndike, which led him to recognize the importance of word difficulty on the ease with which material could be read. By the early twenties, Thorndike had determined the frequency with which each of a very large sample of words appears in print and had used this to provide a measure of difficulty of each word. Armed with this information, Thorndike went on to modify classic works commonly given to children to read so that the vocabulary of these works would be within the grasp of the children. Ten years later his student, A. I. Gates, began to design readers for the lower grades. These readers involved a very carefully planned vocabulary, each word of which occurred a sufficient number of times in the readers so that the pupil could learn to master it. Since that time, the science and art of designing reading materials has grown. A very early development resulted from the observation that vocabulary difficulty alone was not the only factor that made reading material difficult or easy. Sentence structure had to be taken into account. In order to do this, many formulae were developed that permitted the curriculum developer to measure the reading level of material by compounding such factors as vocabulary difficulty, sentence length, and the number of prepositional phrases (see Klare, 1963). The success of these devices is attested by the fact that today a book is not likely to be published for use in schools unless it has first been thoroughly tested for readability by the application of one of the available formulae for doing this. One may note that parallel research on listenability has also been in progress, but it has had much less impact in view of the fact that printed materials are still more widely used than recorded materials.

The development of word counts and means of determining the words most commonly used had another important impact on education. The data thus provided made it possible to develop dictionaries for elementary schools and junior high schools. Such dictionaries had virtually not existed previously, but word counts made it possible to select systematically the words that should be included in them. This and other applications of word counts, in turn, raised scientific questions concerning the weakness of word counts for such purposes. Some research workers began to argue that the frequency with which a word appears in print is not necessarily a good measure of how easy or difficult a word is for a child to understand. This led to other methods of determining word difficulty, which involved asking children the meaning of words and finding out the percentage of children of each age who understood the meaning of each word.

Many other lines of academic research have also had impact on the development of materials. Studies of sensory and cultural deprivation have provided insight into the learning problems faced by the underprivileged and have suggested the kinds of materials needed to remedy deficits. Studies of perception have made contributions to the design of audiovisual materials. Research on both perception and motor-skill learning has made contributions to the techniques adopted in the materials and procedures used in the teaching of typing. A long list of other examples could also be added to those mentioned. Even before midcentury, research on learning was having a real effect on the design of materials for schools.

A new source of influence began to appear at midcentury through the interest shown by B. F. Skinner in the improvement of education. The second chapter of this book was concerned largely with learning that can be described in terms of the operant conditioning model, and B. F. Skinner thought that he saw in such work a foundation for an entirely new approach to education. Some of the applications of such work to classroom situations has already been reviewed, but its application to problems of material design still has to be considered. Skinner was impressed with the fact that, in shaping the behavior of an animal to perform a complex act, a crucial aspect of the planning was to lay out a step-by-step plan for achieving the goal. He believed that a parallel procedure should be adopted in the teaching of subject matter or academic skills. First the skill to be learned should be specified in as precise a manner as possible. Then the steps for achieving the goal should be described in terms as exact as possible. Because the steps involved in teaching an animal a skill are always small steps, Skinner assumed that small steps should also be used in teaching children. At least it looked that way. Skinner also believed his data on subhuman subjects showed that learning took place efficiently only when the learner performed the component acts himself and was reinforced as immediately as possible for correct performance. The task of the instructor was to arrange for conditions of step-by-step learning and to see that appropriate reinforcements were provided. By the adoption of these procedures, Skinner hoped that children would learn several times more rapidly than by conventional methods. It is now quite obvious that some of Skinner's assumptions were quite questionable and that this limited the validity of his proposed applications.

The main application to education of the concepts derived from operant conditioning was in the field of the design of printed materials, and it involved the development of the programmed textbook. Skinner believed that a crucial problem in the design of printed materials was the ordering of subject matter and the teaching programs that evolved had many of the characteristics of medieval catechisms, which were also built by scholars concerned with problems of ordering subject matter. Skinner originally had the notion that effective teaching could be best carried out by mechanical devices, an idea originally proposed by Sidney Pressey, because these permitted the control of learning in the classroom, and particularly the control of reinforcement, in much the same way that the learning of animals could be controlled by mechanical devices in the laboratory. Such devices offered promise of providing the immediate reinforcement shown to be so important in animal studies. Later the same kinds of materials that were used in the learning programs run through the machines were adapted to book form. In this form there was some sacrifice of immediate reinforcement but a gain in convenience and in the cheapness of the materials involved. The materials still preserved the format of providing the pupil with a small amount of information, then requiring him to make a response utilizing the information, and finally giving him information about the correctness of his response.

Numerous refinements and variations of this plan were developed. For example, some programmed textbooks provide branching programs in which a pupil who encounters a difficulty in one class of problem can be given additional practice with that class of problem before returning to the main track of the program. Also, the quantity of information provided at a time, or as program writers say, in each frame, is also varied from a very small quantity to a very large chunk.

The concept of programmed learning and programmed textbooks has had considerable impact in drawing the attention of curriculum builders to the matter of defining precisely what they want to teach, but the effect on actual classroom practice in public schools has been quite minimal. Glaser (1965) has brought together material showing, quite clearly, that such materials do teach, whether they are presented by machine or in textbook form, but educators have wanted to know whether they teach more or less effectively than traditional methods. Studies of programmed learning have been undertaken in many different subject-matter fields.

As an illustration of this kind of research, let us consider some of the studies summarized by Zoll (1969) that have been undertaken in the field of mathematics teaching. Zoll located thirteen studies comparing programmed learning with conventional teaching methods in mathematical areas. Of these studies, three showed the programmed methods to be superior, three showed the traditional methods to be superior, and seven showed no statistically significant difference between the methods. Just what these thirteen studies show, if they show anything at all, is hard to specify. Perhaps they suggest that there are good programs as well as poor programs, just as there is effective conventional teaching and ineffective conventional teaching. The outcome of a particular study probably depends upon how these circumstances of good and poor programs and good and poor teachers happen to be combined. What one needs to know is the particular characteristics of programmed materials that make them effective and the characteristics that make them ineffective. For example, the present writer's impression of programmed texts is that they have been produced largely by the humorless and dry authors. For some strange reason, those who write such texts seem to be devoid of any literary talent whatsoever, perhaps because literary talent is not included as a condition of learning in the theory on which they are based. If such materials could be produced by individuals who have real skill in presenting material in an interesting way, there might be a payoff in terms of pupil learning! Of course, the format of the programmed text may be one that does not attract persons of fine writing talent and may even repulse them. The literary style of those who write programmed texts today is deplorably like that of the writers of catechisms of the Middle Ages, and both represent a very similar form of instruction.

Programmed learning, and the ideas related to it, led those connected with education to explore the role that the computer might play in teaching, in that the computer offered possibilities of providing a super teaching machine. Such exploration was also spurred on by the false notion that because the computer could provide very rapid reinforcement for correct responses, it surely should be an effective teaching device. Work on computer-assisted instruction was also spurred on by the hopes of manufacturing companies that such devices would provide a new market for a lagging electronics industry. Already by 1968, long before the potential and limitations of computer-assisted instruction had been properly explored, one of the largest corporations in America was claiming through the voice of its president that the corporation's computer system provided more effective instruction than any other method of teaching. If the approach to instruction had been regarded as experimental, much more might have been accomplished in the first decade of its existence, but commercial pressures have often played a much greater role in its use than has a genuine scientific interest in what it can accomplish.

Early results, involving the use of the computer as a teaching device, have not provided particularly promising results, but the early results of any new approach to teaching can hardly be expected to generate a basis for radical reforms, for the difficulties involving the use of the technique have not yet been worked out. For example, Suppes, Jerman, and Bryan (1968) conducted a study involving an attempt to teach elementary-school children mathematics through computer-assisted instruction. The results show slightly better learning on some of the measures for the computer-instructed children. The differences are small and are typical of most findings involving research on new teaching techniques. Whatever happens to be designated as the new technique tends to show up slightly better than what is designated as the old or traditional technique. The reasons for this are fairly obvious. Children and adults engaged in what they believe to be new are generally better energized than those who are engaged in what they believe to be routine. Perhaps the Suppes, et al. study shows only that pupils can learn through computer-assisted instruction, a matter that hardly needed to be demonstrated. It does not provide the kind of knowledge needed for the development of the area, namely, knowledge concerning the aspects of the process that are particularly useful and those aspects that could as well be omitted. In evaluating any experimental results, another fact also has to be taken into account, namely, that computer-assisted instruction is very much more expensive than conventional methods and, although a decline in cost can be expected, there is doubt whether it will, for a long time to come, provide instruction at a cost comparable to that of the teacher.

Despite what has been said here, the computer cannot be written off as an instructional device this early in its development. Some of the applications involving problem-solving training offer particularly interesting possibilities in both technical education and higher education. For example, the University of Illinois College of Medicine has developed a whole series of problems for doctors-in-training that can be presented through a computer. The student sits at a console involving a televisionlike screen and typewriterlike keyboard. The problem appears on the screen, informing him that a patient has been brought into an emergency ward with a particular set of symptoms. The student has to decide which of several options is the appropriate course of action with respect to the patient. He might have the options of, say, taking a history of the patient, hospitalizing him, or treating his symptoms directly and giving him supportive therapy. The student types his answer into the computer. In the particular case, it might be that if the student chose to take a history of the patient, the computer might tell him, "Your patient has died while you were taking his case history." The same answer might also be given if the student decided to have the patient admitted to the hospital. If he chose to give supportive therapy, then, in the particular case, the computer might tell the student, "The patient has begun to rally, his blood pressure is now such and such. What do you do now?" The student at that point has another set of choices, such as preparing the patient for surgery, admitting him to the hospital for observation, conducting various laboratory tests, and so forth. If the student manages to make the right decision at each choice point, then he is able to bring the patient through to the point where he can be discharged with a prognosis.

Such problems can be easily set up on computers. In the past, the student has had to provide his answers in some kind of code. Thus, if the student types the numeral 1, then this means that he would take a case history, the numeral 2 means that he would admit the patient to the hospital, and so forth. Newer computers will not require such coding but will be able to accept ordinary language, and this will open up new possibilities of using the devices for instructional purposes. However, before the reader lets his imagination become overenthusiastic about the use of computers for providing problem-solving experience, note should be made of the fact that there are easier ways of performing exactly the same teaching without any electronic equipment at all. One alternative is to have the various answers listed, and opposite each answer is a blank space. Suppose the student reads the problem and chooses answer 2. He indicates his choice by marking the blank space opposite the answer with a pen that uses a water-like ink. As soon as he does this, invisible print on the paper immediately becomes activated and he reads the result of his decision, "The patient dies." If he had chosen the third answer, and taken appropriate action, the answer might have read, "The patient rallies. Now turn to the next problem and give your answer concerning the steps to take." The marker pen thus does in a very simple manner what the computer did in the previous example, and at considerably less expense.

A particularly significant aspect of the computer has been not so much in its direct applications to classroom teaching, but in the potential it provides for research on teaching. The investigation of classroom phenomena has long been hampered by the fact that the experimenter can generally exercise only the most limited control over teacher behavior. The experimental design may require that one group of teachers is to present pattern-of-behavior X in the classroom and that another group is to present pattern Y, but it is likely to happen that many teachers in each group will present the pattern of behavior of the opposite group. Merely telling the teachers how to behave does not produce the desired behavior, even though the teachers are as cooperative as can be and make a genuine effort to behave in the way called for. Experiments on classroom teaching, because of the difficulty of controlling teacher behavior, tend to provide data of very limited value.

Now this is where the computer, as a teacher, has unique advantages. The computer can be programmed to perform certain instructional acts and no others. It will follow directions, without question, and without the variability that all human behavior ordinarily shows. It will not have good days and bad days. It will follow a routine tirelessly and never lose patience with the student. It will avoid irrelevant discussion, except insofar as it is programmed to pursue dialogue with the learner on side issues. It is never forgetful and can be counted on to provide the information it is supposed to provide and on the appropriate occasions that the experimenter has specified. Nevertheless, the computer is not quite the paragon of perfection in the classroom that the experimenter might wish to have. The computer is limited in the dialogue it can hold with the student and is extremely restricted in the language in terms of which the dialogue can be held. Pupils are well conditioned to give verbal responses to other people, but may feel awkward about holding a conversation with an electronic device. Pupils who have spent their lives in learning in a social medium may have difficulty in adjusting to learning in a situation devoid of interpersonal interactions.

The impact of the thinking underlying operant conditioning has been largely a rethinking of the whole problem of the ordering of subject matter, but other kinds of psychological research are now having an impact on the curriculum. All preschool curricula developed during the last decade, and some curricula at higher levels, have been influenced by research originally initiated and later developed by Jean Piaget in Geneva and now being extended on a wide front in America. Of particular significance for curriculum development have been the detailed descriptions of the tasks that can be undertaken by children at particular levels of development. The ability to perform many of these tasks appears to be clearly a prerequisite for the performance of some of the operations that the child subsequently learns to perform. Thus learning related to categorizing tasks, in which a child learns to classify objects in different ways, seems to be a step toward the learning of conservation concepts. The significance of categorizing and classifying tasks, within Piaget's concept of intellectual development, is such that these tasks have now been introduced into all modern educational programs for the preschool child. At the level of concrete operations, which corresponds roughly to the level of the elementary-school child, Piaget has provided a very extensive list of the intellectual operations that the child can be expected to perform, and such a list has had considerable influence on some experimental attempts to develop new curricula. Of course, many of the operations that Piaget includes in his list for this stage have long been included in the elementary-school curriculum. Division and subtraction are two of these operations. The impact of Piaget's thinking and experimental findings is also evident at higher levels in the design of science curricula. The incorporation of the concepts of Piaget into the design of curricula represents significant educational innovation based on psychological research. Much still needs to be learned about the extent to which such ideas provide a sound foundation for curriculum planning, but the ideas are at least derived from the study of children. There are fewer hazards in generalizing from such data than there are in generalizing from research based on subhuman animals.

These few pages on the impact of psychological research on the design of teaching materials have been presented to indicate that the research of the laboratory scientist is immensely influential in the educational sphere. Those who say that research on learning is an enterprise far removed from the real world of education and with little influence on it simply do not know their educational history. One would have a hard time in locating any curricula materials printed in America that did not show the marks left upon them by laboratory research.

Teacher Behavior

Psychological research has probably had far more impact on educational materials than on the way in which teachers behave. Indeed, some models of instruction that find their base in operant conditioning and behavior modification have virtually taken the position that the materials for instruction have to be so fully and thoroughly developed that the teacher will have little to do except hand them out to the students. Many articles have appeared developing such a theme and one even carries the title, "Bye, bye, teacher." Such a view of teaching imagines the classroom as a well-ordered place in which material to be learned is handed out in convenient small packages, complete with directions, so that the pupil merely has to open up the materials and proceed with them. The assumptions underlying such an educational philosophy are that we know exactly what the pupils should learn, that learning occurs through well-designed materials, and that the teacher has little to contribute to the learning process apart from his managerial skills. This general viewpoint has contributed to education by exploring the development of packaged materials that can be used in such a program. Indeed, most so-called *development projects* in education are engaged in the production of packaged materials.

The program of Individually Prescribed Instruction at the Oakleaf School, near Pittsburgh, provides an example in which the use of packaged materials is used as the very core of the educational program. The package, in that program, is generally the single worksheet through which the pupil undertakes a unit of work appropriate to his particular level. All the pupils in the same grade may be working on different sheets at any given time—a fact that reflects the magnitude of the problem of keeping track of what pupils have accomplished to date and what they are trying to accomplish with the sheets on which they are occupied. Teacher aids check the work of the pupils, while the teachers help those that encounter particular difficulties. The program is individualized in that each pupil works at his own rate to achieve particular objectives, but it is not individualized in that all pupils are expected to achieve the same series of objectives in sequence. Thus the program is individualized with respect to rate of achievement, but not with respect to the goals to be achieved. If all pupils stayed in the school long enough to master the entire program provided, then the pupils emerging would be very uniform in what they can do. Whether such uniformity of educational products is desirable is a matter for debate that cannot be engaged in here.

In such a program, the problems faced by the teacher in keeping track of the pupils and their accomplishments is considerable. The problem becomes even more acute in the few schools that also individualize objectives to some extent and have a system of study booths rather than classrooms. For all such programs, the traditional record-keeping system involving the grade book and the cumulative pupil record, consisting of a single card in a file drawer, does not provide the records necessary for the guidance of learning. New methods are slowly emerging for this purpose, focused on the computer. The system emerging appears to require that the teacher have, in the classroom, a computer terminal, through which the teacher can enter requests for information about pupils he identifies, and which provides a screen or teletype on which the information can be read out. Most people have seen such a device at air terminals, where the clerk can request the computer to give information about a passenger's reservation and the complete details will be printed out on a surface that looks like a television screen. In the case of such a computer terminal in a classroom, the teacher would have to provide the computer with information about each pupil's accomplishment, and could obtain back, at any time, the complete record for any pupil. Insofar as the acquisition of knowledge by the pupil can be represented by a single track along which the pupil can progress, the information outputs may not be too complicated. For example, the computer could inform the teacher that pupil number 23 had mastered all units up to Unit 167 of the sequence of 287 units involved in the entire program. However, the fact is that no subject-matter field can be represented by a sequence of units that have to be mastered in order. Also, if different pupils are working toward different objectives, then the data that the computer has to store may become very complicated indeed.

The operant conditioning model of learning, with its ideal of step-by-step planning, requires that the teacher be able to keep track of what the learner is mastering. The teacher makes decisions based on data, and the computer can provide the data. Whether the teacher will use the data effectively remains to be seen. Business enterprises have long sought to provide their executives with direct access to computer data so that decisions can be better undertaken, but studies of such systems have shown that the executive has a way of disregarding the data provided. In the case of the pupil, working through a linear set of worksheet units, the decision-making process is much simpler than that involved in the business world, for when Unit 173 is completed, the decision inevitably follows that the pupil should work on Unit 174. The computer could make such a decision without the intervention of the teacher, for it is a mechanical and empty decision. Indeed, within such a system, the decision-making functions of the teacher are very limited.

The entire model of education that derives from the operant model of learning provides very limited scope for professional teacher activities, except where the pupil encounters learning difficulties. The latter should rarely occur, if one is to believe writers on the subject, for such writings maintain that pupil-learning difficulties are eliminated in the experimental development of the program by rewriting those units which do not move the pupil smoothly forward. Such is the theory of this type of educational program, but most psychologists know well that broad educational theories based on narrow research rarely work out in the way the formulators of the theories expect.

The bypassing of the teacher that occurs in the operant model of schooling makes the assumption that the school has very limited and traditional functions to perform through a very traditional curriculum, and that these can be performed with little professional intervention on the part of the teacher. To some extent, this conception of education is a product of a conception of the pupil that views him as passively molded by circumstances. Such a representation of the pupil is not the only one found at the frontiers of psychological research. Other models exist that provide a far more significant role for the teacher.

Although the operant conditioning approach has very little to say about the function of the teacher, the kind of psychological research that emphasizes man as an exploring, information-organizing, and discovering creature has much to say about how teachers should act. The latter has been a productive view of man, as is quite evident from the chapters on motivation, perception, and development in this volume. There seems little doubt that man *is* an exploring, information-organizing, and discovering creature, and the classroom must provide him with opportunities to function in that kind of way. Some classroom models have attempted to build on this concept of man and have had a long history under various names. In recent times the term *discovery learning model* has been used to refer to this particular model of education, but the model of classroom learning is very similar to that described in the work of John Dewey.

This type of model has much to say about the role of the teacher. Exploratory behavior is an open-ended activity and its results cannot be precisely predetermined. A student expresses an interest in finding out about computers and is helped by his teacher, but who can say where that exploration will end? An extreme example of the unpredictable long-term consequences of exploration in an educational setting is found in the case of the chemistry student at Oberlin College who conducted an original experiment which resulted in the first production of metallic aluminum. Who could have guessed that the same student would have gone on to found the Aluminum Company of America? Most explorations of students will have far less dramatic outcomes, but they may still have unforeseen consequences, such as the development of a lifelong hobby or the emergence of a vocational choice.

A school program that recognizes the importance of man's outgoing, active approach to his environment calls upon the teacher to make many and significant decisions during the course of the school day. The decisions called for do not have the somewhat empty character of those called for in the operant type of program, most of which could just as well be made by the computer. In the program in which much of the activity is initiated by the pupil rather than by the materials, the teacher has to spend much time in helping the child undertake the explorations he wants to undertake. This does not mean that the curriculum has no structure, for there has to be some structure to a curriculum, but it is the exposure to the curriculum that stimulates the child to seek explorations of related phenomena. The teacher can encourage pupil-initiated exploratory activity by encouraging pupils to ask questions. The questions can lead to the study of new books and new ideas, the conduct of experiments, and the collection of data. Teachers can encourage exploratory activity also by asking significant questions. The latter is a very difficult undertaking for the teacher. Many surveys of classroom behavior have shown that the questions asked by teachers typically refer to commonplace matters, which the pupils can answer by remembering what they read in the textbook. So-called recitation procedures generally involve the asking of commonplace questions by the teacher and the giving of commonplace answers by the children. The breaking of this rather unproductive question-answer routine represents a very difficult challenge to teacher education. In addition, the teacher must have a knowledge of the kinds of materials to bring into the classroom to stimulate exploratory activity on the part of the pupil and a knowledge of the materials and equipment available through which the pupil can answer the questions he raises.

This conception of man, if it is implemented in an educational program, necessarily leads to the production of adults who show great differences in their interests, skills, and knowledge. The outcomes are to be contrasted with an educational program in which all pupils move at differing speeds toward the same outcome. One may well suspect that an educational program that brings about large individual differences in its products may result in a society much more difficult to live in and govern than one in which the schools succeed in manufacturing quite uniform components, if this is possible, which will fit easily into a planned and organized social and industrial system. The present writer would be inclined to speculate that man is so clearly a creature that explores, initiates his own behavior, and has such immense potential for establishing his own unique pattern of development, that even the most regimented of school programs, like many of those now emerging, may not result in the smoothly running industrial society envisaged by the planners of these programs.

The operant conditioning model of the classroom has the obvious advantage, from the administrators' point of view, that it requires less skill on the part of the teacher. The second kind of model for classroom planning considered here calls for real skill on the part of the teacher, who needs a rich academic background if his role in the model is to be well performed. There are probably no short cuts to a really effective education, and a program that reduces education in the classroom to the distribution of carefully packaged modules of material may be based on such a limited conception of man that it may provide an equally limited educational experience.

The Technology of Education

Some of those engaged in research on education and research on learning have embraced the idea that education will not develop until it is supported by a scientifically based technology, much as industrial manufacturing has developed in its present form only because it has been built on the foundation of such a technology. Whether the central deficiency of education lies in its lack of a suitable technology has been a topic of debate for nearly half a century, but today the debate has been largely replaced by vigorous efforts to build such a technology. In order to provide a basis for discussing some of the issues involved, let us begin by considering what is meant by a technology.

Man learned, just a few thousand years ago, how to extract metal from ores. This extraction process was perhaps acquired first through the accidental discovery that when certain heavy rocks were tossed into glowing embers, a piece of metal could sometimes be found on the following day. Men learned to build larger fires and to throw into them larger quantities of ore, and thus developed what are referred to as primitive technologies, that is to say, effective procedures for producing a particular kind of processed material. The early technologies had no scientific base, but they led to quite extraordinary accomplishments. As early as Roman times, there were iron smelting plants producing as much as one thousand tons of metal a year. Primitive technologies related to the production of metals were not the first to appear, for the still earlier developed technologies, involving ceramics, had produced not only objects of great utility, but also objects of marvelous beauty.

If one views a technology as a well-established procedure for achieving some quite practical goal, then one must view traditional education as having also been based on a primitive technology. The development of catechisms as teaching devices during the Middle Ages was an attempt to provide a simple routine that could be counted upon to produce a particular effect on the learner. As the centuries rolled by, education slowly evolved a number of procedures for ensuring that the educational product would meet certain standards. Drill procedures, recitation procedures, with the teacher and pupil engaging in questioning and answering one another, examination procedures, and procedures involving the use of threat and the use of praise, all could be viewed as being part of a primitive technology of education. This primitive technology, like the primitive technologies developed by the ancient world, had no scientific basis, but represented an accumulation of knowledge based on centuries of experience.

The primitive technologies related to the production of metals resulted in the production of ingots that varied greatly in quality. The technologies represented rules of thumb that generally worked quite well, but sometimes the metal produced was soft and malleable and sometimes it had the quality of steel. There was no way of predicting exactly what the product would be, because of the existence of many uncontrolled factors that could not be identified until the advent of the scientific era. The primitive technology of education also produced great variability of product with respect to quality.

Just as the primitive technologies of manufacturing and industry have been replaced by scientifically based procedures that provide a high degree of product control, so too is it anticipated by many that a scientifically based technology of education will emerge that will provide a high degree of control over the educational product. The scientific bases of the industrial technologies were chemistry and physics, and the anticipation has been that the scientific bases of educational technology will be the behavioral sciences, including psychology, sociology, and anthropology. Although Pressey (1932), close to half a century ago, wrote about the coming industrial revolution in education and the development of a technology of education that such a change implied, only in recent times has there been much support for such a movement.

The concept of the development of a technology of education is somewhat different from that of providing a scientific basis for guiding the decisions the teacher has to make. A technology would, presumably, establish specific and well-defined procedures through which particular goals could be reached, together with packages of materials through which the goal could be achieved. The concept of an educational technology parallels closely the concept of an industrial technology and carries with it the anticipation that there will be a uniformly good product emerging. Such anticipations must be regarded as more in the world of dreams than the world of reality, for industry has not been very successful at producing a uniformly good product. Nevertheless, the development of a technology of education does have some real potential for providing improved materials for schools and even improved ways of presenting those materials. A number of enterprises, some commercial and some nonprofit corporations, have been engaged in the developments related to the building of a technology of education.

How far the analogy between the schools on the one hand and industrial and manufacturing enterprises on the other can be pushed remains to be seen. There are certain fundamental differences between the two kinds of institutions, which may limit the use of the analogy. The raw materials of industry are passive and conform to the processes performed upon them in any well-planned enterprise, but the raw materials that enter the schools are active and influence those who attempt to shape their behavior. The school community cannot be divided into those who do the shaping and those who constitute the materials to be shaped. The analogy of the school to the factory is, at the best, a poor one, and generally very misleading. Children are active, exploring, information-gathering, and information-organizing creatures, whose education is far more difficult to plan than the manufacturing model of education would suggest. Finally, many people would doubt whether a uniform human product is desirable. Might it not be that the most effective educational system would be one that produced infinite variability in the human product?

References

ABELSON, R. P., et al. (eds.). *Theories of Cognitive Consistency: A Sourcebook*. Chicago: Rand McNally & Co., 1968.

ADAMS, J. A. *Human Memory*. New York: McGraw-Hill Book Company, 1967.

AINSWORTH, M. D. S., and S. M. BELL. "Attachment, Exploration and Separation: Illustrated by the Behavior of One-Year-Olds in a Strange Situation." *Child Development*, 41 (1970), 45–67.

ALLPORT, F. H. *Theories of Perception and the Concept of Structures*. John Wiley and Sons, Inc., 1955.

AMMONS, H., and A. L. IRION. "A Note on the Ballard Reminiscence Phenomenon." *Journal of Experimental Psychology*, 48 (1954), 184–186.

AMMONS, R. B., R. G. FARR, E. BLOCH, E. NEUMANN, M. DEY, R. MARION, and C. H. AMMONS. "Long-Term Retention of Perceptual-Motor Skills." *Journal of Experimental Psychology*, 55 (1958), 318–328.

ANNETT, J. "The Role of Knowledge of Results in Learning: A Survey." *Technical Report:* NAVTRADEVCEN 342-3, U.S. Naval Training Device Center, Port Washington, New York (1961).

———. *Some Aspects of the Acquisition of Simple Sensori-motor Skills*. Unpublished Ph.D. Phil. thesis, Oxford University (1959).

ARBIB, M. A., G. F. FRANKLIN, and N. NILSSON. "Some Ideas on Information Processing in the Cerebellum," in E. R. Caianiello (ed.), *Neural Networks*. New York: Springer Publishing Company, 1968, pp. 43–58.

ARCHER, E. J. "Concept Identification as a Function of Obviousness of Relevant and Irrelevant Information." *Journal of Experimental Psychology,* 63 (1962), 616–620.

ARONFREED, J. "The Problem of Imitation," L. P. Lipsitt and H. W. Reese (eds.), *Advances in Child Development and Behavior,* Vol. 4. New York: Academic Press, 1969, pp. 209–319.

ARONSON, E., and J. MILLS. "The Effect of Severity of Initiation on Liking for a Group," *Journal of Abnormal and Social Psychology,* 59 (1959), 177–181.

ASH, P., and N. JASPEN. "The Effects and Interpretation of Rate of Development, Repetition, Participation, and Room Illumination on Learning from a Rear-Projected Film," *Technical Report,* Special Devices Center, Office of Naval Research, 269-7-39, 1953.

ASHER, J. J. "Vision and Audition in Language Learning," *Perceptual and Motor Skills,* 19 (1964), 255–300. (Monograph Supplement No. 1–V19, 1964).

ATKINSON, J. W., and N. T. FEATHER (eds.). *A Theory of Achievement Motivation.* New York: John Wiley & Sons, Inc., 1966.

ATKINSON, R. C. "Information Delay in Human Learning," *Journal of Verbal Learning and Verbal Behavior,* 8 (1969), 507–511.

ATKINSON, R. W., and T. D. WICKENS. "Human Memory and the Concept of Reinforcement," in R. Glaser (ed.), *The Nature of Reinforcement.* (in publication.)

ATWATER, S. K. "Proactive Inhibition and Associative Facilitation As Affected by Degree of Prior Learning," *Journal of Experimental Psychology,* 46 (1953), 400–404.

AUSUBEL, D. P. *Psychology of Meaningful Verbal Learning.* New York: Grune & Stratton, 1963.

———, and F. G. ROBINSON. *School Learning: An Introduction to Educational Psychology.* New York: Holt, Rinehart and Winston, 1969.

AYLLON, T., and N. H. AZRIN. *The Token Economy.* New York: Appleton-Century-Crofts, 1968.

BAHRICK, H. P., S. CLARK, and P. BAHRICK. "Generalization Gradients as Indicants of Learning and Retention of a Recognition Task." *Journal of Experimental Psychology,* 75 (1967), 464–471.

BAILEY, C. J. "The Effectiveness of Drives as Cues." *Journal of Comparative and Physiological Psychology,* 48 (1955), 183–187.

BALLARD, P. B. "Obliviscence and Reminiscence." *British Journal of Psychology, Monograph Supplement,* 1:2, 1913.

BANDURA, A. *Principles of Behavior Modification.* New York: Holt, Rinehart, and Winston, 1969.

BANDURA, A., J. E. GRUSEC, and F. L. MENLOVE. "Vicarious Extinction of Avoidance Behavior." *Journal of Personality and Social Psychology,* 5 (1967), 16–23.

BARTLETT, F. C. *Remembering*. Cambridge, England: Cambridge University Press, 1932.

BAUMRIND, D., and A. E. BLACK. "Socialization Practices Associated with Dimensions of Competence in Preschool Boys and Girls." *Child Development*, 38 (1967), 291–327.

BENOWITZ, M. L., and T. V. BUSSE. "Material Incentives and the Learning of Spelling Words in a Typical School Situation." *Journal of Educational Psychology*, 61 (1970), 24–26.

BERLYNE, D. E. *Conflict, Arousal, and Curiosity*. New York: McGraw-Hill Book Company, 1960.

———. "Complexity and Incongruity Variables As Determinants of Exploratory Choice and Evaluative Ratings." *Canadian Journal of Psychology*, 17 (1963), 274–290.

———. *Structure and Direction in Thinking*. New York: John Wiley & Sons, Inc., 1965.

———. "The Reward Value of Light Increment Under Supranormal and Subnormal Arousal." *Canadian Journal of Psychology*, 23 (1969) 11–16.

BERSCHEID, E., and E. WALSTER. "Attitude Change, Part II," in J. Mills, (ed.), *Experimental Social Psychology*. New York: The Macmillan Co., 1969, pp. 121–231.

BILODEAU, I. MCD. "Accuracy of a Simple Positioning Response with Variation in the Number of Trials by which Knowledge of Results is Delayed." *American Journal of Psychology*, 69 (1956), 434–437.

———. "Information Feedback." In E. A. Bilodeau (ed.), *Acquisition of Skill*. New York: Academic Press, 1966, Chap. 6.

———, and H. SCHLOSBERG. "Similarity in Stimulating Conditions as a Variable in Retroactive Inhibition." *Journal of Experimental Psychology*, 41 (1951), 199–204.

BJORK, R. A. "Positive Forgetting: The Noninterference of Items Intentionally Forgotten." *Journal of Verbal Learning and Verbal Behavior*, 9 (1970), 255–268.

BLACK, R. W. "Shifts in Magnitude of Reward and Contrast Effects in Instrumental and Selective Learning." *Psychological Review*, 75 (1968), 114–126.

BOSCO, J. J. *Social Class and the Processing of Visual Information*. First Report, Project No. 9-E-041. U.S. Department of Health, Education, and Welfare, Office of Education, 1970.

BOURDON, R. D. "Imitation: Implications for Counseling and Therapy." *Review of Educational Research*, 40 (1970), 429–457.

BOURNE, L. E., JR. *Human Conceptual Behavior*. Boston: Allyn and Bacon, 1966.

———, and E. J. ARCHER. "Time Continuously on Target as a Function of Distribution of Practice." *Journal of Experimental Psychology*, 51 (1956), 25–33.

———, and C. V. BUNDERSON. "Effects of Delay of Informative Feedback and Length of Postfeedback Interval on Concept Identification." *Journal of Experimental Psychology*, 65 (1963), 1–5.

———, and D. E. GUY. "Learning Conceptual Rules. II: The Role of Positive and Negative Instances." *Journal of Experimental Psychology*, 77 (1968), 488–494.

BOWER, G. H. "Chunks as Interference Units in Free Recall." *Journal of Verbal Learning and Verbal Behavior*, 8 (1969), 610–613.

———, M. C. CLARK, A. M. LESGOLD, and D. WINZENZ. "Hierarchical Retrieval Schemes in Recall of Categorized Word Lists." *Journal of Verbal Learning and Verbal Behavior*, 8 (1969), 323–343.

BOWER, T. G. "The Visual World of Infants." *Scientific American*, 215 (1966), 80–92.

BRADY, J. V. "Ulcers in 'Executive' Monkeys." *Scientific American*, 199 (Oct., 1958), 95–103.

BROADBENT, D. E. *Perception and Communication*. New York: Pergamon Press, 1958.

———. "The Well Ordered Mind." *American Educational Research Journal*, 3 (1966), 281–295.

———, and M. GREGORY. "Perception of Emotionally Toned Words." *Nature*, 215 (1967), 581–584.

BRODY, A. L. "Statistical Learning Theory Applied to an Instrumental Avoidance Situation." *Journal of Experimental Psychology*, 54 (1957), 240–245.

BROOKSHIRE, K. H. "Quantitive Differences in Learning Ability and Function," in M. H. Marx (ed.), *Learning Interactions*. New York: The Macmillan Co., 1970, pp. 299–347.

BROWN, R., and C. FRASER. "The Acquisition of Syntax," in C. N. Cofer (ed.), *Verbal Behavior and Learning*. New York: McGraw-Hill Book Company, 1963, pp. 158–209.

———, and D. MCNEILL. "The 'Tip of the Tongue' Phenomenon." *Journal of Verbal Learning and Verbal Behavior*, 5 (1966), 325–337.

BRUNER, J. S., J. J. GOODNOW, and G. A. AUSTIN. *A Study of Thinking*. New York: John Wiley & Sons, Inc., 1956.

BRYAN, J. H., and P. LONDON. "Altruistic Behavior by Children." *Psychological Bulletin*, 73 (1970), 200–211.

BRYAN, W. L., and N. HARTER. "Studies in the Physiology and Psychology of the Telegraphic Language." *Psychological Review*, 4 (1897), 27–53.

BUCHER, B., and O. I. LOVAAS. "Use of Aversive Stimulation in Behavior Modification," in M. R. Jones (ed.), *Miami Symposium on the Prediction of Behavior, 1967: Aversive Stimulation*. Coral Gables, Florida: University of Miami Press, 1968, pp. 77–145.

BUGELSKI, B. R. *The Psychology of Learning*. New York: Holt Rinehart and Winston, 1956.

BYERS, J. L. "Verbal and Concept Learning." *Review of Educational Research*, 37 (1967), 494–513.

———, and R. E. DAVIDSON. "Relevant and Irrelevant Information in Concept Attainment." *Journal of Experimental Psychology*, 76 (1968), 277–281.

CAIN, L. F., and R. DE V. WILLEY. "The Effect of Spaced Learning on the Curve of Retention." *Journal of Experimental Psychology*, 25 (1939), 209–214.

CAMPBELL, B. A., and F. D. SHEFFIELD. "Relation of Random Activity to Food Deprivation." *Journal of Comparative and Physiological Psychology*, 46 (1953), 320–322.

CAMPBELL, J. P., and M. D. DUNNETTE. "Effectiveness of T-Group Experiences in Managerial Training and Development." *Psychological Bulletin*, 70 (1968), 73–104.

CARLTON, P. L. *Response Strength as a Function of Delay in Reward and Physical Confinement*. Unpublished Master's thesis, University of Iowa, 1954.

CASTANEDA, A., B. R. MCCANDLESS, and D. S. PALERMO. "The Children's Form of the Manifest Anxiety Scale." *Child Development*, 27 (1956), 317–326.

CHAN, A., and R. M. W. TRAVERS. "The Effect on Retention of Labeling Visual Displays." *American Educational Research Journal*, 3 (1966), 55–67.

CHOMSKY, N. "Language and the Mind." *Psychology Today*, 1 (1968), 48–51 and 66–68.

———. *Language and Mind*. New York: Harcourt, Brace and World, 1969.

CLARK, D. C. "Teaching Concepts in the Classroom: A Set of Teaching Prescriptions Derived from Experimental Research." *Journal of Educational Psychology*, 62 (1971), 253–278.

COFER, C. N., and M. H. APPLEY. *Motivation: Theory and Research*. New York: John Wiley & Sons, Inc., 1964.

COLE, M., and I. MALTZMAN (eds.). *A Handbook of Contemporary Soviet Psychology*. New York: Basic Books, Inc., 1969.

COOK, T. W. "Distribution of Practice and Size of Maze Pattern." *British Journal of Psychology*, 27 (1937), 303–312.

CORCORAN, D. W. J. "Acoustic Factor in Proofreading." *Nature*, 214 (1967), 851–852.

COSTIN, F. "Dogmatism and Learning: A Follow-Up of Contradictory Findings." *Journal of Educational Research*, 59 (1965), 186–188.

CROSSMAN, E. R. F. W. "A Theory of the Acquisition of Speed-Skill." *Ergonomics*, 2 (1959), 153–166.

CROWNE, D. P., and D. MARLOWE. *The Approval Motive*. New York: John Wiley & Sons, Inc., 1964.

DAY, H. "Role of Specific Curiosity in School Achievement." *Journal of Educational Psychology*, 59 (1968), 37–43.

DEESE, J. *Psycholinguistics*. Boston: Allyn and Bacon, 1970.

DELLAS, M., and E. L. GAIER. "Identification of Creativity." *Psychological Bulletin*, 73 (1970), 55–73.

DENNY, J. P. "Effects of Anxiety and Intelligence on Concept Formation." *Journal of Experimental Psychology*, 72 (1966), 596–602.

DEROSA, D. V., D. S. DOANE, and B. RUSSELL. "The Influence of First-List Organization upon Second-List Free-Recall Learning." *Journal of Verbal Learning and Verbal Behavior*, 9 (1970), 269–273.

DEUTSCH, C. P. "Education for Disadvantaged Groups." *Review of Educational Research*, 35 (1965), 140–146.

DEWEY, J. *How We Think*. Boston: D. C. Heath and Company, 1910.

DIAMOND, S., R. S. BALVIN, and F. R. DIAMOND. *Inhibition and Choice*. New York: Harper & Row, 1963.

DICK, A. O., and S. O. DICK. "An Analysis of Hierarchical Processing in Visual Perception." *Canadian Journal of Psychology*, 23 (1969), 203–211.

DIGGORY, J. C. *Self-evaluation: Concepts and Studies*. New York: John Wiley and Sons, Inc., 1966.

DINSMOOR, J. A. "Escape from Shock as a Conditioning Technique." in M. R. Jones (ed.), *Miami Symposium on the Prediction of Behavior, 1967: Aversive Stimulation*. Coral Gables, Florida: University of Miami Press, 1968, pp. 33–75.

DI VESTA, F. J., and R. T. WALLS. "Multiple- Versus Single-Problem Training and Variations of Solution Rules in the Formation of Learning Sets." *Journal of Educational Psychology*, 59 (1968), 191–196.

DOUGLASS, H. R., and C. KITTELSON. "The Transfer of Training in High School Latin to English Grammar, Spelling, and Vocabulary." *Journal of Experimental Education*, 4 (1935), 26–33.

DREGER, R. M., and K. S. MILLER. "Comparative Psychological Studies of Negroes and Whites in the United States: 1959–1965." *Psychological Bulletin Monograph Supplement*, 70:3 (1968), Pt. 2, pp. 58.

EBBINGHAUS, H. *Uber das Gedächtnis*. Leipzig: Duncker and Humblot, 1885.

ECCLES, J. C., M. ITO, and J. SZENTAGOTHAI. *The Cerebellum as a Neuronal Machine*. New York: Springer-Verlag, 1967.

EHRLICH, H. J., and D. LEE. "Dogmatism, Learning, and Resistance to Change." *Psychological Bulletin*, 71 (1969), 249–260.

EPSTEIN, W. *Varieties of Perceptual Learning*. New York: McGraw-Hill Book Company, 1967.

ESTES, W. K. "An Experimental Study of Punishment." *Psychological Monographs*, 57:263 (1944).

EYSENCK, H. J. "Reminiscence, Drive, and Personality Theory." *Journal of Abnormal and Social Psychology,* 53 (1956), 328–333.

FANTINO, E., D. KASDON, and N. STRINGER. "The Yerkes-Dodson Law and Alimentary Motivation." *Canadian Journal of Psychology,* 24 (1970), 77–84.

FEATHER, B. W. "Semantic Generalization of Classically Conditioned Responses." *Psychological Bulletin,* 63 (1965), 425–441.

FESTINGER, L. *A Theory of Cognitive Dissonance.* New York: Harper & Row, 1957.

FITTS, P. M., and J. R. PETERSON. "Information Capacity of Discrete Motor Responses." *Journal of Experimental Psychology,* 67 (1964), 103–112.

———, and M. I. POSNER. *Human Performance.* Belmont, Calif.: Brooks-Cole, 1967.

FLANDERS, J. P. "A Review of Research on Imitative Behavior." *Psychological Bulletin,* 69 (1968), 316–337.

FLAVELL, J. H. *The Developmental Psychology of Jean Piaget.* Princeton, N.J.: D. Van Nostrand, Inc., 1963.

FLEISHMAN, E. A., and J. F. PARKER, JR. "Factors in the Retention and Relearning of Perceptual-Motor Skill." *Journal of Experimental Psychology,* 64 (1962) 215–226.

FORLANO, G. *School Learning with Various Methods of Practice and Rewards.* New York: Teachers College, Columbia University, Teachers College Contributions to Education, No. 688, 1936.

FOWLER, H. J. *Curiosity and Exploratory Behavior.* New York: The Macmillan Company, 1965.

———. "Cognitive Learning in Infancy and Early Childhood." *Psychological Bulletin,* 59 (1962), 116–152.

FREEBERG, N. E., and D. T. PAYNE. "Parental Influence on Cognitive Development in Early Childhood: A Review." *Child Development,* 38 (1967), 65–87.

FREEDMAN, J. L. "Increasing Creativity by Free-Association Training." *Journal of Experimental Psychology,* 69 (1965), 89–91.

FREEMAN, D. "Human Aggression in Anthropological Perspective," in J. D. Carthy, and F. J. Ebling (eds.), *The Natural History of Aggression.* New York: Academic Press, 1964, pp. 109–119.

GAGNE, R. M. *The Conditions of Learning.* New York: Holt, Rinehart & Winston, 1965, 2nd ed., 1970.

———. "Contributions of Learning to Human Development." *Psychological Review,* 75 (1968), 177–191.

———, and E. C. SMITH, JR. "A Study of the Effects of Verbalization on

Problem Solving." *Journal of Experimental Psychology,* 63 (1962), 12–18.

GANZER, V. J. "Effects of Audience Presence and Test Anxiety on Learning and Retention in a Serial Learning Situation." *Journal of Personality and Social Psychology,* 8 (1968), 194–199.

GARDNER, E. *Fundamentals of Neurology.* Philadelphia: W. B. Saunders Company, 1968.

GELLER, A., M. E. JARVIK, and F. ROBUSTELLI. "Incubation and the Kamin Effect." *Journal of Experimental Psychology,* 85 (1970), 61–65.

GERARD, H. B., and G. C. MATHEWSON. "The Effects of Severity of Initiation on Liking for a Group: A Replication." *Journal of Experimental Social Psychology,*" 2 (1966), 278–287.

GERLACH, V. S., R. E. SCHUTZ, R. L. BAKER, and G. E. MAZER. "Effects of Variations in Test Directions on Originality Test Response." *Journal of Educational Psychology,* 55 (1964), 79–83.

GIBSON, E. J. "Improvement in Perceptual Judgments as a Function of Controlled Practice or Training." *Psychological Bulletin,* 50 (1953), 401–431.

———. *Principles of Perceptual Learning and Development.* New York: Appleton-Century-Crofts, 1969.

GIBSON, J. J. *The Senses Considered as Perceptual Systems.* Boston: Houghton Mifflin Company, 1966.

———, and E. J. GIBSON. "Perceptual Learning: Differentiation or Enrichment?" *Psychological Review,* 62 (1955), 32–41.

GLASER, R. *Teaching Machines and Programmed Learning II.* Washington, D.C.: National Education Association, 1965.

GLUCKSBERG, S., and J. H. DANKS. "Functional Fixedness: Stimulus Equivalence Mediated by Semantic-Acoustic Similarity." *Journal of Experimental Psychology,* 74 (1967), 400–405.

GOLDIAMOND, I. "Perception, Language, and Conceptualization Rules," in B. Kleinmuntz (ed.), *Problem Solving,* New York: John Wiley & Sons, Inc., 1966, pp. 183–224.

GORDON, I. J. *Early Childhood Stimulation Through Parent Education.* Final Report to the Children's Bureau, Social and Rehabilitation Service, Department of Health, Education and Welfare, Pt15-R-306, PHS-R-306 (01), 1969.

GOSS, A. E., and C. F. NODINE. *Paired-Associates Learning.* New York: Academic Press, 1965.

GRIMES, J. W., and W. ALLINSMITH. "Compulsivity, Anxiety, and School Achievement." *Merrill-Palmer Quarterly,* 7 (1961), 247–271.

GUETZKOW, H., E. L. KELLY, and W. J. MCKEACHIE. "An Experimental Comparison of Recitation, Discussion, and Tutorial Methods in College Teaching." *Journal of Educational Psychology,* 45 (1954), 193–207.

GUILFORD, J. P. "Three Faces of Intellect." *American Psychologist,* 14 (1959), 469–479.

HABER, R. N. "Repetition, Visual Persistence, Visual Noise and Information Processing," in K. N. Leibovic (ed.), *Information Processing in the Nervous System,* New York: Springer-Verlag, 1969, pp. 121–140.

———, and R. B. HABER. "Eidetic Imagery: I. Frequency." *Perceptual and Motor Skills,* 19 (1964), 131–138.

HALLE, M., and K. STEVENS. *Speech Recognition: A Model and a Program for Research.* IRE Transactions, 1962, IT-8, 155–159.

HAMBLEN, A. A. *An Investigation to Determine the Extent to Which the Effect of the Study of Latin upon a Knowledge of English Derivations Can be Measured by Conscious Adaptation of Content and Methods to the Attainment of This Objective,* unpublished Doctoral dissertation, University of Pennsylvania, 1925.

HAMILTON, J. and J. STANDAHL. "Suppression of Stereotyped Screaming Behavior in a Profoundly Retarded Institutionalized Female." *Journal of Experimental Child Psychology,* 7 (1969), 114–121.

HAMMER, G. J., and G. M. NATALE. "Initial Learning of a Motor Skill without Motor Involvement." *Journal of Business Education,* 39 (1964), 282–283.

HARBY, S. F. "Comparison of Mental Practice and Physical Practice in the Learning of Physical Skills." *Technical Report,* Special Devices Center, Office of Naval Research, 269-8-27, 1952.

HARLOW, H. F. "The Formation of Learning Sets." *Psychological Review,* 56 (1949), 51–65.

———. "Learning Set and Error Factor Theory," in S. Koch (ed.), *Psychology: A Study of a Science,* Vol. 2. New York: McGraw-Hill, 1959, pp. 492–537.

HARRE, R. "The Formal Analysis of Concepts," H. J. Klausmeier and C. W. Harris (eds.), *Analyses of Concept Learning,* New York: Academic Press, 1966, pp. 3–18.

HARTMAN, T. F. "Dynamic Transmission, Elective Generalization, and Semantic Conditioning," in W. F. Prokasy (ed.), *Classical Conditioning.* New York: Appleton-Century-Crofts, 1965, Chapter 5, pp. 90–106.

HARTSHORNE, H., and M. A. MAY. *Studies in the Nature of Character,* Vol. 1. New York: The Macmillan Company, 1928.

HARTUP, W. W., and B. COATES. "Imitation of a Peer as a Function of Reinforcement from the Peer Group and Rewardingness of the Model." *Child Development,* 38 (1967), 1003–1016.

HEBB, D. O. *Organization of Behavior.* New York: John Wiley & Sons, Inc., 1949.

———. *Textbook of Psychology.* Philadelphia: W. B. Saunders Company, 1958.

———. *Textbook of Psychology,* Second Edition. Philadelphia: W. B. Saunders Company, 1966.

———. "Concerning Imagery." *Psychological Review,* 75 (1968), 466–477.

———, and W. R. THOMPSON. "The Social Significance of Animal Studies," G. Lindzey and E. Aronson (eds.), *The Handbook of Social Psychology,* Vol. 2. Second Edition. Reading, Mass.: Addison-Wesley Publishing Co., Inc., 1968, pp. 729–774.

HECKHAUSEN, H. *The Anatomy of Achievement Motivation.* New York: Academic Press, 1967.

HERRIOT, P. *An Introduction to the Psychology of Language.* London: Methuen & Co., Ltd., 1970.

HERRNSTEIN, R. J., and D. H. LOVELAND. "Complex Visual Concept in the Pigeon." *Science,* 146 (1964), 549–551.

HETHERINGTON, E. M., and L. E. ROSS. "Discrimination Learning by Normal and Retarded Children Under Delay of Reward and Interpolated Task Conditions." *Child Development,* 38 (1967), 639–647.

HEWETT, F. M. "The Autistic Child Learns to Read," *Slow Learning Child: The Australian Journal on the Education of Backward Children,* 13 (1966), 107–120.

HILGARD, E. R., R. P. IRVINE, and J. E. WHIPPLE. "Rote Memorization, Understanding, and Transfer: An Extension of Katona's Card-Trick Experiments." *Journal of Experimental Psychology,* 46 (1953), 288–292.

HILGARD, E. R., and D. G. MARQUIS. "Conditioned Eyelid Responses in Monkeys, with a Comparison of Dog, Monkey, and Man." *Psychological Monographs,* 47:212 (1936), 186–198.

HOLDING, D. H. *Principles of Training.* New York: Pergamon Press, 1965.

HOLLANDER, E. P., and J. W. JULIAN. "Contemporary Trends in the Analysis of Leadership Processes." *Psychological Bulletin,* 71 (1969), 387–397.

HONZIK, M. P. "Environmental Correlates of Mental Growth: Prediction from the Family Setting at 21 Months." *Child Development,* 38 (1967), 337–364.

HOWE, M. J. A. *Introduction to Human Memory.* New York: Harper & Row, 1970.

HUBEL, D. H. "The Visual Cortex of the Brain." *Scientific American,* 209 (Nov. 1963), 54–62.

HULL, C. L. *Principles of Behavior.* New York: Appleton-Century-Crofts, 1943.

Human Factors Research, Inc. *Human Vigilance.* Santa Barbara Research Park, Goleta, Calif. Human Factors Research, Inc., 1968.

HUNT, D. E. "Adolescence: Cultural Deprivation, Poverty, and the Drop-out." *Review of Educational Research,* 36 (1966), 463–473.

HUNT, J. MC V. *Intelligence and Experience.* New York: The Ronald Press Company, 1961.

HUTTENLOCHER, J. "Effects of Manipulation of Attributes on Efficiency of Concept Formation." *Psychological Reports,* 10 (1962), 503–509.

INSKO, C. A. *Theories of Attitude Change.* New York: Appleton-Century-Crofts, 1967.

IRION, A. L. "A Brief History of Research on the Acquisition of Skill," in E. A. Bilodeau (ed.), *Acquisition of Skill.* New York: Academic Press, 1966, Chap. 1.

JASPEN, N. "Effect on Training of Experimental Film Variables: Audience Participation." *Technical Report,* Special Devices Center, Office of Naval Research, 269-7-11, 1950.

JENKINS, W. O., and J. C. STANLEY, JR. "Partial Reinforcement: A Review and Critique." *Psychological Bulletin,* 47 (1950), 193–234.

JENSEN, A. R. "Social Class, Race, and Genetics." *American Educational Research Journal,* 5 (1968), 1–42.

JOHNSON, D. M. "Solution of Anagrams." *Psychological Bulletin,* 66 (1966) 371–384.

———, G. L. PARROTT, and R. P. STRATTON. "Production and Judgment of Solutions to Five Problems." *Journal of Educational Psychology,* Monograph Supplement, 59 (1968), No. 6, Part 2, 1–21.

JOHNSON, D. M., and R. P. STRATTON. "Evaluation of Five Methods of Teaching Concepts." *Journal of Educational Psychology,* 57 (1966), 48–53.

JONES, J. G. "Motor Learning Without Demonstration of Physical Practice." *Research Quarterly,* 36 (1965), 270–276.

JONES, R. A., and BREHM, J. W. "Attitudinal Effects of Communicator Attractiveness When One Chooses to Listen." *Journal of Personality and Social Psychology,* 6 (1967), 64–70.

JONES, R. E., JR. "Effects of Delay of Informative Feedback, Post-Feedback Interval, and Feedback Presentation Mode on Verbal Paired-Associates Learning." *Journal of Experimental Psychology,* 77 (1968), 87–93.

JUDSON, A. J., C. N. COFER, and S. GELFAND. "Reasoning as an Associative Process: II. 'Direction' in Problem Solving as a Function of Prior Reinforcement of Relevant Responses." *Psychological Reports,* 2 (1956), 501–507.

KALE, S. V., J. H. GROSSLIGHT, and L. J. MCINTYRE. "Exploratory Studies in the Use of Pictures and Sound for Teaching Foreign Language." *Technical Report,* Special Devices Center, U.S. Navy SPECDEVCEN, 269-7-53.

Katona, G. *Organizing and Memorizing.* New York: Columbia University Press, 1940.

———. "Organizing and Memorizing: A Reply to Dr. Melton." *American Journal of Psychology,* 55 (1942), 273–275.

KATZ, D. "Consistency for What? The Functional Approach," in R. P. Abelson, et al. (eds.), *Theories of Cognitive Consistency: A Sourcebook.* Chicago: Rand McNally and Company, 1968, Chap. 8, pp. 179–191.

———, and E. STOTLAND. "A Preliminary Statement to a Theory of Attitude Structure and Change," in S. Koch (ed.), *Psychology: A Study of a Science,* Vol. 3. New York: McGraw-Hill, 1959, pp. 423–475.

KEELE, S. W. "Movement Control in Skilled Motor Performance." *Psychological Bulletin,* 70 (1968), 387–403.

KENDLER, H. H., and T. S. KENDLER. "Vertical and Horizontal Processes in Problem Solving." *Psychological Review,* 69 (1962), 1–16.

KENDLER, T. S. "Verbalization and Optional Reversal Shifts Among Kindergarten Children." *Journal of Verbal Learning and Verbal Behavior,* 3 (1964), 428–436.

KIESLER, C. A., B. E. COLLINS, and N. MILLER. *Attitude Change.* New York: John Wiley & Sons, Inc., 1969.

KIMBLE, G. A. "A Letter to Art Melton," in J. F. Voss (ed.), *Approaches to Thought.* Columbus, Ohio: Charles E. Merrill Books, Inc., 1969, 333–337.

KLARE, G. R. *The Measurement of Readability.* Ames, Iowa: Iowa State University Press, 1963.

KLEINMUNTZ, B. *Problem Solving.* New York: John Wiley & Sons, Inc., 1966.

KLEINSMITH, L. J., and S. KAPLAN. "Paired-Associate Learning as a Function of Arousal and Interpolated Interval." *Journal of Experimental Psychology,* 65 (1963), 190–193.

KOHLBERG, L. *Stage and Sequence: The Developmental Approach to Moralization.* New York: Holt, Rinehart and Winston, 1969.

———. "Development of Moral Character and Moral Ideology," in M. L. Hoffman and L. W. Hoffman (eds.), *Review of Child Development Research,* Vol. 1. New York: Russell Sage Foundation, pp. 383–431.

KREBS, D. L. "Altruism—An Examination of the Concept and a Review of the Literature." *Psychological Bulletin,* 73 (1970), 258–302.

KRUGMAN, A. D. "A Comparative Study of the Effect of Induced Failure, Induced Success, and a Neutral Task upon the Retentive Process of Anxiety and Normal Subjects." *Dissertation Abstracts,* 18 (1958), 662.

KUBINIEC, C. M. "The Relative Efficiency of Various Dimensions of the Self-Concept in Predicting Academic Achievement." *American Educational Research Journal,* 7 (1970), 321–336.

LAVERY, J. J. "The Effect of One-Trial Delay in Knowledge of Results on the Acquisition and Retention of a Tossing Skill." *American Journal of Psychology,* 77 (1964) 437–443.

LEBO, D., and E. LEBO. "Aggression and Age in Relation to Verbal Expression in Nondirective Play Therapy." *Psychological Monographs,* **71**: 449, (1957).

LEE, W. S. "A Study of the Effectiveness of Sensitivity Training in an Inservice Teacher Training Program in Human Relations." *Dissertation Abstracts,* **28**:(5A) (1967), 1680.

LEITENBERG, H. "Is Time-Out from Positive Reinforcement an Aversive Event?" *Psychological Bulletin,* **64** (1965), 428–441.

LEITH, G. O., L. A. BIRAN, and J. A. OPPOLLOT. "The Place of Review in Meaningful Verbal Learning." *Canadian Journal of the Behavioral Sciences,* **1** (1969), 113–118.

LENNEBERG, E. H. "On Explaining Language." *Science,* **164** (1969), 635–643.

LEUBA, C., L. BIRCH, and J. APPLETON. "Human Problem Solving During Complete Paralysis of the Voluntary Musculature." *Psychological Reports,* **22** (1968), 849–855.

LEVENTHAL, G. S. "Reward Magnitude, Task Attractiveness, and Liking for Instrumental Activity." *Journal of Abnormal Psychology,* **68** (1964), 460–463.

LEWIN, K., R. LIPPITT, and R. K. WHITE. "Patterns of Aggressive Behavior in Experimentally Created 'Social Climates.'" *Journal of Social Psychology,* **10** (1939), 271–299.

LEWIS, D. J. "Partial Reinforcement: A Selective Review of the Literature Since 1950." *Psychological Bulletin,* 57 (1960), 1–28.

LINTZ, L. M. "The Delay-Retention Effect with Auditory Presentations." *Child Development,* 39 (1968), 933–943.

LIU, I. M. "A Theory of Classical Conditioning." *Psychological Review,* **71** (1964), 408–411.

LOGAN, F. A. *Incentive.* New Haven, Conn.: Yale University Press, 1960.

———. "Incentive Theory and Changes in Reward," in K. W. Spence, and J. T. Spence (eds.), *The Psychology of Learning and Motivation,* Vol. 2. New York: Academic Press, 1968, pp. 1–30.

LOGAN, T. H., and K. H. WODTKE. "Effects of Rules of Thumb on Transfer of Training." *Journal of Educational Psychology,* 59 (1968), 147–153.

LONGSTRETH, L. E. "Tests of the Law of Effect Using Open and Closed Tasks." *Journal of Experimental Psychology,* 84 (1970), 53–57.

LORGE, I. L. *The Inflence of Regularly Interpolated Time Intervals upon Subsequent Learning.* New York: Columbia University, Teachers College Contributions to Education, No. 438 (1930).

———, and E. L. THORNDIKE. "The Influence of Delay in the After Effect of a Connection." *Journal of Experimental Psychology,* **18** (1935), 186–194.

MACAULAY, J., and L. BERKOWITZ (eds.). *Altruism and Helping Behavior.* New York: Academic Press, 1970.

MADSEN, K. B. *Theories of Motivation.* Cleveland: Howard Allen, 1961.

MAIER, N. R. F. *Problem Solving and Creativity.* Belmont, Calif.: Brooks Cole Publishing Company, 1970.

———. "Assets and Liabilities in Group Problem Solving." *Psychological Review,* 74 (1967), 239–249.

———. *Frustration: The Study of Behavior Without a Goal.* New York: McGraw Hill Book Co., 1949.

MALTZMAN, I. "On the Training of Originality." *Psychological Review,* 67 (1960), 229–242.

MANDLER, G. "Transfer of Training as a Function of Degree of Response Overlearning." *Journal of Experimental Psychology,* 47 (1954), 411–417.

MARKOWITZ, N., and K. E. RENNER. "Feedback and the Delay-Retention Effect." *Journal of Experimental Psychology,* 72 (1966), 452–455.

MARLOWE, D., and K. J. GREGEN. "Personality and Social Interaction," in G. Lindzey and E. Aronson (eds.), *Handbook of Social Psychology,* Vol. 3. Reading, Mass.: Addison-Wesley Publishing Co., 1969, Chap. 25, pp. 590–665.

MARTIN, E. "Transfer of Verbal Associates." *Psychological Review,* 72 (1965), 327–343.

MCCLELLAND, D. C. *The Achieving Society.* Princeton, N.J.: D. Van Nostrand, Inc., 1961.

MCGUIRE, W. J. "The Nature of Attitudes and Attitude Change." in G. Lindzey and E. Aronson (eds.), *The Handbook of Social Psychology,* Vol. 3. Reading, Mass.: Addison-Wesley Publishing Co., 1969, Chap. 21, pp. 136–314.

MCKEACHIE, W. J., R. L. ISAACSON, J. E. MILHOLLAND, AND Y. LIN. "Student Achievement Motives, Achievement Cues, and Academic Achievement." *Journal of Consulting Psychology,* 32 (1968), 26–29.

MCLAUGHLIN, B. " 'Intentional' and 'Incidental' Learning in Human Subjects." *Psychological Bulletin,* 63 (1965), 359–376.

MEADE, R. D. "An Experimental Study of Leadership in India." *Journal of Social Psychology,* 72 (1967), 35–43.

MEDNICK, S. A., and J. L. FREEDMAN. "Stimulus Generalization." *Psychological Bulletin,* 57 (1960), 169–200.

MEEKER, M. N. *The Structure of the Intellect.* Columbus, Ohio: Charles E. Merrill Books, Inc., 1969.

MELTON, A. W. "Implications of Short-Term Memory for a General Theory of Memory." *Journal of Verbal Learning and Verbal Behavior,* 2 (1963), 1–21.

———, and W. J. VON LACKUM. "Retroactive and Proactive Inhibition in Retention: Evidence for a Two-Factor Theory of Retroactive Inhibition." *American Journal of Psychology,* 54 (1941), 157–173.

MILGRAM, N. A., and J. S. NOCE. "Relevant and Irrelevant Verbalization in Discrimination and Reversal Learning by Normal and Retarded Children." *Journal of Educational Psychology,* 59 (1968), 169–175.

MILLER, G. R., and ROKEACH, M. "Individual Differences and Tolerance for Inconsistency." in R. P. Abelson, et al. (eds.), *Theories of Cognitive Consistency: A Sourcebook.* Chicago: Rand McNally & Company, 1968, Chap. 60, pp. 624–632.

MILLER, N. E., and J. DOLLARD. *Social Learning and Imitation.* New Haven, Conn.: Yale University Press, 1941.

MILLS, J. *Experimental Social Psychology.* New York: The Macmillan Company, 1969.

MISCHEL, W., and E. STAUB. "Effects of Expectancy on Working and Waiting for Larger Rewards." *Journal of Personality and Social Psychology,* 2 (1965), 625–633.

MONTAGUE, W. E., J. A. ADAMS, and H. O. KIESS. "Forgetting and Natural Language Mediation." *Journal of Experimental Psychology,* 72 (1966), 829–833.

MOWRER, O. H. *Learning Theory and Behavior.* New York: John Wiley & Sons, Inc., 1960(a).

MURRAY, E. N. "Stimulus Generalization in Relation to Anxiety." Ph.D. thesis, University of Pittsburgh, University Microfilms, Ann Arbor, 1965, 66–8159.

MURRAY, H. A. *Explorations in Personality.* New York: Oxford University Press, 1938.

MYERS, K. E., R. M. W. TRAVERS, and M. E. SANFORD. "Learning and Reinforcement in Student Pairs." *Journal of Educational Psychology,* 56 (1965), 67–72.

NAKAMURA, C. Y., and G. BOROCZI. "Effect of Relative Incentive Value on Persistence and Response Speed." *Child Development,* 36 (1965), 547–557.

NEIMARK, E. D., and W. K. ESTES. *Stimulus Sampling Theory.* San Francisco: Holden-Day, 1967.

NEISSER, U. *Cognitive Psychology.* New York: Appleton-Century-Crofts, 1967.

NEWELL, A., J. C. SHAW, and H. A. SIMON. "Elements of a Theory of Human Problem Solving." *Psychological Review,* 65 (1958), 151–166.

NEWMAN, H. H., F. N. FREEMAN, and K. J. HOLZINGER. *Twins: A Study of Heredity and Environment.* Chicago: University of Chicago Press, 1937.

NUTTIN, J. *Reward and Punishment in Human Learning.* New York: Academic Press, 1968.

OLSON, W. C. *Child Development.* Boston: D. C. Heath & Co., 1959.

OSGOOD, C. E. "The Similarity Paradox in Human Learning: A Resolution." *Psychological Review,* 56 (1949), 132–143.

———. "Psycholinguistics," in S. Koch (ed.) *Psychology: A Study of a Science,* Vol. 6. New York: McGraw-Hill Book Company, 1963, pp. 244–316.

OVERING, R. L. R., and R. M. W. TRAVERS. "Effect upon Transfer of Variations in Training Conditions." *Journal of Educational Psychology,* 57 (1966), 179–188.

———. "Variation in the Amount of Irrelevant Cues in Training and Test Conditions and the Effect Upon Transfer." *Journal of Educational Psychology,* 58 (1967), 62–68.

PAIGE, J. M., and H. A. SIMON. "Cognitive Processes in Solving Algebra Word Problems." In B. Kleinmuntz (ed.), *Problem Solving,* New York: John Wiley & Sons, Inc., 1966, pp. 51–118.

PAIVIO, A. "Mental Imagery in Associative Learning and Memory." *Psychological Review,* 76 (1969), 241–263.

———, and K. CSAPO. "Concrete Image and Verbal Memory Codes." *Journal of Experimental Psychology,* 80 (1969), 279–285.

———, and E. J. ROWE. "Noun Imagery, Frequency, and Meaningfulness in Verbal Discrimination." *Journal of Experimental Psychology,* 85 (1970), 264–269.

PALERMO, D. S. "Imagery in Children's Learning: Discussion." *Psychological Bulletin,* 73 (1970), 415–421.

PARKE, R. D. "The Role of Punishment in the Socialization Process," in R. A. Hoppe, G. A. Milton, and E. C. Simmel (eds.), *Early Experiences and the Process of Socialization.* New York: Academic Press, 1970, Chap. 5, pp. 81–108.

PAUL, G. L. *Insight vs. Desensitization in Psychotherapy.* Stanford, Calif.: Stanford University Press, 1966.

PAUL, I. H. "Impressions of Personality, Authoritarianism, and the *Fait-Accompli* Effect." *Journal of Abnormal and Social Psychology,* 53 (1956), 338–344.

PENFIELD, W. "Memory Mechanisms." *Transactions of the American Neurological Association,* 76 (1951), 15–31.

PENNEY, R. K. "Reactive Curiosity and Manifest Anxiety in Children." *Child Development,* 36 (1965), 697–702.

PHILLIPS, J. L. JR. *The Origins of Intellect: Piaget's Theory.* New York: W. H. Freeman, 1969.

PIAGET, J. *The Moral Judgment of the Child.* London: Rowledge and Kegan Paul, Ltd., 1932.

PIHL, R. O., and J. GREENSPOON. "The Effect of Amount of Reinforcement on the Formation of the Reinforcing Value of a Verbal Stimulus." *Canadian Journal of Psychology,* 23 (1969), 219–226.

POND, F. L. "Influence of the Study of Latin on Word Knowledge." *School Review,* 46 (1938), 611–618.

PORRO, C. R. "Effects of the Observation of a Model's Affective Responses to her own Transgressions on Resistance to Temptation in Children." *Dissertation Abstracts,* 28(B), (1968), 3064.

POSTMAN, L. "Short-term Memory and Incidental Learning," in A. W. Melton (ed.), *Categories of Human Learning.* New York: Academic Press, 1964, pp. 145–201.

———. "Experimental Analysis of Learning to Learn." *Psychology of Learning and Motivation,* 3 (1969), 241–297.

———. J. S. BRUNER, and E. MCGINNIES. "Personal Values as Selective Factors in Perception." *Journal of Abnormal and Social Psychology,* 43 (1948), 142–154.

POULTON, E. C. "Tracking Behavior." in E. A. Bilodeau (ed.), *Acquisition of Skill.* New York: Academic Press, 1966, Chap. 8.

PRESSEY, S. L. "A Simple Apparatus which Gives Tests and Scores—and Teaches." *School and Society,* 23 (1926), 373–376.

———. "A Third and Fourth Contribution Toward the Coming 'Industrial Revolution' in Education." *School and Society,* 36 (1932), 668–672.

———. "Education's (and Psychology's) Disgrace: and a Double-Dare." *Psychology in the Schools,* 6 (1969), 353–358.

PROKASY, W. F. *Classical Conditioning.* New York: Appleton-Century-Crofts, 1965.

PUBOLS, B. H. "Incentive Magnitude, Learning and Performance in Animals." *Psychological Bulletin,* 57 (1960), 89–115.

RABIN, A. I. *Growing up in the Kibbutz.* New York: Springer Verlag, 1965.

RACHMAN, S. "Systematic Desensitization." *Psychological Bulletin,* 67 (1967), 93–103.

RANSON, S. W., and S. L. CLARK. *Anatomy of the Nervous System.* Philadelphia: Saunders, 1959.

RAPH, J. B. "Language Development in Socially Disadvantaged Children." *Review of Educational Research,* 35 (1965), 389–400.

RAY, O. S. "Personality Factors in Motor Learning and Reminiscence." *Journal of Abnormal and Social Psychology,* 59 (1959), 199–203.

REESE, H. W. *The Perception of Stimulus Relations.* New York: Academic Press, 1968.

RENNER, K. E. "Delay of Reinforcement." *Psychological Bulletin,* 61 (1964), 341–361.

RICHARDSON, A. "Mental Practice: A Review and Discussion: II" *The Research Quarterly,* 38 (1967), 263–273.

———. *Mental Imagery.* New York: Springer Publishing Company, Inc., 1969.

———, and R. CANT. "Eidetic Imagery and Brain Damage." *Australian Journal of Psychology,* **22** (1970), 47–52.

RICHARDSON, L. F. *Statistics of Deadly Quarrels.* Pittsburgh: Boxwood, 1960.

RIEBER, M. "Delay of Reward and Discrimination Learning in Children." *Child Development,* 35 (1964), 559–568.

RIKLAN, M., and E. LEVITA. *Subcortical Correlates of Human Behavior.* Baltimore: Williams and Wilkins, 1969.

RIMLAND, B. "Effectiveness of Several Methods of Repetition of Films." *Technical Report,* Special Devices Center, Office of Naval Research, 269-7-45, 1955.

ROCK, R. T. *The Influence upon Learning of the Quantitative Variation of After-Effects.* Teachers College Contribution to Education, No. 650. New York: Teachers College, Columbia University, 1935.

ROSCHAL, S. M. "Effects of Learner Representations in Film-Mediated Perceptual-Motor Learning." *Technical Report,* Special Devices Center, Office of Naval Research, 269-7-5, 1949.

ROSEKRANS, M. A. "Imitation in Children as a Function of Perceived Similarity to a Social Model and Vicarious Reinforcement." *Journal of Personality and Social Psychology,* 7 (1967), 307–315.

ROSENKRANS, M. A., and W. W. HARTUP. "Imitative Influences of Consistent and Inconsistent Response Consequences to a Model on Aggressive Behavior in Children." *Journal of Personality and Social Psychology,* 7 (1967), 429–434.

ROSENBERG, M. J. "Cognitive Reorganization in Response to the Hypnotic Reversal of Attitudinal Affect." *Journal of Personality,* **28** (1960), 39–63.

ROSENFELD, H. M. and D. M. BAER. "Unnoticed Verbal Conditioning of an Aware Experimenter by a More Aware Subject." *Psychological Review,* **76** (1969), 425–432.

ROSENSHINE, B. *Teaching Behaviors and Student Achievement.* Study undertaken for the International Association for the Evaluation of Educational Achievement. (mimeographed) 1970.

ROUGHEAD, W. G., and J. M. SCANDURA. " 'What is Learned' in Mathematical Discovery." *Journal of Educational Psychology,* 59 (1968), 283–289.

ROWETON, W. E., and G. A. DAVIS. "Effects of Preresponse Interval, Post-informative Feedback Interval, and Problem Difficulty on the Identification of Concepts." *Journal of Experimental Psychology,* 78 (1968), 642–645.

RYAN, S. M., A. G. HEGION, and J. H. FLAVELL. "Nonverbal Mnemonic Mediation in Preschool Children." *Child Development,* **41** (1970), 539–550.

RYAN, T. J., and P. WATSON. "Frustrative Nonreward Theory Applied to Children's Behavior." *Psychological Bulletin,* 69 (1968), 111–125.

SAFER, M. A., and L. B. KORNREICH. "The Interaction of Social Class and Type of Reinforcement in Discrimination Learning." *Psychonomic Science,* 11 (1968), 206.

SANDERS, A. F. "Attention and Performance." Proceedings of a Symposium Held at Driebergen, August 17–20, 1966 under the auspices of the Institute for Perception RVO–TNO, Svesterberg, The Netherlands. Amsterdam, Netherlands: North Holland, 1967.

SASSENRATH, J. M., and G. D. YONGE. "Delayed Information Feedback, Feedback Cues, Retention Set, and Delayed Retention." *Journal of Educational Psychology,* 59 (1968), 69–73.

SCANDURA, J. M., and J. H. DURNIN. "Extra-scope Transfer in Learning Mathematical Strategies." *Journal of Educational Psychology,* 59 (1968), 350–354.

SCHWITZGEBEL, R. L. "Short-Term Operant Conditioning of Adolescent Offenders on Socially Relevant Variables." *Journal of Abnormal Psychology,* 72 (1967), 134–142.

SCOTT, J. P. *Early Experience and the Organization of Behavior.* Belmont, Calif.: Brooks Cole Publishing Company, 1968.

SEARS, D. O. "The Paradox of De Facto Selective Exposure Without Preferences for Supportive Information," in R. P. Abelson, et al. (eds.), *Theories of Cognitive Consistency: A Sourcebook,* Chicago: Rand McNally & Co., 1968, pp. 777–787.

SEARS, R. R. "Relation of Early Socialization Experiences to Self-Concepts and Gender Role in Middle Childhood." *Child Development,* 41 (1970), 267–289.

———. E. E. MACCOBY, and H. LEVIN. *Patterns of Child Rearing.* New York: Harper & Row, 1957.

SHEA, M. "Formulation of a Generalization Surface for the Simultaneous Variation of Stimulus and Response Similarity." *Journal of Experimental Psychology,* 80 (1969), 353–358.

SHEPARD, R. N. "Recognition Memory for Words, Sentences, and Pictures." *Journal of Verbal Learning and Verbal Behavior,* 6 (1967), 156–163.

SHUELL, T. J. "Clustering and Organization in Free Recall." *Psychological Bulletin,* 72 (1969), 353–374.

———, and G. KEPPEL. "Learning Ability and Retention." *Journal of Educational Psychology,* 61 (1970), 59–65.

SIEGEL, S. "The Physiology of Conditioning," in M. H. Marx (ed.), *Learning Interaction.* New York: The Macmillan Co., 1970, Part VI, pp. 367–415.

SILBERMAN, H. F. "Effects of Praise and Reproof on Reading Growth in a Non-laboratory Classroom Setting." *Journal of Educational Psychology,* 48 (1957), 199–206.

SIMONS, H. W., N. N. BERKOWITZ, and R. J. MOYER. "Similarity, Credibility, and Attitude Change." *Psychological Bulletin,* 73 (1970), 1–16.

SKINNER, B. F. *The Behavior of Organisms.* New York: Appleton-Century-Crofts, 1938.

———. *Science and Human Behavior.* New York: The Macmillan Company, 1953.

———. *Verbal Behavior.* New York: Appleton-Century-Crofts, 1957.

———. "An Operant Analysis of Problem Solving," in B. Kleinmuntz (ed.), *Problem Solving.* New York: John Wiley & Sons, Inc., 1966, pp. 225–258.

SMITH, C. P. (ed.). *Achievement-Related Motives in Children.* New York: Russell Sage Foundation, 1959.

SMITH, J., V. ANDERSON, T. CUNNINGHAM, and W. SJOBERG. "A Comparison of Auditory and Visual Discrimination Learning in Retardates." *American Journal of Mental Deficiency,* **72** (1967), 445–449.

SMITH, M. E. *An Investigation of the Study of the Development of the Sentence and the Extent of the Vocabulary in Young Children.* University of Iowa Studies of Child Welfare, 3, No. 5, 1926.

SMITH, M. P., J. R. MEANS, and S. FISHKIN. "Effects of Naming Upon Learning and Transfer of Learning in the Mentally Retarded." *American Journal of Mental Deficiency,* **72** (1968), 637–647.

SOLLEY, C. M., and G. MURPHY. *Development of the Perceptual World.* New York: Basic Books, Inc., 1960.

SOLOMON, R. L. "Punishment." *American Psychologist,* **19** (1964), 239–253.

———, and L. S. WYNNE. "Traumatic Avoidance Learning: Acquisition in Normal Dogs." *Psychological Monographs,* **67** 354 (1953), 1–19.

———, and L. S. WYNNE. "Traumatic Avoidance Learning: The Principles of Anxiety Conservation and Partial Irreversibility." *Psychological Review,* **61** (1954), 353–385.

SPEAR, P. S. "Motivational Effects of Praise and Criticism on Children's Learning." *Developmental Psychology,* 3 (1970), 124–132.

SPENCE, J. T., and M. C. DUNTON. "The Influence of Verbal and Nonverbal Reinforcement Combinations in the Discrimination Learning of Middle- and Lower-Class Preschool Children." *Child Development,* 38 (1967), 1177–1186.

SPENCE, K. W. *Behavior Theory and Conditioning.* New Haven, Conn.: Yale University Press, 1956.

———. *Behavior Theory and Learning.* Englewood Cliffs, N. J.: Prentice-Hall, Inc., 1960.

SPERLING, G. "The Information Available in Brief Visual Presentations." *Psychological Monographs,* 74:498 (1960).

STAATS, A. W. "An Integrated-Functional Learning Approach to Complex Human Behavior," in B. Kleinmuntz (ed.), *Problem Solving,* New York: John Wiley & Sons, Inc., 1966, pp. 259–339.

———. *Learning, Language, and Cognition.* New York: Holt, Rinehart and Winston, 1968.

START, K. B. "Intelligence and the Improvement in a Gross Motor Skill After Mental Practice." *British Journal of Educational Psychology*. 34 (1964a), 85–90.

———. "Kinaesthesis and Mental Practice." *Research Quarterly*, 35 (1964b), 316–320.

STEIN, Z., and M. SUSSER. "Mutability of Intelligence and Epidemiology of Mild Mental Retardation." *Review of Educational Research*, 40 (1970), 29–85.

STOLUROW, L. M. *Teaching by Machine*. OE-34010, Cooperative Research Monograph No. 6. Washington, D. C.: U. S. Government Printing Office, 1961.

STONES, E., and J. R. HESLOP. "The Formation and Extension of Class Concepts in Primary School Children." *British Journal of Educational Psychology*, 38 (1968), 261–271.

STORMZAND, M. J., and M. V. O'SHEA. *How Much English Grammar?* Baltimore: Warwick and York, 1924.

SULLIVAN, E. V. "Piagentian Theory in the Educational Milieu: A Critical Appraisal." *Canadian Journal of Behavioral Science*, 1 (1969), 129–155.

SUPPES, P., M. JERMAN, and D. BRYAN. *Computer Assisted Instruction: Stanford's 1965–66 Arithmetic Program*. New York: Academic Press, 1968.

THOMAS, H. "Visual-Fixation Responses of Infants to Stimuli of Varying Complexity." *Child Development*, 36 (1965), 629–638.

THOMAS, S., W. B. BROOKOVER, J. M. LAPERE, D. E. HAMACHEK, and E. L. ERICKSON. "An Experiment to Modify Self-Concept and School Performance." *Sociological Focus on Education*, 3 (1969), 55–67.

THORNDIKE, E. L. *Fundamentals of Learning*. New York: Teachers College, Columbia University, 1932.

———. *The Psychology of Wants, Interests, and Attitudes*. New York: Appleton-Century-Crofts, 1935.

TOPPEN, J. T. "Money Reinforcement and Human Operant (Work) Behavior: II. Within-Subject Comparisons." *Perceptual and Motor Skills*, 20 (1965), 1193–1199.

TRABASSO, T., and G. H. BOWER. *Attention in Learning*. New York: John Wiley & Sons, Inc., 1968.

TRAVERS, R. M. W. *A Study of the Advantages and Disadvantages of Using Simplified Visual Presentations in Instructional Materials*. Final Report on Grant No. OEG-1-7-070144-5235, U. S. Office of Education, 1969.

———. *Man's Information System*. San Francisco: Chandler Publishing Co., 1970.

———, and K. E. MYERS. "Efficiency in Rote Learning Under Four

Learning Conditions." *The Journal of Educational Research,* 60 (1966), 10–12.

———. I. E. REID and R. K. VAN WAGENEN. *Reinforcement: A Review of Related Research.* Final Report, U. S. Department of Health, Education and Welfare, Contract No. 2-10-010, 1963.

———. "Research on Reinforcement and Its Implications for Education." *Journal of Teacher Education,* 15 (1964), 223–229.

TREICHLER, F. R., and S. J. WAY. "Task Variables and the Effects of Response-Contingent Stimulus Change on Discrimination Performance." *Journal of Experimental Psychology,* 76 (1968), 671–673.

TULVING, E. "The Effects of Presentation and Recall of Material in Free-Recall Learning." *Journal of Verbal Learning and Verbal Behavior,* 6 (1967), 175–184.

———. "Theoretical Issues in Free Recall," in T. R. Dixon and D. J. Horton (eds.), *Verbal Behavior and General Behavior Theory,* New York: Prentice-Hall, Inc., 1968, pp. 1–66.

TURNER, L. H., and R. L. SOLOMON. "Human Traumatic Avoidance Learning." *Psychological Monographs,* 76:559 (1962), 1–32.

ULRICH, R. E., R. R. HUTCHINSON, and N. H. AZRIN. "Pain-Elicited Aggression." *Psychological Record,* 15 (1965), 111–126.

UNDERWOOD, B. J. "Associative Transfer in Verbal Learning as a Function of Response Similarity and Degree of First-List Learning." *Journal of Experimental Psychology,* 42 (1951), 44–53.

———. "The Representativeness of Rote Verbal Learning," in A. W. Melton (ed.), *Categories of Human Learning.* New York: Academic Press, 1964, pp. 47–78.

———. "Attributes of Memory." *Psychological Review,* 76 (1969), 559–573.

U. S. DEPARTMENT OF HEALTH, EDUCATION AND WELFARE. *Minimal Brain Dysfunction in Children.* Public Health Service Publication No. 1415, 1966.

U. S. DEPARTMENT OF HEALTH, EDUCATION AND WELFARE. *Minimal Brain Dysfunction in Children.* Public Health Service Publication No. 2015, Washington, D. C., 1969.

VACCHIANO, R. B., P. S. STRAUSS, and L. HOCHMAN. "The Open and Closed Mind." *Psychological Bulletin,* 71 (1969), 261–273.

VALENSTEIN, E. S. "The Anatomical Locus of Reinforcement," in E. Stellar and J. M. Sprague (eds.), *Progress in Physiological Psychology,* Vol. 1, New York: Academic Press, 1966, pp. 149–190.

———. V. C. COX, and J. W. KAKOLEWSKI. "Reexamination of the Role of the Hypothalamus in Motivation." *Psychological Review,* 77 (1970), 16–31.

VAN ALLEN, R. K. "Improvement in Appearance and Grooming in a Token-Economy Setting as a Function of Reinforcement Contingency." *Canadian Journal of Behavioral Science*, **2** (1970), 157–161.

VAN WAGENEN, R. K., and E. E. MURDOCK. "A Transistorized Single-Package for Toilet Training of Infants." *Journal of Experimental Child Psychology*, 3 (1966), 312–314.

VIANELLO, M. A. B., and S. H. EVANS. "Note on Pitch Discrimination Learning." *Perceptual & Motor Skills*, **26** (1968), 576.

VIAUD, G. *Intelligence: Its Evolution and Forms*. London: Hutchinson & Company, 1968.

VOGEL-SPROTT, M., and V. BURROWS. "Response Suppression in Humans as a Function of Contingent and Non-contingent Punishment: Signal Properties of Stimuli." *Canadian Journal of Psychology*, **23** (1969), 66–74.

VON SENDEN, M. *Space and Sight*. (Translated by Peter Heath). New York: The Free Press, 1961.

VON WRIGHT, J. M. *An Experimental Study of Human Serial Learning*. Ph.D. Phil. thesis, Oxford University, 1955.

———. "A Note on the Role of 'Guidance' in Learning." *British Journal of Psychology*, 48 (1957), 133–137.

VOSS, J. F. *Approaches to Thought*. Columbus, Ohio: Charles E. Merrill Books, Inc., 1969.

WALLACE, J. "Role Reward and Dissonance Reduction." *Journal of Personality and Social Psychology*, 3 (1966), 305–312.

WALLS, R. T. and T. S. SMITH. "Development of Preference for Delayed Reinforcement in Disadvantaged Children." *Journal of Educational Psychology*, **61** (1970), 118–123.

WALTERS, R. H., R. D. PARKE, and V. CANE. "Timing of Punishment and the Observation of Consequences to Others as Determinants of Response Inhibition." *Journal of Experimental Child Psychology*, **2** (1965), 10–30.

WARD, L. B. "Reminiscence and Rote Learning." *Psychological Monographs*, **49**: 220, 1937.

WARDEN, C. J. "The Distribution of Practice in Animal Learning," *Comparative Psychological Monographs*, **1**:3, 1923.

WARREN, R. M. "Verbal Transformation Effect and Auditory Perceptual Mechanisms." *Psychological Bulletin*, **70** (1968), 261–270.

WATSON, J. B. *Behaviorism*. New York: People's Institute, 1924.

WEST, L. J. "Vision and Kinesthesis in the Acquisition of Typewriting Skill." *Journal of Applied Psychology*, **51** (1967), 161–166.

———. *Acquisition of Typewriting Skills*. New York: Pitman Publishing Company, 1969.

WHITE, R. K., and R. LIPPITT. *Autocracy and Democracy*. New York: Harper & Row, 1960.

WICKELGREN, W. A. "Auditory or Articulatory Coding in Verbal Short-Term Memory." *Psychological Review*, 76 (1969), 232–235.

WICKENS, D. D. "Encoding Categories of Words: An Empirical Approach to Meaning." *Psychological Review*, 77 (1970), 1–15.

WITTROCK, M. C. "Verbal Stimuli in Concept Formation: Learning by Discovery." *Journal of Educational Psychology*, 54 (1963), 183–190.

———. "The Learning by Discovery Hypothesis," in L. S. Shulman and E. R. Keislar (eds.), *Learning by Discovery*, Chicago: Rand McNally & Co., 1966, pp. 33–75.

WOHLWILL, J. F. "Amount of Stimulus Exploration and Preference as Differential Functions of Stimulus Complexity." *Perception and Psychophysics*, 4 (1968) 307–312.

WOLFE, J. B. "Effectiveness of Token Rewards for Chimpanzees." *Comparative Psychological Monographs*, 12, (Serial No. 60), (1936) 72.

WOLFORD, G. L., D. L. WESSEL, and W. K. ESTES. "Further Evidence Concerning Scanning and Sampling Assumptions of Visual Detection Models." Perception and Psychophysics, 3 (1968), 439–444.

WOLPE, J. *Psychotherapy By Reciprocal Inhibition*. Stanford, Calif.: Stanford University Press, 1958.

WOODBURNE, L. S. *The Neural Basis of Behavior*. Columbus, Ohio: Charles E. Merrill Books, Inc., 1967.

WOODROW, H. "The Effect of Type of Training upon Transference." *Journal of Educational Psychology*, 18 (1927), 159–172.

WOODRUFF, A. D. "The Use of Concepts in Teaching and Learning." *Journal of Teacher Education*, 15 (1964), 81–99.

WOODWORTH, R. S. *Dynamics of Behavior*. New York: Holt, Rinehart and Winston, 1958.

WORTHEN, B. R. "Discovery and Expository Task Presentation in Elementary Mathematics." *Journal of Educational Psychology*, Monograph Supplement, 59 (1968), No. 1, Part 2, 1–13.

YARBUS, A. L. *Eye Movements and Vision*. New York: Plenum Press, 1967.

ZIGLER, E. "Learning, Development, and Social Class in the Socialization Process," in M. H. Marx (ed.), *Learning Interactions*, New York: The Macmillan Company, 1970, pp. 193–287.

ZIMBARDO, P. G., M. WEISENBERG, and I. FIRESTONE. "Communicator Effectiveness in Producing Public Conformity and Private Attitude Change." *Journal of Personality*, 33 (1965), 233–256.

ZOLL, E. J. "Research in Programmed Instruction in Mathematics." *Mathematics Teacher*, 62 (1969), 103–110.

ZUBEK, J. P. *Sensory Deprivation*. New York: Appleton-Century-Crofts, 1969.

Index of Names

Index of Subjects